A SOCIOLOGY OF FOOD & NUTRITION

The Social Appetite

Edited by John Germov
and Lauren Williams

Second Edition

OXFORD
UNIVERSITY PRESS

OXFORD
UNIVERSITY PRESS

253 Normanby Road, South Melbourne, Victoria 3205, Australia

Oxford University Press is a department of the University of Oxford. It furthers the University's objective of excellence in research, scholarship, and education by publishing worldwide in

Oxford New York

Auckland Bangkok Buenos Aires Cape Town Chennai
Dar es Salaam Delhi Hong Kong Istanbul Karachi Kolkata
Kuala Lumpur Madrid Melbourne Mexico City Mumbai Nairobi
São Paulo Shanghai Taipei Tokyo Toronto

OXFORD is a trade mark of Oxford University Press
in the UK and in certain other countries

First published 1999
Reprinted 2000, 2001
Second edition published 2004

National Library of Australia
Cataloguing-in-Publication data:

A Sociology of Food and Nutrition: The Social Appetite

2nd Edition

Bibliography.
Includes index.
ISBN 0 19 551625 7.

1. Food habits - Social aspects. 2. Food - Social aspects.
3. Nutrition - Social aspects. I. Williams, Lauren. II.
Germov, John.

394.12

Typeset by OUPANZS
Printed through Bookpac Production Services, Singapore

Foreword

For almost two decades, the study of food and eating has been one of the fastest-growing areas in sociology. The essays collected in this second edition of *A Sociology of Food and Nutrition: The Social Appetite* bear ample witness to the vitality and wide scope of the new sub-discipline of the sociology of food. It is plainly an academic speciality whose time has come. Yet it is worthwhile to ask two questions:

- Why did sociologists, until fairly recently, pay little attention to food and eating, which are, after all, universal human activities requiring social organisation, and which are indeed more urgent necessities for people's survival even than sex?
- And why is the subject now so much the centre of sociological attention?

The lack of systematic attention given to food in the sociological classics is striking. Look up the word 'diet' in an index to the works of Karl Marx, and you will find that it refers to a political assembly. To be fair, Marx's collaborator Friedrich Engels recorded a great deal of nauseating details about the food of the poor in *The Condition of the Working Class in England* in 1845, and the nutritional aspects of poverty continued to receive attention in such empiricist classics as the works of Charles Booth and Seebohm Rowntree in the United Kingdom. After his experiences in the Russian Revolution, Pitirim Sorokin wrote a remarkable study of *Hunger as a Factor in Human Affairs*, although it remained unknown until its publication in English in 1975. At the other end of the social scale, in 1899 Thorstein Veblen drew attention in *The Theory of the Leisure Class* to lavish food and drink as means of social display by the wealthy. And a little later Norbert Elias wrote the famous section of *The Civilising Process* dealing with changing table manners among the European secular upper classes (though he said little about food as such). For the beginnings of serious theoretical interest in food, one can look to Herbert Spencer and Émile Durkheim, both of whom paid attention to the remarkable way in which all human groups taboo—and feel revulsion towards—the consumption of particular potential sources of nourishment, which are factually available to them but which they strictly avoid eating. Spencer's and Durkheim's interests were subsequently pursued more by their anthropological than by their sociological progeny. By the 1960s and 1970s, food was at the centre of structuralist theory, especially in the writings of Claude Lévi-Strauss and Mary Douglas. In the 1980s, food was in turn central to anthropology's turning away from structuralism. Marvin Harris—a controversial maverick among anthropologists—published *Good to Eat*, a hard-hitting polemic against structuralism, in which he sought to crack the tough old nut of explaining food avoidances, such as the Jewish taboo on pork and the Hindu taboo on beef, in materialist, developmental, and instrumental terms (the possibility of which Douglas had denied). And Sidney Mintz, in *Sweetness and Power*, showed how the British and American sweet tooth had been created in connection with the growth of sugar plantations and long-distance commerce in sugar.

By this time, sociologists were listening. But why had they neglected food as a topic for research for so long? Prestige has always played a part in the popularity of research topics. For most of the twentieth century, the prestigious topics tended to be stratification and class inequality, politics and power, industry, organisations and bureaucracy. All were in some sense masculine concerns. The inequality between the sexes was taken for granted, while that between social strata was not: work was mainly a man's world, the home and the kitchen a woman's. Leisure, culture, consumption—and food—were widely considered to be peripheral and even frivolous concerns. I would certainly not wish to present the women's movement of recent decades as the sole cause of the new interest in the study of the social aspects of food and eating. There is more to it than that. The shift from the primacy of production to the primacy of consumption was noted as early as 1950 by David Riesman in his classic *The Lonely Crowd*, and the thought was developed further by Daniel Bell and other theorists of post-industrial and post-modern society in the 1970s and 1980s. Whatever one calls it—post-industrial, post-modern, or consumer society—its rise cannot be entirely reduced to the changing balance of power between the sexes. Sport, for instance, was traditionally a mainly masculine preserve, yet it was once considered just as peripheral and frivolous an interest as eating and cooking. It probably suffered because it was seen as separate from the 'serious' world of work. But feminism has undoubtedly had a profound effect on the sociological enterprise as a whole. It is especially evident in the emergence not just of a vibrant sociology of food, but also of the sociologies of the body and of consumption—all of them intertwined with each other, as this book demonstrates.

One sign of the times is that sociological studies of food have in various ways come to be important vehicles for developing theoretical arguments (and the prestige of theorising and of an upper caste of theorists within sociology should never be underestimated). In *All Manners of Food*, I sought among other things to apply Elias's theory of civilising processes to the social shaping of appetite, as well as extending his account of court society to understanding the development of differences in culinary cultures between England and France. More ambitiously, in *Distinction*—voted in 1998 to be one of the ten most influential sociological books of the twentieth century—Pierre Bourdieu demonstrated how the field of food links up with many other areas of 'taste' (music, literature, furnishings, art ...) in the deployment of cultural capital. Claude Fischler, in *L'Homnivore*, showed the long-term significance of human omnivorousness in the development of society. George Ritzer made a sociological best-seller out of *The McDonaldization of Society*, in which the hamburger chain becomes a metaphor for the hyper-rationalisation of contemporary society as a whole. Alan Warde's *Consumption, Food and Taste* tackles, through modern food habits, the central issues of 'consumer society'. In *Sociologies of Food and Nutrition*, Wm. Alex McIntosh has produced a textbook through which students could be introduced to most of the main issues of current social theory solely through the study of food. And Anne Murcott, from *The Sociology of Food and Eating*, a 1983 collection of essays in which leading British sociologists associated mainly with other areas of the discipline were invited to turn their attention to their hitherto hidden interests in food, through to *The Nation's Diet* which was the outcome in 1998 of a large-scale government funded study, has over many years striven to bring the sociology of food and eating in from the cold.

A Sociology of Food and Nutrition pulls together all of these strands in one volume. John Germov and Lauren Williams have persuaded many of the leading sociologists of food and nutrition from around the world to contribute chapters, and they are grouped to form a coherent treatment of the major issues: gender, the body, culture and class, public policy in the face of the industrialisation of food supply, and food in the context of the emerging global society.

Stephen Mennell
University College Dublin
October 2003

Contents

Preface

A Sociology of Food and Nutrition: The Social Appetite introduces readers to the field of food sociology. The second edition expands on the successful format of the first, with new chapters, updated material, and new pedagogic features. The book is designed to be used as both a general reader, bringing together many of the key authors in the field and focusing on topics that dominate the literature, and a teaching text on the social aspects of food and nutrition. To fulfil this second function, each chapter has:

- an overview section containing a series of questions and a short summary of the chapter, designed to grab the reader's interest and encourage a questioning and reflective approach to the topic
- key terms (concepts and theories) listed at the start of the chapter, highlighted in bold in the text, and defined in a glossary at the end of the book
- a summary of the main points
- discussion questions
- further investigation (essay-style) questions
- further reading and recommended chapter-specific web sites.

What's new?

The book has been completely revised in response to reader feedback and the latest research findings to ensure that it is completely up to date with current developments in the field. Specifically, the second edition includes:

- **A revised introductory chapter:** The first chapter clearly maps out the field of food sociology, introduces the sociological perspective via the sociological imagination template, and provides an overview of the structure and content of the book.
- **A new book structure:** This book is an example of what Wm. Alex McIntosh calls 'sociologies of food'—it is not dominated by one thesis or one theory or method, but rather presents a 'potlatch' of topics organised under key sociological themes. In the first edition we structured the book according to three key trends in the literature. While we still view these trends as significant, we have added new chapters to broaden the book's scope, reorganised some material, revised some of the terminology, and added a new section, so that the book is now structured in the following way:
    - Part 1: An Appetiser (which features the revised and expanded introductory chapter)
    - Part 2: The Food System: Globalisation, McDonaldisation, and Agribusiness

  - Part 3: Food and Public Health Nutrition: Discourses, Politics, and Policies
  - Part 4: Food and Social Differentiation: Consumption and Identity
  - Part 5: Food and the Body: Civilising Processes and Social Embodiment (referred to as self-rationalisation in the previous edition of this book).
- **New chapters on the following topics:** agribusiness, biotechnology, and genetically modified food (Chapter 4); supermarket power and commodity chain analysis (Chapter 5); the public health nutrition workforce (Chapter 8); the social construction of eating disorders (Chapter 16); and body acceptance (Chapter 18).
- **Further investigation questions and web resources:** A further investigation section of essay-style questions and a chapter-specific list of web sites has been added to every chapter.
- **Appendix:** The list of web sites, books, and journals has been updated and expanded.
- **New *Social Appetite* web site:** This professionally designed web site provides access to various supplementary resources, including lists of relevant web sites, books, teaching resources, journals, associations, documentaries, and films. The web site is at au.oup.com/content/General.asp?Content=compsite.

The interdisciplinary nature of studying food and nutrition

The central importance of food in social life means that its study is the province of diverse academic disciplines. In such a field as the study of food and nutrition, there is much that we can learn through interdisciplinary exchange. This book aims to draw together readings from what might be seen as opposing disciplines: sociology and nutrition. Interdisciplinary collaboration is a lengthy and challenging process involving active debate over philosophical assumptions and methodologies, as well as the overcoming of jargon and territorial defences, not to mention the academic structures of universities.

As editors, we have worked through the challenges of interdisciplinary collaboration in compiling this book. John Germov is a sociologist and Lauren Williams is a dietitian with a science background, and we both work as university academics. Our interdisciplinary collaboration resulted from having to share an office because of a lack of university office space. Our office became a place of daily intellectual exploration as we probed the perspectives of sometimes opposing disciplines through discussion and debate. This debate informed the development of a new sociology subject at the University of Newcastle called 'The Sociology of Food', run for both dietetic and sociology students. In establishing the subject, the search for an appropriate textbook led to the creation of this book. With student learning and interdisciplinary collaboration in mind, we broadened the scope of the book to make it relevant to readers across health, nutrition, and social science disciplines.

Part of the value of our collaboration has been the extension of our networks, reflected in the range of people who have contributed to this book. Most are either sociologists or dietitians and all share an interest in the sociology of food and nutrition. Many of the contributing authors have published widely in the field and are based in either the UK, USA, or Australia. Most chapters provide a review of the relevant literature, while others present empirical findings, particularly where sociological data are scant.

Our aim in writing this book is to reach a broad readership so that those interested in food, nutrition, and wider issues of consumption and social regulation can discover the relevance of studying the social context of food; this, we hope, will lead to future interdisciplinary collaboration. We encourage readers interested in the social context of food and nutrition—both inside and outside the discipline of sociology—to break down disciplinary barriers and to facilitate the coalescence of a variety of perspectives through ongoing debate and discussion of the issues presented in this book. Despite our enthusiasm for food sociology and interdisciplinary collaboration, it would be folly to claim that this book provides all the answers for understanding food and eating. The study of food is rightly the province of many disciplines. Had the university placed a geographer in our office, there would no doubt have been more input from that disciplinary field in this text.

We trust that *A Sociology of Food and Nutrition* inspires people from many disciplines to add a sociological perspective to their understanding of why we eat the way we do.

Suggestions, comments, and feedback

We are always interested in receiving feedback on the book and suggestions for future editions. You can contact us at the Social Appetite Web Site at au.oup.com/content/General.asp?Content=compsite.

Bon appetit!

John Germov and Lauren Williams
University of Newcastle, Australia
January 2004

Acknowledgments

We would like to thank the contributing authors for being so professional in their dealings with us and for their high-quality chapters. Our gratitude to the book's original publisher, Jill Henry, for her belief in the book. For the second edition, we are grateful to Debra James and the OUP staff, especially Tim Campbell. We are indebted to Jane Watson (nee a'Beckett) for assistance with the first edition, and Annette Murphy for the second edition.

We thank our students, whose interest in and enthusiasm for the sociology of food and nutrition was the original stimulus for this book. And we thank the lecturers who have used the first edition of the book for providing feedback and encouraging us to produce a second edition.

On a personal note, thanks go to our family and friends: John's father, Ivan, and sister, Roz; Lauren's parents, Jan and Merve, and sisters, Julie and Kim, who have coped so well with their own challenges in recent times; and our partners, Sue Jelovcan and Greg Hill, who have each supported both of us in a multitude of ways.

* * * * *

Unless otherwise stated, all quotations used on the Part openings are from Ned Sherrin's *Oxford Dictionary of Humorous Quotations* (1995, Oxford University Press, Oxford).

The editors and publisher are grateful to the following copyright holders for granting permission to reproduce various extracts and photographs in this book: the International Size Acceptance Association for permission to reproduce their poster; the *Australian Journal of Nutrition and Dietetics* and Colin Binns for the extract from Binns's 'A Letter from America', *Australian Journal of Nutrition and Dietetics*, vol. 47, no. 2, 1990, p. 58; The Body Shop International PLC for the photograph of the 'Ruby' advertising campaign; *Cleo* magazine for the covers of the January 1973, 1983, and 1993 issues; Pine Forge Press for the extract from George Ritzer's book *The McDonaldization of Society*, pp. xii–xiii, © 1993 by Pine Forge Press, New York; South End Press for the extract from P. Idemudia and S. Kole's chapter 'World Bank Takes Control of UNCED's Environmental Fund', in K. Danaher (ed.), *50 Years is Enough: The Case Against the World Bank and the International Monetary Fund*, South End Press, Boston, 1994; *Who Weekly* magazine for the cover of the 27 May 1996 issue.

Every effort has been made to trace the original source of all material reproduced in this book. Where the attempt has been unsuccessful, the author and publisher would be pleased to hear from the copyright holder to rectify any omission.

John Germov and Lauren Williams
University of Newcastle, Australia
January 2004

Contributors

John Coveney works in the Department of Health at Flinders University in Adelaide, where he lectures to students in nutrition and dietetics, medicine, and environmental health. His research projects have included an examination of the emergence of the discipline of nutrition in Australia, especially in terms of public health (written as a doctoral thesis), an ethnographic exploration of family food habits, and a critical analysis of environmental issues related to the food supply. He is the author of a number of publications, including the book *Vegetarian Food and Children* (with Rhonda Mooney).

Pat Crotty is the publisher of the monthly online magazine *Quotidian: Australian Food and Society* (www.quotidian.net), a miscellany of opinion and reporting on food in society, health, and history, with a social justice and Australian slant. She has been a dietitian, a public health nutritionist, and an academic at Deakin University. Her interests are at the intersection of nutrition and the social sciences, especially the social construction of dietary advice. She has explored the Mediterranean diet as a case study. Her book *Good Nutrition: Fact and Fashion in Dietary Advice* was published in 1995. She has been a member (2001–03) of the National Health and Medical Research Council's Working Party to review the Dietary Guidelines for Australians.

Jane Dixon has social work qualifications and a doctorate in food sociology. She is a public health social scientist at the National Centre for Epidemiology and Population Health at the Australian National University. Her most recent book is *The Changing Chicken: Chooks, Cooks and Culinary Culture* (2002). Between 1998 and 2000, Jane coordinated the government-funded Health Inequalities Research Collaboration, where she co-edited *The Social Origins of Health and Well-being* (2001). Before holding this position, she was a Senior Lecturer in the School of Social Science and Planning at the Royal Melbourne Institute of Technology. An interest in the politics of everyday life permeates her writings on community development in health and the human services and food systems and culinary cultures.

John Duff is a Lecturer in Sociology at Edith Cowan University in Perth, Australia. His research interests include the political economy of health care systems and health policy, and the sociology of ecological sustainability. He recently completed a PhD on the formulation of nutrition policy in Australia. His work now includes comparisons with other coutries (particularly South–East Asian countries), which place Australia's policies in an international context. His current research projects include a comparison of health payment systems in Australia and Singapore, and a study of the adoption of sustainable timber production on

Australian farms. Recent publications include 'Public Health Equity Goals: Households and Food Production in Nutrition Research' (*International Journal of Sociology and Social Policy*, in press); *Nutrition Research: Setting the Agenda for the 'New' Public Health* (PhD thesis, University of Western Australia); and 'Eating Away at the Public Health: A Political Economy of Nutrition', in C. Waddell and A. Petersen (eds), *Just Health: Inequality in Illness, Care and Prevention* (1994).

John Germov is a Senior Lecturer in Sociology in the School of Social Sciences at the University of Newcastle, Australia, and is currently President of the Australian Sociological Association (TASA). His research interests include workplace change, professions, social determinants of health, health policy, food sociology, and the area of his doctoral research, managerialism in the public health sector. John's other books include *Second Opinion: An Introduction to Health Sociology* (1998, 2002), *Get Great Marks for Your Essays* (1996, 2000), *Surviving First Year Uni* (2002, with L. Williams), and *Get Great Information Fast* (1998, with L. Williams). He has published a number of articles and book chapters on food sociology, health sociology, legal aid, education, and medical fraud. John is currently an Executive Committee Member of the International Sociological Association.

Janet Grice (formerly Norton) is a Post-doctoral Research Fellow in the School of Social Science at the University of Queensland. She previously worked at the Institute for Sustainable Regional Development at Central Queensland University (CQU), where she completed several studies on the social aspects of biotechnologies. Her doctoral thesis, completed at CQU in 1999, dealt with the Australian public's perceptions of agri-food biotechnologies. Her research interests include biotechnologies in agriculture, consumer attitudes towards the genetic engineering of food, and the role of science in society. Her current research deals with the social construction of 'safe' foods. Her first (co-edited with Geoffrey Lawrence and Richard Hindmarsh) book was *Altered Genes: Reconstructing Nature—The Debate* (1998).

Julie Hepworth is a Senior Lecturer in the Department of Psychology at Queen Margaret University College, Edinburgh. She is a Chartered Health Psychologist and teaches courses in health psychology, research methods, and gender and health. Her research areas include the psychosocial aspects of chronic illness, theoretical approaches to health psychology, and the practice of psychology in public health and medicine. She is the author of the book *The Social Construction of Anorexia Nervosa*, as well as articles on eating disorders, menopause, hepatitis C, and research participation. Recent publications include those in *Social Science & Medicine* (2003, vol. 56, pp. 1643–52), *Sociology of Health and Illness* (2003, vol. 25, no. 2, pp. 185–207), and *Psychology, Health & Medicine* (2002, vol. 7, no. 4, pp. 469–76).

Roger Hughes is a Senior Lecturer in Public Health Nutrition at Griffith University, Australia. His research work focuses on public health nutrition intervention, and includes determinant analysis and intervention development and evaluation. Some of his particular research themes are breastfeeding promotion, workforce development, and program evaluation.

Joanne Pakel Ikeda is the Cooperative Extension Nutrition Education Specialist and a Lecturer in the Department of Nutritional Sciences at the University of California, Berkeley (UCB). She teaches nutrition education and counselling to dietetics students, and health education to teachers in the Graduate School of Education at UCB. Her research is on the foodways and the quality of the diets of minority populations living in California. She has done community participatory research with Mexican-American, Native American, Vietnamese-American, and Hmong-American communities throughout California. Her publications include 'Hmong American Food Practices, Customs, and Holidays'; 'Practicing Pediatrics in a Culturally Diverse Society' (with James Wright, MD, FAAP); and 'Nutrition Education in a Culturally Pluralistic Society' (*Networking News*, no. 17, pp. 5–7).

Karen S. Kubena is a Professor in the Human Nutrition Section of the Department of Animal Science, Texas A&M University. She also serves as Associate Dean for Academic Programs at the College of Agriculture and Life Sciences. Her research interests have included nutrition through the life cycle, the metabolism of magnesium, and the role of dietary fat in cardiovascular disease. Dr Kubena is a registered dietitian and teaches courses in nutrition and the life cycle and nutrition and disease. A member of the editorial boards for the *Journal of the American Dietetic Association* and *Magnesium Research*, Karen is also a member of the American Society for Nutritional Sciences, the American Society for Clinical Nutrition, and the American Dietetic Association.

Geoffrey Lawrence is Professor of Sociology and Head of the School of Social Science at the University of Queensland. He has had over twenty-five years' involvement in agri-food research, studying and researching in Australia (at Central Queensland University and Charles Sturt University), the USA (Cornell and Madison-Wisconsin) and the UK (Essex University). He is the co-editor of the *Journal of Sociology of Agriculture and Food*, associate editor of the *Journal of Environmental Policy and Planning*, and is on the board of the *Journal of Sociology*. His most recent co-authored/co-edited works are *Environment, Society and Natural Resource Management* (2001), *Altered Genes II* (2001), *A Future for Regional Australia* (2001), *Globalization, Localization and Sustainable Livelihoods* (2003), and *Recoding Nature* (2003).

Mark Lawrence is a Senior Lecturer in Food Policy and Regulation at Deakin University, Melbourne. His research interests include analysing food and nutrition policy, monitoring the use of products at the food–drug interface, and developing, implementing, and evaluating policy interventions to support food security and obesity prevention. His recent publications include *Folate Fortification: A Case Study of Public Health Policy-making* (PhD thesis) and *Using*

Domestic Law in the Fight Against Obesity: An Introductory Guide for the Pacific (World Health Organization report).

Terry Leahy is a Senior Lecturer in Sociology in the School of Social Sciences at the University of Newcastle, Australia. Among other things, he teaches the subject 'Environment and Society'. He is at present engaged in a study of the attitudes of Australians to environmental issues and environmental politics; this study is being conducted through in-depth interviews with individuals and focus groups. He has a long-standing interest in permaculture and intends to go on to conduct research into the use of permaculture in developing countries. One of his publications in the area of environment and society is 'Some Problems of Environmentalist Reformism' (*People and Physical Environment Research*, 1994, vol. 46, pp. 3–13).

Wm. Alex McIntosh is a Professor in the Departments of Sociology and Rural Sociology at Texas A&M University and is also a member of the Faculty of Nutrition. His book *Sociologies of Food and Nutrition* was published by Plenum in 1996. He contributed 'World Hunger as a Social Problem' to *Eating Agendas* (1995), 'Social Support, Stress, and Platelet Status of the Elderly' to *Applied Social Science* (1996), and 'An Application of the Health Belief Model to Reduction in Fat and Cholesterol Intake' to *Wellness Behavior* (1995).

Stephen Mennell is a Professor of Sociology at University College Dublin (the National University of Ireland, Dublin). From 1990 to 1993 he was a Professor of Sociology at Monash University, Melbourne. His many books include *All Manners of Food: Eating and Taste in England and France from the Middle Ages to the Present* (1985, 1996), *Norbert Elias: Civilisation and the Human Self-image* (1989, 1992), *The Sociology of Food: Eating, Diet, and Culture* (1992, with A. Murcott and A. H. van Otterloo), *The Norbert Elias Reader: A Biographical Selection* (1998, with J. Goudsblom), and *On Civilization, Power, and Knowledge: Selected Writings of Norbert Elias* (1998, with J. Goudsblom).

Elizabeth Murphy is a Senior Lecturer in the School of Social Studies at the University of Nottingham. She is director of a project, funded by the UK Economic and Social Research Council, entitled 'A Longitudinal Study of the Food Choices Made by Mothers on Behalf of Infants and Young Children'. She is the joint author of 'Food Choices for Babies' in *The Nation's Diet: The Social Science of Food Choice*. She has also recently directed a review of the application of qualitative methods to health care research. Her previous research has been concerned with lay concepts of health and illness and, in particular, chronic illness.

Jeffery Sobal is a nutritional sociologist who is an Associate Professor in the Division of Nutritional Sciences at Cornell University, New York, where he teaches courses that apply social science concepts, theories, and methods to food, eating, and nutrition. His research interests include the sociology of obesity and body weight, the food and nutrition system, and the food choice process. His recent work on body weight focuses on the relationship between marriage and weight and the construction of body weight as a social problem. He co-edited the book *Eating Agendas: Food and Nutrition as Social Problems* with Donna Maurer in 1995.

William C. Whit is the author of *Food and Society: A Sociological Approach* (1995). He is a co-founder of the Association for the Study of Food and Society (1986) and the editor of its newsletter. He is Associate Professor of Sociology at Grand Valley State University in Allendale, Michigan.

Deidre Wicks, formerly Senior Lecturer in Sociology at the University of Newcastle, Australia, is an independent social researcher now residing in Galway, Ireland. She is also an Associate Investigator in the Australian Longitudinal Study on Women's Health (ALSWH) at the Research Centre for Gender and Health, University of Newcastle. She has published in the areas of nursing and history, in particular writing the book *Nurses and Doctors at Work: Rethinking Professional Boundaries* (1999). Her current interests include work on the aspirations of a large cohort of young women in the ALSWH, and issues surrounding vegetarianism.

Lauren Williams is a Lecturer in Nutrition and Dietetics at the University of Newcastle, Australia. She has tertiary qualifications in science, dietetics, health promotion, and social science, and completed a PhD in the area of public health, examining weight gain in women at menopause. Lauren has long held an interest in the social aspects of nutrition and has undertaken collaborative research projects with sociologists, the most recent being in the area of women's dieting and body acceptance. Lauren previously worked in the health system, mostly in the area of community and public health nutrition, and continues to see clients as an Accredited Practising Dietitian (APD).

Acronyms and Abbreviations

ABS	Australian Bureau of Statistics
AGPS	Australian Government Publishing Service
ANZFA	Australia New Zealand Food Authority
ATSIC	Australian and Torres Strait Islander Commission
BMI	body mass index
BSE	bovine spongiform encephalopathy
Bt	*Bacillus thuringiensis*
CAC	Codex Alimentarius Commission
CHD	coronary heart disease
CJD	Creutzfeld-Jakob disease
COMA	Committee on Medical Aspects (UK)
CSA	Commodity Systems Analysis
CSIRO	Commonwealth Scientific and Industrial Research Organisation (Australia)
DAA	Dietitians Association of Australia
DES	diethyl stilboestrol
DGs	Dietary Guidelines
DHSS	Department of Health and Social Security (UK)
DNA	Deoxyribonucleic acid
EC	European Community
EPOS	electronic point of sales
ESRC	Economic and Social Research Council (UK)
FAO	Food and Agriculture Organization (United Nations)
FDA	Food and Drug Administration (USA)
FSANZ	Food Standards Australia New Zealand
g	gram
GM	genetically modified
GMO	genetically-modified organism
HFCS	High Fructose Corn Syrup
HMSO	Her Majesty's Stationery Office (UK)
HVFs	high value foods
IMF	International Monetary Fund
IT	information technology
JIT	Just-in-Time
JSCRS	Joint Select Committee on the Retailing Sector
KFC	Kentucky Fried Chicken
MAFF	Ministry of Agriculture, Fisheries and Food (UK)

mg	milligram
ml	millilitre
MRC	Medical Research Council (UK)
NAFTA	North American Free Trade Agreement
NFA	National Food Authority (Australia)
NGO	non-government organisation
NHMRC	National Health and Medical Research Council (Australia)
NLEA	Nutrition Labeling and Education Act (USA)
NTDs	neural tube defects
OMH	Office of Minority Health (USA)
OST	Office of Science and Technology (UK)
RDA	recommended dietary allowance
RDI	recommended dietary intake
SSHM	Society for the Social History of Medicine (UK)
USFDA	United States Food and Drug Administration
WHO	World Health Organization
WTO	World Trade Organization

Part 1
An Appetiser

We were compelled to live on food and water for several days.

W. C. Fields, *My Little Chickadee* (1940 film)

Beulah, peel me a grape.

Mae West, *I'm No Angel* (1933 film)

Good to eat, and wholesome to digest, as a worm to a toad, a toad to a snake, a snake to a pig, a pig to a man, and a man to a worm.

Ambrose Bierce, *The Enlarged Devil's Dictionary* (1967)

The aim of this book is to introduce a multidisciplinary readership to sociological enquiries into food, regardless of whether or not they have a sociology background. The first chapter maps the field of food sociology and provides an overview of the chapters in the book. It also provides a sociology 'refresher' for those with little or no sociology background, highlighting the distinctive features of the sociological perspective through the analytical framework of the sociological imagination template and giving numerous examples of the application of sociology to the study of food and nutrition. We trust that this section, by providing a taste of things of come, will whet your *social* appetite for exploring the sociology of food and nutrition.

1

Introducing the Social Appetite: Towards a Sociology of Food and Nutrition

John Germov and Lauren Williams

Overview

- Why do we eat the way we do?
- What is sociology and how can it be applied to the study of food and nutrition?
- What are the major social trends in food production, distribution, and consumption?

This chapter provides an overview of the sociological perspective as it applies to the study of food by introducing the concept of the social appetite. We explain how food sociology can help to conceptualise the connections between individual food habits and wider social patterns to explore why we eat the way we do. The chapter concludes by reviewing the major themes discussed in this book, highlighting the social context in which food is produced, distributed, and consumed.

Key terms

agency	food security/insecurity	social appetite
agribusiness	functional foods	social construction
body image	genetic modification	social differentiation
civilising process	globalisation	social structure
cosmopolitanism	McDonaldisation	sociological imagination
culinary tourism	public health nutrition	structure/agency debate
eating disorders	reflexive modernity	thin ideal
figurations	risk society	

Introduction: The social construction of food and appetite

> But food is like sex in its power to stimulate imagination and memory as well as those senses—taste, smell, sight ... The most powerful writing about food rarely addresses the qualities of a particular dish or meal alone; it almost always contains elements of nostalgia for other times, places and companions, and of anticipation of future pleasures.
>
> Joan Smith, *Hungry for You* (1997, p. 334).

We all have our favourite foods and individual likes and dislikes for certain tastes. Consider the tantalising smell of freshly baked bread, the lusciousness of chocolate, the heavenly aroma of espresso coffee, the exquisite sensation of semi-dried tomatoes, and the simple delight of a crisp potato chip. Food is one of the great pleasures of life and the focal point around which many social occasions and leisure events are organised. While hunger is a biological drive and food is essential to survival, there is more to food and eating than the satisfaction of physiological needs. There are also 'social drives', based on cultural, religious, economic, and political factors, that affect the availability and consumption of food. The existence of national cuisines, such as Thai, Italian, Indian, and Mexican (to name only a few), indicates that individual food preferences are not formed in a social vacuum. The link between the 'individual' and the 'social' in terms of food habits begins early: 'While we all begin life consuming the same milk diet, by early childhood, children of different cultural groups are consuming diets that are composed of completely different foods, [sometimes] sharing no foods in common. This observation points to the essential role of early experience and the social and cultural context of eating in shaping food habits' (Birch et al. 1996, p. 162).

Therefore, despite similar physiological needs in humans, food habits are not universal, natural, or inevitable; they are **social constructions**, and significant variations exist, from the sacred cow in India, to kosher eating among the orthodox Jewish community, to the consumption in some countries of animals that are kept as pets in other countries, such as dogs and horses. In Australia, the kangaroo may be on the coat of arms, but it is also a highly prized meat that is increasingly eaten in restaurants. Many indigenous peoples continue to consume traditional food; Australian Aboriginals, for example, consume 'bush foods' not often eaten by white Australians, such as witchetty grubs, honey ants, galahs, and turtles. Some cultures prohibit alcohol consumption, while others drink alcohol to excess, and many cultures have gendered patterns of food consumption (see Box 1.1). As Claude Fischler (1988) notes, food is a bridge between nature and culture, and food habits are learnt through culturally determined notions of what constitutes appropriate and inappropriate food, and through cultural methods of preparation and consumption, irrespective of the nutritional value of these foods and methods (see also Falk 1994).

Box 1.1 Gendered food habits

Gendered patterns of food habits can be observed in many cultures (DeVault 1991; Counihan 1999). Daily examples can be found in the widespread use of gender stereotypes in the advertising of certain food products. In Australia, over many years, the 'Meadowlea mum' commercials depicted a blissful mum who prepared home-cooked meals with margarine to serve her happy family. The Australian Meat and Livestock Corporation ran a popular 'feed the man meat' campaign complete with sing-a-long jingle, once again depicting dutiful mothers, this time preparing hearty meat-based meals for their growing sons and hard-working husbands. In 2003 in Australia, the hamburger chain Hungry Jack's promoted the short-lived 'Beefy big bloke burger'. The burger was in fact a long roll comprising manufactured meat, cheese, and sauce, and was advertised using working-class-looking 'beefy blokes' who apparently had little need for vegetables and few concerns about the fat content of their food. The Hooters restaurant chain, which originated in the USA in 1983, has over 330 stores, the selling point of which are the 'Hooters Girls'—young, attractive, large-breasted female waitresses dressed in a uniform of orange shorts and a white tight-fitting tank top. The company blatantly uses the sex appeal of scantily clad women to attract customers, 70% of whom it claims are men aged 25 to 54.

The sociology of food and nutrition, or food sociology, concentrates on the myriad sociocultural, political, economic, and philosophical factors that influence our food habits—what we eat, when we eat, how we eat, and why we eat. Sociologists look for patterns in human interaction and seek to uncover the links between social organisation and individual behaviour. Food sociology focuses on the social patterning of food production, distribution, and consumption—which can be conceptualised as the **social appetite**. The chapters in this book explore the various dimensions of the social appetite to show the ways in which foods, tastes, and appetites are socially constructed. However, the sociological perspective does not tell the whole story, which is rounded out by many other disciplines, including anthropology, history, economics, geography, psychology, **public health nutrition**, and social nutrition (including the study of food habits, food ideology, or 'foodways'). As Stephen Mennell notes in the Foreword to this book, sociological approaches are a relatively recent addition to the study of food. Despite the delayed interest, the last two decades have witnessed a significant surge in food sociology literature (see the Appendix for an extensive list of publications).

Studying food via the sociological imagination template

Before we can discuss how sociology can contribute to the study of food and nutrition, we need to provide an overview of the sociological perspective (with which some readers will already be familiar). In brief, sociology examines how society is organised, how it influences our lives, and how social change occurs. It investigates social relationships at every level, from interpersonal and small-group interactions to public policy formation and global developments. Sociology critiques explanations that reduce complex social phenomena to biological, psychological, or individualistic causes.

A sociological study of food habits examines the role played by the social environment in which food is produced and consumed. This does not mean that individual choice and personal taste play no role. Rather, because social patterns of food habits exist, a sociological explanation is helpful in understanding the social determinants of why we eat the way we do. If food choice

Box 1.2 The social construction of food and taste

Food is central to social life and it is perhaps this centrality that has resulted in potent food symbolism and connections with key social events, reflected in well-known books and films. The film *Eat, Drink, Man, Woman* explores the importance of food to family life and personal identity. *Babette's Feast* contrasts a pious lifestyle of moral austerity with the sensuality and carnality of food as a feast of sight, aroma, texture, and taste—a spiritual experience of worldly pleasure. *The Wedding Banquet* conveys the social meaning of food in the context of marriage rituals. Linda Jaivin's book *Eat Me* mixes erotica with the sensuality of food in what could be termed a new genre of 'food porn' if it were not for the long tradition of food advertisements that conflate the pleasures of sex and food—just think of any number of adverts about chocolate or ice-cream. Food is often used as a metaphor in daily speech, through sayings such as 'sweetheart', 'honey', 'bad seed', 'couch potato', 'breadwinner', and 'cheesed off', to name a few. Imagine some of the food rituals and food symbolism involved in the following social situations:

- a birthday celebration
- a wake
- a wedding banquet
- a religious feast or fast
- an occasion when you might exercise virtue and restraint in eating
- an occasion when you crave 'naughty but nice' food, your favourite food, or comfort food.

were totally based on individual or natural preferences for certain tastes, few people would persevere with foods such as coffee or beer, which are bitter on first tasting. These foods are said to be an 'acquired taste', and we 'acquire' them through repetition that is socially rather than biologically driven.

Charles Wright Mills coined the term **'sociological imagination'** to describe the way that sociological analysis is performed, defining it as 'a quality of mind that seems most dramatically to promise an understanding of the intimate realities of ourselves in connection with larger social realities' (1959, p. 15). Interpreting the world with the sociological imagination involves establishing a link between personal experiences and the social environment—that is, being able to imagine or see that the private lives of individuals can have a social basis. When individuals share similar experiences, a social pattern emerges that implies that such experiences have a common, social foundation. For example, food and eating are imbued with social meanings and are closely associated with people's social interaction in both formal and informal settings. Box 1.2 provides some everyday examples of the social construction of food, especially food symbolism, to highlight the value of exploring the social appetite.

To help operationalise the concept of the sociological imagination, Evan Willis (1999) outlined a four-part model consisting of historical, cultural, structural, and critical factors. When these four interrelated features of the sociological imagination are applied to a topic under study, they form the basis of sociological analysis. Figure 1.1 is a useful template to keep in mind when you want to apply a sociological perspective to an issue—simply imagine superimposing the template over the topic you are investigating and consider the following sorts of questions:

- **Historical factors:** How have past events influenced the contemporary social appetite (that is, current social patterns of food production, distribution, and consumption)?
- **Cultural factors:** What influence do tradition, cultural values, and belief systems have on food habits in the particular country, social group, or social occasion you are studying?

Figure 1.1 The sociological imagination template

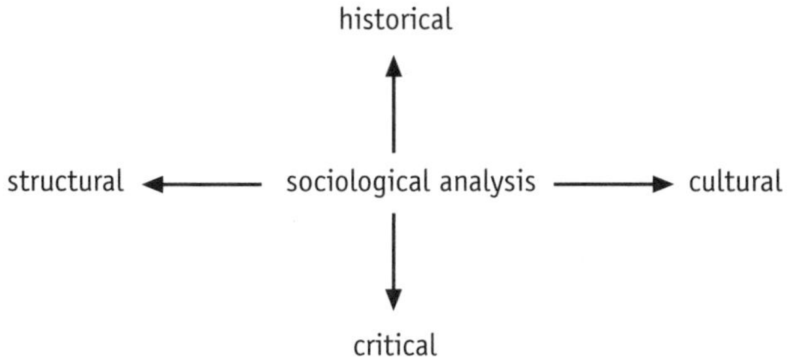

Source: Derived from Willis (1999)

- **Structural factors:** How do various forms of social organisation and social institutions affect the production, distribution, and consumption of food?
- **Critical factors:** Why are things as they are? Could they be otherwise? Who benefits?

Applying the sociological imagination template can challenge your views and assumptions about the world, since such 'sociological vision' involves constant critical reflection. By using the template, the social context of food can be examined in terms of an interplay between historical, cultural, structural, and critical factors. It is important to note, however, that the template necessarily simplifies the actual process of sociological analysis, because, for example, there a wide variety of research methods and social theories through which sociological analysis can be conducted. In practice, there can be considerable overlap between the four factors, and so they are not as distinctly identifiable as is implied by Figure 1.1. For instance, it can be difficult to clearly differentiate between historical factors and cultural factors, or structural factors and cultural factors, as they can be interdependent. Cultural values are often intricately intertwined with historical events and may also be the product of, or at least be reinforced by, structural factors. Nevertheless, the sociological imagination template is a useful reminder that the four factors—historical, cultural, structural, and critical—are essential elements of sociological analysis (see Box 1.3).

Box 1.3 Aboriginal food and nutrition: Applying the sociological imagination template

Until the colonisation of Australia by Europeans, Aboriginal and Torres Strait Islander people lived a healthy hunter–gatherer lifestyle. However, today they suffer from disproportionately high rates of many nutrition-related health conditions, such as Type 2 diabetes, iron-deficiency anaemia, low birth-weight and restricted child growth, cardiovascular disease, and overweight and obesity (Lee 2003). Applying the sociological imagination template highlights a number of issues.

Historical factors

Many indigenous communities were dispossessed of their hunting and fishing areas and forced to live on rations in missions and reserves. The historical legacy of these developments on Aboriginal food and nutrition was a change from a traditional nutrient-dense diet (bush foods) to a contemporary diet high in saturated fat and sugar and low in fruit and vegetables.

Cultural factors

While bush foods such as galahs, turtles, goannas, honey ants, and witchetty grubs represent only a small proportion of the food consumed by

Aboriginal people today, they remain an important part of indigenous culture, identity, and food preferences, particularly in rural and remote regions. Maintaining this cultural heritage and incorporating bush foods into nutrition-promotion strategies could help ameliorate the nutritional problems in indigenous communities.

Structural factors

Unemployment, low education levels, and poverty are disproportionately experienced by indigenous people. **Food insecurity** and the limited food supply in rural and remote areas (particularly in terms of access to fruit and vegetables, and fresh food in general), remain key factors in explaining and addressing the nutrition-related health problems experienced by indigenous people.

Critical factors

The *National Aboriginal and Torres Strait Islander Nutrition Strategy and Action Plan* (NATSINSAP), released in 2001 as part of the *Eat Well Australia* public health nutrition framework, is a significant attempt to address indigenous food and nutrition problems through a range of food-supply, food-security, and nutrition-promotion initiatives (SIGNAL 2001a, 2001b; for good overviews of this topic see NHMRC 2000; Lee 2003). Beyond public health nutrition approaches, a number of employment-generation schemes for indigenous communities have been attempted. For example, in recent years a 'bush tucker' industry has developed, marketing traditional foods (such as bush tomatoes and indigenous oils and spices) to the general community. While still in its infancy, the industry has received indirect government support through funding obtained from the Aboriginal and Torres Strait Islander Commission (ATSIC), though considerably more funds are needed for industry development, which could result in it becoming a significant source of employment for indigenous people.

Food sociology and the structure/agency debate

A key sociological question concerns the relative influence over human behaviour (in this case food choice) of personal preferences and social determinants. To what extent are our food choices the result of social shaping as opposed to individual likes and dislikes? This represents a central concern of any sociological study, and is often referred to as the **structure/agency debate**. The term **social structure** refers to recurring patterns of social interaction by which people are related to each other through social institutions and social groups.

For example:

- The type of economy we have influences the type of agricultural production system adopted (with the consequent environmental implications, as discussed in Chapter 3).
- The increase in immigration, transport, communication, and multinational companies in the last century has influenced the eating patterns of many countries (see Chapters 11 and 13).
- Changing social values have increased the prominence of certain social groups with distinct eating patterns, such as vegetarians (see Chapter 12).

In this sense we are very much products of our society, in that certain forms of social organisation, such as laws, education, religion, economic resources, and cultural beliefs, influence our lives. However, as self-conscious beings, we have the ability to participate in and change the society in which we live. The term **'agency'** refers to the potential of individuals to independently exercise choice in and influence over their social world and their daily lives. While we are born into a world that is not of our making and must learn the 'social rules' to survive and prosper, we are not simply automatons responding to some preordained social program. Human agency produces the scope for difference, diversity, and social change.

It is important to note that structure and agency are inextricably linked—they should not be viewed as representing an either/or choice or as inherently positive or negative. The social structure may liberate individuals by ensuring access to inexpensive food, while the exercise of agency by individuals may be constraining on others—for example, someone may steal your food! As George Ritzer puts it, '[a]ll social action involves structure, and all structure involves social action' (1996, p. 529). Rather than thinking of social structure as a fixed entity, Anthony Giddens suggests conceiving it as 'recurrent social practices' (1989, p. 252). The interdependence of structure and agency is succinctly expressed by Norbert Elias's (1978) concept of **figurations**, which are 'social processes involving the "interweaving" of people. They are *not* structures that are external to and coercive of relationships between people; they *are* those relationships' (Ritzer 1996, p. 512). The figurational approach conceptualises structure and agency as dynamic and as operating through people's daily practices and routines. Elias uses the example of sporting games to explain his concept of figurations: individuals playing a game of football are aware of the rules of the game and the roles they must play—the players are interdependent as the game would not work otherwise—yet they all still possess agency and indeed their choices and actions are crucial for the game to work. Another example is the experience of dining out in restaurants. While diners exercise their agency by choosing food from the menu, social conventions of manners and public eating mean that individuality is suppressed and diners conform to expected modes of interaction, custom, and fashion (see Finkelstein 1989). It is in this dynamic and interdependent way that Elias's concept of figurations suggests we should think about structure and agency. The concept of figurations avoids the tendency towards dichotomous thinking in the structure/agency debate; figurations are the social patterns of human relationships, and reflect particular social, cultural, economic, and political arrangements. Ultimately, they are contingent on the particular time and culture in which they occur, often changing in response to conflict and competition between social groups, and in response to wider socioeconomic and political factors.

Exploring the social appetite: What's on the menu?

The chapters in this book have been grouped into four themes that dominate the sociological literature: the food system, food and public health nutrition, food and social differentiation, and food and the body. However, we do not propose that this classification scheme is an exhaustive or static depiction of the sociology of food, nor do we dispute that there are grey areas, and areas of overlap between the themes. Nonetheless, we believe these to be the dominant themes in the social appetite of advanced capitalist societies. The themes are discussed briefly here to provide an overview of the structure and content of the book.

The food system: Globalisation, McDonaldisation, and agribusiness

> If commercial interests make people's tastes more standardised than they conceivably could in the past, they impose far less strict limits than did the physical constraints to which most people's diet was subject … the main trend has been towards *diminishing contrasts and increasing varieties* in food habits and culinary taste.
>
> Stephen Mennell, *All Manners of Food* (1996, pp. 321–2)

Table 1.1 Share of export food trade by country, in value terms (2001)

Rank	*Country*	*Share (%)*
1	USA	12.6
2	France	7.9
3	Netherlands	6.5
4	Germany	6.2
5	Canada	5.0
6	Belgium	4.5
7	Spain	4.4
8	Italy	4.0
9	Brazil	3.9
10	China	3.6
11	Australia	3.3

Source: Adapted from Department of Agriculture, Fisheries and Forestry (2003, p. 9)

The increasing mass production and commodification of food over the last century has resulted in food being one of the largest industries across the globe, with world food trade estimated to be over US$404 billion per year (DAFF 2003). Australia is the eleventh largest food exporter in the world overall, and seventh largest exporter of minimally processed foods such as grains, nuts, shellfish, fruit, and vegetables (see Table 1.1).

Food is a major source of profit, export dollars, and employment, and thus concerns a range of stakeholders, including corporations, unions, consumer groups, government agencies, and health professionals. To conceptualise the size of the food industry or food system, various models have been proposed, such as food chains, food cycles, and food webs (see Sobal et al. 1998 for an excellent review).

Box 1.4 The McDonaldisation of the World: The 'Beeg Meck' in Russia

The McDonaldisation of food is a global phenomenon and represents the expansion of agribusiness through the standardisation of food production and the homogenisation of food consumption. Ritzer, in *The McDonaldization of Society*, first published in 1993, used the term 'McDonaldisation' as a modern metaphor for '*the process by which the principles of the fast-food restaurant are coming to dominate more and more sectors of American society as well as the rest of the world*' (2000, p. 1, italics in original). McDonald's is a prototype organisation that has been able, through rigid methods of managerial and technical control, to achieve a highly rationalised form of food production: no matter where in the world you come across a McDonald's restaurant, you can be assured of encountering the same look, the same service, the same products, and the same tastes. Not only are there now many other food chains based on the same formula, but, as Ritzer states, there are also fewer and fewer places where you can avoid the McDonald's experience:

> There, in the heart of Moscow, stood the new McDonald's. Musovites are attracted to it in droves for a variety of reasons, not the least of which is the fact that it is *the* symbol of the rationalization of America and its coveted market economy. The rationality of McDonald's stands in stark contrast to the irrationalities of the remnants of communism. Long lines and long waits (so much for fast food) are common, but one sunny Saturday in May the line stretched as far as the eye could see. In fact, teenagers were offering, in exchange for a few roubles, to get you a 'Beeg Meck' in no more than 10 or 15 minutes. Russians are in a headlong rush toward McDonaldization, seemingly oblivious to its potential problems.

Ritzer 1993, pp. xii–xiii

Figure 1.2 The Australian food system and beyond

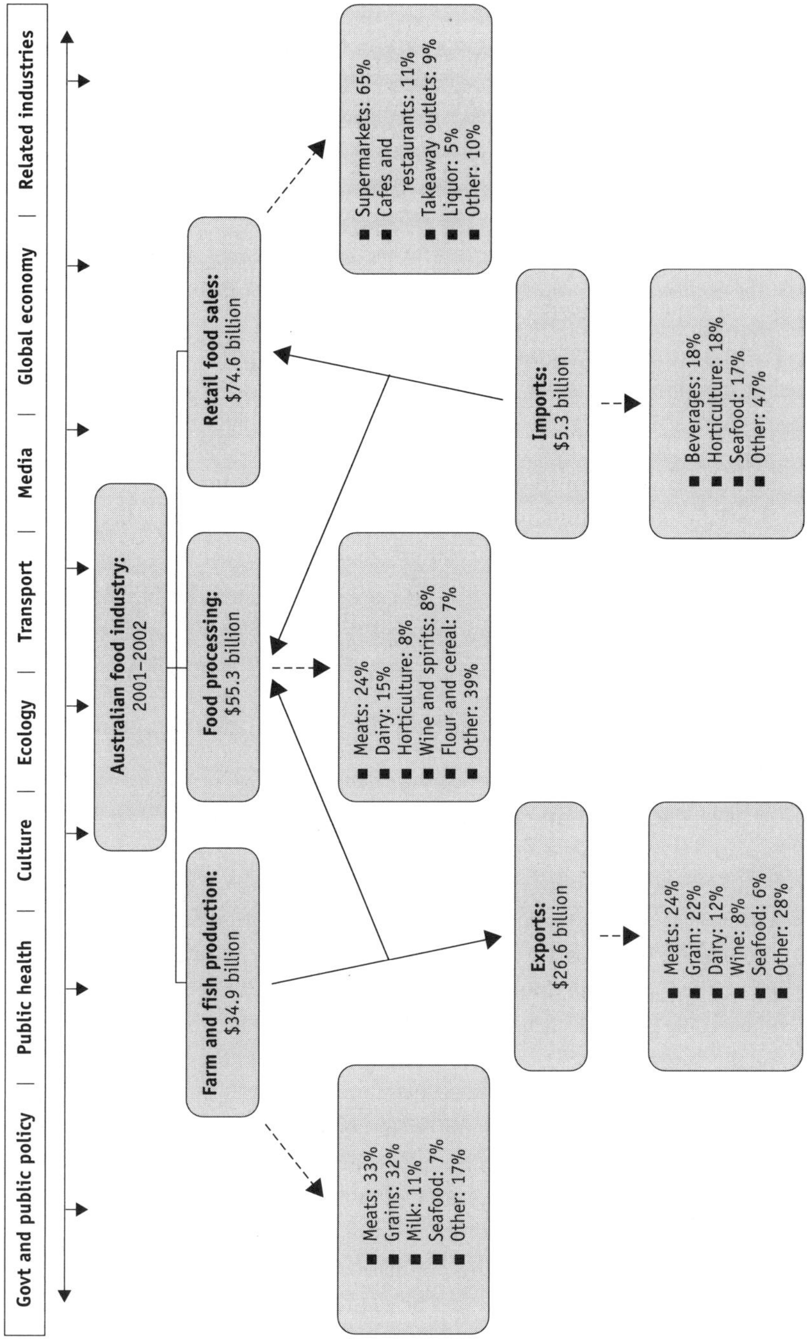

Source: Adapted from Department of Agriculture, Fisheries and Forestry (2003, p. 1)

Figure 1.2 provides a snapshot of the Australian food system, using a food web model to highlight the economic value of the key sectors of farm and fishery production, food processing, and food retailing (supermarkets, restaurants, takeaway shops, and liquor outlets), including exports and imports. Around 45% of all retail spending in Australia in 2001–02 was on food and liquor, accounting for almost $75 billion. Food exports were valued at $26.6 billion, and food processing accounted for $55.3 billion (and at June 2001 employed over 187,000 people) (DAFF 2003).

Food system models invariably simplify the operations involved in the production, distribution, and consumption of food, often failing to take account of the global, political, cultural, and environmental concerns, or the related stakeholders and industries, such as the media, waste-management, advertising, transport, and health sectors. These broader global, social, political, and ecological factors are noted in Figure 1.2, and this book is dedicated to examining these influences more fully. Part 1 of the book explores some of the key sociological issues affecting the food system, particularly the impact of **globalisation**, **McDonaldisation** (see Box 1.4), and **agribusiness** (see Schlosser 2001). Specifically, this part investigates the inequitable distribution of food as the basis of world hunger, the environmental impact of current agricultural practices, the increasing power of food corporations stemming from the **genetic modification** of food, and the dominating influence of supermarket chains on how food is produced and consumed.

Food and public health nutrition: Discourses, politics, and policies

> The only way to keep your health is to eat what you don't want, drink what you don't like, and do what you'd rather not.
>
> Mark Twain, *Following the Equator* (1897)

Given that food is a major industry and source of profit, it should come as little surprise that it is also an area rife with politics and debates over public policy, particularly over food regulation relating to hygiene standards, the use of chemicals, pesticide residues, the legitimacy of advertising claims, and various public health nutrition (PHN) strategies. PHN focuses on the population as a whole and aims to ensure the availability of safe and nutritious food, to improve the health and nutritional status of the general community as well as vulnerable subgroups of the population (such as the poor, indigenous groups, and children) (SIGNAL 2001a). PHN strategies are wide-ranging, from addressing food hygiene and **food security** to promoting improved nutritional knowledge and dietary behaviours among the population at large (SIGNAL 2001a, 2001b).

As Table 1.2 shows, there has been a vast array of national and international PHN developments in the last two centuries. Australia was an early leader in the field, with a number of pioneering food laws, such as the *Pure Food Act*

1905 (Vic.), which was used as a model by other countries to address food hygiene problems, set production standards, and regulate the adulteration of food. Recent years have witnessed a significant increase in PHN developments, such as the *World Declaration and Plan of Action for Nutrition* (WHO & FAO 1992), issued jointly by the World Health Organization (WHO) and the United Nations' Food and Agriculture Organization (FAO). The declaration aims to address global food security and lessen the impact of diet-related illness, though there has been little progress since its inception, with over 799 million people estimated to be undernourished in developing countries in 2002 (FAO 2002). At a national level, many countries have introduced food and nutrition policies, dietary guidelines, food standards codes, and health promotion strategies, such as *Eat Well Australia* (SIGNAL 2001a).

Table 1.2 Key public health nutrition legislation, reports, and events

Year	*Legislation, reports, and events*
1838	*Adulteration of Bread Act 1838* (NSW)
1863	*Act to Prevent the Adulteration of Articles of Food and Drink 1863* (Vic.)
1901	Under the Australian Constitution, food regulation is a state/territory matter
1905	*Pure Food Act 1905* (Vic.): other Australian states follow suit over the next 5 years
1936	National Health and Medical Research Council (NHMRC) established: its brief is to improve individual and public health, foster health research, training, and consideration of ethical issues, and develop health standards, such as the Dietary Guidelines and Recommended Dietary Intakes (RDIs)
1961	Codex Alimentarius Commission established by the United Nation's Food and Agriculture Organisation (FAO): produces voluntary international food standards and codes of practice
1971	*Dietary Allowances for Use in Australia* (developed by NHMRC)
1979	*Dietary Goals and Guidelines for Australians*
1980	*US Dietary Guidelines*
1980–89	All Australian states and territories enact new Food Acts based on the Model Food Act agreed upon by a Conference of Health Ministers: the Acts cover labeling, hygiene, and regulation
1986	First Australian *Food Standards Code* (NHMRC)
	Ottawa Charter for Health Promotion (WHO)
1991	*National Food Authority Act 1991*
	Recommended Dietary Intakes for Use in Australia (currently under review)
	Sundsvall Statement on Supportive Environments for Health (WHO)
1992	*World Declaration and Plan of Action for Nutrition* (WHO & FAO)
	Australian Food and Nutrition Policy
	Dietary Guidelines for Australians (2nd edn)

1994	*Australia's Food and Nutrition* (Lester 1994)
1995	*Dietary Guidelines for Children and Adolescents* (Aust.)
1997	*Australia New Zealand Food Authority Act (No. 2) 1997*: National Food Authority (NFA) becomes Australia New Zealand Food Authority (ANZFA) to reflect increased cooperation on food regulation with New Zealand
	Acting on Australia's Weight: A Strategic Plan for the Prevention of Overweight and Obesity (NHMRC report)
	Jakarta Declaration on Leading Health Promotion into the 21st Century (WHO)
1997–99	National Nutrition Survey: various reports on data collected in 1995 (ABS)
1998	Australian Guide to Healthy Eating
1999	*Dietary Guidelines for Older Australians*
2000	*Australia New Zealand Food Standards Code* (revised)
	ANZFA's *Safe Food Australia* guidelines
2001	ANZFA becomes Food Standards Australia New Zealand (FSANZ)
	Eat Well Australia, a national public health nutrition strategy including the *National Aboriginal and Torres Strait Islander Nutrition Strategy and Action Plan*
2003	*Dietary Guidelines for Adult Australians* (3rd edn) and *Dietary Guidelines for Children and Adolescents in Australia* (2nd edn)
	Expert Report on Diet, Nutrition and the Prevention of Chronic Disease (WHO & FAO)
	A Growing Problem: Trends and Patterns in Overweight and Obesity Among Adults in Australia (AIHW)

Sources: Commonwealth of Australia (2001); SIGNAL (2001a, 2001b); Wahlqvist & Kouris-Blazos (2002)

An examination of the development and implementation of food policy exposes some of the individualistic assumptions and corporate interests that have swayed the good intentions of government authorities and health professionals attempting to address public health nutrition. An example of the influence of the food industry can be seen in the *Australia New Zealand Food Standards Code*, the revised and retitled version of which was phased in from the year 2000. During the code's revision, there was intense political lobbying regarding the labelling of genetically modified (GM) food and the right of food manufacturers to make specific health claims on certain products, often referred to as **functional foods** (see Chapter 6). After initial indications from regulatory agencies that GM food would not need to be labelled in Australia, a public backlash ensued and the decision was overturned, with a similar policy adopted to that of the European Union, but the opposite to what has occurred in the USA, where labelling of GM food is not mandatory.

The importance of a food standards code cannot be understated in terms of regulating industry and setting appropriate public health standards, though it would be naive not to realise that outcomes in this field are often a compromise. Take, for example, the humble meat pie and the food standard related to

Box 1.5 The Aussie meat pie and the definition of 'meat'

The quintessentially Australian meat pie—one of the earliest fast foods in Australia—was actually inherited from the British. Its popularity reflected the wide availability of meat in Australia, its simple flavours (meat and gravy encased in pastry), and its ability to be eaten with the hands, which made it a popular convenience food, especially at sporting occasions such as the football. The industrialisation and mass production of the meat pie has caused much speculation about its actual ingredients, particularly about how much meat and what types of meat it contains. The Australian Consumers' Association (2002) reported in its magazine, *Choice*, that meat pies may contain a minimum of 25% actual meat. However, it is the definition of 'meat' that is of particular interest. Standard 2.2.1 (Meat and Meat Products) of the Australian New Zealand Food Standards Code defines meat as 'the carcass of any buffalo, camel, cattle, deer, goat, hare, pig, poultry, rabbit or sheep, slaughtered other than in a wild state'. So not only can a meat pie include very little actual beef, but it can include animal rind, fat, gristle, connective tissue, nerve tissue, blood, and blood vessels under the label of 'meat' (offal must be listed separately in the ingredients list). This means that muscle meat—what people normally consider to be meat—may not even be included in a meat pie. Furthermore, meat content is measured by the presence of protein and this can be 'beefed up' by adding soy products (ACA 2002).

the definition of 'meat', which makes it possible for buffalo, camel, deer, and gristle, animal rind, and connective tissue to find their way into a meat pie (see Box 1.5). The chapters in this part of the book examine the role of food regulations in relation to functional foods, the corporate influences on dietary guidelines, public health nutrition as an influential field of professional practice, and food discourses and policies relating to the feeding of infants and children.

Food and social differentiation: Consumption and identity

> Tell me what you eat, and I shall tell you what you are.
>
> Jean Anthelme Brillat-Savarin, *The Physiology of Taste* (1825)

As Deborah Lupton notes, food is often defined as 'good or bad, masculine or feminine, powerful or weak, alive or dead, healthy or non-healthy, a comfort or punishment, sophisticated or gauche, a sin or virtue, animal or vegetable' (1996, pp. 1–2). These opposing attributes illustrate the social meanings, classifications, and emotions that people can attach to food and use to define who they are. As Pierre Bourdieu (1979/1984) noted, traditional modes of social distinction based on class have persisted. Therefore, the theme of food and social differentiation encapsulates food habits that are influenced by various forms of social group membership, whether based on traditional social cleavages or new social movements.

People in Western societies are presented with a large number of consumption choices, which can be used to construct their self-identity. People can seek to differentiate themselves from others or, alternatively, convey their membership of a particular social group through their food consumption (among other things). Ordering a vegetarian meal, eating a meat pie, dining at a trendy cafe, and eating an exotic cuisine may be used and interpreted as social 'markers' of an individual's social status or group membership. Thus, food and eating experiences can be used as a form of social differentiation, whereby particular food choices are used to construct and reinforce individuals' self-identity and social group membership (see Box 1.6). This part of the book addresses the relationship between social groups, food consumption, and identity formation, with chapters on class-based food habits, vegetarianism, culture and ethnicity, and ageing.

Box 1.6 The 'slow food' and 'true food' social movements

The Slow Food Movement began in Italy in 1986 as a response to the mass production and globalisation of food. It claims to have over 60,000 members worldwide and it aims to 'counter the tide of standardization of taste' by promoting and cataloguing traditional, regional, and national cuisines, including endangered animal breeds, vegetable species, and cooking techniques. Using the emblem of the snail and calling themselves 'eco-gastronomes', members take a stand against the fast-food industry and work to protect food traditions, historic sites (cafes and bistros), and agricultural heritage (biodiversity, artisan techniques, and sustainable agriculture). The Slow Food Movement promotes its aims by funding research, conferences, and festivals, by publishing material, and by lobbying governments and corporations. Along similar lines but for vastly different reasons, the 'True Food Network', coordinated by Greenpeace, campaigns specifically against genetically engineered food, and, in addition to its lobbying efforts, produces consumer guides on obtaining food free of genetic modification. For more information about these social movements and their food ideologies, see the following web sites:
Slow Food: www.slowfood.com/
True Food Network: www.greenpeace.org.au/truefood/

Food and the body: Civilising processes and social embodiment

> You are what you eat.
>
> Anonymous

The adage 'you are what you eat' was originally intended as a nutrition slogan to encourage healthy eating, but today the meaning has changed as the focus has moved away from the internal health of the body to the external 'look' of the body. The final theme explored in the book concerns the impact of health, nutrition, and beauty discourses on body management. The name of the well-known company Weight Watchers symbolises the body discipline and surveillance that is now commonly practised in Western societies in efforts to conform to a socially acceptable notion of beauty and **body image**—a process that can be referred to as 'social embodiment', whereby the body is both an object and a reflective agent (Connell 2002). Attempts to regulate the body are gendered through the social construction of the **thin ideal** for women. While external pressures from the media and corporate interests play a key role in the construction and maintenance of such discourses, they are also internalised and reproduced by individuals—an example of what Elias termed **'civilising processes'**, whereby social regulation of individual behaviour is no longer achieved through external coercion but through moral self-regulation.

Attempts to rationally manage and regulate the human body mean that for many people the pleasures of eating now coexist with feelings of guilt. While food companies encourage us to succumb to hedonistic temptations, health authorities proclaim nutritional recommendations as if eating is merely an instrumental act of health maintenance. The social-control overtones of such an approach are clearly evident in the 'lipophobic' (fear of fat) health advice given by some health professionals. Changes in the advice of health authorities over the decades and the simplification of scientific findings into media slogans, mixed with the contra-marketing efforts of food companies, have served to create confusion over whether certain foods, particularly those marketed as 'low fat' or 'lite', are in fact health-promoting (see Box 1.7). While some people have become disciplined adherents to the new health propaganda, others have become increasingly sceptical of nutrition messages—particularly in light of the 'French paradox', or the fact that the French have lower rates of cardiovascular disease than Australians and Americans despite having a higher intake of saturated fat, which undermines simple causative links between fat consumption and heart disease (Renaud & Logeril 1992; Drewnowski et al. 1996). This part of book discusses the discourses related to eating and the disciplining of the body in the context of gender, dieting, body image, eating disorders, and obesity stigmatisation.

Box 1.7 'Lite' foods, balance, and increasing obesity rates

Despite the increasing consumption of low-fat foods, rates of overweight and obesity continue to rise in many Western countries—a fact that should caution against any simplistic beliefs that low-fat foods can be used to control weight (Allred 1995). The latest estimates suggest that over 300 million adults worldwide are obese, three million of them Australians (Dixon & Waters 2003; WHO 2003). Using data derived from height and weight measurements, in 1999–2000, of those Australian adults aged 25–64 years, 17% of men were obese (up from 9% in 1980) and 20% of women were obese (up from 8% in 1980). Internationally, this places Australia's obesity rate approximately 4 percentage points below the rate of the USA and UK, but about double the rate in Italy and France (Dixon & Waters 2003).

While so-called 'light foods' are marketed for dieting and weight-maintenance purposes, Claude Fischler (1995) argues that people seek increased pleasure through the inclusion of light foods in addition to, rather than as a replacement for, other foods in the diet (possibly allowing them to eat more). For example, it is not uncommon for people to use artificial sweetener in their coffee so that they can have a slice of chocolate mud cake, or to purchase diet cola with a hamburger, giving a sense of dietary 'balance'. The commonsense notion of a 'balanced' diet is highly variable, but may be defined as a balance between 'good' and 'bad' choices, hedonism and discipline, healthy and unhealthy food (Fischler 1988).

Future directions: Reflexive modernity and the rise of food cosmopolitanism

There is no sincerer love than the love of food.

George Bernard Shaw, *Back to Methuselah* (1930)

While the meal-in-a-pill idea never quite took off (see Belasco 2000), the belief in technological progress in the sphere of food has always been viewed as a double-edged sword. The original TV series of *Star Trek* made much fun of the tasteless food of the future. Brightly coloured marshmellow-like cubes, with each colour representing a different taste (green for peas, yellow for chicken, and so on) pointed to a highly technological future in which food had lost all connection with its origins. In the newer series of *Star Trek*, the unappetising cubes had been surpassed by 'replicator' technology through which matter is instantly reconstituted into any food or cuisine from across the universe. While the technological reality of the early twenty-first century is less impressive, there have been significant improvements in agricultural methods, storage, mass production, and transport that have given people—in developed countries at least—access to a growing variety of foods and cuisines from across the globe. Yet with the industrialisation and globalisation of food have come ecological problems, food safety concerns, the threat of standardisation and homogenisation of taste, rising rates of obesity, and the persistence of food insecurity in both developed and developing countries.

A walk down the aisle of any supermarket reveals food products that were not widely available even two decades ago. French cheese, Russian caviar, Indian spices, Thai coconut cream, Belgium chocolate, and Australian macadamia nuts are a small indication of the extent of social change in food habits. In restaurants and cafes in major urban areas, people can now partake of global cuisines such as Chinese, Indian, Thai, Italian, Greek, and French. In fact, **culinary tourism**, the promotion of gastronomic experiences and events as a key feature of tourism (such as regional food festivals and foodstuffs), has become increasingly popular (Rojek & Urry 1997), particularly amid calls for a return to authenticity and regionality in food and cooking (Symons 1993).

The processes of mass production and globalisation have resulted in such a pluralisation of food choices and hybridisation of tastes and cuisines that a form of food **cosmopolitanism** is emerging (Tomlinson 1999; Beck 2000). The popular description of modern Australian cuisine as 'Australasian' is just one example of this cosmopolitan trend, which implies that a more complex scenario has emerged than the dire prediction of McDonaldisation suggests. Anthony Giddens and Ulrich Beck both argue that contemporary social life is characterised by **reflexive modernity** (Beck et al. 1994). According to Giddens, people's exposure to new information and different cultures undermines traditions, so that 'lifestyle choice is increasingly important in the constitution of self-identity and daily activity' (1991, p. 5). For Fischler this can result in the omnivore's paradox, whereby when faced with such food variety and novelty 'individuals lack reliable criteria to make … decisions and therefore they experience a growing sense of anxiety' (1980, p. 948), or what he playfully refers to as gastro-anomie. In the face of food-borne diseases, such as 'mad cow disease', resulting from modern industrial and agricultural processes, the wide variety of food choices coexist with increased risk and anxiety over what to eat (Lupton 2000), the constant management of which Beck (1992) describes as characteristic of a **risk society**.

While this book represents an academic enquiry into food, we would like to acknowledge the passion, delight, and pure hedonism with which food is intimately associated. In that light and in the spirit of cosmopolitanism, we end this chapter with the following excerpt from Marcel Proust, which encapsulates the central role of food as part of *la dolce vita*:

> She sent for one of those squat, plump little cakes called 'petites madeleines', which look as though they had been moulded in the fluted valve of a scallop shell. And soon, mechanically, dispirited after a dreary day with the prospect of a depressing morrow, I raised to my lips a spoonful of the tea in which I had soaked a morsel of the cake. No sooner had the warm liquid mixed with the crumbs touched my palate than a shiver ran through me and I stopped, intent upon the extraordinary thing that was happening to me. An exquisite pleasure had invaded my senses, something isolated, detached, with no suggestion of its origin. And at once the vicissitudes of life had become indifferent to me, its disasters innocuous, its brevity illusory—this new sensation having had the effect, which love has, of filling me with a precious essence; or rather this essence was not in me, it *was* me. I had ceased now to feel mediocre, contingent, mortal. Whence could it have come to me, this all-powerful joy? I sensed that it was connected with the taste of the tea and the cake, but that it infinitely transcended those savours, could not, indeed, be of the same nature. Where did it come from? What did it mean? How could I seize and apprehend it?
>
> Marcel Proust, *Swann's Way* (1913/1957)

Summary of main points

- Food sociology challenges individualistic accounts of people's eating habits that assume that personal likes and dislikes primarily govern food choice.
- The 'social appetite' refers to the social context in which food is produced, distributed, and consumed, the context that shapes our food choices.
- Sociology examines how society works, how it influences our lives, and how social change occurs. It adopts a critical stance by asking questions such as these: Why are things as they are? Who benefits? What are the alternatives to the status quo?
- Evan Willis suggests that the sociological imagination—or thinking sociologically—is best put into practice by addressing four interrelated facets of any social phenomena: historical, cultural, structural, and critical factors.
- The concept of figurations allows us to conceptualise human behaviour—in particular the way we eat—in terms of the interplay between social structure and human agency.
- Food cosmopolitanism is an increasing feature of contemporary social life in developed societies.

Discussion questions

1 How can food and taste be socially constructed? Give examples.
2 What is meant by the term 'social appetite'?
3 Consider the social meanings and symbolism in the examples of the social appetite in Box 1.1. What other examples can you think of?
4 Think of the influences that have shaped your own food habits and likes and dislikes by imagining a social occasion at which food is consumed (such as a birthday party or Christmas celebration). Apply the sociological imagination template to explore the significance of the occasion, noting for each factor the influences on your food consumption:
   - Historical: When did you first eat that way? What past events have influenced the social occasion?
   - Cultural: What customs or values are involved? Who prepares and serves the food, and with whom is it consumed? Why?
   - Structural: In what setting does the food event occur? What role do wider social institutions or organisations play?
   - Critical: Has the particular event changed over time or not? Why?

Further investigation

1 Food choice is not simply a matter of personal taste, but reflects regional, national, and global influences. Discuss.
2 Given that social patterns of food production, distribution, and consumption exist, to what extent are individuals responsible for their food choices?

Further reading and web resources

An extensive list of books and web sites can be found in the Appendix, but as a starting point here are some publications by the contributors to this book, followed by some distinctly Australian contributions.

Almas, R. & Lawrence, G. (eds) 2003, *Globalization, Localization and Sustainable Livelihoods*, Ashgate, Aldershot, UK.

Coveney, J. 2000, *Food, Morals, and Meaning: The Pleasure and Anxiety of Eating*, Routledge, London.

Crotty, P. 1995, *Good Nutrition? Fact and Fashion in Dietary Advice*, Allen & Unwin, Sydney.

Dixon, J. 2002, *The Changing Chicken: Chooks, Cooks and Culinary Culture*, University of New South Wales Press, Sydney.

Hepworth, J. 1999, *The Social Construction of Anorexia Nervosa*, Sage, Thousand Oaks, Calif.

McIntosh, Wm. A. 1996, *Sociologies of Food and Nutrition*, Plenum Publishing, New York.

Maurer, D. & Sobal, J. (eds) 1995, *Eating Agendas: Food and Nutrition as Social Problems*, Aldine de Gruyter, New York.

Mennell, S. 1996, *All Manners of Food: Eating and Taste in England and France from the Middle Ages to the Present*, 2nd edn, University of Illinois Press, Chicago.

Mennell, S., Murcott, A. & van Otterloo, A. H. 1992, *The Sociology of Food: Eating, Diet and Culture*, Sage, London.

Whit, W. C. 1995, *Food and Society: A Sociological Approach*, General Hall, New York.

Australian sources

Australian Bureau of Statistics (ABS) (various years), *National Nutrition Survey*, ABS, Canberra.

Bannerman, C. (ed.) 1998, *Acquired Tastes: Celebrating Australia's Culinary History*, National Library of Australia, Canberra.

Commonwealth of Australia 2001, *Food Regulation in Australia: A Chronology*, Department of the Parliamentary Library, Canberra.

Department of Agriculture, Fisheries and Forestry 2003, *Australian Food Statistics 2003*, Department of Agriculture, Fisheries and Forestry, Canberra.

Dyson, L. E. 2002, *How to Cook a Galah: Celebrating Australia's Culinary Heritage*, Lothian Books, Melbourne.

Finkelstein, J. 1989, *Dining Out: A Sociology of Modern Manners*, Polity Press, Cambridge.

Lester, I. H. 1994, *Australia's Food and Nutrition*, Australian Government Publishing Service, Canberra. Available online at www.aihw.gov.au/publications/health/afn94/index.html.

Probyn, E. 2000, *Carnal Appetites: Food, Sex, Identities*, Routledge, London.

Riddell, R. 1989, *Food and Culture in Australia*, Longman Cheshire, Melbourne.

Santich, B. 1995, *What the Doctors Ordered: 150 Years of Dietary Advice in Australia*, Hyland House, Melbourne.

Symons, M. 1993, *The Shared Table: Ideas for an Australian Cuisine*, Australian Government Publishing Service, Canberra.

—— 1982, *One Continuous Picnic: A History of Eating in Australia*, Duck Press, Adelaide.

Wahlqvist, M. L. (ed.) *Food and Nutrition: Australasia, Asia and the Pacific*, 2nd edn, Allen & Unwin, Sydney.

Web sites

See the Appendix for a large list of food-related web sites. Some key sites can be accessed from the supporting web site for this book: go to au.oup.com/content/General.asp?Content=compsite.

References

ACA—*see* Australian Consumers' Association.

Allred, J. 1995, 'Too Much of a Good Thing?', *Journal of the American Dietetic Association*, vol. 95, pp. 417–18.

Australian Consumers' Association 2002, 'Meat Pies? Well, Sort of …', *Choice*, April, pp. 8–10.

Beck, U. 1992, *Risk Society: Towards a New Modernity*, Sage, London.

Beck, U. 2000, 'The Cosmopolitan Perspective: On the Sociology of the Second Age of Modernity', *British Journal of Sociology*, vol. 51, pp. 79–106.

Beck, U., Giddens, A., & Lash, S. 1994, *Reflexive Modernization: Politics, Tradition and Aesthetics in the Modern Social Order*, Polity Press and Blackwell Publishers, Cambridge.

Belasco, W. 2000, 'Future Notes: The Meal-in-a-Pill', *Food and Foodways*, vol. 8, no. 4, pp. 253–71.

Birch, L. L., Fisher, J. O. & Grimm-Thomas, K. 1996, 'The Development of Children's Eating Habits', in H. L. Meiselman & H. J. H. MacFie (eds), *Food Choice, Acceptance and Consumption*, Blackie Academic and Professional, London.

Bourdieu, P. 1979/1984, *Distinction: A Social Critique of the Judgement of Taste* (trans. by R. Nice), Routledge, London.

Connell, R. W. 2002, *Gender*, Polity Press, Cambridge.

Counihan, C. M. (ed.) 1999, *The Anthropology of Food and Body: Gender, Meaning and Power*, Routledge, New York.

DAFF—*see* Department of Agriculture, Fisheries and Forestry.

Department of Agriculture, Fisheries and Forestry 2003, *Australian Food Statistics 2003*, Department of Agriculture, Fisheries and Forestry, Canberra.

DeVault, M. L. 1991, *Feeding the Family: The Social Organization of Caring as Gendered Work*, University of Chicago Press, Chicago.

Dixon, T. & Waters, A.-M. 2003, 'A Growing Problem: Trends and Patterns in Overweight and Obesity Among Adults in Australia, 1980 to 2001', Bulletin No. 8, Australian Institute of Health and Welfare (Cat. No. AUS 36), Canberra.

Drewnowski, A., Henderson, S. A., Shore, A. B., Fischler, C., Preziosi, P. & Hercberg, S. 1996, 'Diet Quality and Dietary Diversity in France: Implications for the French Paradox', *Journal of the American Dietetic Association*, vol. 96, pp. 663–9.

Elias, N. 1978, *The Civilizing Process* (trans. by E. Jephcott), Blackwell, Oxford.

Falk, P. 1994, *The Consuming Body*, Sage, London.

FAO—*see* Food and Agricultural Organisation.

Finkelstein, J. 1989, *Dining Out: A Sociology of Modern Manners*, Polity Press, Cambridge.

Fischler, C. 1988, 'Food, Self and Identity', *Social Science Information*, vol. 27, no. 2, pp. 275–92.

—— 1980, 'Food Habits, Social Change and the Nature/Culture Dilemma', *Social Science Information*, vol. 19, pp. 937–53.

—— 1995, 'Sociological Aspects of Light Foods', in P. D. Leathwood, J. Louis-Sylvestre & J.-P. Mareschi (eds), *Light Foods: An Assessment of their Psychological, Sociocultural, Physiological, Nutritional, and Safety Aspects*, International Life Sciences Institute Press, Washington, DC.

Food and Agricultural Organisation (FAO) 2002, *State of Food Insecurity in the World 2002*, FAO, Rome.

Giddens, A. 1991, *Modernity and Self-identity: Self and Society in the Late Modern Age*, Stanford University Press, Stanford, California.

Lee, A. 2003, 'The Nutrition of Aboriginal and Torres Strait Islander Peoples', in National Health and Medical Research Council (NHMRC), *Dietary Guidelines for Adult Australians*, NHMRC, Canberra.

Lupton, D. 1996, *Food, the Body and the Self*, Sage, London.

—— 2000, 'Food, Risk and Subjectivity', in S. J. Williams, J. Gabe & M. Calnan (eds), *Health, Medicine and Society*, Routledge, London, pp. 205–18.

Macinnis, P. 2002, *Bittersweet: The Story of Sugar*, Allen & Unwin, Sydney.

Mennell, S. 1996, *All Manners of Food: Eating and Taste in England and France from the Middle Ages to the Present*, 2nd edn, University of Illinois Press, Chicago.

Mills, C.W. 1959, *The Sociological Imagination*, Oxford University Press, New York.

Mintz, S. 1985, *Sweetness and Power: The Place of Sugar in Modern History*, Penguin, New York.

—— 1998, 'Sweet Polychrest', *Social Research*, vol. 66, no. 1 (titled 'Food: Nature and Culture', ed. by A. Mack), pp. 85–101.

National Health and Medical Research Council 2000, *Nutrition of Aboriginal and Torres Strait Islander Peoples: An Information Paper*, NHMRC, Canberra.

NHMRC—*see* National Health and Medical Research Council.

Proust, M. 1913/1957, *Swann's Way* (trans. by C. K. Scott Moncrieff), Penguin Books, Harmondsworth.

Renaud, S. & de Logeril, M. 1992, 'Wine Alcohol, Platelets, and the French Paradox for Coronary Heart Disease', *Lancet*, vol. 339, pp. 1526–32.

Ritzer, G. 2000, *The McDonaldization of Society*, 3rd edn, Pine Forge Press, Thousand Oaks, California.

—— 1996, *Sociological Theory*, 4th edn, McGraw-Hill, New York.

Rojek, C. & Urry, J. (eds) 1997, *Touring Cultures: Transformations of Travel and Theory*, Routledge, London.

SIGNAL—*see* Strategic Inter-Governmental Nutrition Alliance.

Smith, J. (ed.) 1997, *Hungry for You: From Cannibalism to Seduction—A Book of Food*, Vintage, London.

Sobal, J., Khan, L. K. & Bisogni, C. 1998, 'A Conceptual Model of the Food and Nutrition System', *Social Science & Medicine*, vol. 47, no. 7, pp. 853–63.

Strategic Inter-Governmental Nutrition Alliance 2001a, *National Aboriginal and Torres Strait Islander Nutrition Strategy and Action Plan, 2000–2010*, National Public Health Partnership, Canberra.

—— 2001b, *Eat Well Australia: A Strategic Framework for Public Health Nutrition 2000–2010*, National Public Health Partnership, Canberra.

Symons, M. 1993, *The Shared Table: Ideas for an Australian Cuisine*, Australian Government Publishing Service, Canberra.

Tomlinson, J. 1999, *Globalization and Culture*, Polity, Cambridge.

Turner, B. S. 1997, 'From Governmentality to Risk: Some Reflections on Foucault's Contribution to Medical Sociology', in A. Petersen & R. Bunton (eds), *Foucault, Health and Medicine*, Routledge, London, pp. ix–xxi.

Veblen, T. 1899/1975, *The Theory of the Leisure Class*, Allen & Unwin, London.

Warde, A. 1997, *Consumption, Food and Taste*, Sage, London.

WHO & FAO—*see* World Health Organization & Food and Agriculture Organization.

Willis, E. 1999, *The Sociological Quest*, 3rd edn, Allen & Unwin, Sydney.

World Health Organization 2003, *Obesity and Overweight (fact sheet)*, WHO, Geneva

World Health Organization & Food and Agriculture Organization 1992, *World Declaration and Plan of Action for Nutrition*, WHO, Geneva.

World Health Organization & Food and Agriculture Organization 2003, *Expert Report on Diet, Nutrition and the Prevention of Chronic Disease*, WHO, Geneva.

Part 2

The Food System: Globalisation, McDonaldisation, and Agribusiness

> We are who we are because we are all things to all people all the time everywhere.
>
> Ike Herbert, head of Coca-Cola USA, 1990, quoted in Mark Pendergrast, *For God, Country and Coca-Cola* (1993, p. 398)

> People often feed the hungry so that nothing may disturb their own enjoyment of a good meal.
>
> Somerset Maugham, *A Writer's Notebook* (1949)

In this part of the book we discover why something as innocuous as choosing certain foods can be a politicised act with global consequences. Food is a highly profitable commodity and the pursuit of profit has significant implications for the way food is produced and distributed. Yet food is also an essential commodity—people must literally eat to live—and it therefore has fundamental humanitarian value. In developed countries, the wide availability of food is taken for granted by most, except those in poverty. The unequal distribution of food is also played out on a global scale, and for a large proportion of the world's population hunger is a way of life, with acute periods of starvation occurring in times of famine or political unrest.

The chapters in Part 2 cover the major influences on the food system, in terms of globalisation, McDonaldisation, and agribusiness, by focusing on world hunger, the environment, the development of genetically modified food, and the power of supermarkets in the food commodity chain. Specifically, this section consists of four chapters:

- Chapter 2 outlines a range of perspectives that attempt to explain the persistence of world hunger, and discusses the viability of proposed strategies for ensuring that every human has enough food.
- Chapter 3 explains how the dominant mode of agricultural production in developed countries, driven by the profit imperative, causes environmental degradation; it also examines a number of environmentally sustainable alternatives.

- Chapter 4 highlights the global nature of agribusiness by exploring the use of biotechnology to develop genetically modified foods.
- Chapter 5 examines the increasing power of supermarket chains over Australia's food system and their influence on culinary culture and food habits via a case study of the rise in popularity of chicken meat.

2

World Hunger

William C. Whit

Overview

- How did the world come to tolerate hunger in the midst of plenty?
- How widespread is hunger? What causes it?
- How can the problem of world hunger be fixed? Will it ever be?

This chapter examines a number of different perspectives that attempt to explain world hunger. It documents the extent of hunger and then provides a typology of conservative/neo-liberal, liberal, and Western neo-Marxist analyses and proposed solutions. While conservatives express qualified satisfaction with present arrangements, liberals propose reforms that work within present world socioeconomic systems. Only neo-Marxists propose real structural change that would actually result in access to food for every human.

Key terms

biotechnology
capitalism
class
colonialism
commodification
conservatism
cultural relativism
developed world/ developing world
ethnocentric
globalisation
green revolution
liberalism
materialist
multinational oligopolies
neo-liberalism
neo-Marxism
socialism
state
transnational corporations

Introduction

Most people believe that there is just not enough food to go around. Yet:

> The world is producing, each day, two pounds of grain, or more than 3000 calories for every man, woman and child on earth … 3000 calories is about what the average American consumes. And this estimate … does not include the many other staples such as beans, potatoes, cassava, range-fed meat, much less fresh fruits and vegetables. Thus, on a global scale, the idea that there is not enough food to go around just doesn't hold up.
>
> Food and Agriculture Organization, quoted in Lappe & Collins 1977, p. 13

What is more:

> Forty years ago the Nazis killed six million people. At the Nuremberg trials those responsible claimed they could not personally be blamed, that it was the 'system', that the decisions were made higher up. This was not accepted: they were condemned. Today it is a question of perhaps 20 million dying *every year*. These deaths from starvation are also the result of a system of deliberate policies. What can we say of those, in government, business or international agencies, who operate this system, which results in these deaths?
>
> Buchanan 1982, p. 113

Amid a variety of attempts to define hunger, the following definition probably best suits our purposes: hunger is 'inadequacy of dietary intake relative to the kind and quantity of food required for growth, activity, and maintenance of good health' (Millman & Wikates 1990, p. 3). Most importantly, hunger is generally involuntary and usually chronic.

According to the Food and Agricultural Organization (FAO) of the United Nations, in the **developing world**, the 'number of undernourished people is actually growing … [and] literally millions of people, including six million children under the age of five, die each year as a result of hunger … one in seven children born in the countries where hunger is most common will die before reaching the age of four' (FAO 2002, p. 1). These countries and regions include Sub-Saharan Africa, the Near East and North Africa, Latin America and the Caribbean, India, the Pacific, and China. The total number of undernourished people in the developing world now stands at 799 million and is increasing (FAO 2002).

In addition to depriving people of energy to work, malnutrition causes specific nutritional deficiencies. Before the twentieth century, these usually took the form of:

- beri-beri—a lack of B vitamins (often the result of eating white, rather than brown, rice)

- scurvy—vitamin C deficiency (often resulting from a failure to consume enough fresh fruit)
- pellagra—a niacin deficiency (often the result of eating a diet based on corn and sorghum)
- rickets—lack of exposure to adequate sunlight (which converts ergosterol in the skin and activates vitamin D).

Scrimshaw 1990

But today's hunger-induced vitamin deficiencies often have other effects. Generally, malnourished or food-deprived people:

- give birth to infants who are underweight, often resulting in stunted growth (24 million infants, or 16% of the world's infants).
- are underweight for their age (168 million children, or 31% of the world's children under 5 years of age) (Chen 1990, p. 9).
- suffer from iodine deficiency (210 million people, or 4% of the world's population). Most of those who are iodine deficient are Asian. Chen writes that '190 million suffered from goiter, the enlargement of their thyroid glands (and emic goiter), which may be accompanied by reduced mental function, lethargy, and inbred fetal and infant mortality' (1990, p. 11). This also decreases resistance to infections.
- suffer from iron deficiency (700 million people, or 13% of the world's population). Nevin Scrimshaw (1990, p. 359) estimates that one-third of the population of developing countries are affected, resulting in lowered learning ability, work performance, and resistance to infection, plus fatigue, dizziness, and breathlessness after exertion (FAO 2002, p. 24).
- suffer from vitamin A deficiency. Often coming in the aftermath of pervasive diarrhoea in the developing world, vitamin A deficiency causes partial or total blindness, and increases the 'risk of respiratory infection and the incidence of complications from measles' (Chen 1990, p. 11). Between 100 and 140 million children suffer from vitamin A deficiency (FAO 2002, p. 24).

The most extreme cases of hunger involve protein or calorie malnutrition (also known as 'protein-energy malnutrition') and usually affect small children. One type of protein-energy malnutrition is *kwashiorkor,* which is the 'name used to describe the disease that occurs when a child is displaced from the breast by another baby. It involves moderate to severe growth failure and muscles that are poorly developed and lack tone ... resulting in a large pot belly and swollen legs and face. The child has profound apathy and general misery; he or she whimpers but does not cry or scream' (Bryant et al. 1985, pp. 289–90). *Marasmus* is a condition resulting from a lack of calories. It involves extreme growth failure and generally occurs in a child's first year. The child appears extremely emaciated.

If, as Francis Moore Lappe and Joseph Collins claim, there is enough food for everyone, how does hunger persist? We must understand that, as Millman writes, 'the history of hunger is embedded in the history of plenty' (1991, p. 3). The overriding issue in relation to contemporary hunger is that adequate nutrition can be derived from grains, but 40% of the grain grown in the world is fed to livestock to produce high-priced meat (*The Politics of Food* 1987). In a global transnational capitalist system impelled by profit, food goes to those who can afford to pay for it. Often they are the fast-food customers in the **developed world**. Only the few remaining **socialist** societies seek to provide food as a fundamental right, and with the increasing **commodification** of food in these societies, hunger may become a problem once again.

Box 2.1 Breastfeeding

No one disputes the superior health benefits of mother's milk over cow's milk. As Sara Millman of Brown University's Alan Shaw Feinstein World Hunger Program writes, 'Breast-feeding nourishes very young children, minimises the exposure to environmental contaminates, provides some defense against infection and contributes to a relatively favorable pattern of birth spacing that in turn can have an important positive effect on the health of both your children and their siblings' (1991, p. 91).

In unsanitary and very low-income conditions, breast milk provides a child with many immunities through antibodies from the mother. And it prevents the diarrhoea that is almost universal in the developing world. This malady kills many babies by preventing the absorption of nutrients from food. Unfortunately, the **multinational oligopolies** have sought a new market for infant formula in the developing world. They advertise on radio and billboards. They make sure that samples of infant formula are dispensed in hospitals. In 1977, Nestlé Corporation was employing 4,000–5,000 'mothercraft advisors in nurse-like uniform' (Lappe & Collins 1977, p. 315). They were often given salaries and commissions.

This advertising has combined with the use of infant formula by many middle-class and working mothers to make it a status symbol of Western life. Just as eating McDonald's is a status symbol for the USA's urban poor, so feeding one's baby on Western infant formula has become a mark of status in the developing world. Unfortunately, the living conditions of those on a low income make infant formula a cause of death. If not used, a mother's natural milk dries up, necessitating the continued use of formula milk, and the cost of formula may consume up to half a poor family's food budget. Because of the expense, uneducated families may dilute the formula with water to make it go further. This situation soon leads to serious malnutrition and death. While infant formula instructions advise strict sterility, this is often not possible in places with polluted water supplies and limited cooking facilities. In addition, many of the developing world's poor are illiterate. Because they cannot read, they cannot follow the directions. And even if they could, they often lack the education to understand the importance of a germ-free environment. In this context, infant formula becomes 'nutricidal'.

In 1974, the British group War on Want began an international campaign against Nestlé with its pamphlet 'Nestlé kills babies' (Lappe & Collins 1977, p. 311). The worldwide boycott of Nestlé forced the corporation to curtail this kind of infanticide. But recently Nestlé has started marketing formula in the developing world again, and the boycott has been reinstituted.

Conservative analyses and prescriptions

In *Food, Poverty, and Power*, Anne Buchanan (1982) reproduces a cartoon that reads, 'Starvation is God's Way of Punishing Those Who Have Little or No Faith in Capitalism'. **Conservative** analysts of world hunger have generally seen a (Judaeo-Christian) form of divine providence in the suffering of the poor: 'The poor ye shall always have with you' (Matthew 26: 11). This is an **ethnocentric** position that generally justifies the suffering from hunger on some combination of victim-blaming, theological, value-based, and demographic grounds.

Garrett Hardin (1978) provided the classic demographic justification for doing nothing. His argument rests on an analogy between the Earth and a lifeboat. Each has a limited carrying capacity. Overloading causes catastrophe for all. Therefore, those in the developed world who now control 'lifeboat Earth' should not permit alleviation of hunger. To do so would create too many people (overloading the lifeboat) and decrease the quality of our lives. This argument relies on ethical assumptions that the present world system is 'right' and that we in the West, as the world's dominating force, have a responsibility to keep the 'lifeboat' from overloading with other (minority) 'races' and **classes**.

Demographically, Hardin implores us to 'guard against boarding parties' (1978, p. 75), which could take the form of much higher reproductive rates in developing countries. His work is informed by Thomas Malthus's 1798 *An Essay on the Principle of Population*, which took the position that, at the then current rate of growth, population size—and the corresponding demand for food—would soon outstrip food production. According to Malthus, food production grows arithmetically while population grows geometrically. In this context, Garrett Hardin argues against a world food bank, which would create a means of sustaining people who might otherwise perish from 'natural' causes. He detects the profit motive of private business in the USA's food aid efforts.

In addition, he identifies a desire for cheap labor as the motive in **liberal** demands for increased immigration quotas (1978, p. 79).

The second major conservative argument for the continuation of hunger and malnutrition is one that subverts the **cultural relativism** upon which liberal social scientists tend to pride themselves. Consequently, conservatives maintain that an unprejudiced attitude would see us respect the peasant values of the developing world rather than imposing our values on them. And, they argue, those peasant values are one source of hunger and malnutrition—an essentially victim-blaming account. In addition, Hardin believes that the issue of hunger is one of 'slovenly rulers' and incompetent governments that do not plan for lean years. In *Famine in Peasant Societies*, Ronald Seavoy (1986) continues the values-based argument. He characterises the peasant mentality as 'survivalist'. Peasants work only to subsist (not to grow rich) and to allow for indolence. In fact, the 'peasants will not be motivated by commercial social values until political power is used to destroy the communal institutions that protect the subsistence compromise' (1986, p. 378).

Claire Cassidy (1982) proposes a similar value- or culture-grounded argument in her analysis of weaning customs that may 'potentiate' malnutrition in non-industrialised societies. In the context of her general (liberal) concern for the hungry and malnourished, she shows that many peasant customs (such as early weaning and a preference for large families) have a latent function of 'potentiating' malnutrition, while their manifest function is to socialise and display love for children. Cassidy also echoes Hardin's argument when she says that malnutrition serves to limit population growth and eliminate those biological organisms that are not strong enough to endure the malnutrition and hardships caused by certain socieites' inadequate food supply. She writes: 'the experience of malnutrition in early childhood may also be adaptive in the sense that it biases developmental plasticity toward the hunger-resistant' (1982, p. 333). She refers to this process (echoing Edward Banfield in *The Unheavenly City*, 1974) as 'benign neglect'.

While Hardin truly is a conservative, Cassidy justifies her excursion into conservative territory by her interest in providing more successful nutrition programs. She argues that if nutritionists understand the role of values in developing societies, they can structure truly effective programs for alleviating hunger. While Seavoy and Cassidy rightly explore the role of values in 'traditional' societies, they both fail to come to terms with the aetiology of values and the manner in which they change.

'Value longevity' has been the traditional conservative explanation of most social customs. Banfield argues that the values of the lower class inhibit self-improvement—and those values are passed down through the 'culture of poverty' in North America. Values such as 'a taste for excitement', 'immediate gratification', and 'timelessness' will go on forever among the poor. Therefore, one should do nothing. From a critical **materialist** perspective, values are responses to material situations. The fact that people in 'traditional' societies hold many values in common reflects a collective response to the common conditions of pre-commercial horticultural or agrarian society.

Having large families is a good example. Ronald Seavoy argues that 'large families are desired in peasant societies because child labor allows parents to enjoy indolence' (1986, p. 20). Leisure values motivate high birth rates. In contrast, materialists argue that high birth rates function in poor societies as a system of social security. By having a large number of (especially male) children, parents increase the chances of being adequately supported in old age. Demographers speak of the 'fertility transition'. About 40 years after a country 'develops', the birth rate generally drops. From a materialist point of view, there is a new material reality to adapt to. Developed societies generally have social-security systems that fulfil the function of large families. In addition, developed societies are often predominantly urban. Children, who are positively functional for an agrarian society (they can do many farming tasks), are an economic burden in the city.

Drawing on traditional sociology, we can use the notion of 'cultural lag' (a term coined by William Ogburn) to explain the values aspect of this transition. Because values are an adaptive response, they change slowly. Generally, one's personal values are formed mostly by the onset of adulthood. These values form the basis of one's adult personality. But when material conditions change (a social-security system is implemented, or immigrants come to a different society, for instance), the second generation is the locus of a change in values. Having grown up with a social-security system an in an urban environment, it makes more adaptive 'sense' to have (and to value) a small family.

As for Banfield's analysis of the 'culture of poverty', how does one explain the continuing tendency of some people in the developed world to have large families? First, many poor families in the West are still rural. Extra hands are still needed on farms. And among the urban poor, welfare payments alone provide such a limited retirement income that some people still believe that a large family will be of benefit in old age. In fact, low-income families are more mutually supporting than middle-class families (again, out of material necessity—more support is needed).

In summary, conservatives such as Hardin (1978) generally support hunger as being useful in a potentially overpopulated world. They justify their position on the grounds of protecting the existing elite and of the defective value systems of the malnourished and hungry. They 'blame the victims' of poverty and malnutrition. The conservative solution to world hunger is to allow it to continue. While thinking themselves to be personally compassionate, conservatives support institutional economic exploitation and neglect of the problems of the poor, hungry, and malnourished. Their prescription for social change is to have none—even at the cost of 20 million lives a year.

Liberal analyses and prescriptions

Liberals traditionally lean towards technological manipulation and political 'reforms'. Perhaps the best-known sociologists who view technology as the key to human evolution are Gerhard and Jean Lenski (1982). They analyse human development from the perspective of food-growing technologies. They identify four categories of food production technology: hunting and gathering, horticultural, agrarian, and industrial. In the area of hunger, Esther Boserup provides the technological explanation. Blending demography with technologies in food production, she argues that 'population growth itself stimulates agricultural innovation and leads to production increases that more than keep up with population' (Crossgrave et al. 1990, p. 224).

The technology of food production is the key. Instead of being a contained 'lifeboat', the lifeboat (the world's resources) may now be expanded as a result of a technological fix. The **green revolution** and **biotechnology** (as well as some birth control) are the current technological focuses of liberal hopes to solve world hunger. Like conservatives, liberals (and **neo-liberals**, whose theories and policies return to the original 'liberal' principles advanced by philosophers such as Locke, Mills, and Smith, only now with a capitalist slant) assume the essential goodness of the world economic system. However, unlike conservatives, they maintain that with a bit of technological tinkering and spin-doctored policy reform, the world can alleviate food shortages.

Historically, the USA and its **transnational corporations** have structured and profited from international trade policies ostensibly committed to alleviating world hunger. In the last half century there has evolved a globalised system that has effectively enriched many US transnational corporations in the North and actively inhibited development in most of the countries of the South.

Using Bretton Woods institutions, founded in 1944, the Northern nations worked through the International Monetary Fund (IMF) and what became the World Bank. For the USA, this organisation lent funds so the Southern countries could purchase US surplus grain (under Public Law 480). As Dan Morgan writes:

> PL 480 was advertised as an aid program for foreign countries, but above all it provided assistance to American farmers and the grain trade. Foreign governments received authorization from the US government to purchase, with American loans, certain quantities of American farm commodities and foreigners handled the actual transactions, contracting with private exporters to obtain the goods. But payment for these

> goods actually went straight from the US Treasury to commercial banks in the United States and then to the private exporters. The foreign governments had the obligation to repay the loans, but the terms provided grace periods and long maturities.
>
> Morgan 1980, pp. 147-8.

Formal **globalisation** is now the defining dynamic. In the mid 1980s, the IMF and the World Bank made 'structural adjustment' programs the vehicle for a process of free-market 'liberalisation' that was applied across the board to developing Southern economies seeking loans (Bello 2001, p. 6). Motivated by its ability to facilitate developing countries repaying their loans, the program forced the elimination of much governmental social expenditure (a universal safety net) and decreased wages and indigenous state-directed development. Increasing trade 'liberalisation' was imposed.

Compounding the problems caused by the dumping of Northern grain surpluses into the markets of indigenous Southern producers, structural adjustment programs undercut and ruined local economies, destroyed genetic crop directly, and eliminated the possibility of serious development of indigenous agricultural and food products. In India, the substitution of wheat and soybeans for such indigenous grains as jawar, bajra, dal, sesame, linseed, and millet eliminated entire sections of the local economies. In addition, it created more expensive tastes for imported grains. As Bello writes, 'Northern producers that make a mockery of free trade in agriculture fight for developing country markets to support the increasingly productive [and heavily subsidized] US agricultural sector' (Bello 2001, p. 4).

Evolving out of the Global Agreement on Trade and Tariffs (GATT) in the Uruguay Round in 1995, trade-related investment measured (TRIMs), and trade-related property rights (TRIPs), the World Trade Organization (WTO) has proved the most devastating reversal for the countries of the South. Not only is the 'consensus' decision making of the WTO manipulated by the G7/G8 countries (United States, Canada, Germany, France, Britain, Italy, Japan, and Russia), but the WTO has supported policies that even further reduce any possibility of development by the countries of the South. Among these is the acceptance of US patent laws on biological creations based on genetic material often pirated from the biodiversity of the South. This means that only transnational corporations can receive the profits from patents in crops that were formerly grown locally in developing countries.

For instance, because bio-engineered seed is somewhat more productive (though more expensive), Monsanto has included a 'terminator' gene to forestall small farmers' universal practice of saving seeds for the next year's crops. The increased productivity eliminates little farmers, with their diverse varieties of seed, from competition. Instead of re-circulating profits into the local economy, the proceeds are funnelled into the coffers of transnational corporations that own the patents. As a result, local farmers fall into debt, hunger, and death. For example, record numbers of farmer suicides (500 a year) have been documented in the Warangal district of India (Shiva 2000, p. 95). No matter what liberal illusion the ruling states in the West and their transnational corporations attempt to create, the actual result is that they increase poverty, hunger, and death.

Western neo-Marxist analyses and prescriptions

By way of introduction, it should be made clear that a Western **neo-Marxist** analysis of the world hunger problem is not an analysis from the perspective of the former Soviet Union or Eastern Bloc. It has very little to do with the 'state capitalist' or 'coordinator' societies that existed in Eastern Europe before the current movement towards **capitalism**. Instead, a modern Western neo-Marxist analysis participates in the intellectual tradition that has variously also been called 'critical sociology', 'dialectical, materialistic, political economy', 'world systems theory', and 'radical' analysis. All relate to an intellectual position from which one looks at the political structure in relation to the economy before one looks at the societal norms, ideas, values, and ideologies. This perspective assumes that the more important aspects of the social system are to be found in the qualitative analysis of the economy and the manner in which politics and ideology generally flow from it.

Western neo-Marxists have usually been critical of the authoritarian and anti-democratic practices of many supposedly 'socialist' regimes, such as the former Soviet Union. At the same time, it is only in countries that have claimed to be socialist that we have seen serious attempts to create economic structures that depart from the contemporary norm of global capitalism.

In the developing world, it is only in these socialist countries that effective attempts have been made to alleviate the problem of hunger. Politically, these countries range from the autocratic, one-party dictatorship of China through communist Cuba to the innovative, freely elected communist-party government in the State of Kerala in India. While Western neo-Marxists may have criticisms of the political character of some of these states, they also appreciate their success in solving the problem of hunger as a result of the economic structures they have instituted.

From this perspective, the economic system is composed of two parts: ownership patterns and technology. In the world capitalist system, the basic ownership pattern is that private capitalist elites in transnational corporations in the North own most of the productive apparatus in the world. Workers (including agricultural workers) sell their labour power to them in one form or another. The profit that accumulates in this process flows predominantly to the elites of both the developed Northern Hemisphere and the developing Southern Hemisphere. These elites have similar interests in extracting surplus value from workers—regardless of the costs to their countries or their own environments. In this world system, capitalist transnational oligopolies own and control most of the significant productive apparatus that related to food. These technologies involve land, farming machinery, farm chemicals, seed, and knowledge. These oligopolies also conduct research, biased towards their interests, on future profitable technologies of food production.

Political economists approach food shortages from a historical perspective in which the problem of food, poverty, and hunger is rooted in **colonialism** (see Friedman 2002). Most indigenous peoples knew how to produce enough food for themselves. The groups that did not perished. In the eighteenth century new capitalists encircled the globe. Great Britain, France, and Spain staked out claims to a large part of the world's land. Although this process was often ideologically justified in terms of bringing Christianity and Western civilisation to the 'heathens', it actually brought mountainous profits to the entrepreneurs who invested in it. Some critics of colonialism are fond of saying that the missionaries brought the Bible to the new lands. When they were through, the 'natives' had the Bible, and the missionaries had the land.

This political-economy perspective characterises the government (or state) as generally subservient to the demands of its leading class—that is, the capitalists. The capitalist class provides the funds to finance the election campaigns of people who will represent their interests and who will goad their governments into providing legitimacy and protection for their foreign ventures. These 'democracies' are designed to appear democratic, but in fact they act predominantly in the interests of the capitalist class. In what is now the Southern developing world, the colonial plantation pattern often dominated. For instance, sugar became the principal product imported into Great Britain from the British Caribbean. It both enriched the capitalist class and impoverished the diet of the British industrial working class (Mintz 1985; Whit 1995, Chapter 3). Government-sanctioned slavery created much of the early capital of the imperial European powers by means of the triangular trade in sugar and slaves.

The nineteenth century brought many struggles for political independence throughout the developing world. The subsistence economies of these countries had already been reorganised as plantations, and they did not return to subsistence economic production. Instead, the pattern of ownership switched from colonialism to neo-colonialism. Instead of having British administrators (as in India), local governments ruled in name while private foreign companies employing local elites dominated the economies, especially the agricultural sector. Instead of producing food for the local populations, imperial nations often employed local administrators to produce export crops. Tea (in India) and sugar (in the Caribbean) continued to be sent back to the imperial countries for processing. Thus developed a division of land and labour that characterised relations between the developed and the developing world to this day. Raw materials (which have lower profits) come from the developing world. The developed world imports raw materials and processes them. It is in the latter processes that the greater share of profit is to be found.

Andre Gunder Frank (1969) termed this process 'the development of underdevelopment'; the developed world essentially inhibits indigenous development and keeps the developing world producing raw materials for export. In those instances where food crops are processed locally, foreign stockholders generally own the processing companies, so that the profits are repatriated to the capitalist elites of the developed world. The new development in the twentieth century was the growth of transnational world oligopolies in the food sector: 'Companies such as Cargill, Continental Grain (both American) and Bunge (Argentina), Dreyfus (France) and Andre-Garnac (Switzerland) have an almost total monopoly on the US grain trade' (Bennet & George 1987, p. 177).

It is important to recognise a pervasive pattern in the developed world's treatment of colonial and subsistence food-production patterns. This pattern is analysed most extensively in the publications of the Institute for Food Development Policy, formerly headed by Frances Moore Lappe and Joseph Collins. Their 1977 book *Food First* traced the development of this pattern in country after country in the developing world. We shall refer to this analysis as the 'Lappe–Collins paradigm'.

According to this paradigm, transnational corporations enter a developing country in search of what all capitalists seek: high profits. Because most of the developing world is not highly industrial, the choice area of profit generation is the agricultural sector. Whereas before the oligopolists' entry peasants may have been successfully producing the nutritionally adequate subsistence crops that they have always eaten, the newcomers now gain control over the land on which this production has taken place. In the best of cases, they buy it. But sometimes they simply employ local thugs to murder or move the owners (*The Politics of Food* 1987). Regardless, the company gains control of the land. Because the world market is their target, they grow whatever agricultural commodity will sell the most profitably on the world market. It may be flowers for Europe, coffee for North America, or bananas, strawberries, sugar, vegetable oils, or oranges. A very important need in the developed world is grain to feed cows. The beef of the developing world is a major part of the United States's fast-food industry (Heller 1985). Because land in the developing world comes relatively cheap, there is little ecological concern. Although it is true of capitalist agriculture generally that it has tended to ruin the land (Whit 1995, Chapter 8), in the developing world the land has been exploited particularly severely. In Costa Rica, a leading exporter of beef to the USA, land is overgrazed and therefore environmentally ruined. As a result, many governmental administrators and local owners are cutting down rainforests to convert them to grazing land. Rainforests contain a large number of potential medical substances that have yet to be researched. R. W. Franke and B. H. Chasin report that one-quarter of Central American rainforests have been destroyed and only half a million of several million plant species have been saved: 'The relationship between ecological destruction and food production is ... direct and close. Whenever an environment is degraded, deprived of its basic resources—or even one of the key resources—the environment becomes part of the world food crisis, and the people who live there become its victims' (Franke & Chasin 1980, p. 4).

The lot of the original farmers is even more discouraging. Whereas a country may have previously had a stable rural labouring population, now they are displaced. Of those who choose to stay on the land, some are hired back to work for the corporation that now owns it. Because they no longer produce their own food, they must purchase food they previously produced. This practice often gets them further into debt. It is reminiscent of the system of debt peonage in the USA after the formal demise of slavery. Both the displaced and the remaining agricultural workers end up hungry.

Displaced workers flee to the city as beggars, prostitutes, and thieves. Those workers who are employed by the new large-scale, capitalist farming enterprises usually make only subsistence wages, often not enough to even feed their families. And, if the international market decreases the value of their agricultural product, they become landless wanderers. This also happens when the soil is depleted from the use of farming technologies that are only geared to short-term profit.

The Lappe–Collins paradigm takes a variety of forms throughout the developing world. Different crops require different soil conditions. Sometimes the political structure is controlled to provide protection for capitalism (as in Chile after Allende, and in Nicaragua after the Sandinistas). Sometimes there is a need for more labour-intensive agriculture. Nevertheless, as Lappe and Collins have shown (1977), the paradigm applies in almost every country in the developing world.

In this context, food aid and financial aid are viewed somewhat cynically. Unlike the neo-liberal position, which sees aid as potentially helpful, Western neo-Marxist globalisation analysts are suspicious of Western trade and aid. They note the political and economic debts that come with aid. And they note the manner in which such institutions as the World Bank, the IMF, and the WTO generally sponsor agricultural endeavours that fit the Lappe-Collins paradigm of cash crops for transnational export profits. This usually breeds dependency, poverty, and hunger in developing countries. Eventually it may generate a world workers' movement and agricultural workers' movement, as Marx hoped. Modern Western neo-Marxist prescriptions vary, but generally they focus on food, security, and empowerment. They want people to be able, with the aid of appropriate, environmentally safe technology, to grow food for sustenance. They want to stop ecological destruction, especially of rainforests and of areas adjacent to deserts. They want to develop local industries to process their own agricultural produce. If cash crops are produced and sold on the world market, Western neo-Marxists want the profit to be used for the development of the country growing the crops, rather than shipped to the developed world or used by developing-world elites for luxuries.

Environmental concerns

Serious questions have been raised about the way that alleviating hunger can degrade the environment. Judged in absolute terms, pollution is a problem in the developing world. But the question is, by what standard should one judge countries in the process of developing? The capitalist industrialised world is hardly blameless (see Chapter 3). The pollution of early Western industrial cities is infamous. And today, as Idemudia and Kole write, 'Western populations (which make up only 16% of the world's population and 24% of its land) consume approximately 80% of the world's resources. In fact, the average North American consumes more energy commuting to work than the average African uses in an entire year. Furthermore, it is estimated that Western countries are responsible for producing over 75% of the world's environmental pollution' (1994, p. 108).

Additionally, indigenous ('undeveloped') people were generally self-sufficient with regard to food without causing significant destruction of their environment. In fact, before the invention and use of petroleum-based fertilisers, pesticides, and herbicides, most food was organically grown. Traditional peoples were experts at maximising yield through intercropping, crop rotation, and labour-intensive planting, weeding, and harvesting. Fertiliser was organic and did not, for the most part, pollute.

Smil (1993) raises questions about the enduring environmental degradation resulting from development in China. They pollute by using soft coal and chemical fertilisers. What these critics often fail to mention, as Mittal notes, is that 'per capita consumption in China is currently just one tenth of the developed countries' (quoted in Agarwal et al. 1999, p. 8), while the US, with 5% of the world's population, accounts for a quarter of the global greenhouse gas emissions (Mittal 2001, p. 1). Though China does not approach Cuba's level of sustainable agriculture (see Box 2.2), it does continue to utilise such widespread traditional Chinese practices as fertilising with (minimally processed) human excrement ('night soil'), recycling, and composting. And the Chinese use substantial labour-intensive agriculture, with planting, weeding, and harvesting by hand.

In Asia, the relatively recent development of Taiwan, South Korea, Singapore, and Hong Kong resulted from a combination of heavy US subsidies and very active government involvement (as in Japan) in the economic

Box 2.2 Cuba

A unique and intriguing example of solving the hunger problem with predominantly organic agriculture is socialist Cuba. In 1960, at the beginning of the United States's 40-year trade embargo, Cuba was pushed into an alliance with Eastern Europe. Using **'socialist'** state farms, Cuba traded sugar and tobacco for oil as part of the socialist division of labour. Cuba used oil for fertilisers, pesticides, and herbicides typical of industrialised agriculture.

When Eastern Europe self-destructed, Cuba was devastated. Its predominant form of agriculture failed and, in 1993, hunger (which had been alleviated) reappeared. Cuba declared a 'Special Period' and its people used their considerable ingenuity to reinvent a new socialist agriculture that was a synthesis of traditional/organic and scientific approaches, often rooted in their own discoveries and biotechnologies. Using oxen and horses for traction, Cuba systematically redeveloped traditional techniques of intercropping and hand weeding. From the previously small organic farming movement, they employed four varieties of *Bacillus tharingiesis* (Bt) (a natural pesticide), applying them to vegetables, root crops, tubers, tobacco, cabbage, citrus, plantains, potatoes, and pastures. They developed produce from the neem tree for pest control in avocado, peppers, garlic, rice, eggplant, onion, citrus, cabbage, beans, corn, melons, cucumbers, tobacco, and tomato, as well as for control of the ecoparasites, tics, mites, poultry lice, and scabies on rabbits and pigs (Funes et al. 2002, p. 124).

In terms of fertilisers, Cuba has improved on traditional farming by using cattle, sheep, and poultry manure as 'bioearth' organic composts and worm-casing humus. They have converted byproducts of their massive sugar production into a caheza (filter cake mud) and applied it to pineapples, coffee, plantains, garden vegetables, and rice.

Overcoming the traditional Western separation between city and country (and the associated costs of transporting food), Cuba has established backyard urban gardens with animals and the highly innovative, cooperatively farmed *organiponicos* (urban gardens). They have created these organiponicos in vacant lots of 1 to 5 acres in a pattern of raised seed beds (50 yards long by 3 feet wide) that can be drip watered with PVC pipe and hand weeded. They are intercropped with up to thirty crop varieties that complement each other. Insects attracted to one plant feed on the pests that attack other plants. Fresh produce from the organiponicos is sold in adjacent and nearby urban farmer's markets. Profits are shared.

By the end of 2002, Cuban socialism had again solved the hunger problem—but this time with diversified sustainable agriculture that is not dependent on the international 'aid' agencies for loans or chemical inputs. In spite of US attempts to inhibit it, Cuba trades with most nations. Currently, because of the success of their sustainable agriculture, as well as the growing niche in the world market for organic sugar produce, Cuba is in the process of converting some acreage to organic export crops.

Though they may have been forced to innovate, they have now become an alternate model of what socialism can accomplish without the international aid organisations controlled in large part by US interests. It is possible that certain other poor countries who have been trying to develop with 'liberal' aid programs will default on their massive debts and choose instead to follow the autonomous model of socialist development that Cuba has pioneered.

sphere—much like socialism. However, with recent US demands that it be allowed to dump its surplus rice into these markets, there are problems with food self-sufficiency. Environmentally, this state-directed, capitalist model has also had bad effects. In Taiwan, virgin broadleaf forests are sacrificed and replaced by fast-growing conifers (Bello & Rosenfeld 1990, p. 195). Today, 'Taiwan is among the top users of chemical fertilizers per square inch in the world' (Bello & Rosenfeld 1990, p.198). This heavy use of fertilisers contributes to 'soil acidification, zinc loss, and decline in soil fertility. Fertiliser overuse is a major contributor to water pollution … [and] has devastating effects on surface waters … [and] groundwater, which is the source of drinking water for many Taiwanese' (Bello & Rosenfeld 1990, p. 198).

Environmental destruction besets many other countries following a capitalist path to development. In various forms, the Lappe-Collins paradigm details an orientation towards 'mining' rather than preserving the soil. Transnational companies can then move on to other soil, leaving the old soil decimated of nutrients and full of pollutants. It is undoubtedly true that all development involves some environmental damage. Therefore, one should not criticise socialist developmental paths to the exclusion of the practices of other countries that pollute the environment as much or more.

Hunger amid plenty: The developed world

Fundamental to the discussion of hunger in the advanced, industrialised world is the distinction between destitution and poverty (or between 'absolute' and 'relative' poverty). *Destitution* (absolute poverty) is the lack of the basic necessities of life. *Poverty* is a relative concept. It refers to a situation in which a minimum of food is available. The food may not be of adequate quality or quantity compared with the norms of the society. And the social-psychological context of acquiring food may entail unacceptable rituals of degradation. 'Poverty' refers to inequality. Relative to what is normal in a given society, people in poverty have significantly less. What is new in contemporary societies is that poverty occurs in societies that could provide adequate food for all.

Poverty can serve certain functions for those in society who are not poor. The poor do menial jobs, buy damaged and outdated goods, are scapegoated as deviants, and provide jobs for a cadre of social workers (Gans 1972/1996, pp. 22–5). From a more theoretical position, capitalist owners and stockholders have always benefited from what Marx termed the 'reserve army of the unemployed'. Having people in need of jobs forces people already in jobs to accept their low wages. It makes their jobs less secure. Therefore, in spite of their rhetoric, governments of capitalist countries have generally been willing to tolerate a good deal of unemployment.

Paralleling the three positions on world hunger—conservative, liberal, and neo-Marxist—are three comparable positions on hunger in the capitalist industrialised countries. The conservative position is characterised by the denial of real poverty and homelessness. Early in the Great Depression, the governments of the most developed countries tried to solve the new poverty through private efforts. Soup kitchens and private, voluntary charity were common in that era. Poverty was characterised as a private problem rather than a public issue. Since that time, according to Riches:

> the state has responded to the problem of hunger by denying its existence, by neglecting its legislated and public responsibilities, by framing the issue of welfare costs in terms of fraud and abuse and by 'blaming the victim.' [The state's position] ... is publicly to deny the hunger its policies are creating and to do whatever they can to de-politicize it as an issue. Unfortunately they are frequently aided in this process by the voluntary community.
>
> Riches 1997b, pp. 170–2

From a liberal perspective, a fundamental dilemma exists between mobilising volunteers for direct feeding efforts and applying political pressure to change an advanced, industrial, capitalist system in a manner that would create institutional resources to actually solve domestic hunger and poverty. The Great Depression provided the first real challenge to the myth that all people who are able to work hard can earn enough to adequately feed themselves and their families. From a liberal perspective, the occasional anomaly of hunger should be approached in a way that does not undermine the fundamental motivational structures of capitalist industrialism. Therefore, soup kitchens and breadlines sponsored by churches and private, voluntary welfare organisations provided the first defence against increasing (relative) poverty and hunger.

But ultimately, with 25% unemployment in the USA, the national government began the process of constructing a social safety net. The 'New Deal' in the USA involved projects in which the government became the employer of last resort. Income from public service jobs (Public Law 320) allowed for the purchase of food without undermining the profitability of the capitalist market. The food-stamp program followed. Since a 'rediscovery' of poverty and hunger in the 1960s, the USA has settled into a recent pattern that has eliminated parts of the social-security network while maintaining the illusion that poverty, hunger, and homelessness are not fundamental dynamics of the existing social system. At the same time, the income gap between rich and poor has widened, and much of the middle class is sinking downwards.

Contemporary neo-Marxists note that from the 1980s to the present, the changes in the advanced capitalist industrial economy have included the automation and de-skilling of many manufacturing jobs, creating what has been termed a 'new American poverty'. As industry automates and de-skills, previously well-paid workers are pushed into menial service jobs in the secondary labour market, without social security benefits. There, with much less income, they constitute the new poor. Workers in the fast-food industry are a good example.

In addition, the world economy, aided by the North American Free Trade Agreement (NAFTA) and the WTO, allows manufacturing operations to move to developing countries, where the labour pay rates are significantly lower (McDonald 2002). As in the early stages of the Great Depression, food banks and soup kitchens have stepped in to aid the domestic hungry. Across the industrialised world, a system of direct feeding (not income maintenance) has been employed. As Riches (1997a) writes, 'The story of hunger in late twentieth century Canada is directly related to the rise of charitable food banks as the primary institution providing emergency food assistance to those in need' (pp. 48–9). By 1991, Canada had 292 food banks, supplying 'over 1200 grocery programs and 580 meal programs in more than 300 communities' (p. 49). And J. Wilson writes: 'I think the future of food banks in Australia is, regrettably, one of continued expansion' (1997, p. 40).

Among Western neo-Marxists, there is deep ambivalence about the role of voluntary associations in assuaging the social problem of hunger in an advanced, automated capitalist society. In addition to the problems of 'donor fatigue' and insufficient free food, such solutions avoid tackling the issue of the kind of social change that would guarantee that all citizens have sufficient food.

By devoting energy to direct provisioning, food banks and soup kitchens take over functions that had been, and perhaps should be, fulfilled by the state. Riches writes this of food banks: 'Far from being an emergency response they have become an institutionalized extension of a failing public welfare system' and 'they are not solving the problem of hunger' (1997b, p. 173). Even more significant are reflections on the food systems of contemporary developed societies. According to Riches, with an international capitalist economy supplying the world's food:

> the real goal is local food security. This necessitates going beyond issues of social security reform and requires developing a comprehensive set of politics, focused on rethinking full employment, supporting green economic renewal, ... developing food self-reliance and understanding food policy as health promotion. It requires participatory, 'bottom up' development informed by the principles and practices of community development with local food security as the primary objective.
>
> Toronto Food Policy Council 1994, quoted in Riches 1997a

Conclusion

Conservatives look on both world hunger and developed-world domestic hunger as natural and, in a sense, good. Like evolution, hunger weeds out the weak and rewards the strong. If people in the developed world begin with a significant head start, they are not to blame for that. The liberal position is 'reformist' and, while spin-doctored as well-intentioned, is self-serving. It wishes that the developed world would become altruistic and contribute enough money and technology to bring an end to hunger while maintaining the essential viability of transnational globalisation. But the liberal position overlooks the stake the capitalist transnational corporations have in underdevelopment and dependency. Profit maximisers need hungry and needy people to perform low-paid tasks. And these low-pay workers, a 'reserve army of the unemployed', put pressure on better-paid workers to work without seriously questioning their own pay. Transnational corporations need developing-world land that can be inexpensively farmed ('mined') without ecological considerations being taken seriously. And they need the multitude of dictatorial and puppet regimes that the USA supports throughout the world to keep these countries safe for exploitation.

The Western neo-Marxist position is the only one that provides an adequate analysis of world hunger. But its solution would involve some variety of local socialist (government-directed) development that guarantees all citizens food before undertaking the accumulation of capital required for 'development'.

China, Cuba, North and SouthVietnam, Sri Lanka, and the Indian democratic socialist state of Kerala provide a range of examples of this model.

Summary of main points

- Hunger exists in a world that produces enough food for everyone.
- Though variously defined, 'hunger' can be identified by degrees of undernourishment, including vitamin and mineral deficiencies and protein or calorie malnutrition.
- World hunger appears differently through different conceptual lenses. Conservatives are inclined to tolerate or even approve of world hunger. Liberals want to ameliorate world hunger by reforming what they regard as basically sound institutions. Western neo-Marxists want to change society fundamentally to eliminate world hunger.
- Though the developing countries of the world damage the environment, their pollution is not even close to that produced by the industrialised world now or in the past.
- In Cuba, Kerala, North and South Vietnam, and China, socialist priorities have made it possible for all citizens to obtain an adequate diet of basic foodstuffs.

Discussion questions

1 How do conservatives look at world hunger?
2 What are the assumptions underpinning the 'lifeboat Earth' argument?
3 What are the limitations of the liberal reformist view of world hunger?
4 Is it possible to maintain a capitalist economic system and feed the hungry?
5 Are transnational corporations the root cause of world hunger?
6 What is the relationship between hunger in the developing world and hunger in the developed world?

Further investigation

1 Lappé, Collins, and Rosset (1998) (see further reading) argue that there are twelve myths of world hunger. Choose any three of these myths and discuss with reference to explanations of the persistence of world hunger.
2 Global capitalism is the primary cause of world hunger. Discuss.
3 According to Andre Gunder Frank (1969), the 'first world' is responsible for the 'development of underdevelopment'. Discuss.

Further reading and web resources

Books

Bello, W. (ed) 2002, *The Future in the Balance,* Food First Books, Oakland, California.

Danaher, K. (ed.) 1994, *50 Years is Enough: The Case Against the World Bank and the International Monetary Fund*, South End Press, Boston.

Franke, R. W. & Chasis, B. H. 1991, *Karala,* Institute for Food and Development, San Francisco.

Lappe, F. M., Collins, J. & Rosset, P. 1998, *World Hunger: Twelve Myths*, 2nd edn, Grove Press, New York.

McIntosh, W. M. A. 1996, *Sociologies of Food and Nutrition*, Plenum Press, New York.

Poppendieck, J. H. 1998, *Sweet Charity? Emergency Food and the End of Entitlement*, Viking Penguin, New York.

Journals

New Internationalist: www.oneworld.org/ni/

Documentaries

The Global Banquet, 2002, Old Dog Productions, Manyknoll World Productions, Pine Bush, New York, 58 minutes.

The Politics of Food, 1987, Yorkshire Television, Leeds, four 52-minute episodes. A critical analysis of world hunger, aid, and development.

Web sites

Food and Agriculture Organization (FAO) of the UN: www.fao.org/UNFAO/e/wmain-e.htm
The FAO aims to improve nutrition, agricultural productivity, and general living standards across the globe.

Food and Agriculture Organization USA: www.fao.org/documents/
Provides access to many online publications related to food security.

FoodFirst: www.foodfirst.org/
A nonprofit think-tank and advocacy center that aims to address hunger and poverty; founded by Frances Moore Lappé and Joseph Collins.

The Hunger Site: www.thehungersite.com
A simple and effective site that enables visitors to make free food donations by simply clicking a button each day (made possible through sponsorship and advertising by various organisations).

The HungerWeb: www.brown.edu/Departments/World_Hunger_Program/
A US site at Brown University dedicated to eradicating hunger by promoting the exchange of ideas, information, and research on its causes and solutions.

UN System Network on Rural Development and Food Security: www.rdfs.net/

World Hunger Education service: www.worldhunger.org/
Publishes the online journal *Hunger Notes* and provides access to a wealth of information on world hunger.

References

Agarwal, A., Narinaub, S. & Sharma, A. (eds) 1999, *Green Politics*, New Delhi Center for Science and Environment, New Delhi, India.

Banfield, E. C. 1974, *The Unheavenly City Revisited*, Little Brown & Co., Boston.

Bello, W. 2001, 'The Iron Cage: The WTO, The Bretton Woods Institutions and the South', in W. Bello (ed.), *The Future in the Balance*, Food First Books, Oakland, California, pp. 3–34.

Bello, W. & Rosenfeld, S. 1990, *Dragons in Distress*, Institute for Food and Policy, San Francisco.

Bennet, J. & George, S. 1987, *The Hunger Machine: The Politics of Food*, Polity Press, London.

Bryant, C., Courtney, A., Markesbery, B. & DeWalt, K. 1985, *The Cultural Feast*, West, New York.

Buchanan, A. 1982, *Food, Poverty, and Power*, Spokesman, Nottingham.

Cassidy, C. 1982, 'Protein-Energy Malnutrition: A Culture Bound Syndrome', *Culture, Medicine and Psychiatry*, vol. 6, pp. 325–48.

Chen, R. 1990, 'The State of Hunger in 1990', *The Hunger Report*, 1–26 June.

Crossgrave, W., Egilman, D., Heywood, P., Kasperson, J., Messer, E. and Wessen, A. 1990, 'Colonialism, International Trade, and the Nation State', in L.F. Newman (ed.), *Hunger in History: Food Shortage, Poverty and Deprivation*, Basil Blackwell, Cambridge.

FAO—*see* Food and Agricultural Organization.

Food and Agricultural Organization 2002, 'The State of Food Insecurity in the World', <http://www.fao.org/docrep/+8200e04.htm> accessed June 2003.

Frank, A. G. 1969, *Latin America: Underdeveloped or Revolution*, Modern Reader, New York.

Franke, R. W. & Chasin, B. H. 1980, *Seeds and Famine: Ecological Destruction and the Development Dilemma in the West African Sahel*, Universe Books, New York.

Friedman, H. 2002, 'The International Political Economy of Food', in C. M. Counihan (ed.) *Food in the USA*. Routledge, New York.

Funes, Fernando et al. 2002, *Sustainable Agriculture and Resistance: Transforming Food Production in Cuba*, Food First Books, Oakland, California.

Gans, H. 1972/1996, 'The Positive Functions of Poverty', in G. Massed (ed.), *Readings for Sociology*, W. M. Norton, New York.

Hardin, G. 1978, 'Lifeboat Ethics: The Case Against Helping the Poor', in J. D. Gussow (ed.), *The Feeding Web*, Bull Publishing, Berkeley, California.

Heller, P. 1985, *Hamburger I: MacProfit*, video documentary, Icarus Films, New York.

Idemudia, P. & Kole, S. 1994, 'World Bank Takes Control of UNCED's Environmental Fund', in K. Danaher (ed.), *50 Years is Enough: The Case Against the World Bank and the International Monetary Fund*, South End Press, Boston.

Lappe, F. M. & Collins, J. 1977, *Food First: Beyond the Myth of Scarcity*, Houghton Mifflin, Boston.

Lappe, F. M., Collins, J. and Rosset, P. 1998, *World Hunger: Twelve Myths,* 2nd edn, Grove Press, New York.

Lenski, G. & Lenski, J. 1982, *Human Societies*, McGraw-Hill, New York.

McDonald, J. M. 2002, 'NAFTA and Basic Food Production: Dependence and Marginalization on Both Sides of the US/Mexico Border', in C. M. Counihan (ed.), *Food in the USA*, Routledge, New York.

Millman, S. 1991, *The Hunger Report: Update 1991*, Alan Shawn Feinstein World Hunger Program, Providence.

Millman, S. & Wikates, R. 1990, 'Toward Understanding Hunger', in L. Newman, W. Cosgrove, R. Kates, R. Mattew & S. Millman (eds), *Hunger in History*, Basil Blackwell, Cambridge, pp. 3–8.

Mintz, S. 1985, *Sweetness and Power*, Viking Penguin, New York.

Mittal, A. 2001, 'Foreword', in W. Bello (ed.), *The Future in the Balance,* Food First Books, Oakland, California.

Morgan, D. 1980, *Merchants of Grain*, Penguin Books, New York.

The Politics of Food 1987, documentary series, four 52-minute episodes, Yorkshire Television, Leeds.

Riches, G. 1997a, 'Hunger in Canada: Abandoning the Right to Food', in G. Riches (ed.), *First World Hunger*, Macmillian, London, pp. 46–77.

—— 1997b, 'Hunger, Welfare and Food Security: Emerging Strategies', in G. Riches (ed.), *First World Hunger*, Macmillan, London, pp. 165–78.

Scrimshaw, N. 1990, 'World Nutritional Problems', in L. Newman, W. Cosgrove, R. Kates, R. Mattew, & S. Millman (eds), *Hunger in History*, Basil Blackwell, Cambridge, pp. 353–73.

Seavoy, R. 1986, *Famine in Peasant Societies*, Greenwald Press, New York.

Shiva, V. 2000, 'War Against Nature and the People of the South', in S. Anderson (ed.), *Views from the South*, Food First Books and the International Forum of Globalization, Milford, Connecticut.

Smil, V. 1993, *China's Environmental Crisis,* M. E. Sharpe, New York.

Whit, W. 1995, *Food and Society: A Sociological Approach*, General Hall, New York.

Wilson, J. 1997, 'Australia: Lucky Country/Hungry Silence', in G. Riches (ed.), *First World Hunger*, Macmillan, London, pp. 14–35.

3

Food, Society, and the Environment

Terry Leahy

Overview

- In what ways do current agricultural practices damage the environment?
- What are the major causes of environmental damage?
- Are ruralisation and sustainable agriculture viable solutions?

The dominant mode of agricultural production in developed countries results in significant environmental damage and in the long run is unsustainable. The major problems are caused by monoculture, fertilisers, pesticides, overgrazing, tree clearing, irrigation, and the use of fossil fuels. This chapter considers, in particular, the problem of nutrient loss, whereby nutrients in the soil are embodied in plants and animals and exported when they leave the farm. Environmental damage is ultimately the result of the capitalist imperative of profit-making, because unsustainable agricultural practices make short-term economic sense. However, the predicted demise of cheap oil in the next few decades may create economic incentives to pursue more sustainable alternatives. While it may be necessary to replace capitalism in the long term, solutions based in community action and state regulation can make sense now. Experiments in sustainable agriculture today can be regarded as hybrids—social alternatives that link features of capitalism to features of the gift economy.

Key terms

agribusiness
alienated labour
capitalism
cash crops
community-supported agriculture
gift economy
greenhouse effect
monoculture
organic
permaculture
polyculture
ruralisation
social structure
sustainable agriculture

Introduction

As we go about producing and consuming food, we set in train a long series of environmental problems. Current agricultural methods, while highly efficient, are unsustainable because the environmental damage they cause reduces the productivity of the land for future agricultural use. Major environmental problems are caused by **monoculture**, fertilisers, pesticides, overgrazing, overfishing, tree clearing, irrigation, and the use of fossil fuels (see Box 3.1). What sociology can offer is the insight that these problems develop as a consequence of specific **social structures**. Environmental problems, which are often unintended, are in many ways created by the structures of **capitalism**, both locally and globally. Therefore, any attempt to significantly address environmental degradation through alternative methods of food production and distribution are likely to have enormous consequences for social organisation.

Box 3.1 Some key environmental problems in the agricultural production of food

- The gradual destruction of forests, wetlands, and other wild areas to create land for agriculture.
- The destruction of wildlife through practices that prevent wild species from co-existing on farms: clearing of trees, destruction of hedgerows, erosion of waterways, destruction of understorey, use of toxic pesticides that kill insects and the animals that eat them, use of herbicides that kill weeds and other wild plants, elimination of wild animals seen as vermin, and breaking-up of wild areas into isolated pockets.
- A loss of biodiversity in crop species—with particular varieties being singled out for commercial use for the sake of convenience in packaging, sales, and distribution—putting us at danger of coming to depend on single varieties that can be destroyed by disease.
- Soil erosion through ploughing and subsequent exposure of bare soil to rain or wind, through the use of herbicides that destroy weed cover for soils, and through the removal of tree cover on slopes.
- The destruction of soil humus—the small organisms and decaying plant matter that make a living soil—by ploughing and exposure to sunlight as well as chemical inputs (fertilisers, pesticides, and herbicides).
- Salinity in dry-land agriculture, which is killing many pastures, crops, and wild plant species; generally caused by overclearing.
- Overuse of water in irrigation areas, also causing salinity.
- Overfishing, leading to an inability to maintain existing levels of fish stocks.

- Fishing techniques that destroy other sea animals or habitat—for example, the use of dynamite on coral reefs, long-line fishing that kills sea birds, and fish nets that trap dolphins and turtles.
- The use of toxic chemicals in agriculture that have an impact on both humans and wildlife. Many of these are not broken down in the soil, remaining toxic for decades. Accidental poisoning by chemicals is most common in developing countries, but even in the rich countries links have been made between areas with particular crops and associated chemicals and higher rates of cancer or other diseases.
- Genetic modification of crops, with the possibility of mistakes and accidents producing super weeds. Genetic modifications designed to make crops resistant to herbicides can encourage the use of herbicides, with their associated environmental problems.
- The oil dependence of modern agriculture—in agricultural inputs, processing, and transportation as well as in farm production itself.
- Resistance of plant and insect pests to chemical pesticides and herbicides, leading to the use of more chemicals.
- The elimination of predator insects (insects that prey upon the insects that damage crops) with insecticides. When both the pests and the predators are destroyed by spraying, the pests can return to cause more damage while the predators are absent. This problem is exacerbated by the use of herbicides that kill the weeds that host predator insects.
- The use of large parts of the surface of the globe to produce luxury products for rich consumers—for example, beef, sugar, coffee, tea, and chocolate. One result is the use of agricultural land for such purposes at the expense of food crops for less affluent consumers. Another consequence is the continual expansion of the area used by agriculture, at the expense of wild ecosystems.

A case study: Nutrient loss in Australian agriculture

There is much about Australian agriculture that causes environmental problems. Concentrating on one issue, nutrient loss, will illustrate how intractable these problems can be. Australia is heavily dependent on export agriculture for its affluent lifestyle. The gross value of agricultural production in Australia for the year 2000–01 was $34,000 million (ABS 2002a). More than half of Australia's farm produce is exported (ABS 2002b) and these exports are a key element of the Australian economy as a whole. Approximately one-quarter of Australia's exported goods are products derived from agriculture (ABS 2002c). Because of this focus on export, Australian agriculture is vital to many people living in other countries—it has been estimated that Australia produces the food and fibre requirements for 55 million people (Roberts 1992; McLennan 1996).

All agricultural products ultimately depend for their growth on the presence of key nutrients in the soil. Chief among these are compounds based on three elements: nitrogen, phosphorus, and potassium. What happens in the case of export agriculture is that these elements are embodied in plant or animal products that are exported to another country. They are effectively lost to Australian soils. While the export of products overseas dramatises this issue, the problem is endemic in all modern agriculture. Agricultural products are also exported from the country to the city with no nutrient recycling.

To get some indication of the scope of nutrient loss we can look at the extent to which nutrients are removed in crops and the extent to which they are replaced through the use of fertilisers. To take a typical example, in 1988 in Queensland (Australia), the estimated losses of nutrients in wheat and barley were as follows: approximately 64,000 tonnes of nitrogen, of which 11,000 tonnes were replaced by fertilisers; 6500 tonnes of phosphorus, of which 2000 tonnes were replaced by fertilisers; and 8000 tonnes of potassium, of which 68 tonnes were replaced by fertilisers (Roberts 1995). The result is the long-term depletion of Australian soils. The CSIRO has estimated that Australia exports about $600 million worth of nitrogen, phosphorus, and potassium every year in its grain and livestock commodities (Campbell 1991). We can look at this estimated cost in comparison with the costs of losses from other problems of soil degradation. The total cost of the following major problems in Australian agriculture—dry-land salinity, wind and water erosion, soil acidification, soil-structure decline—is estimated at a quarter of the cost of nutrient loss in crops and livestock leaving the farm (Roberts 1995).

Artificial fertilisers: The economic problems

Within the scientific paradigm of modern agriculture, the obvious solution to nutrient loss is the replacement of soil nutrients with artificial fertilisers. As is clear from the figures presented above, this is already being done to a certain extent, with $1000 million being spent every year on fertilisers (Roberts 1995). Yet it seems that this is not nearly enough. Looking at the Queensland figures for grain production, a rough calculation shows that 78,000 tonnes of nutrients are being removed and only 13,000 tonnes are being replaced with fertilisers. Another 65,000 tonnes of nutrients are required. We could end up spending $5000 million every year on fertiliser to secure the replacement of nutrients by this method. Who could pay for this? Few of the profits of agriculture go to the farmer—much goes to supermarket chains, export businesses, transport companies, and so on. Australian farmers are in much the same situation as farmers overseas. Whereas 50 years ago farmers in Europe and the USA received 45–60% of the money consumers paid for food, they now receive only 7% in the UK and 3.5% in the USA (Ainger 2003). Thus farmers themselves would not be able to foot the bill for increased use of fertilisers.

Large **agribusinesses** get most of the profit from Australian farming. To give some indication of this, in 1988 five of Australia's largest exporters of agricultural products were Japanese companies that together accounted for $7000 million in agricultural exports (Lawrence & Vanclay 1992). A system of environmental taxes could be imposed on companies that are making profits from food production—while leaving farmers untouched. But the international reality of trade is that Australia competes with other countries to sell agricultural products. For the most part, these countries are either developing countries in which labour costs are cheap compared to those in Australia or rich countries in which agriculture is heavily subsidised (for example, EU countries and the USA). Australia cannot risk a tax on international agribusinesses.

This leaves only the Australian taxpayer as a candidate to fund fertilisers to restore soil nutrients. Yet this solution is politically unlikely. The real wages of many sections of the Australian population have been in a steady, if slow, decline since the mid 1970s. The major political parties compete to reassure the electorate that they will not increase taxes. The parties that openly proclaim an intention to raise taxes to engage in serious environmental repair get no more than 10% of the vote. Even if Australian taxpayers were actually to pay $5000 million annually to replace nutrients by this method, we could wonder about the implications of this for the economy. What it would mean is that Australian agriculture would have been propped up by subsidies. While agriculture today is a profitable export industry accounting for a quarter of Australia's exports in goods, it would have become a drain on the public purse.

Therefore, nutrient loss is unlikely to be arrested through the use of artificial fertilisers in Australia. The most likely scenario is that nutrients will continue to be exported in agricultural products at a greater rate than they are being replaced by fertilisers. The profitability of the Australian agricultural industry, a key part of Australia's economy, will ensure that export agriculture continues. Yet in the long term the industry is undoing its own future by mining the soil for nutrients it cannot afford to replace.

Artificial fertilisers: The environmental problems

Would a replacement of nutrients through artificial fertilisers actually solve the environmental problems of export agriculture in the long run? The problems created by these fertilisers can be helpfully divided in two:

1 the polluting of soil and waterways
2 the energy costs and sustainability of long-term use of artificial fertilisers.

One effect of adding nitrogen is acidification of soils. In Australia, some soils are naturally acidic, but in many areas acidity is the outcome of the use of fertilisers. The result of acidification is reduced agricultural productivity, since most crops and pastures do better in neutral soils. Twenty-four million hectares of Australian agricultural land are affected by acidification (Campbell 1995). A related effect of the use of fertilisers is the pollution of waterways. The addition of soluble nutrients to soils increases nutrient levels in streams, rivers, and oceans. Algae builds up in waterways, using up all the available oxygen and starving fish and water plants of oxygen—creating a dead waterway.

The second problem with artificial fertiliser use is the cost in energy and the implications of this for the long-term sustainability of agriculture. Looking at the energy costs of modern agriculture in general, we can take the situation in the USA as an extreme case of high-energy agriculture. Three units of energy are used in farming for every unit of food energy consumed. As for the energy costs of transporting and processing food, there are ten units of energy needed for every unit consumed. In the United States, 17% of total energy use goes into food production and distribution. If every country in the world was using energy at this rate to produce food, all fossil fuel reserves would have been exhausted by 1996 (Soule & Piper 1992). Where crops are fertilised, a large part of the energy used on farms goes into the production of fertilisers. For example, in 1987 in Colorado, the energy used to make fertilisers for wheat farming was 63% of the total energy used, with fuel energy used on the farm being a further 20% (Mannion 1995). Therefore, modern agriculture is massively dependent on cheap supplies of fossil fuel energy, with oil being the central requirement. The most obvious use is oil-based transport of food, but the use of artificial fertilisers, pesticides, and herbicides also depends on oil energy.

One reason that all this is a problem is the **greenhouse effect**. The Intergovernmental Panel on Climate Change has argued that to stabilise greenhouse gases we would need to cut carbon dioxide emissions (and fossil fuel use) by between 60% and 80%. Unless this is done, the most likely result over the next century is a devastating global climate change that would seriously increase the costs of agriculture —even if there was no overall decline in useable agricultural sites (Maslin 2002). This would be just the beginning of the problems caused by the greenhouse effect. Even according to the most optimistic scientific forecasts, the results of the greenhouse effect will be catastrophic.

A further problem is that we are very likely to run out of accessible oil reserves in the next 10 to 20 years. The peak of oil discoveries was in the 1960s, and ever since then less and less oil has been discovered. At the same time the world's consumption of oil has been rapidly increasing. Accordingly, an estimate can be made of when oil is going to become less readily available and much more expensive. Most forecasts are of dates between 2003 and 2020 (Campbell 1997; AEN 2001). Continuing with any method of producing food that depends on the use of oil is not making good use of the time we have between now and when this 'oil crunch' takes place (Gunther 2002). In other words, what would make most sense at the present time is to use the latitude that cheap oil gives us to begin setting up the physical and social structures that are going to be necessary to live in an agricultural economy that does not depend on oil (Holmgren 2002).

Fertility without artificial fertilisers

How can the problem of nutrient loss from crops be confronted without relying on oil? In the case of nitrogen, the answer seems fairly obvious. Certain plants can fix nitrogen from the air, storing it in their roots. This property of 'leguminous' plants is used already in **organic** and other **sustainable agricultures** and also in much commercial agriculture. Leguminous plants are grown in rotation with pasture crops or grain crops, to improve soil humus and add nitrogen. In Australia, one of the most commonly used legumes is subterranean clover (for examples from other countries, see Furuno 2001 and Pretty 2002). If this is all so easy, one may wonder why all Australian farmers do not abandon the use of artificial nitrogenous fertilisers and move to leguminous crops. The answer is that annual applications of nitrogen in fertiliser have generally been enough to maintain yields. It has not seemed economically necessary to add more fertiliser. The low cost of fertiliser has made this a cheaper option than the replacement of nitrogen through 'green manure' crops, which have to be planted and later slashed.

Phosphorus presents a more intractable problem. This element must be present in the soil; it cannot be recovered by plants from the air the way that nitrogen can. At present, oil is being used to mine phosphate ores and convert these to fertilisers for use on farms. As more phosphate is mined, ores become more difficult to access and more energy is required to extract them. It has been estimated that, if current usage rates continue, phosphate ores may last for 130 years. However, a different picture emerges if we consider costs and assume that energy prices will rise by 5% per annum and that the cost of extraction will rise by 3% per annum. Within 75 years the price of phosphate would increase by 140 times, pricing it quite out of the reach of most farmers (Gunther 2002). Without the use of phosphate ores, there is only one way to replace the phosphates removed in crops and animals exported from the farm: by recycling the nutrients from both animal and human waste. This was, in fact, the practice of many ancient societies.

Recycling soil nutrients and ruralisation

Gunther (1998) has considered these issues at some length and described various possible scenarios for Sweden. The problem with recycling human and animal waste (and nutrients) to farms is that a large amount of transport energy would have to be used to move this material from cities to the country. In one of Gunther's scenarios, all phosphorus is recycled from the city of Stockholm to agricultural land, rather than being lost as sewage dumped in landfill or exported to lakes and seas, as now. He found that the energy costs of treating phosphorus would double. This is not a sustainable solution given the impending oil crunch. The problems of recycling phosphorus are even more acute for Australian export agriculture. Australia would have to re-import the treated composted faeces, the used wool, and the urine from 55 million overseas customers of Australian agriculture. All of this extra transport would use fossil fuels. The extra cost would certainly make it uneconomic to continue with export agriculture.

Gunther's recommendation is that agricultural products should be produced close to consumers, with villages of 200 people supplied by farms of 40 hectares. In good agricultural land, these villages could end up being a bit more than a kilometre apart. This is a program of **ruralisation**, in which urban populations are relocated. The local farms would have to produce a diverse range of foods, as food would not be imported into the village. The increased costs associated with this diversity and with the technology of nutrient recycling would be paid for through a system of subscription farming in which consumers guaranteed to buy the food of farmers at up to a third higher price than farmers now receive for their crops. The endless middle of distributors, transporters, processors, and retailers would be cut out. The energy costs of redistributing and recycling phosphorus would be 1% of those incurred now to merely treat waste sewage and manure. The energy costs of producing artificial fertilisers would vanish—soil fertility would come from waste recycling or legume crops. Gunther outlines the following principles for this recycling:

- Animal feed has to be produced on the same farm as it is used on, or in the vicinity, allowing the manure to be returned to the land where the feed was produced.
- Nutrients actually exported as human food should be returned as uncontaminated as possible, preferably as human urine and (composted) faecal matter (Gunther 2002, p. 266).

In such a system, leakage of phosphorus could be virtually eliminated.

Social implications of ruralisation

Looking at the Australian situation, what would be the social implications of such a ruralisation programme? One of the most obvious changes would be the loss of a key export industry. Australia would have to reduce imports to maintain a trading balance. Jobs in the agriculture industry, and not just in farming, would vanish as production for export disappeared. Even that part of the food industry producing and distributing food for Australians would contract if consumers dealt directly with farmers through subscription agriculture. Nevertheless, in the short term much employment would be generated relocating people from urban areas to the country and setting up the infrastructure for sustainable agriculture. But of course the expenditure for all this would have to come from taxpayers, meaning a decline in real incomes. This would in turn cause a reduction in spending in all other areas of consumption, with consequent losses of employment in those industries—for example, entertainment, restaurants, and tourism. Whatever way you look at it, the consequences would be massively disruptive for most Australians. More than half the population would have to move house and change their jobs and even their type of employment. They would be lucky if their income did not drop substantially and if they escaped a transitional period of unemployment.

Unfortunately, much worse than this will be experienced in the long term if current practices continue; if in the next 20 years the price of oil escalates, agriculture, dependent on oil, could fall apart. Many Australians could starve without any infrastructure having been set up to create an alternative sustainable agriculture system. However, this doomsday scenario is not a current political issue. The political choice is whether to make massive alterations to 'business as usual', disrupting lifestyles and livelihoods, by making a voluntary cut in standards of living to fund a transition to a new agricultural model.

Ironically, in view of the life-and-death predicament, most people living in rich countries would be appalled by the implications of the ruralisation scenario for 'hygiene'. The proposal that human manure should be collected and composted at the local level and then spread on crops would meet with massive opposition; most people would find it disgusting. To suggest that this was something we should facilitate by reorganising our whole settlement pattern would be taken as a sure sign of lunacy. But human waste can in fact be composted for between 6 and 12 months to remove all disease-bearing organisms and all parasites (such as worms and helminths). This can even be done in a backyard with two large compost bins (Jenkins 1994).

Socially, the ruralisation scenario could appear as death to the intellect, with claustrophobic hamlets of just 200 people. But there could be other ways of organising life in such villages. People could visit or stay with other households and move about between villages using a system of solar-powered trains, bicycle transport, sailing ships and airships, and could use electronic communication. There would be much to enjoy in living in a landscape with safe sustainable agriculture and the integration of wildlife through agro-forestry and wildlife parks. Such an environment could be like a less dense urban landscape, rather than a set of isolated rural villages (Trainer 1995).

One additional problem of this scenario would be faced in Australia. If Australia supplies food and wool to 55 million consumers in other countries, how would these consumers fare without the Australian agricultural export industry? Beef could fairly be regarded as a luxury product; overseas consumers could switch to environmentally cheaper sources of protein. The same could not be said of wheat, which Australia exports to such countries as Indonesia, China, and Iraq. Either cereal production in these countries would have to intensify—without the

Box 3.2 The social context of population pressures on the environment

There is little doubt that world population growth over the coming decades, peaking at between 9 and 11 billion, will place a serious strain on food and environmental resources. And population pressures create serious problems related to the environmental consequences of agriculture. One is that much agriculture is used not to feed hungry and growing populations, but to feed rich consumers with luxury goods. For example, in much of Central America and South America, rainforests are being cleared. Some of this rainforest land is being cleared by poor farmers who have been displaced from their original farms, where they used to live, by agribusiness, which has taken over the farms to grow crops for overseas consumers. The rest of the rainforest land is cleared for cattle ranchers who sell their beef to consumers in rich countries. Another motive for rainforest destruction is tropical timber exports to rich countries (Romeiro 1987; Anderson 1990; Mannion 1995; Gutberlet 1999; Barraclough & Ghimire 2000). None of these changes can be attributed simply to overpopulation. If anything, there is an overpopulation of rich consumers.

Concern over population pressures on agriculture generally fails to consider why there is an overpopulation crisis. The countries whose population has expanded rapidly in the last 100 years had stable populations for millennia before that. A common explanation of these changes points to the social pressures on population created by global capitalism (Pepper 1995). Capitalism is an economy system founded on growth, particularly the global exchange of agricultural products for cash. Colonial rulers and capitalist entrepreneurs have found it in their interest to intensify the production of agricultural products intended for the world market. In the process they have displaced the subsistence peasantry and turned them into wage labourers whose only economic security is what they can earn—whether in cities or the countryside. The overall effect has been that people do not feel secure about their economic future. It is now in the interest of poor people to invest in bearing and raising children who can earn money to support their parents in their old age. This has been a key cause of population growth over the last century. One solution is a land tenure system that gives people long-term intergenerational ownership of adequate land and control of their own food security (see Chapter 2). We cannot blame a growing population (in the developing world) for global environmental problems, most of which originate in rich, developed countries.

use of fossil fuels—or these consumers would have to migrate to Australia. The most likely scenario in a world deeply affected by the oil crunch would be that Australian voters would abandon overseas consumers to their fate.

The argument so far has taken nutrient removal to be a key environmental issue. Artificial fertilisers are not adequately replacing nutrients lost in crops. In the next few decades, the oil and mineral requirements of artificial fertilisers will become very much more expensive. The only sound solution to this environmental crisis is widespread relocation of urban populations to agricultural areas and a change to largely self-sufficient local agricultural production—with recycling of all food, human, and animal wastes. But the massive social impact of such changes and the likely political barriers to their implementation make them impractical solutions.

Low-input agriculture: Food yields, profitability, and sustainability

The conventional view of **sustainable agriculture** is that it is an inefficient way of producing food, particularly for a growing global population, and that it is unprofitable for farmers. However, much recent research supports the use of low-input agriculture. Jules Pretty (1998, 1999, 2002) has summarised the evidence in support of sustainable agriculture, arguing it 'can be achieved' in all regions of the world:

- in the diverse, complex and 'resource-poor' lands of the Third World, farmers adopting regenerative technologies have doubled or trebled crop yields, often with little or no use of external inputs;
- in the high input and generally irrigated lands, farmers adopting regenerative technologies have maintained yields while substantially reducing inputs;
- in the industrialized agricultural systems, a transition to sustainable agriculture could mean a fall in per hectare yields of 10-20% in the short term, but with better levels of financial returns to farmers.

Pretty 1999, p. 19

The results have been most extraordinary in regions where agriculture provides a meagre sustenance and production is for local consumption only. In Honduras, green manures—the growing of an intercrop of legumes—along with soil conservation measures were able to increase yields of maize by 300%. In India, in a community owning 168 hectares of crop land, soil and water conservation measures increased yields of sorghum on rain-fed fields by 350% and on irrigated fields by 176% (Pretty 1999, p. 214). Chemical inputs and high-yielding seeds are much too expensive for these farmers. Less costly changes using sustainable technologies can produce very large gains.

For developing countries, where profitable **cash crops** are usually grown using high-input agriculture, yields can also be good with sustainable technologies. In China, 1200 eco-farms use only 30% of the average amount of artificial inputs to grow rice. They recycle waste as compost and cultivate fish. Yields are 110% of those typical of the area. In Mexico, an estate of 320 hectares grows organic coffee without artificial inputs. Yields are 66–72% of those in nearby conventional high-input plantations; despite this, the economic returns are good because a premium price is being paid for organic produce (Pretty 1999, p. 212).

In rich countries, yields and economic returns from sustainable farming are also good. In twenty farms surveyed in the mid-west of the USA, inputs of pesticides and fertilisers were totally eliminated while sustainable techniques—rotations of cereal crops with legumes and reduced ploughing—were used to build soil quality, reduce insect attacks, and add nitrogen. Yields of maize per hectare on these farms were 92% of local averages, yields of soybeans 95%, and yields of wheat 57% (Pretty 1999, p. 207). Crop yields on eight biodynamic farms in Switzerland were 95–100% of those on conventional farms in the same region. No artificial fertilisers or pesticides were used and financial returns per hectare were the same as on conventional farms (Pretty 1999, p. 209). The premium price for organic produce could explain their economic success.

Economic barriers to sustainable agriculture

With results like this, one may wonder why farmers are not rushing to sustainable agriculture. There are some economic barriers to more widespread adoption. Usually, sustainable agriculture increases labour costs if labour is hired off the farm. Sustainable agriculture can increase the workload of the farming family—because of labour-intensive technologies, a whole new body of information and technology, and new crops (see Campbell 1991).

Pretty's analysis (1998, 1999) implies a trade-off between the cost of inputs and falling yields as inputs are reduced. Particularly good studies have been done in Europe. These studies show that, with 75% pesticide use, yields may fall to as low as 83% of yields on high-input farms. Yet yields can drop as much as 20% while financial returns increase, because the cost of inputs has been reduced. Still, if farmers completely abandon artificial pesticides and fertilisers, yields can drop below this to the point where farmers end up getting less economic return (Pretty 1998, pp. 96–100). This economic equation works out quite differently for the developing countries. Lower labour costs and lower prices for farm produce may mean that even lower levels of inputs still make economic sense, if sustainable technologies are used.

Another issue is that sustainable technologies usually cost money to set up, even if they save money in the long run. Farmers may not have the resources on hand to start this process. And initial yields may be much lower than those that are achieved after 5 to 10 years. Soil biota and predator insects take time to establish themselves after high-input agriculture has been removed.

Finally, the economic consequences of moves to sustainable agriculture have to be considered in their off-farm context. There are economic losers in sustainable agriculture, such as fertiliser and chemical companies, supermarket chains, and seed companies. These large players in national economies can use their influence to prevent government regulation, to prevent taxation of the pollution caused by high-input agriculture, and to prevent subsidies to sustainable agriculture. They are in a good position to conduct an information war against agricultural alternatives through their contacts with farmers and banks and through research and propaganda. This leads us to the social structures that have been responsible for environmental problems in agriculture; after examining them, we will consider alternative social structures for a more sustainable agriculture.

Capitalism as a basic cause of environmental damage

One common analysis of environmental problems points to capitalism as a central feature of contemporary society; it is argued that the capitalist economic structure works against environmental sustainability. Andrew McLaughlin (1993) gives a compelling summary of the major points of this argument:

- Social decisions about how to use non-human nature are generally made by markets.
- The future is discounted.
- Capitalism creates growth and depends on growth.

We shall consider each of these points in turn. In a capitalist system, non-human nature can be privately owned. Decisions about how it will be used will depend on profits. There can be a mismatch between what is profitable and what is sustainable. For example, it costs money to halt soil erosion, so in any given year profits will be higher if one does nothing (McLaughlin 1993, p. 32). It can be more profitable to cut corners than to pay for the sustainable option. The economic system makes it very difficult for owners and managers to choose a more expensive strategy. Companies compete to attract investment by providing profits to shareholders. The costs of their operations must be cut as low as possible so as to provide money to improve production systems and pay out profits. They cannot increase the price of their goods substantially, because then they would lose their place in the market. McLaughlin does not hold out much hope for the political regulation of markets. The assumption of the capitalist system is that owners of non-human nature will have full rights to use their property to make the maximum profit. Any restriction on these rights has to be fought for as a special case, usually after environmental damage has become too obvious to ignore. The wealth of owners makes them a very powerful lobby group.

The second feature discussed by McLaughlin is the discounting of the future. Within an economy where money can be invested to earn interest, there is a bias towards investments that will pay off in a short time. Because of the many unpredictable variables of the market, politics, and nature, an expected profit may not be realised. So investors and their accountants regularly discount expected profit in the long-term future. Hence, an investment that will pay off in the near future makes more sense. The effect is a mismatch between what makes sense economically (a short-term pay-off) and what makes sense in terms of the long time taken by natural processes. Ecological damage that increases profits now—though at the expense of long-term profits—becomes economically rational. This is the explanation for the decisions of Queensland farmers to cut native vegetation to increase pasture now, even though it seems probable that in the long term this will reduce pasture through salinity.

The third feature of capitalism that McLaughlin considers is the capitalist system's tendency to rely on economic growth. Competition between companies means that it makes sense to cut the costs of production by a constant refurbishing of production technology. The aim is to install new technology that can produce more at less cost, with less labour input. The effect is to constantly increase the number of products that can be produced. To continue to make a profit in these circumstances, companies have to increase their markets and the number of products sold. The end result is a galloping increase in the use of raw materials and the output of wastes into the environment. An example in agriculture is the constant expansion of agricultural production to supply rich consumers with luxury goods, such as tea, coffee, chocolate, meat, out-of-season vegetables and fruits, and even cut flowers. Another example is the expansion of packaging, transport, and promotion activities to make these sales possible.

Cultural and political pressures inherent in capitalism also favour this trend. If market growth does not continue, unemployment increases, leading to political instability. To increase markets, capitalist firms promote consumption as the epitome of the good life, leading to cultural pressure to continue growth. Another factor is **alienated labour** within capitalist societies. To maintain their control over production and profitability, firms control work through hierarchical systems of authority. They also direct the distribution of products, which are owned by the company and cannot be distributed by those who produce them. So decisions about work are taken out of the hands of ordinary workers; they have little power and control, and work often seems boring and pointless. Consumption offers itself as one of the few areas in which people can make choices and express themselves creatively (Cardan 1974; Roszak 1992).

This ties into the way consumers look at food. Expensive, well-packaged, luxurious food seems the appropriate moral reward for a life of thankless labour.

Food is one of the few morally legitimate pleasures (Pont 1997). Foods that are transported from developing countries—at great cost to the environment—are the height of luxury and acceptability. Meat and dairy products are seen as an appropriate reward for hard masculine labour and as necessary for healthy growth; sugar is seen as a sweet pleasure and an apt reward for appropriate femininity; coffee, tea, and chocolate are all stimulating but legitimate drugs, an aid to concentration at work or a reward after work. Elaborate and decorative packaging, flawless food products untainted by pest attacks, and a wide range of foods from every place in the globe are seen as rewards that consumers deserve for all their hard work. These factors make it difficult to get consumers to direct their food purchasing habits to environmental ends. They make it unlikely that affluent consumers will willingly embrace tough environmental regulation of farming and trade, or support strong government initiatives to fund sustainable farming. Such regulations would mean that consumers would pay more for food, pay more in taxes, or have less choice of foods.

The gift economy as a utopian alternative to capitalism

The aspects of capitalism that lie behind environmental damage are unlikely to disappear without a radically different social organisation. Proposing the **gift economy** as such an alternative, I will explain this model and why it might be more environmentally benign than capitalism. Many contemporary reforms to agriculture are based on hybrid social structures that combine aspects of capitalism with aspects of a gift economy.

In a gift economy there is no money and no wage labour. Instead, people produce things for their own consumption or as gifts for other people. It would be a vast extension of the kinds of voluntary work now done by citizen groups such as the Lions' Clubs and Cleanup Australia. It would *not* be a return to some pre-industrial tribal model of society. Clubs and associations would still produce technologically complex goods and services. People would be motivated to give by desire for status and the pleasure of giving. The standard of living would be the effect of multiple gift networks (Vaneigem 1983; Pefanis 1991; Leahy 1994). There is no state in a gift economy utopia. Coordination of activity is conducted by linked collectives of producers and consumers, and by collectives of researchers and media and administrative workers.

This utopia could lead to benign outcomes for the environment. Taking farming as an example, producers would see no advantage in overusing their land. They would seek to conserve their agricultural and environmental resources—to live well in the future and to be able to continue gaining social recognition by giving farm produce to the community. In a capitalist economy it makes sense for entrepreneurs to market anything that can be sold. It also makes sense for consumers to purchase these goods, since they are already tied to a life of forced labour. These factors cause overproduction and overuse of land and other resources. In a gift economy, people's efforts in production would be tempered by the desire to enjoy a leisured existence and a beautiful and healthy environment. Their own material wealth would depend on the desire of others to give, and thus there would be little incentive to continually seek to increase their productive effort—in contrast to the expansionist tendencies of capitalism.

Creativity and choice, which now only find an outlet in leisure, would be turned to creating effective and environmentally benign production processes. A sustainable agriculture based on **polycultures**, with an emphasis on perennial crops, would be the ideal complement to such an economic system. Creating and harvesting a stable polyculture is an enjoyable way to appreciate the bounties of nature as well as a sustainable mode of agricultural production

Box 3.3 Permaculture and community-supported agriculture

Sustainable agriculture can take the forms of **permaculture** and **community-supported agriculture**. 'Permaculture', a term coined by Bill Mollison and David Holmgren, means a system of permanent agriculture—an agriculture that is sustainable because it shares many features with natural forest systems (Mollison & Holmgren 1978; Mollison 1988). The emphasis is on using perennial crops, such as tree crops, to replace food that is now grown through annual cropping. Soil erosion is reduced because there is no annual ploughing and pests and weeds are controlled by mixing a variety of species in a polyculture. Instead of having large areas set aside for pasture, permaculturists favour the integration of animals and mixed crops into domestic and community gardens. Harvesting crops is labour-intensive, as machinery cannot be used to gather crops from a diverse polyculture. Permaculturists favour the development of agricultural systems that supply a local community with diverse products. They oppose the large-scale transport of agricultural products (Mollison & Holmgren 1978; Trainer 1995).

'Community-supported agriculture' refers to organic-farming enterprises that are supported by a community group of consumers in the form of a food-growing/buying cooperative. As subscribers, they pay in advance for a box of fruit and vegetables every week. This food is grown organically by a local farm developed specifically to serve the cooperative. These farms are usually located in urban areas on unused patches of land owned by local councils or governments. The box of food can sometimes be more expensive than the mass-produced food available at the supermarket, but is guaranteed to be locally and organically grown.

(Mollison & Holmgren 1978; see also Mollison 1988; Soule & Piper 1992; French 1993; Hart 1996; Fern 1997; and see Box 3.3). In terms of values, the gift economy operates with an ethic of generosity and egalitarianism. Pleasure is taken from giving to those who are in need. This ethic also applies to the natural world, with other species being regarded as having ethical value and worthy of care and concern.

Hybrids of the gift economy and capitalism: Some case studies

Sustainable agriculture is entering society today despite the constraints of the capitalist economy. It makes sense to characterise these experiments and reforms as hybrids of the gift economy and capitalism. Pretty, in the section of his book *Regenerating Agriculture* that is devoted to case studies, describes the strategies of the Union of Indian Communities of Oaxaca State in Mexico (1999, p. 232). This union was first organised by Indian communities in 1982. In these communities, the main cash crop is coffee, grown on the slopes. A key problem for the farmers growing the coffee had been the role of intermediaries. These entrepreneurs marketed the coffee, controlled credit, and supplied the community with basic necessities. As in many developing countries, most of the profits from the cash crop were appropriated by these middlemen. The basic aim of the union was to deal with this problem by marketing the coffee directly, cutting out the intermediaries.

In 1985 the union decided to move to organic production of coffee. This was done partly to avoid the outlay on costly chemical inputs and partly to (it was hoped) increase yields. A key element in the decision was the fact that international 'fair trade' organisations supported this move to organics and were prepared to pay a premium price for organic coffee. By 1995, some 3000 families in thirty-seven communities had become members of the union. Pretty explains that the new methods of coffee production have required more management supervision and labour input from farmers. In compensation, there has been a 30–50% improvement in yields. While current yields are high compared with previous yields for these communities, they are still less than the yields of large coffee estates, which generally use high-input agriculture.

The organic method used by the union is to grow coffee in the secondary forest, leaving an overstorey of leguminous trees that help to protect and fertilise the coffee and stabilise the soil. The coffee is planted on the contour, with slashed weeds and pruned branches being laid down. The pulp left over after coffee beans are removed is composted, while previously it had been discarded in the waterways. This retention of organic matter aids soil fertility and prevents water pollution. Other additives to the soil are lime, green waste, and animal manure. All these practices create a sustainable coffee plantation, as the long-term fertility of the soil is enhanced. The environmental problems of the input industry are also avoided. The union has created its own organisation for transport, storage, processing, and export of the coffee. Some of the profits from the coffee are used by the union for community-building projects. They have put the money into local schooling, a public transport system that services mountainous areas, a medical insurance system, and several shops that market goods at reasonable prices for local people.

In this scenario, there are aspects of a pure capitalist market economy combined with aspects that challenge capitalism. Looking at the capitalist aspects first, the cooperative is a consortium of growers who are maximising their income by cutting out intermediaries. The coffee is being sold on the world market to rich consumers who are paying a cheap price—in terms of their own labour—for a product that has cost much labour to produce. They are paying a premium price because the product has some quality that as consumers they value; it is a niche market. Much of the social infrastructure of the cooperative is run according to the logic of the capitalist economy. Services such as the bus service and the medical insurance system are paid for by consumers as commodities. So are the items sold in the community shops. The money to pay for these services and goods come from work done growing a cash crop. This work is a form of alienated labour—it is unlikely that it would continue if the farmers had some easier way to access the products that their cash can buy.

Environmentally, the coffee farming has some features in common with other examples of capitalist agriculture. Rainforest is being replaced by a forest dominated by one commercial species, at the expense of biodiversity. The power of consumers from wealthy countries creates this biological destruction from a distance—money for consumer goods has to be made in this way by poor landowners in a developing country. This ecological problem is compounded by the use of fossil fuels to transport coffee across the globe.

There is also much about this enterprise that challenges capitalism. The union has been created by members of an ethnic group that is discriminated against in Mexico—the indigenous Indians. It is a form of social and political empowerment for this group, which 'business as usual' has impoverished. The union is a democratic organisation in which a cooperative of people of roughly equal economic status have joined together to make decisions to the benefit of them all. Under the usual operation of market capitalism, cash incomes from the sale of farm products would be appropriated privately and spent by individual families. Here, many of the fruits of the economic activity are being shared by the community and, in fact, given by the farmers' cooperative as a subsidy for community services—education, health, transport, and so on. This strategy is a partial appropriation of the means of production by a community group. While farms themselves are still owned by individual families, marketing and distribution have come under collective control and are managed for the collective good.

What also makes this situation a hybrid is the role of the fair trade organisation and its alliance of consumers and members. The organisation itself is committed to redressing the imbalance of power between wealthy consumers in rich countries and the poor in developing countries. Its strategy is to pay a higher price to the farmers directly, so that the profits of farming go to them rather than to the owners of shares in multinational food companies. This transaction is a form of gift from wealthy consumers and the organisers and members of the fair trade organisation. It marks a decision to shift resources to those who need them rather than to appropriate as much as possible for personal satisfaction. In this sense, it is a departure from the rationality of self-interest that is the hegemonic ethos of capitalism.

The decision to encourage free trade partners to farm organically is another hybrid aspect of this strategy. It is an attempt by consumers to have some influence over the methods of production. So it is a departure from the systematic tendency of capitalism to put all such decisions in the hands of shareholders and the managers acting rationally on their behalf to increase profits. The strategy possibly has another hybrid aspect: if consumers prefer organics because they are concerned about the environment, it is another form of gift—a gift to nature and to future generations of humans.

My second example is taken from Pretty's book on agricultural reform in Europe (1998). Initial research in Switzerland into low-input farming produced some positive results. Consequently, 200 experimental farms were set up in 1990. In these experiments, pesticides were gradually eliminated and fertiliser inputs were reduced to 20% of the levels that were common in intensive agriculture in Switzerland. Yields fell by 5–15%. Despite this, economic returns went up, as the cost of inputs had fallen by 8–17%. A 4-year rotation of maize, wheat, clover-pasture, and potatoes got the best economic results using 45% of the usual input of nitrogenous fertiliser and half of the usual input of pesticides. These results were so striking that the Swiss public demanded changes and in 1996 the government went ahead with new regulations and a system of subsidies for sustainable agriculture (Pretty 1998, p. 103).

These new regulations make a distinction between three levels of sustainable agriculture, and the government gives larger subsidies to farms that make a more serious attempt to create sustainable agriculture. The lowest level of support is for farms that preserve specific biotypes, such as hedgerows or meadows. The next level of support is for farms that employ 'integrated agriculture' in order to reduce artificial inputs—for example, a mixed farm in which animal manure is used on crops or fertility is enhanced by crop rotations. On these farms, pesticide applications must be reduced to specified low-risk levels. The most support is given to organic farms; organic certification requires farmers to do without any chemical inputs.

Under these regulations, implementation is not supervised by government bureaucracies but by more accountable and local bodies—by farmers' unions, farm advisors, local governments, and NGOs (non-government organisations). These reforms have been quite effective, with 20% of Swiss farms participating in the scheme at one of the three levels. There are 11,000 that protect a biotype, 9000 practising integrated agriculture, and 1500 that are organic.

What are some of the capitalist aspects of this strategy? Farms are still privately owned, marketing their products to paying consumers. Much has been done to ensure that farmers continue to make a profit. For example, the initial research favours integrated agriculture as the most economically effective option. This has been at the expense of some environmental goals; integrated-agriculture farms still use half of the chemical inputs of conventional farms. Economic incentives to move to sustainability are undoubtedly helping, but they are not wholly paying for changes to sustainable agriculture. We can see this in the fact that there are still 80% of farmers who have not been persuaded that it makes economic sense to move in this direction. We can see it also in the way that the more economically difficult farming options are being taken on few farms—of Switzerland's 75,000 farms, only 1500 are fully organic. Thus, most farmers are still making economically rational decisions to maximise income, so there is a limit on the environmental reforms that are practicable. As well, Swiss voters are only paying an *incentive* to promote this change, rather than funding it fully, which suggests that most voters want to avoid the large increases in taxation that would be required to publicly fund substantial environmental reform.

On the other hand, elements of the gift economy are also operating here. Voters are making a decision to give some of their income to environmental reforms. These subsidies are a gift to future generations and to the environment and other species. This decision goes beyond the narrowly defined economic interests of the Swiss people as consumers. As consumers, individuals are expected to use their income to buy the maximum possible number of consumer goods and services for their private use, compensating themselves for the constraints of wage labour and expanding the market in the process. The altruistic and collectivist use of income breaks that pattern. It involves consumers in an attempt to control the means of production in agriculture, to have an influence through the political process on the way agricultural land is used. In terms of the implementation of these regulations, we can also see a move towards community control of agricultural land through voluntary bodies and unions of farmers.

Conclusion: Future directions

Looking at a large number of examples of changes towards sustainable agriculture (see, for example, Pretty 2002 and www.farmingsolutions.org), the concept of capitalist–gift economy hybrids can be used to understand and describe the ways in which these changes fit within the capitalist economic structure but nevertheless move beyond it and point to an alternative economic model. Many of the hybrids incorporate some degree of control of agricultural production by either the producers themselves or by the community at large. This is reflected in the following initiatives and strategies:

- participatory planning of sustainable farming strategies
- land reform and the redistribution of ownership away from large landowners
- participatory and democratic education
- consumer unions that attempt to influence farming practices
- voter alliances that support controls over agriculture for the sake of the environment.

Hybrid models also tend to include some degree of 'gift' as a mode of distribution of products—that is, forms of distribution that are designed to benefit particular people rather than to make the highest possible profit. This is reflected in community control of the products and/or profits of agriculture, distribution of agricultural products for the subsistence of the community, and gifts of wealth from rich consumers to poor producers. Many hybrids are an expression of care and concern for the natural world and for future generations of humans. In a sense, they are gifts to the planet. This applies in the case of voters who support taxes that will benefit the environment, consumers who decide to pay a higher price for products that are more environmentally friendly than rival products, farmers and marketers who are attracted to sustainable farming as an expression of their love for the natural world, and volunteers who engage in non-market sustainable farming in community gardens or alternative-lifestyle farms.

Hybrids can tap into people's need for meaningful and creative work. This is most obviously the case for those whose labour is voluntary. However, in cases where people are labouring for money, it also seems likely that they choose work in sustainable agriculture to express themselves creatively (take, for example, organic farmers who are passionate about organic food). Such a livelihood may be chosen even when it is not the most economically rational choice. Finally, hybrids can prefigure the alliances and networks of participatory democratic structures that can organise production and distribution in a gift economy—for example, the links between agricultural educators in universities and farmers learning to apply organic farming techniques, and the links between consumers of organic food and the marketers and farmers who produce it.

The success of sustainable forms of agriculture, particularly in addressing nutrient loss, ultimately depends not only upon the actions of concerned individuals and communities, but also on state regulation in the form of incentives, subsidies, and planning. The experiments in sustainable agriculture discussed in this chapter show that viable social alternatives are available that effectively link features of capitalism to features of the gift economy.

Summary of main points

- Nutrient loss is a problem for all agriculture that exports nutrients to cities or overseas. It is a major problem for Australian export agriculture.
- While artificial fertilisers are often seen as the answer to nutrient loss, the cost of nutrient replacement is very high and the coming 'oil crunch' makes this an infeasible long-term solution.
- Ruralisation and recycling of all food wastes can be seen as an environmentally sound solution, but the social, economic, and political implications of these solutions are likely to limit their application.
- Nutrient loss is but one of many environmental problems associated with contemporary agricultural practices. These problems are frequently seen as a necessary price that must be paid to feed a growing world population.
- While sustainable agriculture produces good yields and makes economic sense to a certain extent, there are still economic barriers to its widespread implementation.
- Capitalism can be seen as a basic social cause of the environmental damage produced by agriculture; the gift economy is a utopian alternative.
- Experiments in sustainable agriculture can be seen as hybrids of the gift economy and capitalism, and they offer potentially viable solutions to environmental problems.

Discussion questions

1. What are some environmentally damaging agricultural practices?
2. Why is nutrient loss such an intractable problem from a social and economic point of view?
3. Why do current agricultural practices make economic sense, despite the damage they do to the environment?
4. In what ways do consumers contribute to the environmental degradation caused by food production and consumption?
5. Is the gift economy a realistic alternative to capitalism? Is it a desirable alternative?
6. How useful is it to understand sustainable agriculture initiatives as a social and economic mix of capitalism and the gift economy?

Further investigation

1 Capitalist agricultural practices are the prime cause of environmental degradation. Discuss.
2 Explore some examples of community-supported agriculture in your region. What are the benefits and limitations of such approaches?
3 Sustainable agriculture makes social and economic sense. Discuss.

Further reading and web resources

Books

Almas, R. & Lawrence, G. (eds) 2003, *Globalization, Localization and Sustainable Livelihoods*, Ashgate, Aldershot, UK.

Campbell, A. 1991, *Planning for Sustainable Farming: The Potter Farmland Plan Story,* Lothian Books, Melbourne.

Fern, K. 1997, *Plants for a Future: Edible & Useful Plants for a Healthier World,* Permanent Publications, Clanfield, UK.

French, J. 1993, *The Wilderness Garden: Beyond Organic Gardening*, Aird Books, Melbourne.

Furuno, T. 2001, *The Power of Duck: Integrated Rice and Duck Farming,* Tagari, Sisters Creek, Australia.

Holmgren, D. 1994, *Trees on the Treeless Plains,* Holmgren Design Services, Hepburn, Australia.

Just Food Project of Friends of the Earth Brisbane 2002, *Towards a Community Supported Agriculture*, Friends of the Earth, Brisbane.

Mollison, B. 1988, *Permaculture: A Designers' Manual* , Tagari Publications, Tyalgum, Australia.

Pretty, J. 2002, *Agri-Culture: Re-connecting People, Land and Nature,* Earthscan, London.

Trainer, T. 1995, *The Conserver Society: Alternatives for Sustainability,* Zed Books, London.

Journals

New Internationalist: www.newint.org

Organic Gardener

Web sites

Farming Solutions: www.farmingsolutions.org
Stories, news reports, and data on sustainable agriculture.

Growing Diversity: www.grain.org/gd
Grassroots initiatives to preserve agricultural biodiversity.

Holmgren Design Services: www.holmgren.com.au

Organic Consumers Association (USA): www.organicconsumers.org

Organic Europe: www.organic-europe.net/

Permaculture International: www.permacultureinternational.org

The Simpler Way (Ted Trainer's site): www.arts,unsw.edu.au/tsw/

Terry Leahy's Site: www.octapod.org/gifteconomy

Articles on agriculture and other topics.

USDA Alternative Farming Systems Information Center: www.nal.usda.gov/afsic/csa/

References

ABS—*see* Australian Bureau of Statistics.

AEN—*see* Australian Energy News.

Ainger, K. 2003, 'The New Peasants' Revolt', *New Internationalist*, vol. 353, pp. 9–12.

Anderson, A. B. (ed.) 1990, *Alternatives to Deforestation: Steps Toward Sustainable Use of the Amazon Rain Forest*, Columbia University Press, New York.

Australian Bureau of Statistics 2002a, *Year Book Australia, Special Article: Understanding Agricultural Exports Data* (cat. no. 1301.0), Australian Bureau of Statistics, Canberra.

—— 2002b, *International Trade in Goods and Services* (cat. no. 5368.0), Australian Bureau of Statistics, Canberra.

—— 2002c, *Agricultural Commodities, Australia* (cat. no. 7121.0), Australian Bureau of Statistics, Canberra.

Australian Energy News 2001, 'Oil Production Curve Causes Concern', *Australian Energy News*, issue 22, December <www.industry.gov.au/resources/netenergy/aen> accessed March 2003.

Barraclough, S. L. & Ghimire, K. B. 2000, *Agricultural Expansion and Tropical Deforestation: Poverty, International Trade and Land Use*, Earthscan, London.

Campbell, A. 1991, *Planning for Sustainable Farming, The Potter Farmland Plan Story*, Lothian Books, Melbourne.

Campbell, J. 1997, *The Coming Oil Crisis*, Multiscience and Petroconsultants, Brentwood, UK.

Cardan, P. 1974, *Modern Capitalism and Revolution*, Solidarity, London.

Fern, K. 1997, *Plants for a Future: Edible & Useful Plants for a Healthier World*, Permanent Publications, Clanfield, UK.

French, J. 1993, *The Wilderness Garden: Beyond Organic Gardening*, Aird Books, Melbourne.

Furuno, T. 2001, *The Power of Duck: Integrated Rice and Duck Farming*, Tagari, Sisters Creek, Australia.

Gunther, F. 1998, 'Phosphorus Management and Societal Structure', *Vatten*, vol. 98, no. 3.

Gunther, F. 2002, 'Fossil Energy and Food Security', *Energy and Environment*, vol. 12, no. 4, pp. 253–75.

Gutberlet, J. 1999, 'Rural Development and Social Exclusion: A Case Study of Sustainability and Distributive Issues in Brazil', *Australian Geographer*, vol. 30, no. 2, pp. 221–37.

Hart, R. A. 1996, *Forest Gardening: Rediscovering Nature and Community in a Post-Industrial Age*, Green Books, Devon, UK.

Holmgren, D. 2002, *Permaculture: Principles & Pathways Beyond Sustainability*, Holmgren Design Services, Hepburn, Victoria.

Jenkins, J. C. 1994, *The Humanure Handbook: A Guide to Composting Human Manure*, Jenkins Publishing, Grove City, Pennsylvania.

Lawrence, G. & Vanclay, F. 1992, 'Agricultural Production and Environmental Degradation in the Murray-Darling Basin', in G. Lawrence, F. Vanclay & B. Furze, *Agriculture, Environment and Society: Contemporary Issues for Australians*, Macmillan, Melbourne.

Leahy, T. 1994, 'Some Problems of Environmentalist Reformism', *People and Physical Environment Research*, vol. 46, pp. 3–13.

McLaughlin, A. 1993, *Regarding Nature: Industrialism and Deep Ecology*, State of NY Press, Albany.

McLennan, W. 1996, *Australian Agriculture and the Environment*, Australian Bureau of Statistics, Canberra.

Mannion, A. M. 1995, *Agriculture and Environmental Change: Temporal and Spatial Dimensions*, John Wiley & Sons, Chichester, UK.

Maslin, M. 2002, *The Coming Storm: The True Causes of Freak Weather,* ABC Books, Sydney.

Mollison, B. 1988, *Permaculture: A Designers' Manual* , Tagari Publications, Tyalgum, Australia.

Mollison, B. & Holmgren, D. 1978, *Permaculture One*, Corgi Books, Uxbridge.

Pefanis, J. 1991, *Heterology and the Postmodern: Bataille, Baudrillard and Lyotard,* Allen & Unwin, Sydney.

Pepper, D. 1995, *Eco-Socialism: From Deep Ecology to Social Justice*, Routledge, UK.

Pont, J. J. 1997, *Heart Health Promotion in a Respectable Community: An Inside View of the Culture of the Coalfields of Northern New South Wales*, PhD thesis, University of Newcastle.

Pretty, J. 1998, *The Living Land: Agriculture, Food and Community Regeneration in Rural Europe,* Earthscan, London.

Pretty, J. 1999, *Regenerating Agriculture: Policies and Practice for Sustainability and Self-Reliance,* Earthscan, London.

Pretty, J. 2002, *Agri-Culture: Re-Connecting People, Land and Nature,* Earthscan, London.

Roberts, B. 1992, *Land Care Manual,* New South Wales University Press, Kensington.

Roberts, B. 1995, *The Quest for Sustainable Agriculture and Land Use,* University of New South Wales Press, Sydney.

Romeiro, A. R. 1987, 'Alternative Developments in Brazil', in B. Glaeser (ed.), *The Green Revolution Revisited: Critique and Alternatives*, Unwin Hyman, London.

Roszak, T. 1992, *The Voice of the Earth*, Simon and Schuster, New York.

Soule, J. D. & Piper, J. K. 1992, *Farming in Nature's Image: An Ecological Approach to Agriculture,* Island Press, Washington DC.

Trainer, T. 1995, *The Conserver Society: Alternatives for Sustainability*, Zed Books, London.

Vaneigem, R. 1983, *The Revolution of Everyday Life*, Left Bank Books and Rebel Press, London.

4

Agribusiness, Biotechnology, and Food

Geoffrey Lawrence and Janet Grice

Overview

- What is 'agribusiness' and what role does it play in food production?
- What types of biotechnologies are used in the food and agricultural industries and what do consumers think of them?
- What is the future of genetically modified foods?

This chapter deals with the connections between agriculture and food production, highlighting, in particular, the global nature of the agri-food sector and its commitment to biotechnology. It examines consumer attitudes to food biotechnologies and argues that the growing consumer wariness about genetically engineered foods (together with a surge in interest in organic foods) may alter the current pro-biotechnology trajectory of the agri-food sector.

Key terms

agribusiness	food safety	neo-liberalism
agri-food	genetic engineering	substitutionism
appropriationism	genetically modified organisms (GMOs)	transgenic organisms
biotechnology	globalisation	vertical integration
capitalism	horizontal integration	
DNA		

Introduction

Why would scientists wish to take a gene from a fish (the flounder) and insert it into a tomato? Why would they select a gene from a chicken and put it in a potato? The answers, according to food industry scientists, are that, in the first case, the tomato will have a better flavour and longer shelf life, and in the second case, the potato will be able to develop increased resistance to disease. Geneticists are also attempting to produce a variety of wheat that is resistant to pests: it will need fewer, if any, chemical sprayings to control insect infestations. How would this work? A gene from the soil bacterium *Bacillus thuringiensis* produces a substance toxic to insects but not to humans. If inserted and expressed in the plant it provides continuous pest control. In another experiment, scientists have developed a pig with the capacity to grow more quickly on less food and produce leaner pork. The pig has been genetically altered so that it contains extra hormone genes derived from human **DNA**.

For science and industry, the benefits that will be derived from the **genetic engineering** of plants and animals outweigh the risks and concerns. The food processing industry, in particular, will benefit financially if foods can be processed more easily, have a longer shelf life, travel without damage, and exhibit characteristics desired by consumers.

What of the consumers? Going by studies undertaken in Australia and abroad, there appears to be growing consumer resistance to genetically modified foods (GM foods). Why, then, would major segments of the **agri-food** industry be so convinced of the desirability of going down a 'biotech' path in the production of foods? Answers to this question can be found in an understanding of **agribusiness** and its role in farming and food production.

The agribusiness sector

'Agriculture' is often conceived as the on-farm production of foods and fibres. Farmers grow the products necessary to sustain life, which are then distributed and marketed locally, nationally, and globally. Farmers in this sense are viewed as largely independent producers, making on-farm decisions with a very firm understanding of the marketplace but with relative autonomy in deciding what they produce and how they produce it. For the American John Davis—who coined the term 'agribusiness' in the 1950s—such a view of farming is antiquated. Farming must be seen as part of a wider network of production relations. Agribusiness is 'the sum of all farming operations, plus the manufacture and distribution of all farm production supplies, plus the total of all operations performed in connection with the handling, storage, processing and distribution of farm commodities' (Davis 1956, p. 109).

What Davis was highlighting, well over 40 years ago, was the full integration of farming into wider circuits of capitalist production—a process that accelerated in the USA and other Western nations after World War II as the corporate sector began to horizontally and vertically integrate its activities. **Horizontal integration** is the purchasing of like companies (for example, a flour mill purchasing other flour mills), while **vertical integration** is the purchase of unlike companies that can form strategic production linkages (for example, a flour mill purchasing a biscuit or bread manufacturer or a supermarket chain). Both are strategies to increase the size of operations, to draw closer connections between affiliates, to increase the level and efficiency of production, and to raise profits. Both lead, in the agri-food industries, to the progressive integration of farming into corporate business operations. How is this achieved?

On the *upstream* side, the corporate sector, including companies such as John Deere, ConAgra, Syngenta, DuPont (Pioneer), Aventis, and Dow, and firms in the finance industry, supply the inputs used by farmers—the tractors, headers, ploughs, fertilisers, seeds, insecticides, and irrigation pipes—and the credit to purchase them. On the *downstream* side of farming, companies such as Goodman Fielder, George Weston, Kraft, Bunge, Simplot, Kelloggs, Smith's Snackfood, McDonald's, Woolworths, and Coles take agricultural produce and store it, process it, package it, transport it, and sell it through a host of outlets, including supermarkets. The influence of firms involved in upstream and downstream activities has had a significant impact on farming. In entering contract relations with firms in the corporate sector, farmers find they are effectively bound by these relations. The food corporations can demand that certain seeds be used, that certain varieties of potato or tomato or pineapple be grown instead of others, that crops be harvested at specific times, that particular chemical sprays be used, that company-determined pay rates for employees be enforced, and that certain standards be reached before produce is accepted by the company (Burch & Rickson 2001). This gives the corporate sector ultimate control over food production in the developed world.

Globalisation and agribusiness

The 'seedling to supermarket' arrangements described above not only allow control throughout the marketing of foods and fibres, but also ensure profits are made along the production chain. In the US, the agribusiness/food sector is the second most profitable industry after pharmaceuticals and has annual sales of US$400 billion (Magdoff et al. 2000, p. 2). Cargill, the largest grain trader in the world, operates out of the US but has 800 offices/production plants in seventy countries, employing some 70,000 workers. ConAgra, also based in the US, owns fifty-six companies operating in twenty-six countries with a workforce of 58,000, and it had profits of over US$7 billion in 2002 (McMichael 2000, p. 103; *New Farm*, p.1). Both these companies are vertically integrated and both are examples of corporations that have used their market positioning to secure transnational advantage. Another example is Tyson Foods. According to McMichael (2000, p. 103), Tyson sends US chicken meat to Mexico for processing, taking advantage of cheap labour (one-tenth the cost of labour in the US) to prepare chicken for the Japanese market.

Other firms have been accused of exploiting unprotected child labour in their profit-making endeavours (McMichael 2000, p. 99), some have 'bargained' for lower payments for contract production (with the threat of withdrawal if the growers refused the offer) (Burch & Rickson 2001), and others have taken advantage of lower environmental standards in certain countries to produce foods more cheaply—hardly something that will contribute to long-term sustainability (Constance et al. 2003). For an export country like Argentina, the presence of the agri-food transnational corporations has contributed to relative food price increases, the removal of farmers, and increased unemployment and income loss among the lower-income sectors of society (Teubal & Rodriquez 2003). Agri-food change in the wine industry in South Africa has brought workers 'little improvement, either in the form of wages, or living conditions' (Ewert 2003, p. 167).

Another, closer-to-home, example of transnational behaviour concerns Arnotts. Most Australians eat or at least know of biscuits from the Arnotts range—it has been associated with the 'image' of Australia, having, as Pritchard (1999, p. 296) puts it, 'iconic national status'. In 1993, the US-based Campbell Soup Company bid for Arnotts. While there was strong opposition, institutional backers pushed for, and gained, a 60% hold in Arnotts. By 1997 the company was wholly owned by Campbell's. Since this total acquisition, Arnotts has been 'used' for local profit generation (and repatriation), rather than as part of a Supermarket to Asia strategy to place the Australian food industry's products in the Asian market (Pritchard 1999). Decisions are made in the US for (predominantly) US shareholders.

Other examples of the transformative pressures put on food commodity chains by agribusiness abound. Both directly and through agro-political organisations, agribusiness has pressured governments in places such as Australia and New Zealand to deregulate the agricultural sector, allowing corporate takeovers of what were once state-controlled or cooperative ventures (Le Heron & Roche 1999; Pritchard 1999). Hand-in-hand with deregulation of the agricultural sector and **neo-liberal** policies that foster corporate financial advantage have come mergers, takeovers, partnerships, and joint ventures, leading to the concentration of the activities of particular agri-food industries in a small number of firms. In the latest and most comprehensive account of the

US agri-food sector, Heffernan (1999) reports that four companies in the beef-packing industry are responsible for some 79% of US output. Similarly, the top four companies are responsible for 62% of flour milling, 57% of pork production, and 49% of chicken production. Such market concentration gives the top four firms enormous economic and political clout.

Trade in undifferentiated commodities (raw sugar, unprocessed wheat, generic beef, wool, and so forth) has previously been undertaken through statutory authorities and producer boards—particularly in places such as New Zealand, Canada, and Australia. However, as deregulation has occurred, agribusinesses have taken over much of this trade, converting raw materials into 'durable' foods so as to add value to exports. There is obviously financial benefit in global trading, but there is a growing realisation that consumers—particularly in the West—are demanding not more food, but better food, or so-called *high-value foods* (HVFs). These foods include poultry meat, fruits, vegetables, and fish, dairy, and organic products that can be shifted around the world to meet consumer demand (Bonanno et al. 1994; Watts & Goodman 1997). HVFs are not standardised bulk commodities but 'quality' products that serve niche markets. In their aptly titled book *From Columbus to ConAgra*, Bonanno and colleagues (1994) describe the changes that have occurred in the US. Their argument is that flexibility is the major driving force in corporate expansionism. By exercising Just-in-Time principles (delivery-on-demand of agricultural products, rather than the need to store) many firms have moved away from the 'durable' manufactured, processed, canned, and frozen foods to fresh foods and other HVFs. These foods are sourced globally so as to save on labour costs as well as to guarantee year-round supply—largely for consumers interested in purchasing foods that are identified with health and good living (Watts & Goodman 1997).

It is the global organisation of production that is the defining characteristic of both forms of trade—in durable and fresh foods. The so-called 'world steer' is now understood to be the agricultural equivalent of the 'world car'. As the fast-food industry has grown, beef has become a world commodity, with 'components' manufactured (grown) and assembled (in the case of the beef animal, disassembled) in various locations around the globe. Cattle ranching takes place in locations such as Central America, Australia, Argentina, and South Africa. Semen is sent from the US to 'enhance' breeding. This is supplemented by antibiotics and other veterinary medicines manufactured by transnational pharmaceutical companies—with origins in places like Switzerland and Germany. Beef is fattened with grains often imported from the US, and the meat is sent to the US, Russia, the Philippines, Mexico—and indeed to any country proud to display the Golden Arches—as a generic product to be 'ground' for hamburger meat (see descriptions in Rifkin 1992, pp. 192–3; McMichael 2000, pp. 101–2).

The two processes that have underpinned—and help us explain—agribusiness expansion are **appropriationism** and **substitutionism** (Goodman et al. 1987; Goodman & Redclift 1991). Appropriationism is the progressive use of manufactured inputs in agriculture. What were once farm-derived inputs (seeds kept from the year before, silage stored from the past season, 'natural' fertilisation of the soil via crop rotation, and the use of horses to haul machinery) have been appropriated by off-farm industries that now supply the seeds, fertilisers, and machinery as farm inputs. In so doing, agribusiness makes money from these sales, while providing farmers with the technical means to increase output. A contemporary example is the 'redesigning' of plants and animals so that they conform to the corporate agenda of having farmers purchase seeds that will only respond the company's proprietary chemicals (discussed below). Another is the development of tomato varieties specifically suited to particular mechanical harvesting equipment (Pritchard & Burch 2003, p. 34).

The second process—substitutionism—is the replacement of costly and/or unreliably supplied inputs with 'generic ingredients' in the food processing industry. As Friedmann (1991, p. 74) has argued, what food processors want 'is not sugar, but sweeteners; not flour or cornstarch, but thickeners; not palm oil or butter, but fats; not beef or cod, but proteins. Interchangeable inputs, natural or chemically synthesized, augment control and reduce costs better than older mercantile strategies for diversifying sources of supply…' Substitutionism allows for greater corporate control over agriculture because of the ability of firms to substitute components in food production. Firms can use 'sugar' made from the cornstarch, for example, rather than that derived from cane or beet—particularly if it is cheaper, more readily available, and has other positive characteristics, such as being easy to manufacture (see discussion below). The firms have the capacity to bypass particular farmers, particular commodities, and particular regions in sourcing generic food ingredients, again placing more control in the hands of agribusiness.

Agri-food biotechnologies

Why might biotechnologies be so desired by agribusiness? Biotechnologies have been employed for centuries to make cheeses, bake breads, and brew beers. Traditional **biotechnology** is the harnessing of natural biological processes to produce foods, beverages, and medicines. One example is the use of micro-organisms to ferment substances (such as grapes into wine). In more recent times, through the application of advanced cell-biology techniques, other processes have been made possible. Biotechnologies applied in the agri-food sector today include large-scale fermentation, cell culture and fusion, cloning, gene marker technology, DNA sequencing, diagnostic probes, and genetic engineering (Norton 2002, p.4). It is this last component of biotechnology—genetic engineering—that is proving both profoundly transformative and controversial. Genetic engineering involves the manipulation of genes, and components of genes, to alter the characteristics of bacteria, plants, and animals.

Entirely new **transgenic organisms** can be created by the cross-species insertion of genetic material. As well as the examples given at the beginning of the chapter, there are others of considerable interest to agri-food industries:

- Scientists are experimenting with placing a gene from a waxmoth into a potato (to increase resistance to bruising); a gene from a trout into a catfish (to encourage faster growth of the catfish); and a gene from a pea plant into rice (to add new protein to rice grains). These are but a few examples; there are thousands of other transgenic foods being developed throughout the world.
- In the area of animal production, the natural hormone bovine somatotropin has been extracted from cattle, synthesized biogenetically, and injected into cows, increasing milk production by 30%.
- Scientists hope to be able to insert a gene responsible for root-nodule formation in legumes into non-leguminous crop plants such as wheat and barley. If successful, this process would enable those crops to 'fix' their own nitrogen, potentially reducing the amount of fertiliser that farmers need to apply.
- Experiments have been successfully performed to make commercial crops resistant to herbicides. Chemicals can be sprayed to rid the soil of weeds, while still allowing the crops to grow without damage or loss of vigour.
- Enzymes from bacteria, yeast, fungi, and plants are being extracted and biogenetically engineered and 'grown' in fermentation tanks to provide the food industry with substances that speed up food-manufacturing processes and impart new characteristics to food (Lawrence et al. 2001; Norton 2002).

While some of these innovations would appear, *prima facie*, to be desirable in a world of food scarcity, there are many critics who argue that these sorts of experiments will have negative animal-welfare implications, have the potential to create health problems, and will not help feed the world's poor (Ho 1998; Hindmarsh & Lawrence 2001; McMichael 2003). So why persist? By looking a little more closely at the last two examples listed above, the advantages of genetic engineering for agribusiness will become obvious.

Appropriationism

Herbicide resistance provides an excellent case of appropriationism. Agribusiness companies have genetically engineered seeds that will tolerate spraying with particular herbicides. The most well-known case is that of Monsanto and its proprietary herbicide, Roundup. This herbicide is toxic to most herbaceous plants, including soybeans. Scientists have engineered a soybean plant that will not only resist Roundup, but will actually need to be sprayed with it in order to reach peak production. The company is developing a total seed-and-herbicide package that it can sell to farmers. The plant is a productive one, weeds can be removed more readily, and the farmer could potentially increase profits by growing the Roundup Ready seeds. However, the farmer cannot keep the seed and grow it the next year. If that occurs, the farmer can be sued by the company for breaching intellectual property laws that protect the seed's genetic makeup. When contracts are signed with Monsanto, farmers are forbidden from cultivating other varieties, using herbicides other than those produced by Monsanto, and exchanging the seeds with neighbours. The farmer must also allow Monsanto officials to inspect paddocks and fields for 3 years (de la Perriere & Seuret 2000, p. 16). A number of other seed companies—AstaZeneca, Novartis, Du Pont/Pioneer, and Aventis—have developed what has been called 'terminator technology'. They are attempting to put a complete stop to any seed replanting by the farmer by inserting a 'terminator' gene in the seed that is purchased from the companies. Seeds produced from plants with the 'terminator' gene are rendered sterile (Crouch 2001, p. 31).

By 1998, only 4 years after the first authorisations allowing the sowing of genetically modified (GM) crops, some 30 million hectares of GM cotton, soybeans, tomatoes, potatoes, and canola had been planted. By 2001 there were 50 million hectares planted with GM crops—mostly in the US, Canada, Argentina, and China (Pretty 2002, p. 128). The US leads the way, with some 25% of its corn production, 35% of its soybean production, and 50% of its cotton production using GM pesticide-resistant and/or herbicide-resistant seeds (de la Perriere & Seuret 2000, p. 41). It is estimated that the global market for GM crops will be approximately US$20 billion by 2005 (de la Perriere & Seuret 2000, p. 41).

In the case of herbicide-resistant canola, it is now acknowledged there are serious risks of cross-pollination, with spontaneous hybridisation occurring between the genetically engineered crop and its close relatives—including wild radish and hoary mustard. This might result in the growth of 'superweeds' that can resist herbicide treatment, as well as other impacts. For example, given that canola pollen can travel up to two kilometres from the crop, neighbouring farmers wanting to grow and sell 'non-GM' canola will find it virtually impossible to protect their crop. Organic honey producers will not know whether bees have taken pollen from the GM crop—thus preventing the honey from being labelled 'organic' (and, hence, taking away the opportunity of obtaining premium prices for the product) (Allen 2000, p. 65; Fitzsimons 2000, pp. 192–3). There are other major concerns about genetic engineering of crops and animals:

- **Genetically modified organisms (GMOs)** are complex and 'unstable' and have the potential to affect the environment in ways not able to be predicted by science. Even GM advocates are urging caution in the release of GM fish, for fear that these fish will invade the habitats of native species and eliminate them (see report in *Associated Press* 2003, p. 1)
- Insect resistance will inevitably occur, reducing the ability of GM crops to survive infestations. Scientists will then look for alternative insect-resisting

genes to insert into crops and insects will eventually become resistant to them. The problem is linked to large-scale monocropping (planting vast areas exclusively or almost exclusively with one variety), yet monocropping is likely to accelerate as agriculture becomes increasingly industrialised (de la Perriere & Seuret 2000, pp. 43–4; Magdoff et al. 2000).

- Organic producers who have relied on natural biological controls, such as the soil bacterium *Bacillus thuringiensis* (Bt), will face major problems as insects become resistant to plants genetically engineered with Bt (de la Perriere & Seuret 2000, pp. 43–4)
- GM products could seriously compromise the treatment of human and animal diseases. Some GM crops have antibiotic-resistant genes that, if they transferred to bacteria, could make those bacteria immune to drugs, thus undermining current treatments.
- Science has yet to understand the extent of the allergic reactions that people and animals may experience from ingesting GM foods. Allergies relate to particular proteins produced by plants. The recombination of plant genetic material can lead to allergic reactions that have the potential to harm or kill those eating the novel foods (Conner 2000).

Despite these and other concerns, the vertical integration of firms in the seed and chemical industries has provided enormous potential for appropriationist strategies. In the end, the farmers are dependent upon the corporations for all of the inputs for farming—apart, of course, from their own labour power.

Substitutionism

Substitutionism occurs as the food industry seeks to use biotechnology to produce generic inputs rather than rely upon specific crops. The best example is that of sugar. Historically, sugar has been extracted from cane and from beet. Today, through the application of a genetically engineered enzyme to cornstarch, what is called *high-fructose corn syrup* (HFCS) is produced. Corn is wet milled to extract starch, and an enzyme is added to extract glucose—with enzymatic isomerisation turning glucose into fructose. The liquid fructose becomes an input into the industrial food process, where it is used in soft drink and other food manufacturing processes. It is highly regarded by the food industry because it provides an excellent substrate for yeast; blends easily with acids, flavourings and other sweeteners; retains moisture; and allows for greater all-round control in food processing (*Food Resources* 2003, p. 1). It was first used in the 1960s, but consumption soared when raw-sugar prices rose in 1974–75. By 1986, HFCS accounted for over half the caloric-sweetener market in the US (Llambi 1994, p. 200), and it is currently used extensively throughout the world.

According to Goodman and Redclift (1991, p. 190), because sweeteners can now be made from corn, wheat, sorghum, and potatoes and can be used interchangeably in food production, corporate firms have more flexibility than they used to. They can literally pick which field crops they will use to make not only industrial sugars, but also proteins, starches, and oils. Their prediction, at the beginning of the 1990s, that 'agri-food systems gradually will merge with the chemical and pharmaceutical industries to form a "bio-industrial processing complex"' (Goodman & Redclift 1991, p. 109) has become a reality at the beginning of the twenty-first century (see Wilkinson 2003). Heffernan (1999) has stated that the recent joint venture between Cargill (a company with worldwide seed interests) and Monsanto (one of the leaders in biotechnology) will allow the development of seed packages in the manner described above, while Buttel (1999, p. 8) has declared that the world's private and public agri-food research and development systems 'have become globalized and "biotechnologized", with their center of gravity now pivoting around a highly concentrated chemical-seeds-biotechnology complex dominated by seven multinational corporations'.

This does not mean there are not 'spaces' for actors to protest, or for alternative food regimes (such as organics) to emerge (Hendrickson & Heffernan 2003). In fact, there is evidence that, as a result of the contradictory forces that are part of global industrial expansion, homogenisation is being accompanied by differentiation, centralisation is being matched by decentralisation, and integration is occurring alongside fragmentation (Burch & Rickson 2002; Pritchard & Burch 2003). Nevertheless, what is argued above is that biotechnology is being used to enhance both appropriationism and substitutionism in the agri-food industries. Despite some public opposition, biotechnologies continue to be applied widely in agriculture, and are now found in, or are used to produce, over 30,000 varieties of food (*AfroCentric News*, 2003, p. 3). And yet, at the same time, it can be argued that 'Agricultural biotechnology has been, so far, a massive pyramid scheme financed by hopes of great wealth down the road. Few, if any, companies that invested heavily in biotechnology have recovered that investment through sales of a genetically-engineered product' (Charles 2001, p. 295). Monsanto profited from the sales of its herbicide, Roundup, but has since become a subsidiary of the Swedish-owned firm Pharmacia. Others have profited by selling their holdings 'at a good price when the next wave of speculative money came along' (see Charles 2001, p. 296).

Public perceptions of GMOs and GM foods

A number of studies around the world (but largely confined to Western nations) confirm that there is growing public suspicion of GMOs. While people seem to be quite at ease with the application of biotechnologies in the pharmaceuticals industry (to manufacture synthetic chemicals for human and animal health), or to help clean up the environment (bio-remediation) or to grow novel plants for export (for example, developing a 'blue rose' for the international marketplace) they are much less convinced of the benefits of eating GM food. Public surveys in Australia, Brazil, Canada, Japan, the UK, and the US indicate that consumers have a generally negative view of GM foods, with respondents considering that the risks of such foods outweigh any benefits (see Norton 1999). Consumers appear to be increasingly concerned about the health and safety aspects of food production and manufacture. There is growing suspicion that artificial chemicals in foods (preservatives, flavour enhancers, and so forth) are responsible for ill-health, and the public appears to view genetic manipulation as yet another form of 'interference' that compromises naturalness. GM foods are products that consumers believe they and their families could well do without (INRA 2000, p. 50).

In Australia, researchers have established that there is no 'blanket' dislike for genetic engineering—it all depends on the sort of manipulation taking place. Genetic engineering of plants gains more acceptance than for animals, and for animals more than for humans (Norton et al. 1998). While one Australian survey received quite positive responses to questions about genetic engineering (Kelley 1995), a close analysis of the questions indicated they were worded so as to elicit favourable responses (Hindmarsh et al. 1995). The majority of respondents to another Australian survey believed it was morally wrong to insert human genetic material in other species (for example, pigs) and they believed that there would be long-term health problems associated with the ingestion of GMOs. They believed that accidental releases would result in environmental damage, and that, on the whole, the benefits of genetic engineering were outweighed by the risks (Norton et al. 1998). There was over 95% agreement that particular transgenic foods should be labelled, 93% agreement that consumers should be consulted before the release of GM foods, and 92% support for government control of GM foods (Norton et al. 1998). In Europe, people have argued for the right to choose whether or not they would eat GM foods (in other words, that all GM foods be labelled as such) and have called for their banning until they are proven to be harmless (European Commission 2001).

Furthermore, it appears that it is not—as some scientists suggest—only a matter of 'educating' the public about the benefits of GM foods: consumer acceptance is premised on concern for **food safety**. And it seems that the more people are learning about GM foods (and worrying about food safety), the less confident they are becoming about those foods (Norton 1999). Importantly, women are more wary than men of GM foods—and it is women, by and large, who purchase the family's food supplies (Norton 1999).

Busch and colleagues (1991) have argued that three issues are of importance when consumers purchase food commodities—consent, knowledge, and fairness. With GM foods, consent and knowledge are linked to labelling, which allows people to make informed decisions about food purchases. Yet many GM foods in the marketplace are not properly labelled, and it is now believed that foods containing small amounts of GM substances (1% or less) will never be labelled; they are deemed to be 'substantially equivalent' to normal foods (Phelps 2001). In relation to the third criterion—fairness—people are coming to see that it is big business that will benefit from the sale of GM products, not consumers (Norton & Lawrence 1996). In other words, consumers have reason to be wary of ingesting foods that are developed to fulfil the profit-making needs of corporations rather than the desires of consumers for healthy and nutritious foods. Nutritionists Young and Lewis (1995, p. 930) have argued that advances in genetic engineering:

> have been based on relatively little knowledge of basic human nutritional needs. More importantly, these advances have been predicated with no understanding of dietary nutrient interactions. Changing nutrient composition of foods through biotechnology may alter nutrient interactions, nutrient-gene interactions, nutrient availability, nutrient potency, and nutrient metabolism. Biotechnology has the potential to produce changes in our foods and in our diet at a pace far greater than our ability to predict the significance of those changes ...

The point is that scientists, food industry officials, and the public simply do not know what problems will be caused by the genetic manipulation of foods. The scientists and food industry seem to believe that the benefits of experimentation with and releasing of GMOs will outweigh any risks. The public is beginning to question this assessment.

Conclusion: The future of GM foods

Any critical assessment of agribusiness must start with recognition of the fact that there has been, since the 1950s, a strong technological push in commercial agriculture and food production. Within the commercial agriculture sector, producers have found it necessary to purchase the latest seeds, fertilisers, tractors, and management techniques to stay economically viable. Farmers have sought any new inputs that would help to boost productivity or efficiency or both. Genetically engineered inputs promise a continuation of this trend. The agribusiness sector has found a receptive market among farmers for its latest GM seed/pesticide/fertiliser packages. For many farmers, and for the agribusiness-input industries, the use of GM seeds is simply a continuation of the productive, 'high-tech' approach to farming that has increased food production enormously over the past 20 years. For the food industry, the use of genetically engineered enzymes, bacteria, plants, and animals promises to speed up production, create novel products of great benefit to society, and literally 'feed the world' with genetically enhanced plants and animals.

So why would there be any opposition to such a glowing future? There are basically six reasons why there has been, and will continue to be, strong challenges from throughout the world:

- GM foods do not seem to provide obvious benefits to consumers. Rather, they seem to benefit the companies selling GM seed/fertiliser/insecticide packages to farmers, and the companies using GMOs to catalyse chemical reactions in foods that are part of the food processing industry. What advantage will the 'end users' (consumers) of the new foods and fibres derive? This has not been well explained by proponents of biotechnology.
- Genetic engineering has not been proven safe and beneficial. There are major concerns about the unknown health effects of genetic interactions when GM foods are ingested, and when the release of genetically engineered plants and animals allows novel genes to become widespread in the environment.
- Some important industries, both traditional and new (such as 'commercial organics'), will be compromised by the release of GMOs. Will farmers growing non-GM cotton, canola, corn, and soybeans be able to segregate their crops? Will those wanting to label their products as 'non-GMO', be able to do so, when the extent of 'genetic pollution' from GMO crops is unable to be monitored?
- There is evidence that, throughout the world, large supermarket chains are banning GMOs and stacking their shelves with organic produce—a certain sign that consumer resistance to GMO is not going away, and a reflection of people's desire for natural 'clean and green' foods (Burch et al. 2001).
- The release of GMOs will make it harder for countries to claim that they are producing food in a sustainable manner. There are likely to be arguments (some decades hence) that a GMO-based agricultural production system is not sustainable, particularly when GMO products are perceived to corrupt 'natural' products and natural production systems (see Campbell & Coombes 1999; McKenna & Campbell 2002). If this occurs, foods from a GMO-based agri-food regime might be deemed unacceptable as imports, thereby severely limiting the exportation of foods from those nations that have gone down the GMO path.
- The idea that GMOs will 'feed the world' is viewed as nothing more than a cynical justification for the perpetuation of corporate control of food (Crouch 2001). The 'green revolution' technologies of the 1960s and 1970s were going to feed the world but failed. Why? Because the world food problem has less to do with the volume of production than with the patterns of distribution. We have enough food *now* to feed the world, but there is little political will to ensure that it is available to those in need. Biotechnology cannot address what is essentially a global geopolitical problem, even if the rhetoric of 'food for all' can be used as an ideological device to promote corporate involvement in food production (McMichael 2000, 2003).

It is important to understand the intensity of the opposition to GMOs. There are literally thousands of organisations around the world opposed to the introduction of GM inputs to agriculture and to the further development and commercialisation of GM foods (Tokar 2001, pp. 420–42; Phelps 2001). A genetically engineered future for foods should not, therefore, be taken as a given.

What has been argued in this chapter is that two dominant processes—appropriationism and substitutionism—are helping to fashion agri-food industries in a manner that increases the profits, and level of control, of the corporate sector in relation to food production. There is no conspiracy here. Companies are attempting to meet demand for particular products, satisfy shareholders' desires for strong returns on invested capital, and employ the latest technologies in an effort to save costs and increase productivity. This logic is entirely consistent with the behaviour of most firms within the system of **capitalism**. The problem for the agri-food firms is that the powerful techniques that they are now harnessing—biotechnologies in general, and genetic engineering in particular—are different from older forms of food production and processing and have uncertain (and potentially harmful) outcomes. Not surprisingly, there is growing consumer resistance to their application in the food sector.

What is the future of GM foods? Writers are divided on this question. For some, agribusiness will use its power to 'enforce' the adoption of GM foods—even in countries, such as those of Europe, where there is quite strong rejection of GMOs. This, they argue, will be achieved through the World Trade Organisation (WTO), a body that has the power to overrule what are considered to be unfair barriers to trade. If the WTO decides that the Europeans must accept genetically modified foods (and that banning them would be an unacceptable trade block), then it is clear that a major hurdle will have been overcome by the corporate food sector (McMichael 2003).

For other writers, the level of protest against GM foods will be such that those dealing with GMOs at point of sale (that is, the supermarkets) will determine that it is in their own interest to remove GM foods from their shelves. As stricter (mandatory) labelling is put in place, consumers will be able to gauge immediately which foods are GM and which are not. If, as many expect, there is a near total rejection of GM foods, it will not take the supermarkets long to remove these products and replace them with alternatives that are in higher demand. Many people are predicting a very rosy future for organic products as consumer rejection of GM food grows, and as the organics industry becomes better organised and more market savvy (Campbell & Coombes 1999; Lockie et al. 2002).

There is, of course, a third possibility—that the two trajectories (growth in the application of GMOs and growth in organics and other 'clean and green' options) will be followed simultaneously. Indeed, this option appears the most likely to come to pass. If it does, we can be certain that there will be a heightened battle between the agri-food corporations and the organic and other 'clean and green' producers for the hearts, minds, and stomachs of consumers.

Summary of main points

- The term 'agribusiness' refers to corporate involvement in the 'upstream' provision of farm inputs and the 'downstream' processing and sale of farm products.
- Aided by biotechnologies, agribusinesses in the 'upstream' sector are developing chemical and seed 'packages' to sell to farmers; on the 'downstream' side, they are contracting farmers to provide both generic inputs into the food processing industry and fresh foods for the supermarkets.
- The two key processes driving agribusiness penetration into the farming and food industry sectors are appropriationism and substitutionism. Both allow for increased profit-making, as well as higher levels of control, for the agribusiness sector.
- There is substantial public resistance to genetically engineered foods.
- Recent evidence suggests that while agribusiness as a whole remains enchanted with GMO technology, some major players in the food industry—in particular the supermarkets—are seeking to minimise the presence of GMOs in their stores.
- There is little doubt that there will be significant battles between consumer/non-GMO farmer groups and the agribusiness sector over the next decade.

Discussion questions

1. Is agribusiness really a 'juggernaut', or can its biotechnology trajectory be altered or stopped?
2. Why would people in the 'third world' oppose genetic engineering when the new technology promises a more abundant food supply?
3. Appropriationism and substitutionism are seen to be the two key processes driving agribusiness expansion. Are there any others?
4. Of the following genetic engineering procedures, which ones would you approve and why?
   a) Placing a gene from a cornflower plant into a rose so that the rose flower is deep blue.

b) Placing a hormone of human origin into a pig so that the pig demands less feed, matures quickly, and produces lean meat.
c) Adding a fish gene to a tomato so that the tomato has more flavour and colour and can be harvested without bruising.
d) Placing a gene from a soil bacterium into a wheat plant so that the wheat plant requires less chemical pesticide sprays.

5 As a consumer, will you purchase genetically modified foods?

Further investigation

1 Genetic engineering is the new green revolution for the twenty-first century. Discuss.
2 Choose a specific genetically modified food that is available in your community and investigate its advantages and disadvantages for agribusiness and consumers.

Further reading and web resources

Books

Almas, R. & Lawrence, G. (eds) 2003, *Globalization, Localization and Sustainable Livelihoods*, Ashgate, Aldershot, UK.

Dixon, J. 2002, *The Changing Chicken: Chooks, Cooks and Culinary Culture*, University of New South Wales Press, Sydney.

Hindmarsh, R. & Lawrence, G. (eds) 2003, *Recoding Nature: Critical Perspectives on Genetic Engineering*, University of New South Wales Press, Sydney.

Hindmarsh, R., Lawrence, G. & Norton, J. (eds) 1998, *Altered Genes: Reconstructing Nature—The Debate*, Allen & Unwin, Sydney.

Ho, M-W. 1998, *Genetic Engineering, Dream or Nightmare? The Brave New World of Bad Science and Big Business*, Gateway Books, Bath, UK.

Web sites

Australian Agri-food Network: www.sct.gu.edu.au/sci_page/research/agri

Australian Consensus Conference on Gene Technology in the Food Chain: www.abc.net.au/science/slab/consconf/default.htm

Food Standards Australia New Zealand: www.foodstandards.gov.au

Gene Technology in Australia, CSIRO: genetech.csiro.au/

International Federation of Organic Agriculture Movements: www.ifoam.org/

International Journal of Sociology of Agriculture and Food: www.acs.ryerson.ca/%7Eisarc40/

Office of the Gene Technology Regulator: www.ogtr.gov.au/

References

AfroCentric News, 16 January 2003, pp. 1–4, <www.afrocentricnews.com/html/food.html>.

Allen, T. 2000, 'The Environmental Costs of Genetic Engineering', in R. Prebble (ed.) *Designer Genes: The New Zealand Guide to the Issues, Facts and Theories about Genetic Engineering*, Dark Horse, Wellington, pp. 61–8.

Associated Press, 15 January 2003, p. 1.

Bonanno, A., Busch, L., Friedland, W., Gouveia, L. & Mingione, E. (eds) 1994, *From Columbus to ConAgra*, University Press of Kansas, Kansas.

Burch, D. & Rickson, R. 2001, 'Industrialised Agriculture: Agribusiness, Input-dependency and Vertical Integration', in S. Lockie & L. Bourke, L. (eds), *Rurality Bites: The Social and Environmental Transformation of Rural Australia*, Pluto Press, Sydney, pp. 165–77.

Busch, L., Lacy, B., Burkhardt, J. & Lacy, L. 1991, *Plants, Power and Profit: Social, Economic and Ethical Consequences of the New Biotechnologies*, Basil Blackwell, London.

Buttel, F. 1999, 'Agricultural Biotechnology: Its Recent Evolution and Implications for Agrofood Political Economy', *Sociological Research Online*, vol. 4, no. 3, pp. 1–17, <www.socresonline.org.uk/socresonline/4/3/buttel.html>.

Campbell, H. & Coombes, B. 1999, 'Green Protectionism and Organic Food Exporting from New Zealand: Crisis Experiments in the Breakdown of Fordist Trade and Agricultural Policies', *Rural Sociology*, vol. 64, no. 2, pp. 302–19.

Charles, D. 2001, *Lords of the Harvest: Biotech, Big Money and the Future of Food*, Perseus Publishing, Cambridge, Massachusetts.

Conner, T. 2000, 'Crops: Food, Environment and Ethics', in R. Prebble (ed.) *Designer Genes: The New Zealand Guide to the Issues, Facts and Theories About Genetic Engineering*, Dark Horse, Wellington, pp. 141–52.

Constance, D., Bonanno, A., Cates, C., Argo, D. & Harris, M. 2003, 'Resisting Integration in the Global Agro-food System: Corporate Chickens and Community Controversy in Texas', in R. Almas & G. Lawrence (eds), *Globalization, Localization, and Sustainable Livelihoods*, Ashgate, Aldershot, UK, pp. 103–18.

Crouch, M. 2001, 'From Golden Rice to Terminator Technology: Agricultural Biotechnology will not Feed the World or Save the Environment', in B. Tokar (ed.) *Redesigning Life: The Worldwide Challenge to Genetic Engineering*, McGill-Queen's University Press, Montreal, pp. 22–39.

Davis, J. 1956, 'From Agriculture to Agribusiness', *Harvard Business Review*, vol. 34, pp. 107–15.

de la Perriere, R. & Seuret, F. 2000, *Brave New Seeds: The Threat of GM Crops to Farmers*, Zed Books, London.

European Commission 2001, *Eurobarometer 55.2, Europeans, Science and Technology*, European Opinion Research Group, Brussels.

Ewert, J. 2003, 'Co-operatives to Companies: The South African Wine Industry in the Face of Globalization' in R. Almas & G. Lawrence (eds), *Globalization, Localization, and Sustainable Livelihoods*, Ashgate, Aldershot, UK, pp. 153–69.

Fitzsimons, J. 2000, 'The Nuclear-free Issue of the 21st Century', in R. Prebble (ed.), *Designer Genes: The New Zealand Guide to the Issues, Facts and Theories About Genetic Engineering*, Dark Horse, Wellington, pp. 187–96.

Food Resources, 16 January 2003, p.1.

Friedmann, H. 1991, 'Changes in the International Division of Labor: Agrifood Complexes and Export Agriculture', in W. Friedland, L. Busch, F. Buttel, & A. Rudy (eds), *Towards a New Political Economy of Agriculture*, Westview, Boulder, pp. 65–93.

Goodman, D. & Redclift, M. 1991, *Refashioning Nature: Food, Ecology and Culture*, Routledge, New York.

Goodman, D, Sorj, B. & Wilkinson, J. 1987, *From Farming to Biotechnology*, Basil Blackwell, Oxford.

Heffernan, W. 1999, *Consolidation in the Food and Agriculture System* (report to the National Farmers' Union), University of Missouri Department of Rural Sociology and the National Farmers Union, Colorado.

Hendrickson, M. & Heffernan, W. 2003, 'Opening Spaces through Relocalization: Locating Potential Resistance in the Weaknesses of the Global Food System', *Sociologia Ruralis*, vol. 42, no. 4, pp. 347–69.

Hindmarsh, R. & Lawrence, G. (eds) 2001, *Altered Genes II: The Future?* Scribe, Melbourne.

Hindmarsh, R., Lawrence, G. & Norton, J. 1995, 'Manipulating Genes or Public Opinion?' *Search*, no. 26, pp. 117–21.

Ho, M-W. 1998, *Genetic Engineering: Dream or Nightmare? The Brave New World of Bad Science and Big Business*, Gateway Books, UK.

INRA (Europe) & European Consumer Safety Organisation 2000, 'Eurobarometer 52.1: The Europeans and Biotechnology', <www.europa.eu.int/comm/research/eurobarometer-en.pdf>.

Kelley, J. 1995, *Public Perceptions of Genetic Engineering: Australia, 1994*, Department of Industry, Science and Technology, Canberra.

Lawrence, G., Norton, J. & Vanclay, F. 2001, 'Gene Technology, Agri-food Industries and Consumers', in R. Hindmarsh & G. Lawrence (eds), *Altered Genes II: The Future?*, Scribe, Melbourne, pp. 143–59.

Le Heron, R. & Roche, M. 1999, 'Rapid Regulation, Agricultural Restructuring, and the Reimaging of Agriculture in New Zealand', *Rural Sociology*, vol. 64, no. 2, June, pp. 203–18.

Llambi, L. 1994, 'Opening Economies and Closing Markets: Latin American Agriculture's Difficult Search for a Place in the Emerging Global Order', in A. Bonanno, L. Busch, W. Friedland, L. Gouveia & E. Mingione (eds), *From Columbus to ConAgra: The Globalization of Agriculture and Food*, University of Kansas Press, pp. 184–209.

Lockie, S., Lyons, K., Lawrence, G. & Mummery, K. 2002, 'Eating "Green": Motivations Behind Organic Food Consumption in Australia', *Sociologia Ruralis*, vol. 42, no. 1, April, pp. 20–37.

McKenna, M. & Campbell, H. 2002, 'It's Not Easy Being Green: The Development of "Food Safety" Practices in New Zealand's Apple Industry', *International Journal of Sociology of Food and Agriculture*, vol. 10, no. 2, pp. 110–41.

McMichael, P. 2000, *Development and Social Change: A Global Perspective*, 2nd edn, Pine Forge, Boston.

McMichael, P. 2003, 'The Power of Food', in R. Almas & G. Lawrence (eds), *Globalization, Localization, and Sustainable Livelihoods*, Ashgate, Aldershot, UK, pp. 69–85.

Magdoff, F., Foster, J. & Buttel, F. (eds) 2000, *Hungry for Profit: The Agribusiness Threat to Farmers, Food and the Environment*, Monthly Review Press, New York <www.monthlyreview.org/hungry.html>.

New Farm, 15 January 2003, p.1, <www.newfarm.org.newfarm/news/11502/foundation_seeds.shtml>.

Norton, J. 1999, *Science, Technology and the Risk Society: Australian Consumers' Attitudes to Genetically-engineered Foods*, unpublished PhD thesis, Central Queensland University, Rockhampton.

Norton, J. 2002, *Potential of Biotechnologies to Enhance Sustainable Development of the Central Queensland Region* (Occasional Paper 3/2002), Institute for Sustainable Regional Development, Central Queensland University, Rockhampton.

Norton, J. & Lawrence, G. 1996, 'Consumer Attitudes to Genetically-engineered Food Products: Focus Group Research in Rockhampton, Queensland' in G. Lawrence, K. Lyons, & S. Momtaz (eds), *Social Change in Rural Australia*, Rural Social and Economic Research Centre, Central Queensland University, Rockhampton, pp. 290–311.

Norton, J., Lawrence, G. & Wood, G. 1998, 'The Australian Public's Perceptions of Genetically-Engineered Foods', *Australasian Biotechnology*, vol. 8, no. 3, pp. 172–81.

Phelps, B. 2001, 'Opposing Genetic Manipulation: The GenEthics Campaign', in R. Hindmarsh & G. Lawrence (eds), *Altered Genes II: The Future?* Scribe, Melbourne, pp. 187–202.

Pretty, J. 2002, *Agri-Culture: Reconnecting People, Land and Nature*, Earthscan, London.

Pritchard, B. 1999, 'Australia as the Supermarket to Asia? Governments, Territory, and Political Economy in the Australian Agri-food System', *Rural Sociology*, vol. 64, no. 2, pp. 284–301.

Pritchard, B. & Burch, D. 2003, *Agri-food Globalization in Perspective: International Restructuring in the Processing Tomato Industry*, Ashgate, Aldershot, UK.

Rifkin, J. 1992, *Beyond Beef: The Rise and Fall of the Cattle Culture*, Penguin, New York.

Teubal, M. & Rodriguez, J. 2003, 'Globalization and Agro-food Systems in Argentina', in R. Almas & G. Lawrence (eds), *Globalization, Localization, and Sustainable Livelihoods*, Ashgate, Aldershot, UK, pp. 119–34.

Tokar, B. 2001, *Redesigning Life: The Worldwide Challenge to Genetic Engineering*, McGill-Queen's University Press, Montreal, Canada.

Watts, M. & Goodman, D. 1997, *Globalising Food*, Routledge, London.

Wilkinson, J. 2003, 'The Final Foods Industry and the Changing Face of the Global Agro-food System', *Sociologia Ruralis*, vol. 42, no. 4, pp. 329–46.

Young, A. & Lewis, G. 1995, 'Biotechnology and Potential Nutritional Implications for Children', *Pediatric Nutrition*, vol. 42, no. 4, pp. 917–30.

5

Adding Value(s): A Cultural Economy Analysis of Supermarket Power

Jane Dixon

Overview

- What activities comprise the sphere of food distribution and exchange?
- How have retail traders wrested power from primary producers and food processors (secondary producers and manufacturers) in the Australian food system?
- How can a cultural economy approach illuminate the balance of power in commodity and food systems?

This chapter focuses on a relatively neglected part of the food system, the distribution and exchange of food commodities and food-related services. The dynamics of this sphere are explored through a case study of the role that supermarkets have played in building the popularity of chicken meat. The power of these highly profitable retail traders is explained using the concept of cultural economy activities. The influence of supermarket chains over many aspects of Australia's food system and culinary culture sheds light on the changing nature of expertise and values underpinning household food-consumption patterns.

Key terms

agri-food	cultural economy	food system
Commodity Systems Analysis (CSA)	ethnography	Just-In-Time (JIT)
cultural capital	flexible accumulation	time famines

Introduction

In the late 1960s, Australians ate 40 kilograms of red meat and only 8 kilograms of chicken per year. Forty years later, chicken is set to overtake beef as the nation's preferred meat (Dixon 2002). This trend can be partly attributed to the changing demographic mix: since the 1960s, different ethnic groups have arrived in Australia with culinary cultures that either do not use much meat (Italians), or use mostly pork and chicken (many Asian and Pacific Islander subgroups). (See Michael Symons's (1993) treatment of the influence of migrants to Australia's culinary culture.) The other significant influence on meat consumption has been the way a large proportion of the population has come to justify their consumption patterns using a mixture of values that coalesce in the idea of 'healthy convenience' (Gofton & Ness 1991). Largely promoted by Australia's two major supermarket chains, 'healthy convenience' reflects the twin concerns of food that does not contribute to heart disease and other diseases (often associated with red meat and full-fat dairy products) with a desire for food that allows the household manager, most often the family cook, to use time and money wisely.

One explanation for the rapid shift from red to white meat is that consumers have displaced producers in exercising the balance of power in the **food system**. Whereas housewives used to uncritically buy what was provided by beef and sheep meat producers, their expressed concerns for their family's health and their demands for 'shortcuts' and more flexible meal options signalled the growing influence of the consumer. While studies of post-1950s changes to national food systems and shopping practices generally conclude that the newly reflexive consumer is powerful (Gabriel & Lang 1995; Miller 1995; Falk & Campbell 1997), research that is based on interviews with consumers often challenges this argument. Accounts by consumers of their mundane routines and decision-making considerations portray consumption as an endless series of compromises: poorer families are forced to rely on relatively expensive foods of dubious nutritional value (Charles & Kerr 1986); women are concerned about the nutritional goodness of foods (Murcott 1993; CSIRO 1994); and working mothers are concerned that lack of time to cook during the week forces them to rely on processed and convenience foods (Dixon 2002).

The pressures of money and the perception of **time famines**, a term used by Gofton (1990), combine with the constant promotion of new products and media coverage of the latest evidence from nutrition science to unsettle shoppers and undermine confident shopping—the behaviour that most challenges marketplace authority (Douglas 1997). Lack of confidence among shoppers and the constant need to be flexible fuel volatile consumption patterns that producers have trouble interpreting. Translating consumer demands into products has become a highly specialised and expensive facet of food enterprises and supermarkets have assumed leadership in communicating consumer wants to producers. However, supplying the latest market intelligence is only one of the ways in which supermarket chains influence what is happening in the food system. Their promotional activities—for example, categorising and advertising certain foods as 'fresh produce' and 'home-meal replacement'—influence the way that consumers think about food commodities far more effectively than the marketing campaigns of commodity producers, who are often distrusted as sources of product endorsement (Tansey & Worsley 1995; Dixon et al. forthcoming).

Until recently, most research on food systems has ignored the dynamics between production and consumption. Owing to the discipline-bound nature of the social sciences, most political economists only consider consumers in relation to government regulations (like shopping-hours deregulation, food-safety measures, and monitoring of the consumer price index). And with few exceptions (Warde 1992; Fine & Leopold 1993), sociologists of consumption take food production for granted. While consumer scientists (see Marshall 1995) consistently insist on the importance of the supply chain—delivering goods to market (availability)—and the value chain—the cultural norms surrounding the goods (acceptability)—systematic analyses of what happens between the two chains, between production and consumption, are rare.

How availability and acceptability align with one another, so that the goods on offer are sufficiently desirable to lead to their transfer from one owner to another, lies at the heart of the sphere of distribution and exchange. In this sphere, cultural processes are enlisted to facilitate economic exchange and, in turn, economic processes influence the value sets and practices that make up cultural systems. ('Value sets' are also referred to as 'regimes of value', a term coined by Appadurai (1986).)

This chapter explores the interdependence of production and consumption by following the commodity path of chicken meat between the farm and the dinner table. For 30 years, supermarkets have been instrumental in fostering the everyday availability and acceptability of a meat that was traditionally associated with special occasions. The chapter begins by laying out the methodological approach adopted for data collection and in so doing outlines the elements that comprise the sphere of distribution and exchange.

The study of distribution and exchange: The case of chicken meat

One of the most influential approaches to the study of power in food systems emerged in the mid 1980s. **Commodity Systems Analysis (CSA)** encouraged researchers to explore a wide range of processes that contribute to the final form of a commodity, including production practices, science application, the labour process on the farm and in the factory, and marketing and distribution networks (Friedland 1984). William Friedland, who developed CSA, has since added further foci for study, including what he calls 'the commodity culture', which refers to the cultural forms found among commodity producers and consumers (Friedland 2001). While CSA acknowledges that primary producers are significantly influenced by distributors—including marketing boards and wholesale traders—the activities of marketing and distribution networks have remained a minor part of the overall schema.

Between 1996 and 1998, I adapted the CSA approach by adding the distinctive sphere of consumption, influenced by Warde (1994). Data were collected on the post–World War II history of chicken meat production and consumption in Australia, with a view to answering the question: have consumers displaced producers as the driving force behind the chicken meat commodity complex? (A full account of the study can be found in *The Changing Chicken* (Dixon 2002).) Chicken meat was chosen because, along with margarine, it showed the most marked increase in consumption of any food between 1970 and 1990 (Skurray & Newell 1993).

The Australian chicken meat industry has grown spectacularly over the last quarter century, with approximately six and a half million chickens coming to market each week. These chickens are being produced by a relatively small number of chicken farmers (about 820) and processing plants (about ninety), who together employ a modest number of labourers (about 13,000) (Fairbrother 2001). State governments regulate farmer pay rates and conditions, and hence provide a measure of stability for the industry. As a consequence, contract farmers have an incentive to invest in the latest technology, and developments in bird breeding have made today's birds convert feed into flesh more rapidly. Some claim this to be Australia's most successful **agri-food** industry (Fairbrother 1988; Cain 1990). Furthermore, there has never been an intermediary marketing board (as there is for eggs and red meat); farmers are contracted directly to processors, enhancing even further the smooth flow of product onto the market.

The efficiency of the production side of the complex has helped to keep wholesale prices low, and some credit chicken's cheapness relative to other meats with its success. However, my focus group research showed that the esteem with which chicken is held by consumers is more complex. Among the explanations provided were a personal liking of chicken meals; the fact that chicken is healthier than red meat; the fact that it is easy to prepare and easy to chew, which was a particularly important attribute with children; and, above all, the versatility of chicken, which extended to its acceptance by vegetarian family members. It was a particularly 'family friendly' food. Interestingly, chicken emerged from the group discussions with several negative features: removing chicken fat was viewed with disgust and the use of growth hormones and the conditions under which chickens were raised caused anxiety. Despite these misgivings, chicken was purchased because it helped ease the pressures on the family cook. This finding makes sense in the context of the general concerns shared by family food providers in an era when so many women are part of the labour force. Social and market research indicates that, at the end of a busy day, women look for opportunities for casual eating (Mackay 1992), relief from the burden of cooking (Santich 1995), and assistance in making food-related decisions (De Vault 1991; Fischler 1993). As is often remarked upon, food is associated with both physical and metaphysical risks, and the anthropological conundrum that food must be 'good to think' before it is 'good to eat' (Harris 1986) provides employment for thousands of consumer scientists, marketers, and advertisers.

Given consumer misgivings about this most popular of foods, it seemed imperative to understand how chicken was made 'good to think', and this entailed examining the operations of actors in the middle of the chicken commodity system. It was not sufficient to understand the exchange of material goods—money and meals; the processes and effects of the trade in cultural goods, such as time, 'quality', rituals, and authority, appeared to be equally important.

For insights into the distribution and exchange of foods and food-related services, anthropology is particularly helpful. Anthropologists teach us that merchants have long provided a dual function: they deliver goods to the market and they deliver stories about the goods—they imbue them with both mystery and relevance. As Appadurai has noted, 'over the span of human history, the critical agents for the articulation of the supply and demand of commodities have been not rulers but of course, traders' (Appadurai 1986, p. 33).

Recently, economic and retail geographers have begun to focus on those actors who are responsible for mediating the relationship between producers and consumers (Wrigley & Lowe 1996; Freidberg 2003), and they have dubbed retailers 'the new masters of the food system' (Flynn & Marsden 1992). Using in-depth interviews, **ethnographic** techniques, and syntheses of secondary sources, my research revealed that supermarkets, fast-food chains, nutrition educators, and other producers of food knowledge all contribute to making chicken meat desirable. It also showed how large retailers blur the boundaries between production and distribution through their direct and indirect influence over product development. The next two sections explore how, in relation to chicken meat, 'retail capital is increasingly mediating the producer-consumer relation' (Lowe & Wrigley 1996).

Supermarkets and the chicken meat supply chain

Australian supermarkets are becoming increasingly influential in the production of what are called 'high-value foods' (HVFs), including chicken meat products, because this is where the highest profits are to be made. HVFs are generally fresh, minimally processed foods, such as fruit and vegetables, dairy products, shellfish, and poultry. They are characterised by heterogeneity, associations with 'quality', and niche markets (Watts & Goodman 1997, p. 11). Displacing more traditional HVF providers—the greengrocer, butcher, 'continental deli', and fish monger—has required applying vast amounts of retail capital to the restructuring of supermarket operations, and this multi-faceted process is described below.

Concentration and operation of retail capital

In 1999, a Parliamentary Joint Select Committee on the Retailing Sector (JSCRS) noted that Australia has one of the most concentrated supermarket sectors of any country. At that stage, the three major chains, Woolworths/Safeway, Coles, and Franklins, accounted for 80% of grocery sales and 60% of the fresh food market (JSCRS 1999). With the recent sale of Franklins stores to the other two majors as well as to minor chains, like the Independent Grocers of Australia (IGA), the share of the market controlled by Woolworths and Coles has grown. When retail capital is concentrated in so few firms, it confers purchasing power and thus market power on those who control it. In other countries, governments regulate the extent to which major chains can dominate food retailing, but despite lobbying from farmer's organisations for this kind of regulation in Australia, the JSCRS refused to cap retail-firm concentration, arguing that this would be to the detriment of thousands of small shareholders, including families. The relaxed attitude by governments toward retailers is not unique to Australia: Hughes (1996) identified benign regulatory environments in the USA and UK as well. Even so, Australia has a much higher degree of retail concentration than these two countries.

The Australian ruling was significant for chicken meat producers for two reasons. First, it consolidated the monopoly conditions of the market, where there a few product buyers and many sellers. In contrast, red meat producers, while increasingly beholden to supermarkets, still sell a majority of their products through the thousands of independent butchers. They can walk away from the supermarkets when offered too little for their products, whereas the biggest customers for the major chicken meat producers are the supermarkets, and chicken meat producers could not survive by selling only to butchers and fast-food chains.

Second, supermarkets are no longer content to make profits by moving goods between the factory and wholesale operation and from the wholesale point to retail operation. They are increasingly reinvesting their own capital in food processing and value-adding activities, thus directly competing with traditional food processors. In the case of chicken meat, the major chains have set up specialist poultry sections like Coles's All Things Poultry. Supermarkets employ staff to perform the labour previously undertaken by the staff of the chicken processor: they cut up the raw meat and add the herbs, spices, and sauces. On the basis of this enhanced capacity to compete directly with processors, supermarkets dictate terms to the dependent processor. Through labour substitution, the supermarkets have increased their bargaining power: if the processor cannot or will not produce the cuts the supermarket orders, the supermarket turns to its own operation. To use market jargon, processors have become price-getters not price-setters.

Retail concentration provides a few actors with large cash flows ready for investment in restructuring how the retail sector operates. 'Retail restructuring' is the term given to a wide range of activities designed to position retailers at the forefront of commercial and social life. The most notable activities over the last three decades include organisational and technological transformations in retail distribution, reconfiguring of labour practices within retailing, and redesigning of the retail–supply interface.

Supermarkets at the forefront of technological transformations

In terms of technological innovation, the introduction by supermarkets of the cool chain cannot be underestimated. The cool chain, developed by the UK supermarket firm Marks & Spencer, involves getting produce to stores in an unfrozen but chilled state, ready for storage in the supermarkets' refrigerated cabinets. This particular food technology was fundamental in the 1970s to encouraging housewives to buy a chicken more often than for the weekend roast. Market research had revealed to Marks & Spencer that while chilled birds were more expensive than frozen ones, housewives preferred them for their 'convenience'. Chilled birds did not have to thawed and they tasted better, and the 'flood of water released by frozen birds during thawing made them seem a poor buy in comparison with chilled birds' (Senker 1988, p. 167).

The cool chain is by no means the sole revolutionary technology that has been introduced by the supermarkets. Improved stock ordering has been made possible through computerised technologies and the bar-coding of products. For over a decade, supermarket checkout tills have supplied a central computer with a continual flow of data on what products are leaving every store. Their EPOS (electronic point of sale) systems have in turn allowed supermarkets to make the most of **Just-in-Time (JIT)** systems, whereby the goods producer has to anticipate the amount of stock that will be demanded by the retail customer and have the warehousing facilities to hold the stock until it is ordered. This shifting the risk of holding stock that may or may not be sold has further consolidated the power of the retailer over the secondary producer (Foord et al. 1996).

Reconfiguring labour processes

As to changing labour practices, supermarkets and other parts of the food service sector prefigured what has since become known as **flexible accumulation**, based on having a labour force and processes that allow for both flexible production and flexible specialisation (Mathews 1989). The food service sector was among the first to dispense with a full-time male workforce in favour of a part-time and casual workforce of women and young people (Murray 1989). The adoption of a flexible workforce had a twin effect: it lowered the wages bills, thus boosting the profits of the large retailers, and it allowed retailers to introduce employee multi-skilling. Unlike the butcher, whose skills are acquired in an apprentice-like relationship with a master butcher over several years, the women employed in the delicatessen and specialist poultry sections of supermarkets can be sent away for 2 days of training in meat preparation or a 3-day course in safe food handling, and can have similarly short exposures to marketing, budgeting, and staff training. Because they possess generic skills, employees with specialist talents can be deployed to different sections of the supermarket at different times.

Because of the large volumes in which they trade, their technological sophistication and trained staff (albeit relatively inexpensively trained), supermarkets have an advantage over small family-run businesses on a number of fronts. They can charge lower prices on items produced in-house, they can afford to open for longer hours, and, because of the precarious nature of casual employment, employees desperate to keep their jobs are willing to accept new job demands with minimal training (Ryan & Burgess 1996). These are exactly the same factors operating in favour of fast-food chains like KFC, another significant purveyor of chicken meat products (Lyons 1996).

As Goodman and Redclift (1991) note, a circular logic operates between the food sector's dependence on women's employment and women's demand for convenience foods. With a majority of mothers doing two jobs—one as a paid employee and the other as the family food provider—the food service sector has effectively engineered demand for its products. The evolving 'home meal replacement' category of heat-and-serve and ready-to-eat meals being championed by the supermarkets is the logical outcome of family meal providers experiencing 'time famine'.

With their economies of scale, cheap labour, and large amounts of investment capital, supermarkets have been able to develop their fresh food operations to a point where in-store bakeries and fruit-and-vegetable, meat, and fish sections compete directly with small, owner-operated specialist food businesses. In many locales, these shops are losing customers because they appear to be lacking in variety, convenience, and specials—a feature loved by the post-war generation, who were brought up to value thrift in food purchasing. Furthermore, the Australian experiment with shopping-hours deregulation has made family owner-operated stores even less competitive, thus further diminishing competition between different retail forms. Unsurprisingly, a less competitive food sector has not delivered lower food prices (Baker & Marshall 1998).

Redesigning the retail–supply chain interface

The chicken meat complex is an exemplar of changes being experienced by other commodity complexes. At the heart of the control of retail-supplier chains lie three conditions: the designation of 'preferred suppliers', improved stock-handling procedures, and retailer knowledge of the manufacturing process (Burch & Goss 1999).

The first factor has long been integral to Australia's chicken meat commodity complex. For over 30 years, Woolworths has been supplied by Inghams, the nation's largest poultry processor, and Coles has a preferential supply arrangement with Steggles, the second largest processor (which was previously owned by Goodman Fielder and is now owned by Barrter Enterprises, the third biggest processor until this purchase). These preferential supply arrangements, which have never been subject to a formal inquiry by the nation's competition regulatory authority, have created what is known in the chicken meat industry as a three-tier system. The first tier consists of the two suppliers to the two major supermarket chains; the second tier of medium-sized processors also supplies supermarkets, but is as dependent for survival on their contracts with fast-food chains and specialist poulterers; and the third tier of small processors ekes out a precarious existence trying to supply butchers, food caterers, and the shortfall created by the other two tiers.

The adoption of EPOS systems to facilitate improvements in stock handling have already been mentioned. This retailer-controlled stocktaking system has been accompanied by a form of organisational interdependence called 'relational contracting'. Relational contracts are based on interactive, flexible, and stable supply networks. They rarely involve formal written documents; regular face-to-face and telephone exchanges are used to negotiate price, quality standards, and ingredients. Usually the contact originates with the product manufacturer, who rings stores and tells them what product is available.

However, a few years ago the chicken meat industry became a test site for eliminating the part of the process that involved negotiation. In what was called the 'cross-docking' of poultry, the Coles supermarket chain began to fax their daily orders through to their preferred processors, and it was incumbent on the latter to meet the order, whether they had the stock or not. The rationale of the new ordering system was to achieve a marketing system that stressed economies of coordination, achieved 'through minimising stock holding and transport costs, reducing paperwork … reducing the need for market searching by the retailer etc' (Dawson 1995, p. 80). While the larger chicken meat processors were content with the new arrangements (they no longer had to employ telephone sales staff or truck drivers to deliver to scores of outlets), this form of supply disadvantages smaller processors, whose plants are not geared to deliver a range of products with just 24 hours' notice. If the business media is correct, the relentless pursuit of cost savings in supply chains is set to intensify. By adopting integrated

IT systems that directly link cash registers with product suppliers, Woolworths anticipates saving $4.5 billion in the next 5 years (Kohler 2003, p. 14).

Dawson (1995) points out that the ability to drive these forms of marketing systems creates new kinds of channel power, which reinforces retailer power relative to the power of suppliers and consumers. Those firms that profit from the new supply arrangements grow bigger and other firms are forced out, which in turn decreases the choice of firms for producers to sell to and the spiral of size, profitability, and concentration increases.

Retail power is further illustrated by other events that have affected the chicken meat commodity complex. During the years when the new supply chain arrangements were being put into place, chicken meat producers were successfully fighting government plans to force chicken meat imports on the industry and to deregulate the arrangements that allowed chicken farmers to collectively bargain over the amounts they were paid for growing birds (Dixon & Burgess 1998). As chicken farmers and processors were successfully repelling government 'reforms' justified by global free-trade pressures and national competition policy, they were succumbing without protest to retailer-led restructuring of their industry.

Supermarkets and the chicken meat value chain

Just as supermarkets exert considerable influence over the production sphere of the chicken meat commodity complex, they are also extremely active in shaping the practices of food consumption. Here the general strategy is one of selling 'a way of life' that provides a supportive context to the exchange of goods and services. Selling a way of life involves using particular language, images, and practices in anticipation that consumers will accept and adopt them. Australian supermarkets' efforts to influence shopping and consumption practices are best explained in two social histories of Australian supermarkets, *Shelf Life* (Humphery 1998) and *Basket, Bag and Trolley* (Kingston 1994). Together they show how supermarket chains have for 80 years been proactive in shaping the consumer experience so as to maximise their profits. As supermarkets moved beyond their variety-store heritage during the 1960s, they became purveyors not simply of groceries but of three C's: 'convenience, cleanliness and consumer choice' (Humphery 1998, p. 105). Clearly they hoped that Mrs Housewife, an identity they helped to forge from the 1920s onwards, would forego and forget the super-convenient practice of boys delivering the weekly grocery order on bicycle or (in later years) buying her fish and vegetables from the back of a truck that meandered through suburban streets. In place of having her consumables bagged and delivered, Mrs Housewife had to learn how to participate in the consumer culture of self-service. This required a dedicated promotional effort by the supermarkets, who had to associate the shift in labour with the march of economic progress (Humphery 1998, p. 105).

In what follows, I describe how the table chicken has assisted supermarket chains to acquire the requisite **cultural capital** to continue to amass financial capital. Whereas the previous section showed how producer–retailer relations are being refashioned, this section analyses the constant reworking of the consumer–retailer interface.

Supermarkets as the heart of the household: Providing 'healthy convenience'
The humble chicken has played a significant role in the fortunes of supermarket chains. This most acceptable food has allowed supermarkets to constantly rework their identity as a family-friendly institution whose mission is to help consumers negotiate their busy lives. Nowhere is this better illustrated than in the logo that the Franklins' chain adopted in the mid 1990s when trying to recruit staff to the 'Franklins Family': a giant rooster bestriding the space rocket of progress.

The cool chain, described earlier, brought benefits over and above bringing new products onto the market. The sale of chilled as opposed to frozen chickens allowed supermarkets to portray themselves as being at the cutting edge of progress, a position reached through their foresight with new technologies. As Hollander (2003) argues, cool chains enhanced the legitimacy of supermarkets, which had become increasingly reliant on produce from far-flung reaches, to metaphorically 'freshen' the meaning of a first-world food system.

The introduction of this particular technology coincided with the advent in the 1970s of social movements concerned with health and the environment, which together encouraged consumers to desire goods that had had minimal contact with the industrial process and were 'close to nature'. What could be more natural than unfrozen and, by dint of marketing prowess, 'fresh' products? Arguably, it was their success with chicken that provided supermarkets with an opportunity to actively promote themselves as offering opportunities for a fresh and healthy life. Company annual reports reveal that, in the mid 1990s, the three major chains all promoted themselves through the discourse of 'fresh produce'. And it seems that the symbolic importance of 'freshness' has not diminished, with Woolworths codenaming its present restructuring efforts Project Refresh (Kohler 2003, p. 14).

While supermarkets were establishing fresh-produce sections, they were also competing with small suburban takeaway and fast-food shops to supply the traditional Friday night meal. Rather than attempt the more labour-intensive fish and chips or hamburger, supermarkets introduced rotisserie chicken counters. Whole cooked chickens, with potatoes and coleslaw, consolidated their reputation for offering not only healthy convenience but meal solutions to families at the end of a busy week. Furthermore, by lowering the price of these chickens, or giving two-for-the-price-of-one deals just prior to store closing time, they communicated to Mrs Housewife that if she valued thrift then here was the place to get it. The supermarket practice of loss leading—whereby selected items are sold for less than they cost the retailer, to entice consumers to visit the store and then buy more profitable items—is an important vehicle for communicating the value-for-money ethos so esteemed by many consumers. Over the years, the range of goods used as loss leaders has been quite consistent (Coca-Cola, margarine, and bacon, for example) and, from the time of the frozen chicken onwards, chicken has featured prominently.

A recent example of supermarkets using their association with chicken to position themselves in the household consciousness is the establishment of dedicated poultry sections, like All Things Poultry, in higher-income areas. Here the intention is to draw middle-class consumers away from small independent poulterers. Generating customer allegiance to these in-store specialists will, the supermarkets hope, develop customer loyalty over the long term.

Fashioning the discourse around home-meal replacement (HMR)

Many food retailers offer to solve a nation's problems of not having enough time, being confused about nutrition, and lacking food-preparation skills by providing what the food service sector calls 'meal solutions'. The Friday night 'roto bird' described above was preceded by frozen TV dinners in the 1960s, which were a forerunner to cook-chilled meals that require minimal effort from the household cook. Not only was the first TV dinner in the US a chicken dish (SwansonTV Brand dinners), but Chicken Kiev and Chicken Cordon Blue ushered in the heat-and-serve cook-chill revolution. Apparently, cook-chilled meals were viewed as 'a pleasure, a relief, a welcome technical fix for the working woman's double burden: feeding the family as well as the bank balance' (Raven et al. 1995, p .5). Coles supermarkets have set up 'Dine In Tonight' sections—with the slogan 'simply heat & serve'—in their higher-income-area stores. In other outlets they have rebadged their delicatessen sections 'Deli fresh', with the slogan 'we will spend hours to allow you to serve in minutes' (Dixon 2002). Both sections provide gourmet dishes ready for the home microwave, the wide-scale adoption of which for rapid thawing and heating of dishes has been essential to the investment of large sums for research and development related to HMR.

Meal-replacement strategies do not simply mean product innovation; they also involve redefining what is meant by the terms 'home', 'meal', and 'replacement'. And consumer acceptance has been contingent upon a subtle effort to alleviate the guilty feeling of housewives that they were failing in their primary job by not feeding their families with foods prepared at home (Strickland 1996). The supply by the food service sector—including supermarkets, fast-food chains, takeaway shops, cafes, and restaurants—of the close-to-ready main meal of the day, several days of the week, is a market niche that is being vigorously fought over (Strickland 1996). At this stage, supermarkets have the edge over fast-food chains in this niche because they have a longer association with offering healthy choices, thanks to their early appropriation of the 'fresh food' title.

Product differentiation to foster chain differentiation

There is plenty of evidence that supermarkets do not act purely in response to consumer demands, but that their product offerings influence those demands. For example, specialist sections selling HVFs are an integral part of supermarkets' strategy to use product differentiation to foster different communities of consumption. Product-differentiated retail systems emerge when a single chain segments its stores on the basis of store layout and services and the mix of distinctive product ranges (Harvey 1998). To determine the best ambience and product mix, supermarkets use psychographic mapping techniques, which allow market researchers to determine the lifestyles and attitudes of consumers in the catchment areas surrounding stores. The information gleaned from these techniques complements the scanner data acquired when shoppers use their store loyalty cards. As a result, supermarkets know how to micro-market their offerings: which stores should promote themselves as catering to older Australians of a conservative outlook who still like 'meat and three veg'; which should cater to young urban professionals for whom cooking is down-time; and where to introduce novel products for shoppers attracted to multicultural food experimentation, encouraged by celebrity chefs.

Each of the chains is particularly keen to attract consumers who are time-poor and who are willing to spend more on value-added foods, where the biggest profits are to be made. Coles and Woolworths are locked in a battle to assemble product and service portfolios that will appeal to the consumer market segment for whom quality is more important than price. They want this group to identify with their firm and to dismiss the other as not complementary to their social status. In this way, chicken (and other HVFs) is not only of economic and cultural value to housewives, it performs a similar function for those who trade in it. Being able to go to the specialist in-store poulterer to order a duck or stuffed chicken for Saturday night's dinner party bestows a form of cultural capital on a shopper. Similarly, the trader is earning its own cultural capital through being patronised by a high-status consumer.

Elaborating the sphere of distribution and exchange

In his study of fast food in France, Fantasia (1995, p. 201) notes that '[t]here is a vantage point situated at the intersection of economic and cultural sociology from which we can discern ever more clearly the material dimensions of culture and the non-material dimensions of goods'. That point is the sphere of distribution and exchange. Within this sphere are numerous actors, including those who work in what Sassen (1991) calls the 'producer services'—accountants, lawyers, IT specialists, psychographic researchers, market analysts, advertisers, and public relations experts. Corporations are dependent on these services to make money. Other experts, including nutritionists, health educators, home economists, and celebrity chefs, constitute what can be called a 'consumer services' sector (Dixon 2002). Their function is to facilitate consumption practices. The combined producer and consumer services sector assists consumers and producers to make decisions in relation to market, lifestyle, and household management. They help align the spheres of production and consumption. Supermarkets and fast-food chains use these producer and consumer services to strategically invest their capital in cultural production, in order to shape consumption discourses and practices.

Commercially employed food-knowledge producers constitute a wider phenomenon, as identified in the sociological literature. They are responsible for undermining older forms of social authority in favour of their own expert authority. Thus, as the authority of the mother, family cook, and government-employed home economist diminishes, so expert authority is increasingly being marshalled by the market (Dixon, in press). The alliance between Coles and the Dietitians Association of Australia on the 7-a-day fruit and vegetable campaign is a notable example. Another partnership between supermarkets and professional authorities is the promotion by supermarket of eggs endorsed by the RSPCA as produced by free-range hens. While Australian supermarkets are relative newcomers to the art of promoting themselves as ethical traders (Freidberg 2003), they will surely add this skill to their repertoire so as to renew their credentials as the pre-eminent family-friendly food-retailing institution.

On another front, they have formed a valuable partnership with the federal government to spearhead the Supermarket to Asia initiative. The Australian Supermarket Institute has joined forces with the Australian Food Council, which represents the biggest food processors, and the National Farmers Federation to implement the decisions by the government's Supermarket to Asia Council. Participation with government on such endeavours helps the market players to project an image of integrity and trustworthiness to the consuming public. In this sense, the government is legitimising the market while blurring the distinction between public and commercial interests (Pritchard 1999).

Conclusion: Towards a cultural economy approach

In 2002, the edited collection *Cultural Economy* appeared on the market. In their introduction, the editors describe the many ways in which cultural and economic processes interact to influence the way in which markets and organisations operate (du Gay & Pryke 2002). They point out the twin dangers of denying the relative autonomy of cultural and economic processes and of privileging one set of processes over the other. As they put it, to do **cultural economy** is to acknowledge that 'economic and organizational life is built up, or assembled from, a range of disparate, but inherently cultural, parts [and is concerned with] the extent to which economic and organizational relations in the present are more thoroughly "culturalized" than their historical predecessors' (du Gay & Pryke 2002, pp. 11–12).

My appreciation of the value of 'doing' cultural economy came from an understanding of the inadequacies of assuming that the production sphere involved economic activities only and that the consumption sphere was the sole province of cultural practices (this is explained more fully in Dixon 1999). What was needed was an approach that was broad enough to account for value-adding processes that apply to more than material production. In practical terms, I required a theoretical framework that would allow me to collect and analyse data on the reasons why the desirability of particular practices, like home cooking and backyard food production, wax and wane and differ among subpopulations. My study of the chicken meat commodity complex made me aware that the cultural adding of value by both producers and consumers was too often hidden by the market's promotion of the economic value of goods and services.

Scott Lash (1990, p. 240) credits Pierre Bourdieu (1979/1984) with being the foremost exponent of cultural economy, because much of his work interprets society and culture in the light of the interaction between symbolic and financial capital. Many other works are cited as examples of this approach in the book *Cultural Economy,* including Lash and Urry's *Economies of Signs and Space,* Featherstone's 1987 article 'Lifestyle and Consumer Culture' and Appadurai's (1986) edited book *The Social Life of Things*. Not mentioned is Halperin's (1994) *Cultural Economies: Past and Present*, which builds on the work of Karl Polanyi (in the 1940s) to develop a model for charting the contributions of cultural and political systems to the allocation of productive resources.

The essence of the cultural economy approach, as described in these works, is the detailed and systematic analysis of the economic basis for group practices/lifestyles and of how these influence the decisions of economic actors. Using the lexicon of nutrition and consumer scientists, doing cultural economy entails making a politically critical examination of the relationships between the acceptability, availability, and adoption of practices and commodities.

The table chicken case study highlights the symbiotic relationship between cultural production and capital-production activities. The growing popularity of chicken cannot be explained without exploring the cultural economy processes that have positioned it within a more general commodity context centred on 'healthy convenience'. Chicken has been a key ingredient in the marketing of convenience foods to suit the lifestyles of over-committed family cooks: beginning with the frozen TV dinner, followed by the hot rotisserie chicken, the cook-chill meal, and more recently heat-and-serve gourmet meals. The story of the table chicken is indicative of how Australia's culinary dynamism and the balance of power in the national food system are shifting away from primary producers towards large retail traders—the supermarkets.

Summary of main points

- Since the 1970s, supermarkets have played the major role in positioning chicken to become Australia's preferred meat. Simultaneously, they have used chicken meals to portray themselves in the consumer consciousness as a valued social institution.
- With assistance from a range of producer and consumer services, supermarkets have claimed the balance of power in the food system because they trade not simply in goods and services but in practices, ideas, and values. A range of professional services position large retail traders at the intersection of production and consumption within a nation's culinary culture.
- Using extensive insights into the socioeconomic and psychosocial characteristics of the population, supermarkets are constantly able to 'refresh' the relevance of the products and services that they sell, and by association they renew their own centrality to the nation's food system and culinary culture.
- The nascent appreciation of the value of 'doing cultural economy' will grow as the critical importance of the sphere of distribution and exchange is realised.

Discussion questions

1 Describe the activities that comprise the spheres of food production, distribution, exchange, and consumption.
2 In what ways has chicken meat become both 'good to think' and 'good to eat'?
3 When undertaking a cultural economy analysis of a commodity system, what steps would you take?
4 Do fast-food chains operate similarly to supermarket chains? What are their points of difference?
5 Describe the contradictions in the notion of 'healthy convenience'.
6 How do supermarkets acquire cultural capital?

Further investigation

1 Take a popular commodity grouping, like breakfast cereal, and describe the ways in which primary and secondary producers, supermarkets and specialist retail outlets, and consumers add value to the commodity.
2 Write a social history of the changes to small, family-run food retailers since the 1950s.

Further reading and web resources

Books

Bourdieu, P. 1979/1984, *Distinction: A Social Critique of the Judgement of Taste*, Routledge, London.

Dixon, J. 2002, *The Changing Chicken: Chooks, Cooks and Culinary Culture*, University of New South Wales Press, Sydney.

Du Gay, P. and Pryke, M. 2002, *Cultural Economy*, Sage, London.

Humphery, K. 1998, *Shelf Life: Supermarkets and the Changing Culture of Consumption*, Cambridge University Press, Cambridge.

Wrigley, N. & Lowe, M. 1996, *Retailing, Consumption and Capital: Towards the New Retail Geography*, Longman, Essex.

Web sites

Agri-food Chains Online: www.agribusiness.asn.au/ChainsNet

Agri-food Research Network: www.usyd.edu.au/geography/staff/bpritchard/AFRN

References

Appadurai, A. 1986, *The Social Life of Things*, Cambridge University Press, Cambridge.

Baker, R. & Marshall, D. 1998, 'The Hilmer Paradox: Evidence from the Australian Retail Grocery Industry', *Urban Policy and Research*, vol. 16, no. 4, pp. 271–84.

Bourdieu, P. 1979/1984, *Distinction: A Social Critique of the Judgement of Taste,* Routledge, London.

Burch, D. & Goss, J. 1999, 'Global Sourcing and Retail Chains: Shifting Relationships of Production in Australian Agri-foods', *Rural Sociology*, vol. 64, no. 2, pp. 334–50.

Cain, D. 1990, *History of the Australian Chicken Meat Industry 1950–1990*, Australian Chicken Meat Federation, Sydney.

Charles, N & Kerr, M. 1986, 'Issues of Responsibility and Control in the Feeding of Families', in S. Rodmell & A. Watt (eds), *The Politics of Health Education: Raising the Issues*, Routledge and Kegan Paul, London, pp. 57–75.

CSIRO—*see* Commonwealth Scientific and Industrial Research Organisation.

Commonwealth Scientific and Industrial Research Organisation 1994, *Information Needs and Concerns in Relation to Food Choice*, CSIRO, Adelaide.

Dawson, J. 1995, 'Food Retailing and the Food Consumer', in D. W. Marshall (ed.), *Food Choice and the Consumer*, Blackie Academic & Professional, London, pp. 77–104.

DeVault, M. 1991, *Feeding the Family: The Social Organization of Caring as Gendered Work*, University of Chicago Press, Chicago.

Dixon, J. 1999, 'A Cultural Economy Model for Studying Food Systems', *Agriculture and Human Values*, vol. 16, pp.151–60.

—— 2002, *The Changing Chicken: Chooks, Cooks and Culinary Culture*, University of New South Wales Press, Sydney.

—— in press, 'Authority, Power and Value in Contemporary Industrial Food Systems', *International Journal of Sociology of Agriculture and Food*.

Dixon, J. & Burgess, J. 1998, 'When Local Elites Meet the WTO: Chicken as Meat in the Sandwich', *Journal of Australian Political Economy*, no. 41, pp. 104–33.

Dixon, J., Sindall, C. & Banwell, C. forthcoming, 'Exploring the Intersectoral Partnerships Guiding Australia's Dietary Advice', *Health Promotion International*.

Douglas, M.1997, 'In Defence of Shopping', in P. Falk & C. Campbell (eds), *The Shopping Experience*, Sage, London, pp. 15–30.

Du Gay, P. & Pryke, M. 2002, *Cultural Economy*, Sage, London.

Fairbrother, J. 1988, 'The Poultry Industry: Technology's Child Two Decades on', *Food Australia*, November, pp. 456–62.

—— 2001, *Submission to the Department of Foreign Affairs and Trade on Forthcoming Multilateral Trade Negotiations in the World Trade Organisation*, Australian Chicken Meat Federation, Sydney.

Falk, P. & Campbell, C. 1997, *The Shopping Experience*, Sage, London.

Fantasia, R. 1995, 'Fast Food in France', *Theory and Society*, vol. 24, no. 2, pp. 201–43.

Featherstone, M. 1987, 'Lifestyle and Consumer Culture', *Theory, Culture & Society*, vol. 4, no. 1, pp. 55–70.

Fine, B. & Leopold, E. 1993, *The World of Consumption*, Routledge, London.

Fischler, C. 1993, 'A Nutritional Cacophony or the Crisis of Food Selection in Affluent Societies', in P. Leatherwood, M. Horisberger & W. James (eds), *For a Better Nutrition in the 21st Century*, Vevey/Raven Press, New York, pp. 57–65.

Flynn, A. & Marsden, T. 1992, 'Food Regulation in a Period of Agricultural Retreat: The British Experience', *Geoforum*, vol. 23, pp. 85–93.

Foord, J., Bowlby, S. & Tillsley, C. 1996, 'The Changing Place of Retailer-supplier Relations in British Retailing' in N. Wrigley & M. Lowe (eds), *Retailing, Consumption and Capital: Towards the New Retail Geography*, Longman, Essex, pp. 68–89.

Freidberg, S. 2003, 'Cleaning up Down South: Supermarkets, Ethical Trade and African Horticulture', *Social & Cultural Geography*, vol. 4, no. 1, pp. 27–43.

Friedland, W, 1984, 'Commodity Systems Analysis: An Approach to the Sociology of Agriculture', *Research in Rural Sociology and Development*, vol. 1, pp. 221–35.

—— 2001, 'Reprise on Commodity Systems Methodology', *International Journal of Sociology of Agriculture and Food*, vol. 9, no. 1, pp. 82–103.

Gabriel, Y. & Lang, T. 1995, *The Unmanageable Consumer*, Sage, London.

Gofton, L. 1990, 'Food Fears and Time Famines', in M. Ashwell (ed.), *Why We Eat What We Eat: The British Nutrition Foundation Bulletin*, vol. 15, no. 1, pp. 78–95.

Gofton, L. & Ness, M. (1991) 'Twin Trends: Health and Convenience in Food Change or Who Killed the Lazy Housewife', *British Food Journal*, vol. 93, no. 7, pp. 17–23.

Goodman, D. & Redclift, M. 1991, *Refashioning Nature: Food, Ecology & Culture*, Routledge, London.

Goodman, D. & Watts, M. 1997, *Globalising Food: Agrarian Questions and Global Restructuring*, Routledge, London.

Halperin, R. 1994, *Cultural Economies: Past and Present*, University of Texas Press, Austin.

Harris, M. 1986, *Good to Eat: Riddles of Food and Culture*, Allen & Unwin, London.

Harvey, M. 1998, 'UK Supermarkets: New Product and Labour Market Segmentation and the Restructuring of the Supply-demand Matrix', paper presented to the International Working Party on Labour Market Segmentation Conference, Trento, Italy.

Hollander, G. 2003, 'Re-naturalizing Sugar: Narratives of Place, Production and Consumption', *Social & Cultural Geography*, vol. 4, no. 1, pp. 59–74.

Hughes, A. 1996, 'Forging New Cultures of Food Retailer-manufacturer Relations?', in N. Wrigley & M. Lowe (eds), *Retailing, Consumption and Capital: Towards the New Retail Geography*, Longman, Essex, pp. 90–115.

Humphery, K. 1998, *Shelf Life: Supermarkets and the Changing Culture of Consumption*, Cambridge University Press, Cambridge.

Joint Select Committee on the Retailing Sector 1999, *Fair Market or Market Failure: A Review of Australia's Retailing Sector*, Parliament of Australia, Canberra.

JSCRS—*see* Joint Select Committee on the Retailing Sector.

Kingston, B. 1994, *Basket, Bag and Trolley: A History of Shopping in Australia*, Oxford University Press, Melbourne.

Kohler, A. 2003, 'Sam Walton's Long Shadow', *The Weekend Australian Financial Review*, July 26–27, p. 14.

Lash, S. 1990, *Sociology of Postmodernism*, Routledge, London.

Lash, S. & Urry, J. 1994, *Economies of Signs & Space*, Sage, London.

Lowe, M. & Wrigley, N. 1996, 'Towards the New Retail Geography', in N. Wrigley & M. Lowe (eds), *Retailing, Consumption and Capital: Towards the New Retail Geography*, Longman, Essex, pp. 3–30.

Lyons, K. 1996, 'Agro-industrialization and Social Change within the Australian Context: A Case Study of the Fast Food Industry', in D. Burch, R. Rickson & G. Lawrence (eds), *Globalization and Agri-food Restructuring: Perspectives from the Australasia Region*, Avebury, Aldershot, UK, pp. 239–50.

Mackay, H. 1992, *The Mackay Report: Food*, Hugh Mackay, Sydney.

Marshall, D. (ed.) 1995, *Food Choice and the Consumer*, Blackie Academic & Professional, London.

Mathews, J. 1989, *Tools of Change: New Technology and the Democratisation of Work*, Pluto Press, Sydney.

Miller, D. 1995, 'Consumption as the Vanguard of History', in D. Miller (ed.) *Acknowledging Consumption: A Review of New Studies*, Routledge, London, pp. 1–57.

Murcott, A. 1993, 'Talking of Good Food: An Empirical Study of Women's Conceptualizations', *Food and Foodways*, vol. 5, no. 3, pp. 305–18.

Murray, R. 1989, 'Fordism and post-Fordism', in S. Hall & M. Jaques (eds), *New Times: The Changing Face of Politics in the 1990s*, Lawrence and Wishart, London.

Pritchard, B. 1999, 'Australia as the Supermarket to Asia? Governments, Territory and Political Economy in the Australian Agri-food System', *Rural Sociology,* vol. 64, no. 2, pp. 284–301.

Raven, H., Lang, T. & Dumonteil, C. 1995, *Off Our Trolleys? Food Retailing and the Hypermarket Economy*, Institute for Public Policy Research, London.

Ryan, S. & Burgess, J. 1996, 'The Supermarket Co.', in J. Burgess, P. Keogh, D. Macdonald, G. Morgan, G. Strachan & S. Ryan (eds), *Enterprise Bargaining in Three Female Dominated Workplaces in the Hunter: Processes, Participation and Outcomes* (Employment Studies Centre Working Paper Series No. 26), University of Newcastle, Australia.

Santich, B. 1995, '"It's a Chore!" Women's Attitudes Towards Cooking', *Australian Journal of Nutrition and Dietetics,* vol. 52, no. 1, pp. 11–13.

Sassen, S. 1991, *The Global City*, Princeton University Press, Princeton, New Jersey.

Senker, J. 1988, *A Taste for Innovation: British Supermarkets' Influence on Food Manufacturers*, Horton Publishing, Bradford, UK.

Skurray, G. & Newell, G. 1993, 'Food Consumption in Australia 1970–1990', *Food Australia*, vol. 45, no. 9, pp. 434–8.

Strickland, K. 1996, 'Fast Food Chains Latch onto Health', *The Australian*, February 5, p. 3.

Symons, M. 1993, *The Shared Table,* Australian Government Publishing Service, Canberra.

Tansey, G. & Worsley, T. 1995, *The Food System: A Guide*, Earthscan Publications, London.

Warde, A. 1992, 'Notes on the Relationship between Production and Consumption', in R. Burrows & C. Marsh (eds), *Consumption and Class: Divisions and Change*, Macmillan, London, pp. 15–31.

—— 1994, 'Consumers, Identity and Belonging: Reflections on Some Theses of Zygmunt Bauman', in R. Keat, N. Whiteley & N. Abercrombie (eds), *The Authority of the Consumer*, Routledge, London, pp. 58–73.

Watts, M. & Goodman, D. 1997, 'Agrarian Questions', in D. Goodman & M. Watts *Globalising Food*, Routledge, London, pp. 1–32.

Wrigley, N. & Lowe, M. 1996, *Retailing, Consumption and Capital: Towards the New Retail Geography*, Longman, Essex.

Part 3

Food and Public Health Nutrition: Discourses, Politics, and Policies

Food is an important part of a balanced diet.

Fran Lebowitz, *Metropolitan Life* (1978)

Food is an area that brings the best and worst of politics into play; the formation of public policy and attempts to influence it by vested interest groups take place at national and international levels. The chapters in this part address the politics of food in terms of food regulations, food and nutrition policy used for health promotion, the emergence of public health nutrition as a specialist field, and the food discources and policies relating to the feeding of infants and children. Part 3 is divided into five chapters:

- Chapter 6 discusses the emergence of 'functional foods', which allegedly produce specific health benefits, and the implications these have for public-health and food-regulation policy in the face of powerful agribusinesses.
- Chapter 7 examines the role of food policy in the form of dietary guidelines, exposing some of the individualistic assumptions and corporate interests that have impacted on the good intentions of government authorities and health professionals in attempting to address public health nutrition, in terms of food production and consumption.
- Chapter 8 explores the development of the public health nutrition workforce and examines how workforce composition influences practice.
- Chapter 9 discusses the maternal ideologies and health-related discourses surrounding the choice of method for infant feeding.
- Chapter 10 examines food discourses in the context of the family and the feeding of children.

6

Future Food: The Politics of Functional Foods and Health Claims

Mark Lawrence and John Germov

Overview

- What are 'functional foods' and how is their development related to health claims?
- What has politics got to do with the regulation of functional foods and health claims?
- What are the costs and benefits of functional foods for individuals, food manufacturers, and society?

Future eaters will be faced with an increasingly medicalised food supply, with new products being marketed as health-promoting or disease-preventing foods—otherwise known as 'functional foods'. This chapter reviews the controversies associated with the research and development of functional foods and their promotion using health claims, describes the political issues, assesses the assumptions that have emerged, and explores options for the future. The functional foods debate provides a valuable case study of public policy relating to food and health. From a sociological perspective, it reflects a coalescence of the interests of food manufacturers and medical scientists in seeking to exert control over the composition and marketing of food. At a broader political level, the debate takes place within a climate characterised by the globalisation of food trade, a reduction in public sector spending, and market deregulation. The increasing medicalisation of the food supply is discussed as having significant social implications, of which consumers, health professionals, and government authorities should be aware.

Key terms

active micro-organisms	health claims	novel foods
biotechnology	healthism	phytochemicals
economic liberalism	medical–food–industrial complex	public health
food security	medicalisation	public policy
functional foods	new public health	risk factors
genetic engineering		social structure

Introduction

For millennia, people have been searching for miracle foods that could make them healthier, enhance performance, or immunise against disease. Hippocrates (460–360 BC) is quoted as saying 'Let your food be your medicine, and your only medicine be your food' (Bender & Bender 1997). However, a nutrition truism has been that no food in isolation can promote health or prevent disease, with the exception of breast milk in the first few months of life. Such potent influences on health were considered the domain of therapeutic products. Now, certain food manufacturers and some medical scientists are arguing that advances in food science are generating the technological capacity to develop food products that can help promote health and prevent disease. These foods are referred to by a number of names, such as 'nutraceuticals' or '**functional foods**'. 'Functional foods' is the most common term used in the literature, even though there remains a lack of consensus on a definition and the term is not officially recognised by regulatory agencies. The term 'functional food' is generally used to describe food products that it is claimed will deliver a health benefit beyond providing sustenance and nutrients (National Food Authority 1994, 1996; American Dietetic Association 1999).

Medical scientists have speculated that the health benefits of functional foods may be conferred by a variety of production and processing techniques, such as:

- fortifying food products with specific nutrients
- adding **phytochemicals** and **active micro-organisms** to conventional foods to formulate **novel foods**
- employing **genetic engineering** techniques.

Examples of food products that are candidates for future classification as functional foods are listed in Box 6.1.

Designer foods are not new—selective breeding and food fortification have existed for some time. However, the increasing sophistication of molecular biology and **biotechnology** is now enabling scientists to investigate, in considerable detail, the functional characteristics of food ingredients and their effects on the human body. Some scientists predict that the increased genetic

Box 6.1 Functional food candidates and related health claims

- Yoghurts and fermented milk drinks: some of these contain strains of 'good' bacteria such as *Acidophilous* and *Bifidus* that help improve gut function and digestion and promote general wellness.
- 'Energy drinks': these soft drinks with added guarana (a source of caffeine) and vitamins supposedly help enhance mental and physical performance.
- Breakfast cereals: some cereals contain either psyllium fibre, which it is claimed helps lower cholesterol levels, or folate, which it is claimed helps prevent neural tube defects in foetuses.
- Margarines: these contain phytochemicals (plant sterols and stanol esters) that it is claimed help lower cholesterol levels.
- Eggs, bread, and milk: these may contain omega 3 polyunsaturated fatty acids, derived from fish oil, which allegedly help lower cholesterol levels.

knowledge about humans, diseases, and food ingredients, combined with advances in food technology, will make it possible to construct functional foods that prevent and even treat diseases (Thomas & Earl 1994).

The existence and promulgation of functional foods are dependent upon there being food regulations permitting the use of health claims on food product labels and in advertising. According to the international food standards agency, the Codex Alimentarius Commission (Codex), a **health claim** 'means any representation that states, suggests, or implies that a relationship exists between a food or a constituent of that food and health' (CAC 2003, p. 38). Food manufacturers state candidly that if they are not allowed to promote the potential health benefits of their products to consumers, research into and development of functional foods is unlikely to proceed. In the USA, researchers have described health claims as the 'engine that powers' functional food development (Hasler et al. 1995). In this context, functional foods and health claims may be regarded as forming a strategic agenda on the part of some manufacturers who want to enable a specific form of development of the food supply. Effectively, the concept of functional foods will take on meaning in terms of health claims policy.

Most countries do not permit the use of health claims. The rationale for the general prohibition on health claims is the fundamental **public health** principle that it is the total diet, not individual food products, that determines health. Conventional wisdom holds that there is no such thing as a good or bad food, only good or bad diets. However, certain food manufacturers and, to a lesser extent, some medical research scientists have invested substantial resources in aggressively lobbying food regulators to permit the inclusion of health claims on food products. Many countries and Codex are now reviewing their food regulation policies in relation to this topic. In recent years, the USA, Canada, Sweden, and Japan have developed regulatory frameworks that permit certain health claims to be made, albeit within strict guidelines.

The interrelated nature of functional foods and health claims presents one of the most complex and political issues facing food regulators. The lack of definition of functional foods and the prohibition on health claims in most countries have resulted in a lack of information on which to base policy decisions. Stakeholders have tended to initiate and frame this **public policy** debate using opinions and speculation, relying on the liberal use of 'ifs', 'buts', and 'maybes'. Now that some countries are beginning to develop health claims policies it is possible to assess many of the arguments and assumptions associated with the debate. The purpose of this chapter is to place the debate in a clear context, review the current developments, challenge the assumptions that have emerged from the often adversarial debate between the different stakeholders, and explore the future options.

Why are functional foods and health claims political?

The concept of functional foods is political because it engages the competing values, interests, and beliefs of different stakeholders regarding the relationship between food and public health. In particular, the debates concern the nature of substantiation requirements and the impact of functional foods on population health and safety. A variety of interventions are required to promote and protect public health, but most interventions can be categorised into two broad health paradigms:

- the health promotion paradigm, which aims to promote health in populations as a whole
- the medical paradigm, which aims to reduce **risk factors** and treat disease in individuals.

Proponents of interventions aligned with the health promotion paradigm generally subscribe to the view that the most powerful determinants of health are the social, economic, and cultural circumstances in which people live (Blane et al. 1996; Marmot & Wilkinson 1999). This view is supported by the fact that populations with lower socioeconomic status suffer a disproportionate burden of ill health and disease (National Health Strategy 1992; Germov 2002). Therefore, interventions to promote the health of populations need to address the underlying social, economic, and cultural determinants. Such interventions are ecological in scope, preserving the integrity and sustainability of environmental resources—including the food supply—that are essential for health (World Health Organization 1991). In the health promotion paradigm, the relationship between food and health is understood in holistic terms of balance, variety, and moderation in dietary intake. The priority interventions are those that promote **food security** among the population.

By contrast, proponents of interventions aligned with the medical paradigm generally subscribe to the view that the population's health can best be promoted by preventing and treating disease in individuals. These interventions aim to address the risk factors and genetic factors associated with disease by focusing on changing dietary intake. In this context, food is regarded as a commodity that may be modified to assist the dietary reform process. Selected characteristics of these two paradigms are summarised in Table 6.1.

Table 6.1 Selected characteristics of health promotion and medical paradigms

	Health promotion paradigm	*Medical paradigm*
Focus	Population	Individual
View of health	Positive resource for living; Social responsibility	Absence of disease; Individual responsibility
View of food	Prerequisite for health	Product to prevent or treat disease
Cause of illness	Risk-imposing factors: social inequality, work, culture, etc.	Biology and risk-taking behaviour

Table 6.1 simplifies each paradigm for the purposes of comparing key features and highlighting differences. While both paradigms coexist and can be complementary, in practice the medical paradigm dominates the organisation and delivery of health care, as well as health research and policy. Despite this dominance, numerous critics of the medical paradigm highlight its implicit individualism, which leads to a concentration on curing individuals once they are sick, and on using health education messages in an attempt to change individual behaviour (Naidoo 1986; Tesh 1988; Richmond 2002). The health promotion paradigm is derived from the **new public health** movement, which, among other things, focuses on changing the social environment to provide for a secure food supply to promote health and prevent the onset of disease across the population.

Opponents of functional foods and health claims argue, from the perspective of the health promotion paradigm, that it is the total diet that is important for health, not so-called 'magic bullet' approaches, which are primarily about differentiating products on commercial grounds to enable manufacturers to indulge in marketing hyperbole. Moreover, these critics express concern that the marketing of such products is based on scaremongering, because it exploits consumer confusion and anxiety about the relationship between food and health to create a demand and then blurs the distinction between food and drugs to capitalise on this created demand. Supporters of functional foods respond, from the perspective of the medical paradigm, that these foods may reduce health care expenditure and that health claims are a legitimate nutrition education tool that will help to inform consumers of the health benefits of certain food products.

Extrapolating scientific evidence from one paradigm to another can be problematic and may falsely raise expectations. For example, caution is needed in applying the findings of medical research from trials on individuals to generate public health policy intended for the total population. The application of correlations established under controlled experimental settings to the 'real world'—where people consume varied diets and adopt a wide range of lifestyles—can clearly distort the variables investigated in an experimental or clinical setting. It is more appropriate to look at expectations regarding functional foods and health claims within the context in which they were developed: in relation to the potential effects on certain individuals. It needs to be emphasised that it is not science *per se* that is at fault, but rather the misinterpretation and misapplication of scientific investigation, which is unintentionally facilitating what Illich (1975) called the **medicalisation** of life.

Medicalising food and healthism

The functional foods and health claims agenda presents a novel challenge. There are few precedents upon which to base an assessment of whether it is likely to have any acute public health and safety consequences. The concerns that are raised relate to the general theme of 'medicalising' the food supply—producing food that approximates drugs.

The medicalisation of food involves treating food like a drug with therapeutic properties that are able to prevent disease. Such a view represents a pathologised and reductionist approach to health promotion and food consumption. The likely outcome is that the individual will be blamed for any diet-related illness, since the mode of prevention simply becomes a matter of food consumption choices. A preoccupation with the consumption of individual foods for their hypothetical health benefits ignores the fact that disease causation is multifactorial and the outcome of wider social influences. Therefore, universal claims of the health benefits resulting from consumption of functional foods are meaningless and give a misleading message by overemphasising diet risk factors at the expense of others (for example, smoking and hypertension are also risk factors for heart disease, along with diet).

Peter Conrad (1992) defines 'medicalisation' as the process of adopting medical terminology and treatment for non-medical, social problems. The medical paradigm is necessarily individualistic, but in the arena of health education such individualism merges with an ideology of **economic liberalism** that assumes the only requirement is the delivery of a health education message—it is then up to the individual to choose whether to change their lifestyle. An alternative approach to an emphasis on individual risk-taking is to change the **social structure** that induces 'risk-imposing behaviour' (see Ratcliffe et al. 1984). For example, regulations regarding advertising and minimum production standards for fat content in food—such as labelling requirements that remove the ambiguity of labels such as 'lite', 'low-fat', and 'cholesterol-free'—could be introduced. Such a population-based public health approach is likely to have a greater impact on individual health than is an exclusive focus on health education.

The other implicit message of the educative approach—effectively a 'buyer beware' stance—is what Richard Crawford (1980) terms **'healthism'**. Healthism is the belief that health attainment and maintenance are primary human values. The key philosophical principle underpinning healthism is self-responsibility. This belief is based on an idealised 'health consumer' who consciously responds to health education messages by modifying his/her individual—in this case through choices relating to food consumption. Such a conceptual model does not account for the manipulation of 'choices', or for obstacles to exercising choice, such as the social inequalities suffered by marginalised groups (especially as functional foods are likely to be marketed as premium, and thus high-priced, goods, restricting access for low socioeconomic groups).

The political context of the policy debate

The diminishing authority of food authorities

Food regulation in Australia and New Zealand is governed by the statutory authority Food Standards Australia New Zealand (FSANZ) (see Box 6.2). FSANZ's prime objective is to protect public health and safety via food standards (or rules) governing food manufacturing, product labelling, food hygiene, food additives, contaminants, residues, and new technologies like genetic modification. However, food regulation has developed within a climate of reduced public sector expenditure and deregulation. The nature and strength of food regulations were examined in Australia in the 'Blair Review', which had a clear deregulatory bias, as was evident in its first objective: 'while protecting public health and safety, to: reduce the regulatory burden on the food sector, and examine those regulations which restrict competition, impose costs or confer benefits on business' (Food Regulation Review 1998, p. 4). There appears to be an inherent contradiction in proposing to liberalise public policy to enhance the profitability of the food industry while also prioritising public health and safety. Essentially, private sector funding is required to fully implement the food regulations. This option is clearly attractive to governments, but it may also be seen as an abrogation of the responsibility for nutrition education, monitoring, and evaluation, and to shift the funding of such services from the public to the private sector. This is particularly the case in states and territories with conservative governments that promote themselves as 'business friendly'. Yet this raises fundamental questions about whether it is appropriate for public money to be spent on services to complement a policy initiated for the private sector's benefit. Alternatively, if there is a reliance on private sector contribution, who is responsible for public sector services intended to protect public health and safety?

Box 6.2 Food regulation in Australia and New Zealand

Public health, including food regulation, is a responsibility of state and territory governments in Australia. Recognition of the need for a unified approach to food regulation resulted in these governments adopting the Australian *Food Standards Code* in 1986, which was followed by the establishment of the National Food Authority (NFA) in 1991. Increased cooperation with New Zealand on food policy led to the renaming of the NFA as the Australia New Zealand Food Authority (ANZFA) in 1997, which was again renamed in 2001 as Food Standards Australia New Zealand (FSANZ). In 2000, the *Australia New Zealand Food Standards Code* was introduced and it came into full effect on 20 December 2002 (Commonwealth of Australia 2001; Healy et al. 2003). Similar food authorities exist in many countries, such as the UK Food Standards Agency and the US Food and Drug Administration.

The rise of the medical–food–industrial complex

The functional foods and health claims agenda reflects a coalescence of the interests of food manufacturers and medical scientists in seeking to exert control over the composition and marketing of food. Moreover, certain government agencies appear united with food manufacturers in their support of functional foods (Downer 1994; Hindmarsh 1996). The impetus for their support appears to be the potential economic gain, particularly the export dollars that the pundits predict the development of functional foods will bring.

From an economic perspective, the functional foods and health claims agenda represents a critical dilemma for food regulators. Responding to the requests of the private sector and establishing a health claims regulatory framework will potentially generate significant public sector administrative costs and will create a demand for 'protective' services, including nutrition education, monitoring and evaluation, enforcement, and interpretation—all of which will drain the public purse.

Allowing health claims would present both opportunities and challenges to the various stakeholders. New players from the pharmaceutical industry may emerge. Food manufacturers with substantial research and development budgets will be better placed than primary producers, including fruit and vegetable producers, to take advantage of regulatory change. The increased investment in research and development that is anticipated to result from a regulatory change endorsing functional foods and health claims agenda would boost opportunities for medical researchers. The opportunities for public health practitioners and social scientists are less clear.

Together these stakeholders constitute a new '**medical–food–industrial complex**'. The corporate agenda is minimal regulation and limited public debate in pursuit of rapid returns on capital investment. Certain government bodies are supporting these developments because of the predicted economic benefits, and medical scientists are either captives of the promise of substantial research funding or advocates of the individualistic medical paradigm critiqued above.

Case studies of functional food

The most significant health claims activity is occurring in the USA, as a consequence of the Food and Drug Administration's (FDA's) *Nutrition Labeling and Education Act 1990* (NLEA). The final regulations implementing the NLEA were issued in 1993, and this has resulted in extensive changes to food labelling in the USA: manufacturers are now allowed to use model health claims for those food products that satisfy specified qualifying and disqualifying criteria (USDHHS 1993a, 1993b). By 2003, the FDA had approved fourteen health claims for foods and food ingredients. These claims related to the following products, among others:

- whole oat products (lowered cholesterol levels and reduced heart disease risk)
- foods containing psyllium (lowered cholesterol levels and reduced heart disease risk)
- margarines made with plant stanol or sterol esters (lowered cholesterol levels and reduced heart disease risk)
- sugarless chewing gums and lollies made with sugar alcohols (do not promote tooth decay)
- folate-fortified food products (help reduce the risk of neural tube defects, or NTDs).

Key Australian developments in functional foods are summarised in Table 6.2; the most significant events have been the pilot folate/NTD health claim (discussed below) and the *Review of Health and Related Claims* report (ANZFA 2001). The report recommended that health claims be allowed in Australia—approved on a case-by-case basis and subject to significant substantiation requirements. This recommendation is currently under review, and in the meantime Standard 1.1A.2,

Table 6.2 Functional foods and health claims in Australia: Key developments

Year	*Key developments: Reports, legislation, and key events*
1986	Australian Food Standards Code adopted—includes Standard A1(19), prohibiting health claims.
1994	*Discussion Paper on Functional Foods* (NFA 1994).
1996	*Concept Paper on Health and Related Claims* (NFA 1996).
1998	Pilot of new health claim framework—folate/NTD health claim allowed on certain foods.
1998	Standard A18: Food Produced Using Gene Technology adopted, but subsequently revised due to consumer pressure (see First Australian Consensus Conference 1999).
1999	Evaluation of health claims pilot completed; folate/NTD health claim subsequently extended until February 2004, with an application pending to extend it until 2006.
2000	GM labelling regulation adopted: Food Produced Using Gene Technology (Standard 1.5.2). All GM foods must be labelled, unless GM ingredients are less than 1%, as an unintended consequence of production (Brent et al. 2003).
2001	ANZFA (2001) *Inquiry Report—Proposal P153: Review of Health and Related Claims* recommends the adoption of new health claims standard allowing health claims to be approved in Australia on a case-by-case basis (currently under review).
2001	Standard 1.5.1 on Novel Foods and Standard 2.6.4 on Formulated Caffeinated Beverages added to the *Australia New Zealand Food Standards Code.*
2002	Standard 1.1A.2, the Transitional Standard—Health Claims, added to the *Australia New Zealand Food Standards Code*; to remain in place for a two-year transitional period. The standard incorporates clause 19 of Standard A1 of the old code, which includes the general prohibition on health claims, with the addition of the pilot folate/NTD health claim.

the Transitional Standard—Health Claims, has been added to the *Australia New Zealand Food Standards Code*, which maintains the general prohibition on health claims (with the exception of the pilot folate/NTD health claim).

The growing number of candidate functional food products in the marketplace and the increasing recognition of health claims in the USA provide a number of case studies that can be examined to help us assess the various assumptions and arguments in the functional foods/health claims debate. Five case studies are discussed below to illustrate the nature and range of candidate functional foods and functional ingredients: folate, psyllium, phytosterols, the fat substitute olestra, and so-called 'energy drinks'. These case studies reveal the potential benefits and risks associated with functional foods and health claims.

Folate and neural tube defects (NTDs)

Folate is one of the water-soluble B group vitamins. During the 1980s and 1990s, the findings from thirteen of fourteen epidemiological trials provided evidence that an increase in a mother's folate intake during the periconceptional period may help reduce the risk of her giving birth to a baby with an NTD (Medical Research Council 1991; Czeizel & Dudas 1992). The actual biological mechanism that underlies this preventative action is not yet understood. It would appear that folate is likely to be compensating for a congenital defect affecting a biochemical pathway involved in folate metabolism in certain susceptible women.

There are challenges for policy-makers in translating the epidemiological findings about the relationship between folate and NTDs into public health policy. First, the genetic condition that predisposes some women to giving birth to a baby with an NTD is not fully understood and cannot be detected. Second, a significant proportion of pregnancies are unplanned. Consequently, those interventions that may best target individuals—nutrition education and the promotion of folate-supplement consumption—may not achieve maximum coverage. By contrast, folate fortification of staple food products can reach all individuals at risk. However, such fortification exposes everyone in the population to raised levels of folate in the food supply.

The policy response of several governments to the epidemiological evidence has been to encourage folate fortification of staple foods, to reduce the risk of NTDs. This policy has created a unique opportunity for the functional foods and health claims lobby. For example, in Australia in November 1998, these developments resulted in an exemption being made to the existing prohibition on health claims to permit a pilot study of a folate-related health claim (ANZFA 1998). The use of a health claim to complement the folate-fortification intervention is intended, first, to assist the targeted individuals by informing them of the benefit of consuming fortified products, and, second, to provide manufacturers with an incentive to implement government policy (where fortification is a voluntary recommendation) and invest in research and development (USDHHS 1996; Lawrence 1997). This will result in a win–win situation for governments and food manufacturers. A further benefit is that it may help to mitigate the concern that fortification is a non-specific intervention; a health claim on a folate-fortified food product could inform those individuals who wish to avoid such products. This informing function is important, as the long-term safety implications of consuming raised levels of folate are uncertain. There is some evidence of adverse side effects, such as a 40% increase in the chance of multiple births, associated with folate supplementation (Czeizel et al. 1994; Lumley et al. 2003). Furthermore, a review of the folate trial noted that the health claim was only relevant to a small percentage of women, perhaps 5% of whom are in a peri-conceptional phase of life at any given time (ANZFA 2001). What is essentially a population-wide intervention is being used to address a medical condition in specific individuals (Lawrence 2003).

With increased understanding of the folate–NTD relationship and of the dietary habits of targeted individuals, and with advances in molecular biology, it may be possible to refine the 'dosage' of folate (and other nutrients) in food products and to better identify at-risk individuals. Folate fortification is setting expectations that certain food products will approximate the actions of therapeutic agents.

Psyllium and risk of coronary heart disease

Psyllium is a very rich source of soluble fibre and has been included as an ingredient in some breakfast cereals. Feeding trials have indicated that a psyllium-based breakfast cereal reduced cholesterol levels by approximately 9% when consumed as part of a low-fat diet (Anderson et al. 1988; Greenberg et al. 1994). A food manufacturer urged the United States Food and Drug Administration (FDA) to allow the following health claim regarding the relationship between psyllium and coronary heart disease (CHD) (USDHHS 1993a): 'Low-fat diets that include foods high in soluble fiber from psyllium may help lower blood cholesterol levels, which are among the risk factors for heart disease'.

The following questions are raised by this scientific data, and by any health claims resulting from it:

1 How relevant are the findings to the majority of the population? The feeding trials involved middle-aged men who were hypercholesterolaemic (i.e. had a high cholesterol level). Is it appropriate to extrapolate these findings to men who are not hypercholesterolaemic, or to women? Is it desirable to expose children to products that might lower their cholesterol levels?
2 Are there special considerations that need to be taken into account? The studies reported that between three and five serves of the breakfast cereal per day were required to achieve the 9% reduction in cholesterol levels.

Despite these unresolved issues, in early 1998 the FDA approved a health claim stating that the consumption of grain products that contain psyllium may help to reduce the risk of heart disease.

Phytosterols and cholesterol reduction

Phytosterols (plant stanol or sterol esters) are naturally occurring components in edible vegetable oils. Phytosterols were initially approved for use in Australia in a limited range of edible oil spreads (margarines). Evidence from clinical trials indicates that high doses of plant sterols or stanols may lower serum cholesterol concentrations by 8–15% (Law 2000). Phytosterols reduce serum cholesterol by inhibiting the absorption of dietary and biliary cholesterol. The dietary phytosterol contribution from edible oil spreads required to lower cholesterol levels is significantly higher than would otherwise typically be consumed. Edible oil spreads with added phytosterols are primary candidates for health claims.

There are safety concerns about exposure to high levels of dietary phytosterols. For example, at the dosage levels required to lower serum cholesterol concentrations, phytosterols have been reported to lower plasma alpha- and beta-carotene levels by up to 19% (Barker et al. 1999). In addition, public health practitioners have raised concerns about the broader public health implications associated with the marketing and widespread use of such products. They question whether it is appropriate to market such products to children, to pregnant and lactating women, to people with normocholesterolaemic levels, and to people on cholesterol-lowering medication. Also, they highlight the contradictions implicit in promoting a high-fat product as a commodity that will help reduce risk of heart disease when high fat intakes are associated with obesity, itself a risk factor for heart disease. In mid 2001, in an indictment on the marketing of such products, the UK Advertising Standards Authority ruled that two competing edible oil spreads (margarines) made misleading claims. Specifically, it was argued that the manufacturers of the two competing margarine brands were involved in a 'bidding war' to talk up the claimed health benefits of their respective products. The ruling stated that Benecol claimed it could reduce cholesterol by 14%, while Flora Pro-activ went one better with a claim of 15% cholesterol reduction (Just-food.com 2001).

In June 2001, the Food Standards Ministerial Council of Australia and New Zealand approved vegetable oil-derived plant sterol esters as a novel food ingredient in edible oil spreads and required that such products carry an advisory statement. The advisory statements should recommend that 'these products are not appropriate for infants, children and pregnant and lactating women and that people using cholesterol reducing medication should seek medical advice before using the spreads' (FSANZ 2001a). Permission was not given for the use of the phytosterol esters in a broader range of foods products, because of the lack of evidence relating to their safety and efficacy. However, FSANZ is currently considering applications to extend the use of phytosterols to fibre-increased bread, breakfast-cereal bars, low-fat milk, and low-fat yoghurt.

Food products with added phytosterols sit in the grey area between food and drugs. On the one hand, they have the appearance of a food product; on the other hand, they have been developed to serve a physiological role beyond the provision of nutrients. The achievement of this physiological role requires a dosage and advisory statement of usage. Food products with added phytosterols represent an example of the potential benefits and risks associated with functional foods. Although there is no evidence that such products offer any health benefit to the population at large, or to individuals who do not have raised cholesterol levels, they may (as a component of a healthy diet) provide some medical benefit to individuals with raised cholesterol levels. From a public health and safety perspective, the regulation of food products with added phytosterols needs to ensure that the potential public health and safety risks do not outweigh the potential medical benefits for certain individuals.

Olestra: The rise (and fall?) of artificial fat

Olestra is the generic name for a fat substitute originally discovered in 1968 by researchers working for the multinational company Procter and Gamble. Olestra is derived from a sucrose (table sugar) molecule combined with a number of fatty-acid residues and cannot be metabolised by gut enzymes and bacteria; thus it passes through the body without being absorbed or digested. In 1996, the FDA approved olestra for use in snack foods, such as chips and crackers. This synthetic fat was promoted as allowing consumers to eat as many 'fatty' foods as they desired without gaining weight or suffering health problems. Olestra has been tentatively supported by the American Dietetic Association (1998) for its potential to address obesity problems in the United States. It was hoped that olestra would follow the successful path of artificial sweeteners such as aspartame and saccharine into the American diet; however, this has not proved to be the case.

Olestra has a number of serious side-effects. Products using olestra require fortification because, as olestra passes through the body, it can bind with fat-soluble vitamins, lessening their absorption if present in the intestines. There are also dosage issues. Relatively modest consumption can result in some unpleasant side-effects, such as:

- severe diarrhoea
- anal leakage and faecal incontinence
- abdominal cramping.

Because of these side-effects, the FDA made the use of olestra subject to specific labelling conditions and fortification requirements. All products containing olestra must carry the following label: 'This product contains olestra. Olestra may cause abdominal cramping and loose stools. Olestra inhibits the absorption of some vitamins and other nutrients. Vitamins A, D, E, and K have been added.' Olestra is not approved in Australia and has been rejected for use in Canada.

'Energy drinks': Formulated caffeine beverages

'Energy drinks' are generally carbonated soft drinks that contain ingredients that allegedly enhance physical and mental performance, most notably caffeine and/or guarana (a herb containing caffeine), along with a range of vitamins, such as niacin, cobalamin, and amino acids. Until recently, there were no Australian regulations relating to the sale of such products. In fact, energy drinks were introduced into the Australian market without prior approval, thanks to a regulatory loophole that allowed their importation from New Zealand under the Trans Tasman Mutual Recognition Arrangement. A number of health professionals and consumer groups, most notably the Australian Consumers Association, raised concerns about energy drinks because of the high levels of caffeine and their potential detrimental health effects on children, the prime market for such products. Not only did many of the products not state that they contained caffeine, there was suspicion of deliberate deception

Table 6.3 Comparison of caffeine levels of energy drinks and other foods

Food	*Caffeine level*
Energy drink	80 mg per 250 mL
Instant coffee	60–80 mg per 250 mL cup
Coca-Cola	36 mg per 375 mL can
Tea	10–50 mg per 250 mL cup
Milk chocolate	20 mg per 100 g

Source: FSANZ (2001b)

by manufacturers who promoted guarana as a 'natural' ingredient that was primarily responsible for the energy-enhancing effects. High consumption of caffeine, particularly when 'hidden' in a sweetly flavoured drink, can result in dehydration, raised diastolic blood pressure, heart palpitations, and anxiety. Table 6.3 compares the significant caffeine levels of energy drinks with some other common foods (FSANZ 2001b).

Concerns over energy drinks prompted a new food standard to be introduced in 2001: Formulated Caffeinated Beverages (Standard 2.6.4). This standard requires all energy drinks to be labelled with the following information:

- the amount of caffeine per serving size and per 100 mL
- advisory statements asserting that the food contains caffeine and is not recommended for children, pregnant or lactating women, or individuals sensitive to caffeine, and that users '[c]onsume no more than [amount of one-day quantity (as cans, bottles or mL)] per day'.

While energy drinks make no specific health claims, the inclusion of vitamins and herbs with alleged functional properties is used to support spurious health-like claims such as 'improves mental alertness', 'enhances concentration', and 'provides a natural energy boost'. Such products expose the difficulties of food regulation in the health claims area, particularly when novel foods are released onto the market.

Analysing the functional foods and health claims debate

The competing values, interests, and beliefs of the stakeholders in the functional foods and health claims argument can be summarised in the following four debates:

1. 'Functional foods promote health and prevent disease' versus 'Functional foods are a public health and safety risk'.
2. 'Health claims are a legitimate way to inform consumers' versus 'Health claims are a marketing tool that fosters confusion about the links between food and health'.

3 'The general prohibition of health claims is ambiguous and should be removed' versus 'The removal of the general prohibition undermines public health strategies'.
4 'Food regulation policy permitting health claims stimulates research and food innovation' versus 'Health claims promote novel foods to generate profits for multinational companies under false health pretences'.

Now that there are several case studies of the application of health claims to functional foods, the arguments and assumptions of the different stakeholders can be assessed.

Debate 1: Functional foods—Disease prevention or safety risk?

It is too early to evaluate the public health and safety impact of the recent permissions to use health claims on certain food products. However, what can be examined is the capacity of functional food and health claim developments to contribute to the success of the priority public-health nutrition-policy initiatives for Australia. These initiatives are outlined in the *Eat Well Australia* policy document (Commonwealth Department of Health and Ageing 2001). The four priority initiatives are as follows:

1 promoting vegetable and fruit consumption
2 promoting healthy weight
3 promoting good nutrition for mothers and infants
4 promoting good nutrition for vulnerable groups, with particular emphasis on addressing structural barriers to safe and healthy food.

It is not immediately clear how functional foods and health claims will contribute to the achievement of any of these four priority initiatives.

A critical component of the decision-making process associated with the passage of the *Nutrition Labeling and Education Act 1990* (NLEA) in the USA was the publishing of a regulatory-impact analysis in the form of an economic costs and benefits study. In 1993, the FDA estimated that allowing manufacturers to make food-label changes in response to the NLEA—most importantly, placing nutrient-content claims and health claims on product labels—would, over a 20-year period, result in at least 12,600 lives saved and 79,000 life-years saved (USDHHS 1993b). This analysis rests on a litany of assumptions, including that consumers will:

- read and understand health claims
- be motivated to change their behaviour
- be able to change their behaviour
- have a health improvement as a direct consequence of the change in behaviour.

This exercise was confined to the medical paradigm, with little attempt made to assess the broader public health impact of the policy change. The analysis unproblematically predicted that consumer uncertainty and ignorance 'will' decrease and that many consumers 'will inadvertently eat a better diet' as a consequence of the NLEA. The FDA's own research (Levy 1996; Levy et al.

1997) is now confounding the assumptions central to this costing exercise. The validity of the assumptions has also been questioned by Allred (1995), who highlights the interesting correlation between the increased consumption of low-fat foods and the increasing weight of the American population—clearly cautioning against the adoption of a simplistic, quick-fix technical approach to individual and public health problems.

There are many aspects of the relationship between food and health that remain poorly understood. It is premature to start predicting the public health impact of novel changes to the composition or structure of the food supply. The reduction of nutritional analysis to the analysis of single foods or nutrients, and of single outcomes, is problematic, as the introduction of one intervention can have broader and more profound effects, particularly by distorting nutrient metabolism. For example, the interaction between nutrients may affect their bio-availability, as occurs when excessive calcium intake interferes with iron absorption (Hallberg et al. 1992).

Conventional risk-assessment procedures for novel ingredients and products are generally limited to short timeframes and consider the ingredient or product in isolation. Comprehensive information on the broader public health impact of products in combination with other foods and over extended periods of time is required—especially consumer research on how people react to functional foods (Norton & Lawrence 1996; First Australian Consensus Conference 1999). Therefore, there are certain stakeholders who believe that it is premature to introduce a health intervention without knowing its likely impact on dietary behaviour and nutritional intake.

Debate 2: Health claims—Consumer education or marketing hyperbole?

Information regarding the impact of health claims on consumers' understanding of diet and health is limited to that available from studies that have evaluated the NLEA in the USA. Preliminary research using focus-group testing indicated that consumers were sceptical of health claims and felt 'bombarded' by diet and health information (Levy 1996). Different wordings and different presentation styles for improving the effectiveness of communication of FDA-approved health claims were then tested in consumer research conducted by the FDA (Levy et al. 1997). The results of this testing did not support the view that the use of health claims is an effective public health intervention to change people's food choices and achieve healthier diets.

Public health researchers have reported that some sections of the community are becoming sceptical about diet and health messages and that in some cases a backlash against dietary recommendations has occurred (Patterson et al. 2001). Nevertheless, marketing analysts provide many examples of food products, such as grape juice and breakfast cereals, which have shown a significant increase in sales when a health claim has been displayed on the product label

(Leighton 2002). In the future, adequate monitoring will be required to assess whether health claims contribute to informing consumers or to distorting consumers' food-consumption patterns as a consequence of their use to market certain food products.

Debate 3: The general prohibition of health claims—Ambiguous or a key public health strategy?

Does regulatory review solve problems, or does it open the door to an ongoing process of change? Being a political process, the review of food regulation policy is subject to lobbying and advocacy. The most vociferous voices often do not reflect the broad interests of the community. Yet there is a strong temptation to 'oil the squeaky wheel' in order to avoid confrontation. In the case of functional foods and health claims, there are concerns that this could compromise public health principles. Prohibition provides an unambiguous policy position. As such, it provides clear parameters for all stakeholders to work within. The review of the black-and-white prohibition policy inevitably leads to the creation of a grey area. The challenge associated with revising the policy position is to avoid uncertainty and excessive resource demands upon regulators and the public purse in relation to interpretation and enforcement procedures. In addition, the effects of any potential functional-food regulation will need careful consideration in relation to existing theories of public and private law regarding liability and obligation (Preston & Lawrence 1996). What, for example, would be the legal response if a person consumed a functional food expecting to prevent an NTD birth but then tragically conceived a baby with an NTD?

Debate 4: Health claims policy—Stimulating research and innovation or profit under false pretences?

An implicit assumption of the functional foods and health claims agenda is that the food supply needs to be 'fixed' on public health grounds. This assumption is itself based on a series of other assumptions, including that:

- the current food supply is deficient
- diets are inadequate
- a 'technological fix' will solve the problem.

Some stakeholders have criticised current food-regulation policy in relation to health claims as being both 'old and outdated', arguing that it does not do enough to encourage research and development opportunities or to prevent abuse. However, this regulatory policy is based on the fundamental scientific principle that it is the total diet, not individual foods, that determine health. This principle is as relevant today as it was when the regulatory policy was first prepared.

Food manufacturers are able to take advantage of many opportunities to include nutrition information on their food labels and in advertising. For example, Codex and most countries have regulations permitting the use of nutrient-content claims on food labels to describe the level of a nutrient contained in a food—allowing manufacturers to describe a product as 'low fat' or a 'source' of a particular vitamin (CAC 1996). In addition, food manufacturers are encouraged to use nutrient-function claims, which describe the physiological role of the nutrient in the growth, development, and normal functioning of the body—for example, 'Contains folic acid: folic acid contributes to the normal growth of the fetus' (CAC 1996). Problems arises when it is not clear whether a claim is a legal nutrient-function claim or an illegal health claim. This is more an issue of the interpretation of the regulations rather than a flaw in the logic underpinning them, and there is a need for food regulators to clearly specify which nutrient claims are permissable.

Future directions: Challenges and possibilities

The pre-eminent political challenge facing policy-makers as they attempt to move the functional food/health claims debate forward is that of managing the competing values, interests, and beliefs of the different stakeholders. A good way to approach the debate is to acknowledge the nature and scope of these competing characteristics. Such an acknowledgment helps one to avoid the unconstructive pretence—or naïve assumption—that functional foods and health claims are purely about public health and are somehow apolitical. Some food-marketing advisers are becoming more frank about the commercial motivation behind health claims. For example, in his analysis of health claims, Tillotson advises the developers of health claims that 'the overriding purpose of the claim is commercial—to sell a *food product*. Any collateral public health or consumer education that occurs is necessarily secondary' (2003, p. 60, italics in original).

The use of 'scenarios' is an effective way to move the debate beyond a stalemate between those for and those against functional foods and health claims. The scenarios technique is a powerful tool that involves stakeholders working together to construct different outcomes, based on certain common assumptions, in order to consider public policy options. The preferred scenario is identified to provide the consensus outcome to be worked towards. This procedure combines the key strategies of communication, clear setting of expectations, and cooperation in planning. The scenarios process has been successfully employed in health promotion (Hancock 1997).

The 'best case scenario' would deliver a win–win situation by ensuring the protection of public health and safety while still providing a secure framework within which manufacturers could pursue research and development. Conversely, a 'worst case scenario' may arise from the so-called 'fundamental conflict' of the health claims debate: the difference in ethical standards of the marketing and science communities (Miller 1991). This scenario has been termed 'quick-fix nutrition'; it provides marketers with increased leverage to

Table 6.4 Selected characteristics of potential scenarios relating to functional foods and health claims

Best case scenario ('win–win')	*Worst case scenario ('quick-fix nutrition')*
Promote consumer confidence in and understanding of the food supply	Exacerbation of confusion, anxiety, and mistrust of the food supply
Food promoted within the total diet as a resource for health	Defensive eating: diet is viewed as a collection of foods and nutrients designed to ward off specific diseases
Opportunities for research and development of innovative products	A 'power race' of indiscriminate food fortification and health claims between manufacturers
Clarification of regulations	Blurring of regulations
Strengthened enforcement	Escalation of regulatory abuse
Increased opportunities for nutrition education, monitoring, and evaluation	Large stakeholders dominate nutrition information, with public funds diverted to compensate for distorted messages

employ dubious messages (Yap et al. 1997). Selected characteristics of these scenarios are summarised in Table 6.4.

So how can a win-win scenario be facilitated? The immediate priority is for food regulators to develop a coherent public health policy framework for conceptualising the relationship between food and health. Food regulators need to explain, for example, exactly what they mean by the policy objectives of 'protecting public health and safety' and 'providing sufficient information to enable consumers to make informed decisions'. A policy framework that articulates these policy objectives in practical terms will enable functional foods and health claims to be placed into perspective.

The relationship between food and health is complex, and thus does not lend itself to simple cause-and-effect explanations. Unfortunately, there is often a temptation for 'experts' to overstate or simplify their findings, and for the media to take scientifically rigorous research out of context and to distort it; precision in conducting scientific investigations and the intention of accurately informing a lay audience can get subverted. Alan Petersen and Deborah Lupton (1996) argue that medical and epidemiological findings are often oversimplified by the media and by health authorities, such that tentative conclusions come to be presented to the public as unquestionable 'facts'.

Health claims are not a panacea for consumer misunderstanding. The food label is just one tool that can complement broader nutrition-education initiatives.

It would be simplistic to assume that providing more information on the label will necessarily help. While some consumers assiduously read food labels, others are clearly overwhelmed when confronted with the bewildering array of messages, often couched in technical language. As the NLEA acknowledges, potential health claims need to be considered as a component of an integrated and comprehensive nutrition-education strategy (Kulakow et al. 1993). It is within this broader educational context that health claims may have a role. Otherwise, the marketing of functional foods will oversimplify the diet–disease link.

A policy approach consistent with a comprehensive nutrition-education strategy would be to maintain the general prohibition on health claims, with particular health claims only being permitted as exemptions to this prohibition on a case-by-case basis. Such an exemption would be made if the applicant satisfied special criteria, including scientific substantiation requirements, qualifying and disqualifying criteria, usage instructions, and safety assessment.

Scientific substantiation will be essential to the success of functional foods and health claims. Invariably, substantiation is conducted within a medical-research setting, in which findings relate to risk factors in individuals; the broader public health impact is not measured. This places health claims regarding functional foods within the medical paradigm. They may offer individuals greater choice in constructing their diets, or they may be directly beneficial to individuals who are at risk of specific diseases. In the case of psyllium, studies have concluded that a psyllium-enriched breakfast cereal can be a useful adjunct to the dietary treatment of hypercholesterolaemia (Stoy et al. 1993; Roberts et al. 1994). In this context, a health claim targeted at specific individuals may be warranted; however, it is not clear how a health claim relevant to the population as a whole could be substantiated. Regulatory requirements would need to specify strict criteria for the marketing of psyllium-enriched products, to protect against prevarication and to ensure that the products were directed only to the intended users.

The elements of a regulatory framework that accommodates functional foods and health claims from a public health policy perspective have been proposed elsewhere (Lawrence & Rayner 1998). This framework details the scientific substantiation criteria for functional foods and emphasises the integral role of nutrition education, and of monitoring and evaluation, in the implementation of such a policy. Ultimately, any policy approach that permits functional foods and health claims must address the following questions:

- Who will fund the monitoring and evaluation, the nutrition education, and the enforcement of the regulations?
- What are the respective roles of government, food manufacturers and public health practitioners?

Consumer groups have asked why the converse of health claims cannot be considered in any review of the current prohibition—that is, if the policy rationale for the review of health claims is achieving public health goals, then why not build in warning statements about disease outcomes as well? If the manufacturers of certain food products are permitted to make dietary-guideline-type claims—as, for example, in the model NLEA claims—then manufacturers should also be required to include 'disease claims' on their labels where there is evidence that a product may be inconsistent with dietary-guideline recommendations. Here is an example of a possible disease claim: 'This is a high sugar food; high sugar foods eaten frequently cause tooth decay'.

Conclusion

The debate about functional foods and health claims provides a valuable case study of the public policy process in relation to food and health. This chapter has shown that the debate is fundamentally political in nature. How the relationship between food and health is defined and who is best placed to inform consumers have become the moral questions around which this public policy debate has been framed. At a technical level, the debate concerns the appropriateness of using medical research data, most often derived from trials on individuals, to justify changes to public health policy intended for society as a whole. Here the concern is whether food as a form of technological intervention can solve health problems that are essentially socially generated. At a broader policy level, the debate is a component of the political economy of food: in the current political climate of deregulation and falling public sector spending, the food supply is being transformed from a public health resource into a valuable commercial commodity.

Significant controversy exists regarding the need to change the conventional public policy prohibiting the use of health claims, the nature and quality of the evidence, who is driving the change and for whose benefit, and what the consequences will be for individuals and society as a whole. As we have argued in this chapter, there is insufficient empirical evidence to sustain an argument that functional foods and health claims will significantly or equitably promote public health, or that they will reduce health care costs. The medical paradigm, within which the change is being sought, is inadequate to deal with—and substantially improve—health at a population-wide level. Rather, there may be benefits for certain individuals, particularly those with the resources and skills to appropriately incorporate functional foods into their diet. The most significant, sustainable, and equitable health benefits for the population as a whole will result from those initiatives that focus on the social, economic, and ecological circumstances in which public health is created (Germov 2002).

The challenge for food regulators will be to provide a secure framework for manufacturers to conduct their product research, development, and marketing, while upholding the protection of public health and safety. It would be less disingenuous and more constructive to frame the issue in terms of a commercial and medical paradigm. The rationale for regulatory change would then be that of offering individuals more choice to construct a diet consistent with medical advice and to assist at-risk individuals to reduce risk factors and help prevent disease. This outcome could be achieved by reaffirming the general prohibition on health claims—so as to uphold public health principles—while permitting exemptions on a case-by-case basis for products that have been scientifically substantiated. Adequate and timely resourcing will need to be secured both to manage the implementation and enforcement of the regulations and to conduct complementary nutrition education, monitoring, and evaluation.

Summary of main points

- Functional foods and health claims, are complementary initiatives that, some stakeholders argue, will represent the potential health-promoting or disease-preventing properties of individual food products. Currently there is no universally accepted definition of the term 'functional food'.
- The conventional analysis of food and health states that it is the total diet that is important for health; individual products that have a direct health effect are considered to be drugs.
- The functional foods and health claims debate is political because it engages the competing values, interests, and beliefs of different stakeholders regarding the food–health relationship.
- The scientific arguments for the public health benefits of functional foods are couched in the medical paradigm, in which medical research findings are used to argue for certain public health policy decisions.
- The functional foods and health claims issue is an important component of the corporatisation of food. Food manufacturers predict that functional foods will be profitable, value-added products. Policy decisions associated with this issue will have a significant influence on the composition and marketing of food products.
- The political environment in which food regulation policy is being developed is characterised by a desire to take economic advantage of opportunities emerging from the globalisation of food trade and by the powerful influence of the doctrine of economic liberalism (leading to deregulation and reduced public sector spending).
- Food is a fundamental public health resource for society. There is insufficient evidence to suggest that functional foods and health claims would significantly, sustainably, or equitably promote health or reduce health care costs at a population-wide level. Instead, they may offer benefits for some individuals. The most significant health benefits for the population as a whole will result from initiatives that focus on the social, economic, and ecological environment.

Discussion questions

1 Would you or do you consume functional foods? Why?
2 What positive and negative implications for public health do functional foods and health claims have?
3 Who are the key stakeholders in the functional foods debate and what are their respective views?
4 It has been argued that nutrition education is ineffective, idealistic, and inappropriate for promoting public health nutrition, and thus functional foods can improve public health without requiring individuals to substantially change their dietary behaviour. What is your opinion?
5 Functional foods have been referred to as illusory 'magic bullets' and health claims as little more than marketing tools that facilitate the medicalisation of the food supply and create consumer confusion. What is your view?
6 Is it inevitable that the social and cultural agenda of food and health and the economic agenda of food and trade will be in conflict? How might public policy-makers resolve this dilemma?
7 If functional foods and health claims were to be permitted, what do you think should be the respective roles of the public and private sectors in nutrition education, monitoring, and evaluation?

Further investigation

1 Do you believe that there is a role for functional foods and, if so, what are the characteristics of a regulatory framework that facilitates this role while still protecting public health and safety? (Consider scientific substantiation, nutrition education, monitoring, and enforcement.)
2 What are the potential costs and benefits of functional foods and health claims for food manufacturers, society, and individuals?
3 Food regulation is a political process. What does the functional foods and health claims debate reveal about the operation of the food regulatory system and the role of different stakeholders in and their influence on the decision-making process?
4 What do you expect would be the impact (positive and/or negative) of the introduction of functional foods and health claims in the coming decade? Consider your answer in terms of the impact on:
- consumers
- food manufacturers
- public health
- public health practitioners
- the food supply
- the food regulatory system.

Further reading and web resources

Books

Cannon, C. 1987, *The Politics of Food*, Century Hutchinson, London.

Nestle, M. 2002, *Food Politics*, University of California Press, Berkeley.

Articles

Briggs, D. R. and Lennard, L. B. 2002, 'New and Emerging Developments in Food Production' and 'Food Law', in M. L. Wahlqvist (ed.) *Food and Nutrition: Australasia, Asia and the Pacific*, 2nd edn., Allen & Unwin, Sydney, pp. 115–51.

Gussow, J. D. & Akabas, S. 1993, 'Are We Really Fixing up the Food Supply?', *Journal of the American Dietetic Association*, vol. 93, no. 11, pp. 1300–4.

Web sites

Australian Consensus Conference on Gene Technology in the Food Chain: www.abc.net.au/science/slab/consconf/default.htm

Australian Consumers Association: www.choice.com.au

Biotechnology Australia: www.biotechnology.gov.au/

Codex Alimentarius Commission: www.codexalimentarius.net

Dietitians Association of Australia: www.daa.asn.au

Food and Agriculture Organization: www.fao.org

Food Standards Australia New Zealand: www.foodstandards.gov.au

Gene Technology in Australia, CSIRO: genetech.csiro.au/

Institute of Food Science & Technology: www.ifst.org

Office of the Gene Technology Regulator: www.ogtr.gov.au/

Physicians and Scientists for Responsible Application of Science and Technology: www.psrast.org/

Public Health Association of Australia: www.phaa.net.au

United Kingdom Food Standards Agency: www.food.gov.uk

United States Food and Drug Administration: www.fda.gov

World Health Organization: www.who.org

References

ANZFA—*see* Australia New Zealand Food Authority.

Allred, J. 1995, 'Too Much of a Good Thing?', *Journal of the American Dietetic Association*, vol. 95, pp. 417–18.

American Dietetic Association 1998, 'Position Statement of the American Dietetic Association: Fat Replacers', *Journal of the American Dietetic Association*, vol. 98, p. 463–8.

—— 1999, 'Position Statement of the American Dietetic Association: Functional Foods', *Journal of the American Dietetic Association*, vol. 99, p. 1278.

Anderson, J., Zettwoch, N., Feldman, T., Tietyen-Clark, J., Oeltgen, P., & Bishop, C. 1988, 'Cholesterol-lowering Effects of Psyllium Hydrophilic Mucilloid for Hypercholesterolemic Men', *Archives of Internal Medicine*, no. 148, pp. 292–6.

Australia New Zealand Food Authority 1998, *ANZFA News: The Monthly Newsletter of the Australian and New Zealand Food Authority*, no. 4, August.

—— 2001, *Inquiry Report—Proposal P153: Review of Health and Related Claims*, Australia and New Zealand Food Authority, Canberra.

Baker, V. A., Hepburn, P. A., Kennedy, et al. 1999, 'Safety Evaluation of Phytosterol Esters: Part 1. Assessment of Oestrogenicity Using a Combination of In Vivo and In Vitro Assays', *Food Chemical Toxicology*, vol. 37, pp. 13–22.

Bender, D. & Bender, A. 1997, *Nutrition: A Reference Handbook*, Oxford University Press, New York.

Blane, D., Brunner, E. & Wilkinson, R. (eds) 1996, *Health and Social Organization: Towards a Health Policy for the Twenty-first Century*, Routledge, New York.

Brent, P., Bittisnich, M., Brooke-Taylor, S., Galway, N., Graf, L., Healy, M. & Kelly, L. 2003, 'Regulation of Genetically Modified Foods in Australia and New Zealand', *Food Control*, vol. 14, pp. 409–16.

CAC—*see* Codex Alimentarius Commission.

Codex Alimentarius Commission 1996, *Report of the Twenty-fourth Session of the Codex Committee on Food Labelling, Ottawa, Canada, 14–17 May 1996* (ALINORM 97/22), Food and Agriculture Organization of the United Nations, World Health Organization, Geneva.

—— 2003, *Report of the Thirty-first Session of the Codex Committee on Food Labelling, Ottawa, Canada, 28 April–2 May 2003* (ALINORM 03/22A), Food and Agriculture Organization of the United Nations, World Health Organization, Geneva.

Commonwealth of Australia 2001, *Food Regulation in Australia: A Chronology*, Department of the Parliamentary Library, Canberra.

Commonwealth Department of Health and Ageing, 2001, *Eat Well Australia*, National Public Health Partnership, Canberra.

Conrad, P. 1992, 'Medicalization and Social Control', *Annual Review of Sociology*, vol. 18, pp. 209–32.

Crawford, R. 1980, 'Healthism and the Medicalisation of Everyday Life', *International Journal of Health Services*, vol. 10, no. 3, pp. 365–88.

Czeizel, A. & Dudas, I. 1992, 'Prevention of the First Occurrence of Neural-tube Defects by Periconceptional Vitamin Supplementation', *New England Journal of Medicine*, vol. 327, pp. 1832–5.

Czeizel, A., Metneki, J. & Dudas, I. 1994, 'Higher Rate of Multiple Births after Periconceptional Vitamin Supplementation', *New England Journal of Medicine*, vol. 330, no. 23, pp. 1687–8.

Downer, A. H. 1994, 'Functional Foods: What's in it for the Australian Food Industry', *Food Australia*, vol. 46, no. 9, pp. 414–15.

First Australian Consensus Conference 1999, *Gene Technology in the Food Chain: Lay Panel Report,* Australian Museum, Canberra, March 10–12.

Food Regulation Review ('Blair review') 1998, *Food: A Growth Industry*, Australian Government Publishing Service, Canberra.

Food Standards Australia New Zealand 2001a, 'Media Releases & Publications', <www.foodstandards.gov.au/mediareleasespublications/mediareleases/mediareleases2001/foodstandardsministe118.cfm>.

—— 2001b, 'Standard 2.6.4: Formulated Caffeinated Beverages', *Australia New Zealand Food Standards Code*, Food Standards Australia New Zealand, Canberra.

FSANZ—*see* Food Standards Australia New Zealand.

Germov, J. 2002, 'Class, Health Inequality and Social Justice', in J. Germov (ed.), *Second Opinion: An Introduction to Health Sociology*, 2nd edn., Oxford University Press, Melbourne, pp. 67–94.

Greenberg, E., Baron, J., Tosteson, T., et al. 1994, 'A Clinical Trial of Antioxidant Vitamins to Prevent Colo-rectal Adenoma', *New England Journal of Medicine*, vol. 331, pp. 141–7.

Hallberg, L., Rossander-Hulten, L., Brune, M. & Gleerup, A. 1992, 'Inhibition of Haem-Iron Absorption in Man by Calcium', *British Journal of Nutrition*, vol. 69, pp. 533–40.

Hancock, T. 1997, *Health Promotion Future: Workshop of the Fourth International Conference on Health Promotion*, Aikenhead Centre, St Vincent's Hospital, Jakarta, 13–14 August.

Hasler, C., Huston, R. & Caudill, E. 1995, 'The Impact of the Nutrition Labeling and Education Act on Functional Foods', in R. Shapiro (ed.), *Nutrition Labeling Handbook*, Marcel Dekker, New York.

Healy, M., Brooke-Taylor, S. & Liehne, P. 2003, 'Reform of Food Regulation in Australia and New Zealand', *Food Control*, vol. 14, pp. 357–65.

Hindmarsh, R. 1996, 'Bio-Policy Translation in the Public Terrain', in G. Lawrence, K. Lyons & S. Momtaz (eds), *Social Change in Rural Australia*, Rural Social and Economic Research Centre, Queensland.

Illich, I. 1975, *Medical Nemesis*, Penguin Books, New York.

Just-food.com 2001, 'UK: Flora Pro-activ, Benecol Found Wanting by Advertising Standards Authority', <www.just-food.com/news_detail.asp?art=36712&c=1>.

Kulakow, N., Baggett, W. & McNeal, G. 1993, 'Putting the E into NLEA!', *Nutrition Today*, September/October, pp. 37–40.

Law, M. 2000, 'Plant Sterol and Stanol Margarines and Health', *British Medical Journal*, vol. 320, pp. 861–4.

Lawrence, M. 1997, 'Highlight Interview', *Food Australia*, vol. 49, no. 3, p. 106.

—— 2003, 'Folate Fortification: A Case Study of Public Health Policy-making in a Food Regulation Setting', in V. Lin, B. Gibson & J. Daly (eds), *Evidence-based Health Policy*, Oxford University Press, Melbourne.

Lawrence, M. & Rayner, M. 1998, 'Functional Foods and Health Claims: A Public Health Policy Perspective', *Journal of Public Health Nutrition*, vol. 1, no. 2, pp. 75–82.

Leighton, P. 2002, 'Selling Wellness leads to Greener Pastures', *Functional Foods & Nutraceuticals*, November, pp. 24–6.

Levy, A. 1996, 'Summary Report on Health Claims Focus Groups', in *Final Report of the Keystone National Policy Dialogue on Food, Nutrition and Health*, Keystone Center, Denver and Washington, DC.

Levy, A., Derby, B. & Roe, B. 1997, *Consumer Impacts of Health Claims: An Experimental Study*, US Food and Drug Administration Center for Food Safety and Applied Nutrition, Washington, DC.

Lumley, J., Watson, L., Watson, M. & Bower, C. 2003, 'Periconceptional Supplementation with Folate and/or Multivitamins for Preventing Neural Tube Defects (Cochrane Review)', in *The Cochrane Library*, issue 1.

Marmot, M. & Wilkinson, R. G. (eds) 1999, *Social Determinants of Health*, Oxford University Press, Oxford.

Medical Research Council Vitamin Research Group 1991, 'Prevention of Neural Tube Defects: Results of the Medical Research Vitamin Study', *Lancet*, no. 338, pp. 131–7.

Miller, S. 1991, 'Health Claims: An Ethical Conflict?', *Food Technology*, vol. 45, May, pp. 130–56.

Naidoo, J. 1986, 'Limits to Individualism', in S. Rodmell & A. Watt (eds), *The Politics of Health Education: Raising the Issues*, Routledge & Kegan Paul, London.

National Food Authority 1994, *Discussion Paper on Functional Foods*, Australian Government Publishing Service, Canberra.

—— 1996, *Review of the Food Standards Code: Concept Paper on Health and Related Claims*, Australian Government Publishing Service, Canberra.

National Health Strategy 1992, *Enough to Make You Sick: How Income and Environment Affect Health*, Australian Government Publishing Service, Canberra.

Navarro, V. 1998, 'Book Review of Private Medicine and Public Health: Profits, Politics and Prejudice in the American Health Care Enterprise by Lawrence D. Weiss', *Contemporary Sociology*, vol. 27, no. 4, pp. 419–20.

NFA—*see* National Food Authority.

Norton, J. & Lawrence, G. 1996, 'Consumer Attitudes to Genetically-engineered Food Products: Focus Group Research in Rockhampton, Queensland', in G. Lawrence, K. Lyons & S. Momtaz (eds), *Social Change in Rural Australia*, Rural Social and Economic Research Centre, Rockhampton, Australia.

Patterson, R., Satia, J., Kristal, A., Neuhouser, M. & Drewnowski, A. 2001, 'Is There a Consumer Backlash Against the Diet and Health Message?', *Journal of the American Dietetic Association*, vol. 101, no.1, pp. 37–41.

Petersen, A. & Lupton, D. 1996, *The New Public Health: Health and Self in the Age of Risk*, Allen & Unwin, Sydney.

Preston, C. & Lawrence, M. 1996, 'Regulatory and Legal Aspects of Functional Foods: The Australian Perspective', *Nutrition Reviews*, vol. 54, no. 11 (supp.), pp. 156–61.

Ratcliffe, J., Wallack, L., Fagnani, F. & Rodwin, V. 1984, 'Perspectives on Prevention: Health Promotion vs Health Protection', in J. deKervasdoue, J. R. Kimberly & V. G. Rodwin (eds), *The End of an Illusion: The Future of Health Policy in Western Industrialized Nations*, University of California Press, Berkeley.

Relman, A. S. 1980 'The New Medical Industrial Complex', *New England Journal of Medicine*, no. 303, pp. 963–70.

Richmond, K. 2002, 'Health Promotion Dilemmas', in J. Germov (ed.), *Second Opinion: An Introduction to Health Sociology*, 2nd edn., Oxford University Press, Melbourne.

Roberts, D., Truswell, A., Bencke, A., Dewar, H. & Farmakalidis, E. 1994, 'The Cholesterol Lowering Effect of a Breakfast Cereal Containing Psyllium Fibre', *Medical Journal of Australia*, no. 161, pp. 660–4.

Stoy, D., LaRosa, J., Brewer, B., Mackey, M. & Meusing, R. 1993, 'Cholesterol Lowering Effects of Ready-to-Eat Cereal Containing Psyllium', *Journal of the American Dietetic Association*, vol. 93, no. 8, pp. 910–12.

Tesh, S. N. 1988, *Hidden Arguments: Political Ideology and Disease Prevention Policy*, Rutgers, New Brunswick, New Jersey.

Thomas, P. & Earl, R. (eds). 1994, *Opportunities in the Nutrition and Food Sciences: Research Challenges and the Next Generation of Investigators*, National Academy Press, Washington, DC.

Tillotson, J. E. 2003, 'Does Nutrition Sell? Do Health Claims Work? Part 2', *Nutrition Today*, vol. 38, no. 1, p. 6–10.

US Department of Health and Human Services 1993a, 'Food and Drug Administration, Final Rules to Amend the Food Labeling Regulations', *Federal Register*, vol. 58, no. 3, pp. 2533–2620.

—— 1993b, 'Food and Drug Administration, Regulatory Impact Analysis of the Final Rules to Amend the Food Labeling Regulations', *Federal Register*, vol. 58, no. 3, pp. 2927–41.

US Department of Health and Human Services and Food and Drug Administration 1996, 'Food Labeling; Health Claims and Label Statements; Folate and Neural Tube Defects, and Food Standards: Amendments of Standards of Identity for Enriched Grain Products to Require Addition of Folic Acid, Final Rules', *Federal Register*, vol. 61, no. 44, pp. 8749–8807.

USDHHS—*see* US Department of Health and Human Services.

World Health Organization 1991, *The Sundsvall Statement on Supportive Environments for Health*, World Health Organization, Geneva.

Yap, M., Petrina, L. & Pritchard, S. 1997, 'Food and Nutrition' (conference working paper), in *Health Promotion Futures, New Players for a New Era: Leading Health Promotion into the 21st Century*, Fourth International Conference on Health Promotion, Aikenhead Centre, St Vincent's Hospital, Jakarta, 13–14 August.

7

Setting the Menu: Dietary Guidelines, Corporate Interests, and Nutrition Policy

John Duff

Overview

- Are dietary guidelines an effective means of influencing food production and consumption?
- To what extent do corporate interests work against the public interest in the area of nutrition policy?
- What alternative nutrition policies could be pursued?

Food and nutrition have become central to public health policy because of their potential to improve public health. A common form of nutrition policy in developed countries is the use of dietary guidelines to achieve population-based targets (that nonetheless are used to direct individual decisions about food and diet). This approach to policy, based on rational individualism, fails to account adequately for the systematic influence of food producers, processors, and marketers on the food supply, which in turn structures and shapes the choices that individuals are able to make. Food corporations take a strong interest in the development and wording of dietary guidelines, which are a site of ideological contest, and of potential conflict between corporate interests and public health goals. This chapter illustrates this conflict by using the example of Australian nutrition policy to show that its focus on changing individual behaviour, while neglecting the role of the food industry, can only provide a partial resolution of nutrition problems.

Key terms

agency
biomedical model
dietary guidelines
ideological contest
individualism
McDonaldisation
new public health
public health
rational individualism
structuralism

Introduction: Why do people choose the food they do?

Food and nutrition have become central to **public health** policy because of their potential to improve public health. Current public health policy on food and diet, however, focuses so much on individual choices that it pays too little attention to the way those choices are structured. The main thrust of public health policy on nutrition in developed countries is to encourage individuals to change the choices that they make in relation to food and diet, while the way these choices are structured remains relatively unexamined. The production and marketing of food are significant examples of structural influences on food choices. While a great deal can be achieved by focusing on individual choices, if we ignore the food industry and its interests we get, at best, only a partial understanding of the problems of nutrition and public health policy.

The concern with nutrition policy is part of a more general issue in the social sciences: the question of how we explain social phenomena. Two different, but complementary, approaches are **structuralism** and **individualism**. The corresponding aspects of social behaviour are frequently described as structure (the way our society shapes our decisions in everyday life) and **agency** (the way our everyday decisions shape our society) (Giddens 1984).

Explanations of why people choose to eat what they do, for example, frequently focus on individual behaviour, motivation, preferences, and knowledge. Such explanations fail to account for structural aspects of social life, over which individuals exert no direct control. Marvin Harris (1998), in his *Good to Eat: Riddles of Food and Culture*, highlights the influence of culture on our food preferences, and on shared notions of what is good to eat and what is repulsive. In similar fashion, Mary Douglas (1982) explains how the symbolism attached to food makes it seem quite 'natural' to combine foods the way we do, and quite bizarre to break these rules (for example, by serving ice-cream with roast beef). This chapter will examine a different structural influence on food choices: food production and marketing. Understanding structural influences helps us to appreciate that the question 'Why do individuals choose to eat the way they do?' is much more complex than it seems at first.

The problem

There are two reasons that food and nutrition have become central to current Australian public health policy, which has a strong focus on prevention (like the policy of many other developed countries). The first is that diet-related causes account for more deaths in affluent industrialised countries than do any other cause (Lester 1994). The second is that the cost-effectiveness of nutrition programs makes them a very attractive preventative strategy in public health. Compared with the cost of building health care facilities and staffing them, or increasing the literacy of a population, the benefits of public health policy directed to nutrition education and promotion seem greatly to outweigh the cost.

Australia provides a good case study of the interaction between public health policy and nutrition-related deaths. Its population has had inexpensive meat and dairy products in abundance, and over the past century has become increasingly sedentary in its habits. From the 1930s to the 1960s, there was a steady rise in the rate of deaths from cardiovascular disease. From the 1960s to the present, Australia has seen a steady reduction in the proportion of deaths attributable to coronary heart disease (Russell & Dobson 1994; Mathers et al. 1999, p. 34; AIHW 2002, p. 38). This reduction in the rate of deaths from heart disease is an example of what a public health program that encourages dietary changes can achieve. Twenty years of promoting diet and exercise regimes conducive to better health appear to have been effective, and offer a model worthy of emulation.

The desire of public health policy advisers to reduce the costs of preventable deaths is evident in most reports on diet-related diseases. A report by the Nutrition Taskforce, established by the Australian government to investigate diet-related diseases, emphasised 'the enormous costs to the Australian community, both in economic terms and in terms of human suffering' (English 1987, p. 48). Using extrapolations from 1977 United States figures, they estimated potential savings resulting from disease prevention in Australia in 1984–85 of around A$5 billion in the cost of health care. A 1993–94 estimate of the cost of cardiovascular disease alone put direct medical costs at $A3.9 billion, about 12.5% of total health expenditure (Mathers et al. 1999, p. 83). A more recent research trend has been to measure the costs of diet-related diseases in 'Years Lost to Disability' instead of just dollars (Mathers et al. 1999).

With the costs of diet-related diseases in mind, public health policy aims to promote better nutrition and more exercise to bring about a dramatic reduction of illness and death. Policy-makers monitor rates of death, particularly from cardiovascular causes. Specific targets have been set for reductions both in death rates and in associated risk factors (Commonwealth Department of Human Services and Health 1994). Baseline data for 1992 in Australia, for example, reveal that around 50% of men and women have an 'ideal' body mass index (BMI)—that is, a BMI between 20 and 25. A target of 60% was set for the year 2000. Strategies to achieve this target included reducing the average consumption of fat as a proportion of total energy in the food supply from 34% to 32%, and reducing the proportion of adults not engaged in regular physical activity from 36% to 25%. The targets for the prevalence of ideal BMI were not achieved by the year 2000 (AIHW 2002). Poor nutrition and lack of physical activity remain prominent in the list of risk factors associated with lifestyle (AIHW 2002, p. 120). Public health policy promises to make a real difference by promoting healthy lifestyles.

The nutrition goal of new public health

It is easy to see that the problem of cardiovascular diseases is a worthwhile focus for public health policy. If such policy were effective, the health of the population would improve and the social and economic costs of ill-health would diminish. There are difficulties, however, in understanding precisely how people make decisions about food and diet, and why there are group differences in consumption patterns. Consequently, there are difficulties in understanding how policy can most effectively influence those decisions. Influences on food choices are diverse. They include, among other things, the culture of food preferences in different social groups, varying ability to pay for food, the significance food assumes in the lives of people, the convenience factor, and differences in knowledge about food and diet. Research responding to the aims of the **new public health** movement is trying to address this lack of understanding.

New public health measures focus not only on health problems in a narrow sense, but also on the broader social, political, and economic conditions that produce differences in health among different groups. Research explaining these differences in terms of individual characteristics will lead to policies that attempt to remedy individuals' 'ignorance' or the 'low priority' they give to health. Such policies are typically top-down, relying on education programs to change lifestyle, or on regimes of supplementary professional assistance for disadvantaged groups. Privileged individuals are most likely to have the resources to benefit significantly from these programs, which, as a result, may do little to diminish health inequality. Policies that emphasise individual choices but ignore the social circumstances that present different groups with different choices must, in the final analysis, be regarded as flawed (Donahue & McGuire 1995).

Rational individualism: Dietary guidelines as nutrition policy

Researchers and policy-makers can call on two distinct paradigms when explaining the way we make food choices. The first is **rational individualism**, which emphasises the voluntary aspect of choices, and the second is a form of structuralism that emphasises the way that food production, processing, and marketing shapes the choices open to us.

Rational individualism is most evident in the use of expert advice to guide individual decisions about food. Nutrition scientists' advice on nutrition and diet presumes an idealised consumer of food who applies the technical rationality of nutrition science to the body in order to maximise health. Bryan Turner (1992) described modern dietetics as 'science of diet expressed, in practice, as a medical regimen' that subjects the body to disciplined government and regulation. Those who do not follow the 'medical regimen' then appear as if they are not acting in their own best (health) interests—that is, not acting rationally.

The beginnings of nutrition policy in industrialised countries can be found in the development of **dietary guidelines** to help individuals make rational choices based on sound knowledge. In 1979 the Australian Department of Health formalised this approach with the publication of *A Food and Nutrition Policy* (Langsford 1979). The policy consisted of broad dietary goals, which were soon followed by more specific prescriptions about diet (CDH 1981). Nutrition education became the favoured vehicle of policy implementation. The information provided was **biomedical**, with few links to the culture of food and eating or to the political or economic structure of food production and marketing.

The centrepiece of Australia's first food and nutrition policy was a list of eight policy goals, similar to those introduced around the same time in the USA, the UK, and elsewhere (United States Congress 1977; Turner & Gray 1982; Milio 1990; Pinstrup-Andersen 1993). The aim was to change 'poor eating habits', identified through epidemiological studies as the source of much illness and avoidable death (Langsford 1979, p. 100). The eight dietary goals, and the corresponding guidelines that were issued 2 years later (CDH 1981), are set out in Table 7.1.

The individualistic orientation of the 1979 policy could hardly be clearer (Langsford 1979, p. 103):

> The individual must accept responsibility for life-style decisions, which affect both his [sic] nutritional and health status. Nutritional health is not a gift or a right. It has to be earned chiefly by sensible habits of food selection, exercise and rest. The consumer has

Table 7.1 Australian dietary goals and guidelines

Dietary goals	*Dietary guidelines*
Increase breastfeeding.	Promote breastfeeding.
Provide nutrition education on a balanced diet for all Australians.	Choose a nutritious diet from a variety of foods.
Reduce the incidence of obesity.	Control your weight.
Decrease total fat consumption.	Avoid eating too much fat.
Decrease refined sugar consumption.	Avoid eating too much sugar.
Increase consumption of complex carbohydrate and dietary fibre (i.e. wholegrain cereals, vegetables, and fruit).	Eat more bread and cereals (preferably wholegrain) and vegetables and fruit.
Decrease consumption of alcohol.	Limit alcohol intake.
Decrease consumption of salt.	Use less salt.

Sources: CDH (1981); Langsford (1979)

the responsibility to become informed on nutritional matters and to fit that knowledge into practice when selecting both foods to include in his diet and their quantity.

These guidelines for adults have been revised twice (NHMRC 1992, 2003a) and a set has been developed for children and adolescents, with particular advice about physical activity, fats, alcohol, calcium, and iron (NHMRC 1997, 2003b). In 1999, guidelines were published for older Australians (NHMRC 1999). All these guidelines are under constant review (Howe & Nestel 2000).

Tables of food composition and recommended dietary intakes (RDIs)

Vital adjuncts to the dietary guidelines are tables of food composition and recommended dietary intakes (RDIs). Food-composition tables provide information on 'micronutrients' (vitamins and minerals), 'macronutrients' (protein, fat, carbohydrate, and alcohol), and energy (Lester 1994, p. 72). The tables are compiled to provide information on the levels of these nutrients that can be monitored in the diet of particular populations:

> Using these tables it should be possible to:
>
> (a) obtain an approximation of the nutrient content of daily or weekly dietary intakes;
>
> (b) select many combinations of foods which would provide a varied and adequate diet.
>
> Corden & Thomas 1971, p. 7

Nutritionists (for example, Sumner et al. 1983) have long pointed out that rational planning for micronutrients becomes difficult because of changes produced by processing, storing, and cooking. The complexity of the information required to take all these contingencies into account makes the tables of limited practical value. The 1971 edition of the tables primarily lists the basic foods from which meals in households are made. There is little reference to snack foods, and almost none to the 'fast foods' and prepared and precooked meals that have since proliferated. A major revision in 1989 (Cashel et al. 1989) pointed out the limitations of the previous tables. These included the following:

- the use of nutrient composition data from other countries where different foods are known by similar names
- the effects of different agricultural practices in different countries
- the omission of fast foods, for which food values can differ with brands.

The new tables have given priority to providing information about foods that are of concern to consumers and health professionals, especially foods from takeaway outlets. A simplified version has been published for community use and includes brand-name fast foods; it is also available through several computer dietary-analysis packages (English & Lewis 1992). The problem of consumers being unable to monitor the nutritional content of foods they eat has partly been addressed by the requirements of the Australia New Zealand Food Standards Code (Curran 2002). The code stipulates that, from December 2002, all packaged food should have a nutrition information panel setting out nutrition values in a standard form (Polya 2001).

RDIs, which had their origins in the crude calculations of the nineteenth-century 'dietaries' for prisons and hospitals, make highly specific recommendations for dietary intake of a huge array of food components. An Australian table of recommended dietary allowances was first compiled in 1954 (Palmer 1982, p. 157). In 1981 the Australian National Health and Medical Research Council (NHMRC) Nutrition Committee recommended a revision of the tables, which are now under regular review. Expert panels (see, for example, Rutishauser 1982 and Wood 1985) went on to establish upper and lower limits for listed nutrients on the basis of laboratory and epidemiological analyses. The focus of RDIs has been steadily shifting from the prevention of nutritional deficiency to limiting the reach of chronic diseases and promoting a high quality of physical and mental health (Howe & Nestel 2000). To be effective, the use of RDIs need to be sensitive to the differing needs of segments of the population (defined by gender, age, or ethnicity). For this reason, a set of dietary guidelines has been published for older Australians (NHMRC 1999) and for children and adolescents (NHMRC 2003b). Lynne Cobiac (2000) argues that there need to be specific RDIs for indigenous Australians and Maori, for example, to bring about positive changes to their health.

The food composition tables and the RDIs provide the backbone of rational regulation of diets. The problem confronting health professionals and policy-makers is to ensure that people are guided by this formal knowledge of nutritionists, and to ensure compliance with dietary guidelines. Consumers also receive information from other sources, ranging from alternative health workers to industry advertising. Not only does the model of the ideal rational food consumer pay little attention to other influences on eating, but it also gives nutrition science a privileged status, as a typical study of nutrition knowledge shows: 'This survey has shown that many high school students … leave school with insufficient knowledge to put into perspective the variety of information on food and nutrition presented by the health professions, the media and the food industry' (Crawford & Selwood 1983, p. 33).

It is in the interest of food producers to provide information about their products, and to do so in a form that is consistent with RDIs, since they can use the status of science to enhance their marketing. The claims made about foods are regulated: nutrition information must be supplied in an approved form on mandatory nutrition information panels attached to food packaging (Curran 2002). Food producers try to counteract negative attitudes to processed foods by presenting them in a good light. This can be done in two ways:

- Assuring consumers that each food item is of a high quality. This may require showing that the food meets all legislated requirements.

- Showing that the food has a place in an 'approved' diet. This is done by relating it to the RDIs; linking a product to the RDIs of the health professionals gives the appearance of an endorsement.

RDIs are designed to guide nutrition advisory programs. They provide the benchmark against which a given population's consumption of food constituents is measured. In some cases, the dietary advice may be to increase some food factor up to the lower limit of the RDI, while in other cases it may be to reduce it to an upper limit (Darnton-Hill & English 1990). A consideration of salt in the Australian diet will demonstrate the limitations of rational strategies designed to help individuals regulate the types and amounts of food they consume.

Salt in the Australian diet

Common salt is a sodium compound. The RDIs recommend an upper limit to sodium intake because of health risks associated with high intake. The discretionary consumption of salt (sodium chloride) in the diet—that is, salt added by individuals in cooking and eating meals—accounts for only a minor portion of total sodium consumption. This is because most sodium in the present-day diet occurs naturally in food or is added during processing. United States figures showed that discretionary use of sodium accounted for between 10% and 40% of total sodium use (Bullock 1982); studies have put the figure nearer to 6% for Australia (Crawford & Baghurst 1990, p. 103). Someone who eats common foods such as bread and breakfast cereals would need to adopt a sophisticated information gathering and processing regime to regulate sodium intake. Where constituents such as salt and sugar are added to resolve technical problems of large-scale food production, individuals' rational decisions about what to eat come into direct conflict with the rational decisions of producers about the production process. Individuals who eat a lot of bread, for example, to increase their consumption of complex carbohydrates, would necessarily consume larger amounts of sodium than they may otherwise choose to do.

The official RDI reference paper for sodium steps delicately around this issue. The earlier reference paper on sodium (Bullock 1982) pointed out that discretionary use of salt accounted for most of the differences between individuals, because of the common background levels attributable to bread and other manufactured foods. Although the average sodium consumption in Australia was, at the time, substantially above the RDI, the paper concluded that 'it is not considered practical to recommend an intake which would require major changes in the usual diet. It is considered that the recommended range of intake should be one which can be achieved by elimination of intake of discretionary sodium without appreciable alteration in the consumption of staple foodstuffs' (Bullock 1982, p. 184).

We can draw two conclusions from this focus on discretionary sodium. The first is that nutrition researchers regard structured determinants of sodium intake, especially food production and processing, to be less easily managed than individual consumer decisions. Consequently, high sodium intake is interpreted, and acted on, as a failure of personal control over diet. Putting information on food labels about sodium levels in processed foods completes the shift of the onus onto individuals.

The second conclusion is that as discretionary use diminishes, sodium consumption becomes increasingly invisible and cannot easily be monitored by individuals. Because of this, dietary surveys that try to estimate sodium consumption levels are quite unreliable. This may account for conflicting findings about sodium intake levels. Two studies that relied on people answering questions about how much salt they ate found figures towards the lower end of the RDI range for sodium, while one smaller study that measured sodium levels in urine produced a figure 60% above the upper limit of the RDI (Lester 1994, p. 170). People were aware of the salt they had chosen to eat, but were less aware of the salt they had not chosen to eat. For this reason, an analysis of sodium intake was not initially included in the food and nutrient database derived from the Australian *1995 National Nutrition Survey* (ANZFA 1999; see also ABS 1997, 1999). Food Standards Australia New Zealand (which replaced the Australia New Zealand Food Authority in 2001) subsequently released a 'sodium file' based on other sources of information, with explanatory notes on how to use it.

The structure of food production, processing, and marketing

Public health strategies regarding nutrition are based largely on a biomedical model of diet that requires individual consumers to comply voluntarily with dietary advice. The efficacy of those strategies is, however, weakened by the effects of industrialised agriculture and food production on dietary patterns in the developed economies of the West.

Michael Symons (1993, p. 9) regards the changes in eating patterns as a direct consequence of the commercialisation of food. He identifies three main phases in the development of 'industrial cuisine'. The first, starting in the eighteenth century, saw the flow of capital into enclosures in the UK and into colonial plantations, with the colonisation of Australia being part of that development. The second phase, from the late nineteenth century, involved the flow of capital into food preservation and retailing, with the establishment of familiar food brand-names. The third phase has seen the concentration of capital in global food companies that dilute national differences and often grow, process, prepare, and serve whole, brand-named meals. Food technology dedicated to improving profitability 'commands the entire technical battery of growing, preserving, processing, distribution and cooking' (Symons 1993, p. 11), and, as George Ritzer (2001, p. 166) argues in his theory of **McDonaldisation**, it displaces local food cultures.

Geoffrey Lawrence (1987), in his analysis of changes in Australian agriculture, shows how the technical demands of capital-intensive feed-lotting of cattle and pigs, of factory production of chickens, and of potato production for chains such as McDonald's change the nature of food available for consumption. The growing global uniformity of food 'choice' supports the view that consumer decisions follow, rather than shape, the technologies of food.

Harvey Levenstein (1988) analysed the transformative power of the food industry in *Revolution at the Table*, an account of changes in American food and eating over the past century. In the nineteenth century, Levenstein argues, smaller producers found themselves competing against more highly capitalised companies using new processing technologies. Companies such as Heinz took the view that their substantial investment in new technologies was threatened by the public's distrust of processed foods—generated by smaller operators. The small companies were accused of using inconsistent raw materials or dangerous additives to keep costs down. The large manufacturers led the movement to involve the state in defining and policing food standards to counteract public distrust of processed foods.

The success of large-scale agriculture, processing, and marketing depended not only on a carefully nurtured trust in manufactured food, but also on changes in traditional eating habits. The technical demands of large-scale production and the need for consumption patterns to change as food technology changes have been major forces in the transformation of diet over the past 200 years. Stuart Ewen (1976, p. 64) is sceptical of an explanation that simply sees dietary change as being a result of labour-saving meal solutions. Ewen shows how home production of food by many American migrant groups was targeted by mass producers in search of disciplined mass markets. He records the efforts of American advertisers, often using patriotism, to persuade European migrants to abandon home production in favour of manufactured American goods. Levenstein (1988, pp. 42–3) supports Ewen's analysis: 'Because of the rise of the giant food processing industries, by 1914 the United States was on the verge of becoming a country in which traditional rules no longer held ... The great changes in business organisation would play a major role in dictating what Americans would consume'.

At a broader level, and covering a longer period, Sidney Mintz (1986) makes the same point by exploring the symbiotic development of sugar, tea, and cocoa in European cuisine as a result of the colonisation of the New World. The increasing scale and capital-intensification of agriculture has continued to transform national diets by changing the food supply itself. Developments such as genetic engineering (Hindmarsh et al. 1998), 'designer' low-fat meat, and the falling cost of foods once restricted to the wealthy offer the prospect of increased choice. The important point is that the choice may be a product not so much of consumer pressure as of the changes to the production process.

In *The McDonaldization of Society*, George Ritzer (1993) analyses the fast-food chain as the most highly developed example of the 'industrialised cuisine', showing how the demands for efficiency in fast-food franchises effectively reduce, rather than expand, choice. Taken as a whole, fast food may provide a wide range of options, but this is generally not the case in any one outlet, and there are limited choices about how the food is cooked. Corporate manipulation of the culture of food and eating—with marketing illusions more important than the food they seek to promote—is driven increasingly by the need to maintain profitability, rather than by consideration of local customs. The restriction of food choices through the streamlining of production processes, and the use of oil and salt to maintain appearance and taste throughout the production process, alter what constitutes a meal, how it is eaten, and what proportions of different ingredients are used.

Industrialised food has so come to dominate the way we eat that Ritzer feels compelled to give the following advice: 'At least once a week', he writes, 'pass up a lunch at McDonald's and frequent a local greasy spoon. For dinner, again at least once a week ... cook a meal from scratch' (Ritzer 1993, p. 184). Colin Binns, when he was Chairperson of the Australian NHMRC Nutrition Committee, explained why this might be a difficult task. He wrote this of his shopping experience while visiting the 'McDonaldised' USA:

> A stroll down the aisles of our local supermarket in Boston reveals a bewildering array of health claims, all on lavishly packaged, processed food products. The leaders in the claims appear to be any foods which contain even a sprinkling of oat bran, although recent research has shown that enthusiasm to have been a little premature. The fresh fruit and vegetables cringe in the back corner, unpromoted, unloved and probably unprofitable. 'Plain rice? Sure, we stock it. It's usually over there.' But we didn't mean the precooked 'instant' rice, and it took us three trips to buy one of our staple foods. Without a car and therefore without a choice where to shop, one gains a new perspective on purchasing food.
>
> Binns 1990, p. 58

Any analysis of food habits that concentrates on 'individual choice' and ignores the way the globalised food industry transforms not only diets but even what constitutes a meal is far from complete.

Corporate interests and nutrition policy

The food industry is vulnerable to the charge that it contributes to mortality and morbidity by actively seeking to increase consumption of the foods on which profits depend, regardless of the nutritional consequences. The lengthy libel suit brought by McDonald's in the UK shows how sensitive food companies are on this issue (McLibel 1997). The companies have no wish to be seen as being responsible for excessive food consumption, or for promoting profitable diets before healthy ones. The analysis of diet in terms of constituent nutrients, which is a consequence of the institutionalised use of tables of food composition and RDIs, makes the broader structures of food production more difficult to see, and makes it easier for food companies to project an image of being 'good' public health citizens. They present themselves as providing an ever-increasing range of pure food items, leaving individuals, guided by health workers, to accept responsibility for assembling the constituents into diets suited to their needs.

Good diets, according to this line of reasoning, have two requirements: information about the constituents of different foods, and the knowledge to assemble these foods according to sound dietary principles. Constituents can be regulated by the state, through bodies such as Food Standards Australia New Zealand, but diets remain the responsibility of individuals. The constant changes in foods brought about by developments in agriculture and food technology mean that anyone intent on regulating the amount of any nutrient in their diet must be forever taking in and acting on new information.

The Commonwealth Department of Health (1981) considered models in other countries when developing the Australian dietary guidelines. The United States Department of Agriculture, which is responsible for providing dietary advice to the US public, first established dietary guidelines in 1917 (Nestle 1993). Foods were grouped as a guide to meeting all nutritional needs, while encouraging the consumption of US farm products. Not surprisingly, the guidelines enjoyed the support of the primary producers. In 1977 the US Department of Agriculture issued the first of a new generation of guidelines, *Dietary Goals for the United States*, as a public health response to the chronic illnesses attributed to overconsumption (United States Congress 1977; Nestle 1993). These guidelines, unlike the earlier ones, encouraged a reduction in the consumption of some high-fat farm products, particularly meat, eggs, and dairy products. Marion Nestle, in her analysis of the debate over the US guidelines, follows the recommendations about meat through successive publications to 1990. Changes of wording between editions resulted from negotiations between conflicting interests. Nestle's analysis shows the influence of commercial interests on dietary guidelines.

The statement 'decrease consumption of meat', in the first edition of the US *Dietary Goals* in 1977, provoked an immediate response from meat interests, who demanded that the word 'decrease' be removed. Over successive revisions, the guideline was transformed into an encouragement to eat meat. A second edition in 1977 stated 'Choose meats ... which will reduce saturated fat intake', which in the 1980 revision became 'Choose lean meat'. Nestle reports that early in the Reagan administration the human nutrition research unit in the United States Department of Agriculture, which had done much of the developmental work for the *Dietary Goals*, was disbanded. In 1990 the statement became 'have two or three servings of meat … with a daily total of about 6 ounces' (Nestle 1993, p. 491).

Similar changes have been made to the Australian guidelines: the words 'avoid too much' in the 1981 guidelines became 'choose a diet low in' in a review by the NHMRC (1992). There is little direct evidence that this change of wording was brought about by lobbying from producer interests, but it is clear that food producers take an active interest in the scientific basis of nutrition guidelines. Meat and Livestock Australia (2002) made a submission to the Joint WHO/FAO Expert Consultation on Diet, Nutrition and the Prevention of Chronic Diseases, arguing that there is no clear evidence to justify the recommendation to 'moderate consumption of red meat'. A key argument in the submission was that reduced meat sales would be bad for regional economies that depend on the livestock industry.

In 1987 the Nutrition Taskforce of the Australian Better Health Commission recommended that there be a review of the Australian guidelines, which had been in use since 1981, noting the support of the representative of the Food Council of Australia for the review (English 1987, p. 66). The review of the guidelines was published by the NHMRC in 1992. For the first time, the guidelines were set out in order of importance (see Table 7.2). The breastfeeding

Table 7.2 Dietary guidelines, 1981 and 1992

Dietary guidelines (1981)	*Revised dietary guidelines (1992)*
Promote breastfeeding.	Enjoy a wide variety of nutritious foods.
Choose a nutritious diet from a variety of foods.	Eat plenty of breads and cereals (preferably wholegrain), vegetables (including legumes), and fruits.
Control your weight.	Eat a diet low in fat, and in particular, low in saturated fat.
Avoid eating too much fat.	Maintain a healthy body weight by balancing physical activity and food intake.
Avoid eating too much sugar.	If you drink alcohol, limit your intake.
Eat more bread and cereals (preferably wholegrain) and vegetables and fruit.	Eat only a moderate amount of sugars and food containing added sugars.
Limit alcohol intake.	Choose low fat foods and use salt sparingly.
Use less salt.	Encourage and support breastfeeding.

Sources: CDH (1981) and NHMRC (1992)

guideline was placed last, because of the relatively small number of people to whom it applies at any one time (NHMRC 1992).

The words 'avoid', 'less', and 'too much' disappeared from the guidelines in the 1992 revision. There are several explanations for this. The first is the reliance of Australian nutritionists on the US policy statements as a 'resource'. To the extent that this is the case (and the 1992 review does cite US and other policies), lobbying by agricultural and food interests in the USA extends its influence to Australia (and other countries). The second is the attempt to overcome the negative approach of the original guidelines, which look like a list of 'bad' foods. Representatives of the food industry criticised the negativity of the 1981 guidelines. Their argument (Cartwright 1991, p. 310) is that the food industry uses the *Dietary Guidelines for Australians* for product development, and negative statements are not helpful in this respect. Nutritionists were in general agreement with the shift from negative to positive statements. They believe that negative messages can diminish their efforts when compared with the positive messages people receive from advertising and from popular food journalism.

Professional, industrial, and research nutritionists met in 2000 to consider 'Dietary Guidelines for a New Millennium' (Howe & Nestel 2000), resulting in a third edition of the Australian guidelines (NHMRC 2003a). Although this edition emphasises the scientific evidence underlying its recommendations, it also gives prominence to two sociopolitical issues. The first of these is ecological sustainability. The guidelines acknowledge the growing deregulation of and concentration of ownership in the food industry, but state that these developments makes it possible for policy-makers to speak more directly to industry. They assert that dietary guidelines can also be effective in shaping demand for foods from more ecologically sustainable systems of production. The second issue given prominence is equity. A number of studies in Britain and Australia have concluded that following the guidelines without fundamentally altering traditional dietary patterns may be beyond the means of the most disadvantaged segments of the population (Baghurst 2003). A challenge for future editions of the guidelines will be to suggest ways of restructuring diets to achieve greater nutritional equity across socioeconomic groups.

An emphasis on lifestyle as well as on specific nutrients is evident in the very structure of the recommendations in the third edition of dietary guidelines (NHMRC 2003a). The foods to be 'enjoyed' have been grouped into a more coherent set of categories, and water has been added to the list. 'Care' is encouraged with respect to foods that contribute most to overconsumption and obesity. In addition, the guidelines give advice about physical activity and weight control, linked to different lifestyles. Breastfeeding is given a higher profile by being considered separately from recommendations about food groups, and is taken up more fully in a parallel set of dietary guidelines for children and adolescents (NHMRC 2003b). The most notable addition to the guidelines is

Table 7.3 Dietary guidelines, 2003

Dietary guidelines for Australian adults (2003)
Enjoy a wide variety of nutritious foods:
• Eat plenty of vegetables, legumes, and fruits.
• Eat plenty of cereals (including breads, rice, pasta, and noodles), preferably wholegrain.
• Include lean meat, fish, poultry, and/or alternatives.
• Include milks, yoghurts, cheeses, and/or alternatives.
• Reduced-fat varieties should be chosen, where possible.
• Drink plenty of water.
And take care to:
• Limit saturated fat and moderate total fat intake.
• Choose foods low in salt.
• Limit your alcohol intake if you choose to drink.
• Consume only moderate amounts of sugars and foods containing added sugars.
• Prevent weight gain: be physically active and eat according to your energy needs.
• Care for your food: prepare and store it safely.
• Encourage and support breastfeeding.

Source: NHMRC (2003a)

advice on caring for food. This advice addresses the health risks that have emerged as diagnosis of food-related illnesses has improved, as more food is being imported and exported across the world, as production methods have transformed, and as buying pre-cooked foods and eating out have become more common. The guidelines, set out in Table 7.3, are not in order of importance, but designed to help health professionals use the information in advising individuals and in shaping policy.

Researchers such as Colin Binns (2000) have concluded that the Australian diet has been moving towards conformity with the dietary guidelines, especially with the decreases in the consumption of fats and alcohol. Despite this, there is a clear trend, in the United States (Harris 2000) as well as in Australia, towards obesity. The use of dietary advice (and of nutrition labels that extol certain foods as 'low fat'), seems to have resulted in increased energy consumption overall, or at least an increased consumption of high-energy foods (Sullivan 2000). The most recent guidelines are attempting to correct these trends.

Conclusion

At the time that food producers began reacting so strongly to the Australian dietary guidelines, few people had even heard of these guidelines (M. Lawrence 1987, p. 57). How, then, is the strong concern over the wording of nutrition policy to be explained? Nutrition policy is a site of **ideological contest** that tests out the proposition that the interests of food producers are compatible with the interests of public health nutrition. The ideological contest is evident in the defensive position of food producers, who are sensitive about being depicted as hostile to public health goals.

The conflict over the wording of the guidelines reflects their strategic importance in increasing food sales. As discussed in Chapter 5, nutritionists have expressed concern about a form of 'public education' used by both public health agencies and food producers that deflects attention from the whole diet onto foods about which a particular claim can be made. Sindall and others (1994) refer to a 'nutrition power race', in which producers fortify foods so as to be able to make positive claims about vitamins or minerals, or modify production so a food can be represented, in terms matching the guidelines, as 'low fat' or 'low salt'.

The conflict between public health and corporate interests is evident in the thwarted attempts to regulate advertising, particularly television advertising, directed at children. About a third of the advertising budget of the top 100 advertisers in Australia in 1993 was spent on food and drink advertising. This included A$45 million for McDonald's, A$36 million for Kelloggs, A$30 million for Pepsico, A$12 million for the Australian Meat and Livestock Corporation, and A$11.5 million for the Australian Dairy Corporation (Sindall et al. 1994, p. 159). An earlier study documented the concentration of television advertising for children on precisely the foods already well overrepresented in children's diets (Morton 1990). The *Dietary Guidelines for Children and Adolescents* provide information showing that a third to a half of the fat intake of boys and girls aged 10–15 years comes from heavily advertised snack foods (NHMRC 1997). Successive attempts to build regulation of this advertising into policy have been unsuccessful (NHMRC 1981, 1989).

The guidelines produced in the 1970s in Australia and the USA were a first response to diet-related morbidity and mortality. Their intent, however modest, was to alter patterns of food consumption at the population level. The increased consumption of fruit, vegetables, and cereals recommended by the guidelines implied a reduction in the consumption of processed, or 'value-added', foods, for which brand-names could be established and maintained. Likewise, the recommended decrease in the consumption of fatty foods was in conflict with the interests of meat producers and processors, while the recommended decrease in fats, sugar, and salt was a challenge to manufacturers to alter the many food processes in which they were essential or cost-effective components.

While the intent of the guidelines was to bring about real changes in eating patterns, and by implication in the food supply, the means of implementation was primarily at the level of knowledge—that is, nutrition education programs. Food producers have been able to affect this policy strategy in two significant ways: by placing an ideological emphasis on individual choice, and thus steering the public health debate away from the question of the food supply itself, and by exercising a high degree of control over the shape of the food supply. Taken together, these mean that policy focusing on individual choices does too little to address the structure of food production and marketing that shapes these choices.

Summary of main points

- Diet-related illness accounts for more deaths in industrialised countries than any other cause.
- 'New' public health policy has the goal of reducing the rate of avoidable deaths using preventative measures that address the social and economic conditions that cause ill-health.
- Nutrition policy has relied on dietary guidelines, which assume an idealised consumer making rational decisions based on scientific information. Those who do not make the 'right' decisions are seen as failing to act in their own best interests.
- The way in which the production, processing, and marketing of food is structured has a substantial influence on the choices available to us.
- Nutrition policy that does not take the structure of food production, processing, and marketing into account is not an adequate basis for 'new' public health strategies.

Discussion questions

1 Why does nutrition policy rely so heavily on dietary guidelines? Are dietary guidelines equally useful to affluent and economically disadvantaged segments of the population?
2 In what ways do the production, processing, and marketing of food (including its cost) affect the choices adults and children make about food?
3 Does labelling of food make it easier for us to make rational dietary choices?
4 What are the advantages and disadvantages of a mandatory nutrition panel printed on all packaged food?
5 Economically disadvantaged groups generally experience higher-than-average rates of diet-related illness and death. What might be some of the reasons for this?
6 Large food companies are sometimes accused of being responsible for people eating too much of the foods that are bad for their health. Can such accusations be justified, given that individuals choose what they eat?

Further investigation

1 What might explain the fact that there has been a trend towards obesity in the population while conformity with dietary guidelines has been increasing?
2 What are the advantages and disadvantages of close cooperation between government health authorities and the food industry in setting and overseeing standards of food content and food labelling?

Further reading and web resources

Books

Coveney, J. 2000, *Food, Morals, and Meaning: The Pleasure and Anxiety of Eating*, Routledge, London.
Harris, M. 1986, *Good to Eat: Riddles of Food and Culture*, Simon & Schuster, New York.
Levenstein, H. 1988, *Revolution at the Table: The Transformation of the American Diet*, Oxford University Press, New York.
Milio, N. 1990, *Nutrition Policy for Food-rich Countries: A Strategic Analysis*, Johns Hopkins University Press, Baltimore.
Ritzer, G. 2001, *Explorations in the Sociology of Consumption: Fast Food, Credit Cards and Casinos*, Sage, London.
Santich, B. 1995, *What the Doctors Ordered: 150 Years of Dietary Advice in Australia*, Hyland House, Melbourne.
Symons, M. 1993, *The Shared Table: Ideas for an Australian Cuisine*, Australian Government Publishing Service, Canberra.

Journals

Asia Pacific Journal of Clinical Nutrition
Australian and New Zealand Journal of Public Health
Food Australia
Food Standards News: The Newsletter of Food Standards Australia New Zealand
Health Promotion International
International Journal of Health Services
International Journal of Sociology of Agriculture and Food
Journal of the American Dietetic Association
Milbank Quarterly: A Journal of Public Health and Health Care Policy
Nutrition and Dietetics: The Journal of the Dietitians Association of Australia
Social Science and Medicine
Sociology of Health and Illness

Web sites

Food and Agriculture Organization (FAO) of the UN: www.fao.org/WAICENT/faoinfo/economic/esn/Nutri.HTM
An FAO site on food and nutrition.

Food Standards Australia New Zealand (FSANZ): www.foodstandards.gov.au/
FSANZ is an independent statutory authority that develops food standards for composition, labelling, and contaminants, including microbiological limits, which apply to all foods produced or imported for sale in Australia and New Zealand.

Hardin MD: www.lib.uiowa.edu/hardin/md/nutr.html
A medical site with a page dedicated to Internet resources in the field of nutrition.

The International Union of Nutrition Sciences: www.iuns.org/
Includes a page with links to nutrition guidelines in different countries, and to books, monographs, reports, and theses.

McSpotlight: www.McSpotlight.org/
A site that grew up around the year-long libel case brought by McDonald's in the UK against two activists who distributed pamphlets accusing McDonald's of being bad for public health and the environment.

United States Food and Drug Administration (USFDA) Center for Food Safety and Applied Nutrition: vm.cfsan.fda.gov/list.html
The USFDA is influential in its evaluations of food safety.

References

ABS—*see* Australian Bureau of Statistics.

ANZFA—*see* Australia New Zealand Food Authority.

AIHW—*see* Australian Institute of Health and Welfare.

Australia New Zealand Food Authority 1999, *Ausnut* (Electronic Resource), Australian Food and Nutrient Database for Estimation of Dietary Intake Australia New Zealand Food Authority, Australia New Zealand Food Authority, Canberra.

Australian Bureau of Statistics 1997, *1995 National Nutrition Survey: Summary of Results*, Australian Bureau of Statistics, Canberra.

—— 1999, *National Nutrition Survey: Foods Eaten, Australia 1995*, Australian Bureau of Statistics, Canberra.

Australian Institute of Health and Welfare 2002, *Australia's Health 2002*, Australian Institute of Health and Welfare, Canberra.

Baghurst, K. 2003, 'Appendix B: Social Status, Nutrition and the Cost of Healthy Eating', in National Health and Medical Research Council, *Dietary Guidelines for Australian Adults*, AusInfo, Canberra.

Binns, C. 1990, 'A Letter from America', *Australian Journal of Nutrition and Dietetics*, vol. 47, no. 2, p. 58.

Binns, C., Leong, J. & Lee, M. 2000, 'Dietary Guidelines in Australia', *Australian Journal of Nutrition and Dietetics*, vol. 57, no. 3, pp. 131–3.

Bullock, J. 1982, 'Sodium (Na)', *Journal of Food and Nutrition*, vol. 39, no. 4, pp. 181–6.

Cartwright, I. 1991, 'How to Develop a Corporate Nutrition Policy', *Food Australia*, vol. 43, no. 7, pp. 308–10.

Cashel, C., English, R. & Lewis, J. 1989, *Composition of Foods, Australia*, Australian Government Publishing Service, Canberra.

CDH—*see* Commonwealth Department of Health.

Cobiac, L. 2000, 'Australia's RDIs [Recommended Dietary Intakes]: Into the New Millennium', *Australian Journal of Nutrition and Dietetics*, vol. 57, no. 3, pp. 134–5.

Commonwealth Department of Health 1981, 'Dietary Guidelines for Australians', *Journal of Food and Nutrition*, vol. 38, no. 3, pp. 111–19.

Commonwealth Department of Human Services and Health 1994, *Better Health Outcomes for Australians: National Goals, Targets and Strategies for Better Health Outcomes into the Next Century*, Australian Government Publishing Service, Canberra.

Corden, M. & Thomas, S. 1971, *Simplified Food Composition Tables: Composition of Selected Raw and Processed Foods Expressed in Common Household Portions*, 3rd edn, Australian Government Publishing Service, Canberra.

Crawford, D. & Baghurst, K. 1990, 'Diet and Health: A National Survey of Beliefs, Behaviours and Barriers to Change in the Community', *Australian Journal of Nutrition and Dietetics*, vol. 47, no. 4, pp. 97–106.

Crawford, D. & Selwood, T. 1983, 'The Nutritional Knowledge of Melbourne High School Students', *Journal of Food and Nutrition*, vol. 40, no. 1, pp. 25–34.

Curran, M. 2002, 'Nutrition Labelling: Perspectives of a Bi-national Agency for Australia and New Zealand', *Asia Pacific Journal of Clinical Nutrition*, vol. 11, no. 2, pp. S72–S76.

Darnton-Hill, I. & English, R. 1990, 'Nutrition in Australia: Deficiencies, Excesses and Current Policies', *Australian Journal of Nutrition and Dietetics*, vol. 47, no. 2, pp. 34–41.

Donahue, J. & McGuire, M. 1995, 'The Political Economy of Responsibility in Health and Illness', *Social Science and Medicine*, vol. 4, no. 1, pp. 47–53.

Douglas, M. 1982, 'Food as a System of Communication', in M. Douglas, *In the Active Voice*, Routledge & Kegan Paul, London, pp. 82–104.

English, R. 1987, *Towards Better Nutrition for Australians: Report of Nutrition Taskforce of the Better Health Commission*, Australian Government Publishing Service, Canberra.

English, R. & Lewis, J. 1992, *Food for Health: A Guide to Good Nutrition with Nutrient Values for 650 Australian Foods*, Australian Government Publishing Service, Canberra.

Ewen, S. 1976, *Captains of Consciousness: Advertising and the Social Roots of the Consumer Culture*, McGraw-Hill, New York.

Giddens, A. 1984, *The Constitution of Society: Outline of the Theory of Structuration*, Polity Press, Cambridge.

Harris, M. 1998, *Good to Eat: Riddles of Food and Culture*, Waveland Press, Prospect Heights, Illinois.

Harris, S. S. 2000, 'Dietary Guidelines for Americans: Recommendations for the Year 2000', *Food Australia*, vol. 52, no. 6, pp. 212–14.

Hindmarsh, R., Lawrence, G. & Norton, J. (eds) 1998, *Altered Genes: Reconstructing Nature—The Debate*, Allen & Unwin, St Leonards, Australia.

Howe, P. & Nestel, P. 2000, 'Dietary Guidelines for a New Millennium', *Australian Journal of Nutrition and Dietetics*, vol. 57, no. 3, pp. 128–9.

Langsford, W. 1979, 'A Food and Nutrition Policy', *Food and Nutrition Notes and Reviews*, vol. 36, no. 3, pp. 100–3.

Lawrence, G. 1987, *Capitalism and the Countryside: The Rural Crisis in Australia*, Pluto Press Australia, Leichardt.

Lawrence, M. 1987, 'Making Healthier Choices Easier Choices: The Victorian Food and Nutrition Project', *Journal of Food and Nutrition*, vol. 44, no. 2, pp. 57–9.

Lester, I. 1994, *Australia's Food and Nutrition: A Report of the Australian Institute of Health and Welfare in Collaboration with the NHMRC Expert Panel on National Food and Nutrition Monitoring and Surveillance Strategy*, Australian Government Publishing Service, Canberra.

Levenstein, H. 1988, *Revolution at the Table: The Transformation of the American Diet*, Oxford University Press, New York.

Mathers, C., Vos, T. & Stevenson, C. 1999, *The Burden of Disease and Injury in Australia*, Australian Institute of Health and Welfare, Canberra.

McLibel 1997, 'Quotes from Dave Morris following the Judgment in the Mclibel Trial 21st June 1997', <www.McSpotlight.org/>.

Meat and Livestock Australia 2002, 'Submission to Joint WHO/FAO Expert Consultation on Diet, Nutrition and the Prevention of Chronic Diseases', <www.who.int/hpr/nutrition/CommentsExpertConsultationReportOrgs/MeatLivestockAustralia.pdf>.

Milio, N. 1990, *Nutrition Policy for Food-rich Countries: A Strategic Analysis*, Johns Hopkins University Press, Baltimore.

Mintz, S. 1986, *Sweetness and Power: The Place of Sugar in Modern History*, Penguin Books, New York.

Morton, H. 1990, 'Television Food Advertising: A Challenge for the New Public Health in Australia', *Community Health Studies*, vol. 14, no. 2, pp. 153–61.

NHMRC—*see* National Health and Medical Research Council.

National Health and Medical Research Council (Australia) 1981, 'Report of the Working Party on Television Advertising of Foods Directed to Children', in *Report of 92nd Session, Canberra, October 1981*, Australian Government Publishing Service, Canberra, pp. 223–99.

—— 1989, *Implementing the Dietary Guidelines for Australians: Report of the Subcommittee on Nutrition Education*, Australian Government Publishing Service, Canberra.

—— 1992, *Dietary Guidelines for Australians*, Australian Government Publishing Service, Canberra.

—— 1997, *Dietary Guidelines for Children and Adolescents*, Australian Government Publishing Service, Canberra.

—— 1999, *Eat Well for Life: A Practical Guide to the Dietary Guidelines for Older Australians*, National Health and Medical Research Council, Canberra.

—— 1999, *Dietary Guidelines for Older Australians*, National Health and Medical Research Council, Canberra.

—— 2003a, *Dietary Guidelines for Australian Adults*, AusInfo, Canberra.

—— 2003b, *Dietary Guidelines for Children and Adolescents in Australia; Incorporating the Infant Feeding Guidelines for Health Workers*, AusInfo, Canberra.

Nestle, M. 1993, 'Food Lobbies, the Food Pyramid, and US Nutrition Policy', *International Journal of Health Services*, vol. 23, no. 3, pp. 483–96.

Palmer, N. 1982, 'Recommended Dietary Intakes for Use in Australia', *Journal of Food and Nutrition*, vol. 39, no. 4, pp. 157–8.

Pinstrup-Andersen, P. 1993, 'Household Behavior and Government Preferences: Compatibility or Conflicts in Efforts to Achieve Goals of Nutrition Programs', in P. Pinstrup-Andersen (ed.), *The Political Economy of Food and Nutrition Policies*, published for the International Food Policy Research Institute by Johns Hopkins University Press, Baltimore, pp. 116–30.

Polya, R. 2001, *Food Regulation in Australia: A Chronology*, Department of the Parliamentary Library, Canberra.

Ritzer, G. 1993, *The McDonaldization of Society: An Investigation into the Changing Character of Contemporary Social Life*, Pine Forge Press, Newbury Park, California.

—— 2001, *Explorations in the Sociology of Consumption: Fast Food, Credit Cards and Casinos*, Sage, London.

Russell, M. & Dobson, A. 1994, 'Age-Specific Mortality from Cardiovascular Disease and Other Causes, 1969 to 1990', *Australian Journal of Public Health*, vol. 18, no. 2, pp. 160–4.

Rutishauser, I. 1982, 'Vitamin B-6', *Journal of Food and Nutrition*, vol. 39, no. 4, pp. 158–67.

Sindall, A., Wright, J. & O'Dea, K. 1994, 'Food Production, Human Nutrition and the Impact of Health Messages: A Public Health Perspective', *Proceedings of the Nutrition Society of Australia*, vol. 18, pp. 156–66.

Sullivan, D. 2000, 'Dietary Guidelines for a New Millennium: Total Fat—More or Less?', *Australian Journal of Nutrition and Dietetics*, vol. 57, no. 4, pp. 222–4.

Sumner, J., Eu, S. & Dhillon, A. 1983, 'Ascorbic Acid Retention in Foods', *Journal of Food and Nutrition*, vol. 40, no. 1, pp. 43–8.

Symons, M. 1993, *The Shared Table: Ideas for Australian Cuisine*, Australian Government Publishing Service, Canberra.

Turner, B. S. 1992, 'The Government of the Body: Medical Regimens and the Rationalization of Diet', in B. Turner, *Regulating Bodies: Essays in Medical Sociology*, Routledge, London, pp. 177–95.

Turner, M. & Gray, J., (eds) 1982, *Implementation of Dietary Guidelines: Obstacles and Opportunities*, British Nutrition Foundation, London.

United States Congress 1977, *Eating in America: Dietary Goals for the United States. Report of the Select Committee on Nutrition and Human Needs*, US Senate and MIT Press, Cambridge, Massachusetts.

Wood, B. 1985, 'Thiamin', *Journal of Food and Nutrition*, vol. 41, no. 3, pp. 110–18.

8

The Public Health Nutrition Workforce: A Sociological Review

Roger Hughes

Overview

- What is public health nutrition? What is the public health nutrition workforce?
- How can a sociological analysis of the public health nutrition workforce help us to identify factors that affect its capacity and performance?
- Why is the sociological perspective important in examining the development of the public health nutrition workforce?

The public nutrition workforce represents a social organisation of human resources with the specific purpose of providing services that address the determinants of nutrition-related health issues and in the process prevent disease and enhance health and well-being. This chapter focuses on the public health nutrition workforce to illustrate the importance of sociological scholarship in building the capacity of society to combat population health problems. It will explore the historical, cultural, and structural determinants of workforce performance and provide a critical analysis of the factors that currently limit the capacity of this workforce to effectively address public health nutrition issues. As a result, it will cover a range of issues relevant to students and practitioners who have an interest in developing careers in this important field of nutrition practice.

Key terms

competencies	ecological model	primary prevention
continuing competency development	health promotion	public health nutrition
dietitian	medical model	public health nutritionist
	population health	

Introduction

Readers of this book with plans to become a nutrition professional such as a **dietitian** or a nutritionist might wonder about the relevance of sociological studies to their own competency development. Those who are already experienced nutrition professionals will, on reflection, acknowledge the importance of the sociological perspective as one of the approaches to developing knowledge that can be applied to solving nutrition-related problems. For many, this realisation has come more from experience and learning in the workplace than from formal education methods and mediums such as courses and textbooks. This may be because the existing workforce received inadequate sociological education in their training, or it may simply reflect a reality that learning about sociological phenomena requires the learner to be imbedded in the phenomena and to learn from experience.

The sociological imagination template, introduced in Chapter 1, provides a framework for interpreting the **public health nutrition** workforce, its historical development, the cultural factors that influence its effectiveness and actions, and the structural factors that limit or enhance the workforce's capacity to effectively address food and nutrition problems in society. This sociological perspective enables a critical analysis and interpretation of the workforce development needs that has implications not only for students but also for the contemporary workforce.

Before a sociological analysis of the public health nutrition workforce can be adequately performed, a definition of 'public health nutrition' needs to be developed and the composition of the workforce described and delineated.

Defining 'public health nutrition'

Common use of 'public health nutrition' as a term to describe a field of practice or the workforce employed in this field is a recent development. However, the application of prevention principles to prevent diet-related disease has a centuries-long history. Eighteenth century English naval officer Captain James Cook's attempt to prevent the vitamin-C-deficiency disease scurvy by promoting the consumption of vitamin-C-rich foodstuffs among his sailors is a famous example of a public health nutrition intervention involving food supply changes, supported by policy and enforced with the threat of punitive action. Enforcing the consumption of lime juice and sauerkraut through the threat of 50 lashes for malingerers is a strategy rarely available to contemporary health promoters. While population-based approaches have been a mainstay of nutrition work for decades in many countries, the popular use of the title **'public health nutritionist'** for nutrition practitioners has only recently been adopted in countries such as Australia and the UK. In Australia, some of the earliest public health nutrition activities related to food legislation, particularly aimed at eliminating food adulteration—for example, the *Adulteration of Bread Act 1838* (NSW) and the *Pure Food Act 1905* (Vic.) (Commonwealth of Australia 2001).

Preventative and population-based approaches to dealing with nutrition issues to enhance public health have recently become more accepted in those Western countries that have experienced spiralling increases in the social and financial burden associated with diseases of affluence, such as heart disease, some cancers, and diabetes. This acceptance is linked to a realisation that countries cannot afford to sustain the cost of treatment of these diseases, and that investment in effective prevention makes good sense economically as well as socially. There is evidence that countries worldwide are putting more money and effort into the development of the public health nutrition workforce (Landman 2001), in order to deal with the spiralling social costs of these largely preventable health problems.

During the last decade there have been various attempts in the international literature to define 'public health nutrition' as a field of nutrition practice distinct from the well-established professional practice of clinical nutrition and dietetics (Hughes & Somerset 1997; Rogers & Schlossman 1997; Landman et al. 1998; Yngve et al. 1999; Johnson et al. 2001). This literature has developed from considerable effort and debate among professionals and organisations in response to health-service policy shifts consistent with the public health, **health promotion**, and primary health care movements. It has also been in response to efforts to raise people's awareness of public health nutrition as a distinct profession or mode of practice delineated from clinical practice paradigms (Hughes & Somerset 1997; Landman et al. 1998). This has not passed without controversy and debate within the nutrition community (Ash et al. 1997; Niall & O'Dea 1997; Tapsell 1997; Yeatman 1997; Mackerras 1998).

In the late 1990s the Nutrition Society in the UK identified the need for a definition of 'public health nutrition' to make explicit the broad vision, intention, character, and commitment to popular service values associated with the field (Landman et al. 1998). Statements that define a field of practice or a type of work are important in workforce development because they help describe the work needed, and in turn provide direction about the type of worker and competency mix required for that work. Definitions serve as a statement of intent, philosophy, and method, important for communication of what the field entails. They have implications for marketing, development of professional identity, and systematic workforce development.

Table 8.1 lists the definitions found in the international literature since 1997 and includes the definition adopted for the national public health nutrition strategy in Australia (SIGNAL 2001a, 2001b). This definition differs from the others in that it makes a point of specifying what public health nutrition is

Table 8.1 Definitions of 'public health nutrition'

Publication and country	*Definition*
Hughes & Somerset 1997 (Australia)	'Public Health Nutrition is the art and science of promoting population health status via sustainable improvements in the food and nutrition system. Based upon public health principles, it is a set of comprehensive and collaborative activities, ecological in perspective and intersectoral in scope, including environmental, educational, economic, technical and legislative measures.'
Rogers & Schlossman 1997 (USA)	'The term "public nutrition" has been defined as a new field encompassing the range of factors known to influence nutrition in populations, including diet and health, social, cultural, and behavioural factors; and the economic and political context. Like public health, public nutrition would focus on problem solving in a real-world setting, making its definition an applied field of study whose success is measured in terms of effectiveness in improving nutrition situations.'
Landman et al. 1998 (UK)	'Public health nutrition focuses on the promotion of good health through nutrition and the primary prevention of diet-related illness in the population. The emphasis is on the maintenance of wellness in the whole population.'
Yngve et al. 1999 (EU)	'Public health nutrition focuses on the promotion of good health through nutrition and physical activity and the prevention of related illness in the population.'
Johnson et al. 2001 (USA)	'Public health nutrition practice includes an array of services and activities to assure conditions in which people can achieve and maintain nutritional health, including surveillance and monitoring nutrition-related health status and risk factors, community or population based assessment, program planning and evaluation, leadership in community/population interventions that collaborate across disciplines, programs and agencies, and leadership in addressing the access and quality issues around direct nutrition services to populations.'
SIGNAL 2001a (Australia)	'Public health nutrition focuses on issues affecting the whole population rather than the specific dietary needs of individuals. The impact of food production, distribution and consumption on the nutritional status and health of particular population groups is taken into account, together with the knowledge, skills, attitudes and behaviours in the broader community.'

not (in the words, 'rather than the specific needs of individuals') in order to delineate public health nutrition from clinical dietetic modes of service.

Close assessment of the descriptors used in these definitions reveals a number of consistent elements, suggesting that there is a consensus developing internationally about how public health nutrition as a field of practice is seen. This observation has recently been tested as part of an international Delphi study (see Box 8.1) among an international panel of public health nutrition experts to assess the level of agreement about how 'public health nutrition' is defined (Hughes 2003a). This study, conducted among twenty-four public health nutrition experts from Portugal, Spain, Sweden, Finland, Iceland, England, Switzerland, Belgium, South Africa, the USA, and Australia, identified key descriptors of public health nutrition, as an alternative to a prescribed definition. The agreed descriptors of this field of practice included the following:

- being population-based
- applying public health principles
- focusing on **primary prevention**, health promotion, and wellness
- using a food and nutrition systems approach that utilises environmental, political, behavioural, and inter-sectoral strategies.

Box 8.1 The Delphi Technique

The Delphi Technique is a research strategy that was developed by the RAND Corporation as a forecasting tool in the 1960s to measure or develop agreement about issues. It uses multiple survey rounds among an anonymous group of experts. Controlled feedback between survey rounds is provided by the researcher in the form of statistical summaries of the previous round's results, and this is followed by further ratings by experts. This process continues until there is stability in responses and consensus is achieved.

Source: Rowe & Wright (1999)

In order to be able to conduct an analysis of the public health nutrition workforce, it is necessary to first examine and delineate the composition of the public health nutrition workforce.

Workforce composition

The public health nutrition workforce is a social organisation of human resources with the role of enhancing public health by addressing the determinants of nutrition-related health problems. This emphasis on identifying, understanding, and addressing the determinants of public health problems is consistent with the **ecological model** of public health, a model that underpins much of the public health movement internationally (Gebbie et al. 2002).

Numerous factors, such as workforce composition, level of collaboration, **competencies**, practice methods, information access, resource allocation, and organisational issues, are likely to affect the capacity of the workforce to effectively address population nutrition problems (Hughes 2003b). It is important to consider the composition of this workforce, so that specific workforce development initiatives can be targeted at those groups within the workforce with the greatest opportunity to effect the desired outcomes or with the greatest need.

An inclusive and simplistic approach would be to argue that the public health nutrition workforce includes all those who make a contribution to organised efforts to prevent diet-related disease and promote health. This could include nutritionists, dietitians, teachers, nurses, medical practitioners, town planners, food-industry staff, and advertisers, to name a few. This approach is not very helpful if the objective is to identify and target factors that influence the workforce's capacity and development needs. It also does not fit the realities of workforce organisation, in which workers are usually categorised on the basis of work tasks and roles, employing agency, professional background, credentials, or competencies.

Previous attempts to conceptualise the composition of the public health, health promotion, and public health nutrition workforces in Australia (PHAA 1990; NHMRC 1996; Campbell et al. 1997) have resulted in the recognition of multiple workforce tiers that consistently differentiate between specialist and generalist categories. There is a developing consensus, at least in Australia, that the public health workforce can be categorised into a number of workforce categories or tiers, with different professional backgrounds, development needs, roles, and functions, but all part of, and contributing to, the collective capacity of the workforce (PHAA 1990; Campbell et al. 1997).

One approach is to consider the workforce in terms of its employers. It is naive to assume that organised efforts to influence population or societal dietary behaviour only originates in the health sector or that such efforts have health promotion as their driving agenda. Marion Nestle's recent exposé of the food industry in America highlights the significant influence of this sector on **population health** and nutrition (Nestle 2002). Nestle demonstrates that the food industry spends huge amounts of money each year on lobbying and on marketing foods that can only be classified as 'junk food'. The industry employs an army of workers (including nutrition professionals) to ensure that their market is protected and expanded. Should nutritionists working in the food industry be considered part of the public health nutrition workforce, despite the fact that they are employed by an industry whose primary objective is shareholder profits rather than the public good?

The first argument worth considering is that nutritionists employed in the food industry can promote public health from within this sector, by, for example, reducing the fat or salt content of food products (and thus changing to the food supply) or running nutrition education/marketing programs that increase consumer awareness about healthy diets and products (Tapsell & de Groot 1999). The counter argument is that nutritionists in the food industry are confronted with a conflict of interests (corporate profit versus public health) in their role (Niall & O'Dea 1997) and that this conflict means that, in reality, the ability of nutrition professionals 'embedded' in the food industry to promote public health is limited. Another classification system only includes those workers employed by public organisations (tax-funded health systems, charities, etc.) (Mackerras 1992). A recent attempt to assess consensus among an international panel of public health nutritionists showed that half of the panel of twenty-four experts from the USA, Europe, and Australia disagreed with this classification system (Hughes 2003a).

An alternative approach is to consider what group in the workforce is the lead group in terms of employment, competency mix, and capacity to initiate population-level action. There have been only a few specific studies published that describe national public health workers specialising in nutrition or occupying designated public health nutrition positions—in the US (Kaufman et al. 1986; Haughton et al. 1998), Canada (Gatchell & Woolcott 1992), and Britain (Adamson & Cowburn 1996). These studies consistently identify practitioners with dietetic professional backgrounds as the dominant professional group occupying designated public health nutrition work roles. The reasons for this will be considered in the sociological analysis of the workforce that follows.

A historical perspective

Little has been published on the historical development of the public health nutrition workforce. In any case, the relative stage of workforce development tends to vary between countries. The United States, for example, has a relatively large and well-developed public health nutrition workforce that has developed over the past 50 years, whereas in countries such as Australia and the UK the development of public health nutrition as a professional grouping or a specific workforce is in its infancy.

Current public health nutrition in many countries is more appropriately described as an offshoot of the public health workforce or the dietetic profession. There are, however, indications that there is a desire for recognition of public health nutritionists as a professional group distinct from other public health and dietetic professionals. In the UK, the Nutrition Society has established a registration program for public health nutritionists that confers registration as a credential of competency in this field (Landman 2001).

If we limit our discussion of the public health nutrition workforce to the designated workforce (that is, those workers with designated positions with a full-time work mandate for preventative and population-based practice), the historical development of the public health nutrition workforce is closely linked to that of the dietetic profession.

A cultural perspective

It is often difficult to separate historical from cultural perspectives because they are interrelated. In the case of the public health nutrition workforce, it can be argued that, in Australia at least, public health nutritionists as distinct nutrition practitioners have evolved out of the dietetic profession in response to changes in the professional, policy, and funding environments. This relates to the dominance of dietetic training as a background for work in public health nutrition, identified in workforce enumeration studies internationally (Gatchell & Woolcott 1992; Haughton et al. 1998; Hughes 2003c). This suggests that dietetic professional culture would have a strong influence on the culture of the public health nutrition workforce. In many cases it probably has. Values such as a commitment to the public good, social justice, ethical practice, evidence-based practice, and advocacy for the public are strong features of the public health nutrition workforce culture and are consistent with those of dietetics and health professions generally.

Some differences, however, can be observed in the public health nutrition workforce as a result of this evolution of practice from clinical practice based on a **medical model** to public health practice based on an ecological model. Many of the contemporary public health nutrition workers in Australia report having 'evolved' through work as clinical dietitians to public health nutrition work because of frustration with the (perceived) ineffectiveness of a treatment paradigm for preventable diseases. Evolution in this sense does not imply that public health nutrition is a more advanced version of practice, but a product of natural selection of career paths based on interests and circumstances. This evolution influences work culture, as is illustrated by the following quote from a high-level Australian public health nutritionist: 'I got pretty sick of going to ICU every morning and realising that much of the problems presenting there were preventable…' (quoted in Hughes 2003f).

Public health nutritionists appear to have moved on from the philosophies they learned during professional socialisation as a dietitian. There is evidence that individual professionals are rejecting the medical model and embracing what they consider to be a more holistic, socially empowering, and appropriate approach to public health improvement: 'I could see solutions to problems like obesity come through public health efforts in communities … the clinical model is a limited model for dealing with complex social phenomena like obesity' (Hughes 2003f).

Qualitative investigation of the career paths of advanced public health nutrition practitioners in Australia (Hughes 2003d) has also shown that this evolution has largely been opportunistic and unplanned. This reflects the lack of coordinated workforce development at a national level in Australia.

Public health nutrition is a field of practice that is currently in the process of defining and delineating its professional boundaries. There is, for example, whispered debate in Australia about the appropriateness of employment stipulations requiring applicants for public health nutrition positions to be qualified in dietetics: why not instead hire people with a demonstrated competency in public health nutrition and recruit people from diverse backgrounds rather than from a specific professional group? Part of the problem is that there has been no consensus about which public health nutrition competencies are required for effective practice, and a lack of clarity about what constitutes effective practice.

Clearly, the culture of the public health nutrition workforce is still evolving, borrowing heavily from dietetics and public health but responding to events as they arise.

A structural perspective

Structural factors relevant to the analysis of the public health nutrition workforce include the policy and strategic environment within government, the size of the workforce, employment requirements, workforce organisation, and systems for workforce development.

Policy and strategic framework

Government policy is a structural determinant of the workforce's activity, structure, and development. Figure 8.1 outlines the public health nutrition policy and strategic framework in Australia. The first national public health nutrition policy, the *Food and Nutrition Policy* (FNP) was released in 1992. This policy provided general guidelines and priorities for federal, state, and territory governments. The aim of the FNP was to 'make healthy food choices easy choices' (CDHHCS 1992, p. 1). It recognised the importance of social justice, quality of the food supply, community participation, involving all stakeholders, and supporting ecologically sustainable development. This policy was followed by the establishment of the National Public Health Partnership (NPHP), a national coordinating body constituted by representatives of federal, state, and territory government agencies. The public health nutrition arm of the NPHP is the Strategic Inter-Governmental Nutrition Alliance (SIGNAL), which was responsible for the development of the National Public Health Nutrition Strategy (known as *Eat Well Australia*, or EWA, and released in 2001). This strategy includes the *National Aboriginal and Torres Strait Islander Nutrition Strategy and Action Plan* (NATSINSAP). *Eat Well Australia* is a strategic plan for public health nutrition until 2010,

Figure 8.1 Public health nutrition policy and strategic framework in Australia

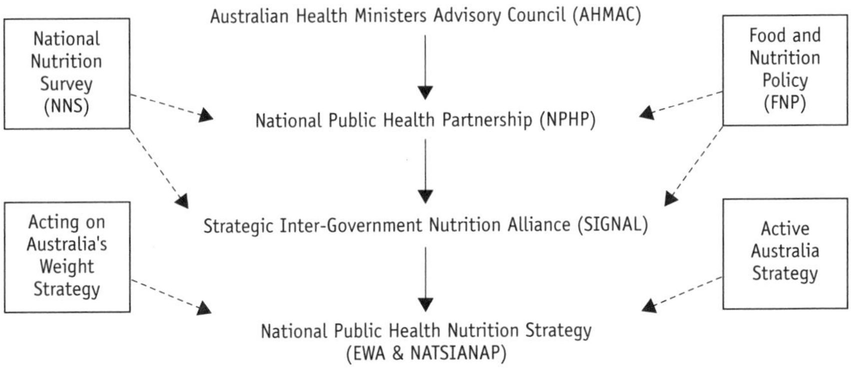

and is complemented by related strategies such as *Acting on Australia's Weight* (NHMRC 1997) and *Active Australia*, which outline strategic approaches to preventing overweight and obesity and improving health and well-being.

EWA aims to provide 'a coherent national approach to the underlying causes of the preventable burden of diet-related disease and early death, providing a set of interlinked initiatives for the prevention and management of these diseases' (SIGNAL 2001b, p. 2). EWA is a population-wide strategy and includes, but does not solely focus on, at-risk groups. It consists of three broad action areas and thirteen strategic directions:

Health gain

- Promoting vegetable and fruit consumption
- Promoting healthy weight
- Promoting good nutrition for mothers and infants
- Promoting good nutrition for school-aged children
- Improving nutrition for vulnerable groups
- Addressing structural barriers for safe and healthy food

Capacity building

- Investing in public health nutrition research
- Improving the effectiveness of interventions
- Building human resource capacity
- Communicating with the public

Strategic management

- Steering and developing *Eat Well Australia*
- Developing nutrition policy and resources
- Monitoring progress in food and nutrition

SIGNAL 2001a

This strategic framework influences the workforce because it guides the actions of employers, such as state-government health departments (many of which have developed a state version of the national strategy), and influences resource allocation.

Size and characteristics of the workforce

Workforce scholarship in the US (Gebbie & Merrill 2001; Kennedy & Moore 2001) has recently focused on enumerating and profiling the public health workforce in order to plan for workforce development. There have been only a few specific studies published that describe national public health workers specialising in nutrition in the US (Kaufman et al. 1986; Haughton et al. 1998), Canada (Gatchell & Woolcott 1992), and Britain (Adamson & Cowburn 1996). Until recently the information about the public health nutrition workforce in Australia was limited to grey literature (unpublished reports) (Steele 1995; Anthony & Cooper 1998) and information gleaned from workforce studies in the nutrition and dietetics and public health fields. Workforce studies in nutrition and dietetics in Australia (Scott & Binns 1988, 1989; Williams 1993; Hughes 1998; AIHW 2000; Meyer et al. 2002) make little reference to public health nutrition practice.

Box 8.2 Summary of data relating to compositional analysis of the public health nutrition workforce in Australia, the USA, and Canada

- The public health nutrition workforce is seen by most within the public health nutrition community as multi-disciplinary, with many 'players'.
- There are multiple workforce tiers, each tier having different roles, competency needs, and mandates for public health nutrition action.
- A key constituent of the public health nutrition workforce is the nutrition 'specialist'.
- Practitioners who have a dietetics background and who work in community health settings are the dominant workforce constituent in Australia and in most countries for which there are available data.
- Most employers recruiting health professionals to public health nutrition positions in Australia stipulate dietetic qualifications.
- Other key workforce constituents include individual care dietitians, health promotion officers, academics, managers, nurses, and home economists.
- The existing Australian community and public health nutrition workforce is predominantly female and most workers have entry-level dietetic qualifications as their highest qualification.

- Inconsistent and variable position nomenclature is used for the 'designated' public health nutrition workforce tier. Use of the title 'public health nutritionist' is increasing.
- Almost half of the workers are in temporary or part-time positions and most are employed in the government health sector.
- Public health nutrition work is only a part of the role of most of those in the community and public health nutrition workforce in Australia, with most having clinical responsibilities also. This is a potential limitation on the capacity for public health nutrition effort.
- The public health nutrition workforce is dynamic and evolving. Some 35% of the Australian workforce reported that they expected to change jobs in the next 2 years and only 18% expected to be in their current job for another 5 years or more.
- The workforce responsible for addressing public health nutrition in Australia is small relative to the size of the problems, and self-reported capacity is low.

Sources: Kaufman et al. (1986); Gatchell & Woolcott (1992); Steele (1995); Adamson & Cowburn (1996); Campbell et al. (1997); Hughes (2003b, 2003c, 2003d)

In order to garner more information about the public health nutrition workforce in Australia, a mixed-method study of the public health nutrition workforce was recently conducted (Hughes 2003b). Data from this study—and various studies done in other countries—relevant to the analysis of the composition and nature of the public health nutrition workforce are summarised in Box 8.2.

Table 8.2 (see p. 182) provides data from a recent study attempting to enumerate and delineate between different public health nutrition workforce groups, and illustrates the relatively small number of positions dedicated to public health nutrition work. This suggests that the current workforce in Australia is less than 40% of projected need based on established staff-to-population ratios used in the US (Dodds & Kaufman 1991).

Employment requirements

Employers' expectations of and requirements for public health nutrition positions are important structural factors influencing the composition and nature of the workforce. Position descriptions are an instrument of human resource management used by employers to define the roles and responsibilities, credentials, and competency requirements of a position. They define a position and express the organisational expectations of the position, and are the standard against which employers recruit, and assess the performance of, the public health nutrition workforce (Hughes 2003e). They also provide an organisational mandate

Table 8.2 Calculations of adjusted national full-time-equivalent positions dedicated to public health nutrition (PHN) practice: Australian Public Health Nutrition Workforce Study, November 2001–February 2002

Position	***A*** *Number*	***B*** *Mean hours worked*	***C*** *FTE positions (AxB/38)*	***D*** *Assumed proportion of work dedicated to PHN practice*	***E*** *FTE positions dedicated to PHN practice (CxD)*	***F*** *Total FTE positions, adjusted for survey response rate (E/0.87)*
PHN in regional/ zonal	15	33.0	13.0	1.0	13.0	14.9
PHN in NGO	10	36.1	9.5	1.0	9.5	10.9
PHN in state health department	18	36.2	17.1	1.0	17.1	19.7
Community dietitian/nutritionist in community health	81	30.3	64.6	0.5	32.3	37.1
Community dietitian/nutritionist in hospital	14	31.7	11.7	0.5	5.9	6.8
Project officer in health promotion	20	33.9	17.8	1.0	17.8	20.5
Regional dietitian/nutritionist	16	34.3	14.4	0.5	7.2	8.3
Hospital-based dietitian with community role	13	32.8	11.2	0.5	5.6	6.4
Nutritionist in academic institution	11	31.6	9.1	0.5	4.6	5.3
Nutritionist on project grant	11	27.3	7.9	1.0	7.9	9.1
Nutritionists working with food industry	2	31.0	1.6	1.0	1.6	1.8
Other*	19	33.0	16.5	0.5	8.3	9.5
Total	****239**		**194.4**		**130.8**	**150**

FTE = full-time equivalent; PHN = public health nutrition; NGO = non–government organisation
* Includes eleven staff from Food Standards Australia New Zealand
** One missing response (total response sample = 240)

Source: Hughes 2003c

for a particular type of practice. The importance of this codified mandate was recently demonstrated in a study of the Victorian public health nutrition workforce: community-based dietitians reported being limited in their capacity to

Box 8.3 Employers' expectations about public health nutrition workforce functions, credentials, and competencies

Most common functions

- team building
- program planning
- program evaluation
- providing nutrition advice/support
- program implementation
- human resource management
- needs assessment
- strategy design
- training other professionals
- continuing professional development
- conducting local research
- community development
- dietary education of individuals
- grantsmanship (submission writing)
- quality management

Most common credentials (listed in at least 33% of position descriptions)

- dietetic qualifications
- eligibility for DAA membership
- current drivers license

Most common competency requirements (listed in at least 33% of position descriptions)

- experience in and knowledge of public health nutrition intervention management (planning, implementation, and evaluation)
- consultation and negotiation skills
- interpersonal communication skills
- ability to work in a multi-disciplinary manner
- knowledge of public health nutrition issues and strategies
- being an independent and self-directed worker
- cultural competency

Source: Hughes 2003e (based on analysis of forty-six position descriptions reviewed between February and August 2002)

perform public health nutrition roles because position descriptions and organisational expectations did not provide support for services that were not clinical in nature (Hughes & Woods 2003). Box 8.3 summarises the results of a recent review of public health nutrition position descriptions in Australia that identified consistent job roles (functions) and key selection criteria (credentials and competencies). The fact that dietetic qualifications are required for most of the positions in this study suggests that:

- This credential is valued by employers as a benchmark of competency and workforce preparation.
- These position descriptions (or this credential requirement) are based on dietetic position descriptions, and/or
- The professionals or employers who develop these instruments of staff recruitment are dietitians.

The development of a position description implies that the person developing it has adequate knowledge of the work required and the competency requirements needed to effectively do this work. This assumption is questionable. Regardless of the limitations of analysis based on position descriptions, this structural factor limits the access of nutritionists not trained as dietitians to public health nutrition work, because of the widespread dietetic credential requirement. This may explain the dominance of dietetic professionals in the designated public health nutrition workforce, which will be discussed further in the critical-perspective section that follows.

Workforce organisation

The organisation of the public health nutrition workforce—in terms of location, setting of practice, accountability, and funding source—may have important effects on its composition, practice culture, and overall effectiveness. Profiling studies of the Australian public health nutrition workforce indicate that the publicly funded health sector is the main employer, with most of the workforce employed and located in community health services and reporting to health managers without nutrition qualifications (Hughes 2003c). The workers in this setting experience considerable pressure from managers and the community to provide clinical services that address the short-term needs of individuals, reflecting the traditional culture of community health services in many parts of Australia. This limits their ability to plan and develop interventions that address long-term population needs (Hughes & Woods 2003).

Recent workforce developments in some Australian states have placed new public health nutritionists in public health units that have a mandate for public health surveillance, planning, intervention, and evaluation at a zonal or state level (Lee 2002). This organisational positioning of practitioners in a practice culture consistent with public health is likely to be more conducive to an effective public health nutrition effort.

Systems for workforce development

There are a number of systems that are used to recruit and develop workforces, one of which has already been discussed (position descriptions). Other examples include codifications or statements of the core functions and competencies required for effective practice.

Core function statements have recently been developed for the broad area of public health work in a number of countries (NPHP 2001; CLBAPHP & HRSA 2002) to help define the core or essential functions of the public health workforce. The following list of core public health nutrition functions (Box 8.4) has been developed in Australia (Hughes 2003b) based on a mix of research methods, including literature review, position description auditing, national workforce surveying, practitioner consultation, and consensus development. These functions

Box 8.4 Proposed core public health nutrition workforce functions

Research and analysis

- Monitor, assess, and communicate population nutritional health needs and issues.
- Develop and communicate intelligence about determinants of nutrition problems, policy impacts, intervention effectiveness, and prioritisation through research and evaluation.

Building capacity

- Develop the various tiers of the public health nutrition workforce and its collaborators through education, disseminating intelligence, and ensuring organisational support.
- Build community capacity and social capital to formulate and implement solutions to nutrition problems.
- Build organisational capacity and systems to facilitate and coordinate effective public health nutrition action.

Intervention management

- Plan, develop, implement, and evaluate interventions that address the determinants of priority public health nutrition problems.
- Enhance and sustain population knowledge and awareness of healthy eating so that dietary choices are informed choices.
- Lobby for food- and nutrition-related government policy and action that protects and promotes health.
- Promote, develop, and support healthy growth and development throughout all life stages.
- Promote equal access to safe and healthy food so that healthy choices are easy choices.

represent the consistent function categories identified following triangular analysis of data from these different methods.

Workforce practices are a factor affecting human resource contributions to the structural capacity of the public health system (Handler et al. 2001). Box 8.5 presents a hypothetical practice scenario to illustrate how these core functions are applied in practice and how the public health nutrition mode of practice differs from the traditional clinical dietetic approach. As the scenario demonstrates, the practice approach used to address nutrition problems will influence the effectiveness of the work. A large workforce that practices in a way that is inconsistent with disease prevention (for example, one-on-one dietary counselling to prevent obesity) may have low overall effectiveness in disease prevention, because of poor reach and/or efficacy.

Competencies: The architecture for workforce development

This public health nutrition scenario in Box 8.5 illustrates the extensive interaction with stakeholders in communities that is required to successfully implement solutions to nutrition problems. Public health nutritionists have to be in touch with their community, trusted, culturally competent, and committed to community development—all qualities that depend on their having advanced social skills—in order to be able to understand and effectively interact with community members.

Public health workforce development scholarship over the last few years has emphasised the importance of developing a competent public health workforce as a precursor to increasing societal capacity to protect and promote public health (CDC & ATSDR 2001; Kennedy & Moore 2001; Lichtveld et al. 2001; Gebbie et al. 2002; Riddout et al. 2002). As a result, there has been an emphasis on developing competency standards to provide the architecture for workforce development in the fields of public health (Healthwork UK 2001; CLBAPHP & HRSA 2002), preventive medicine (Lane et al. 1999; Gebbie et al. 2002), health promotion (Howat et al. 2000; PrecisionConsultancy 2000) and health education (NCHEC 2002). This has also been of interest to public health nutrition scholars (Rogers & Schlossman 1997; Landman et al. 1998; Pew Health Professions Commission 1998; Dodds & Polhamus 1999; Nutrition Society 2000).

Competencies reflect the knowledge, skills, and attitudes required to be able to effectively perform the required work. Table 8.3 lists the broad competency domains considered by an international group of public health nutrition experts as essential for effective public health nutrition practice (Hughes 2003f). There is a strongly held view among advanced public health nutrition practitioners in Australia that competencies in the nutritional sciences are essential and distinguish the public health nutritionist from the rest of the public health workforce (Hughes 2003g).

Box 8.5 A comparison of the traditional and public health nutrition approaches to dietetics

The traditional dietetic approach

Tony is a dietitian employed by the Gosford Community Health Centre. Data produced by the Area Health Epidemiology Unit has identified a recent increase in the prevalence of overweight and obesity in the area population and this finding is supported by an increasing rate of referral of overweight and obese clients to the health centre by general practitioners (GPs). Tony's initial response is to work with the other staff in the Community Health Centre to establish a multi-disciplinary weight-reduction clinic, linking with the local Division of General Practice. This results in a streamlined service that provides services for an average of sixty individuals a week and that occupies three days a week of his time. He notices that each individual needs an average of six visits spread over two to three months to successfully stabilise their weight and sustain changes to related behaviours (the desired outcome), so there are ten outcomes per week. Realising that this method requires significant resources for the limited population reach, he reorganises the service into a group-education format, increasing the client service rate to 120 per week for the same time investment and for twice as many outcomes per week (20). At this rate he will achieve about 1000 outcomes per year.

The public health nutrition approach

Tess is a public health nutritionist working for the Central Coast Area Health Service of New South Wales and has decided to develop a public health nutrition response to the spiralling rates of overweight and obesity in her community. The following account describes how each of the core functions listed in Box 8.4 applies to this scenario.

Tess decides to act after analysing recently collected data from her epidemiology unit that shows that the rates of overweight and obesity are increasing at an alarming rate, particularly among school-aged children. Her first step is to consult key stakeholders in her community and form a representative taskforce to assist in planning a community-wide intervention to address the problem. At the same time as this taskforce is being established and commencing discussions, Tess lobbies her local public health unit to provide research support and some seed funding for the community taskforce to develop and implement its initial strategies.

With the public health epidemiologist, Tess summarises the available public health data about overweight and obesity in a report that is used to inform the taskforce's deliberations and to communicate this information to the local health workforce. The taskforce then undertakes a determinant analysis (consultation, research, and discussion to identify determinants of overweight and obesity in their community) assisted by Tess and staff from the public health unit. This analysis finds that sedentary lifestyles and increasing reliance on takeaway food are the major direct determinants of increasing adiposity. Indirect determinants include a lack of community facilities for exercise—such as safe pathways, organised sport, and affordable gym access. The increasing reliance on takeaway food is considered to be the result of time poverty among working parents, limited food preparation skills, the saturation of the local community environment with fast-food advertising, and the high number of fast-food outlets.

The taskforce develops a community strategy with the help of Tess, who informs them about earlier interventions and their effectiveness and other possible options. This strategy forms the basis of a submission for funding from the state government to develop a community-wide obesity-prevention strategy. Among other things, the strategy mix includes:

- working with local government to:
  - develop policies and invest in safe pathways
  - regulate fast-food outlet locations through town planning
- a train-the-teacher program in district schools and health centres, so that teachers and health workers can implement a healthy meal preparation skills development program for students, parents, and other community members.
- developing a community sports organisation to coordinate community-wide physical activity for people of all ages (assisted by the Department of Sport and Recreation)

On receipt of the government funding, Tess works with the taskforce and community stakeholders to implement the program, making a concerted effort to keep the stakeholders engaged in and informed about the project. The project team also develops community organisation systems and seeks funding to sustain the project after the government funding ends. On completion of the intervention funding, Tess works with stakeholders to evaluate the intervention and reports widely on its outcomes and lessons.

Comparison of approaches

The difference between these two approaches relates not only to the reach of the interventions, but also to the types of changes achieved, the determinants addressed, and the competencies required to successfully implement them.

Table 8.3 Competency domains identified by an international public health nutrition expert panel

Competency domain	*Example units*
Analytical	Nutrition monitoring and surveillance, applied research, needs assessment, evaluation
Sociocultural and political processes	Advocacy, policy development and analysis, building capacity, cultural awareness
Public health services	Intervention planning, strategy design, workforce development, intervention research, health promotion
Communication	Interpersonal and scientific communication skills, media and writing skills, grantsmanship
Management and leadership	Strategic planning, team building and staff management, negotiation, collaboration
Nutrition sciences	Nutrition assessment, food guidance and goals, lifespan nutrition and requirements
Professionalism	Ethics, quality assurance, evidence-based practice, reflective practice, commitment to lifelong learning

Source: Hughes 2003f

Although there is a developing literature about competency standards and the needs of the public health nutrition workforce, few studies have focused on how workforce competencies are best developed. This leads us to the critical phase of the sociological analysis.

A critical perspective

The level of competence possessed by the public health nutrition workforce at any given time is a product of the interaction between and effects of workforce education and training processes and workforce management processes (Kennedy & Moore 2001). Competency development can therefore be temporally compartmentalised into pre-employment education and training (such as university programs) and postgraduate **continuing competency development** (CCD). Postgraduate CCD takes many forms, including further university-based coursework, research higher degrees, and workplace based CCD.

The adequacy of workforce preparation

Given the dominance in the contemporary public health nutrition workforce of workers from a dietetic training background—with most having entry-level dietetics training as their highest qualification (Hughes 2003c)—it is important to consider the adequacy of this preparation for competency in public health nutrition practice. Two recent studies of the CCD needs of this workforce provide evidence that dietetic training is inadequate preparation for effective public health nutrition work (Hughes 2003d, 2003h). This suggests that there may need to be a review of existing competency standards and of how training programs meet those standards relevant to public health nutrition practice.

In response to a question asking public health nutrition workers with dietetic qualifications to list the advantages of dietetic training, the most commonly cited benefits were the strong grounding in nutrition knowledge and the wide range of skills attained, including health promotion skills, basic research skills, and problem-solving skills. The most commonly mentioned disadvantages of dietetic training were its clinical bias and narrow focus, the inadequate training in public health approaches, and the inadequate public health nutrition work experience (Hughes 2003h). In the same study, when respondents were asked to rate the adequacy of dietetic training as preparation for public health nutrition practice, 57% rated it as inadequate to very inadequate.

The (perceived) inadequacy of dietetic training as preparation for public health nutrition work may be due to the fact that dietetic education is designed to produce entry-level graduates, not specialists. It is now recognised that public health nutrition competency is considered to be an advanced qualification, or a specialised practice area, by definition builds on experience and more generic professional proficiencies (Hughes 2003h). It is also recognised that public health nutrition competency development is best facilitated by experiential and problem-orientated learning in a work setting (Pelletier 1997; Hughes 2003h), making it more suited to practice-based learning and consistent with the principles of self-directed learning and adult learning (Kaufman 1990). Another advantage of focusing on the existing workforce is that it has privileged access to work situations that encourage CCD via these learning styles (Hughes 2003c). Evidence from recent Australian studies suggest that competency development amongst the public health nutrition workforce has been largely unplanned, uncoordinated and probably inefficient (Hughes 2003d).

The necessity of integrated learning systems

This therefore suggests a need for integrated learning systems that facilitate CCD among the existing workforce and future workers. A recent study (Hughes 2003h) has shown that the most common motivations to further develop competencies in public health nutrition in the Australian workforce were intrinsic motivations (such as a desire to learn more and a desire to be more effective), which is consistent with the features of adult and self-directed learning (Kaufman 2003). The reported barriers to continuing professional development are similar to those found in American studies of the dietetic workforce (American Dietetic

Association 2000; Manning & Vickery 2000) Time poverty in the workplace and financial constraints may reflect a lack of employer support for CCD and suggest that workforce development strategies should focus on creating a workplace environment that supports and encourages ongoing education and competency development. This means that organisational and cultural change within the workplace may be needed, rather than more CCD courses and training programs.

A practitioner's confidence in their own ability and skills may be an important variable affecting practices (Hughes 2003h). This notion is based on the concept of self-efficacy, which asserts that an individual's judgments of their own ability to deal with certain situations is central to their actions (Kaufman 2003). Self-reported confidence levels may also be used as an indicator of competency development needs and has been used in CCD needs assessment studies in the public health workforce (Corby 1997). The confidence deficits reported most frequently by Australian public health nutritionists in a recent national survey (Hughes 2003h) were in analytical and policy-process competency areas.

Formal training to develop public health nutrition competencies needs to be flexible and student-centred if it is to successfully engage the workforce (Hughes 2003h). Most of this workforce is currently employed in the public health nutrition field and further study must be integrated into their existing work. This will require greater interaction between universities and employers. It also provides an opportunity to apply teaching and learning strategies that reflect contemporary views about health-profession competency development, such as problem-based learning (Vernon & Blake 1993), situated learning (Grant 2002), and self-directed learning and reflective practice (Kaufman 2003). The recent funding of an advanced public health nutrition training program by the Commonwealth's Public Health Education and Research Program (PHERP) may provide the opportunity to develop integrated learning systems that address these issues.

Constraints on workforce development imposed by current recruitment stipulations

The common inclusion of dietetic credentials as a key selection criterion, discussed earlier, is potentially a problem for workforce development in this field. It assumes that dietetic qualifications provide appropriate preparation for public health nutrition work and does not recognise that it is possible to develop competencies in public health nutrition via other routes. The evidence discussed previously seriously challenges this assumption.

Workforce development efficiency: Up-skilling dietitians

Workforce development rarely involves a clean slate that allows the development of a workforce tailor-made for the work needed. The work that the public health nutrition workforce in Australia must perform does not always match the competency or practice mix available among the existing workforce. Hughes (2003c) argues that the existing infrastructure and outcomes associated with dietetic training and the dietetic profession should be built on to improve the public health nutrition workforce's capacity. This would entail targeting dietitians and dietetic graduates for advanced competency development via integrated learning systems—such as linking work with further studies, linking novices with mentors, and developing systems that increase worker access to public health information.

Dietitians as a professional group have been recognised as priority (but not exclusive) targets for ongoing public health nutrition workforce development in Australia. Underpinning this view is a consistent qualifier that workforce development targeting dietitians should not be exclusive or limited to this professional group (Hughes 2003f, 2003g). An inclusive view is consistent with the multi-disciplinary model of public health nutrition workforce development and practice (Rogers & Schlossman 1997).

Conclusion

This chapter has illustrated how sociological analysis can be used to identify and describe the determinants that affect the capacity of the public health nutrition workforce. Consideration of the historical, cultural, structural, and critical factors that affect the actions and effectiveness of the public health nutrition workforce is an important step in effective workforce development. This will ultimately bolster society's capacity to address public health nutrition issues.

Summary of main points

- The public health nutrition workforce is that group within the health workforce that focuses on addressing the determinants of population-level nutrition and health problems, on preventing diet-related disease, and on promoting health and well-being.
- Dietitians are the dominant professional group in the designated public health nutrition workforce. They have also been identified as a priority target for public health nutrition workforce development, in recognition of this existing workplace positioning, their training background, and competency development needs.
- The public health nutrition workforce is influenced by a range of factors that influence its capacity to effectively address public health nutrition issues. The major capacity determinants identified in this sociological analysis were structural, including small workforce size, existing practices that do not align with agreed core functions, inadequacies in workforce preparation, and a lack of consensus on workforce competencies.

Discussion questions

1. What workforce groups (other than dietitians) are important constituents of the public health nutrition workforce?
2. What competency strengths and deficits are these practitioners likely to have that are relevant to effective public health nutrition practice?
3. What strategies, other than further competency development for dietitians, do you think are required to enhance the capacity of the public health nutrition workforce?
4. Review the definitions of 'public health nutrition' given in the chapter. Which of these definitions would you use? Justify your answer.

Further investigation

1. To what extent can a dietitian working in a community health setting reorient their services away from the traditional clinical role to working as a public health nutritionist?
2. What structural and cultural barriers might hamper the reorientation from clinical to public health nutrition work?

Acknowledgments

Thanks to John Germov for the initial work on the *Eat Well Australia* section of the text and the accompanying Figure 8.1.

Further reading and web resources

Books and reports

Commonwealth Department of Housing, Health and Community Services 1992, *Food and Nutrition Policy*, Australian Government Publishing Services, Canberra.

Commonwealth of Australia 2001, *Food Regulation in Australia: A Chronology*, Department of the Parliamentary Library, Canberra.

Lester, I. 1994, *Australia's Food and Nutrition*, Australian Institute of Health and Welfare, Canberra. Available online at www.aihw.gov.au.

National Health and Medical Research Council (NHMRC) 1997, *Acting on Australia's Weight: A Strategic Plan for the Prevention of Overweight and Obesity*, NHMRC, Canberra. Available online at www.nhmrc.gov.au/publications/synopses/n21syn.htm.

—— 2003, *Dietary Guidelines for Adult Australians*, NHMRC, Canberra (including appendices on the Nutrition of Aboriginal and Torres Strait Islander Peoples; Social Status, Nutrition and the Cost of Healthy Eating; and Dietary Guidelines and the Sustainability of Food Systems). Available online at www.nhmrc.gov.au/publications/synopses/dietsyn.htm.

Nestle, M. 2002, *Food Politics*, University of California Press, California.

Strategic Inter-Governmental Nutrition Alliance (SIGNAL) 2001, *Eat Well Australia: A Strategic Framework for Public Health Nutrition 2000–2010*, National Public Health Partnership, Canberra. Available online at www.nphp.gov.au/publications/index.htm#signal.

—— 2001, *National Aboriginal and Torres Strait Islander Nutrition Strategy and Action Plan, 2000–2010*, National Public Health Partnership, Canberra. Available online at www.nphp.gov.au/publications/index.htm#signal.

Wahlqvist, M. & Kouris-Blazos, A. 2002, 'Food and Nutrition Policies in the Asia-Pacific Region: Nutrition in Transition', in M. Wahlqvist (ed.), *Food and Nutrition: Australia, Asia and the Pacific*, 2nd edition, Allen & Unwin, Sydney, pp. 575–98.

Journals

Australia and New Zealand Journal of Public Health

Critical Public Health

FOODChain—The Newsletter of SIGNAL: www.nphp.gov.au/workprog/signal/foodchain.htm

Public Health

Public Health Nutrition

Web sites

Australian Food & Nutrition Monitoring Unit: www.sph.uq.edu.au/nutrition/monitoring/index.htm

Australian Institute of Health and Welfare: www.aihw.gov.au

Codex Alimentarius Commission: www.codexalimentarius.net/

Food and Agriculture Organization: www.fao.org

Food Standards Australia New Zealand: www.foodstandards.gov.au

SIGNAL—Strategic Inter-Governmental Nutrition Alliance: www.nphp.gov.au/workprog/signal/index.htm

National Health and Medical Research Council: www.nhmrc.gov.au

Public Health Association of Australia: www.phaa.net.au

World Declaration and Plan of Action for Nutrition: www.fao.org/docrep/U9920t/u9920t0a.htm

World Health Organization: www.who.org

References

Adamson A. & Cowburn G. 1996, 'Community Nutrition and Dietetics: A Survey of Nutrition Group Members in 1995', *Journal of Human Nutrition and Dietetics*, vol. 9, pp. 339–48.

AIHW—*see* Australian Institute of Health and Welfare.

American College of Preventive Medicine 2002, *Core Competencies and Performance Indicators for Preventive Medicine Residents*, American College of Preventive Medicine, Washington, DC.

American Dietetic Association 2000, 'Report on the American Dietetic Association's Member Needs Assessment/Satisfaction Survey', *Journal of the American Dietititans Association*, vol. 100, pp. 112–16.

Anthony H. & Cooper C. 1998, *Summary Report on Public Health and Community Nutrition Activities Carried Out by Victorian Members of the Dietitians Association of Australia*, Dietitians Association of Australia (Vic. Branch), Melbourne.

Ash S., Capra S., Cummings F., Gibbons K., Roberts N. & Tapsell L. 1997, 'Viewpoint Article: Definitions and Conceptual Framework for Public Health and Community Nutrition' (letter to editor), *Australian Journal of Nutrition and Dietetics*, vol. 54, no. 3, pp. 152–3.

Australian Institute of Health and Welfare 2000, *Profile of Dietitian Labour Force Australia 1996*, Australian Institute of Health and Welfare, Canberra.

Campbell K., Steele J., Woods J. & Hughes R. 1997, *Developing a Public Health Nutrition Workforce in Australia: Workforce Issues*, National Specialty Program in Public Health and Community Nutrition, Melbourne.

CDC & ATSDR—*see* Centers for Disease Control and Prevention & Agency for Toxic Substances and Disease Registry.

CDHHCS—*see* Commonwealth Department of Health, Housing and Community Services.

Centers for Disease Control and Prevention & Agency for Toxic Substances and Disease Registry 2001, *Strategic Plan for Public Health Workforce Development*, US Department of Health and Human Services, Washington, DC.

Commonwealth Department of Health, Housing and Community Services 1992, *Food and Nutrition Policy*, Australian Government Publishing Service, Canberra.

Commonwealth of Australia 2001, *Food Regulation in Australia: A Chronology*, Department of the Parliamentary Library, Canberra.

CLBAPHP & HRSA—*see* Council on Linkages Between Academic and Public Health Practice & Health Resources and Services Administration.

Corby, L. 1997, 'Assessment of Community Development and Leadership Skills Required by Caribbean Nutritionists and Dietitians: Research and International Collaboration in Action', *Journal of Nutrition Education*, vol. 29, no. 5, pp. 250–7.

Council on Linkages Between Academic and Public Health Practice & Health Resources and Services Administration 2002, *Core Competencies for Public Health Professionals: 2002*, CLBAPHP & HRSA, Rockville, Maryland.

Dodds J. & Kaufman M. 1991, *Personnel in Public Health Nutrition for the 1990s: A Comprehensive Guide*, Public Health Foundation, Washington, DC.

Dodds J. & Polhamus B. 1999, 'Self-perceived Competence in Advanced Public Health Nutritionists in the United States', *Journal of the American Dietetic Association*, vol. 99, no. 7, pp. 808–12.

Gatchell S. & Woolcott D. 1992, 'A Demographic Profile of Canadian Public Health Nutritionists', *Journal of the Canadian Dietetic Association*, vol. 53, pp. 30–4.

Gebbie K. & Merrill J. 2001, 'Enumeration of the Public Health Workforce: Developing a System', *Journal of Public Health Management Practice*, vol. 7, no. 4, pp. 8–16.

Gebbie K., Rosenstock L. & Hernendez L. 2002, 'Who Will Keep the Public Health? Educating Public Health Professionals for the 21st Century', Institute of Medicine National Academic Press, Washington, DC.

Grant, J. 2002, 'Learning Needs Assessment: Assessing the Need', *British Medical Journal,* vol. 321, pp. 156–9.

Handler A., Issel M. & Turnock B. 2001, 'A Conceptual Framework to Measure Performance of the Public Health System', *American Journal of Public Health*, vol. 91, no. 8, p. 1235–9.

Haughton B., Story M. & Keir B. 1998, 'Profile of Public Health Nutrition Personnel: Challenges for Population/System-focused Roles and State-level Monitoring', *Journal of the American Dietetic Association*, vol. 98, no. 6, pp. 664–70.

Healthwork UK 2001, *National Standards for Specialist Practice in Public Health: An Overview* (Approved Version), Healthwork UK, London, p. 7.

Howat P., Maycock B. Jackson L., Lower T., Cross D., Collins J. & van Asselt K. 2000, 'Development of Competency-based University Health Promotion Courses', *Promotion & Education*, vol. VII, no. 1, pp. 33–8.

Hughes R. 1998, 'An Omnibus Survey of the Australian Rural Health Dietetic Workforce', *Australian Journal of Nutrition and Dietetics,* vol. 55, no. 4, pp. 163–9.

—— 2003a, 'Definitions for Public Health Nutrition: A Developing Consensus', *Public Health Nutrition*, vol. 6, no. 6, pp. 615–20.

—— 2003b, *Public Health Nutrition Workforce Development: A Blue-print for Australia*, School of Health Science, Griffith University, Gold Coast.

—— 2003c, 'Enumerating and Profiling the Australian Public Health Nutrition Workforce', *Nutrition and Dietetics*, under review.

—— 2003d, 'Competencies for Effective Public Health Nutrition Practice: A Developing Consensus', *Public Health Nutrition*, (in press).

—— 2003e, 'Employers' Expectations of Core Functions and Competencies for the Public Health Nutrition Workforce', *Nutrition and Dietetics*, (in press).

—— 2003f, 'Competency Development in Public Health Nutrition: Reflections of Advanced Level Practitioners in Australia', *Nutrition and Dietetics*, vol. 60, no. 3, pp. 205–11.

——2003g, 'Public Health Nutrition Workforce Composition, Core Functions, Competencies and Capacity: Perspectives of Advanced Level Practitioners in Australia', *Public Health Nutrition*, vol. 6, no. 6, pp. 607–13.

—— 2003h, 'Competency Development Needs of the Australian Public Health Nutrition Workforce', *Public Health Nutrition*, (in press).

Hughes R. & Somerset S. 1997, 'Definitions and Conceptual Frameworks for Public Health and Community Nutrition: A Discussion Paper', *Australian Journal of Nutrition and Dietetics,* vol. 54, no. 1, pp. 40–5.

Hughes R. & Woods J. 2003, *A Needs Assessment for Public Health Nutrition Workforce Development in Victoria: Report 2 of the Victorian Public Health Nutrition Workforce Development Initiative*, Monash University, Melbourne.

Johnson D., Eaton D., Wahl P. & Gleason C. 2001, 'Public Health Nutrition Practice in the United States', *Journal of the American Dietetic Association*, vol. 101, no. 5, pp. 529–34.

Kaufman D. 2003, 'Applying Educational Theory in Practice', *British Medical Journal*, vol. 326, pp. 213–16.

Kaufman M. (ed.) 1990, *Nutrition in Public Health: A Handbook for Developing Programs and Services*, Aspen publishers, Gaithersburg, New York State.

Kaufman M., Heimendinger J., Foerster S. & Carroll M. 1986, 'Survey of Nutritionists in State and Local Public Health Agencies', *Journal of the American Dietetic Association,* vol. 86, pp. 1566–70.

Kennedy V. & Moore F. 2001, 'A Systems Approach to Public Health Workforce Development', *Journal of Public Health Management Practice*, vol. 7, no. 4, pp. 17–22.

Landman J. 2001, 'Training in Public Health Nutrition: Symposium at the 17th International Congress of Nutrition, Vienna', *Public Health Nutrition*, vol. 4, no. 6, pp. 1301–2.

Landman J., Buttriss J. & Margetts B. 1998, 'Curriculum Design for Professional Development in Public Health Nutrition in Britain', *Public Health Nutrition*, vol. 1, no. 1, pp. 69–74.

Lane D., Ross V., Chan D. & O'Neill C. 1999, 'Core Competencies for Preventative Medicine Residents: Version 2', *American Journal of Preventive Medicine*, vol. 16, no. 4, pp. 367–72.

Lee A. 2002, 'Enhanced Investment in Nutrition in Queensland Health', *Foodchain*, vol. 9.

Lichtveld M., Cioffi J., Baker E., Bailey S., Gebbie K., Henderson J., Jones D., Kurz R. 2001, 'Partnership for Front-Line Success: A Call for a National Action Agenda on Workforce Development', *Journal of Public Health Management Practice*, vol. 7, no. 4, pp. 1–7.

Mackerras D. 1992, 'Public Health Nutrition Practice in Houston and Harris County, Texas, USA: Applications in Australia?', *Australian Journal of Nutrition and Dietetics,* vol. 49, no. 4, pp. 122–7.

—— 1998, 'Viewpoint Article: Definitions and Conceptual Framework for Public Health and Community Nutrition' (letter to editor), *Australian Journal of Nutrition and Dietetics*, vol. 55, no. 1, pp. 37–8.

Manning C. & Vickery C. 2000, 'Disengagement and Work Constraints are Deterrents to Participation in Continuing Professional Education Amongst Registered Dietetians', *Journal of the American Dietetic Association*, vol. 100, pp. 1540–2.

Meyer R., Gilroy R. & Williams P. 2002, 'Dietitians in NSW: Workforce Trends 1984–2000', *Australian Health Review,* vol. 25, no. 3, pp. 122–30.

National Commission for Health Education Credentialing NCHEC 2002, *Responsibilities and Competencies for Health Educators*, NCHEC, Allentown, Philadelphia.

National Health and Medical Research Council 1996, *Promoting the Health of Australians: A Review of Infrastructure Support for National Health Advancement: Final Report*, Australian Government Publishing Service, Canberra.

—— 1997, *Acting on Australia's Weight*, Australian Government Publishing Service, Canberra.

National Public Health Partnership 2001, *Public Health Practice in Australia Today: Core Functions*. National Public Health Partnership, Melbourne.

NCHEC—*see* National Commission for Health Education Credentialing.

Nestle M. 2002, *Food Politics: How the Food Industry Influences Nutrition and Health*, University of California Press, Los Angeles.

NHMRC—*see* National Health and Medical Research Council.

Niall M. & O'Dea K. 1997, 'Viewpoint Article: Definitions and Conceptual Framework for Public Health and Community Nutrition' (letter to editor), *Australian Journal of Nutrition and Dietetics*, vol. 54, no. 4, pp. 208.

NPHP—*see* National Public Health Partnership.

Nutrition Society 2000, *How to Specify Levels of Learning Outcome in Public Health Nutrition*, Nutrition Society, London.

Pelletier D. 1997, 'Advanced Training in Food and Nutrition: Disciplinary, Interdisciplinary, and Problem Orientated Approaches', *Food and Nutrition Bulletin*, vol. 18, no. 2, pp. 134–45.

Pew Health Professions Commision 1998, *Recreating Health Professional Practice for a New Century: Forth Report of the Pew Health Professions Commission*, Pew Health Professions Commision, San Fransisco.

PHAA—*see* Public Health Association of Australia.

Public Health Association of Australia PHAA 1990, *Workforce Issues for Public Health: The Report of the Public Health Workforce Study*, Public Health Association of Australia, Canberra.

Precision Consultancy 2000, *Draft Health Promotion Competency Standards*, Precision Consultancy, Melbourne.

Riddout L., Gadiel D., Cook K. & Wise M. 2002, *Planning Framework for the Public Health Workforce: Discussion Paper*, National Public Health Partnership, Melbourne.

Rogers B. & Schlossman N. 1997, '"Public nutrition": The Need for Cross-disciplinary Breadth in the Education of Applied Nutrition Professional', *Food and Nutrition Bulletin*, vol. 18, no. 2, pp. 120–33.

Rowe G. & Wright G. 1999, 'The Delphi Technique as a Forecasting Tool: Issues and Analysis', *International Journal of Forecasting*, vol. 15, pp. 353–75.

Scott J. & Binns C. 1988, 'A Profile of Dietetics in Australia: Part 1—Demography and Educational Characteristics', *Journal of Food and Nutrition*, vol. 45, no. 3, pp. 77–9.

—— 1989, 'A Profile of Dietetics in Australia: Part 2—Employment Characteristics', *Australian Journal of Nutrition and Dietetics,* vol. 46, no. 1, pp. 14–17.

SIGNAL—*see* Strategic Inter-Governmental Nutrition Alliance.

Steele J. 1995, *Towards a Public Health Nutrition Human Resource Infrastructure in Queensland.* Master of Public Health Program, University of Queensland, Brisbane, p. 158.

Strategic Inter-Governmental Nutrition Alliance 2001a, *Eat Well Australia: Strategic Framework for Public Health Nutrition 2000–2010*, National Public Health Partnership & Department of Health and Aged Care, Canberra.

—— 2001b, *Eat Well Australia: An Agenda for Action for Public Health Nutrition 2000–2010,* National Public Health Partnership & Department of Health and Aged Care, Canberra.

Tapsell L. 1997, 'Letter to editor', *Australian Journal of Nutrition and Dietetics,* vol. 54, no. 3, 153–4.

Tapsell L. & de Groot, R. 1999, 'Dietitian-nutritionists in the Australian Food Industry: An Educational Needs Assessment', *Australian Journal of Nutrition and Dietetics,* vol. 56, no. 2, pp. 86–90.

Vernon D. & Blake R. 1993, 'Does Problem-based Learning Work? A Meta-analysis of Evaluation Research', *Academic Medicine*, vol. 68, pp. 550–3.

Williams P. 1993, 'Trends in the New South Wales Dietetic Workforce 1984–1991', *Australian Journal of Nutrition and Dietetics*, vol. 50, no. 3, pp. 116–19.

Yeatman H. 1997, 'Letter to editor', *Australian Journal of Nutrition and Dietetics,* vol. 54, no. 3, pp. 155–6.

Yngve A., Sjostrom M., Warn D., Margetts B., Rodrigo C.& Nissinen A. 1999, 'Effective Promotion of Healthy Nutrition and Physical Activity in Europe Requires Skilled and Competent People: European Master's Programme in Public Health Nutrition', *Public Health Nutrition*, vol. 2(3a), pp. 449–52.

9

Risk, Maternal Ideologies, and Infant Feeding

Elizabeth Murphy

Overview

- What are the current trends in infant feeding in industrialised countries?
- What role do experts play in influencing mothers' infant-feeding practices?
- How can policy responses to concerns about infant feeding be seen as individualising a social problem?

The decline in the frequency and duration of breastfeeding in industrialised countries during the early part of the twentieth century was a matter of concern to policy-makers. While there have been increases in breastfeeding rates in most industrialised countries since 1970, a substantial proportion of mothers continue to feed their babies in ways that experts see as sub-optimal. Currently only one-third of mothers in the UK and less than one-half of mothers in the USA breastfeed their babies for the minimum recommended period in those countries. Rather more Australian mothers breastfeed, but there is still a significant proportion who do not. This situation concerns policy-makers and health professionals because of evidence that breastfeeding promotes the health of babies and protects them against a range of illnesses.

Breastfeeding promotion is emblematic of the many areas of contemporary life in which individuals are presented with expert assessments of risk and called upon to modify their behaviour accordingly. Risk assessment and avoidance have been elevated to the status of moral obligations and, in the case of infant feeding, this obligation is intensified by the intersection of the discourse of risk with that of motherhood. In this chapter, I consider the ways in which, both historically and currently, the 'problem' of infant feeding has been individualised and transformed into a question of maternal morality. I consider how, in infant feeding as in other aspects of child-rearing, experts have been invested with the power to define what counts as 'good mothering'. Drawing upon data from a recent study of infant feeding in Nottingham, England, I discuss the ways in which mothers themselves negotiate the demands placed upon them and, in particular, how they seek to re-establish positive identities in the face of behaviours that place them in moral jeopardy. I show how mothers' accounts of their decisions about infant feeding can be read as displays of morality and responsibility that respond to expectations about what it means to be a good wife or girlfriend, a good woman, and a good mother.

Key terms

deviance
identity
medicalisation
risk discourse

Introduction

> 'One must feel an absolute failure or feel that you are letting your baby down in some way if you don't breast-feed.'
>
> 'You've got to say "yes" or you're some kind of monster.'

One of the most immediate decisions facing a new mother in contemporary industrialised societies concerns how her baby is to be fed. In practice, the decision is limited to a choice between breast milk and infant formula milk. As is illustrated by the above quotes, which are taken from interviews with first-time mothers shortly before their babies were born, this decision raises profound issues of morality and maternal responsibility. Medical opinion and health and nutrition policy are unequivocal: breast is best. Internationally, the World Health Organization (WHO) and the United Nations' Children's Fund are committed to promoting breastfeeding. This pro-breastfeeding stance is reflected in the policies of individual governments. In the UK, for example, exclusive breastfeeding is recommended for the first 4 months of a baby's life (DHSS 1988; DOH 1994), and this is an important element in the government's strategy for improving the health of the nation (DOH 1999). In the USA, the American Academy of Pediatrics (1997) recommends exclusive breastfeeding for 6 months and the Surgeon General has made increasing breastfeeding rates a public health priority (Office on Women's Health 2001). Similarly, guidelines from the Australian National Health and Medical Research Council (NHMRC) emphasise that 'exclusive breastfeeding until around six months should be the aim for every infant' (National Health and Medical Research Council 2003, p. 14).

The promotion of breastfeeding is directed largely towards reducing or eliminating the risks to babies' short-, medium- and long-term health that are attributed to formula feeding. These include the following conditions:

- respiratory and gastro-intestinal infections (Howie et al. 1990; American Academy of Pediatrics 1997)
- allergies such as eczema, asthma, and food intolerance (Saarinen & Kajosaari 1995)
- insulin-dependent diabetes (Virtanen et al. 1991)
- Chron's disease and cancer (Lawrence 1995)
- sudden infant death syndrome (Ford et al. 1993; see also Golding 1993 and British Paediatric Association 1994)
- impaired mother–infant bonding and lowered self-esteem (Lawrence 1995).

In addition, the American Academy of Pediatrics (1997) also credits breastfeeding with the possible enhancement of cognitive development.

Contemporary patterns of infant feeding

In spite of strong scientific support for the benefits of breastfeeding, current rates of breastfeeding are relatively low in most of the industrialised world. In both the UK and the USA, marked increases in rates of breastfeeding were observed between the early 1970s and the mid 1980s. In 1970, only 26% of mothers in the USA initiated breastfeeding, but this had risen to 60% by 1984 (Hartley & O'Connor 1996). Similar, if less extreme, rises occurred in England and Wales: in 1975, the figure was 51% (Martin 1978), but by 1980 it had risen to 67% (Martin & Monk 1982). However, hopes of continued steady growth in the popularity of breastfeeding have not entirely been fulfilled. In 1990, the percentage of mothers in England and Wales who initiated breastfeeding had fallen to 64%. Surveys in 1995 and 2000 (Foster et al. 1997; Hamlyn et al. 2002) reported apparent improvements in breastfeeding incidence (68% in 1995 and 71% in 2000), but once these data were standardised for age and occupational class the improvements disappeared. The situation in the US has been more volatile (Ryan et al. 2002). After a drop in initial breastfeeding rates to 51% in 1990 (Hartley & O'Connor 1996), the most-recent data show a marked upswing to 70% in 2001 (Ryan et al. 2002). In the 1980s, Australia had one of the highest rates of initial breastfeeding in the world (85% at hospital discharge) (Palmer 1985).

Concern about the decline of breastfeeding centres not only on those babies who are never breastfed, but also on those whose mothers breastfeed them for less than the recommended length of time. In 2000, only 29% of British mothers were breastfeeding 4 months after their babies' births (the minimum recommended duration) (Hamlyn et al. 2002). The percentage of women who were *exclusively* breastfeeding their babies for the full 4 months is not known, but is likely to be considerably less than 29%. In the USA, less than

20% of women were still exclusively breastfeeding their babies at 6 months (the minimum recommended duration in that country) (Ryan et al. 2002). Once again, figures for Australia are somewhat higher, with 40–42% of mothers breastfeeding their babies at 6 months (Palmer 1985).

Breastfeeding and the privatisation of risk

As already observed, infant feeding raises profound issues of morality and responsibility. In this sense, breastfeeding promotion is emblematic of the way in which **risk discourses** dominate a wide range of political programmes and professional practices (Giddens 1991). In many areas, from mobile phones to pension provision, individuals are confronted with expert assessments of the risks associated with particular practices and are called upon to modify their behaviour accordingly. These expert risk calculations are particularly prevalent in the health field, where individuals are educated about risks associated with numerous lifestyle choices—including those related to diet, exercise, smoking, alcohol consumption, and certain sexual behaviours—and are urged to modify their lifestyle in the light of this information. This all contributes to the 'privatisation of risk management', which Nikolas Rose identifies as characteristic of contemporary liberal societies (Rose 1996, p. 58).

Within contemporary liberal societies, health is increasingly understood as something that can be chosen (Greco 1993). The citizen no longer simply enjoys good health or suffers from poor health. Rather, health is now constructed as something we foster or undermine through acts of choice. An individual can, through deliberate acts of circumspection and self-control, foster personal well-being. Citizens are obligated to 'adopt a calculative, prudent personal relation to fate now conceived in terms of calculable dangers and avertable risks' (Rose 1996, p. 58).

The obligation to exercise prudence in the light of expert risk assessments of behavioural risks is a strongly moral one (Nettleton 1997; Petersen 1997). Good health is a visible sign of 'initiative, adaptability, balance and strength of will ... a free and rational agent' (Greco 1993, p. 370). Health-compromising practices raise questions about the individual's capacity for mastery and self-control (Ogden 1995). Those who engage in risky behaviours place themselves in potential 'moral danger' (Lupton 1993, p. 425), as they neglect to 'take care of self' (Greco 1993, p. 357). By failing to live up to the liberal ideal of the rational, responsible individual, they invite moral judgment (S. Carter 1995).

The interview excerpts presented above suggest that this moral obligation to exercise prudence in the light of expert assessments of risks is reinforced in the case of infant feeding. I propose that this is for two reasons. First, the potential consequences arising from 'risky' infant-feeding 'choices' (Murphy et al. 1998b) are borne not by the mother, but by the baby, to whom the mother owes a duty of care. As I have argued elsewhere (Murphy 2000), special censure is reserved for those who knowingly put others at risk (drink-drivers, for example). Douglas (1990, p. 7) has gone so far as to suggest that to be put 'at risk' is the equivalent of being sinned against.

Second, the moral obligations associated with infant feeding are intensified by the way in which these contemporary discourses of risk and responsibility are cross-cut and reinforced by an ideology of motherhood that not only holds mothers responsible for how their children turn out (Phoenix & Woollett 1991), but also insists that they need expert advice to carry out their responsibilities successfully (Apple 1987, p. 97). Mothers' main (if not exclusive) function is assumed to be maximising the short- and long-term physical and psychological welfare of their children (Ribbens McCarthy et al. 2000). The location of infant-feeding practices at this intersection between the powerful and mutually reinforcing discourses of risk, responsibility, and motherhood places mothers who feed their babies in ways that go against expert advice in particular moral jeopardy. Later in this chapter I shall examine how such mothers deal with this threat to their **identity**.

Breastfeeding 'failure': A historical perspective

Concern about mothers who 'fail' to breastfeed their babies is not a new phenomenon. However much policy-makers may reminisce about a golden age before the introduction of formula feeding, there is evidence (Arnup 1990; Lewis 1990; Fildes 1992; P. Carter 1995) that anxiety about women's failure to breastfeed their babies is longstanding. In the eighteenth century, this concern focused on women who sent their babies out to be wet-nursed rather than breastfeeding them themselves (Maher 1992; P. Carter 1995). In 1747, William Cadogan, an influential physician, berated women who did not feed their own babies, ascribing the refusal to do so to a woman's reluctance to 'give up a little of the Beauty of her Breast to feed her off-spring' (quoted in P. Carter 1995, p. 7). While Cadogan attributed the popularity of wet-nursing to women's vanity, modern commentators suggest that it had more to do with the insistence of husbands on their sexual privileges. Vanessa Maher (1992) describes how, in the sixteenth, seventeenth, and eighteenth centuries, it was believed that sexual intercourse would 'spoil the milk', and so men prevented their wives from breastfeeding rather than give up their sexual rights.

Katherine Arnup (1990), Jane Lewis (1990), and Valerie Fildes (1992) all show that the failure of women to breastfeed was a source of public and professional anxiety in the early twentieth century in both the UK and Canada. Fildes (1992) reports doctors' concerns about the decline of breastfeeding in the UK in the late nineteenth and early twentieth centuries. Arnup (1990) relates this preoccupation with mothers who did not breastfeed their babies to wider public anxieties about national adequacy. In the UK the discovery, during recruitment for the Boer War, that a substantial proportion of working class men were unfit for military service provoked concerns about the state of the nation's health. In Canada, similar issues arose during the First World War. In both countries, attention focused on evidence of high rates of infant mortality, which were attributed to women's failure to breastfeed their babies.

In Canada the policy response was to establish a complex public health bureaucracy (Arnup 1990). The emphasis was on prevention. Experts were adamant that most infant deaths could be avoided. However, the concept of prevention was somewhat limited. While these reformers acknowledged that a range of factors, including poverty, overcrowding, and malnutrition, were associated with infant mortality, they focused their efforts on the reform of maternal behaviour—in particular, on the promotion of breastfeeding. As Arnup acknowledges, the reformers were undoubtedly right to view breastfeeding as the safest form of infant feeding. However, their exclusive focus on maternal behaviour served to divert attention from the social and material causes of infant mortality and placed the responsibility for infant survival entirely upon mothers' shoulders. This individualising of the problem of infant feeding is, as we shall see, also characteristic of contemporary approaches to promoting breastfeeding.

Lewis (1990) describes how similar concerns arose in England during the same period. Working class women were seen as a particular problem, and their education and reform was presented as the key to improving the health of the nation. Once again, by focusing upon the supposed 'ignorance and carelessness of mothers' (G. Newman 1906, quoted in P. Carter 1995, p. 41), such policies diverted attention away from the wider causes of infant mortality. As Lewis observes, 'The fault lay not in offering mothers information on child rearing, which they welcomed, but in subordinating the material conditions of their lives—the poverty and unsanitary living conditions—which were also at the root of the problem and which early twentieth century medical reports adequately diagnosed, to an individualist solution' (Lewis 1990, p. 6).

Such individualising tendencies were not restricted to infant feeding. Naomi Aronson (1982) has shown how the rise of nutritional science in the late nineteenth century was characterised by the attribution of malnutrition to the shortcomings of the poor rather than to poverty *per se*. By arguing that the cause of poor living standards was the poor's extravagance and mismanagement, rather than their limited access to resources, nutritionists offered politicians an expedient response to the 'labour problem'. The nutritional problems of the poor were to be solved not by relieving poverty, but by educating the poor to shop and cook more economically. Emphasising the contribution that individual behaviour (whether it be household management or breastfeeding) makes to health is politically expedient. In the case of breastfeeding, by emphasising the one aspect of the situation over which mothers might, superficially at least, be said to exercise control, other sources of infant morbidity and mortality are rendered less visible. Infant feeding becomes a problem of individual morality and responsibility.

Contemporary policy responses to the 'problem' of infant feeding

As we have seen, infant-feeding practices continue to be something of an intransigent problem for policy-makers and health care practitioners. In spite of expert consensus about the benefits of breastfeeding, the majority of mothers feed their babies in ways that are deemed sub-optimal. Extensive efforts to educate mothers about the benefits of breastfeeding and the risks of formula feeding have not changed this situation. There is evidence that mothers have heard and understood these expert views and yet do not necessarily follow them (Murphy 1999, 2000). Such non-adherence to expert advice continues to be seen as highly consequential not simply for individual children, but also for national projects of fostering healthy citizenries. Adequate and appropriate nutrition in childhood is held to make a vital contribution to adult health (DOH 1994), and this has many implications for controlling future welfare expenditure.

For contemporary liberal governments, characterised by a reluctance to intervene directly in the private sphere and a commitment to upholding the autonomy of individuals and families, the possibilities for improving children's nutrition are somewhat limited. In the course of the last century, a small number of direct welfare interventions were attempted. For example, in the UK, the universal provision of milk at school was introduced (and subsequently abandoned). More recently in the UK, another centrally directed intervention was introduced through the National Fruit Scheme: every child aged between four and six is entitled to a free piece of fruit each day at school. However, the thrust of government policy continues to be investing mothers with the responsibility for feeding their babies in ways that are deemed to foster short- and long-term health. Thus the individualising approach to health promotion criticised by Arnup, Lewis, and Aronson is perpetuated.

This devolution of responsibility to mothers persists in spite of substantial evidence that both the initiation and the duration of breastfeeding are associated with a mother's social and economic class. Women who are older, better educated, from higher occupational classes, and living with partners on higher incomes are more likely to start breastfeeding and to continue breastfeeding for longer (Wright & Walker 1983; Florack 1984; Simopoulos & Grave 1984; Hitchcock & Coy 1988; Martin & White 1988; White et al. 1992; Bailey & Sherriff 1993; Cooper et al. 1993; Lowe 1993; Pesssl 1996; Piper & Parks 1996; Foster et al. 1997; Hamlyn 2002; Ryan 2002). At one level, these patterns are paradoxical. Those women who can least afford to buy infant formula, and whose babies are in greatest need of the protective and health-promoting qualities of breast milk, are least likely to breastfeed.

The professional and governmental response to evidence of such socioeconomic variations in infant-feeding practices has largely been restricted to educating and 'targeting' mothers. Having identified the population groups that are least likely to breastfeed, health professionals are encouraged to direct their educational and promotional activities towards these groups, in an attempt to persuade these mothers to breastfeed their babies. Educational programs sometimes include 'support' for women in the most disadvantaged groups. However, such support is generally just verbal encouragement and advice, rather than an attempt to modify the conditions under which women feed their babies. Once again, the problem of infant feeding is individualised. While the research informing such targeting exercises frequently refers to the 'determinants' of infant-feeding practices (for example, Salt et al. 1994), these determinants tend to be seen as immutable. Little effort has been made to uncover the processes by which material and social disadvantages constrain the decisions that mothers make about how they will feed their babies, and even less has been done to discover how such disadvantages might be overcome, other than by encouraging individual mothers to compensate for them.

The establishment of successful breastfeeding, which often initially involves frequent feeding sessions throughout the day and night (Quandt 1986), makes heavy demands on a mother's time and energy (Murphy et al. 1998b). For example, the American Academy of Pediatrics (1997) advises that new-born babies may require up to twelve feeds a day, each lasting up to 30 minutes. Securing optimal infant nutrition is only one of the (sometimes competing) tasks that women must perform as they feed their babies (Murphy et al. 1998a). A mother's capacity to meet such demands is inextricably linked to the availability of certain human and material resources. A new mother who is supported by her partner, family, and friends can breastfeed her baby while these others take on responsibility for running the home—and so provide her with the essential time for both feeding and rest. In later weeks, when time between feeds is at a premium, breastfeeding will also be easier for those women who have access to a car and can make necessary trips to the supermarket or the health centre quickly, rather than by public transport. Breastfeeding is a form of work to which a mother may not be able to readily commit herself if it conflicts with her other responsibilities.

Mothers' responses to expert advice on infant feeding

The **medicalisation** of infant feeding can be seen as just one aspect of the growing involvement of professional experts in all aspects of child-rearing and family life throughout the twentieth century. Dorothy Chunn (1990) describes the impact of this new 'cadre of experts': 'Good mothering, parenthood, marital sex were not simply a matter of following biological instinct: they were activities requiring the most specialized knowledge and training' (p. 92). Thus, as Lynn Jamieson and Claire Toynbee (1990) argue, the needs of children are now defined by professionals rather than by parents, and experts have acquired the power to overrule parents' definitions of reality. Parents, and in particular mothers, bear the responsibility of meeting such expert-defined needs, in expert-approved ways, rather than identifying and interpreting their children's needs for themselves. More traditional sources of information, such as family and friends, have been displaced (Arnup 1990). Harriette Marshall shows how modern child-care manuals warn mothers about the dangers of the 'many old wives' tales, horror stories and unfounded advice which continues to surround motherhood' (Gordon Bourne 1979, quoted in Marshall 1991, p. 73). The dominance of science and technology has led to an assumption that lay people, particularly parents, are in need of expert guidance. In infant feeding, as elsewhere, the child's needs and the optimal means of meeting those needs are now defined by experts.

While recognising that infant feeding has become an 'expert domain', we should not exaggerate the power of experts to control infant feeding. Women are not simply passive recipients of expert directives. In practice, their exposure to surveillance and control is limited. While, as outlined above, women's feeding practices are subject to both social and material constraints, nevertheless it is mothers who are in day-to-day control of how babies are fed (Maher 1992). Experts may recommend exclusive breastfeeding, but mothers are free to ignore such advice. The inability of health professionals and other experts to impose their advice upon women is reflected in the relatively small numbers of women who actually meet current recommendations for exclusive breastfeeding. Mothers are able to resist the attempts of health professionals to direct how their babies are fed—and, in many cases, do so.

The force of expert advice about infant feeding lies not in compelling women to conform, but in the way in which it sets the moral context within which women negotiate their identities as mothers. It would be a mistake to assume, just because women do not always follow expert recommendations, that such recommendations have no impact. Their power lies not in their ability to make women do what they would otherwise not have done, but in their authority to define the standards by which mothers' feeding activities are to be judged, by others and indeed by the women themselves.

The categorical nature of expert advice on the benefits of breastfeeding makes a woman's failure to follow it particularly transparent. Either babies are exclusively breastfed for the recommended period or they are not. Failure to breastfeed one's child lays one open to the charge of being a 'poor mother' (P. Carter 1995). However, simply breastfeeding one's child is not in itself constitutive of good mothering. 'Good mothers' not only breastfeed their babies, but they must do so 'successfully', so that the baby thrives. As Oakley comments: 'A baby that is feeding and growing "well" is ... a tangible token of her love and work. Conversely, a baby who gains weight more slowly than it "should", and who perhaps cries a lot and seems unsatisfied is ... a sign of maternal failure' (1979, p. 165). Women may reject expert advice on infant feeding, but they can rarely ignore it. Infant feeding, like other ways in which mothers provide food for their families, is not simply a practical activity; it is a moral undertaking. As Deborah Lupton (1996) observes, the way in which a mother feeds her baby becomes a symbol of her general ability to care for her child.

Dealing with moral jeopardy

The force of expert definitions of breastfeeding and formula feeding as 'good' and 'bad' respectively, and the implications of such definitions for the self-evaluations of mothers, were illustrated in a recent longitudinal study of the decisions that mothers make about how, when, and where to feed their babies (Murphy et al. 1998a, 1998b; Murphy 1999, 2000). As part of this study, thirty-six first-time mothers living within 10 miles of Nottingham, England, were interviewed at six fixed intervals between late pregnancy and their babies' second birthdays. Quota sampling was used to ensure heterogeneity in terms of both the age and occupational class of the women. (Full details of the study's methods can be found in Murphy 1999 and Murphy 2000). The data discussed below are drawn from the first two interviews with each woman, one of which was carried out shortly before the birth of her baby and the other 2 months afterwards.

Antenatally, the majority of women (twenty-nine out of thirty-six) declared an intention to breastfeed their babies; six intended to formula-feed, and one woman intended to combine breastfeeding and formula feeding. At this stage, then, four-fifths of the women we interviewed planned to follow expert recommendations about infant feeding. The women who intended to breastfeed primarily explained their decision in terms of the health benefits to the baby, in ways that reflect current expert opinion. For example, one woman said, 'I just think it's healthy for the baby; it gets all the, the goodness from the breast ... because at the beginning the first lot of milk, it's got all the extra vitamins and nourishment which the baby needs and also, er whatever it is, antibodies, whatever to protect it from diseases and bugs'. These women were able to present themselves unproblematically as 'good mothers' acting in ways that prioritised their babies' needs. Their decisions are entirely in keeping with expert definitions of appropriate maternal behaviour, and their explanations of their decisions can be read as straightforward claims to responsible motherhood.

By contrast, five of the six women who had decided to formula-feed accounted for their decision in ways that suggest that they saw the morality of their decision to formula-feed as problematic. In spite of the self-consciously neutral stance adopted by the interviewers, these women's accounts appeared to be formulated in response to the putative charge that formula feeding is an irresponsible or inappropriate choice, evidence that the woman will be a 'bad mother'. These women treated their decision to formula-feed their babies as an 'untoward act' (Scott & Lyman 1963), and they engaged in defensive justification as they explained it to the interviewers. The sixth woman's discussion of her feeding intentions was significantly different from that of all the other women in the study. This woman acknowledged that breastfeeding was 'supposed to be more good for the baby than bottle feeding', but did not appear to see her decision to formula-feed, or indeed any of the other decisions that she made in relation to her baby, as in need of justification.

The remaining five women who intended to formula-feed acknowledged that their decisions deviated from expert recommendations and sought to justify them, so countering any potential allegations that they were not 'good mothers'. The justifications took a number of different forms. First, the women specifically challenged expert claims that 'breast is best'. Such challenges were often presented in the quasi-scientific language of 'nutrients' and 'vitamins'. For example, one woman said, 'There's the same nutrients in both … they say breast milk is better because it's yours and it's nature … there's definitely the same nutrients in both'. Formula feeding was presented as being more reliable, because 'at least you know how much it's getting'. Breastfeeding mothers ran the risk of underfeeding their babies:

> Like sometimes a woman's had a poor diet through pregnancy or if she has a poor diet when she's had a baby because probably she is rushing around after the baby, then her milk could be poor if she was breastfeeding the baby. So the baby might be starving you know. It might not be getting the right, or gaining weight properly. So I think it's better bottle.

Here, the 'good mother' is implicitly redefined as one who ensures that her baby receives sufficient milk, rather than one who uses a particular type of milk. The women bolstered their claims that formula feeding is a legitimate choice for the responsible mother by pointing to other babies who have been formula-fed and who are 'all perfectly healthy'.

The second way in which this group of women countered the implied charge of irresponsibility was to challenge the authority of experts to define what is in the best interests of their particular child. They appealed to their own authority as mothers ('I don't care what everybody else says, it's what I feel is better for my child') and to the expertise of their family and friends ('I know that might sound a bit daft, but I think my family knows best').

These women also justified their decision to formula-feed in terms of their responsibilities to others. They argued that breastfeeding would exclude their partners or other members of the family. One woman explained, 'But you see, if I was breastfeeding he'd feel left out because he wouldn't be able to feed his baby'. This reminds us that the moral responsibilities of mothers extend to their partners as well as to their babies. Not only did these women feel called upon to demonstrate that they were 'good mothers', but they were also expected (and expected themselves) to be good wives. Harriette Marshall's analysis of child-care manuals shows how a mother is required not only to meet the needs of the new baby, but also to ensure both that her partner plays his new role as father adequately and that he does not feel neglected. For example, she cites Gordon Bourne, who advised women as follows: 'It should be remembered that men are sometimes neglected when their wives are pregnant and therefore require just as much attention as the new arrival. Every woman should make sure that the new member of the family does not mean that her husband has less of her love, time and affection' (Bourne 1979, quoted in Marshall 1991, p. 77). Thus, women must meet the needs of their babies, but they must do so in ways that keep their partners happy. A woman's partner must be insulated from any negative consequences arising from the baby's arrival. It is for women to ensure that both the baby's and the father's interests are safeguarded, however much these are in conflict with one another.

While, as noted above, those women who intended to breastfeed their babies did not appear to feel called upon to justify this decision *per se*, a number were at pains to point out that the way in which they would breastfeed would allow them to still meet their responsibilities to their partners. In particular, they addressed themselves to the possible charge that the decision to breastfeed would exclude their partners. Thus, the factor that women intending to formula-feed invoked to justify their decision became, for some breastfeeding women, a challenge that needed to be addressed. A number of these women described how they planned to express breast milk, so that the baby's father would not feel 'left out'. For example, one woman said, 'I intend, as early as possible, to start expressing and giving it bottles of breast milk so that Ray [her partner] can have that [the opportunity to feed the baby]'. Another said, 'I was worried he'd feel a bit left out, but I've bought a breast pump anyway and I've got some bottles and a sterilising unit'.

Not only do new mothers have to deal with the moral injunction to be 'good mothers' and 'good partners', but they must also be 'good women'. The 'sexualisation' of women's breasts (Newson & Newson 1963) means that breastfeeding women risk being seen as immodest or indiscreet. Thus, those women who intended to formula-feed also appealed to modesty to justify their decision not to breastfeed. For example, one woman explained, 'I'm self-conscious about my body … I'm not going to have to get my boobs out in the middle of Nottingham'. Another referred to a recent experience in which she had observed a woman breastfeeding in public and had been 'quite put off by it'. She insisted that women who wanted to breastfeed their babies should 'hide away'.

Conversely, a number of the women who intended to breastfeed their babies were concerned to distance themselves from any suggestion of brazenness or immodesty. These women stressed the measures they would take to avoid giving offence to others:

> When I'm out in public, I don't like the idea of that ... I couldn't just openly do it in public ... I'd have to be in a corner somewhere tucked away where nobody can see. I won't feed in public like on a bench in a park or anything like that ... I think I'd probably, what do you call it, suction it out ... I'd feel conscious if I was out and the baby wanted to feed, and I'd want some kind of privacy, because it's like flashing your flesh to everyone.

As we have seen, the women who had decided not to breastfeed their babies at all felt vulnerable to the charge that they were 'bad mothers'. The reasons they gave for deciding to formula-feed can be read as a rebuttal of a potential charge of **deviance**. However, it is not only mothers who 'fail' to breastfeed their babies who are faced with the possibility of being considered deviant. There is evidence from a number of studies to suggest that women who prolong breastfeeding, particularly into the baby's second year, are likely to incur social disapproval (Hills-Bonczyk et al. 1994; Kendall-Tackett & Sugarman 1995). In our study, while breastfeeding in itself was not an activity that the women felt required to justify, a number appeared to want to distance themselves from the charge that they might be the 'sort of woman' who would prolong breastfeeding. They referred to such behaviour as 'not very dignified' and 'very, very distasteful'. One woman said, 'Our midwife told us that somebody breastfeeds when they are three. That to me is absolutely revolting, for mother and child, because it's not natural. Well not the way, in the society I've been brought up with. You don't do that sort of thing'.

Of the thirty women who declared an intention to breastfeed their babies, only six met the current UK recommendations for exclusive breastfeeding for a minimum of 4 months. The duration of breastfeeding among the other twenty-four women ranged from 4 hours to 14 weeks, with half the women having stopped by 2 weeks after the birth and twenty-one by 2 months. These women described, in some detail, their disappointment and distress at not feeding their babies for as long as they intended to. They detailed their feelings of failure and the ways in which they felt judged and criticised by both professional and lay people (Murphy 2000)

These women, who had committed themselves to breastfeeding and then reverted to formula feeding, faced particular difficulties in establishing their credentials as responsible and morally adequate mothers when interviewed after their babies were born. They had, in the previous interview, endorsed expert opinion that breast milk was the optimal food for babies and that breastfeeding reduced the risks to the health of babies. In many cases this commitment to breastfeeding had been framed in moral terms. For example, one mother said, 'I think sometimes you've got to be not selfish and consider the baby's health'. These women had presented their decision to breastfeed as a subordination of their own interests and welfare to those of their babies (Murphy et al. 1998). As such, antenatally, they were able to frame their feeding intentions squarely within the ideology of motherhood discussed above. Their subsequent decision to use formula milk raised doubts about their maternal credentials and called for a renegotiation of the moral meaning of their behaviour (Douglas 1990, p. 6). The postnatal interviews became occasions upon which the mothers appeared compelled to reconstruct images of themselves as normal, moral, responsible, and good mothers in the face of doubts provoked by their introduction of formula milk.

In reconstructing their identities as good mothers, these women accounted for their use of formula feeding in a number of ways (Murphy 2000). Whereas, antenatally, they had drawn on expert assessments to assert the superiority of breastfeeding, they now appealed to knowledge based on experience rather than statistics to defend their use of formula. They cited both the experience of friends and relatives and their own experience to support their claim that formula feeding was in the best interests of their child. Babies who were unhappy or failing to thrive were presented as becoming settled and growing well once formula milk was introduced. Many of the mothers described the difficulties that they had encountered that had made the introduction of formula milk inevitable. Such difficulties included the extreme nature of both the baby's hunger and the physical distress caused to the woman herself by breastfeeding. They also pointed to the role played by others in their failure to breastfeed. They told 'atrocity stories' (Webb & Stimson 1976) in which they presented themselves and their babies as the victims of the insensitive, careless, ignorant, or negligent behaviour of others, both professional carers and lay contacts.

As we have seen, the moral obligations confronting a new mother as she feeds her baby are both complex and weighty. In order to be a 'good mother', one must breastfeed one's baby and do so for an extended period. To be a 'good mother' who is also a 'good partner', one must breastfeed one's baby in such a way that one's husband or boyfriend does not feel neglected or displaced. To be a 'good mother' and a 'good wife' who is also a 'good woman' is even more demanding. One must avoid giving offence to others by breastfeeding in public or prolonging breastfeeding beyond the age when it is socially acceptable. The space within which one can simultaneously be a 'good mother', a 'good partner', and a 'good woman' is therefore very limited indeed. Many of the women in the Nottingham study were actively engaged in moral repair work, both before and after their babies' births. In the face of potential threats to their identities as good mothers, partners, and women, they actively sought to re-establish their credentials and to justify their feeding behaviours. Thus moral repair work was just one more of the many obligations put upon these new mothers.

Conclusion

In this chapter, we have looked at the 'problem of infant feeding' from a sociological perspective. We have examined the ways in which nutritional concerns have been translated into a problem of maternal behaviour, so that issues of morality, risk, and individual responsibility have come to preoccupy not only the policy-makers but also mothers themselves. For policy-makers and health practitioners, the problem may appear to be a simple one: babies should be breastfed, but too few mothers actually do so for long enough. Solutions that have been advocated include the education of supposedly ignorant mothers, but this approach has had little success. I would argue that those developing policies to encourage breastfeeding need to recognise that infant feeding is a moral as well as a nutritional matter, and that simply trying to change the knowledge or behaviour of individual women, without paying due attention to the broader cultural and material contexts in which they act, is likely to meet with limited success.

Summary of main points

- Current rates of breastfeeding are low in most countries of the industrialised world, and this causes concern to policy-makers because of evidence of the health benefits of breastfeeding.
- Policy responses have tended to individualise the problem, diverting attention away from the social and economic conditions in which women opt to feed their babies in particular ways.
- Infant feeding, like other aspects of child-rearing, has increasingly become an 'expert domain' dominated by expert assessments of risk. While experts are not able to control how mothers actually feed their babies, they are able to set standards by which women may be judged and may judge themselves.
- Infant feeding is a highly moral practice and failure to breastfeed leaves women vulnerable to the charge that they are not 'good mothers'. However, women who do breastfeed must demonstrate that they do so in ways that do not cause offence to the public or cause their husbands or boyfriends to feel neglected.

Discussion questions

1 What are the current trends in infant feeding in the industrialised world, and why do these cause concern for medical experts and policy-makers?

2 How can policy-makers' responses to concerns about infant feeding be seen as the individualising of a social problem?
3 In what ways can infant feeding be seen as an example of medicalisation?
4 How do experts on infant feeding influence mothers' self-evaluations?
5 In what ways do women's statements about their feeding choices suggest that they are concerned with presenting themselves as 'good mothers', 'good partners', and 'good women'?

Further investigation

1 From a sociological perspective, examine the effectiveness of public policy interventions aimed at increasing rates of breastfeeding.
2 Motherhood is increasingly subject to medicalisation. Discuss.

Acknowledgments

The empirical work discussed in this chapter was funded by the UK Economic and Social Research Council as part of the Nation's Diet Programme (L209252035). I am very grateful to the women and professionals who took part in this study, and to Dr Tony Avery and Lindsay Groom, of the Department of General Practice at the University of Nottingham, who gave me valuable assistance in locating and gaining access to the practices from which the sample was drawn. Special thanks are also due to Susan Parker and Christine Phipps, who carried out the interviews for this study and who made important contributions to an earlier version of this chapter.

Further reading and web resources

Books

Arnup, K., Levesque, A., & Roach Pierson, R. 1990, *Delivering Motherhood: Maternal Ideologies and Practices in the 19th and 20th Centuries*, Routledge, London.

Carter, P. 1995, *Feminism, Breasts and Breast Feeding*, Macmillan, Basingstoke, UK.

Articles

Maher, V. 1992, 'Breast Feeding in Cross-cultural Perspective: Paradoxes and Proposals', in V. Maher (ed.) *The Anthropology of Breast Feeding: Natural Law or Social Construct*, Berg, Oxford.

Murphy, E. 1999, '"Breast is Best": Infant Feeding Decisions and Maternal Deviance', *Sociology of Health and Illness*, vol. 21, pp. 187–208.

Murphy, E. 2000, 'Risk, Responsibility and Rhetoric in Infant Feeding', *Journal of Contemporary Ethnography*, vol. 29, pp. 291–325.

Web sites

Australian Breastfeeding Association: www.breastfeeding.asn.au/

References

American Academy of Pediatrics 1997, 'Breast Feeding and the Use of Human Milk', *Pediatrics*, vol. 100, pp. 1035–9.

Apple, R. D. 1987, *Mothers and Medicine: A Social History of Infant Feeding. 1890–1950*, University of Wisconsin Press, Wisconsin.

Arnup, K. 1990, 'Educating Mothers: Government Advice for Women in the Inter-War Years', in K. Arnup, A. Levesque, & R. Roach Pierson (eds), *Delivering Motherhood: Maternal Ideologies and Practices in the 19th and 20th Centuries*, Routledge, London, pp. 190–210.

Aronson, N. 1982, 'Nutrition as a Social Problem: A Case Study of Entrepreneurial Strategy in Science', *Social Problems*, vol. 29, pp. 474–87.

Bailey, V. F. & Sherriff, J. 1993, 'Reasons for Early Cessation of Breastfeeding in Women from Lower Socio-economic Groups in Perth, Western Australia', *Breastfeeding Review*, vol. 11, pp. 390–3.

British Paediatric Association 1994, 'Is Breastfeeding Beneficial in the UK? Statement of the Standing Committee on Nutrition', *Archives of the Disabled Child*, vol. 71, pp. 376–80.

Carter, P. 1995, *Feminism, Breasts and Breast Feeding*, Macmillan, Basingstoke, UK.

Carter, S. 1995, 'Boundaries of Danger and Uncertainty: An Analysis of the Technological Culture of Risk Assessment', in J. Gabe (ed.), *Medicine, Health and Risk*, Blackwell, Oxford, pp. 133–50.

Chunn, D. 1990, 'Boys Will Be Men, Girls Will Be Mothers', in P. Adler & P. Adler (eds), *Sociological Studies of Child Development*, JAI Press, Greenwich, Connecticut, pp. 87–110.

Cooper, P., Murray, L., & Stein, A. 1993, 'Psychosocial Factors Associated with Early Termination of Breast Feeding', *Journal of Psychosomatic Research*, vol. 37, pp. 171–6.

Department of Health 1994, *Weaning and the Weaning Diet: Report of the Working Group on the Weaning Diet of the Committee on Medical Aspects of Food Policy* (no. 45), Her Majesty's Stationery Office, London.

Department of Health 1999, *Saving Lives: Our Healthier Nation*, The Stationery Office, London.

Department of Health and Social Security 1988, *Present Day Practice in Infant Feeding: Third Report* (no. 32), Her Majesty's Stationery Office, London.

DHSS—*see* Department of Health and Social Security.

DOH—*see* Department of Health.

Douglas, M. 1990, 'Risk as a Forensic Resource', *Daedalus*, Fall, pp. 1–16.

Fildes, V. 1992, 'Breast Feeding in London, 1905–19', *Journal of Biosocial Science*, vol. 24, pp. 53–70.

Florack, E. 1984, 'Breast-feeding, Bottle-feeding and Related Factors', *Acta Paediatrica Scandanavica*, vol. 73, pp. 789–95.

Ford, R. P. K., Taylor, B. J. & Mitchell, E. A. 1993, 'Breastfeeding and the Risk of Sudden Infant Death Syndrome', *International Journal of Epidemiology*, vol. 22, pp. 885–90.

Foster, F., Lader, D., & Cheesbrough, S. 1997, *Infant Feeding 1995*, The Stationery Office, London.

Giddens, A. 1991, *Modernity and Self-identity: Self and Society in the Late Modern Age*, Polity, Cambridge.

Golding, J. 1993, *Breastfeeding and Sudden Infant Death Syndrome: Report of the Chief Medical Officer's Expert Group on the Sleeping Position of Infants and Cot Death*, Her Majesty's Stationery Office, London.

Greco, M. 1993, 'Psychomatic Subjects and the "Duty to be Well": Personal Agency within Medical Rationality', *Economy and Society*, vol. 22, 357–72.

Hamlyn, B., Brookner, S., Oleinikova, K. & Wands, S. 2002, *Infant Feeding 2000: A Survey Conducted on Behalf of the Department of Health*, The Scottish Executive, Social Services and Public Safety in Northern Ireland, & The Stationery Office, London.

Hartley, B. & O'Connor, M. 1996, 'Evaluation of the "Best-start" Breast Feeding Education Program', *Archives of Pediatric and Adolescent Medicine*, vol. 150, pp. 868–71.

Hills-Bonczyk, S., Tromiczak, K., Avery, M., Potter, S., Savik, K. & Duckett, L. 1994, 'Women's Experiences of Breast Feeding Longer than 12 Months', *Birth*, vol. 21, pp. 206–12.

Hitchcock, N. E. & Coy, J. F. 1988, 'Infant Feeding Practices in Western Australia and Tasmania: A Joint Survey, 1984–85', *Medical Journal of Australa*, vol. 148, pp. 114–47.

Howie, P. W., Forsyth, J. S., Ogsten, S. A., Clarke, A., Florey, C. du V. 1990 'Protective Effect of Breast Feeding Against Infection', *British Medical Journal*, vol. 100, pp. 11–16.

Jamieson, L. & Toynbee, C. 1990, 'Shifting Patterns of Parental Authority, 1900–1980', in H. Corr & L. Jamieson (eds), *Politics of Everyday Life: Continuity and Change in Work and the Family*, Macmillan, London, pp. 86–113.

Kendall-Tackett, K. & Sugarman, M. 1995, 'The Social Consequences of Long-term Breast Feeding', *Journal of Human Lactation*, vol. 11, pp. 179–83.

Lawrence, R. 1995, 'The Clinician's Role in Teaching Proper Infant Feeding Techniques', *Journal of Pediatrics*, vol. 126 (supp.), pp. 112–17.

Lewis, J. 1990, '"Motherhood Issues" in Late Nineteenth and Twentieth Centuries', in K. Arnup, A. Levesque & R. Roach Pierson (eds), *Delivering Motherhood: Maternal Ideologies and Practices in the 19th and 20th Centuries*, Routledge, London, pp. 1–19.

Lowe, T. 1993, 'Regional and Socio-economic Variations in the Duration of Breastfeeding in Victoria', *Breastfeeding Review*, vol. 2, pp. 312–15.

Lupton, D. 1993, 'Risk as Moral Danger: The Social and Political Functions of Risk Discourse in Public Health', *International Journal of Health Services*, vol. 23, pp. 425–35.

—— 1996, *Food, the Body and the Self*, Sage, London.

Maher, V. 1992, 'Breast Feeding in Cross-cultural Perspective: Paradoxes and Proposals', in V. Maher (ed.) *The Anthropology of Breast Feeding: Natural Law or Social Construct*, Berg, Oxford, pp. 1–36.

Marshall, H. 1991, 'The Social Construction of Motherhood: An Analysis of Childcare and Parenting Manuals', in A. Phoenix, A. Woollett & E. Lloyd (eds), *Motherhood: Meanings, Practices and Ideologies*, Sage, London, pp. 66–85.

Martin, J. 1978, *Infant Feeding 1975: Attitudes and Practices in England and Wales*, Office of Population Censuses and Surveys, London.

Martin, J. & Monk, J. 1982, *Infant Feeding 1980*, Office of Population Censuses and Surveys, London.

Martin, J. & White, A. 1988, *Infant Feeding 1985*, Office of Population Censuses and Surveys, London.

Murphy, E. 1999, '"Breast is Best": Infant Feeding Decisions and Maternal Deviance', *Sociology of Health and Illness*, vol. 21, pp. 187–208.

—— 2000, 'Risk, Responsibility and Rhetoric in Infant Feeding', *Journal of Contemporary Ethnography*, vol. 29, pp. 291–325.

Murphy, E., Parker, S. & Phipps, C. 1998a, 'Competing Agendas in Infant Feeding', *British Food Journal*, vol. 100, no. 3, pp. 128–32.

—— 1998b, 'Food Choices for Babies', in A. Murcott (ed.), *The Nation's Diet: The Social Science of Food Choice*, Addison Wesley Longman, London, pp. 250–66.

National Health and Medical Research Council 2003, *Dietary Guidelines for Children and Adolescents in Australia, Incorporating the Infant Feeding Guidelines for Health Workers*, Ausinfo, Canberra.

Nettleton, S. 1997, 'Governing the Risky Self: How to Become Healthy, Wealthy and Wise' in Petersen, A. & Bunton, R. (eds), *Foucault, Health and Medicine*, Routledge, London, pp. 207–22.

Newson, J. & Newson, E. 1963, *Patterns of Infant Care in an Urban Community*, Penguin Books, Harmondsworth.

Oakley, A. 1979, *Becoming a Mother*, Martin Robertson, Oxford.

Office on Women's Health 2001, *Breastfeeding* <www.4women.gov/Breastfeeding/>.

Ogden, J. (1995) 'Psychosocial Theory and the Creation of the Risky Self', *Social Science and Medicine*, vol. 40, 409–15.

Palmer, N. 1985, 'Breastfeeding: The Australian Situation', *Journal of Food and Nutrition*, vol. 42, pp. 13–18.

Pesssl, M. 1996, 'Are We Creating Our Own Breast Feeding Mythology?', *Journal of Human Lactation*, vol. 12, pp. 271–2.

Petersen, A. 1997, 'Risk, Governance and the New Public Health', in A. Petersen & R. Bunton (eds), *Foucault, Health and Medicine*, Routledge, London, pp. 189–206.

Phoenix, A. & Woollett, A. 1991, 'Motherhood: Social Construction, Politics and Psychology' in A. Phoenix, A. Woollett & E. Lloyd. (eds), *Motherhood: Meanings, Practices and Ideologies*, Sage, London, pp. 13–27.

Piper, S. & Parks, P. 1996, 'Predicting the Duration of Lactation: Evidence from a National Survey', *Birth*, vol. 23, pp. 7–12.

Quandt, S. 1986, 'Patterns of Variation in Breast Feeding Predictors', *Social Science and Medicine*, vol. 23, pp. 445–53.

Ribbens McCarthy, J., Edwards, R. & Gillies, V. 2000, *Parenting and Step-parenting: Contemporary Moral Tales*, Occasional paper, Centre for Family and Household Research, Issue 4.

Rose, N. 1996, 'Governing the Enterprising Self', in P. Heelas & P. Morris (eds), *The Values of the Enterprise Culture*, Routledge, London.

Ryan, A. S., Wenjun, Z. & Acosta, A. 2002, 'Breastfeeding Continues to Increase into the New Millenium', *Pediatrics*, vol. 110, pp. 1103–9.

Saarinen, U. M. & Kajosaari, M. 1995 'Breast Feeding as Prophylaxis Against Atopic Disease: Prospective Follow-up Study until 17 Years Old', *Lancet*, vol. 346, pp. 1065–9.

Salt, M., Law, C., Bull, A. & Osmond, C. 1994, 'Determinants of Breast Feeding in Salisbury and Durham', *Journal of Public Health Medicine*, vol. 16, pp. 291–5.

Scott, M. & Lyman, S. 1963, 'Accounts', *American Sociological Review*, vol. 33, pp. 46–62.

Simopoulos, A. & Grave, G. 1984, 'Factors Associated with the Choice and Duration of Infant-feeding Practice: Task Force on Infant-feeding Practices', *Pediatrics*, vol. 74 (supp.), pp. 603–14.

Virtanen, S. M., Rasanen, L. & Aro, A. 1991 'Infant Feeding in Finnish Children 7 Years of Age with Newly Diagnosed IDDM', *Diabetes Care*, vol. 13, pp. 415–17.

Webb, B. & Stimson, G. 1976, 'People's Accounts of Medical Encounters', in M. Wadsworth & D. Robinson (eds), *Studies in Everyday Medical Life*, Martin Robertson, London.

White, A., Freeth, S. & O'Brien, M. 1992, *Infant Feeding 1990*, Her Majesty's Stationery Office, London.

Wright, H. & Walker, P. 1983, 'Prediction of Duration of Breast Feeding in Primiparae', *Journal of Epidemiology and Community Health*, vol. 37, pp. 89–94.

10

The Government of the Table: Nutrition Expertise and the Social Organisation of Family Food Habits

John Coveney

Overview

- How have changing social attitudes towards childhood affected nutrition advice about children's eating patterns?
- In what ways can nutrition advice be seen as a form of power?
- Does current child nutrition advice result in positive outcomes for children and parents?

In this chapter, the area of child nutrition is analysed in relation to changing views about family life in Australia over the past 60 years. I look at how the phenomenon of 'picky' or 'fussy' eaters—something largely absent from earlier discourses about the feeding of children—emerged as a problem for parents and professionals in the late twentieth century. I situate the changing attitudes towards the feeding of children in a wider context in which modern social views accord children the status of citizens with rights, responsibilities, and autonomy. Indeed, the new social space that children occupy has been reproduced and reinforced in the advice of experts such as nutritionists. I also examine how the importance of 'food choice' in the eating habits of children is especially foregrounded in texts that advise parents on how to feed the family. Interviews with families are used to reveal the tensions that the new views of childhood—especially the notions of rights, independence, and autonomy—bring to the process of feeding children. The chapter suggests that the feeding of children is made problematic by new social definitions of 'good' parenting that privilege independence for children, a belief that food and mealtimes should be enjoyable, and an imperative that food for children should be nutritious. This problematisation does not necessarily disempower parents. On the contrary, it provides them with yet more opportunities to establish codes of conduct, informed by expertise, for the management of children's feeding behaviour.

Key terms

ethics
ethical responsibilities
Foucaultian perspective
government
normality
state
technologies of government

Introduction

The Australian National Health and Medical Research Council's guidelines on healthy diets for children (NHMRC 2003) represent the latest in a long line of advice from health and nutrition experts about the kinds of food that infants and children should eat. Indeed, expert advice on what children should eat has a long history, the Australian branch of which has been well documented by Nancy Hitchcock (1989a, 1989b). By contrast, expert recommendations about the management of children's social behaviour in relation to food—for example, how to cope with 'difficult' or 'fussy' eaters—has a much shorter history. To be sure, books, articles, and papers on children's nutrition published early last century often contained sections in which these matters were briefly discussed. This advice, however, was quite different, in terms of both content and detail, from that provided today. Current manuals on parenting contain information designed to prepare parents for, and advise them about, what now appears to be an inevitable aspect of childhood: antisocial habits associated with food and feeding difficulties. This is not to say, of course, that children have only recently become so-called 'fussy' or 'picky' eaters. Rather, it is to say that the recognition of this phenomenon as a 'problem'—and its necessary management—has become part of expert advice to parents only quite recently.

The role of the expert in advising parents about the social management of children is not, of course, confined to feeding. According to Nikolas Rose (1990, p. 129), family life in general, and parenting in particular, has become governed by expertise. Expert advice now infuses and shapes the personal investments of parents, especially the ways in which they regulate and evaluate their actions and their goals. Through this process, expert opinion not only informs parents but also provides them with an index of what is considered to be the 'right' way of managing children. Expertise thus becomes the benchmark against which parental behaviour is judged by others and, importantly, by the parents themselves. In other words, parents know they are doing a 'good' job by reference to expert opinion. Expertise outlines and facilitates the production of '**normality**' in childhood, which, in the end, is what most parents aspire to for their children. The popularity of books, journals, articles, and Internet sites concerned with parenting skills is an indication of these aspirations. In trying to understand this popularity, we should not see parents as cultural or 'judgemental dopes' (Heritage 1987) who are beguiled by expert advice against their will or better nature. On the contrary, we should recognise that parents actively seek out this information in order to better handle the complex and often challenging process of bringing up children. And even when parents do not find expert advice especially useful, such advice is still recognised as having a certain validity. Comments like 'They say you should [do such and such], but I find that …' are frequently heard from parents, indicating the recognised authority with which experts speak.

It is the changing nature of 'doing it right', especially with regard to the feeding of children, that is the topic of this chapter and that demonstrates the emergence of the social management of eating, with its inherent problems in modern family settings. The subject is examined in a number of ways. First, expert advice on the feeding of children from earlier this century is compared with that available today. Second, this advice is situated within the larger context of the changes in Australian social life with respect to the family—especially attitudes to raising children—over the last 60 years. This comparison illustrates the new considerations that parents must take into account in relation to the feeding of children. Third, in order to ground the recognition of these changes—and the tensions they bring—in concrete experience, I examine interviews with families in which the feeding of children is discussed.

Setting an analytical context: Government and the family

The theoretical framework of the analysis presented here uses a **Foucaultian perspective** drawn from Michel Foucault, especially as his work has been used by Donzelot (1980) and Rose (1990). Briefly, this work acknowledges that the development of the 'modern family' (small, private, independent) began in the early part of the nineteenth century. This development culminated in the **state** making possible certain advantages and privileges for families that went beyond the provision of regulation and legislation. As Rose says, '"Familialization" was crucial to the means whereby personal capacities and conducts could be socialised, shaped and maximised in a manner that accorded with the moral and political principles of liberal societies' (1990, p. 126).

In this process, however, the state should not necessarily be seen as a centralised bureaucracy from which power emanates. As Rose and Miller (1992) note, it is more productive to analyse political power from the point of view of **government** than of state apparatus. The difference is that government may be understood as a range of diffuse practices: 'tactics, strategies, techniques, programmes, dreams and aspirations of those authorities who shape the beliefs and conduct of the population' (Nettleton 1991, p. 99). As Rose and Miller point out, 'in Europe for many centuries economic activity was regulated, order was maintained, laws promulgated and enforced, assistance provided for the sick and needy, morality inculcated, if at all, through practices that had little to do with the state' (1992, p. 176). In other words, a range of organisations operating outside the apparatus and bureaucracy of the state have been, and still are, responsible for the **technologies of government**.

To give an example, much of the work in the early formation of the domesticated modern family was undertaken through philanthropic activity, especially that concerning health, welfare, and hygiene (Donzelot 1980, p. 55). This assistance was almost always conditional upon families adopting 'good' moral principles, especially marriage, good housekeeping, sobriety, and the moral supervision of children (Rose 1990, p. 127). As such, charitable organisations often worked more closely with families who had middle class tendencies and aspirations. Even in the working classes, it was the 'deserving' families—those who, despite economic and social hardships, displayed certain moral principles—who were the main targets of middle class philanthropy. Charitable organisations would not assist the 'undeserving' poor, whose plight was a product of 'drunkenness, laziness, roving dispositions, and dishonesty' (Finch 1993, p. 44).

Central to the technologies of government is knowledge—expertise or 'know-how'. This knowledge can be applied in programs that specify objects to be governed or managed and the uses to which these objects are to be put. By laying claim to certain bodies of knowledge, programs map out the problems that are to be addressed. Thus programs, through knowledge, become problematising activities that attempt to direct or control the behaviour of others. It is through such technologies of government that power is exercised. As Foucault says, 'power and knowledge directly imply one another; there is no power relationship without the correlative constitution of a field of knowledge, nor any knowledge that does not presuppose and constitute at the same time power relations' (Foucault 1979, p. 27). However, it is important to note that relationships of power are not necessarily negative. Foucault argued that power can be positive: 'It [power] needs to be considered as a productive network which runs through the whole social body, much more than as a negative instance whose function is to repress' (Foucault 1980, p. 119).

One aspect of the productive nature of power is the creation of socially desirable or ethical categories. We can see this in the development of family ideals during the last century, when expert advice from philanthropic organisations was available in the areas of health, hygiene, and 'normality'. The latter quality was especially important for the promotion of happy, healthy family lives. 'Normal' families were those that had high standards of ethical conduct. Unsociable behaviour—debauchery, viciousness, masturbation, insanity, and so on—was considered to be detrimental to the health and harmony of family life (Rose 1990, p. 128). But normality was not merely an observation; it was a valuation that defined a situation as 'that which should be', and the justification of which was increasingly made according to medical, psychological, and other scientific knowledge. A number of proto-state services were established in this way. It was, for example, through the establishment of categories of 'normality' that child health and welfare services first made an appearance earlier this century. In Australia, as in other countries, the early child welfare movement began as a philanthropic venture (Reiger 1986, p. 130). Attendance at the infant welfare clinic—then as now—became an exercise in examining children against a range of normal criteria for feeding, growth and development, and behaviour.

Today it is the reification of what is considered to be 'normal'—in family life in general, and childhood in particular—that imposes on parents an obligation (and fosters in them a commitment) to produce hygienic homes and to raise happy, healthy children. It is in the attainment of 'normality' that parents are judged by others and by themselves in terms of doing the 'right thing'. And it is the quest for the 'normal', especially in relation to child-rearing, which requires parents to seek out expert advice for reassurance or correction of parenting practices. It is important to stress again that it would be a mistake to view this analysis of the construction of the modern family as implying some kind of domination or repression on the part of the state. Quite the opposite: parents actively seek out expert advice about the 'proper way' of raising children, and they do not do so under any 'false consciousness'. They do it as a way of fulfilling their **ethical responsibilities** as parents. We should regard **ethics** as the body of obligations that individuals feel compelled to fulfil, especially in relation to moral codes defined by their social groups. Foucault sees the development of ethics as a 'process in which the individual delimits that part of himself [sic] that will form the object of his moral practice, defines his position relative to the precepts he will follow, and decides on a certain mode of being that will serve as his moral goal. And this requires him to act upon himself, to monitor, test, improve, and transform himself' (Foucault 1992, p. 28).

Moral conduct has, since the seventeenth century, become increasingly governed by expertise in the human sciences. We should thus understand the expert advice examined in this chapter as a form of 'control at a distance' (Rose & Miller 1992); it is a kind of control that requires families to be independent from, and yet cooperative with, the state. This control functions through the production and valorisation of specific forms of conduct, developed and outlined by experts, to which parents will want to aspire in order to recognise themselves as 'good', 'responsible', and 'committed' mothers and fathers, thus fulfilling their ethical responsibilities.

The changing nature of family life

Reporting on a survey of Australian family life undertaken in 1954, Harold Fallding noted that parents at this time saw themselves as pioneering a new era of child-rearing. This new form of parenting had four main elements (Fallding 1957, p. 71):

- a belief that one had to be equipped with knowledge in order to deal with children effectively, not simply repeat the methods used by one's own parents;
- a belief that one should be affectionate and companionable towards children, not the remote authorities that parents had been in previous generations;
- a desire to produce a self-regulated rather than an obedient child; and
- an aim to ensure the full development of the child's capacities rather than prepare him [sic] to be devoted to duty.

Fallding notes that, compared with the position of children in families before World War II, the status of post-war childhood had radically changed. Blind obedience was replaced by cooperation and negotiation between parents and children.

These changes in family life are very noticeable in the different obligations parents had before and after World War II in relation to the feeding of children. We can examine these changes by looking at the expert advice given to parents on the 'correct' ways of feeding children. In the early part of the twentieth century, advice for parents on feeding children focused almost exclusively on food rules and regimes. *The Australian Mothercraft Book* (Mothers and Babies' Health Association 1938), used by infant welfare nurses in the 1930s, lists the sequence in which foods should be introduced into a child's diet upon weaning. Also, special instructions are given on how to 'correctly' cook these foods and how to achieve the 'right' consistency. Specimen diets for older children are also provided, listing those foods that should be given and the times at which they should be offered. However, little is written about the ways in which parents should manage the social arrangement of mealtimes or about how to act if a meal is refused by a child. Another book of the day offering advice about the management of children in the nursery makes this suggestion: 'As a rule it is wise not to coax an unwilling child to take its food … Faddiness about food should in no case be encouraged … The food provided should always be suitable and it should be *assumed that it will be eaten*' (Bennett & Issacs 1931, italics added). Truby King's pre-war book *Feeding and Care of Baby* (1933), which was used extensively by infant welfare nurses in Australia, offers a range of timetables and menus, listing the foods that should be given, but it offers little guidance about the social management of feeding—that is, what to do if food is disliked and refused. King takes a rather 'no nonsense' approach, implicitly assuming that feeding children will be an unproblematic affair.

We should contrast this advice with that given in manuals written in the post-war period, when problems in feeding children started to surface. In his book *Baby and Child Care*, Ben Spock (1955) devotes almost a whole chapter to these feeding problems. Spock starts by noting that 'You don't see feeding problems in puppies or among young humans in places where mothers don't know enough about diet to worry' (1955, p. 448). He continues by stressing the importance of being patient, offering choices, and encouraging independence in eating. As a post-war text on child management, Spock's book stands in stark contrast to those written earlier in so far as feeding children is now a recognised problem. Another topic, that of fatness in children, which was not mentioned to any great degree in earlier texts, is also given special treatment by Spock. He provides advice on how to cope with fat children who 'crave large amounts of rich foods [cakes, biscuits, and pastry]' (p. 457). Obesity in children is now understood as a health problem requiring intervention by parents and doctors. Stressing the difficulties that beset the management of children's weight problems, Spock points out that 'A child has less will-power than an adult. If the mother serves the child less fattening foods it means either that the whole family must go without the richer dishes or that the fat child must be kept from eating the very things his heart craves while the rest of the family enjoy them. There are few fat children reasonable enough to think that's fair' (p. 459).

Note that Spock stresses children's ability to reason and implies that their views should be respected. According to Spock, if a child shows willingness to cooperate in dieting, then he or she should be encouraged to visit the doctor, preferably alone: 'Talking to the doctor, man to man, may give him a feeling of running his own life like a grown up' (p. 459). Essential to Spock's advice, then, is the assumption that reason, independence, and self-regulation in children should be encouraged. Children should not be merely obedient.

The importance of fostering dietary freedom and independence in children becomes explicit in the recommendations of contemporary nutritionists. For example, in her book *The Complete Guide to Feeding Your Child*, Audrey Stewart-Turner (1986) points out that children should be given a choice of nutritious foods to encourage independence in eating. She puts children's capricious attitude to eating on the same footing as the food preferences of adults: 'remember that there are some foods [parents] like to eat more than others or feel like at certain times and not other times!' (p. 67). We are, then, invited to rationalise children's eating behaviours by comparing them with those of adults, who, presumably, know when they are hungry and when they are not and have recognisable and distinct food preferences.

A second example of contemporary advice is a book on child nutrition by Baker and Henry (1987), who recognise that many children are 'picky' eaters. In dealing with this problem, parents should show encouragement rather than use force. According to the authors, negative encounters with food should always be avoided and 'parents should respect children's food preferences and not try to dictate them' (p. 135). A more recent example is the nutrition book by Susan Thompson (1995), which points out that 'Finding the balance between self-expression and freedom on the part of your child, and meeting [parents'] ideas of a healthy diet can be difficult' (p. 14). Thompson paraphrases Ellen Satter—another child nutrition expert—who believes that 'The parent is responsible for what is presented to eat. The child is *responsible* for how much is eaten and even whether he eats' (Satter 1987, italics added). It is the recognition of the right—or responsibility—of children to make choices regarding their diet that is so apparent in modern texts. Such a recognition assumes that children will be accorded a degree of autonomy and social freedom, a notion that is utterly missing from earlier advice by experts.

Part of the rationale for encouraging self-expression and independence in children's food choices is the importance of harmony and happiness when eating. Parents are reminded that a child's happiness around food and eating should be preserved because unpleasant social experiences around food in childhood can lead to eating problems. As Thompson puts it, 'Studies have shown that if parents are rigid and authoritarian about food [amounts], children will lose their ability to control intake. There is a good chance that your child will become overweight, or even underweight if the battle becomes more important than eating' (1995, p. 70). The supposed scientific validity of this advice arises from quasi-experiments in child psychology, the social relevance of which has been questioned (Coveney 2002). However, the argument reaches something of an apogee in the work of Hirschmann and Zaphiropoulos, who, promoting a more child-centred approach to the management of eating, believe that 'by allowing the child to decide when to eat, what to eat, and how much to eat, we can strengthen her self-confidence, self-esteem, and sense of dignity and also avoid the kinds of eating difficulties that have plagued many of us for life' (1985, p. 13). Thus, the social organisation of the feeding of children, mostly taken for granted by experts of an earlier era, now becomes somewhat precarious. It requires sensitivity, so as to avoid rigidity and authoritarianism, the pathological consequences of which have now been established as scientific fact.

To summarise the discussion so far, in modern (i.e. post–World War II) nutrition texts parents have new responsibilities concerning food that explicitly recognise and give importance to an emotional investment in eating. Coping with children's eating habits is now another opportunity for individuals to display prowess in the art of good parenting. This skill is 'in theory intellectually exciting, a test of personal capacities, virtually a profession in its own right; in practice [parenthood] is the site of a constant self-scrutiny and self-evaluation [by the parent] in relation to the norms of responsibility to one's child' (Rose 1990, p. 198). It is through this self-scrutiny of ethical conduct that parents recognise themselves as 'good' mothers and fathers.

However, the concept of children *choosing* food—especially nutritious food—is somewhat problematic, and encouraging self-expression and independence in children comes at a price. Commenting on this, Rosemary Stanton says that 'In Australia and New Zealand, we cannot assume that giving children a free choice of foods will produce an ideally balanced intake of nutrients' (1990, p. 6). Nevertheless, the idea that children should be given certain choices in relation to their diets endures. Stanton continues: 'Whatever your age it makes sense to follow the principles of a balanced diet. With this scheme, nothing is forbidden, but some foods are given a greater or lesser place than others' (p. 8). And yet, the issue of balancing diets and choice in eating is not easily managed. As we have seen, nutrition experts recognise this as 'difficult' because of the need to match the importance of encouraging the child's self-expression with the parent's responsibility to provide a healthy diet. The difficulty of managing this delicate balance has been readily recognised by the food industry, which often promotes certain foods to children as both 'nutritious' and 'enjoyable'. In reality, while many such foods are certainly enjoyable, they are not necessarily nutritious (Australian Consumers Association 1993, p. 21). Thus the freedom to choose—so much a part of the modern consumer ethos—becomes problematic because of the sheer variety of food in the marketplace, and because many foods fall short of current nutritional guidelines. The responsibility now falls to parents, teachers, and others, who are expected to instil in children the notion of 'correct' or 'incorrect' food choices.

Children as citizens

Modern attitudes to food choice did not, of course, arrive unannounced purely in the area of child nutrition. Instead, the recognition given to the new ways in which parents should interact with children can be seen as a manifestation of a new social view of childhood that emerged in the second half of the twentieth century. The growing importance of children in post-war families dramatically influenced their visibility and status. This new status can be seen in a number of developments. For example, in 1959 the United Nations unveiled a *Declaration of the Rights of the Child* (United Nations 1960), which was reformulated and re-released in 1989 as the *United Nations International Convention for the Rights of the Child* (Greenwood 1993). Under this new convention, the Australian government has to report to the United Nations every 2 years on how well it is complying with the convention's principles. The emergence of children's rights in the post-war period required that family life be opened up to closer scrutiny, to ensure that these rights were being respected. The granting of rights to children in effect extended to them a form of citizenship, not in the sense that they could participate in the execution of political power, but in the sense that they had the right to liberty and they had social rights (Rose 1990, p. 122). These rights provided for the exercising of choice by children.

Early-twentieth-century expert discourses on parenting emphasised the importance of avoiding 'molli-coddling' or 'spoiling' children. Frequent parent–child interactions, through play or even just cuddling, were believed to lead to overstimulation of the nervous system, which was thought to be detrimental to proper development (Reiger 1986, p. 148). However, with modern advances in understanding, especially in child psychology, attitudes towards parent–child interaction changed: emotional and cognitive development were to be strongly encouraged through play, discovery, and frequent 'quality' interactions between adults and children. The home itself was believed to be the best place for these activities. The norms of good parenting were predicated less on the amount of discipline and control of children than on the extent to which parents maximised their children's learning and developmental potential: 'With the aid of books, games, toys, records, and other aids now made available for purchase, the intimate environment of the home was to be transformed into a veritable laboratory of cognitive growth' (Rose 1990, p. 196). We might note here that the recognition of children's choice and freedom went hand in hand with the greater economic and material possibilities of the so-called 'boom' after World War II. Choice and variety became key themes in modern consumerism.

On another level, children now had the right to be heard, and they had opinions that were to be taken seriously. The idea of choice and freedom for children in family life was played out in a number of regimes of new parenthood. As we have seen, the eating habits of children became an important site for encouraging the development of choice, self-expression, and eventual independence of children. Thus the notion of choice for children became an important part of family food events.

In the next section I will examine the experiences of individuals who are negotiating the role of parent. On the one hand, this role requires that they provide their children with foods they will enjoy and foods that allow them to display autonomy and self-expression. On the other hand, it requires that they provide a nutritious diet to their children.

A study of family food experiences

This small study involved twelve families with young children from different parts of Adelaide, Australia. Although these families were randomly enlisted in this study, they are not presented here as representative of all families. They are, instead, used to illustrate examples of family life concerned with food. The material presented here was collected and compiled in the following way. In each family, the father and mother were interviewed—sometimes together, sometimes individually. An interview schedule was developed to guide the discussions with participants. The schedule consisted of open-ended questions about everyday routines concerning food preparation, shopping, and other aspects of family food decision-making. All the interviews were audio-taped (with permission) and transcribed. All transcriptions were reviewed and summarised with field notes, so that for each family an overall description of the couple's responses was produced. The interview transcripts were then 'thematised' using NUDIST (version 3.0.4, QSR Melbourne), a software package for handling qualitative data. Reported here are some of the themes that emerged—regarding the parents' food experiences during their own childhood compared with those of today, the management of social arrangements of family meals, and the obligations of parents in relation to nutrition and health.

The first extract discusses the differences between arrangements in family eating when the parents were children and those of today:

ANGUS: I think when I was a kid I was served meat and two veg …

HILARY: The same thing every night virtually.

ANGUS: And I was expected to pretty much eat it, and if I did not eat it I wouldn't get dessert. And that would be legit, like if I didn't eat it I wouldn't get dessert. Whereas these days … you serve meat and two veg or three veg and you say 'If you don't eat it you won't get dessert' and they don't eat it but they still get dessert. And it's not just us …

HILARY: But we're not strict like, we're just not strict.

ANGUS: It's not just us that are soft, I think it's just like everything shifts to the left, you know, society is just a bit more malleable whereas when I was a kid it was a bit more black and white.

These comments are typical; many respondents remembered childhood mealtimes to be more restricted than those of their own children. Many also remembered the hardships that their parents endured, with money often in short supply. This required that food be eaten and not wasted. The lack of mealtime rigidity that now exists for these families ('We are just not strict') may therefore result from a more affluent society, in which choice is not only desirable but a material possibility. In some cases, current family food arrangements were influenced by parents' own food experiences as children, as the following extracts indicate:

GREG: Well I think I quite often believe that a lot that I went through and was made to eat and whatever, that I don't believe you've got to … modern day children, or my children should not be forced to do that.

WENDY: OK, when I was growing up you ate whatever you got the first time, you didn't have to ask for seconds but you finished what was on your plate. Anyway my mother would serve this God-awful stuff, stewed tomatoes on toast with cheese, and it's nauseating … and we would have this I would say at least twice a month, and we had to eat it and I swore I would never do that to my children and I don't.

However, the different expectations parents have of mealtimes today are also the result of a change in parental attitudes; as Angus said, 'society is just a bit more malleable [today] whereas when I was a kid it was a bit more black and white'. Parents today are expected to be more flexible and to offer their children certain freedoms. The extent of the change may be judged by the influence children have over the family menu. This influence is brought out in the following extracts:

STELLA: No. I had virtually no say in what meals went on the table as a child, whereas my kids do have a say in what does go on the table.

GREG: We [parents] try to I suppose change our own [food preferences] around to suit the children always.

Keeping the children happy and providing an enjoyable meal for them was a priority for many of these parents. Mealtimes together were expected to be occasions when the family came together to share not only food but also pleasant experiences. And respondents often justified the choice and freedom they gave to children by reference to a need to avoid unpleasant experiences:

WENDY: I don't see turning the mealtimes into a battleground anyway.

DIANA: I always try to cook something that I know that [husband] is going to get a good meal and at least [son] will have something that he will like.

Sometimes, in order to ensure that mealtimes were positive occasions, parents specifically catered for the food preferences of children and prepared a separate meal for them, even if this meant extra work for the cook:

ALISON: It's a nuisance. It's a great nuisance but I tend to do the things, when I'm cooking two separate things, I'll do things that I know the children will definitely eat. So at least I don't feel I've gone to all this trouble to do two separate things and find that they don't eat what I gave them anyway.

JACK: He [son] has been spoilt by his grandmother and [mother]; he quite often gets different things cooked for him because he doesn't like this and he doesn't like that.

For these families, then, the principles that informed meal preparation and presentation were based on the importance of providing children with a certain degree of choice and freedom. They were also informed by the need to provide a happy and harmonious environment in which the family can eat, thus avoiding a 'battleground' at mealtimes. A third obligation—that of providing nutritious foods—was often believed to be a necessary mealtime consideration. However, because this obligation often jeopardised harmony and choice, it was seen as problematic:

ROSE: We try, I mean if you can get them to eat [healthy food]. Yeah, I would like them to eat meat and three vegetables every night, but they don't always.

CASSIE: I mean, you go to the trouble of trying to prepare something different and something nutritious possibly, you know, and you sort of think 'God, this is a waste of time'.

Some parents took a broader view of the problems that confronted them in feeding the family. Below, Alison recognises the change in the status of children and the way that it has been cultivated in a number of institutions, especially the school.

ALISON: I've been trying to work out why [our children are difficult to feed], and I suspect that they seem to grow up a lot more quickly these days and I think partly because school encourages them to think a lot more for themselves and they are taught that they have rights as children and so they question what we tell them far more, and that includes things like what they're going to eat and what they're not going to eat and how they're going to eat it and where.

As Alison says, children's rights are dealt with explicitly at school, thereby providing children with notions of autonomy and choice. In the next extract, May, who had arrived in Australia from Vietnam 10 years earlier, contrasts the attitudes to children in Australia with those in Vietnam:

MAY: Maybe I [take notice of my children] because I think Vietnamese people you know, their children, when they upset about parent they don't want to say [anything] about them, only keep inside. Because now the children learn Australian school they have their opinion and I think I have to hear [pauses] listen to them, you know; in Vietnam parents very rarely listen to the children.

INTERVIEWER: Is that right?

MAY: Yeah, the children only do what the parent say [and] they have to obey, or have to do anything that the parent wants them to do, you know, and now maybe my children is better than in Vietnam.

Children in Australia are thus constructed through discourses of freedom and choice, and May judged this preferable to the position of children (as she saw it) in Vietnam. She makes the point that children now have to be listened to; their views have to be considered. Autonomy and choice not only construct children as modern subjects, but also assist in the production of 'good parents'—ones who show the right ethical concern for their children's views. The relationship between views on the 'correct' way of feeding children and views on 'good' parenting was demonstrated recently in a study by Heather Morton and colleagues (1996). Mothers of two-year-olds considered themselves to be 'good' parents if, first, they gave their children the 'right' foods and, second, if the children ate with visible pleasure and enjoyment. Parental responsibilities concerning the provision of family foods are, then, informed by what is believed to be 'right'. Mealtimes and menus that are influenced by children's preferences should not therefore be seen as passive capitulation by parents. Instead, they should be considered as examples of parents actively seeking to do the 'right' thing by implementing child-rearing strategies based on negotiation and cooperation, which are designed to encourage autonomy and independence in children and promote happy and harmonious eating occasions.

Conclusion

This chapter set out to examine the way that nutrition advice has mirrored certain social expectations in family life over the course of the last century. It looked at the changing nature of expert advice on how to feed children over the last 60 years and has linked these changes to larger social trends in which the relationship between children and parents has undergone a profound change. The influence of expert knowledge has been granted an important role in this analysis, since changes in social attitudes have generally followed the standards and norms set by experts, whose knowledge is a 'technology of government'. Expert knowledge informs everyday ethical conduct by specifying what are the 'right' and the 'wrong' things to do: it provides the network—the power relationship—within which people act. The area of parenting, which is thoroughly imbued with the psychology of child development and family relationships, is a good example of this kind of power, and the examination of expert advice allows for an understanding of the way that specific acts are articulated so as to shape the desires and aspirations of parents. Of course, parents do not always do what experts say. What is suggested here is that expert discourse, often reified by science, becomes the moral fabric out of which 'normality' is fashioned. This is not to say, however, that expertise is wrong or ill-informed: this chapter has attempted to describe what is, not what should be. It is explanatory rather than critical or judgmental.

The interviews with families reported in this chapter highlighted a number of changes regarding what is considered 'normal' and the labile nature of social phenomena. Participants clearly articulated the changes in family eating habits and the increasing centrality of children. The rigid and often authoritarian family food practices that these parents experienced as children were entirely consistent with the expert advice of the time. Less well articulated—though still identifiable—were the parents' reasons for changing to a more flexible approach to family meals. Statements like 'We are just not strict' and phrases such as 'gone soft' highlight the way that parenting has undergone a change in direction. The new approach, which recognises the need for self-expression and freedom in childhood, assumes that children have autonomy and gives them responsibility for choosing to eat or not to eat. As shown earlier, this is either explicit or implicit in the advice of experts, who are both reflecting and reinforcing the new approaches to raising children. In reality, however, granting children some independence can often be problematic, since the training of children in proper dietary habits can be fraught with difficulties. It is especially difficult for parents to get their children to follow a healthy diet while still providing happy, positive mealtimes. The modern way out of this dilemma is not the traditional authoritarian approach, the pathological consequences of which have been outlined by experts. On the contrary, as in other areas of family difficulty, parents are encouraged to negotiate and reason with children. Such practices are, in fact, part of the role of today's 'good' parent: the listener, the reflective adviser, the 'sounding board' for children's thoughts, desires, and beliefs (Gordon 1975).

The area of child nutrition, then, provides a way of understanding the process by which social priorities influence nutrition advice. The production of children as self-reflecting, self-regulating individuals is encouraged through allowing them to make some choices about their diets. But nutrition expertise can also be seen to inform cultural practice by virtue of the fact that it defines which foods are 'good'. Expertise—in its many guises—thus produces 'good' parents: ones who can recognise themselves as having acquired the modern skills of parenting, in which enjoyment, health, and, importantly, choice are central to the management of feeding the family. As this chapter has shown, this societal development is a relatively recent phenomenon, and can be understood through a cultural analysis of 'good food' and the 'good child'.

Summary of main points

- Social attitudes to childhood have changed over the last 60 years, such that children are now expected to have choice, autonomy, and independence.
- The changing expectations of childhood are reflected in and reinforced by modern advice from nutrition experts about how children's eating habits should be managed.
- Expert advice on feeding the family can be analysed in terms of its government of daily conduct or ethics.
- Applying Foucault's ideas, we can regard expert knowledge on nutrition as a form of power.
- As an example of Foucaultian power, nutrition advice can be seen as positive and productive in that it outlines some of the ethical responsibilities of parents, or the proper and correct ways of behaving.

Discussion questions

1 What are the advantages of analysing the function of the state as 'technologies of government' rather than as a centralised bureaucratic power?
2 Apart from nutritionists, who may have been important in dispersing ideas to parents regarding the proper management of the feeding of children?
3 Brief mention was made in this chapter of the role of the food industry in the provision of food directed at children. Comment further on the sociological impact of food industry's practices in this area.
4 What are the advantages and disadvantages of considering children as 'citizens', especially in terms of their having independence and autonomy?
5 Professional knowledge and expertise is often regarded as superior to lay knowledge, especially in areas like child-rearing. How might professionals be better informed than they currently are about what parents think about child nutrition? What would be the benefits of understanding how parents view parenting practices?

Further investigation

1 Contrast Foucault's view of power, as described in this chapter, with that of a more traditional position in social theory (for example, a

Marxist position). Highlight the implicit assumptions of each position. Comment on the explanatory possibilities that each position provides for the social actor.

2 Compare the information and advice provided by experts on the feeding of children before and after World War II. How might the greater material wealth of families have influenced attitudes to child-rearing?

3 This chapter has combined historical data and empirical data collected through interviews. Discuss the current debates about the collection of qualitative research data, in particular the 'crisis of representation' and the 'crisis of legitimation' (see Altheide & Johnson 1994). How are the solutions proposed expected to overcome some of the purported problems of qualitative research?

Further reading and web resources

Books

Charles, N. & Kerr, M. 1988, *Women, Food and Families*, Manchester University Press, Manchester.

Coveney, J. 2000, *Food, Morals and Meanings: The Pleasure and Anxiety of Eating*, Routledge, London.

Donzelot, J. 1980, *The Policing of Families*, Hutchinson, London.

Rose, N. 1990, *Governing the Soul: The Shaping of the Private Self*, Routledge, London.

Articles

Altheide, D. & Johnson, J. 1994, 'Criteria for Assessing Interpretive Validity in Qualitative Research', in N. Denzin & Y. Lincoln (eds), *The Handbook of Qualitative Research*, Sage, Thousand Oaks, California.

Coveney, J. 2002, 'What does the Research on Families and Food Tell Us?', *Nutrition and Dietetics*, vol. 59, no. 2, pp. 113–19.

Nettleton, S. 1991, 'Wisdom, Diligence and Teeth: Discursive Practice and the Creation of Mothers', *Sociology of Health and Illness*, vol. 13, pp. 98–111.

Rose, N. & Miller, P. 1992, 'Political Power beyond the State: Problematics of Government', *British Journal of Sociology*, vol. 43, no. 2, pp. 173–205.

Web sites

Foucault Info: www.foucault.info/

Governmentality.com: www.governmentality.com/

Michel Foucault Resources (by Clare O'Farrell): www.qut.edu.au/edu/cpol/foucault/

References

Altheide, D. & Johnson, J. 1994, 'Criteria for Assessing Interpretive Validity in Qualitative Research', in N. Denzin & Y. Lincoln (eds), *The Handbook of Qualitative Research*, Sage, Thousand Oaks, California.

Australian Consumers Association 1993, 'Fruit Substitutes for Children', *Choice Magazine*, vol. 34, no. 3, pp. 21–3.

Baker, S. & Henry, R. 1987, *Parents' Guide to Nutrition: Healthy Eating from Birth through Adolescence*, Addison-Wesley, Reading, Massachusetts.

Bennett, V. & Issacs, S. 1931, *Health and Education in the Nursery*, George Routledge & Sons, London.

Coveney, J. 2002, 'What does the Research on Families and Food Tell Us?', *Nutrition and Dietetics*, vol. 59, no. 2, pp. 113–19.

Donzelot, J. 1980, *The Policing of Families*, Hutchinson, London.

Fallding, H. 1957, 'Inside the Australian Family', in A. Elkin (ed.), *Marriage and the Family in Australia*, Angus & Robertson, Sydney.

Finch, L. 1993, *The Classing Gaze: Sexuality, Class and Surveillance*, Allen & Unwin, Sydney.

Foucault, M. 1979, *Discipline and Punish: The Birth of the Modern Prison*, Peregrine Books (Penguin), London.

—— 1980, 'Truth and Power', in C. Gordon (ed.), *Power/Knowledge: Selected Interviews and Other Writings 1972–1977*, Pantheon Books, New York.

—— 1992, *The History of Sexuality: The Use of Pleasure*, vol. 2, Penguin Books, Harmondsworth.

Gordon T. 1975, *Parent Effectiveness Training: The Tested New Way to Raise Responsible Children*, New American Library, New York.

Greenwood, A. 1993, *Children's Rights: The United Nations Convention on the Rights of the Child*, Australian Early Childhood Association, Canberra.

Heritage, J. 1987, 'Ethnomethodology', in A. Giddens & J. Turner (eds), *Social Action Today*, Stanford University Press, Stanford, California.

Hirschmann, J. & Zaphiropoulos, L. 1985, *Solve Your Child's Eating Problems*, Fawsett Columbine, New York.

Hitchcock, N. 1989a, 'Infant Feeding in Australia: An Historical Perspective Part 1: 1788–1900', *Australian Journal of Nutrition and Dietetics*, vol. 46, pp. 62–6.

—— 1989b, 'Infant Feeding in Australia: An Historical Perspective Part 2: 1900–1988', *Australian Journal of Nutrition and Dietetics*, vol. 46, pp. 102–8.

King, T. 1933, *Feeding and Caring of Baby*, Macmillan & Co., London.

Morton, H., Santich, B., & Worsley, T. 1996, 'Mothers' Perception on the Eating Habits of Two-year-olds: A Pilot Study', *Australian Journal of Nutrition and Dietetics*, vol. 53, pp. 100–5.

Mothers and Babies' Health Association 1938, *The Australian Mothercraft Book*, Rigby, Adelaide.

National Health and Medical Research Council 2003, *Dietary Guidelines for Children and Adolescents in Australia, Incorporating the Infant Feeding Guidelines for Heath Workers*, Ausinfo, Canberra.

Nettleton, S. 1991, 'Wisdom, Diligence and Teeth: Discursive Practice and the Creation of Mothers', *Sociology of Health and Illness*, vol. 13, pp. 98–111.

NHMRC—*see* National Health and Medical Research Council.

Reiger, K. 1986, *Disenchantment of the Home: Modernising the Australian Family 1880–1940*, Oxford University Press, Melbourne.

Rose, N. 1990, *Governing the Soul: The Shaping of the Private Self*, Routledge, London.

Rose, N. & Miller, P. 1992, 'Political Power beyond the State: Problematics of Government', *British Journal of Sociology*, vol. 43, no. 2, pp. 173–205.

Satter, E. 1987, *How to Get Your Child to Eat ... But Not Too Much*, Bull Publishing Co., Palo Alto.

Spock, B. 1955, *Baby and Child Care*, Bodley Head, London.

Stanton, R. 1990, *Foods for Under Fives*, Allen & Unwin, Sydney.

Stewart-Turner, A. 1986, *The Complete Guide to Feeding Your Child*, Science Press, Sydney.

Thompson, S. 1995, *A Healthy Start for Kids: Building Good Eating Patterns for Life*, Simon & Schuster, Sydney.

United Nations General Assembly 1960, *Declaration of the Rights of the Child*, Her Majesty's Stationery Office, London.

Part 4

Food and Social Differentiation: Consumption and Identity

Like cannibalism, a matter of taste.

G. K. Chesterton

The chapters in Part 4 are concerned with the role food plays in the process of social differentiation. People can seek to differentiate themselves from others by conveying their collective membership of a particular social group through their food-consumption practices (among other things). Food consumption can symbolise social status, ethnic heritage, social class, religious beliefs, or a chosen lifestyle and self-identity—being a vegetarian, for example. Part 4 consists of four chapters, each of which exemplifies a different mode of social differentiation in terms of food consumption:

- Chapter 11 argues that class differences in food-consumption practices have 'diminished without disappearing altogether'. The differences that do exist have no significant nutritional consequences, so concern about the 'poor diets of the poor' tends to reflect class prejudice rather than an objective assessment of nutritional inequalities.
- Chapter 12 discusses the growing number of people who describe themselves as vegetarian. Vegetarianism is viewed as both a way of defining the self and as a social movement based on ethical considerations about animal rights and the environmental and health implications of raising and consuming animals.
- Chapter 13 explores the pervasive influence of culture on food habits in increasingly multicultural societies.
- Chapter 14 examines the social impact of ageing on food consumption and, in turn, on self-identity and social interaction.

11

Food and Class

Pat Crotty and John Germov

Overview

- Are there class-based differences in food choice?
- What are the underlying implications of equating the working class with poor food choices?
- Are class differences diminishing?

Food is one of the most basic necessities of life and its inequitable distribution on the basis of some form of social stratification may be as old as human society itself. Contemporary concerns about nutrition and health in developed countries have rekindled interest in class differences in diet and eating habits. In the recent past, differences in nutritional intake and food choice between the working class and the middle and upper classes have diminished. Nevertheless there continues to be an active discourse that, to a greater or lesser extent, blames health problems on the 'poor diets of the poor'. The relationship between class and food is examined in three main areas: nutrition, food habits, and symbolic consumption. The findings of nutritional science alone do not explain the concern among nutrition experts about the diet of low-income groups. The possibility that a form of social distinction is created through criticism of working class diets is examined, and the benefits of a broad range of social science perspectives on nutrition inequalities are highlighted. In particular, insights gained from Pierre Bourdieu's concepts of 'habitus' and 'cultural capital', and recent work on cosmopolitanism, are discussed.

Key terms

- class
- cosmopolitanism
- cultural capital
- dichotomous view
- Dietary Guidelines for Australians
- food inadequacy/insufficiency
- food insecurity
- food use
- globalisation
- habitus
- life chances
- life choices
- McDonaldisation
- 'modern' foods
- rationalisation
- reflexive modernity
- social differentiation
- structure–agency debate
- 'traditional' foods

Introduction

> 'Please, sir, I want some more.'
>
> Charles Dickens, *Oliver Twist* (1837–39)

Class-based food consumption is a classic example of the social patterning of taste. The famous line from *Oliver Twist* evokes images of a bygone era of rigid **class** structures, poverty, and food scarcity. Up to the late eighteenth century, subsistence economies and limited means of transportation and storage left European populations susceptible to famines. Food scarcity meant that even the wealthy ate relatively frugally, though the poor subsisted mostly on cereals, pulses, potatoes, some milk, and very small quantities of meat (mostly pork, which was considered of low status and was less expensive). Social status in times of food scarcity was often conveyed by a person's girth—that is, a large body was a sign of wealth and of the ability to overconsume when food was available (Mennell 1996). The 'fat ideal' was the symbol of beauty, as represented in the famous paintings of voluptuous women by Renoir and Bertolucci, among others. Only the wealthy could afford to host feasts and banquets, the 'gastro-orgies' of endless dishes and hearty servings that, though rare, reflected the chasm in living standards between the rich and poor (Mennell 1996).

The working class's lack of sufficient quantities of food was exacerbated by their inability to afford food of good quality. As Friedrich Engels noted in *The Condition of the Working Class in England* (1845/1958, p. 103), 'the working-people, to whom a couple of farthings are important ... cannot afford to inquire too closely into the quality of their purchase ... to their share fall all the adulterated, poisoned provisions'. For example, in the 1800s it was a widespread practice to adulterate milk by watering it down by at least 25% and then adding flour for thickening, chalk for whitening, the juice of boiled carrots for sweetening, and even lamb brains for froth (Atkins 1991; Murcott 1999). The adulteration of food was commonplace in Australia as well, so much so that the earliest public health laws addressed this problem—for example, the *Adulteration of Bread Act 1838* (NSW) and the *Act to Prevent the Adulteration of Articles of Food and Drink 1863* (Vic.) (Commonwealth of Australia 2001). In Britain, enormous differences between the diets of the working class and the middle and upper classes persisted well into the early twentieth century, and the poorest 10% of the population 'barely subsisted' on a diet of tea, butter, bread, potatoes, and a small amount of meat (Nelson 1993). The situation was somewhat different in Australia and the USA, where food scarcity was rare and those who had employment could afford meat regularly (Symons 1982; Levenstein 1988). Nonetheless, the upper classes always ate considerably better and their consumption practices were often used as social markers to reinforce class distinctions—what Thorstein Veblen (1899/1975) termed 'conspicuous consumption'.

Class prejudice has long surrounded food consumption, often associated with the allegedly 'good taste' and 'good manners' of the upper classes compared to the working class. Such pejorative and moralistic overtones are still prevalent, despite the greater access to food in developed countries today. Stories about the problematic diet of the working class are not uncommon in the media. In January 1997 the *Australian* newspaper ran an article with the headline 'Fast-Food Fashion Fuels Nutritional Underclass' (Meade 1997, p. 7). Quoting 'leading experts', the article stated that wealthier and better-educated people made better nutritional choices by purchasing 'nutritionally dense' takeaway foods, such as Indian, Thai, and Japanese food. Those on lower incomes chose McDonald's, KFC, pizza, and hot chips, which are higher in fat and lower in nutritional value; the article claimed that a 'nutritional underclass' was emerging.

It is often assumed in popular and scientific discussions that the 'poor diets of the poor' are substantially responsible for the persistence of health inequalities (see Germov 2002). The diet of the working class is often viewed as uniformly 'unhealthy'. Recommendations are frequently made for the improvement of the working class diet so that it more closely approximates those of the higher social classes, which are often assumed to be uniformly 'healthier'. The food choices and diets of the affluent thus become an inappropriate surrogate standard of 'healthy eating' for low-income groups. It is easier with the hindsight of history to identify the association of upper class prejudices with working class food choice. It is more difficult to do so in one's own time, and, as a consequence, it is particularly important to be vigilant. This chapter seeks to clarify three types of association between class and food, in terms of:

- nutrition
- food habits
- symbolic consumption.

In exploring class differences in developed countries (see Chapter 2 for a discussion of world hunger), we must assess the extent to which modern nutritional science has helped us separate the facts of nutrition from the prejudices

Box 11.1 Class and socioeconomic status: Conceptualising social inequality

Class is a central topic of research and debate in sociology. Due to differences in theoretical perspectives and research methodologies used by sociologists, the terminology used to signify social inequality varies. For example, it is common to find the terms *class* and *socioeconomic status* (SES) used interchangeably, though they are quite different concepts. A basic definition of 'class' can be derived from a hybrid of Marxist and Weberian perspectives, using a three-class model:

- upper class: those who own and/or control scarce economic resources
- middle class: those who own marketable skills and/or qualifications
- working class: those who rely on their unskilled manual and non-manual labour.

The concept of SES refers to a statistical grouping of people into high, medium, and low SES groups according to certain criteria (usually a composite index of income, occupation, and education). In fact, much of the empirical study of social inequality uses the concept of SES because it is perceived as less controversial and easier to operationalise. SES figures can indicate levels of social inequality, but they are abstract categorisations used for statistical analysis (Connell 1977). For example, very few people identify themselves as being a member of a middle SES group. Class, by contrast, is meant to represent people's daily lives and identities, so that being working class or middle class entails holding certain class-based values and living a certain lifestyle. Therefore, the concept of SES should not be substituted for class, because class refers to real groups of people living in a social structure based on an unequal distribution of wealth and power (Connell 1977, 1983; Crompton 1998).

Throughout this chapter, the terms used by the authors of the studies cited have been maintained, terms that in general refer to segments of society who have more or less access to social and economic resources. Some authors have proclaimed that 'class is dead', or at least less influential today than it was in the past (Pakulski & Waters 1996); whether or not this is true, it is important to note that class is not the only basis of **social differentiation** in terms of food consumption. Social research has found a range of demographic factors other than class, income, and occupation as useful in explaining differences in food consumption—for example, gender, ethnicity, age, and the presence of children in the household.

of privilege. In some ways health professionals, especially dietitians, are on a knife-edge in regard to class-based food habits. It is possible to go too far in believing that working class individuals are so 'different' that powerful interventions focused on them are required; but it is important not to become complacent because the gains made in raising general living standards have diminished food poverty (see Box 11.1).

Class differences in nutrition

While there is always concern at some level in developed societies about those who have poor diets, there are times when interest is rekindled by particular circumstances. Wartime is one such occasion, and concern usually centres around the impact of poor diets on the health of young males and their fitness to serve in the armed forces; food shortages and the capacity of the domestic workforce to support agricultural and industrial production may be a focus for government action. More recently, concern about poor diets in developed countries has focused on the relationship between diet and heart disease. Because of the demonstrated higher rates of chronic disease, especially coronary heart disease, among low-income groups, interest in the diets of these groups has increased. This usually takes the form of analysis of the fact that the diets of those in lower social strata conform less well to government nutrition advice on lowering the risks for chronic disease. Research into social stratification and diet has been stimulated and fat consumption has received particular attention because of its association with heart disease. Commonly, when mean levels of nutrients in the diets of people from different income levels are compared, those on lower incomes are found to have a greater proportion of total dietary energy coming from fat.

Dietary patterns consistent with health can be as diverse as those characteristic of subsistence farmers, nomadic herdsmen, and youth from deepest suburbia. However, any food pattern which fails over time—either in terms of quantity (too much or too little) or variety, or both—can have serious consequences because it does not provide the nutrients and energy needed for health, for work, and possibly, in the longer term, for life. One may arrive at a health-sustaining dietary pattern by many paths. Class differences in food habits do not necessarily lead to problematic differences in nutrition. For example, a low-income family may be well nourished in a nutritional sense, but nevertheless experience painful deprivation through lack of access to highly valued foods, the preferred amount of food, or consistent amounts of food. None of these problems will necessarily result in poor nutrition measured against nutrient-intake norms, although they increase the likelihood that this will occur. Moreover, it is important to distinguish between **food insecurity**, **food**

inadequacy/insufficiency (undernutrition), and malnutrition. Food insecurity is a broad concept that concerns the social context of access to food and the ability to acquire it in socially acceptable ways (that is, without stealing, begging, or relying on food aid). It thus goes beyond a focus on nutrition-related disease (malnutrition) or energy deficiency (food inadequacy/insufficiency) and refers to a state in which people are unable to access affordable, nutritious, safe, and culturally acceptable food, and possibly face periods of hunger or regularly fear starvation (NCHS 1994; McComb et al. 2000; FAO 2002). The existence of food aid programs such as food stamps, soup kitchens, food banks, and food cooperatives sponsored by government and non-government welfare organisations are evidence of the continued existence of food poverty in developed countries (Riches 1997).

The work of Kathy Radimer and colleagues in the USA has described in some detail the various aspects of the experience of food insufficiency and food insecurity, including household food-supply depletion and constant worry about this, the monotony of household food, and the experience of unbalanced or 'not proper' eating (Radimer et al. 1997). In a study by Gavan Turrell in Queensland, Australia, a group of recipients in a welfare service who were younger and more likely to be unemployed than other study participants had food practices that made them distinctly different from other groups in the community, including those on low incomes. In Turrell's study, those in the low-income category *not* attending a welfare agency reported practising dietary habits similar to those of the people in higher income categories (Turrell 1996). This is consonant with other Australian data that showed that the diets of low-income sole parents receiving welfare payments but not attending a welfare agency to be not very different from those of more affluent Australians (Crotty et al. 1992). This presents the likelihood, discussed by Turrell, that groups needing the services of welfare agencies are under-represented in nutrition studies and that this may mask some important dietary differences between higher and lower socioeconomic groups (Turrell & Najman 1995).

In summary, it seems that, in Australia at least, there may be cause to differentiate between the working class and specific subgroups in poverty when discussing differences in food behaviour and diet. These groups of particularly disadvantaged people are likely to be among the young, the homeless, the unemployed, students, sole parents, and the elderly. Furthermore, poverty and geographic remoteness are a potent combination in determining access to a quality food supply and this has serious consequences for the health and welfare of Aboriginal communities, in which food insecurity remains a serious problem. These groups should be viewed, at least in terms of diet, as distinctly different from the working class or the general category of low SES groups.

Class differences in food habits

Studies exploring class differences in food habits in developed countries have often used SES measures to suggest that class differences have diminished without disappearing altogether (Prattala et al. 1992; Nelson 1993; Popkin et al. 1996; Dobson et al. 1997a). Those differences that persist have been considered by some to be minor contributors to differential disease rates—for example, Smith and Baghurst (1992) in Australia and Murphy and Bayer (1997) in the United States. Others have seen diet as a major contributor—for example James, Nelson, Ralph, and Leather (1997) for Britain.

In countries like Australia, the nexus between 'undesirable food choices' and 'poor nutrition' is usually assumed and linked with the working class and other groups of low social status. These groups are most frequently categorised by income, occupational category, or educational attainment. However, there is evidence that we should be cautious in generalising about such broad categories. Work by the Division of Human Nutrition at CSIRO in Adelaide has shown that when the diets of those categorised by occupational prestige are assessed for conformity to the ***Dietary Guidelines for Australians*** (NHMRC 1992; see also NHMRC 2003), diets in the upper groups are more frequently closer to the guidelines; but there is considerable overlap between the diets of high- and low-status groups, and the differences between the groups are not great (Smith & Baghurst 1992). The study found there were small differences in nutrient intake between the top and bottom quintiles stratified by occupational prestige. Almost twice the number of diets in the upper occupational-prestige group complied with Australian fat targets compared with those in the lowest group; however, the difference was between 19% complying diets in the highest-status group and 9% in the lowest. Therefore, conformity to the recommendations in the dietary guidelines is rare in every category.

Gavan Turrell and Jake Najman have shown that if the detailed composition of low-income groups is not clarified, important information is disguised. In their study, dietary practices (for example, buying low-fat milk) rather than dietary intakes were examined (Turrell & Najman 1995; Turrell 1996). Comparing a population sample stratified by income and a sample of clients from a welfare centre, the study shows clearly that the low-income group was very similar to the higher-income groups in terms of reported dietary practices, whilst the welfare-service clients were very different from all income groups. Using a score out of 20 based on individuals' reports on how often they chose 'recommended' foods, the mean scores for high-income, medium-income, low-income, and welfare-service groups were 10.4, 9.9, 9.8, and 5.3 respectively (Turrell 1996). Apart from being much younger and more likely to be female, unemployed, and a sole parent, the people in the welfare-service group were least likely to claim they followed recommended food practices such as choosing low-fat and wholemeal varieties of foods. Although they reveal the existence of a particularly disadvantaged group, these Australian data do not support a **dichotomous view**—that is, the assumption that the middle and upper classes have a 'healthy' diet and the working class an 'unhealthy' diet when measured against nutrient-intake and dietary guidelines. Data from other countries support these findings.

Ritva Prattala's conclusions in summarising data for Nordic countries were that social-class differences in diets have diminished since the 1970s and that lower-social-class diets follow those of the upper social classes with a five to ten year time lag (Prattala et al. 1992; Pràttala 1995). Eva Roos and colleagues (1996) investigated who in Finland followed the Finnish national dietary guidelines. They found that there were no substantial differences in nutrient intake by educational or income level, although there were some differences in intake of vitamin C and carotenoids in favour of the higher-status groups. There were, however, interesting differences in foods chosen. In a creative discussion of their results, Roos and her colleagues designate those foods that Finns are consuming in increasing amounts (fruit juices, vegetables and fruit, cheeses, and candies) as **'modern' foods**, and designate those for which consumption is falling (milk, potatoes, bread, and butter) as **'traditional' foods**. They label the foods, in contemporary nutritional terms, as 'healthy' or 'unhealthy', and demonstrate that 'traditional healthy' foods such as potatoes and bread have higher consumption in lower socioeconomic groups and 'modern healthy' foods are consumed in greater amounts by higher-status groups. 'Unhealthy modern' foods such as cheese and candies, and 'unhealthy traditional' foods such as butter, follow the same pattern. Therefore, food habits at all income levels are likely to have both good and bad points when measured against dietary recommendations, and, in the end, may add up to nutrient intakes that are not very different.

In Australia, those foods for which consumption is increasing reflect these trends, with some variations. Foods for which there is good evidence of increasing consumption include fresh fruit, vegetables, and breakfast foods; those that are decreasing include butter, margarine, sugar, and alcohol. Consumption of bread and eggs may be decreasing, and milk consumption may be increasing, but the data on these foods are inconsistent (Dobson et al. 1997b). This introduces the notion of desirable and undesirable eating patterns common to all classes, something usually not recognised in health promotion campaigns or media stories.

These issues have recently been well illustrated by analyses of data from the 1995 Australian National Nutrition Survey (NNS) (ABS 1997). Mishra, Ball, Arbuckle, and Crawford (2002) explored how the dietary patterns of Australian women and men varied according to SES. Their study used a sample of 6680 participants drawn from the NNS who completed a food frequency questionnaire (FFQ) that assessed the consumption of 100 food items over the previous 12 months. Using employment status as an indicator of SES, the authors found that low-employment-status men (compared to men of higher status) consumed more 'tropical fruits' (such as grapes, pineapple, and mango), 'protein foods' (such as bacon, sausage, and fried fish), and offal and canned fish. High-status men consumed more breakfast cereals and wholemeal bread. Low-employment-status women consumed more 'traditional vegetables' (such as peas, carrots, and potatoes), pasta, and rice than their high-status counterparts, who ate more 'ethnic vegetables' (zucchini, mushrooms, and capsicum) and breakfast cereals. While such consumption patterns bear some similarity to the notion of traditional and modern foods discussed earlier (though distinguishing between 'traditional' and 'ethnic' vegetables is problematic), there appear to be contradictory class trends, such as the greater consumption of tropical fruit by men of low employment status and the gretater consumption of pasta and rice by women of low employment status. Such findings show the complexity of attempting to measure and identify class-related food consumption patterns and lend credence to the 'diminishing contrasts' thesis.

Table 11.1 1995 Australian NNS results: Comparison of most disadvantaged areas (quintile 1) with all other areas (quintiles 2–5)

Measure	*Quintile 1 (most disadvantaged)*	*Quintiles 2–5*
Median intake of all food and beverages	2541 grams per day	2672 grams per day
Reported running out of food over past 12 months	8.9%	4.1%
Eat cereals and cereal products	93.0%	95.1%
Consume milk products/dishes	91.7%	94.0%
Eat seed and nut products/dishes	10.0%	12.8%
Use fats and oils	74.2%	76.2%
Usually eat less than two serves of fruit a day	49.7%	45.2%
Use whole milk	41.9%	37.6%
Trim fat off meat	69.6%	73.8%
Consume alcohol	27.0%	34.3%
Median consumption of alcoholic beverages	571 grams per day	393 grams per day

Sources: Adapted from Wood et al. (2000a, pp. 8, 15 & 21), ABS (1999), and Baghurst (2003)

Further analysis of the NNS data using an index of relative disadvantage for geographical areas, the Socio-Economic Index for Areas (SEIFA), has allowed a comparison of the diets of those in the most disadvantaged quintile (quintile 1, the poorest 20% of the population) with the diets of those in the upper four quintiles (Wood et al. 2000a, 2000b; see also Baghurst 2003 for a good summary of the data). The sample for the study consisted of 2052 people in quintile 1 and 9203 people in quintiles 2–5. The main findings are summarised in Table 11.1.

In the most disadvantaged areas people were found to have a lower median intake of all food and beverages (2541 grams for quintile 1 versus 2672 grams for the upper four quintiles). Furthermore, 8.9% of people in quintile 1 reported 'running out of food and having no money to buy more at some time during the last 12 months', compared to 4.1% for the other quintiles, indicating that food insecurity is a significant problem in Australia (affecting around 5% of the total Australian population) (Wood et al. 2000a, p. 8). People living in the most disadvantaged areas tend to consume slightly lower amounts of cereals, milk products, seed and nut products, fats and oils, and fruit and vegetables. They are also less likely to trim fat off meat or use low-fat milk. While fewer consume alcohol, among those that do the median alcohol intake is considerably higher. However, in terms of overall food intake, the differences between people living in the most disadvantaged areas compared to all other areas are relatively small and unlikely to account for class-based health inequalities. It is also important to note that NNS data is likely to under-represent the most disadvantaged members of society and that SEIFA comparisons are crude measures of social inequality. Nonetheless, the results suggest that poverty rather than class may be a better indicator of food and nutrition inequality.

Anne Murcott (2002) has argued for a range of sociological approaches to food inequality. Whilst supporting the utility of the 'political arithmetic' approach of the quantitative studies upon which most of the discussion in this chapter is based, she notes the potential value of qualitative research methods, which are used less often. Such approaches can illuminate differences in lay understandings of food and nutrition and can provide in-depth insights into the everyday reality of class-based **food use**. A fine illustration of such an approach is a study by Carol Devine and colleagues (2003). Their study, based on interviews with fifty-one New York adults of low or moderate income, shows how workers themselves see the relationship between work and household food choices. It amply illustrates the complexity of the interaction between personal perceptions, availability of resources (which is related to SES), family roles (especially gender roles), and job characteristics. Their study reveals the complex network of influences on food choice, and particularly shows how the food choices of those who experienced shift work, multiple jobs, and inflexible hours were affected by family responsibilities and a lack of time and energy.

Other qualitative studies have reached similarly interesting findings. A UK study by Dobson, Beardsworth, Keil, and Walker (1994) of forty-eight low-income families found that food expenditure was treated flexibly in order to meet the costs of unexpected bills. Not only was the food budget elastic, but when money was scarce food shopping was undertaken more frequently so as to avoid a build-up of food supplies that might be consumed too quickly and cause a food shortage later in the week. A lack of experimentation with novel ingredients and meals was also common, because experimentation carried with it the risk of wastage if family members found the new foods unpalatable (see also Charles & Kerr 1988; DeVault 1991). Food poverty was generally well hidden by families, by avoiding guests for dinner or specially saving for such events. The authors cite the example of children being visited by their friends only once their mothers had saved money to provide brand-name snacks. In one instance, a mother filled an empty Coca-Cola bottle with low-cost cola to serve her son's friends, to 'save face' and effectively hide their food poverty (Dobson et al. 1994; Beardsworth & Keil 1997, pp. 93–4).

Class and symbolic consumption: Cultural capital and habitus

Pierre Bourdieu, particularly through his book *Distinction*, has had a considerable influence on sociological studies of class and food. *Distinction* (1979/1984) examined how the upper classes used particular lifestyles and taste preferences as modes of distinction to symbolically express their domination over the working class. In studying the consumption practices of the French, Bourdieu argued that distinct class-related 'tastes' in art, film, literature, fashion, and food were the major means through which class differences were produced and reproduced. Class distinctions were thus made obvious through different consumption practices, which acted to reinforce class identity and group membership. According to Bourdieu, in terms of food consumption the working class had 'a taste for the heavy, the fat and the coarse', while the upper classes preferred 'the light, the refined and the delicate' (1979/1984, p. 185). In an age of food abundance, the upper classes were concerned with health and refinement, eating exotic ingredients and 'foreign foods' and valuing the artistry, aesthetics, and novelty of food and its preparation. The working class were distinctly different, and in 'the face of the new ethic of sobriety for the sake of slimness ... industrial workers maintain an ethic of convivial indulgence' (p. 179). Thus food habits are social markers of class identity.

The upper and middle classes use food consumption, among other things, as a symbolic way of differentiating themselves from the working class through an appreciation of etiquette, modest serves, and aesthetic factors, as reflected in common notions of 'good' and 'bad' taste. Bourdieu sought to explain how such class distinctions were formed and reproduced through the concepts of **habitus** and **cultural capital**. 'Habitus', an expansion of the notion of habit, refers to 'a disposition that generates meaningful practices and meaning-giving perceptions' (p. 170). In particular, Bourdieu conceptualised it as the internalised and taken-for-granted personal dispositions we all possess—such as our accent, gestures, and preferences in food, fashion, and entertainment—which convey status and class background. 'Cultural capital' refers to a particular set of values and knowledge, possessed by the upper classes, upon which social hierarchies are formed. In this sense, cultural capital is similar to an economic asset in that it confers privilege and high social status. As Alan Warde states, 'consumption ... is a means whereby social classes display their "cultural capital" and their place in a hierarchical system of social distinction ... generated by the habitus, a learned set of dispositions that underpin and generate social and cultural judgements in both familiar and novel social situations' (1997, p. 10).

Bourdieu's conceptual schema attempts to transcend the **structure–agency debate** by presupposing that 'social reality exists both inside and outside of individuals, both in our minds and in things' (Swartz 1997, p. 96). Thus people act according to their class dispositions (habitus), which ultimately lead to the reproduction of class lifestyles (Swartz 1997). Simon Williams (1995) has used the work of Bourdieu to clarify some of the connections between class, health, and lifestyle. The relative importance of **life chances** and **life choices** has been of interest to a number of social theorists. Williams notes that the relative importance of behaviours and lifestyles, compared with wider social determinants of health, is still debated and that the relationship between the two is complex. For example, a belief that one is not able to control one's health may be engendered by frequent illness experiences—a more likely occurrence for the working class. In other words, personal experiences of particular living and working conditions shape beliefs about diet, health, and illness. Thus, life chances are inextricably intertwined with life choices.

Bourdieu's insights provide a theoretical explanation of why a dichotomous view of diet and class lingers on, even in the face of contrary evidence. As he states, 'Tastes in food also depend on the idea each class has of the body and of the effects of food on the body, that is, on its strength, health and beauty ... some of which may be important for one class and ignored by another, and which the different classes may rank in very different ways' (1979/1984, p. 190). Those who have more cultural capital—that is, those groups who are better able to create notions of 'good taste'—can legitimate forms of consumption to which they have more access. They are able to define their bodies, their lifestyles, and their preferred food habits as superior, worthy of respect, and 'classier' (Williams 1995). Thus Indian and Thai takeaway are better than McDonald's hamburgers and fish and chips from the corner store; what is more, they are chosen by better-educated and better-paid people.

While Bourdieu's ideas are insightful, they should not be adopted uncritically. The ideas presented in *Distinction* were based on a study of French society at a particular time; the data was collected over 30 years ago. Bourdieu himself acknowledged that all theorising is culturally and historically contingent. Therefore, how well his ideas apply today, particularly in countries such as Australia, the USA, and the UK, requires empirical investigation. Despite his attempt to provide an explanation that integrated structure and agency, Bourdieu appears to accord habitus a particularly fixed and determining quality that belies the internal differentiation among the working class, not to mention the influence of other identity-forming characteristics, such as ethnicity and gender (Swartz 1997; Mennell 1996). Indeed, a number of authors suggest that class is diminishing in importance; it may well be that a person's habitus today reflects a much wider range of dispositions than in the past.

Are class differences in food use diminishing?

In *All Manners of Food*, Stephen Mennell (1996) suggests that **globalisation** and **rationalisation** processes have precipitated a decline in class differences in food consumption. Since the mid 1800s, the industrialisation and mass production of food have continued unabated; canned food, in particular, played a significant role early on in making food relatively cheap and widely accessible (Levenstein 1988; Burnett 1989). Food shortages and rationing during the Depression and World War II further lessened class differences in food habits (Hollingsworth 1985; Braybon & Summerfield 1987). This period is sometimes seen as a time when dietary restrictions made affluent diets 'healthier', and contributed to lower rates of some diseases (such as diabetes). It is at least as plausible that the diets of the poorest sections of the population were improved by wartime organisation of the food supply, which ensured that what was available was distributed with reasonable equity. While those with more resources always had more options, the homogenising influence on diets across classes was considerable.

Post-war affluence in developed countries had a further homogenising influence on food habits, with post-war migration and international trade resulting in the exchange of foods between cultures, as foods from the USA and Europe began to be widely introduced in countries such as Australia. By the 1990s, the standardising influence exerted by the food industry was such that George Ritzer (1993) coined the concept of **McDonaldisation** to describe it. According to Mennell, 'If commercial interests make people's tastes more standardised than they conceivably could be in the past, they impose far less strict limits than did the physical constraints to which most people's diet was subject… the main trend has been towards *diminishing contrasts* and *increasing varieties* in food habits and culinary taste' (1996, pp. 321–2, italics in original). In an age of plenty, significant class-based differences in food consumption become difficult to sustain. The mass production of food has increased the consumption choices available to people through the greater number of food products and outlets, and the greater access to cuisines from across the globe.

Some authors have gone as far as suggesting that a new form of **cosmopolitanism** has emerged, referring to the worldwide hybridisation of cultures, tastes, and cuisines, which has left class distinctions as somewhat antiquated and peripheral to people's everyday lives. Globalisation, particularly via the media, international trade, and travel, has resulted in a cosmopolitanisation of food (Tomlinson 1999; Beck 2000). People have greater access to, and openness towards, cultures other than their own, and, particularly in terms of food, are able to incorporate multicultural aspects into their lifestyle. Cosmopolitanism does not imply an overarching trend towards uniformity and homogeneity, but rather a plurality of lifestyles reflecting multiple food discourses. The work of Anthony Giddens and Ulrich Beck suggests that such developments are characteristic of the contemporary age we live in, which they describe as **reflexive modernity** (Beck et al. 1994). According to Giddens, our exposure to information and other cultures makes us open to reflection and change, so that 'lifestyle choice is increasingly important in the constitution of self-identity and daily activity' (1991, p. 5).

While there has been an evening out of disparities between classes in terms of diet, differences persist, as this chapter has shown. A lively and interesting discussion has developed around the social patterning of food choices, even where there seems to be equitable access to a wide variety of foods and little difference in income. Mark Tomlinson and Alan Warde (Tomlinson & Warde 1993; Tomlinson 1994) examined data from the Family Expenditure Surveys of 1968 and 1988, both involving 7000 English households. They note that most of the literature on food and class focuses on the supposed link between nutritional problems and 'poverty and ignorance'—an approach that they believe obscures symbolic differences in food choice. Within the data set they studied, households belonging to four different classes (differentiated by occupational group) but with the same level of disposable income per household head per week, were identified. There were important differences in the food-purchasing patterns of the classes. The higher-class groups spent more per head per week on food, spent more on eating out in restaurants, on takeaway food, and on 'street food'. The 'manual' group spent more than all other groups on food eaten at work. In these studies, the 'modern' foods were fruit juices, wine, cereal, and fresh vegetables and fruit.

Some clues to factors other than class that may help explain patterns of food choice are offered by market researchers (Gerhardy et al. 1995). In examining what variables can be used to differentiate households according to food consumption, Gerhardy and colleagues studied a limited number of foods through 2-week food diaries in 102 households in Newcastle upon Tyne in the UK. Household class was not a good discriminator; other factors, such as the presence of children and the educational level of the main food preparer, were more useful. The researchers noted that paying attention to household composition, especially the presence of children, is more informative, particularly for foods consumed at breakfast and lunch. Other explanatory factors are demonstrated in a study by Margaret Wichelow and Tony Prevost (1996) that examined the diets of a random sample of 9000 British adults through an FFQ collected for the 1984–85 Health and Lifestyle Survey. They did not look at nutritional adequacy or diet, but, using thirty-nine foods, they discerned four dietary patterns that explained much about how different groups—defined demographically, geographically, and by lifestyle factors—consume 'patterns' of food. They identified the following four patterns:

1. low-fat, high-fruit-and-vegetable pattern
2. high-carbohydrate pattern consistent with a traditional meal structure of meat and vegetables plus another course
3. high-fat pattern
4. high-refined-carbohydrate pattern.

Keeping in mind that these patterns were not discussed in terms other than food choices, there are a large range of associations reported. For example, pattern 1 was favoured more by the middle-aged than by the very young or old, and was strongly associated with high SES and the southeast region of England. However, of particular interest is the authors' statement that demographic factors alone explain a high proportion of the variation in patterns 1 and 3. Therefore, where one lives and one's stage of life in terms of age and family formation may play a significant role in influencing dietary patterns. Mennell's 'diminishing contrasts and increasing varieties' trend may indeed be an apt description.

Conclusion: Class and social differentiation

Human history is littered with examples of groups attempting to create social distinctions by separating themselves from others, through cultural, political, and sometimes violent means (Lamont & Fournier 1992). Yet social distinctions do not remain static and are always culturally and historically contingent. As Peter Corrigan notes, 'there is a permanent tension between "distinguished" goods and the popularization which threatens their distinguished status. Goods, then, are involved in endless definitions and redefinitions of social status' (1997, p. 17). The widespread consumption of 'ethnic foods' by the working class, such as Chinese, Indian, Mexican, and Italian food, indicates that even the hallmark distinctions of 'traditional' and 'modern' food are on the wane.

What will happen when the working class catches up with the consumption of 'modern' foods such as fruit juice, cheese, and fresh fruit and vegetables and forsake traditional foods such as potatoes and butter? Prattala, discussing Swedish data, suggests that when class differences level off in terms of particular foods, 'social classes are likely to differ in the way they talk about food, set their tables and combine their foods into dishes and meals. Without any changes in nutrient content a snail becomes an escargot!' (Prattala 1995, p. 20). And maybe hot chips and *pommes frites* will be seen as equivalent.

Food habits are one of the most prominent examples of social differentiation in the form of class distinction. In relation to current nutrition guidelines, higher classes more frequently follow recommendations than the working class, but the proportion of diets achieving these standards is small in all classes. Aside from various subgroups who experience food insecurity due to poverty, concerns about working class diets appear misplaced in terms of nutrient intake and tend to reflect class biases in terms of symbolic consumption. Thus, a 'nutritional underclass' is unlikely to emerge, which leads us to the rather unhappy possibility that nutritionists and others are 'doing distinction' when they adopt a dichotomous view of class and food use.

There remain many issues open for discussion in the area of food use, nutrition, and class; this chapter has only briefly covered some of the behavioural, social, and cultural complexities of this important area. The literature on developed countries suggests that differences in food choice and nutrient intake by class, however measured, have diminished without disappearing altogether. To what extent the remaining differences explain health differentials, and therefore the potential value of dietary change programs directed at the poor, is more controversial. The contemporary tendency toward dichotomous thinking about food habits and class is in need of review. At the same time, there is cause to be increasingly concerned about subgroups of the population who seem quite distinct and experience significant food insecurity. There is further cause for concern that the difficulties experienced by the most disadvantaged are not well addressed by health professionals or government policy.

Summary of main points

- In developed countries, there is mounting evidence that differentials in diet between the upper and working classes are diminishing and that those that persist are not great.
- The common assumption that the 'poor diets of the poor' (i.e. poor working class food habits) are responsible for health inequalities is ill-informed.

- The Australian data suggest there are likely to be subgroups within the population that experience poverty and have diets very different from those of other groups due to food insecurity, and this is where nutrition interventions may need to be targeted.
- There may be differences in food use that are not class-related but are related to demographic factors, such as region, age, ethnicity, gender, and presence of children in the household; these factors may have good explanatory power for understanding food habits.
- The idea of creating distinction helps us to improve on simplistic traditional interpretations of the links between food habits, health, and class; the available data suggest that the relationships are more complex than has usually been supposed.

Discussion questions

1 Class differences in food consumption can be distinguished by 'modern' foods and 'traditional' foods. What are some examples of each in your society? What factors might make 'traditional' and 'modern' foods culturally specific or international?

2 What are some other forms of food consumption by which class distinctions or social differentiation can be observed?

3 What are the implications for public policy of the fact that those households most likely to benefit from improved diets are the least able to respond to current dietary guidelines?

4 People who use the services of welfare agencies are probably the most at risk of having limited food choices, insufficient food, and nutritionally inadequate diets. What groups in society may be represented in this category?

5 How might life chances and life choices converge to produce healthy food habits and diets among low-income groups?

6 How can Bourdieu's concepts of cultural capital and habitus help to explain class differences in food consumption? In light of the arguments of Mennell, are Bourdieu's ideas relevant to your society?

Further investigation

1 The higher morbidity and mortality rates of the working class are due to the 'poor diets of the poor'. Discuss.

2 Class differences in food consumption are diminishing as a result of food abundance and cosmopolitanism. Discuss.

3. One of the major differences in expenditure on food between the working class and the upper classes is the amount of money spent on food eaten away from home. Discuss.
4. Readily accessible shops, affordable transport, community services, supportive social relationships, and family-friendly workplaces are some of the things that influence food use. Living in a disadvantaged area may compound individual and household disadvantage. How can nutritionists become more focused on the local food supply?

Further reading and web resources

Books

Kempson, E. 1996, *Life on a Low Income*, Joseph Rowntree Foundation, York.

Kohler, B. M., Feichtinger, E., Barlosius, E. & Dowler, E. (eds) 1997, *Poverty and Food in Welfare Societies*, Edition Sigma, Berlin.

Mennell, S. 1996, *All Manners of Food: Eating and Taste in England and France from the Middle Ages to the Present*, 2nd edn, University of Illinois Press, Chicago.

Warde, A. 1997, *Consumption, Food and Taste: Culinary Antinomies and Commodity Culture*, Sage, London.

Articles

Bacon. J. 2002, 'Traditional Food and Tourist Food' [interview with dietitian Jenny Bacon on food supply changes in small towns in Victoria (Australia) affected by the rural decline], <www.quotidian.net/intJB1.html>.

Baghurst, K. 2003, 'Appendix B: Social Status, Nutrition and the Cost of Healthy Eating', in National Health and Medical Research Council, *Dietary Guidelines for Australian Adults*, AusInfo, Canberra.

Web sites

Australian Food and Nutrition Monitoring Unit: www.sph.uq.edu.au/nutrition/monitoring/index.htm

Provides access to the unit's publications on food and nutrition monitoring in Australia.

Demos (UK): www.demos.co.uk/

Demos is an independent policy think-tank. This site provides access to reports on a range of topics, including food poverty, such as *Foodstuff: Living in an Age of Feast and Famine* and *Inconvenience Food: The Struggle to Eat Well on a Low Income.*

Food and Society (USA): www.wkkf.org/Programming/Overview.aspx?CID=19

A Food Systems and Rural Development initiative of the W. K. Kellogg Foundation. The initiative supports the development of community-based food systems that are health-promoting and locally owned and controlled.

Quotidian—Australian Food and Society: www.quotidian.net

A website by Pat Crotty presenting a miscellany of opinions anc society, health, and history, with a social justice slant; focuses most

Ryerson Centre for Studies in Food Security (Canada): www.r publication.htm

Provides access to a wide range of publications on food poverty and ...od security.

Sustain (UK): www.sustainweb.org/poverty_index.asp

Contains information on the Food Poverty Project, which deals with local, national, and international programs to reduce health inequality, particularly policies that address food poverty.

References

ABS—*see* Australian Bureau of Statistics.

Atkins, P. J. 1991 'Sophistication Detected or, the Adulteration of the Milk Supply, 1850–1914', *Social History*, vol. 16, no. 3, pp. 317–39.

Australian Bureau of Statistics 1997, *1995 National Nutrition Survey: Summary of Results*, Australian Bureau of Statistics, Canberra.

—— 1999, *National Nutrition Survey: Foods Eaten, Australia 1995*, Australian Bureau of Statistics, Canberra.

Baghurst, K. 2003, 'Appendix B: Social Status, Nutrition and the Cost of Healthy Eating', in National Health and Medical Research Council, *Dietary Guidelines for Australian Adults*, AusInfo, Canberra.

Beardsworth, A. & Keil, T. 1997, *Sociology on the Menu*, Routledge, London.

Beck, U. 2000, 'The Cosmopolitan Perspective: On the Sociology of the Second Age of Modernity', *British Journal of Sociology*, vol. 51, pp. 79–106.

Beck, U., Giddens, A. & Lash, S. 1994, *Reflexive Modernization: Politics, Tradition and Aesthetics in the Modern Social Order*, Polity Press and Blackwell Publishers, Cambridge.

Bourdieu, P. 1979/1984, *Distinction: A Social Critique of the Judgement of Taste*, Routledge, London.

Braybon, G. and Summerfield, P. 1987, *Out of the Cage: Women's Experiences in Two World Wars*, Pandora, London.

Burnett, J. 1989, *Plenty and Want: A Social History of Food in England from 1815 to the Present Day*, 3rd edn, Routledge, London.

Charles, N. & Kerr, M. 1988, *Women, Food and Families*, Manchester University Press, Manchester.

Commonwealth of Australia 2001, *Food Regulation in Australia: A Chronology*, Department of the Parliamentary Library, Canberra.

Connell, R. W. 1977, *Ruling Class, Ruling Culture*, Cambridge University Press, Cambridge.

—— 1983, *Which Way is Up? Essays on Sex, Class and Culture*, Allen & Unwin, Sydney.

Corrigan, P. 1997, *The Sociology of Consumption: An Introduction*, Sage, London.

Crompton, R. 1998, *Class and Stratification: An Introduction to Current Debates*, 2nd edn, Polity Press, Cambridge.

Crotty, P. A., Rutishauser, I. H. E. & Cahill, M. 1992, 'Food in Low–income Families', *Australian Journal of Public Health*, vol.16, no.2, pp. 168–74.

DeVault, M. L. 1991, *Feeding the Family: The Social Organization of Caring as Gendered Work*, University of Chicago Press, Chicago.

Devine, C. M., Connors, M. M., Sobal, J. & Bisogni, C. A. 2003, 'Sandwiching it in: Spillover of Work onto Food Choices and Family Roles in Low- and Moderate-income Urban Households', *Social Science and Medicine*, vol. 56, pp. 617–30.

Dobson, B., Beardsworth, A., Keil, T. & Walker, R. 1994, *Diet, Choice and Poverty: Social, Cultural and Nutritional Aspects of Food Consumption among Low-income Families*, Family Policy Studies Centre and Joseph Rowntree Foundation, London.

Dobson, A., Porteous, J., McElduff, P. & Alexander, H. 1997a, 'Whose Diet has Changed?', *Australian and New Zealand Journal of Public Health*, vol. 21, no. 2, pp. 147–54.

Dobson, A., Porteous, J., McElduff, P. & Alexander, H. 1997b, 'Dietary Trends: Estimates from Food Supply and Dietary Data', *European Journal of Clinical Nutrition*, vol. 51, pp. 193–8.

Engels, F. 1845/1958, *The Condition of the Working Class in England*, Basil Blackwell, Oxford.

FAO—*see* Food and Agricultural Organisation.

Food and Agricultural Organisation, 2002, *State of Food Insecurity in the World 2002,* Food and Agricultural Organisation, Rome.

Gerhardy, H., Hutchins, R. K. & Marshall, D. W. 1995, 'Socio-economic Criteria and Food Choice Across Meals', *British Food Journal*, vol. 97, no. 10, pp. 24–8.

Germov, J. 2002, 'Class, Health Inequality and Social Justice', in J. Germov (ed.), *Second Opinion: An Introduction to Health Sociology*, 2nd edn, Oxford University Press, Melbourne, pp. 67–94.

Giddens, A. 1991, *Modernity and Self-Identity: Self and Society in the Late Modern Age*, Stanford University Press, Stanford, California.

Hollingsworth, D. 1985, 'Rationing and Economic Constraints on Food Consumption in Britain since the Second World War', in D. J. Oddy and D. S. Miller (eds), *Diet and Health in Modern Britain,* Croom Helm, Kent, pp. 255–73.

James, W. P. T., Nelson, M., Ralph, A. & Leather, S. 1997, 'The Contribution of Nutrition to Inequalities in Health', *British Medical Journal*, vol. 314, pp. 1545–9.

Lamont, M. & Fournier, M. (eds) 1992, *Cultivating Differences: Symbolic Boundaries and the Making of Inequality*, University of Chicago Press, Chicago.

Levenstein, H. A. 1988, *Revolution at the Table: The Transformation of the American Diet*, Oxford University Press, New York.

McComb, J., Webb, K. & Marks, G. C. 2000, 'What Do We Mean by "Food Access" and "Food Supply"?', *Food Chain*, March, pp. 3–4.

Meade, A. 1997, 'Fast-food Fashion Fuels Nutritional Underclass', *The Weekend Australian*, January 25–26.

Mennell, S. 1996, *All Manners of Food: Eating and Taste in England and France from the Middle Ages to the Present*, 2nd edn, University of Illinois Press, Chicago.

Mishra, G., Ball, K., Arbuckle, J. & Crawford, D. 2002, 'Dietary Patterns of Australian Adults and their Association with Socioeconomic Status: Results from the 1995 National Nutritional Survey', *European Journal of Clinical Nutrition*, July, vol. 56, no. 7, pp. 687–94.

Murcott, A. 1999, 'Scarcity in Abundance: Food and Non-food', *Social Research*, vol. 66, no. 1, pp. 305–39.

—— 2002, 'Nutrition and Inequalities: A Note on Sociological Approaches', *European Journal of Public Health*, vol. 12, pp. 203–7.

Murphy, S. & Bayer, O. 1997, 'Evaluating Dietary Quality among Low-income Groups in the United States', in B. M. Kohler, E. Feichtinger, E. Barlosius & E. Dowler (eds), *Poverty and Food in Welfare Societies,* Edition Sigma, Berlin, pp.113–23.

National Center for Health Statistics 1994, *Consensus Workshop on Dietary Assessment: Nutrition Monitoring and Tracking the Year 2000 Objectives*, National Center for Health Statistics and US Department of Health and Human Services.

National Health and Medical Research Council, 1992, *Dietary Guidelines for Australians*, Australian Government Publishing Service, Canberra.

—— 2003, *Dietary Guidelines for Australian Adults*, AusInfo, Canberra.

NCHS—*see* National Center for Health Statistics.

Nelson, M., 1993, 'Social Class Trends in British Diet, 1860–1980', in C. Geissler & D. Oddy (eds), *Food, Diet and Economic Change Past and Present*, Leicester University Press, Leicester, pp.101–20.

NHMRC—*see* National Health and Medical Research Council.

Pakulski, J. & Waters, M. 1996, *The Death of Class*, Sage, London.

Popkin, B. M., Siega-Riz, A. M. & Haines, P. 1996, 'A Comparison of Dietary Trends Among Racial and Socioeconomic Groups in the United States', *New England Journal of Medicine*, vol. 335, pp. 716–20.

Prattala, R. 1995, 'Social Class and Food in the Nordic Countries', in E. Feichtinger & B. M. Kohler (eds), *Current Research into Eating Practices: Contributions of Social Sciences*, AGEV Publication Series, vol. 10, supplement to ERNAHRUNGS–UMSCHAU, vol. 42, pp. 16–20.

Prattala, R., Berg, M. A. & Puska, P. 1992, 'Diminishing or Increasing Contrasts? Social Class Variation in Finnish Food Consumption Patterns', *European Journal of Clinical Nutrition*, vol. 46, pp. 279–87.

Radimer, K., Allsop, R., Harvey, P. W. J., Firman, D. W. & Watson, E. K. 1997, 'Food Insufficiency in Queensland', *Australian and New Zealand Journal of Public Health*, vol. 21, no. 3, pp. 279–87.

Riches, G. (ed.) 1997, *First World Hunger*, Macmillan, London.

Ritzer. G. (1993) *The McDonaldization of Society*, Pine Forge Press, Thousand Oaks, California.

Roos, E., Prattala, R. Lahelma, E., Kleemola, P. & Pietinen, P. 1996, 'Modern and Healthy?: Socioeconomic Differences in the Quality of Diet', *European Journal of Clinical Nutrition*, vol. 50, pp. 753–60.

Smith, A. M. & Baghurst, K. I. 1992, 'Public Health Implications of Dietary Differences Between Social Status and Occupational Category Groups', *Journal of Epidemiology and Community Health,* vol. 46, pp. 409–16.

Symons, M. 1982, *One Continuous Picnic: A History of Eating in Australia*, Duck Press, Adelaide.

Swartz, D. 1997, *Culture & Power: The Sociology of Pierre Bourdieu*, University of Chicago Press, Chicago.

Tomlinson, J. 1999, *Globalization and Culture*, Polity, Cambridge.

Tomlinson, M. 1994, 'Do Distinct Class Preferences for Foods Exist? An Analysis of Class-based Tastes', *British Food Journal*, vol. 96, no. 7, pp. 11–17.

Tomlinson, M. & Warde, A. 1993, 'Social Class and Change in Eating Habits', *British Food Journal*, vol. 95, no. 1, pp. 3–10.

Turrell, G. 1996, 'Structural, Material and Economic Influences on the Food Purchasing Choices of Socioeconomic Groups', *Australian and New Zealand Journal of Public Health*, vol. 20, no. 6, pp. 611–17.

Turrell, G. & Najman, J. M. 1995, 'Collecting Food-related Data from Low Socioeconomic Groups', *Australian Journal of Public Health*, vol. 19, no. 4, pp. 368–74.

Veblen, T. 1899/1975, *The Theory of the Leisure Class*, Allen & Unwin, London.

Warde, A. 1997, *Consumption, Food and Taste: Culinary Antinomies and Commodity Culture*, Sage, London.

Whichelow, M. J. and Prevost, A. T. 1996, 'Dietary Patterns and their Associations with Demographic, Lifestyle and Health Variables in a Random Sample of British Adults', *British Journal of Nutrition,* vol. 76, pp. 17–30.

Williams, S. J. 1995 'Theorising Class, Health and Lifestyles: Can Bourdieu Help Us?', *Sociology of Health and Illness,* vol. 17, pp. 577–604.

Wood B., Wattanapenpaiboon, N., Ross, K. & Kouris–Blazos, A. 2000a, *1995 National Nutrition Survey: Data for Persons 16 Years and Over Grouped by Socio-economic Disadvantaged Area. Executive Summary of the SEIFA Report*, Healthy Eating Healthy Living Program, Monash University, Melbourne.

—— 2000b, *1995 National Nutrition Survey: Data for Persons 16 Years and Over Grouped by Socio-economic Disadvantaged Area. The SEIFA Report*, Healthy Eating Healthy Living Program, Monash University, Melbourne.

12

Humans, Food, and Other Animals: The Vegetarian Option

Deidre Wicks

Overview

- Why are large numbers of people voluntarily removing meat from their diet?
- What are some of the processes that operate to separate 'meat' from the living animal from which it came?
- What sociological concepts can enhance our understanding of vegetarianism?

This chapter reviews the recent sociological literature on vegetarianism. The focus is on the voluntary rejection of meat, which is explored in relation to theories of oppression and liberation, cultural denial, ecology, aesthetics, and health. The chapter examines the concept of 'life politics' developed by Anthony Giddens, discusses its usefulness for understanding vegetarianism in the late modern period, and concludes by examining the contradictory forces that influence the prevalence of vegetarianism and will determine its survival and possible growth in the future.

Key terms

anti-vivisection	food safety	social construction
biological determinism	globalisation	socialism
civilising process	life politics	speciesism
economic rationalism	modernity	state
emancipatory politics	pacifism	unproblematised
epidemiology	patriarchy	vegetarianism

Introduction

Eating is a highly personal act. But it is also, for most people, a social act. When we eat, how we eat, and what we eat are, for those of us not experiencing genuine scarcity, decisions that are driven by complex motives. While these motives include 'natural' or biological motives—such as hunger—they also include social factors, such as taste, manners, expectations, and obligations. Consequently, the act of eating becomes imbued with social meaning. The connections between nature, culture, eating, and the meaning of food become even more complex when we examine the decision to include or exclude certain foods, such as meat, in the diet. For this very reason, such an examination ought to hold great interest for students of human behaviour and of social movements and social change.

For the purposes of this chapter, we can divide people who do not eat meat into two categories. First, there are those who are forced to exclude meat from their diet. Such people are usually compelled to take this course of action for economic or environmental reasons or a combination of both. Second, there are those who voluntarily exclude meat. This group can itself be divided into people who exclude meat for religious reasons and those who do so for other reasons, such as philosophical and ethical, political, or health reasons. It is this latter group with which we will be primarily concerned in this chapter, not because they are the most important but because they hold the most interest sociologically. These people are at the nexus of the natural and the social, the private and the public. I will examine the key issues that underlie the decision of a growing number of people to voluntarily forgo a nourishing and pleasure-giving food. I will then attempt to interpret these decisions within a framework of recent sociological theory.

Vegetarianism and the social sciences

Despite the potential for rich social observation and analysis, there has been little research and writing on **vegetarianism** in the social sciences, although, as we shall see, there have recently been some very useful exceptions. Why this long period of neglect within a discipline that is always on the lookout for new areas of analysis? It can partly be explained by the social sciences' more general neglect of the whole area of food consumption (Murcott 1983). This in itself is interesting and relates to the more specific reasons for the neglect (or avoidance) of the subject of vegetarianism by social scientists. It is fair to say that sociologists are uncomfortable with and wary of theoretically focusing on 'the natural' or 'the biological' in analysis of social issues, social patterns of behaviour, and social change. There are good reasons for this. In a very real sense, sociology is constructed around opposition to the notion that the social can be reduced to our biological origins and destiny (**biological determinism**). Over several decades, sociological analyses have successfully challenged biologically determinist accounts and rationalisations of inequality in the areas of class, gender, and ethnicity. Clearly these challenges have not just been confined to the pages of books and to debates within universities, but have had profound effects on social attitudes and social policy worldwide.

Yet while behaviour and attitudes concerning discrimination based on class, gender, and ethnicity are regarded as **socially constructed** and therefore socially amenable to change, the issue of what we eat—and therefore our relationship with other living creatures—has remained strangely **unproblematised** and hence implicitly regarded as natural. When searching for reasons for this blind spot in social analysis, it is impossible to ignore the bedrock of Judaeo-Christian teachings, which conveniently mesh with a sociological view of humans as having distinct and unique characteristics that mark them out as superior to all other living creatures. In line with this view, sociologists have reinforced the tendency to deny the animal in humans as well as the social in animals (Noske 1997). Social scientists have, on the whole, been content to leave the study of animals to natural scientists and to criticise their subject–object approach only if it is applied to humans (Noske 1997, p. 78). Whatever the reasons for the past neglect, social scientists are now turning their attention to the area of food in general, and diet choice in particular, for research and analysis.

Historical overview

While vegetarianism is a relatively modern phenomenon, it is informed and underpinned by a collection of rich and varied historical antecedents. Alan Beardsworth and Teresa Keil (1997) provide a useful account of the historical and cultural background of meat rejection, as does Colin Spencer (1995). Suffice to say that one of the earliest coherent philosophies of meat rejection was put forward by the Greek philosopher and mathematician Pythagoras (born approximately 580 BC). The Pythagorean doctrine was based on a belief in the transmigration of souls, which implied a kindred relationship between and a common fate for all living creatures. It also incorporated what would now be called environmental or ecological concerns (Beardsworth & Keil 1997, p. 220). The theme of the connection and relatedness of all creatures (including humans) has surfaced many times throughout the history of Western thought and has been a constant in many Eastern religions and in the belief systems of many indigenous peoples. It is encapsulated in the words of Della Porta: 'When one part suffers, the rest also suffer with it' (quoted in Merchant 1980, p. 104).

Another theme that has emerged at various times and places in history concerns the connection between the rejection of meat and the health of individuals and societies. In Italy in 1558, in England in the seventeenth century, and in Germany, Britain, and the USA in the nineteenth century, various theorists posited a connection between vegetarianism and a long and healthy life (Spencer 1995, p. 274). In the 1830s in the USA, a Presbyterian preacher named Sylvester Graham (famous as the founder of Graham Cracker, makers of a wholemeal biscuit) preached that vegetarianism was the natural diet and that meat was probably not included in the food of the 'first family and the first generations of mankind' (quoted in Fieldhouse 1995, p. 155). These theories were bolstered by the 'conversion' of prominent individuals, such as the co-founder of Methodism, John Wesley, and literary figures such as Percy Bysshe Shelley, Leo Tolstoy, and George Bernard Shaw. Spencer (1995) makes the important point that, as well as the emphasis on health, the vegetarian movement has historically maintained long-standing links with movements such as ethical **socialism**, animal rights, **anti-vivisection** and **pacifism**. Links with other, kindred social movements are still apparent within modern vegetarianism.

What is a vegetarian?

Before studying the extent of modern vegetarianism and the reasons for its voluntary adoption, we must first be clear on what we mean by vegetarianism, which is a 'broader church' than is commonly thought. Essentially, a vegetarian is a person who eats no flesh. There are subcategories, such as lacto-vegetarians and ovo-vegetarians, who eat no flesh but who eat some of the products of animals—in these cases, milk and eggs respectively. A vegan, on the other hand, not only refuses flesh, but also abstains from eating (and sometimes wearing) all animal products. Vegans argue that animal products cannot be separated from animal mistreatment. They point, for instance, to the connections between eating eggs and the keeping of hens in 'battery' cages, and between drinking milk and the breeding and slaughter of 'veal' calves, which are necessary to keep dairy cows in milk (Singer 1975, pp. 179–80; Marcus 2001, pp. 128-132). For the same reason, many vegans also refuse to wear or use products based on animal material—for example, soap, wool, and leather. They make the point that it would be incongruous to be entertained by a vegetarian on a leather lounge. Other variations are vegetarians who will eat free-range eggs but refuse milk, and others who will eat fish but refuse the flesh of other animals.

A fascinating recent study from the UK indicates that there are even more complex permutations to the vegetarian diet and the vegetarian identity. In this study, based on fieldwork in southeast London, Anna Willetts found that the terms 'vegetarian' and 'vegan' covered a varied set of dietary practices, including the ingestion of fish and sometimes chicken and other meat (1997, p. 115). While some vegetarians presented meat-eating as a momentary 'lapse' (as in not refusing a lovingly cooked meat-based casserole at a dinner party), others developed a more fluid definition, as with the woman who said 'I'm often vegetarian apart from the fact that I buy chicken now … I do like chicken curries' (Willetts 1997, p. 117). On the other hand, another woman stated that she did not think of herself as a vegetarian, even though she abstained from meat and fish, because she wore leather shoes and ate dairy products. Both of these statements, and others of a similar kind, do, however, reveal an awareness of a vegetarian identity and a conscious effort to remove animal matter from the diet, partially or completely.

How many are there?

Notwithstanding problems of definition, there have been several attempts to calculate the extent of vegetarianism in a number of countries. Beardsworth and Keil (1997) note that the data available for countries such as the UK and the US are sparse and fragmentary. On the basis of conflicting surveys, they estimate the proportion of self-defined vegetarians in the UK to be between 4% and 6% and conclude that this proportion is steadily rising. Spencer (1995, p. 338) has calculated that the number of people who avoid red meat in the UK has increased from around 2.2 million in 1984 to 8.2 million in 1991, which is 16% of the population. He writes that, 'Historically, of course, in the West, this is the greatest number of vegetarians ever to exist within a meat eating society who are not part of any one idealistic or religious group, who have abstained from meat for a variety of different reasons, though they broadly share the same view of society itself' (1995, p. 338). In the US, the proportion of self-defined vegetarians falls between 3% and 7% (Beardsworth & Keil 1997, p. 225). This does not necessarily mean that all these individuals refrain from eating exactly the same foods. It does mean that a very large and ever-increasing number of people have adopted a vegetarian identity and make a conscious effort to remove animal products from their diet, or at least to restrict them.

The Australian situation appears to be similar, as indicated by the 1995 National Nutrition Survey (ABS 1997). In this survey, 14,000 respondents were asked to report on their type of diet. In the category 'Special Diet', respondents were given the following options: 'Vegetarian', 'Weight-reduction', 'Diabetic', 'Fat-modified', and 'Other(s)'. The highest percentages of self-reported vegetarians were in the 19–24 years category, with males at 2.4% and females at 6.2%. More generally, 2.6% of males and 4.9% of females aged 19 or over classified themselves as vegetarian. It is, however, important to note that a further 10.3% of males and 11.8% of females aged 19 or over placed their diets in the non-specific 'Other(s)' category of 'Special Diet'. As there were no categories for 'partly vegetarian' or 'vegan', it is reasonable to assume that some of these diets were included in the category of 'Other(s)' and so the numbers for different types and degrees of vegetarian diets may well be under-reported. Certainly the categories in the survey can be criticised for being wide and inexact. Yet these figures, like those for the UK and USA, bring out the fact that vegetarianism in the West is no longer just the domain of a few 'cranks' but has become something approaching a mass movement, with millions of adherents worldwide.

Why become vegetarian?

There are many possible reasons for voluntarily abstaining from eating meat, and sociology has provided concepts and theories as well as in-depth studies that help us to more fully understand this phenomenon. The decision to stop eating meat is inevitably tied up with such fundamental questions as these: Who am I? Why am I here? What is my place in relation to others on the planet? These are the important, difficult questions that organised religion and secular philosophy have attempted to answer since the beginning of human history. In the Judaeo-Christian tradition, the answers are based on Old Testament interpretations of the place of humans in relation to other species. The pivotal passage comes from Genesis: 'And God blessed them, and God said unto them, Be fruitful, and multiply, and replenish the earth, and subdue it; and have dominion over the fish of the sea, and over the fowl of the air, and over every living thing that moveth upon the earth' (Genesis 1: 24–8).

The Jewish and Christian religions have, on the whole, chosen to interpret 'dominion' as the right to have power over, to control, and to use all other species for the benefit of the human species. These religious traditions are so pervasive in the West that they constitute the bedrock of morality for the majority of people, including those who do not ostensibly adhere to any organised religion. We are brought up to believe that eating meat is not wrong or, more commonly, that we are not even required to question whether it is right or wrong. This is not to say that Jewish and Christian sects and individuals have not questioned the morality of the killing and eating of animals, but they have usually been treated at best as outsiders and at worst as heretics (Singer 1975; Spencer 1995; Patterson 2002). These individuals and sects have often come to another interpretation of 'dominion', one that emphasises humanity's responsibility to care for and nurture other species on the planet. This interpretation has had a profound influence on the animal rights movement, as well as on the environmental and ecological movements more generally.

Theories of oppression and liberation

There have also been attempts to develop philosophies of animal rights within secular traditions. Probably the best known is 'animal liberation', a philosophy and a social and political movement developed and championed by the Australian philosopher Peter Singer. Though a philosophy, the concept of animal liberation developed by Singer owes a debt to the liberation sociology of the

1960s, which developed concepts of racism and sexism and applied them to situations of race and gender oppression. These are concepts that permit an understanding of inequality that does not rely on the supposed inferior characteristics of particular social groups but that focuses on the ability of the dominant group to accrue unequal benefits by using their power to define the 'other' as inferior and to institutionalise these attitudes in social institutions and practices. Fundamental to this process is an assumption that the interests of the dominant group are more important than the interests of the oppressed group. This understanding of the operation of power paved the way for theories and strategies of liberation for oppressed groups. Singer invokes the analogy of the oppression of women and people of colour and asks us to see traditional attitudes to non-humans as a form of prejudice and an abuse of power no less objectionable than racism and sexism. The key point for Singer in relation to determining 'rights' is not the degree of intelligence, wealth, beauty, or status held by a living creature but rather the degree to which it is capable of suffering (Singer 2000, p. 35). Like Jeremy Bentham before him, Singer argues that the capacity of animals to experience suffering and pleasure implies that they have their own interests, which ought not to be violated. When humans allow the interests of their own species to justify causing pain and suffering to another species the pattern is identical to that of racism and sexism: Singer calls this **speciesism**.

In his book *Animal Liberation* (1975), Singer details the shocking litany of mistreatment inflicted on animals through animal experimentation and meat production and slaughter, particularly that associated with modern, intensive farming methods. This book was one of the first public exposés of many types of cruelty to animals—for instance, the fact that battery hens spend their entire lives in cages no larger than the an A4 page and that the lights in the battery sheds are permanently left on so that their bodies are tricked into producing two eggs instead of one; and the fact that sows are immobilised by iron bars during the weeks following the birth of their piglets so that they can feed but cannot turn to nuzzle their young, and that these naturally intelligent, curious, ruminating animals are kept in tiny, cement-floored stalls that are too small for the sow even to turn around in, let alone exercise in any way. Perhaps even more shocking were Singer's exposés of modern veal-production methods. He detailed the way that day-old calves are removed from their mothers and housed in tiny, dark wooden 'crates', where they live, immobilised, for the next 13–15 weeks. The calves are deliberately made anaemic so that the colour of their flesh remains a desirable pale colour for the pleasure of the consumer. Other miseries experienced by these calves are detailed in Singer's book and make sobering reading for lovers of veal scaloppine. While 'crating' is widespread in Europe and the USA, it is not yet a significant part of Australian veal production; however, there are constant pressures on all sectors of Australian and European farming to become more intensive and 'productive'. It is treatment such as this, in addition to inhumane methods of animal slaughter, which led Singer to the conclusion that intellectual and theoretical consistency (not to mention compassion) demand that we become vegetarian. However, as Matt Cartmill points out in his wonderful book *A View to a Death in the Morning* (1993, p. 224), most humans prize consistency less highly than sausage.

Gender and ethnicity

Another contribution that helps us understand vegetarianism through sociological concepts is Carol Adams's book *The Sexual Politics of Meat* (2002), which draws a connection between the objectification and oppression of women and the treatment of animals. At the beginning of her book, Adams quotes the noted anthropologist Mary Douglas, who suggests in her essay 'Deciphering a Meal' that the order in which we serve foods and the foods that we insist be present at a meal reflect and reinforce our larger culture. Douglas states: 'The ordered system which is a meal represents all the ordered systems associated with it. Hence the strong arousal power of a threat to weaken or confuse that category' (quoted in Adams 2002, p. 47). Adams makes the point that to remove meat from one's diet is to threaten the structure of the larger **patriarchal** culture. She goes on to give numerous examples of the way that meat is seen as a symbol of masculinity and of how the refusal of women to serve meat is frequently perceived as a hostile act—one that can lead to domestic violence.

Adams develops her argument using a concept she terms the 'absent referent' (2002, p. 53). Adams explains that through the act of butchering, animals become absent referents because in name and body they are made absent as animals so that meat can exist. It is not possible to eat meat without the death of an animal. Live animals are therefore the absent referents in the concept of meat. As well as their literal absence as live animals, they are also absent in language. When people eat animals they change the way they talk about them. For instance, they do not use the term 'baby animal', but rather 'lamb' or 'veal' (2002, p. 51). After animals are butchered, they are given new names to disguise the fact that they were once animals. Cows become beef, steak, and mince; pigs become rashers, bacon, ham, and lardoons; lambs become cutlets, chops, and crown roast. Adams develops a unified theory that incorporates sexual violence against women and the butchering of animals through an analysis of the social and political processes of objectification, fragmentation, and consumption (2002, p. 58). She ends by providing the building blocks for a feminist–vegetarian critical theory (2002, p.178).

A more recent contribution to our quest for a sociological understanding of vegetarianism, one that also lies within the tradition of power/oppression/liberation theory, is the work of Charles Patterson (2002), whose project is to understand and elucidate the connection between racism and the treatment of non-human animals. Patterson makes the key point that the construction of a great divide between humans and animals provided a standard by which to judge other people: 'If the essence of humanity was defined as consisting of a specific quality or set of qualities, such as reason, intelligible language, religion, culture, or manners, it followed that anyone who did not fully possess those qualities was "subhuman"' (2002, p. 25). This then opened up the possibility of turning those judged as less than human into slaves, beasts of burden, internees in 'hospitals' and prisons, vermin to be eradicated, specimens to be experimented on, or food to be eaten.

Patterson describes in disturbing detail the way that the practice of vilifying people by designating them as animals serves as a prelude to their persecution, exploitation, and murder (2002, p. 27–50). Equally disturbing—and illuminating—is his exposition of the origins of the technology of institutionalised violence used against animals and the mass slaughter of Jews in concentration camps. He traces a direct line from the design of assembly-line killing at the Chicago slaughterhouse to Henry Ford's application of the same principles in the industrial manufacture of automobiles and to Nazi Germany's assembly-line mass murder of Jews at the death camps (p. 71). Ford himself acknowledged that the inspiration for assembly-line production came from a visit he had made to a Chicago slaughterhouse as a young man (p. 72). What is not so widely known is that Ford was regarded by Hitler as a 'comrade-in-arms' and was presented with the Grand Cross of the Supreme Order of the German Eagle, the highest honour Nazi Germany could bestow on a foreigner. While Patterson provides the most comprehensive and detailed analysis of the connections between animal and human mistreatment, he is not the only one who has explored this subject. Indeed, he quotes Theodor Adorno, one of the sociological founders of modern critical theory, who noted that 'Auschwitz begins wherever someone looks at a slaughterhouse and thinks: they're only animals' (quoted in Patterson 2002, p. 51).

'Sociology of denial'

Through their analyses of the interconnectedness of abuses of power through speciesism, sexism, and racism, sociologists have provided us with ways to understand why individuals have made conscious decisions to become vegetarians. The real question is this: Given the evidence presented above, why are there so few vegetarians? Here also, sociology provides us with tools to assist our understanding. In addition to general concepts such as discourse and ideology, which can be used to elucidate the process of suppressing knowledge and language about the suffering of animals involved in their killing for food, we can draw on the concepts of the recent book *Sociology of Denial*, which looks specifically at the processes used by individuals and groups to 'not see' the pain and terror experienced by others (Cohen 2001, preface).

While Cohen's book focuses solely on human atrocities and suffering, his concepts are equally applicable to the way we deny and ignore the daily realities of the suffering experienced by animals turned into meat. Cohen defines denial as 'the maintenance of social worlds in which an undesirable situation (event, condition, phenomenon) is unrecognised, ignored or made to seem normal' (2001, p. 51). He identifies three different types or levels of denial: personal, official, and cultural. Cultural denial, which is of most interest to us in this context, is neither wholly private nor officially organised by the **state**. According to Cohen, whole societies may slip into collective denial without there being either public sanctions or overt methods of control. Without being told what to think, societies arrive at unwritten agreements about what can be known, remembered, and said (2001, p. 11). Denial and 'normalisation' reflect both personal and collective states in which suffering is not acknowledged. Normalisation happens through routinisation, tolerance, accommodation, collusion, and cover-up.

Cohen uses the example of domestic violence against women to illustrate the social process of cultural denial and the journey toward acknowledgment through political and social action (2001, p. 51). He points out that in the denial phase domestic violence was hidden, normalised, contained, and covered up. It was designated as private and therefore nobody else's business. The denial process relied on people turning a blind eye to women's bruises, using a shared vocabulary of such stock expressions as 'She deserved it' and 'He loses his temper a bit sometimes'. Indeed, Cohen makes the point that cultural denial must draw on shared cultural vocabularies if it is to be credible. These shared vocabularies represent the commitment of groups of people (couples, families, or entire populations) to support and collude in each other's denials (2001, p. 64).

Without conscious negotiation, people know which facts are better not noticed and which trouble-spots to avoid. For instance, people do not consciously repress references to slaughterhouses when they are guests at a barbeque or dinner party where meat is being served. There is, however, an unspoken—indeed unconscious—agreement that such references would be bad manners or in bad taste. This is why the mere presence of a vegetarian at a dinner table can make people uncomfortable. Their presence raises into consciousness all those ideas and images so carefully 'not known' and 'not seen'. The discomfort felt by others at the table can lead to aggression or self-justification directed to the vegetarian. However, *this* is not seen as a breach of good taste or good manners, because the vegetarian is the outsider, the threat to social cohesion. The existence of a self-declared vegetarian at the table punctures the carefully constructed edifice of personal and cultural denial concerning the suffering of animals, suffering that is necessary to produce the meat being eaten.

Mass media

This discomfort and ambivalence is also reflected in the mass media. An extreme example can be found in the television cooking program *The Two Fat Ladies*: the two lead chefs were openly hostile to, patronising to, and dismissive of vegetarians during the entire series of their program. Fashion magazines such as *Vogue* frequently swing between pro- and anti-vegetarian articles. One month they will include a feature announcing that high-profile vegetarians are back on meat, and the next issue may contain pro-vegetarian material, such as an article that begins: 'A meat free diet once went hand-in-hand with grungy looks. But a new wave of smart girls have changed all that' (*Vogue*, December 2002). Meanwhile, the major British broadsheets *The Guardian*, *Sunday Times*, and *Observer* present the usual panoply of meat and fish dishes in their colour magazines, yet frequently present in the same editions graphic descriptions of the horrors of intensive farming of fish and animals. For example, the *Sunday Times* magazine featured a colour picture on its cover of cooked salmon and lemon, with the caption 'Tasty? It should be. It's been dyed, disinfected and bred in a polluted, parasite-infested cage... and they call it healthy food' (30 September 2001). The Christmas edition of the *Observer* Food Monthly contained the usual recipes for Christmas fare and yet had a lead article on the cruelty involved in the intensive rearing of turkeys, which reported (among other things) that many thousand turkeys are inadvertently boiled alive each year (December 2002).

While messages about vegetarianism are mixed and sometimes confused, it can be seen that the edifice of cultural denial, while still pervasive, has been breached and is less secure and monolithic than it once was. The main reason for this has been the activities, both political and intellectual, of animal rights activists, who have worked on many different fronts to increase awareness and change the behaviour of enough individuals to make a social movement. Just as activists against domestic violence began by exposing the mistreatment of victims, animal rights activists have exposed—and continue to expose—forms of cruelty that have either been hidden from view or 'normalised'. And both of these groups of activists aim to create a space that permits the emergence of a new discourse and eventually the development of new laws and institutions and a new concept of what is normal and acceptable. We will return later in the chapter to this complex but key issue of the relationship between individual action and social movements and social change.

Environmental sociology

Environmental sociology has made important contributions to highlighting the adverse impact of meat production on the environment. The facts are persuasive.

Meat production is an inefficient and energy-intensive process, especially when intensive farming methods are used. Grain, which could be used to feed people, is instead fed to cattle, pigs, and fowls, and in the process of conversion of grain to meat a large amount of food energy is wasted. There are two dimensions to the environmental consequences of this process: the effects on humans and the effects on non-human life forms. In terms of the human consequences, it is clear that the high meat consumption in affluent countries has an adverse impact on people in developing countries. This is illustrated by the fact that the European Union is the largest buyer of animal feed in the world, and 60% of this imported grain comes from developing countries. These countries grow the cereals as cash crops (for desperately needed foreign exchange) when they could be growing crops for food, which would halt malnutrition among their own people (Spencer 1995, p. 341). Spencer makes the crucial point that if the world's population is to be fed adequately, a more efficient way of producing protein must be adopted: 'A large percentage of the protein fed to cattle (94%), pigs (88%), and poultry (83%) is lost, mostly in their dung. The world's cattle alone consume a quantity of food equal to the calorific needs of 8.7 billion people, which is nearly double the population of the planet now. To halve the number of livestock reared would dramatically alleviate world hunger' (1995, p. 341).

Jeremy Rifkin (1993) has researched in great detail both the human and non-human consequences of beef production. He argues that if the US land that is currently used to grow feed for livestock was instead used to grow grain for human consumption, 400 million more people around the world could be fed. Cattle occupy a quarter of the world's land mass and consume enough grain to feed hundreds of millions of people. While these figures are staggering, it is important to note, as Beardsworth and Keil (1997) have emphasised, that this argument does not address crucial issues of the distribution of wealth and income. Those who experience malnutrition and starvation tend to be the poor, who lack the resources to produce or buy the food they need for themselves and their families. These structural constraints, and their political and economic roots, are as significant as the increase in the global pool of grain that would result from an increase in vegetarianism (Beardsworth & Keil 1997, p. 231). Any realistic action to reduce world hunger would need to take account of both these dynamics.

Rifkin describes beef as an inefficient food. It requires 5455 litres of water to produce one 250 gram boneless steak in California. In US feed-lots, cattle are kept in small holding areas for their entire lives and fed solely on grain and processed food, and this intensive feeding results in a ten-fold loss of energy. In fact, it takes 8 to 10 kilograms of grain to produce 1 kilogram of meat. Rifkin claims that cattle production is destroying Central American rainforests and North American rangelands and is polluting lakes and waterways. The problem of waste is even more dramatic in countries with small acreage and highly developed farming, such as the Netherlands. Dutch farms produce 94 million tonnes of manure every year, but their soil can only absorb 50 million tonnes (Spencer 1995, p. 331). Even Australia, a country with a vast landmass, is now experiencing serious problems with animal waste run-off. A report by the New South Wales Department of Land and Water Conservation titled *Window on Water: The State of Water in NSW* stated that up to 300 bore sites across New South Wales were found to be badly polluted. It found that groundwater supplies used by 250,000 people for drinking contained dangerously high levels of nitrates. The rise in pollution is attributed to run-off and leakages from piggeries, animal feed-lots, dairies, and septic and sewerage systems. The report also found that the quality of NSW rivers and storage dams was rapidly declining (*Sun-Herald*, 17 August 1997).

The relationship between meat production and environmental degradation can be seen with pristine clarity if we focus on hamburger production. Hamburger chains such as McDonald's make billions of dollars worldwide each year through manipulative and aggressive marketing. This marketing successfully presents their hamburgers as an integral and fun-filled part of today's busy lifestyles. The reality is that the production and consumption of these hamburgers is having a catastrophic effect on the surviving rainforests of the planet. It has been calculated that, after rainforest clearing for cattle grazing, the cost of a hamburger produced in the first year is approximately half a tonne of mature forest, since such forest naturally supports about 800,000 kilograms of plants and animals per hectare. This same area under pasture would yield around 1600 hamburgers. This means that the real price of a hamburger is not an amazing $1.99, but anything up to 9 square metres of rich, highly diversified, and irreplaceable rainforest (Spencer 1995, p. 331).

Pollution due to meat production is not limited to land-based animals. Increased consumption of fish, combined with overfishing, has encouraged the intensive farming of many varieties of fish, including Atlantic salmon, rainbow trout, Atlantic cod, Atlantic halibut, sea bass, sea bream, tilapia, tuna, turbot, shrimps, and prawns (*Observer* 'Food Monthly', May 2003). The environmental problems caused by fish farms are now very serious. For instance, the fish imprisoned in fish cages are an easy target for sea lice, which bore through their skin and feast on their flesh. When the victim dies, the lice, which have multiplied ten-fold, move on and attack other fish, including exhausted wild salmon returning from their spawning ground and young salmon making their first trips to the sea. Norway's Marine Research Institute has calculated that 86% of young wild salmon are eaten alive or fatally infected with viral anaemia by sea lice (*Sunday Times*, 30 September 2001).

The situation is similar in Scotland and Ireland, where lice have gone close to wiping out the wild sea trout. Another hazard concerns salmon escaped from the cages. Not only do escapees compete for spawning sites but they also debase the wild species by interbreeding. Because farmed fish do not originate from a home river, they have no instinct to return to one to breed. Instead, they swim aimlessly about in fjords, sea lochs, and estuaries. Norwegian scientists have calculated that the degree of genetic distinction between farmed and wild fish is being halved every 3.3 generations. The inevitable consequence is that the wild population will eventually be composed entirely of descendents of farmed fish (*Sunday Times*, 30 September 2001). Their salmon instincts will be gone and the wild Atlantic salmon will no longer exist.

The work of sociologists and other social scientists has been significant in alerting people to the environmental hazards of intensively rearing animals for their consumption as meat and has been important in convincing people to adopt a vegetarian diet.

Health sociology

The application of sociology to health and illness is based on several research traditions and methods. One relevant to this chapter is public health research based on large-scale **epidemiological** surveys. Such surveys allow for the analysis of disease patterns and the identification of risk factors associated with the development and distribution of specific diseases. The information gathered in these large-scale studies is then disseminated, first to other researchers and academics and then to the general public through the mass media. This constant flow of information regarding health and risks to health has made many people highly sensitive to risk and many have changed their behaviour, including their eating behaviour, to minimise the risk of developing various chronic and acute diseases. In a Gallup survey in the UK, the main reason adults gave for becoming vegetarian was health (76%), although other reasons, such as animal welfare, followed closely behind (Spencer 1995, p. 338). One health reason is the desire to reduce saturated fat intake and introduce more fibre into the diet. Another is fears about contamination of meat by additives (chemicals and hormones) and bacteria. There is evidence to indicate that both of these reasons are valid.

In relation to the health reasons for adopting vegetarianism, there are at least two major studies worth noting. The 'China Study' began in 1983 and its results were published in 1990. It involved a survey of 6500 Chinese, who each contributed 367 facts about their diet. In general terms, the study found that the fewer animal products eaten, the lower the incidence of disease and death (Berriman 1996, p. 54). More specifically, the study found that in those regions of China where meat consumption has begun to increase, this increase has been closely followed by an increase in the 'diseases of affluence', such as cardiovascular disease (up to fifty times the rate of those on a more traditional

Chinese diet), cancer, and diabetes (Spencer 1995, p. 339). The larger 'Oxford Study' confirms these findings. In this study of 11,000 people, half the people were maintained on their traditional meat-based diet, while the other half consumed either vegetarian or near-vegetarian diets. It was found that the latter group had nearly 40% less cancer and 30% less heart disease and were 20% less likely to die before the age of 80. These figures were adjusted for factors such as smoking and alcohol consumption (Berriman 1996, p. 54).

Public fears over contamination of meat have grown as more information concerning practices associated with intense 'factory farming' have filtered into public awareness. These practices have included the use of antibiotics and growth hormones, which hasten the fattening of animals. One of the most infamous growth promoters is DES (diethyl stilboestrol), which was banned in 1981 after it was found that some small children in Italy had developed sexual features after eating commercial baby food made from veal containing residues of DES. Large amounts of DES had been injected into the calves' rumps (where it remained in the meat) instead of their ears. There has also been concern about the over-reliance on antibiotics, which are necessary when animals are reared in overcrowded conditions. Residues have been found in the organs of animals as a result of this practice, which has been actively encouraged by pharmaceutical companies. Bacterial resistance to antibiotics is now worldwide, and there is concern that this use of antibiotics is adding to the problem (Spencer 1995, p. 223).

These concerns pale, however, in the light of recent scares over bacterial contamination of meat. In the 1980s there were several major salmonella outbreaks in the UK that had their origins in animal products. It has been estimated that 10,000 Britons suffer from food poisoning each week, and 100 people die from it each year. More than 95% of these cases originate in animal or poultry products (Spencer 1995, p. 335). A notable instance occurred in 1996, when an *E. Coli* outbreak that originated in a butcher's shop in Scotland killed twenty people who consumed the meat from this long-established 'family butcher'. Hugh Pennington, Professor of Bacteriology at Aberdeen University, who led the inquiry into the *E. Coli* outbreak, stated that 'Food poisoning in the UK has now reached unacceptable levels. A million cases a year is outrageous' (*Guardian Weekly*, 18 January 1998). His warning came hard on the heels of another warning from the British Medical Association that the public should treat all raw meat as infected, a claim dismissed by the Meat and Livestock Commission as 'scare mongering' (*Guardian Weekly*, 18 January 1998). In Australia, there were several serious outbreaks of food poisoning in 1995 and 1996, including one in South Australia that resulted in the death of a young child. The source of this case was a smallgoods factory that produced 'salami' (in reality, fermented, uncooked meat) that was infected with a strain of *E. Coli*.

In the US, the situation is even worse. Every day, approximately 200,000 people are made sick by a food-borne disease, 900 are hospitalised, and fourteen die (Schlosser 2001, p. 195). According to the Center for Disease Control and Prevention (CDC), each year more than a quarter of the US population suffers from at least one bout of food poisoning. Over the past decade, scientists have discovered more than a dozen new food-borne pathogens; however, the CDC estimates that more than three quarters of the food-related illnesses and deaths in the US are caused by pathogens not yet identified. Eric Schlosser argues that it is the rise of huge feed-lots, slaughterhouses, and hamburger grinders that has provided the means for pathogens to become widely distributed in the nation's food supply. He contends that the meat-packing system that arose to supply the fast-food chains—a system designed to provide massive amounts of uniform ground beef—proved to be an extremely efficient system for spreading disease. Schlosser also makes the point that the enormous power of the giant meat-packing firms, sustained by their close ties and large donations to the Republican Party, has allowed them to successfully oppose any further regulation of their **food safety** practices (2001, p. 196). Worryingly, it appears that some recently discovered food-borne pathogens are carried and shed by apparently healthy animals. It is most likely that meat becomes tainted through contact with an infected animal's stomach contents or faeces during slaughter or processing. A national US study published in 1996 found that '7.5% of the ground beef samples taken at processing plants were contaminated with Salmonella, 11.7% were contaminated with Listeria monocytogenes, 30% with Staph. Aureus and 53.3% with Clostridium perfringens' (Schlosser 2001, p. 197). All of these pathogens cause illness and some can be fatal.

The major food scare and scandal of the last decade has concerned bovine spongiform encephalopathy (BSE), or 'mad cow' disease. This disease causes the development of holes in the cow's brain, the same symptom that affects sheep suffering from the disease scrapie. Most experts now concede that it was the feeding of feed-lot cows with scrapie-infected sheep meat, plus the feeding of calves with contaminated milk substitutes and pellet meal, which caused the disease to occur in cattle (Berriman 1996, p. 47). It is now known that this disease can manifest itself as the brain-destroying Creutzfeld-Jakob disease (CJD) in humans who have consumed infected meat. While the number of human fatalities has been relatively small (129 deaths to date), it is not possible, because of the very long incubation period (up to 20 years), to say that there will be no more human fatalities. Millions of cows have been destroyed in the UK, the Republic of Ireland, and elsewhere in Europe, yet it is clear that the disease is still present in some stock. In Ireland, for instance, despite the fact that the feeding of cattle with meat and bone meal has been banned since 1989, young animals are still found with the disease. Between 300 and 400 cases of BSE are found in the national Irish herd each year (*Irish Times*, 21 December 2002).

In Britain, 180,000 BSE cases had been recorded up to January 2003 (*Financial Times*, 31 January 2003), and there are fears that more people than expected may have contracted the human form of BSE. These fears were raised by the discovery of the infectious agent in a random screening of tonsils and appendixes removed in routine surgery between 1995 and 1999. If the infection rate found in this screening program were to hold true for the whole of the population, it would indicate that approximately 6000 people in Britain have the disease (*Financial Times*, 20 September 2002).

Meanwhile, the World Health Organization has warned that countries outside the European Union, especially in central and Eastern Europe and South-East Asia, are not doing enough to prevent another epidemic of BSE. While most of the 2790 non-UK BSE cases have been in Western Europe, BSE has been reported as far afield as Japan and Israel (*Financial Times*, 31 January 2003). In France, where four people have died from CJD and where imports of British beef have been banned since 1996, the population was alarmed to discover not only that the food chain Buffalo Grill been illegally importing British beef but that two of the BSE fatalities had dined there regularly over many years. As a result, four of the company's managers have been detained as part of a judicial investigation to investigate charges of manslaughter (*Financial Times*, 7 January 2003).

As the facts about BSE emerged, ordinary people in many countries were disgusted to learn that recycled waste from intensive farming—the excreta, feathers, soiled straw, and remains of dead birds and animals—was being pasteurised and processed into pellets and fed to domestic and farm animals, including the naturally herbivorous cow (Spencer 1995, p. 335). While this scare has been focused on the UK, it is important to note that until recently many intensively reared animals in Australia were fed a diet that included 4–10% animal protein, most commonly a rendering of bone, fat, and blood. Not unrelated to this practice was the outbreak of botulism that occurred in two cattle feed-lots in Queensland in 1990 after chicken litter, including carcasses, was used in the feed—a practice now banned (Berriman 1996, p. 47). In the USA, about 75% of cattle were routinely fed the rendered remains of dead sheep and cattle until August 1997. They were also fed millions of dead cats and dogs every year, purchased from animal shelters; this practice is no longer allowed. Current regulations, however, permit dead pigs, horses, and poultry to be rendered into cattle feed. The regulations also allow dead cattle to be fed to poultry (Schlosser 2001, p. 202). The image of an endless recycling of infected animal matter that is able to infect humans is a powerful reminder of the danger of eating meat in the late modern era. According to Spencer (1995, p. 336), there can be little doubt that the increase in public knowledge about factory farming has increased the number of vegetarians.

'The civilising process'

The sociological project of Norbert Elias (1978/2000), embodied in *The Civilizing Process*, is difficult to categorise. There are two aspects of his opus that are of interest in the context of vegetarianism. The first is his theoretical exposition of historical change, which is based on the concept of a link between the long-term structural development of societies and changes in people's behaviour. We will examine this central theme in the final part of this chapter. The second aspect is connected to the first, in that Elias attempts to understand the process of historical change, primarily in Western Europe, through a detailed analysis of changes in personal habits related to such 'natural' functions as eating, washing, spitting, urinating, and defecating (Elias 1978/2000). While these might appear trivial behaviours on which to focus, it is precisely the perceived 'naturalness' of the tasks that makes any changes in the way they are performed visible as social changes. It is Elias's detailed study of a changing aesthetic and changing daily habits in the preparation and consumption of food that is of immediate interest for our sociological understanding of vegetarianism. Elias points out that delicacy and a heightened sense of beauty and ugliness may prompt the refusal of meat.

Through the lens provided by Elias, it is possible to see vegetarianism as a logical development in the **civilising process**, which entails a strong and conscious effort to remove distasteful objects and activities from the sight of society. This process has resulted in activities such as urination, vomiting, and defecation being removed from the public sphere into the private sphere. In relation to meat-eating, it has entailed the removal of the obvious signs of the living and dead animal from public view (2000, p. 102). Where once a whole carcass would be carved at the table, it is now likely to be hidden from view, with the diner being presented with a dainty portion of meat often surrounded and hidden by vegetables and salad. In the same way, from the 1960s onwards, butchers carved the animal carcass at the back of the shop and began to remove pigs' and calves' heads from the window. There was a discernible move towards buying meat cut, sealed, and packaged and towards buying it in a supermarket rather than from the more confronting (and more honest) butcher's shop (Spencer 1995, p. 327).

By following Elias's theory it is possible to see that the complete rejection of meat is the next logical step on this civilising curve. Those who are repulsed by the sight and taste of meat have a 'threshold of repugnance' that is in advance of twentieth-century civilised standards in general. Elias argues that while their contemporaries may consider vegetarians abnormal, they are in fact at the vanguard of a larger social movement of the type that has produced social change in the past (2000, p. 102). These sentiments are echoed in the statement of an interviewee in Willetts's study, a teacher who commented on the large number of his students who were vegetarian: 'I have a prediction that in about a hundred years eating meat will be seen as something you don't mention, something obscene. It might not be outlawed, but you'd have to go to special restaurants to eat it' (Willetts 1997, p. 125). Then again, George Bernard Shaw said something similar over 100 years ago when he made this statement: 'A hundred years hence a cultivated man will no more dream of eating flesh or smoking than he now does of living, as Pepys' contemporaries did, in a house with a cesspool under it' (quoted in Smith 1997). Clearly the civilising process is not linear in its progression and occurs through reaction to action in a complex and uneven way.

Currently, it is possible to discern a simultaneous raising and lowering of the threshold of repugnance in relation to meat-eating. On the one hand, we have dainty, disguised portions of meat presented at the table. On the other, we have the glamorisation of meat through its association with celebrities and celebrity chefs. Of particular note are the cooking programs featuring Nigella Lawson, known as *Nigella Bites*. In these programs, we are visually seduced by the gorgeous house, the fabulous kitchen, and the beautiful chef. When we see raw meat pulverised or squelched through her elegant fingers, somehow the death of the animal disappears or becomes beautiful by association. This is the same Nigella Lawson who was quoted in an interview as claiming that when she was last in southwest France they aborted a pig for her and she 'ate the crispy foetus' (*Observer*, 20 October 2002). The fact that this did not raise a comment is illustrative of the fluid nature of the threshold of repugnance in the new millennium.

At the same time, we have even more famous and respected chefs repudiating meat. Of particular note was the announcement by three-star Michelin chef Alan Passard, in late 2000, that he was going to serve only vegetarian food at his famous Paris restaurant, L'Arpege. Passard said, 'I can no longer stand the idea that we humans have turned herbivore ruminants into carnivores. Personally, it is many years since I have eaten meat.' Later in the same interview he added, 'I can't get excited about a lump of barbecue meat. Vegetables are so much more colourful, more perfumed. You can play with the harmony of colours, everything is luminous. And it has been some time since I have been able to find any culinary inspiration in animal products. I want to become the first three-star chef to use only vegetables, a driving force in the field of vegetable and flower cuisine.' (*Observer* 'Food Monthly', June 2001). There appears to be growing support for *haute cuisine* vegetarian restaurants worldwide. Joia, run by chef Pietro Leemann in Milan, is another example. This restaurant has also produced a glossy cookbook of the same name in which Leemann states: 'Death in cuisine is associated above all with the animal world. In spite of the fact that death accompanies us throughout our life … [m]y cuisine is a hymn to life and to nature' (Leemann 2000).

While these are trends at the top end of the market, it does seem that more people are eating less meat and more meatless dishes. In 1990 in the UK, 28,000 people per week were converted to vegetarianism. And among these 'voluntary abstainers', the class composition was changing. Research undertaken in 1988 and 1990 showed that the converts were from the lower middle classes and low-income groups. No longer just a movement of middle class radicals, vegetarianism is spreading through the class structure, with the numbers of converts thinnest among the high-income groups (Spencer 1995, p. 337). At the same time, the gender balance remains strongly in favour of women. In the UK, the 1995 Realeat Survey indicated that women were showing twice the rate of vegetarianism as men (cited in Beardsworth & Keil 1997, p. 224). Australian data, such as they are, reveal the same gender bias. A 1993 Australian study of 11,000 people also found that the majority of vegetarians were women—17% of women and 12% of men described themselves as some sort of vegetarian ('partly vegetarian', 'mainly vegetarian', 'lacto-ovo vegetarian', 'lacto vegetarian', or 'vegan') (Young & Rubicam 1993). More recently, in a UK survey published by the Federation of Food and Drink (2002), it was stated that the market for vegetarian processed foods in Britain had grown by 8% over the preceding year. A poll of more than 1000 people showed that one in three had bought meat-substitute meals during the period and half said they would consider a meat substitute at a barbecue this summer (*Financial Times*, 24 May 2003).

Do these trends indicate a real and long-lasting shift in eating behaviour? There are times in history when whole groups begin to embrace attitudes and forms of behaviour that are significantly different from what has been considered the social norms. One social theorist who is interested in this phenomenon (and who has clearly been influenced by Norbert Elias) is Anthony Giddens, whose work has explored changes in the ways that people think and act in their daily lives within the period that he calls 'high modernism' or 'late modernism' (the late twentieth and the twenty-first centuries). This work also has some useful insights and concepts for understanding the emergence of vegetarianism in the late modern age (Giddens 1991). In particular, Giddens is interested in the emergence of what he calls **life politics**, which is a politics of lifestyle in the sense that it involves a politics of life decisions or life choices (1991, p. 215). The decisions that are involved in life politics relate to those questions that philosophical thought has always revolved around: Who am I? What am I here for? How should I live? In the deepest sense, the decisions involved in life politics affect self-identity itself (1991, p. 215). Giddens, however, sees this as a reflexive process, one in which self-identity is constructed out of the debates and contestations that derive from the dynamic between the ongoing formation of identity and the changing external life circumstances.

Before making connections between life politics and the growth of vegetarianism, it is important to grasp another concept that is related to the idea of life politics. Giddens argues that in order for people to be in a position to make life choices, they must have attained a certain level of autonomy of action (1991, p. 214). This makes sense: people are only able to make choices when they are in a material and political position to make them. Giddens goes on to argue that the ability to make such choices is unique to the period of high **modernity** and it is built on the political orientations and achievements of the modern period—orientations in which **emancipatory politics** were of central concern. Giddens defines 'emancipatory politics' as 'a generic outlook concerned above all with liberating individuals and groups from constraints which adversely affect their life chances' (1991, p. 210). He goes on to say that emancipatory politics seeks to reduce or eliminate exploitation, inequality, and oppression. In all cases, the objective is either to 'release under-privileged groups from their unhappy condition, or to eliminate the relative differences between them' (1991, p. 211). The aim of liberating people from exploitation is predicated on the adoption of moral values, and these values are often expressed within a framework of justice ('social justice', for example). It is possible, then, according to Giddens, to see emancipatory politics as a politics concerned with the conditions that liberate people in order to make choices. So, while emancipatory politics is a politics of life chances, life politics is a politics of choice (1991, p. 214).

The adoption of a vegetarian diet can be seen as a choice that is part of the life politics of late modernity, and as a choice that involves the application and extension of the emancipatory politics of the modern period beyond the human species. In the modern period, the concepts of oppression and emancipation were extended to apply to all humans, regardless of race and gender. It may be that the conditions of late modernity are conducive to the extension of the concept of emancipation to the animal world. This, of course, is precisely what philosophers such as Singer (1975) have been attempting to achieve. What Giddens shows us is that this attempt can be seen in a social and political context as part of a great social movement—in fact, a 'remoralising' of social life. This gives us a sociological framework for understanding the growing awareness of animal rights and the voluntary adoption, by growing numbers of people, of a meatless diet for reasons connected with animal welfare. If Giddens is correct in stating that 'the concerns of life politics presage future changes of a far-reaching sort: essentially, the development of forms of social order "on the other side" of modernity itself', then it may well be that the growing numbers of voluntary vegetarians are indicative of a real change in social attitudes and behaviour towards animals (Giddens 1991, p. 214).

Conclusion: The future of vegetarianism

While Giddens provides us with a theoretical framework for understanding the emergence of life politics—which, I suggest, includes for many the choice to abstain from eating meat—it by no means enables us to predict the future of vegetarianism as a social movement in Western developed countries. While the data are too fragmentary to generate any predictive certainty (Beardsworth & Keil 1997, p. 240), there are, as we have seen, indications that voluntary vegetarianism is on the rise. It is also true, however, that late modernity applies contradictory pressures to individuals and groups. On the one hand, late modernity has produced a high level of personal autonomy for many in the developed world, particularly the educated middle class. On the other hand, for many of these same people, late modernity has also provided more rushed and busy lives, with little of the promised leisure and pleasure. This period has also seen the development of huge disparities in wealth between different populations both within and between countries. In this environment, life choices may become pragmatic, based more on expediency and survival than on principle. It may be that a remoralising of social life and a heightened sensitivity to personal and political issues results in an 'I should, but … ' attitude, with associated guilt and neurosis becoming defining features of the construction of the self in late modernity.

At a less individual and personal level, the social, economic, and environmental pressures regarding meat consumption are also contradictory. On the one hand, US hamburger chains such as McDonald's continue to grow and penetrate new markets in the developed and developing world (including India, where 'mutton burgers' are sold instead of beef). Companies such as McDonald's use clever marketing strategies (such as easy, cheap, staff-run birthday parties for children) to develop a taste for their bland, mass-produced food. When you look at the exponential growth of McDonald's, it is hard to envisage a successful challenge to their hamburger hegemony. Yet the company is facing a profit squeeze in its major markets as the customer base levels off. After 38 years of growth, McDonald's is in trouble. Sales are sliding and, in late 2002, the group announced that it would make its first loss since going public in 1965 (*Sunday Times*, 12 January 2003).

It is clear that the new millennium will be marked by economic pressures towards increased productivity and an expanded market share for meat-based products. This must inevitably entail a continuation and expansion of intensive farming methods. At the same time, the growth of the ecological and animal rights movements, concerns about health, and the 'remoralising' of private and public life will ensure that these economic strategies are contested by social movements within the political arena. I said at the beginning of the chapter that vegetarianism was at the nexus of the natural and the social. It is now apparent that the issues of meat-eating and vegetarianism are also at the nexus of **economic rationalism**, **globalisation**, and a politics based on personal ethics and ecological awareness. As well as having an ancient and multicultural heritage, vegetarianism can now be seen as one of the key moral and political issues of the late modern period.

Summary of main points

- Vegetarianism is not just a movement of the twentieth century, but has an ancient history encompassing many different cultures.
- Definitions of 'vegetarian' vary widely.
- Sociology has provided many theories, concepts, and methodologies that can help us understand vegetarianism. Of particular note are theories of oppression and liberation and the concept of speciesism; the sociology of denial; environmental sociology; health sociology; and the concept of the civilising process, developed by Norbert Elias.
- There is evidence that the number of voluntary vegetarians is increasing worldwide.
- Recent contributions towards a theory of late modernism may assist our understanding of voluntary meat-rejection in this period.

Discussion questions

1. What is vegetarianism and what are some of the reasons people give for voluntarily choosing not to eat meat?
2. What might be some of the reasons for the long period of neglect of meat-eating and vegetarianism within sociology?
3. What has aesthetics to do with diet in general, and with the rejection of meat in particular?
4. Discuss some of the social processes involved in cultural denial. How does this process work to reinforce meat-eating in Western societies?
5. Discuss the environmental consequences of vegetarianism.
6. Relate Giddens's ideas of life politics and emancipatory politics to the issue of meat-rejection.

Further investigation

1. Turning animals into meat has become hazardous for human and non-human life forms. Discuss this statement in relation to the impact of meat production on the environment.
2. How does the theoretical approach of Norbert Elias help us understand the growth of vegetarianism in modern Western countries?

Further reading and web resources

Books

Beardsworth, A. & Keil, T. 1997, *Sociology on the Menu*, Routledge, New York.

Giddens, A. 1991, *Modernity and Self-Identity*, Polity Press, Cambridge.

Marcus, E. 2001, *Vegan: The New Ethics of Eating*, McBooks Press, New York.

Maurer, D. 2002, *Vegetarianism: Movement of Moment?*, Temple University Press, Philadelphia.

Patterson, C. 2002, *Eternal Treblinka: Our Treatment of Animals and the Holocaust*, Lantern Books, New York.

Singer, P. 1975, *Animal Liberation: A New Ethics for Our Treatment of Animals*, Avon, New York.

Spencer, C. 1995, *The Heretic's Feast*, University of New England, Hanover, NH.

Web sites

McLibel: www.mclibel.com

McSpotlight: www.mcspotlight.org

Vegan.com: www.vegan.com

Vegetarian.com: www.vegetarian.com

Vegetarianism and the Social Sciences—A Bibliography by Donna Maurer: academic-editor.com/vegbib.html

References

ABS—*see* Australian Bureau of Statistics.

Adams, C. 2002, *The Sexual Politics of Meat: A Feminist-Vegetarian Critical Theory*, Continuum, New York.

Australian Bureau of Statistics 1997, *National Nutrition Survey Selected Highlights 1995*, Commonwealth of Australia, Canberra.

Beardsworth, A. & Keil, T. 1992, 'The Vegetarian Option: Varieties, Conversions, Motives and Careers', *The Sociological Review*, vol. 40, pp. 253–93.

—— 1997, *Sociology on the Menu*, Routledge, New York.

Berriman, M. 1996, 'Mad Cow Disease, the Watergate of the Meat Industry', *New Vegetarian and Natural Health*, Winter edition, pp. 47–8.

Cartmill, M. 1993, *A View to a Death in the Morning: Hunting and Nature Through History*, Harvard University Press, Mass.

Cohen, S. 2001, *States of Denial: Knowing about Atrocities and Suffering*, Polity Press, Cambridge.

Elias, N. 1978/2000, *The Civilizing Process*, Blackwell Publishing, Oxford.

Fieldhouse, P. 1995, *Food and Nutrition: Customs and Culture*, Croom Helm, Kent.

Financial Times, 20 September 2002.

Financial Times, 7 January 2003.

Financial Times, 31 January 2003.

Financial Times, 24 May 2003.

Giddens, A. 1991, *Modernity and Self-identity*, Polity Press, Cambridge.

Guardian Weekly, 18 January 1998.

Irish Times, 21 December 2002.

Leemann, P. 2000, *Joia: Colours, Flavours and Consistency in Natural Haute Cuisine*, Editrice Abitare Segesta, Milan.

Marcus, E. 2001, *Vegan: The New Ethics of Eating*, McBooks Press, New York.

Maurer, D. 1995, 'Meat as a Social Problem: Rhetorical Strategies in the Contemporary Vegetarian Literature', in D. Maurer & J. Sobal (eds), *Eating Agendas: Food and Nutrition as Social Problems*, Aldine de Gruyter, New York.

Merchant, C. 1980, *The Death of Nature*, Wildwood House, London.

Murcott, A. (ed.) 1983, *The Sociology of Food and Eating*, Gower, Aldershot.

Noske, B. 1997, *Beyond Boundaries: Humans and Animals*, Black Rose Books, Montreal.

Observer, 20 October 2002.

Observer, 'Food Monthly', June 2001.

Observer, 'Food Monthly', December 2002.

Observer, 'Food Monthly', May 2003.

Patterson, C. 2002, *Eternal Treblinka: Our Treatment of Animals and the Holocaust*, Lantern Books, New York.

Rifkin J. 1993, *Beyond Beef: The Rise and Fall of the Cattle Culture*, Plume, New York.

Schlosser, E. 2001, *Fast Food Nation*, Penguin, London.

Singer, P. 1975, *Animal Liberation: A New Ethics for Our Treatment of Animals*, Avon, New York.

—— 2000, *Ethics into Action: Henry Spira and the Animal Rights Movement*, Rowman & Littlefield Publishers, Maryland.

Smith, J. 1997, *Hungry for You*, Vintage, London.

Spencer, C. 1995, *The Heretic's Feast*, University Press of New England, Hanover.

Sunday Times, 30 September 2001.

Sunday Times, 12 January 2003.

Sun-Herald, 17 August 1997.

Tester, K. 1991, *Animals and Society*, Routledge, London.

Vogue (Britain), December 2002.

Willetts, A. 1997, '"Bacon Sandwiches Got the Better of Me": Meat-eating and Vegetarianism in South-east London', in P. Caplan (ed.), *Food, Health and Identity*, Routledge, London.

Young & Rubicam 1993, *Australian Vegetarian Diets*, Young and Rubicam, Sydney.

13

Culture, Food, and Nutrition in Increasingly Culturally Diverse Societies

Joanne P. Ikeda

Overview

- How do the links between food and health vary among different cultures, particularly between Westernised and traditional cultures?
- What are some of the challenges health professionals trained in biomedicine face in dealing with people from traditional cultures?
- What are the potential benefits of adopting a holistic approach to health in culturally diverse societies?

This chapter describes the issues related to food habits and health that arise when large numbers of people from traditional cultures immigrate to countries where biomedical health values and beliefs dominate. In the past, the unstated assumption was that cultural differences would disappear as a result of assimilation of these populations into the mainstream. However, today most ethnic minorities are committed to sustaining their cultural identity and are reluctant to change their values, beliefs, and practices. As a result, health professionals are challenged to become more cross-culturally sensitive and competent. They are also beginning to reflect on their narrow approach to health, which emphasises physical well-being over other kinds of well-being.

Key terms

biomedicine
culture
cross-cultural competence
cultural sensitivity
ethnocentric
evidence-based medicine (EBM)
family commensality
food security
foodways
placebo effect
psychological well-being
spiritual well-being
shaman

Introduction

The number of migrants in the world has more than doubled since 1975. In 2002, about 175 million people resided in a country other than the one in which they were born (United Nations 2002). The International Organisation for Migration predicts that there will be even greater movements of people during this century—both forced and voluntary. The major factors causing people to move include growing inequity in wealth between and within countries; war, violence, persecution, and discrimination; environmental and man-made disasters; family reunification; and the search for better economic prospects.

The ten countries receiving the most immigrants are the United States, India, Pakistan, France, Germany, Canada, Saudi Arabia, Australia, the UK, and Iran. One of the major effects of immigration on these nations is an increase in racial and cultural diversity. The early twentieth century expectation that all immigrants would assimilate into the local mainstream **culture** has mellowed into an appreciation of diversity in most developed countries. Health professionals in these nations increasingly find themselves working with patients whose beliefs about health and illness are very different from their own. Establishing effective relationships with these patients means learning about their culture and acquiring **cross-cultural competence**.

Cultural views of food and health

In Western culture, health professionals are trained to view food as a source of nutrients, which provide energy, regulate body processes, and furnish essential compounds needed for growth and maintenance of the human body. The assumption is that people will purposely choose foods that contribute to their long-term physical well-being by reducing their risk of chronic disease. There is little doubt that a diet compatible with human biological needs is essential to the survival of the species. However, anthropologists and sociologists have identified many non-biological influences on food choices and food behaviour. When Maslow's hierarchy of needs is applied to food habits, eating for survival evolves into eating to satisfy the need for security, then for belongingness, then for self-esteem, and finally for self-actualisation (Lowenberg 1970, p. 32).

Members of traditional cultures have difficulty relating to the Western biomedical bias, according to which food selection should be based on the physical needs of the body. In these cultures, there is a much greater degree of integration between spiritual beliefs and health beliefs. Healers, or **shamans,** in traditional cultures have been described as physician-priests (Muecke 1983, p. 835). They generally conceptualise well-being as the attainment of harmony and balance in body, mind, and spirit (see Box 13.1) (Bodeker 1996, p. 280). In these cultures, an imbalance in these forces can cause disease. Treating the disease

> **Box 13.1** Healers in non-Western cultures
>
> In Mexican–American communities, healers are known as *curanderos* or *curanderas*; in Hmong communities they are *neng*; Vietnamese have *thay thuoc*; Koreans have *mansin*; Native Americans have *medicine men*. These traditional healers are quite knowledgable about treatment remedies as well as spiritual healing ceremonies specific to their culture. Chinese, Vietnamese, Cambodians, and Laotians refer to the two opposite forces of yang and yin. Yang is masculine and is represented by light, heat, or dryness. Yin is feminine and is represented by darkness, cold, and wetness. Some Filipinos and Mexican Americans also believe that health represents a state of equilibrium between hot and cold, wet and dry.
>
> There are other practices that affect the balance of hot and cold, including bathing, washing one's head, and keeping oneself wrapped in blankets. Herbal remedies are also used to help restore balance. Chinese and South-East Asians also use acupuncture, coining, cupping, pinching, and moxibustion for this purpose. These practices may be implemented or avoided depending on whether the illness is viewed as 'hot' or 'cold'.

means bringing the forces back into balance and harmony. In Chinese, South-East Asian, Filipino, and Hispanic cultures, this is accomplished through avoiding some foods and consuming others. Some foods are considered yang, or 'hot', while others are considered yin, or 'cold'. If an illness is considered yang, then the patient needs to consume yin foods, and vice versa. The categorisation of foods as hot or cold is not necessarily consistent between or within cultures. The best way health professionals can deal with the inconsistency is to ask if the patient is avoiding or favouring any particular foods when treating their condition. For the most part, these practices have little effect on overall nutritional status unless they are prolonged and exclude broad categories of food.

The concept of health in traditional cultures—the achievement of harmony and balance in body, mind, and spirit—initially appears to be very similar to the Western definition of health, which is 'a state of complete physical, mental, and social well-being, and not merely the absence of disease or infirmity' (World Health Organization 1946, quoted in Mosby 1994, p. 835). However, in the field of **biomedicine**, physical well-being has been overemphasised, with only token attention given to social, mental, and **spiritual well-being** (Engel 1977, p. 129). Some experts believe this may be changing. For example, according to Gerard Bodeker, the molecular approach to human biology and the treatment of disease is being called into question by new findings from mind/body medicine and environmental health that support a more holistic view of human health. This view is more consistent with the concepts underlying traditional systems of health and human potential (Micozzi 1996, p. 289). On the other hand, the recent emphasis on **evidence-based medicine (EBM)**, with its focus on reductionist science, may impede efforts to address the complex relationships between spiritual, psychological, social, and physical well-being (Hart 1997; Williams 1997). Nonetheless, there appears to be a need for health professionals to anticipate the impact their efforts will have on all aspects of well-being rather than focusing exclusively on the clinical parameters of health (such as weight, blood pressure, and serum glucose and lipid levels).

Food and social relationships

Food is used to build and maintain social relationships in all cultures. Paul Rozin points out that the basic tasks of growing, harvesting, processing, and preparing food are almost always carried out by groups of people working together. In traditional cultures, the members of a family, or even a group of families comprising a village, cooperate to ensure that their most basic need for food is met. The consumption of food is also a social occasion, with family members and/or villagers gathering together to eat. There is no culture that promotes solitary eating. Food is an extremely valuable social instrument for humans because it promotes social interaction (Rozin 1996, p. 244). In turn, positive social support promotes physical well-being and decreases mortality (McIntosh et al. 1993; Avlund et al. 1998).

The offering of food by one person or group to another is generally viewed as a gesture of friendship. The acceptance of food indicates a willingness to establish or strengthen a bond. Failing to offer food or refusing to partake when it is offered may be viewed as an indication of unwillingness to establish or maintain a relationship. As George Foster and B. G. Anderson point out, we do not share food with our enemies. On the rare occasions when we do, it is well understood that antagonisms are to be laid aside, at least temporarily. Meals are seldom viewed as an appropriate milieu for discord (Foster & Anderson 1978, p. 268). In fact, it is usually the opposite: mealtimes are viewed as occasions for sharing and bonding, and most people believe that a pleasant atmosphere is desirable.

Vanessa Clendenen and her colleagues believe the most powerful factor affecting food intake is social influence. They found that when the subjects in the study dined with others, they ate substantially more, almost twice as much when they ate in pairs or in groups of four as when they ate alone (Clendenen et al. 1994, p. 10). Thus an individual's consumption is modified by the mere presence of another person.

One of the few nutrition programs that has actually documented the beneficial effects of eating in groups on social and **psychological well-being** is the seniors nutrition program authorised by the US *Older Americans Act 1972*. Masako Ishii-Kuntz has found that adults benefit psychologically from close personal relationships, and that the quality of social interaction is positively related to psychological well-being across all stages of adulthood (1990, p. 36). Older people are particularly susceptible to social isolation and loneliness. Loneliness may be defined as 'a feeling and realization of a lack of meaningful contacts with others and a lack or loss of companionship' (Berg et al. 1981, p. 342). Roxanne Smith, Larry Mullins, and their colleagues documented reduced social isolation in older people participating in a senior-citizens nutrition and activities program (Mullins et al. 1993, pp. 37, 342; Smith et al. 1994, p. 21).

Some nutritionists and dietitians will be resistant to the idea that programs such as the seniors nutrition programs should do more than improve dietary intake and nutritional status and reduce the risk of chronic disease. However, others will feel enlightened and liberated by the realisation that their impact is not limited to physical aspects of well-being but can benefit the total health of people. More effort needs to be put into documenting these benefits.

Health professionals rarely acknowledge the role that food plays in building and maintaining social relationships, despite the fact that food is used to establish and strengthen friendships and family relationships in all cultures. People often welcome new neighbours with gifts of food. They hold sit-down dinners for 'special guests'. Office workers bring food to work to be shared on breaks. People hold 'pot-luck dinners', in which all participants bring food to share with each other. Refreshments are served at 'tea time' or 'coffee break' at conventions, symposia, and meetings of all types; this is considered conducive to the establishment of mutually beneficial relationships with others, a process popularly known as 'networking'.

Strong sentiment becomes attached to favourite dishes and foods that are traditionally served at celebrations (Bryant et al. 1985, p. 151). These foods are symbolic of the loving ties that bond family members, and the serving of these foods at other times is used to symbolise the fact that these bonds are permanent. Extended families gather at events such as weddings, funerals, and holidays to share food and maintain kinship relations. The food served at these gatherings often serves as a reminder of the cultural heritage shared by the family members. Many Chinese–American families continue to hold 'red egg and ginger parties' for newborn children who are fourth- and fifth-generation Americans. Californian Native American families still gather for pow-wows, at which traditional dishes made from acorns, as well as 'Indian tacos', are enjoyed by an open fire. *Issei*, *Nisei*, *Sansei*, and *Yonsei*—that is, second-, third-, fourth-, and fifth-generation members of the Japanese–American community—gather annually in San Francisco just before the New Year to pound hot, steamed glutinous rice into *mochi* to be shared by all. Asian–American students at colleges and universities throughout the USA take time off to head home to celebrate the Lunar New Year with their families, who are busy preparing traditional New Year's food. African–American families gather at Grandma's or

Auntie's for a Sunday dinner that may include fried chicken, greens, cornbread, or sweet potato pie.

The USA has long been described as a great 'melting pot', with the implication that immigrant groups were expected to gradually lose their cultural identity and take on the attitudes, beliefs, and values of mainstream American culture—mainstream American culture being that of white, middle class citizens. But two major historical events have altered the popular idea of the USA as a 'melting pot'. First, as part of the civil rights movement in the 1960s, a sizeable minority population asserted their desire and their right to retain and take pride in their cultural identity and heritage. At the same time, the USA experienced a second great wave of immigration, but, instead of coming from the UK, Ireland, Scandinavia, and Europe, the majority of newcomers came from Mexico, Central and South America, China, and South-East Asia. Thus the United States population became much more culturally and racially diverse over a fairly short period of time. This has led to increased acceptance of the idea of the USA as a 'mosaic' of diverse cultures, with various groups committed to retaining their sense of cultural identity and community.

The implications of cultural diversity for health professionals

Cultural influences on **foodways** have received more and more attention as migration has increased the ethnic and cultural diversity of Western societies (Sanjur 1995; Kittler & Sucher 2004; Fee 1998; Curry 2000; Harris-Davis & Haughton 2000). Health professionals have recognised that they need to increase their competence in interacting with patients from other cultures. This need has been acknowledged by a number of their organisations. The American Academy of Pediatrics has issued a policy statement on 'Culturally Effective Pediatric Care: Education and Training' and the American Nurses Association has published a position statement on cultural diversity (American Nurses Association 1991; American Academy of Pediatrics 1999). The Code of Ethics for Nurses in Australia includes the following value statement: 'Nurses respect individuals' needs, values, cultures, and vulnerability in the provision of nursing care' (Australian Nursing Council 2002).

In order to facilitate cross-cultural communication and to address disparities in health status, the USA established an Office of Minority Health (OMH) in 1985. The mission of OMH is to improve the health of racial and ethnic populations through the development of effective health policies and programs that help to eliminate disparities in health. OMH recently published recommendations for national standards for culturally and linguistically appropriate services in health care. (US Department of Health and Human Services 2001). In 1997, the State of New South Wales in Australia established a Multicultural Health Communication Service to assist health professionals to communicate with people from non-English-speaking communities. This office produces resources and translation guidelines and acts as a central referral point for agencies and workers undertaking research with ethnic populations (New South Wales Government 2003).

The American Medical Association has published a 460-page 'Cultural Competence Compendium' for physicians and other health professionals on communicating with patients whose culture is different from their own (Hedrick 1999). In addition, numerous web sites offer advice and resources for health professionals working with diverse populations (see the web resources at the end of this chapter).

It is generally acknowledged that 'one size fits all' programs tend to be ineffective with minority populations, as members of these groups view these programs as being targeted at the dominant mainstream culture and find little advice that is applicable to them. These programs are usually designed from a 'culture-bound' point of view by people who have little experience with cultures other than their own. When confronted with different values, customs, and behaviours, culture-bound individuals tend to assume that their own values, customs, and behaviours are more admirable, sensible, and right—a perspective often referred to as ethnocentrism. They lack **cultural sensitivity** in that they do not have the ability to view the world from another person's point of view without making a judgment about the values, assumptions, and beliefs that structure that person's behaviour.

In recent years, a variety of studies have been conducted on the foodways and dietary intakes of immigrant populations in order to gather information that can be used as a basis for designing culturally appropriate nutrition education programs (Ikeda et al. 1991a; Metcalf et al. 1998; Cruickshank & Sharma 2001; Satia et al. 2001; Varghese & Moore-Orr 2002; Wahlqvist 2002). Most dietitians and nutritionists know that dietary needs can be met in a variety of ways, and usually promote retention of traditional food habits when they are economically feasible. They also recognise that recent immigrants are being exposed to many new and unfamiliar foods and food-preparation practices, and need assistance in deciding if and how to incorporate these foods and practices into their own foodways. By designing and implementing culturally specific nutrition education programs, they are attempting to help new immigrants adapt to a changed food supply and to exposure to Western food habits without sacrificing foodways integral to their cultural identity (Ikeda et al. 1998 & 2002; Hawthorne 2001; Chen & Rankin 2002; Hyman et al. 2002).

Health professionals need to consider how their advice on food choice, preparation, and intake is going to affect a person's ability to maintain social relationships and cultural identity. People may be unwilling to omit certain foods from their diet because doing so would mean sacrificing the social benefits associated with these foods. They may not be anxious to adopt new—and possibly healthier—versions of favourite recipes if traditional preparation methods

Box 13.2 Breastfeeding and cultural diversity

Physicians agree that breastfeeding is the ideal way to feed an infant; however, breastfeeding rates vary tremendously among cultural groups in the USA. Native Americans have some of the highest rates of breastfeeding, while South-East Asians have low rates. Why have some traditional cultures retained this practice while others have essentially abandoned it?

A number of researchers have investigated the reasons why South-East Asian women, who breastfeed in their homeland, are no longer doing so in the USA (Rassin et al. 1994, p. 132; Tuttle & Dewey 1994, p. 282). They found that these women viewed bottle feeding as convenient; the idea that others could help feed the baby was appealing to them. They thought it was the way most American women fed their babies, since it was the only infant-feeding method they had actually observed American women using, with breastfeeding in America almost always done in private. They concluded that it must be the best way to feed a baby. This notion was reinforced by the fact that most American infants appeared larger than South-East Asian babies. These women also associated breastfeeding with the thinness of infants in their homeland, and the death of some of these infants.

In order to promote breastfeeding in this population, health professionals will need to deal with these perceptions. Tuttle and Dewey found that the single most important predictor of an intention to breastfeed among South-East Asians was being advised to breastfeed in prenatal visits (Tuttle & Dewey 1994, p. 282). This was also found to be the case with Mexican–American and non-Hispanic white women (Balcazar et al. 1995, p. 74). Yet a national random survey of physicians in the USA found that they were ill prepared to counsel breastfeeding mothers (Freed et al. 1995, p. 472).

However, that situation may be changing as a result of an international program of the World Health Organization called the Baby-Friendly Hospital Initiative. This program recognises hospitals and birth centres that have taken steps to provide an optimal environment for the promotion, protection, and support of breastfeeding. Unfortunately, only thirty-five hospitals and birth centres in the United States and twenty-five in Australia have earned the Baby-Friendly label, compared to approximately 16,000 facilities in the rest of the world (UNICEF 2003).

symbolise cultural origins or family ties that need to be maintained. They may be reluctant to change their diet because this may place a burden on other family members and they may feel guilty about imposing their needs on the family.

The challenge for health professionals is to help patients to change their diets in ways that do not undermine the sociocultural functions of food. If health professionals are cognisant of the role that food plays in helping people retain their cultural identity, they are more likely to propose a variety of options for improving diet. They will encourage clients to evaluate proposed changes in terms of their potential for successful adoption. Most importantly, they will promote open communication that invites clients to identify barriers to change so that these can be considered when determining a course of action.

The role of food in establishing positive relationships between individuals and family members needs to be exploited. Food offerings between family members are symbols of love and affection. The father who patiently spoons food into the mouth of a toddler is nurturing not only the child's physical well-being, but also the social and emotional development of the child. A mother's breastfeeding of an infant is testimony to the intimacy of the loving relationship between mother and child (see Box 13.2).

Even though fathers do not breastfeed, they are often involved in decisions about infant feeding. Among Mexican Americans, the father's being Hispanic was negatively associated with the mother's use of breastfeeding (Balcazar et al. 1995, p. 74). It is important for health professionals to recognise the influence that the male head of traditional households has on all aspects of family life. It is appropriate to include him in counselling sessions in which changes in diet or lifestyle or both are recommended, since he may have the final word on whether the recommended changes are to be implemented.

Family and cultural diversity

Some years ago, Donald Allen and his colleagues (1970) used a Family Commensality Score to test his hypothesis that family relationships and nutritional factors affect student performance and aspirations. He found that **family commensality**—as measured through questions about meals eaten together by the whole family, the attractiveness and quality of the food, the appetite of the student, and the family member who did the cooking—was the factor most fully correlated to intrafamily and performance factors. Family commensality had significant positive effects on students' academic performance, academic goals, personal problems, money problems, perceptions of the level of family love, and family role performance. Increases in family commensality were also associated with increases in food likes, improvement of dietary adequacy, and more positive perceptions of personal health status (Allen et al. 1970, p. 333).

Family mealtime provides an important opportunity for family members to share news of the day's events, express feelings, and listen to one another. With respect to nutrition, children learn rules of cuisine primarily through their observations and experiences at family mealtimes (Birch 2001). This includes what is and what is not considered edible, as well as the appropriateness and value of consuming foods in different contexts and combinations. Vietnamese children learn that dog is acceptable as food, while Australian children learn that dogs are pets, not food. Japanese children learn that it is acceptable to pick up one's soup bowl and drink from it, whereas American children are told that this is impolite. More than half the world's children learn to use chopsticks as their primary eating utensil. Hmong and Vietnamese children dip their food in fish sauce, a condiment most American children have never tasted. Mexican children become accustomed to hot salsas that would be resolutely rejected by children from other cultures. American children know that peanut butter and jelly is a desirable sandwich filling, whereas most Asian children have never heard of a peanut butter and jelly sandwich. These are just a few examples of how food is culturally defined.

Little research has been done into the relationship between the frequency of participation in family meals and the quality of children's food intake. However, several studies suggest that eating family dinners is associated with having a healthful dietary intake pattern, one with more fruits and vegetables, less fried food and soda, less saturated and trans fat, lower glycemic load, and more fibre and micronutrients, though with no material differences in red meat or snack foods (Gillman et al. 2000; Stockmyer 2001).

Health professionals have traditionally given parents and child-care providers nutritional information on what to feed children. Pamphlets on this topic generally discuss the basic food groups and the number and appropriate size of servings from each group. Advice on handling child-feeding problems has been limited and based on common sense, intuition, and experience. Emerging research on parent–child interactions involving food and eating has provided a foundation for conceptualising and promoting the establishment of a healthy feeding relationship between parent and child. According to Elleyn Satter (1996), there are many benefits of establishing such a relationship. An appropriate feeding relationship supports a child's development and fosters self-esteem. It helps the child to learn to discriminate between different feeding cues and to respond appropriately to them. It enhances the child's ability to consume a nutritionally adequate diet and to regulate the quantity of food they consume. Satter believes that the feeding relationship is characteristic of the overall parent–child relationship and that distortions that show up in feeding are likely to appear in other parent–child interactions.

Support for the promotion of a positive feeding relationship has come from extensive research conducted by Leann Birch and colleagues (Birch &

Davison 2001). According to Birch, her research shows that children can be given a substantial degree of control over their food intake, especially over the quantity of food consumed. Infants are born with the ability to self-regulate energy intake. This ability persists into the preschool years unless parents or other carers attempt to control the child's eating by imposing contingencies and coercive practices. Birch feels that parents can promote healthy self-regulation of eating by offering repeated opportunities to sample healthful foods in non-coercive, positive contexts, so that through associative learning processes some of the foods offered will become preferred (Birch 1996, pp. 2–5). Based on more recent research, Birch warns that coercive child feeding can easily lead to either dietary restraint and dis-inhibition among young girls as well as eating styles characterised by a lack of responsiveness to internal hunger and satiety cues (Carper et al. 2000).

Building on Birch's research, Satter calls for a division of responsibility in the feeding relationship, with parents assuming responsibility for providing a variety of nutrient-dense foods at regular meal and snack times, and children determining whether or not to eat and how much to eat (Satter 2000). Nutritionists and dietitians have made a special effort to help parents establish a positive feeding relationship with their children. They are basing their advice to parents on these recent research findings. However, there is a need to document the effectiveness of these efforts. Has there been an improvement in feeding relationships as a result of this new trend in the counselling of parents? One concern about Birch's research is that most of it has been carried out with mainstream middle class families. Do her findings also apply to children in low-income families, who may experience hunger regularly, or to children from minority groups, whose parenting practices are often quite different from those of the mainstream population?

Anthropologist Katherine Dettwyler has described tremendous cultural variation in the amount of control care-givers exert over food consumption of infants and children around the world (Dettwyler 1989, p. 679). This ranges from cultures that sanction maximum control by care-givers to those that give almost complete autonomy to infants. She raises a number of interesting questions about the effects these different 'styles' of feeding have on nutritional status and on the development of (life-long) attitudes towards hunger, satiety, food, and eating. She points out that parent–child power relationships are usually established around the control of food consumption. Parental authority and children's obedience to and respect for their parents are major values within many traditional cultures. It may be difficult for parents from these cultures to accept the concept that infants and children are capable of internal self-regulation of food intake and should be allowed to eat as much or as little of nutrient-dense foods as they want for meals and snacks. Some parents will be tempted to exert control over the quantity of food consumed by encouraging eating or by limiting consumption. Explaining that children have an innate ability to self-regulate energy intake, and emphasising that parents are responsible for the quality of foods served, may help to mitigate this tendency.

It is also important to make sure that parents do not misinterpret this division of responsibility as meaning that children should be given whatever they want, whenever they want it. This is certainly not what Birch and others are advocating. Although foods with low nutrient density—such as chips, confectionery, biscuits, cakes, and the like—should not become 'forbidden fruits', they should be given infrequently, as occasional adjuncts to nutritious meals and snacks.

People from developing countries who migrate to developed nations often have little experience with the idea that some foods are more nutrient dense than others. In their homeland, 'junk food' did not exist. My colleagues and I use the notion of 'any day foods', 'some day foods', and 'not many day' foods to the Hmong living in California in order to introduce them to the concept of nutrient density and the benefits of limiting consumption of foods of low nutrient density (Ikeda et al. 1991a, 1991b).

Lifestyle and environmental changes

Susan Crockett and Laura Sims have identified dramatic changes in lifestyle and the environment that have brought about significant alterations in children's eating patterns and food choices. Many of the sociocultural and demographic characteristics of the US population of today have combined to affect what children eat, where children eat, and with whom they eat. Decisions that used to be made by parents are now increasingly in the domain of other caregivers and peers (Crockett & Sims 1995, p. 235). The days are long gone when most children shared home-cooked meals around the family dinner table. This is because mothers, who were once the primary teachers of sound eating practices for their children, now face stiff competition from the media and childcare providers. Governments, schools, health professionals, and business groups must understand the reality and complexity of our changed societal eating environment and adjust their programs accordingly.

Surveys in the USA and elsewhere have shown a decline in the number of meals that families eat together (Gilman et al. 2000). However, Audrey Gillespie found that the vast majority of families with young children surveyed in upstate New York ate the evening meal together most of the time, and my colleagues and I reported similar findings after surveying Native American families in California (Gillespie & Achterberg 1989, p. 509; Ikeda et al. 1998, p. 25). Traditional communities tend to maintain a slower-paced lifestyle in which days are not regularly scheduled with activities, and family meals are an integral part of the daily routine. With respect to mainstream families, Gillespie has found that many parents feel that family meals become less important as children get older.

In light of the fact that as many as 11.6 million children in the USA under the age of 13 years are enrolled in child-care programs outside of the home, some attempt needs to be made to extend research on child feeding to cover the work of child-care providers. Marcia Nahikian-Nelms measured the nutrition knowledge and attitudes of child-care providers and observed their behaviour as they interacted with children at mealtimes (Nahikian-Nelms 1997, p. 505). She found that although care-givers believed that they positively influenced children's eating habits, they had poor nutrition knowledge and their behaviour at mealtimes was often inconsistent with their beliefs and with expert recommendations. They often did not sit and eat with the children; they did not model the behaviours they wanted to instil; and they often attempted to influence the amount of food consumed in inappropriate ways. In order to provide more guidance to child-care workers regarding what to feed children and how to help them establish healthy eating habits, the United States Department of Agriculture has set up a Child Care Nutrition Resource System on the internet (US Department of Agriculture 2003).

There is little doubt that school nutrition programs are introducing children from immigrant families to a wide variety of foods that are unfamiliar to their families. Attempts to measure the impact of this trend appear to be non-existent. In most schools, the provision of school meals has an almost mechanical quality and is done as efficiently as possible in order to conserve time and money. Although some school food-service directors have attempted to include 'ethnic' foods on the menu, meals generally consist of more widely popular items, such as pizza and spaghetti.

Food, culture, and psychological well-being

A good deal is known about the relationship between food and mental health. Mental health has been defined as a 'relative state of mind in which a person who is healthy is able to cope with and adjust to the recurrent stress of everyday living in an acceptable way' (Mosby 1994, p. 10). Carol Ryff has argued for a broader definition with respect to psychological well-being. Using the points of convergence within the literatures of developmental psychology, clinical psychology, and mental health, she found that the key dimensions of psychological well-being were self-acceptance, positive relationships with other people, autonomy, environmental mastery, purpose in life, and personal growth. As she states, 'Taken together, these six dimensions encompass a breadth of wellness that includes positive evaluations of one's self and one's life, a sense of continued growth and development as a person, the belief that life is purposeful and meaningful, the possession of good relationships with other people, the capacity to manage one's life and the surrounding world effectively, and a sense of self-determination' (Ryff 1995, p. 99).

Food deprivation

It was noted earlier that the most basic need of humans is to survive, and that in order to survive people must eat food. Food deprivation has a dramatic negative effect on all elements of well-being, especially psychological aspects, as was demonstrated in the classic study on human starvation that was carried out in 1945 by Ancel Keys and his colleagues at the University of Minnesota (see Box 13.3).

Numerous studies in developing countries have described the devastating effects that starvation and hunger have had on the physical, social, and mental well-being of millions of children and adults (Lewis 1992; see also Chapter 2). In developed countries, social welfare systems and special nutrition programs have been established to prevent these problems. However, in the USA, these systems have not totally eradicated the problem of hunger. From 1996 through 1999, adult respondents from nine states participating in the Behavioral Risk Factor Surveillance System survey provided information on their concerns about having enough food (Evenson et al. 2002). Overall, the prevalence of concern about having enough food ranged from 3.1% to 11.8% for individual states. Across all states, low household income was the strongest predictor of concern about having enough food. Nutritionists are troubled by the growing

Box 13.3 The 1945 food-deprivation study

The results of the 1945 study were documented in two volumes, published as *The Biology of Human Starvation* (Keys et al. 1950). In Chapter 38, there is an extensive description of the changes that took place in the male subjects as they became semi-starved. These changes included the following:

- striking changes in physical appearance
- marked reduction in strength and endurance
- constant craving for food
- strong tendency towards introversion
- almost no social interaction during eating, with subjects giving total attention to the food and its consumption
- preoccupation with thoughts of food, with food becoming the principal topic of conversation, reading, and day-dreams
- emotional instability, with transitory and sometimes protracted periods of depression
- heightened irritability
- neglect of personal appearance and grooming
- diminution of the sex drive
- compulsion to overeat or eat constantly once food restrictions were lifted.

hunger and homelessness in the USA, and they are paying a great deal of attention to **food security**, which has become a public policy issue (Kennedy 2002; Olson & Holben 2002).

At the same time that many people are going hungry because of a lack of food, self-imposed semi-starvation among women for the purpose of achieving a thin body has become commonplace in many Western societies (see Chapter 15). This process, better known as dieting, is an attempt, successful or unsuccessful, to restrict calorie intake in order to lose or maintain weight or alter one's body image (Polivy 1996). Janet Polivy points out that the consequences of food deprivation are extraordinarily similar for animals and human beings. It does not matter whether the food restriction for human beings is involuntary (that is, controlled by external forces), or a voluntary choice to restrain one's eating either for the benefit of science (as in the starvation study by Keys and colleagues), or for personal goals (such as those of dieters or patients with eating disorders): people who are food-deprived exhibit a variety of cognitive, emotional, and behavioural changes, and almost all of these changes have negative consequences.

Health professionals, for the most part, have played down the adverse effects that constant dieting has on health. They continue to advise individuals to lower their energy intake in order to achieve and maintain a 'healthy weight' (NIH 1998). Less than 2% of those who attempt to do so actually accomplish this goal, primarily because obesity is the result of powerful biochemical defects in the systems responsible for the control of body weight (Schwartz & Seeley 1997, p. 54). And there is little evidence that weight loss would actually benefit the obese (Lee & Paffenbarger 1996, p. 116; see also Chapter 17). None of this has dampened enthusiasm among health professionals for 'treating' obesity by recommending a restriction of food intake. The situation has become even more serious with evidence that dieting and a 'fear of fat' are damaging all aspects of well-being in children and adolescents (Berg 1997; Ikeda & Mitchell 2001).

This emphasis on thinness is confusing to new immigrants to the USA, many of whom are from developing countries that value fatness as a symbol of wealth and well-being. A study of Mexican–American women showed that mothers of obese children selected a chubby baby as the ideal baby significantly more often than mothers of non-obese children (Alexander et al. 1991, p. 53). Indeed, in remote areas of Mexico, where medical treatment may not be readily available, fatter infants have a better chance of surviving diseases and food scarcity than do thinner infants. Recently immigrated Mexican–American men may take pride in having fat wives and children, as evidence of their ability to provide for their families.

Although mainstream American women may be highly dissatisfied with their weight, this is not the case among women from less-developed countries who have recently immigrated to the USA. When 209 Hmong women living in California were asked about their weight, 60% said that they were 'just right', 25% thought they were 'too thin', and only 15% said they were 'too fat' (Ikeda et al. 1991a, p. 171). However, Perez and his colleagues found that a combination of acculturative stress and body dissatisfaction may render minority women more vulnerable to bulimic symptoms, whereas the absence of acculturative stress among minority women may buffer them against bulimic symptoms, even in the presence of body dissatisfaction (Perez et al. 2002).

Another minority group in the USA, African Americans, are much more tolerant of obesity than Caucasian women. Sheila Parker and her colleagues found African–American females to be more flexible than their white counterparts in their concepts of beauty. They also tended to de-emphasise external beauty as a prerequisite for popularity. African–American girls were more apt to be supportive of each other with respect to 'looking good', as opposed to white girls, who were apt to be envious and competitive with respect to appearance. White girls tended to view appearance as the most critical factor in becoming popular (Parker et al. 1995, p. 103).

A number of nutritionists are advocating a new approach to weight management and health promotion for large people called the 'non-dieting, size acceptance' approach, in the hope of diminishing the adverse effects of rampant body dissatisfaction among girls and women (Miller 1999; Parham 2000; see also Chapter 12).

Emotions and food

Emotions do influence eating behaviour in human beings. Negative emotions have been thoroughly studied and it is well established that they increase food consumption. Positive emotions also seem to increase food intake, but this finding is less conclusive (Canetti et al. 2002). Macht studied the impact of anger, fear, sadness, and joy on hunger (Macht 1999). Subjects reported experiencing higher levels of hunger during anger and joy than during fear and sadness. They also reported that during anger there was an increase of impulsive eating—that is, fast, irregular, and careless eating of any food available. During joy there was an increase of hedonic eating, which is the tendency to eat because of the pleasant taste of the food. Macht's study found that anger and joy had a stronger influence on eating behaviour than sadness and fear.

Spirituality and healing in mainstream and traditional cultures

Traditional cultures have long recognised the importance of spiritual beliefs to the healing encounter. They have created complex ceremonies and rituals to alleviate anxiety and cultivate an expectation of healing. The treatments used by shamans are always linked to the cause of the illness. If the body is out of balance, then balance must be restored. If the soul has been lost, then it must be found. If a taboo has been broken, penance is due. If a noxious object has entered the body, it must be removed. Western health professionals have difficulty accepting the notion that conditions such as soul loss and spirit possession actually exist. Nevertheless, members of traditional cultures may believe that these conditions exist and are the cause of their illness. Galanti points out that 'Whether these etiologies are the true causes of the disease is irrelevant. A patient who believes he or she is ill because of soul loss will not be cured by any amount of antibiotics. The mind is very powerful, as the **placebo effect** demonstrates. The patient's beliefs, as well as the body, must be treated' (1991, p. 102).

Animosity among Westerners towards traditional medicine dates back to colonial times, when healers, who were powerful leaders in their communities, were forbidden by law from practising. The World Health Organization (WHO) recently released its first global strategy on traditional, complementary, and alternative medicines (WHO 2003). Besides reviewing these practices worldwide, the 74-page strategy document outlines steps that governments can take over the next 3 years to improve the safety, efficacy, and availability of these practices. WHO experts suggest that the lack of interaction between traditional healers and medical doctors is a source of lost opportunities (Fink 2002).

Some health professionals have speculated that under-utilisation of Western health services by non-Western populations can be explained by the fact that the traditional health beliefs and practices are rooted deep within these cultures. They are concerned that such beliefs and practices may act as barriers to access to and utilization of services. To examine this hypothesis, Jenkins and his colleagues examined traditional health beliefs and practices among Vietnamese in the San Francisco Bay area and analysed the relationships between these factors and access to health care and use of preventive health services (Jenkins et al. 1996). The results of this study showed clearly that many Vietnamese possessed traditional health beliefs and practices that differed from those of the general population of the USA. Yet the data did not support the conclusion that these traditional beliefs and practices acted as barriers to access to Western medical care or to utilisation of preventive services. Kim conducted a similar study with elderly Korean Americans and found that health-service utilisation among this group varied: some only used Western medicine, some only used traditional Korean medicine (hanbang), and some used both Western and traditional clinics (Kim 2002). Western-trained health professionals can take solace in the fact that patients tend not to abandon biomedical treatment when using traditional medicine.

David Aldridge has argued that spirituality must not be ignored in modern medical practice. He believes that issues of abandonment, suffering, hopelessness, and lack of purpose, as well as problems arising from the process of dying, are essentially spiritual, not solely physiological, psychological, or social (Aldridge 1993, p. 4). Spiritual well-being has been described as having three dimensions: a sense of meaning, purpose, and fulfilment in life; the hope or will to live; and belief and faith in self, others, and a supreme being (Ross 1995).

Steven Hawks believes that spirituality is a vital component of human wellness, and that there may be ways in which health practitioners can enhance spirituality (Hawks et al. 1995, p. 371). More and more research in recent years has examined the relationship between spirituality and health. Health professionals are recognising that religious and spiritual concerns are important for understanding health-related behaviours, attitudes, and beliefs. Chatters (2000) states that 'recent research has validated the multidimensional aspects of religious involvement and investigated how religious factors operate through various biobehavioral and psychosocial constructs to affect health status through proposed mechanisms that link religion and health'.

Interestingly, there have been very few attempts by biomedical researchers to examine the potential relationship between spirituality and the placebo effect. The 'placebo effect' can be defined as any practice that has no clear clinical or physiological aspect but that brings about an observable change in a patient's condition (Brody 1985). Placebo effects have been found with drugs, medical treatments, surgery, biofeedback, psychotherapy, and diagnostic tests (Turner et al. 1994). Judith Turner and others (1994) found that individuals do not consistently demonstrate placebo responses across placebo administrations. However, patients' positive expectations of treatment increase their responsiveness to treatment. Turner also points out that a provider's warmth, friendliness, interest, empathy, and positive attitude towards the patient and towards the treatment are associated with positive effects of placebos as well as of active treatments. Turner admits that confusion and uncertainty exists among physicians and other health professionals about placebo effects. There is a general failure to appreciate the interaction of body processes with thoughts of past experiences and anticipated events and with immediate environmental influences. These factors are inextricably intertwined, and may never be unravelled by biomedical research.

Papakosta and Daras propose a reconceptualisation of the 'placebo effect' as a 'response to the healing situation' and propose harnessing this response so it can be deliberately mobilised (Papakosta & Daras 2001). As mentioned earlier, traditional healers have long recognised the importance of creating an environment that promotes anticipation of healing. They have learned to maximise the body's ability to heal itself, and have unquestioningly accepted this ability without understanding the intricacies of how it operated.

Conclusion

The immigration of large numbers of people from developing nations has resulted in societies that are increasingly culturally pluralistic. The foodways, health beliefs, and health practices of traditional cultures in developing countries are quite different from those of Western societies. There is evidence that health professionals in Western societies are becoming less **ethnocentric** and more understanding, accepting, and respectful of the values, assumptions, and beliefs of members of traditional cultures. Becoming more cross-culturally sensitive, competent, and knowledgable may help Western-trained health professionals to become more open to holistic approaches to health that encompass total well-being.

Summary of main points

- Because of the immigration of large numbers of people from developing countries, cultural diversity is increasing in countries such as Australia, the USA, Canada, and the UK.
- People from developing countries are apt to practise traditional forms of medicine that are more holistic with respect to the concept of health.
- Health professionals, trained in biomedicine, feel an increasing need to become cross-culturally competent since they are now working with patients from very diverse cultures.
- Health professionals are learning to understand and accept the values, assumptions, beliefs, and practices of people from other cultures in order to help these people.
- Health professionals are being encouraged to reconsider the narrow approach to health that promotes physical health over other aspects of well-being.

Discussion questions

1 What are the similarities and differences in the concepts of health in biomedicine and traditional medicine?
2 How does food facilitate social and psychological well-being in all cultures, whether Westernised or traditional?
3 What are some of the barriers that health professionals trained in biomedicine have to overcome in order to effectively treat people from traditional cultures?
4 Are there potential benefits to the adoption of a more holistic approach to health by Western health professionals?
5 Can and should health professionals trained in biomedicine accept and harness the positive benefits of traditional healing while being unable to explain the biomedical basis for these effects?

Further investigation

1. Joanne Ikeda states that 'The challenge for health professionals is to help patients change their diets in ways in which the socio-cultural function of food remains intact'. Discuss.
2. Examine the ethnic composition of your local community. What changes would you make to the health services in your community to ensure that they address cultural diversity?

Further reading and web resources

Books

Hays, P. A. 2002, *Addressing Cultural Complexities in Practice: A Framework for Clinicians and Counselors*, American Psychological Association, Washington, DC.

Articles

Harris-Davis, E. I. & Haughton, B. 2000, 'Model for Multicultural Nutrition Counseling Competencies', *Journal of the American Dietetic Association*, vol. 100, no. 10, pp. 1178–85.

Hawks, S. 1995, 'Review of Spiritual Health: Definition, Role, and Intervention Strategies in Health Promotion', *American Journal of Health Promotion*, vol. 9, no. 5, pp. 371–8.

Web sites

Center for Immigration and Multicultural Studies: cims.anu.edu.au/index.html

Includes a page with sixty links to international sites dealing with immigration and multicultural studies. Sponsored by the Australian National University.

Cross Cultural Health Care Program: www.xculture.org/

Aims to serve as a bridge between communities and health care institutions, to ensure full access to quality health care that is culturally and linguistically appropriate. Sponsored by a grant from the W. K. Kellogg Foundation.

Diversity Rx: www.DiversityRx.org/

Focuses on how language and culture affect the delivery of quality services to ethnically diverse populations. Sponsored by the National Conference of State Legislatures, Resources for Cross Cultural Health Care, and the Henry J. Kaiser Family Foundation.

Ethnic/Cultural Food Guide Pyramids: www.nal.usda.gov/fnic/etext/000023.html

Includes pyramids for Asian, Arabic, Chinese, Cuban, Indian, Italian, Mexican, Portugese, Russian, Thai, Japanese, and Mediterranean diets and more! Sponsored by the Food and Nutrition Information Center (US).

Food and Nutrition Information Center—Cultural and Ethnic Food and Nutrition Education: www.nal.usda.gov/fnic/pubs/bibs/gen/ethnic.html

Provides links to books, book chapters, booklets, journal articles, and online information for myriad cultures. Sponsored by the US Department of Agriculture.

Multicultural Web Links: www.isomedia.com/homes/jmele/mcultlink.html

Links to multicultural book and journal publishers, education sites, resource sites, photographs, and articles. Geared towards k–12 teachers. Sponsored by *Multicultural Book Review*.

Office of Minority Health: www.omhrc.gov/

Offers publications, links to data and statistics, health links, and information on initiatives, cultural competence, health and race, and health disparities. Sponsored by the US Department of Health and Human Services.

Resources for the Anthropological Study of Food Habits: lilt.ilstu.edu/rtdirks/

A wealth of articles on every aspect of the study of food habits. Sponsored by Illinois State University.

References

Aldridge, D. 1993, 'Is There Evidence for Spiritual Healing?', *Advances*, vol. 9, no. 4, pp. 4–21.

Alexander, M. A., Sherman, J. B. & Clark, L. 1991, 'Obesity in Mexican-American Preschool Children: A Population Group at Risk', *Public Health Nursing*, vol. 8, no. 1, pp.53–8.

Allen, D. E., Patterson, Z. J. & Warren, G. L. 1970, 'Nutrition, Family Commensality, and Academic Performance among High School Youth', *Journal of Home Economics*, vol. 62, no. 5, pp. 333–7.

American Academy of Pediatrics 1999, 'Culturally Effective Pediatric Care: Education and Training Issues', *Pediatrics*, vol. 103, no. 1, pp. 167–70.

American Nurses Association 1991, 'Position Statement: Cultural Diversity in Nursing Practice', <www.nursingworld.org/readroom/position/ethics/>.

Australian Nursing Council 2002, 'Code of Ethics for Nurses in Australia', <www.anci.org.au/codeofethics.htm>.

Avlund, K. & Damsgaard, M. T. 1998, 'Social Relations and Mortality: An Eleven Year Follow-up Study of 70-year-old Men and Women in Denmark', *Social Science & Medicine*, vol. 47, no. 5, pp. 635–43.

Balcazar, H., Trier, C. M., & Cobas, J. A. 1995, 'What Predicts Breastfeeding Intention in Mexican-American and Non-Hispanic White Women? Evidence from a National Survey', *Birth*, vol. 22, no. 2, pp. 74–80.

Berg, A., Mellstrom, D., Person, G. & Swanborg, A. 1981, 'Loneliness in the Swedish Aged', *Journal of Gerontology*, vol. 36, pp. 342–9.

Berg, F. M. 1997, *Afraid to Eat: Children and Teens in Weight Crisis*, Healthy Weight Publishing Network, Hettinger, North Dakota.

Birch, L. L. 1996, 'Food Acceptance Patterns: Children Learn What They Live', *Pediatric Basics*, no. 75, pp. 2–5.

Birch, L. L. & Davison, K. K., 2001, 'Family Environmental Factors Influencing Behavioral Controls of Food Intake and Childhood Overweight', *Pediatric Clinics of North America*, vol. 48, no. 4, pp. 893–907.

Bodeker, G. C. 1996, 'Global Health Traditions, Fundamentals of Complementary and Alternative Medicine', in M. S. Micozzi (ed.), *Fundamentals of Complementary and Alternative Medicine*, Churchill Livingstone, New York.

Brody, H. 1985, 'Placebo Effect: An Examination of Grunbaum's Definition', in L. White, B. Tursdky & G. E. Schwartz (eds), *Placebo Theory, Research, and Mechanisms*, Guilford Press, New York.

Bryant, C. A., Courtney, A., Markesbery, B. A. & DeWalt, K. 1985, *The Cultural Feast: An Introduction to Food and Society*, West Publishing Co., St Paul.

Canetti, L., Bachar, E., Berry, E. M. 2002, 'Food and Emotion', *Behavioral Processes*, vol. 60, no. 2, pp. 157–64.

Carper, J. L., Fisher, J. O. & Birch, L. L. 2000, 'Young Girls' Emerging Dietary Restraint and Disinhibition are Related to Parental Control in Child Feeding', *Appetite*, vol. 35, pp. 121–9.

Chatters, L. M. 2000, 'Religion and Health: Public Health Research and Practice', *Annual Review of Public Health*, vol. 21, pp. 335–67.

Chen, J. L. & Rankin, S. H. 2002, 'Using the Resiliency Model to Deliver Culturally Sensitive Care to Chinese Families', *Journal of Pediatric Nursing*, vol. 17, no. 3, pp. 157–66.

Clendenen, V. I., Herman, P. C. & Polivy, J. 1994, 'Social Facilitation of Eating among Friends and Strangers', *Appetite*, vol. 23, pp. 1–13.

Crockett, S. J. & Sims, L. 1995, 'Environmental Influences on Children's Eating', *Journal of Nutrition Education*, vol. 27, no. 5, pp. 235–49.

Cruickshank, J. K. & Sharma S. 2001, 'Cultural Differences in Assessing Dietary Intake and Providing Relevant Dietary Information to British African-Caribbean Populations', *Journal of Human Nutrition & Dietetics*, vol. 14, no. 6, pp. 449–56.

Curry, K. R. 2000, 'Multicultural Competence in Dietetics and Nutrition', *Journal of the American Dietetic Association*, vol. 100, no. 10 pp. 1178–85.

Dettwyler, K. A. 1989, 'Styles of Infant Feeding: Parental/Caretaker Control of Food Consumption in Young Children', *Research Reports: American Anthropologist*, vol. 91, pp. 696–703.

Engel G. 1977, 'The Need for a New Medical Model Challenge for Biomedicine', *Science*, vol. 196, no. 42, pp. 129–36.

Evenson, K. R., Laraia, B. A., Welch, V. L., Perry, A. L. 2002, 'Statewide Prevalence of Concern about Enough Food', *Public Health Reports*, vol. 117, no. 4, pp. 358–65.

Fee, C. H. 1998, 'Increasing Cultural Competence for Effective Client Counseling: An Experimental Course', *Journal of Nutrition Education*, vol. 30, pp. 117–19.

Fink, S. 2002, 'International Efforts Spotlight Traditional, Complementary, and Alternative Medicine', *American Journal of Public Health*, vol. 92, pp. 1734–9.

Foster, G. & Anderson, B. G. 1978, *Medical Anthropology*, John Wiley & Sons, New York.

Freed, G. L., Clark, S. J., Sorenson, J., Lohr, J. A., Cefalo, R., & Curtis, P. 1995, 'National Assessment of Physicians' Breast-feeding Knowledge, Attitudes, Training, and Experience', *Journal of the American Medical Association*, vol. 273, no. 6, pp. 472–6.

Galanti, G. 1991, *Caring for Patients from Different Cultures: Case Studies from American Hospitals*, University of Pennsylvania Press, Philadelphia.

Gillespie, A. & Achterberg, C. 1989, 'Comparison of Family Interaction Patterns Related to Food and Nutrition', *Journal of the American Dietetic Association*, vol. 89, pp. 509–12.

Gillman, M. W. 2000, 'Family Dinner and Diet Quality among Older Children and Adolescents', *Archives of Family Medicine*, vol. 9, pp. 235–40.

Harris-Davis, E. I. & Haughton, B. 2000, 'Model for Multicultural Nutrition Counseling Competencies', *Journal of the American Dietetic Association*, vol. 100, no. 10, pp. 1178–85.

Hart, J. T. 1997, 'What Evidence Do We Need for Evidence Based Medicine?', *Journal of Epidemiology of Community Health*, vol. 51, no. 6, pp. 623–9.

Hawks, S. 1995, 'Review of Spiritual Health: Definition, Role, and Intervention Strategies in Health Promotion', *American Journal of Health Promotion*, vol. 9, no. 5, pp. 371–8.

Hawthorne, K. 2001. 'Effect of Culturally Appropriate Health Education on Glycaemic Control and Knowledge of Diabetes in British Pakistani Women with Type 2 Diabetes Mellitus', *Health Education Research*, vol. 16, no. 3, pp. 373–81.

Hedrick, H. 1999, 'Cultural Competence Compendium', *American Medical Association*, Chicago.

Hyman, I., Guruge, I., Makarchuk M. J., Cameron, J. & Micevski V. 2002. 'Promotion of Healthy Eating among New Immigrant Women in Ontario', *Canadian Journal of Dietetic Practice & Research*, vol. 63, no. 3, pp. 125–9.

Ikeda, J. P., Ceja, R. C., Glass, R. S., Harwood, J. O., Lucke, K. A. & Sutherlin, J. M. 1991a, 'Food Habits of the Hmong Living in Central California', *Journal of Nutrition Education*, vol. 23, no. 4, pp. 168–74.

Ikeda, J. P., Chan, S., Harwood, J. O., Lucke, K. A. & Sutherlin, J. M. 1991b, 'Nutrition Education for the Hmong', *Journal of Nutrition Education*, vol. 23, no. 4, p. 198.

Ikeda, J. P. & Mitchell, R. A. 2001, 'Dietary Approaches to the Treatment of the Overweight Pediatric Patient', *Pediatric Clinics of North America*, vol. 48, no. 4, pp. 955–68.

Ikeda, J. P., Murphy, S., Mitchell, R. A., Flynn, N., Mason, I. J., Lizer, A., Pike, B. & Lamp, C. 1998. 'Foodways and Dietary Quality of Rural California Indian Homemakers', *Journal of the American Dietetic Association*, vol. 98, no. 7, pp. 812–14.

Ikeda, J. P., Pham, L, Nguyen K. P., Mitchell R. A. 2002, 'Culturally Relevant Nutrition Education Improves Dietary Quality Among WIC-eligible Vietnamese Immigrants', *Journal of Nutrition Education & Behavior*, vol. 34, no. 3, pp. 151–8.

Ishii-Kuntz, M. 1990, 'Social Interaction and Psychological Well-being: Comparison across Stages of Adulthood', *International Journal of Aging and Human Development*, vol. 30, no. 1, pp. 15–36.

Jenkins, C. N., McPhee, L. T., Stewart, S. & Ha, N. T. 1996, 'Health Care Access and Preventive Care among Vietnamese Immigrants: Do Traditional Beliefs and Practices Pose Barriers?', *Social Science & Medicine*, vol. 43, pp. 1049–56.

Kennedy, E. 2002, 'The New Face of Food Insecurity and Hunger', *Nutrition Today*, vol. 37, no. 4, pp. 154–5.

Keys, A., Brozek, J., Henschel, A., Mickelson, O. & Taylor, H. L. 1950, *The Biology of Human Starvation*, University Of Minnesota Press, Minneapolis.

Kim, M., Han, H. R., Kim, K. B. & Duong, D. N. 2002, 'The Use of Traditional and Western Medicine among Korean American Elderly', *Journal of Community Health*, vol. 2, pp. 109–20.

Kittler, P.G. & Sucher, K.P. 2004, *Food and Culture*, 4th edn, Wadsworth, California

Lee, M. & Paffenbarger, R. S. 1996, 'Is Weight Loss Hazardous?', *Nutrition Reviews*, vol. 54, no. 4 (supp.), pp. 116–24.

Lewis, S. 1992, 'Food Security, Environment, Poverty, and the World's Children', *Journal of Nutrition Education*, vol. 24, no. 1 (supp.), pp. 3–11.

Lowenberg, M. E. 1970, 'Socio-cultural Basis of Food Habits', *Food Technology*, vol. 24, no. 8, pp. 27–32.

Macht, M. 1999, 'Characteristics of Eating in Anger, Fear, and Sadness', *Appetite*, vol. 33, pp. 129–39.

McIntosh, W. A., Kaplan, H. B., Kubena, K. S., Landmann, W. A. 1993, 'Life Events, Social Support, and Immune Response in the Elderly', *International Journal of Aging and Human Development*, vol. 37, no. 1, pp. 23–6.

Metcalf, P. A., Scragg, R. K., Tukuitonga, C. F., Dryson, E. W. 1998. 'Dietary Intakes of Middle-aged European, Maori and Pacific Islands People Living in New Zealand', *New Zealand Medical Journal*, vol. 111, pp. 310–13.

Micozzi, M. S. 1996, *Fundamentals of Complementary and Alternative Medicine*, Churchill Livingstone, New York.

Miller, W. C. 1999, 'How Effective are Traditional Dietary and Exercise Interventions for Weight Loss?', *Medicine, Science, and Sports Exercise*, vol. 31, no. 8, pp. 1129–34.

Mosby's Medical Nursing and Allied Health Dictionary 1994, 4th edn, Mosby, St Louis.

Muecke, M. A. 1983, 'Caring for Southeast Asian Refugee Patients in the USA', *American Journal of Public Health*, vol. 174, no. 7, pp. 431.

Mullins, L. C., Cook C., Mushel M. & Machin G. 1993, 'A Comparative Examination of the Characteristics of Participants of a Senior Citizens Nutrition and Activities Program', *Activities, Adaptation and Aging*, vol. 17, no. 3, pp. 15–37.

Nahikian-Nelms, M. 1997, 'Influential Factors of Caregiver Behavior at Mealtime: A Study of 24 Child-care Programs', *Journal of the American Dietetic Association*, vol. 97, no. 5, pp. 505–9.

National Institutes of Health 1998, *Clinical Guidelines on the Identification, Evaluation and Treatment of Overweight and Obesity in Adults—The Evidence Report*, National Heart, Lung and Blood Institute, Bethesda, MD.

New South Wales Government 2003, *Multicultural Health Communication*, <www.mhcs.health.nsw.gov.au/>.

NIH. *see* National Institutes of Health.

Office of Minority Health 2001, *National Standards for Culturally and Linguistically Appropriate Services in Health Care*, US Department of Health and Human Services, Washington, DC.

Olson, C. M. & Holben, D. H. 2002, 'Position of the American Dietetic Association: Domestic Food and Nutrition Security', *Journal of the American Dietetic Association*, vol. 102, no. 12, pp. 1840–7.

OMH. *see* Office of Minority Health.

Papakostas, Y. G. & Dara, M. D. 2001, 'Placebos, Placebo Effect, and the Response to the Healing Situation: The Evolution of a Concept', *Epilepsia*, vol. 42, no. 12, pp. 1614–25.

Parker, S., Nichter, M., Nichter, M., Vuckovic N., Sims C. & Ritenbaugh C. 1995, 'Body Image and Weight Concerns among African American and White Adolescent Females: Differences that Make a Difference', *Human Organization*, vol. 54, no. 2, pp.103–13.

Parham, E. 2000. 'Promoting Body Size Acceptance in Weight Management Counseling', *Journal of the American Dietetic Association*, vol. 100, no. 10, pp. 920–5.

Perez, M., Voelz, Z. R., Pettit, J. W. & Joiner, T. E. 2002, 'The Role of Acculturative Stress and Body Dissatisfaction in Predicting Bulemic Symptomatology', <www.interscience.wiley.com>.

Polivy, J. 1996, 'Psychological Consequences of Food Restriction', *Journal of the American Dietetic Association*, vol. 96, no. 6, pp. 589–92.

Rassin, D. K., Richardson, C. J., Baranowski, T., Nadar, P. R., Guenther, N., Bee, D. E. & Brown, J. P. 1994, 'Incidence of Breast-feeding in a Low Socioeconomic Group of Mothers in the United States: Ethnic Patterns', *Pediatrics*, vol. 73, pp. 132–7.

Ross, L. 1995, 'The Spiritual Dimension: Its Importance to Patients' Health, Well-being and Quality of Life and Its Implications for Nursing Practice', *International Journal of Nursing Studies*, vol. 32, no. 5, pp. 457–68.

Rozin, P. 1996, 'Sociocultural Influences on Human Food Selection', in E. Capaldi (ed.), *Why We Eat What We Eat*, American Psychological Association, Washington, DC.

Ryff, C. 1995 'Psychological Well-being in Adult Life', *Current Directions in Psychological Science*, vol. 4, no. 4, pp. 99–104.

Sanjur, D. 1995, *Hispanic Foodways, Nutrition and Health*, Simon & Schuster, Massachusetts.

Satia, J. A., Patterson, R. E., Kristal, A. R., Hislop, T. G., Yasui, Y. & Taylor, V. M. 2001, 'Development of Scales to Measure Dietary Acculturation among Chinese-Americans and Chinese-Canadians', *Journal of the American Dietetic Association*, vol. 101, no. 5, pp. 548–53.

Satter, E. M. 1996. 'Internal Regulation and the Evolution of Normal Growth as the Basis for Prevention of Obesity in Children', *Journal of the American Dietetic Association*, vol. 96, no. 9, pp. 860–4.

Satter, E. M. 2000, *Child of Mine: Feeding with Love and Good Sense*, Bull Publishing, Palo Alto, California.

Schwartz, M. W. & Seeley, R. J. 1997, 'The New Biology of Body Weight Regulation', *Journal of the American Dietetic Association*, vol. 97, no. 1, pp. 54–8.

Smith, R., Mullins L. C., Mushel M. & Roorda, J. 1994, 'An Examination of Demographic, Socio-cultural, and Health Differences between Congregate and Home Diners in a Senior Nutrition Program', *Journal of Nutrition for the Elderly*, vol. 14, no. 1, pp. 1–21.

Stockmeyer, C. 2001, 'Remember When Your Mom Wanted You Home for Dinner?', *Nutrition Reviews*, vol. 59, no. 2, pp. 57–60.

Turner, J., Deyo, R., Loeser, J., Von Korff, M. & Fordyce, W. 1994, 'The Importance of Placebo Effects in Pain Treatment and Research', *Journal of the American Medical Association*, vol. 271, no. 20, pp. 1609–14.

Tuttle, C. R. & Dewy, K. G. 1994, 'Determinants of Infant Feeding Choices among Southeast Asian Immigrants in Northern California', *Journal of the American Dietetic Association*, vol. 94, no. 2, pp. 282–6.

UNICEF 2003, *Baby Friendly Hospital Initiative*, <www.unicef.org/programme/breastfeeding/baby.htm>.

United Nations 2002, *International Migration*, Population Division, Department of Economic and Social Affairs, New York.

US Department of Agriculture 2003, Child Care Nutrition Resource System, <www.nal.usda.gov/childcare/>, National Agricultural Library Food and Nutrition Service.

US Department of Health and Human Services 2001, *National Standards for Culturally and Linguistically Appropriate Services in Health Care*, Office of Minority Health, Rockville, Maryland.

Varghese, S. & Moore R. 2002, 'Dietary Acculturation and Health-related Issues of Indian Immigrant Families in Newfoundland', *Canadian Journal of Dietetic Practice and Research*, vol. 63, no. 2, pp. 72–9.

Wahlqvist, M. L. 2002, 'Asian Migration to Australia: Food and Health Consequences', *Asia Pacific Journal of Clinical Nutrition*, vol. 11, supp. 3, pp. S562–8.

Williams, N. 1997, 'Biologists Cut Reductionist Approach Down to Size', *Science*, vol. 277, no. 5325, pp. 476–7.

World Health Organization 2003, 'WHO Launches the First Global Strategy on Traditional and Alternative Medicine', <www.who.int/inf/en/pr-2002-38.html>.

14

Food and Ageing

Wm. Alex McIntosh and Karen S. Kubena

Overview

- Why are older people at risk of hunger and poor nutrition?
- How do social isolation and stress affect older people's nutrition?
- How do social relationships reduce the risk of hunger and poor nutrition among older people?

Older people are a group at high risk of food insecurity, hunger, and poor nutrition. They are particularly vulnerable because they generally have fewer socioeconomic resources than younger people and are more prone to isolation, disability, and stress. These problems tend to be even more prevalent among older people who are members of ethnic minorities. In addition, many countries, including the USA, have recently reduced funding for food-assistance programs such as food stamps and congregate meals. Private charities have been unable to compensate for these cutbacks. Many older people, however, are able to compensate for their lack of resources and physical isolation through their social networks. Older people who live alone may find mealtime companionship among their friends and neighbours. In addition, relatives and neighbours provide many disabled older people with shopping and cooking assistance.

Key terms

ageism
activities of daily living
disabilities
food insecurity
life chances
nutritional risk
postmodern society
role
social control
social isolation
social network
social support
socioeconomic status (SES)
status
stigma

Introduction

Older people are an important group for sociological study for a number of reasons. First, older people represent one of the fastest-growing segments of the population of most developed countries. The populations of most developed countries are growing older. In the USA, the number of people aged 65 or older constituted 13% of the population in 2000; it has been predicted that, by 2050, over 20% of the population will be in this age group, thanks to better diets as well as better health and health care (FIFARS 2000). The proportion of people aged 85 or above is expected to increase at an even faster rate during this same period. The growth of the older population and their increasing needs will have an impact on every aspect of society.

Second, because of filial obligations supported by laws, traditions, and social norms, older people are a group whose needs continue to be the responsibility of both families and the state. However, as older people live longer, and as financial and time constraints place a greater burden on families and government programs, it will become more and more difficult to meet these obligations.

Third, age is a social category and is related to **status** and **role**, two of sociology's most fundamental concepts. Typical roles include patient, physician, grandmother, and daughter. Age determines a role, 'independent of capacities and preferences' of the incumbent (Moen 1996, p. 171). Status represents the prestige or respect accorded to individuals occupying these social positions. The respect that an individual receives for performing a role is somewhat independent of actual performance; simply occupying the position itself accords a certain amount of prestige. 'Age', 'ageing', and 'elderly' are all words with supposed biological meanings, yet each represents a socially defined category. In fact, much of what passes as biological wisdom in defining 'older people' has more to do with socially generated beliefs and norms. In addition, because age is a social category, it contains an evaluative component. The terms 'age', 'ageing', and 'elderly' are all associated with negative expectations about abilities and quality of life, among other things (Palmore 1990). Ageing is also viewed as a process of declining status; it is seen as biologically driven downward mobility. This is, in part, true. Many older people experience a decline in their health as they age, and many face declining incomes in the form of retirement reimbursements. But ageing also has a negative status because of its relationship to what is currently one of the most desirable statuses in Western society: youth. There is considerable evidence that older people encounter **ageism**, or prejudice and discrimination based on age.

Because of the increasing size of the elderly population and the difficult economic circumstances that many older people face, sociologists and nutritionists have turned their attention to older people's food habits, nutritional status, and health. Several important themes have emerged from their studies.

The first is that of **socioeconomic status (SES)**. It is widely believed that inadequate resources are the reason for **food insecurity** and risk of malnutrition (McIntosh 1996; Weddle et al. 1996). A second theme is **social isolation**. Isolation from others is thought to deprive an individual of help, companionship, and motivation for self-care. The third theme represents the opposite of isolation: social integration and **social support**. A multiplicity of ties to others not only increases contact with other human beings, but also ensures companionship and access to resources such as transportation and help with cooking. Some believe that the nature of an older person's **social network** has greater consequence for them than the help that network provides; others have argued that the greatest impact of help from others lies in how it is perceived by its recipients.

The fourth, and most recent, theme to emerge in the sociology of nutrition is that of stressful life events. All human beings experience change, and some of these changes are upsetting and disrupting (Thoits 1995). Older people are not immune to such events, and they are most likely to experience events such as the death of a loved one. Such stressors have a negative impact on health, including nutritional status. The debate here centres on whether some stressors have a more deleterious effect than others have, and whether some individuals are better equipped than others to deal with negative life changes. Some old people are able to cope with the help of their social support network. Such aid comes into play for another kind of crisis that confronts many older people: reduced functional capacity.

Disability, its effects, and the social responses to it represent a fifth theme in the literature. As people age, the probability of contracting one or more chronic illnesses increases (Verbrugge 1990). A number of such illnesses have symptoms that limit mobility or some other aspect of body functioning (Manton 1989). Some older people are able to cope with these threats to independence through their own efforts. 'Self-care' involves those changes that individuals choose to make as a means of improving health and dealing with symptoms of illness—for example, dietary and exercise modifications. Certain limitations, however, may make it more difficult for some individuals to engage in self-care. In such cases, the social network's services become vitally important.

Sixth, sociologists have renewed their interest in the body as a reflection of various socially defined attributes of worth. These values play a major role in determining individuals' perceptions of themselves. Sociologists refer to this self-perception as 'the self'. Body image, or body self, has increased in importance in the formation of the self. Anthony Giddens (1991) and others have argued that individuals have found it increasingly difficult to affect their political and economic environments and so have turned to the self and the body as things upon which they can have an impact. Much of this concern is directed at manipulating body weight in an attempt to achieve physiologically improbable goals.

Finally, it should be noted that sociological approaches to food and nutrition tend to take a 'social problems' orientation. Concern centres on the social causes and consequences of food insecurity, hunger, malnutrition, overnutrition, and so on.

This chapter reviews the literature that has developed around the themes mentioned above, beginning with the notion that food and nutrition problems may be conceived of as social problems.

Ageing and associated food and nutrition problems

A number of nutritional problems confront older people, and they are usually presented in biological terms. Without doubt, these nutritional problems have clear biological causes and consequences; however, unless social and economic factors are also considered, our understanding of older people's nutrition is incomplete.

People's nutritional needs change as they age (Fiatarone & Evans 1993). Older people have decreased energy requirements but greater protein requirements. General concerns in this area have focused on the inability of some older people to meet their nutrient needs and on the effects of nutrient deficiency on, for example, immune function (Kubena & McMurray 1996). Mobility of elderly individuals is dependent on their having adequate bone mass and normal muscle function. Bone loss and impaired muscle function can be caused by inadequate dietary intake of vitamin D (Jassen et al. 2002) and calcium (Dawson-Hughes & Harris 2002). Increasingly, research is suggesting a role for adequate nutrition in maintaining cognitive functioning (Smith 2002). The lower intake of nutrients among the elderly is partly a result of the decreased income that some receive as they age, but it is also a consequence of misconceptions within this age group regarding their nutrient needs. One source of these misconceptions is the marketing messages of our consumer society. Products and advertisements both provide a contradictory array of information regarding the way that nutrition, health, and ageing are related.

Loosely associated with the declining ability of some older people to meet their nutritional needs are the problems of *hunger* and *food insecurity*. In the USA, the definitions of these terms are less rooted in biology than in norms. 'Hunger' is defined and measured in terms of the inability to buy all the food one would like or of sending one's children to bed hungry. For some, hunger is an acute, emergency situation, the result of a temporary shortfall in resources. For others, hunger is chronic. Some older people, for example, have reported that they commonly run short of money to purchase food during the last week of every month. While there is no evidence that such food insufficiency increases the likelihood of chronic disease, there is evidence that it increases the likelihood of infections such as pneumonia.

Food insecurity is a broader concern, affecting all those who believe that hunger is just around the corner. The food-insecure are those who anticipate deprivation, or the inability to achieve a diet that they consider adequate. Currently, 6% of elderly households are considered to be food-insecure (Nord 2002). Once again, inadequate resources appear to be the driving force behind food insecurity. Low income, costly medical bills, lack of transportation, and the absence of nearby grocery stores have been associated with food insecurity in the elderly (Rowley 2000). Furthermore, several studies of food-insecure elderly people indicate that such people are more likely to experience poorer quality diets, be underweight, and be anaemic (Rose & Oliveria 1997; Klesges et al. 2001; Lee & Frongillo 2001; American Dietetic Association 2002). We suggest that, while those who concern themselves with hunger and food insecurity probably have negative biological consequences in mind, it is, once again, a normative interpretation that has led people to define these conditions as problems. Hunger and food insecurity are thought to be the result of the inequitable distribution of resources and the denial of inalienable rights. According to this position, all people, including older people, have a 'right to food', which is said to incorporate 'the right of everyone to an adequate standard of living' and 'the right to be free from hunger' (Alston 1994, p. 209).

Declining ability may also result from changes in body size. Both being overweight and being underweight, and the associated health problems, can make it more difficult for older people to perform their various roles. In addition, there is strong evidence that body weight affects the probability of death. Older people who are greatly over or under the weight standard for their age, height, and gender have a greater risk of dying than older people closer to standard (Flegal 1996).

Weight is also a highly salient social marker, partly because of the association of slimness with youth but also because what is defined socially as excessive body weight connotes a negative social status. To begin with, the weight itself is considered unattractive. In addition, overweight is perceived to be a marker of more deep-seated undesirable traits, such as greed, dishonesty, and lack of ambition and self-control (see Chapter 17).

Both chronic illnesses and medications affect appetite, the sense of taste, the absorption of nutrients, and the need for nutrients. There are social issues here as well, regarding the decline in social relationships that occurs when an individual becomes disabled and the effect that this decline and the disability has on the individual's ability to shop, prepare meals, and eat. Furthermore, there is some evidence that older people are overmedicated because they are too passive when confronting medical authority.

Access to resources

Socioeconomic status

A person's socioeconomic status (SES) depends on their wealth, prestige, and power; differential access to these things leads to differences in lifestyle and life chances (Gerth & Mills 1946). Those with greater wealth and status enjoy better **life chances** than those with less of these, simply because they can afford better health practices and health care. Greater resources also permit expanded lifestyle choice in such areas as dwellings, food purchases, clothing, and vacations. An individual's SES is usually conceptualised and measured by that individual's education, occupation, and income. Education and occupation are primary determinants of income, and they are also sources of prestige. Gender, ethnicity, and age also influence a person's status. Each of these characteristics affects access to wealth, prestige, and power, and each is associated with distinctive aspects of lifestyle and life chances.

In the USA, old age was commonly associated, until recently, with poverty—as many as 25% of older people were classified as poor (Crystal 1996, p. 394). Increases in social security benefits and other changes have halved this proportion. But great inequities remain among retired people in the USA, with former white-collar workers generally in a better financial position than former blue-collar workers. Furthermore, many of those in the lowest 20% of incomes are still considered to be above the poverty line (Crystal 1996, p. 397). Those in this group tend to lack health insurance, but are not considered poor enough to qualify for means-tested programs like Medicaid or food stamps. Janet Poppendieck (1998) found that while only 10% of the poor are older people, this group constitutes 22% of soup-kitchen clientele.

As previously mentioned, malnutrition exists among poor older people (Weddle et al. 1996). In fact, low SES is related to low levels of nutrition knowledge, poorer eating habits, inadequate diets, and poorer nutritional status (Wolinsky et al. 1990; Quinn et al. 1997; Howard et al. 1998; Guthrie & Lin 2002). Finally, food-insecure elderly people are more likely to be poor and in need of food assistance (Lee & Frongillo 2001).

Ethnicity and class

Ethnicity is a social status that has implications for the distribution of resources. Social scientists argue that the combination of low income and ethnicity constitutes 'double jeopardy'. Others have used this same argument to claim that older people who are members of minorities experience double jeopardy, and it is a relatively short logical leap to argue that poor older people from minority groups are subject to triple jeopardy. Poverty rates have remained highest among older black and Hispanic people, with 26% and 21% living in poverty respectively (Federal Interagency Forum on Aging Related Statistics 2000). The effects of double and triple jeopardy are reflected in older people's nutritional status. Nancy Schoenberg and her colleagues (1997), for example, found rural black people to be at greater **nutritional risk** than urban black people or white people in general.

Class conflict

Social class is no mere marker of the distribution of resources. Because resources are scarce, struggles ensue over their distribution, usually along class lines. Food and medical care are two such resources that politicians frequently consider redistributing according to social categories, such as those of children, older people, women, and veterans. In an era of declining social-welfare funding, struggles over food-stamp eligibility and access to subsidised medical care once again reflect class, generational, and ethnic group interests, among other interests.

In the past, after a great deal of political struggle, a number of programs to benefit older people were established in the USA. Meals on Wheels and Congregate Meals were designed to provide one meal per day containing at least one-third of the recommended daily allowances of most nutrients. Critics have sparked considerable debate over the efficacy of these programs, and some have even questioned their fairness.

Debates aside, budget cuts and decentralisation have left many US states unable to fund feeding programs to meet current needs. Forty-one percent of Meals on Wheels programs report, for example, that they now maintain lengthy waiting lists (Ponza et al. 1997). Many food-pantry and soup-kitchen participants report that they use such food charities because they are unable to access government programs such as food stamps.

Ageism and stigma

Social statuses contain evaluative as well as cognitive components: not only do we hold certain beliefs about people with particular statuses, but we also make judgments regarding the worth of people holding those statuses. Age is a social status, and various age groups reflect differentially valued statuses. Groups accorded negative status and negative evaluations frequently encounter prejudice and discrimination. When it comes to race and gender, these are referred to as 'racism' and 'sexism' respectively. 'Ageism' is their counterpart when it comes to negative evaluations of old age. At present, youth is generally regarded as more valuable in Western societies, and so young people are accorded more status than older people. Perhaps one of the most undesirable statuses to inhabit is that of old age. Numerous negative evaluations are attached to this status. As with many negatively evaluated statuses, the basis of the negative evaluations is socially determined.

The stereotypes associated with ageism are similar to those associated with racism and sexism in that they question the abilities of the status-holder relative to the abilities of others. Those holding negatively evaluated statuses are usually judged, in a biological sense, as having lesser physical and mental abilities, and this negative evaluation is thus considered to be both natural and immutable. Many believe that because some older people have physical or mental limitations, all older people are so limited. These assumptions lead to a denigration of older people's capabilities and worth. It is assumed that older people are unable to care for themselves. Such negative evaluations hinder older people's ability to obtain employment and result in intergenerational struggles over the allocation of resources. Much of the debate over the extent to which current and future resources should be devoted to retirement benefits and to subsidised access to food and medical care has reflected a continuing debate over the worth of older persons. This debate is cast in either equality or equity terms. Equality arguments have endorsed the sharing of resources based on need (Poppendieck 1998). Equity arguments, by contrast, have advocated the sharing of resources based on the size of the contribution each individual makes to society or has made at some time in the past (Gokhale & Kotlikoff 1998).

The unequal distribution of resources is brought about by social as well as economic and political factors. Those persons eligible for aid, including older people, often refuse it because of the **stigma** associated with poverty and welfare. Simply put, those who are less well-to-do are less admired than those who are better off. In the USA, where poverty is viewed as being the result of irresponsible behaviour rather than unequal resource distribution, the working poor are accorded more respect than the non-working poor. The poor who get by on charity and/or welfare receive the least respect. The public associates a wide range of negative characteristics with welfare recipients, culminating in the pejorative label 'the undeserving poor'. Those who provide benefits such as food stamps hold many of these stereotypes, as do a number of those who work for private charities such as food pantries and soup kitchens (Poppendieck 1998).

Social resources

Social networks

A person's social network consists of his or her friends, relatives, spouses, children, co-workers, neighbours, fellow members of voluntary organisations, fellow church members, and so on. These tend to be the individuals with whom a person has the most contact or from whom the person receives the most support or help (Berkman & Glass 2000; Brissette et al. 2000). 'Social support' refers to both instrumental aid (goods and services) and expressive aid (emotional support and companionship). Social support also includes efficacious **social control:** network members may attempt to persuade or cajole an individual to engage in desirable behaviour, such as reducing dietary fat (Brissette et al. 2000).

People who receive social support become ill less frequently and recover more quickly and successfully when they do become ill. The most striking effect of social support appears to be the lessening of the risk of death. Numerous studies have found that those with social support are likely to live longer than those who lack it (Schoenbach et al. 1986; Seeman et al. 1993; Yasuda et al. 1997). More recently, we and our colleagues have found a connection between social support and nutritional health (McIntosh, Kubena & Landmann 1989; McIntosh, Shifflett & Picou 1989; McIntosh et al. 1995).

Social support results in part from the very structure of the social network. There is considerable debate between social-support researchers, however, about the degree to which network characteristics are more important than the aid received or the recipients' subjective evaluations of that aid. Network structure characteristics include the network's size (the number of people in it) and its density (the degree to which network members know and interact with one another). Networks that contain a small number of people who are well acquainted with one another provide greater intimacy and emotional support. At the same time, some studies suggest that larger networks generate more support (Faber & Weiseman 2002). In our study of 424 free-living Houston elderly, we found that those older people with large social networks tended to receive more social support, although men received greater benefits from greater network size than did women. Older men with large networks got more advice about food and cooking, more help with grocery shopping and cooking, and more mealtime companionship than men with smaller networks, and their iron status was better than that of men with smaller networks. Older women with denser networks tended to have more company during meals. Other researchers have found that larger, denser networks are not necessarily beneficial for the elderly when it comes to making healthy changes in their diets. Such networks may block these efforts through social control (Silverman et al. 2002).

Social support and nutrition

Certain kinds of social support appear to be associated with nutritional health, particularly that of older people. Instrumental aid, such as transportation for grocery shopping, help with meal preparation, companionship during meals, loans of food, and advice about cooking, diets, and food, has the potential to maintain or improve the nutritional health of individuals. It is precisely this sort of help that older people frequently need. In Houston, older people with a greater number of companions in their networks had better appetites and more muscle mass (McIntosh, Kubena & Landmann 1989a). Those who received help with shopping, cooking, and housekeeping were at lower nutritional risk (fewer impediments to eating a healthy diet) than those who received little or no such help. And those who had more people in their social network giving them advice about food and nutrition tended to have higher vitamin B-6 status. Elderly people who had a greater number of companions had lower nutritional risk (Hendy et al. 1998).

Social isolation and loneliness

Living alone (social isolation) represents a clear trend among older people. In 1960, about 20% of older people in the USA lived alone, but by 1998 the proportion had increased to 37% (FIFARS 2000). Forty-one per cent of elderly women lived alone; this is partly the result of the mortality differential between males and females—women, on average, live longer than men. Our own data on older people in Houston indicate that 12% of the men and 50% of the women lived alone, and that the propensity to live alone increased with age, especially for women. Others note, however, that many older people live close to one of their children, and approximately 40% keep in daily phone contact with one of their offspring (Moody 1994). Because many older people live alone, they are frequently thought to be at risk of loneliness and poor nutrition. There are documented health consequences of living alone. Those older people who live alone because of the recent death of their spouse, for example, have an increased risk of mortality (Rogers 1996).

Nutrition researchers have argued that without the social contact that typically come with shared living arrangements, the motivation to cook food or to eat regular meals may be reduced. Maradee Davis and her colleagues (1985) found that older people who lived alone were more likely to eat an inadequate diet than those living with a spouse. Similarly, Susan Murphy and others (1990) observed that older women had a higher energy intake if they lived with a spouse. Dellmar Walker and Roy Beauchene (1991) found among older people in Georgia that the greater the loneliness experienced, the poorer the diet in terms of iron, protein, phosphorous, riboflavin, niacin, and ascorbic acid (vitamin C). In New York, older men skipped more meals if they lived alone (Frongillo et al. 1992). In Houston, we measured dietary adequacy by determining the degree to which the dietary intake of older people over a 3-day period met 67% of the recommended dietary allowances (RDAs) for this age group. We found that both older women and older men were likely to fall below 67% of the RDA for a number of nutrients if they lived by themselves. Elderly people who ate a greater number of meals with others each day were less likely to experience nutritional risk (Hendy et al. 1998). In addition, Green and Wang (1995) found that elderly people who skip meals have less adequate diets than those who miss no meals. Meal skipping is more common among those elderly people who live alone. Finally, old people who report being lonely also report forgetting to eat and experiencing loss of appetite (Wylie 2000).

Disability and functioning

All human beings are susceptible to impairments caused by chronic illness, injury, or accident; impairments involve bodily abnormalities that may limit movement of limbs or cause generalised muscular weakness (Jette 1996). They can limit the ability of a person to perform social roles and are often referred to as '**disabilities**'. Older people are more prone to chronic illnesses than people in other age groups, and thus their rates of impairment are higher. Furthermore, as they grow older, greater percentages of older people experience these limitations. Some impairments result in functional limitations or restrictions in performing what are considered to be everyday activities. In the USA, 39% of people aged 70 or older have one or more disabilities that limit **activities of daily living**. Eleven per cent of older people experience difficulties shopping for groceries; 4% have trouble preparing meals; 2% experience problems with eating food (Jette 1996, p. 100). Some elderly people report having to sit down while cooking, while others have trouble manipulating cooking utensils (Wylie 2000).

Disabilities are directly associated with risk of poor nutritional status, and thus some of the tools devised to measure nutritional risk include measures of disability, such as difficulty chewing or swallowing. Certain foods may be avoided as a result of such difficulties, as a study by Mary-Ellen Quinn and others (1997) demonstrated. Other studies have found a relationship between inadequate diet and level of disability (Walker & Beauchene 1991). The Houston study found that older people who had difficulties in using their upper bodies or difficulties in walking tended to have more body fat and less muscle mass. Such people also tended to be less physically active and have less adequate diets. Elderly people with dentures tend to eat more fats, sweets, and snacks (Vitolins et al. 2002).

There is considerable debate over whether disability leads to an increase or decrease in social support. Some studies provide evidence of a shrinking social network and increased social isolation, with the only help with daily activities being supplied by remaining kin. Furthermore, as the burden of such help grows, the care-giver is in danger of experiencing resentment and burnout. Others argue that disabilities actually mobilise social networks into action, increasing the level of support supplied (Kivett et al. 2000). Our own Houston data confirm the latter hypothesis. The greater the level of disability, the more help with grocery shopping, cooking, and other activities of daily living the older person received, regardless of gender (McIntosh et al. 1988). In addition, people with disabilities were less likely to experience the nutritional problems mentioned above when they had social support from others. For example, although those with limited mobility were less likely to eat breakfast and more likely to have lower muscle mass but more body fat, these negative effects were offset, to a degree, by their having more friends in their social network and receiving help with activities of daily living.

Stress, strain, and health

Human beings experience a great number of changes in their lives—marriage, having children, getting and losing jobs, retirement, illness, and so on (Thoits 1995). A number of these changes are welcomed; others are not. The unwelcome changes are thought to be 'stressors'. Stressors are threats, demands, or constraints on individuals that 'tax or exceed their resources for managing them' (Burke 1996, p. 146). One kind of stressor is a 'life event', a discrete, observable event that leads to a major change in life. Divorce, job loss, and the death of a spouse are examples of such potentially life-shattering changes.

There is a well-established link between poor health and stressors (House et al. 1988). Various forms of illness—such as coronary heart disease, hypertension, cancer, and depression—have been found to be associated with various stressful events, such as job loss, marital conflict, and the death of a spouse or close friend (Marmot & Theorell 1988; Umberson et al. 1992). Definitions of 'stress' often emphasise disequilibrium in the organism, which results from exposure to stressors. William Krehl (1964, p. 4) has described nutrition as 'the sum of all the processes by which an organism ingests, digests, absorbs, transports, and utilizes food substances'. Therefore, anything that disrupts nutrient ingestion, digestion, absorption, transportation, or utilisation by the body is a potential stressor.

Research suggests that stressful life events do indeed interfere with nutrition. In our study of older Virginians (McIntosh, Shifflett & Picou 1989), we found that financial worries led to depressed appetite, which in turn was associated with lower intake of energy and protein. More recently, Payette and others (1995) observed a relationship between a high level of self-assessed stress and a lower intake of protein. We found, in Houston, that the two kinds of events that seemed to have the greatest negative effect on older people's nutrition were financial difficulties and general, unspecified problems in relations with various family members. Financial problems had a negative effect on body fat, muscle mass, iron status, and the frequency of eating breakfast among older women, and older men had higher body fat and snacked more if they had recently experienced family troubles.

Social identity and age

All human beings develop a sense of identity, persona, or self. Much of this sense of self derives from social interactions with others. Individuals, however, have some control over the perceptions of others and actively attempt to influence those perceptions. While there is disagreement over the degree to which an individual can 'manage the impressions of others', it is clear that, within limits, this management is achievable.

Western societies, particularly the USA, place a high value on youthfulness. Mass-media programming and advertising have perhaps exacerbated this emphasis, by mostly featuring young actors, presenters, and models (Turrow 1997). But as the older population has grown and its economic fortunes have improved, producers and advertisers have discovered a vast, insufficiently tapped market in older people, especially the so-called 'young-old' (those under 70 years of age). Their approach to older people has been to stress that older people are still as capable, in many ways, as the young. According to Mike Featherstone and Mike Hepworth (1995), this has had a positive effect in that it has helped reduce the perception of older people as less capable human beings. However, it must be pointed out that producers have attempted to market their products in terms of identity manipulation—that is, they have developed products to help older people disguise their age.

Sociologists have increasingly been taking the body's social dimensions seriously. Chris Shilling (1994), for example, has put forward the notion that bodies are judged unequally; thus differentials in body size and shape constitute a form of inequality. Linda Jackson's (1992) review of extant research indicates that body appearance has a significant impact on how others judge an individual. Pierre Bourdieu (1984) has hypothesised that bodies reflect social class in that they represent the owner's relationship to the worlds of necessities and taste. Among the lower classes, a heavy body represents a diet high in fat but low in cost. Bourdieu refers to this as the diet of necessity. Taste makes necessity a virtue. Bodies also reflect 'bodily orientation'. Members of the working class take a more instrumental approach to their body in that they make direct use of their body's capacities in making their living. The implication for eating is that heavy foods in large quantities are desirable because of their perceived contribution to strength. The dominant classes, according to Bourdieu (1979/1984), prefer slender bodies and are willing to defer gratification to achieve them.

In old age, working class individuals may experience a decline in both income and bodily function. A middle class individual may worry about being replaced by a person with a younger body. Upper class individuals may view middle and old age as a time to enjoy the fruits of their labour and may expect to have not only the money but also the physical capacity to do so.

The body in **postmodern society** is said to have become more malleable, in the sense that it can be manipulated in a person's quest for a new or altered identity. Surgery, diets, exercise, and drugs have all been called upon in attempts to make the body appear more youthful (see Chapter 15). Older people are equally inclined to make such attempts (Biggs 1997). Older people are slightly less likely to participate in exercise programs, but after differences in disability levels are accounted for their participation levels are higher than those of many other age groups. Older women have been found to worry about weight gain for appearance as well health reasons. But for these women, 'health tends to be a valid justification for being concerned with one's weight, while an appearance orientation is deemed to be indicative of vanity' (Clarke 2002). Featherstone and Hepworth argue that with increasing age, the physical constraints on the ability to alter appearance grow. As they put it, the body becomes an unchanging mask that its occupant can no longer escape.

Conclusion

While much is known about the effects of SES on nutrition, research is just beginning on how social networks help older people maintain a healthy diet and avoid nutritional risk. Similarly, the negative effects of both stressors and disabilities on older people's nutrition are not fully understood. Finally, older people's efforts to manage their identities through diet and exercise remain an important, but relatively unexplored, area of sociological research.

Summary of main points

- While older people's energy needs tend to be lower than those of people from other age groups, their need for nutrients is as high or higher.
- Older people's nutrition can be compromised by chronic illness, disabilities, and interactions between drugs and nutrients.
- Older people are at greater risk of serious consequences from food-borne illnesses than younger people.
- Older people's nutrition is also negatively affected by poverty, stressful life events, and social isolation.
- Social networks supply aid of various kinds, such as transportation to buy groceries, help with meal preparation, and companionship during meals. Both network structure and the help networks provide have a positive impact on older people's nutrition. Social support helps people overcome the constraints imposed by living alone, functional limitations, and stressful events.
- Older people perceive their weight, as do others in modern society, as a means through which they can recreate their selves. Consumer culture has some influence on the choices that older people and others make when selecting 'selves' to pursue. As they age, however, their ability to control their appearance declines.

Discussion questions

1. What are the main nutritional problems faced by older people?
2. What are the sources of low socioeconomic status and isolation among older people?
3. How do stress and disabilities affect older people's nutrition?

4 How does social support help older people overcome such problems as lack of resources, isolation, disability, and stress?
5 Why are older people concerned with their physical appearance, and what do they do to maintain that appearance?

Further investigation

1 Compare and contrast the effects of social and economic resources on the elderly's nutritional health. How might the absence of both social and economic resources interact to make an elderly person's situation worse?
2 Discuss the normative/moral issues connected to the status of elderly people in society and how the normative order contributes to the elderly's nutritional health.

Further reading and web resources

Books

Blaxter, M. 1990, *Health and Lifestyles*, Routledge, New York.

Kosberg, J. I. & Kayne, L. 1997, *Elderly Men: Special Problems and Professional Challenges*, Springer, New York.

Litwak, E. 1985, *Helping the Elderly: The Complementary Roles of Informal Networks and Formal Systems*, Guilford Press, New York.

Sokolovsky, J. 1997, *The Cultural Context of Aging: Worldwide Perspectives*, Bergin & Garvey, Westport.

Articles

Peters, G. R. & Rappaport, L. R. 1988, 'Food, Nutrition, and Aging: Behavioral Perspectives', *American Behavioral Scientist*, vol. 32, no. 1, special issue, pp. 1–88.

Journals

Ageing and Society
Agriculture, Food, and Human Values
Appetite
The Gerontologist
Journal of Aging and Health
Journal of the American Dietetic Association
Journal of Gerontology
Journal of Health and Social Behavior
Journal of Nutrition Education

Journal of Nutrition for the Elderly
Journal for the Study of Food and Society

Web sites

Association for the Study of Food and Society: www.nyu.edu/education/nutrition/NFSR/ASFS.htm
New England Research Institute: www.neri.org

References

Alston, P. 1994, 'International Law and the Right to Food', in B. Harriss-White & R. Hoffenberg (eds), *Food: Multidisciplinary Perspectives*, Blackwell, New York.

American Dietetic Association 2002. 'Position of the American Dietetic Association: Domestic Food and Nutrition Security', *Journal of the American Dietetic Association*, vol. 102, no. 12, pp. 1840–7.

Berkman, L. F. & Glass, T. 2000, 'Social Integration, Social Networks, Social Support, and Health', in L. F. Berkman & I. Kawachi (eds), *Social Epidemiology*, Oxford University Press, New York.

Biggs, S. 1997, 'Choosing Not to Be Old? Masks, Bodies, and Identity Management in Later Life', *Ageing and Society*, vol. 17, September, pp. 553–70.

Bourdieu, P. 1979/1984, *Distinction: A Social Critique of the Judgement of Taste*, Harvard University, Cambridge, Massachusetts.

Brissette, I., Cohen, S. & Seeman, T. 2000, 'Measuring Social Integration and Social Networks', in S. Cohen, L. G. Underwood & B. H. Gottlieb (eds), *Social Support Measurement and Intervention: A Guide for Health and Social Scientists*, Oxford University Press, New York.

Burke, P. 1996, 'Social Identities and Psychosocial Stress', in H. B. Kaplan (ed.), *Psychosocial Stress: Perspectives on Structure, Theory, Life-Course, and Methods*, Academic Press, San Diego.

Clarke, L. H. 2002. 'Older Women's Perceptions of Ideal Body Weights: The Tensions between Health and Appearance Motivations for Weight Loss', *Ageing and Society*, vol. 22, no. 6, pp. 751–73.

Crystal, S. 1996, 'Economic Status of the Elderly', in R. H. Binstock & L. K. George (eds), *Handbook of Aging and the Social Sciences*, 4th edn, Academic Press, San Diego.

Davis, M. A., Randall, E., Forthofer, R. N., Lee, E. S. & Margen, S. 1985, 'Living Arrangements and Dietary Patterns of Older Adults in the United States', *Journal of Gerontology*, vol. 40, no. 4, pp. 434–9.

Dawson-Hughes, B. & Harris, S. S. 2002, 'Calcium Intake Influences the Association of Protein Intake with Rates of Bone Loss in Elderly Men and Women', *American Journal of Clinical Nutrition*, vol. 75, no. 6, pp. 773–9.

Faber, A. D. & Wasserman, S. 2002. 'Social Support and Social Networks: Synthesis and Review', *Social Networks and Health*, vol. 8, pp. 29–72.

Featherstone, M. & Hepworth, M. 1995, 'Images of Positive Ageing: A Case Study of Retirement Magazine', in M. Featherstone & M. Hepworth (eds), *Images of Ageing: Representations of Later Life*, Routledge, New York.

Federal Interagency Forum on Aging Related Statistics 2000, *Older Americans 2000: Key Indicators of Well-being*, Washington, DC.

Fiatarone, M. & Evans, W. 1993, 'The Etiology and Reversibility of Muscle Dysfunction in the Aged', *Journal of Gerontology*, vol. 47, September, pp. 77–83.

FIFARS—*see* Federal Interagency Forum on Aging Related Statistics.

Flegal, K. M. 1996, 'Trends in Body Weight and Overweight in the US Population', *Nutrition Reviews*, vol. 54, no. 4 (supp.), pp. 97–100.

Frongillo, E. A., Jr, Rauschenbach, B. S., Roe, D. R. & Williamson, D. F. 1992, 'Characteristics Related to Elderly Persons' Not Eating for 1 or More Days: Implications for Meal Programs', *American Journal of Public Health*, vol. 82, no. 4, pp. 600–2.

Gerth, H. & Mills, C. W. 1946, *From Max Weber: Essays in Sociology*, Oxford University Press, New York.

Giddens, A. 1991, *Modernity and Self-identity: Self and Society in the Late Modern Age*, Stanford University Press, Stanford, California.

Gokhale, J. & Kotlikoff, L. J. 1998, 'Medicare from the Perspective of Generational Accounting', paper presented at the Medicare Reform: Issues and Answers conference, Bush School of Government and Public Service, Texas A&M University, College Station, 3 April.

Green, B. L. & Wang, M. Q. 1995, 'The Effects of Missing Meals on the Dietary Adequacy of the Elderly: The 1987–1988 National Food Consumption Survey', *Wellness Perspectives*, vol. 11, no. 4, pp. 64–8.

Guthrie, J. F. & Lin, B.-H. 2002, 'Overview of the Diets of Lower- and Higher-Income Elderly and Their Food Assistance Options', *Journal of Nutrition Education and Behavior*, vol. 34, supp. 1, pp. S31–S41.

Hendy, H. M., Nelson, G. K. & Greco, M. D. 1998, 'Social Cognitive Predictors of Nutritional Risk in Rural Elderly Adults', *International Journal of Aging and Human Development*, vol. 47, no. 4, pp. 299–327.

House, J. S., Umberson, D. & Landis, K. 1988, 'Structures and Processes of Social Support', *Annual Review of Sociology*, vol. 14, pp. 293–318.

Howard, J. H., Gates, G. E., Ellersieck, M. R., & Dowdy, R. P. 1998, 'Investigating Relationships between Nutritional Knowledge, Attitudes and Beliefs, and Dietary Adequacy of the Elderly', *Journal of Nutrition for the Elderly*, vol. 17, no. 4, pp. 35–52.

Jackson, L. A. 1992, *Physical Appearance and Gender: Sociological and Sociocultural Perspectives*, State University of New York, Albany.

Jassen, H. C., Samson, M. M., & Verhaar, H. J. J. 2002, 'Vitamin D Deficiency, Muscle Function, and Falls in Elderly People', *American Journal of Clinical Nutrition*, vol. 75, no. 4, pp. 611–15.

Jette, A. 1996, 'Disability Trends and Transitions', in R. H. Binstock & L. K. George (eds), *Handbook of Aging and the Social Sciences*, 4th edn, Academic Press, San Diego.

Kivett, V. R., Stevenson, M. L. & Zwane, C. H. 2000, 'Very-old Rural Adults: Functional Status and Social Support', *Journal of Applied Gerontology*, vol. 19, no. 1, pp. 58–77.

Klesges, L. M., Pahor, M., Shorr, R. J., Wan, J. Y. & Williamson, J. D. 2001, 'Financial Difficulty in Acquiring Food among Elderly Disabled Women: Results from the Women's Health and Aging Study', *American Journal of Public Health*, vol. 91, no. 1, pp. 68–75.

Krehl, W. A. 1964, 'Nutrition in Medicine', *American Journal of Clinical Nutrition*, vol. 15, no. 2, pp. 191–4.

Kubena, K. & McMurray, D. 1996, 'Nutrition and the Immune System: A Review of Nutrient–Nutrient Interactions', *Journal of the American Dietetic Association*, vol. 96, no. 11, pp. 1156–64.

Lee, J. S. & Frongillo, E. A., Jr. 2001. 'Nutritional and Health Consequences are Associated with Food Insecurity among U.S. Elderly Persons', *Journal of the American Dietetic Association*, vol. 131, no. 5, 1503–9.

McIntosh, W. A. 1996, *Sociologies of Food and Nutrition*, Plenum, New York.

McIntosh, W. A., Kaplan, H. B., Kubena, K. S. & Landmann, W. A. 1995, 'Life Events, Social Support, and Immune Response in Elderly Individuals', in J. Hendricks (ed.), *Health and Health Care Utilization in Later Life*, Baywood, Amityville, New York State.

McIntosh, W. A., Kubena, K. S. & Landmann, W. A. 1989, *Social Support, Stress, and the Diet and Nutrition of the Aged: Final Report to the National Institute on Aging*, Department of Rural Sociology, Texas A&M University, College Station.

McIntosh, W. A., Kubena, K. S., Landmann, W. A. & Dvorak, S. 1988, *A Comparative Assessment of the Social Networks of Elderly Disabled and Non-disabled*, paper presented at the annual meeting of the American Sociological Association, Atlanta, August.

McIntosh, W. A., Shifflett, P. A. & Picou, J. S. 1989, 'Social Support, Stress, Strain, and the Dietary Intake of the Elderly', *Medical Care*, vol. 21, no. 2, pp. 140–53.

Manton, K. 1989, 'Epidemiological, Demographic, and Social Correlates of Disability among the Elderly', *Milbank Memorial Quarterly*, vol. 67, supp. 2, part 1, pp. 13–58.

Marmot, M. & Theorell, T. 1988, 'Social Class and Cardiovascular Disease', *International Journal of Health Service*, vol. 8, no. 4, pp. 1–13.

Moen, P. 1996, 'Gender, Age, and the Life Course', in R. H. Binstock & L. K. George (eds), *Handbook of Aging and the Social Sciences*, 4th edn, Academic Press, San Diego.

Moody, H. R. 1994, *Aging: Concepts and Controversies*, Pine Forge Press, Thousand Oaks, California.

Murphy, S. P., Davis, M. A., Neuhouse, J. M. & Lein, D. 1990, 'Factors Influencing the Dietary Adequacy and Energy Intake of Older Americans', *Journal of Nutrition Education*, vol. 22, no. 6, pp. 284–91.

Nord, M. 2002 'Food Security Rates are High for Elderly Households', *Food Review*, vol. 25, no. 2, pp. 19–24.

Palmore, E. 1990, *Ageism: Negative and Positive*, Springer, New York.

Payette, H., Gray-Donaldson, K., Cyr, R. & Boutier, V. 1995, 'Predictors of Dietary Intake in a Functionally Dependent Elderly Population in the Community', *American Journal of Public Health*, vol. 85, no. 5, pp. 667–83.

Ponza, M., Ohls, J. C. & Millen, B. E. 1997, *Serving the Elderly at Risk, The Older Americans Act Nutrition Programs, National Evaluation of the Elderly Nutrition Program, 1993–1995*, Agency on Aging, National Aging Information Center, Washington, DC.

Poppendieck, J. 1998, *Sweet Charity? Emergency Food and the End of Entitlement*, Viking Penguin, New York.

Quinn, M. E., Johnson, M. A., Poon, L. W., Martin, P. & Nickols-Richardson, S. M. 1997, 'Factors of Nutritional Health-seeking Behaviors: Findings from the Georgia Centenarian Study', *Journal of Aging and Health*, vol. 9, no. 1, pp. 90–104.

Rogers, R. 1996, 'The Effects of Family Composition, Health, and Social Support Linkages on Mortality', *Journal of Health and Social Behavior*, vol. 37, no. 4, pp. 326–38.

Rose, D. & Oliveria, V. 1997. 'Nutrient Intakes of Individuals from Food Insufficient Households in the United States', *American Journal of Public Health*, vol. 87, no. 12, pp. 1956–61.

Rowley, T. D. 2000, *Food Assistance Needs of the South's Vulnerable Populations*, Southern Rural Development Center, Mississippi State University, Starkville, Mississippi.

Schoenbach, V. J., Kaplan, B. H. & Kleinbaum, D. G. 1986. 'Social Ties and Mortality in Evans County, Georgia', *American Journal of Epidemiology*, vol. 123, no. 4, pp. 577–91.

Schoenberg, N. E., Coward, R. T., Gilbert, G. H. & Mullens, R. A. 1997, 'Screening Community-dwelling Elders for Nutritional Risk: Determining the Influence of Race and Residence', *Journal of Applied Gerontology*, vol. 16, no. 2, pp. 172–89.

Seeman, T. E., Berkman, L. F., Kohout F., LaCroix, A. & Blazer, D. 1993, 'Intercommunity Variations in the Association between Social Ties and Mortality in the Elderly: A Comparative Analysis of Three Communities', *Annual Review of Epidemiology*, vol. 3, pp. 325–35.

Shilling, C. 1994, *The Body and Social Theory*, Sage, Newbury Park, New York State.

Silverman, P., Hecht, L. & McMillin, J. D. 2002, 'Social Support and Dietary Change among Older Adults', *Ageing and Society*, vol. 22, no. 1, pp. 29–59.

Smith, A. D. 2002, 'Homocystine, B vitamins, and Cognitive Deficit in the Elderly', *American Journal of Clinical Nutrition*, vol. 75, no. 6, pp. 785–6.

Thoits, P. A. 1995, 'Stress, Coping, and Social Support Processes: Where are We? What Next?', *Journal of Health and Social Behavior*, vol. 36 (supp.), pp. 53–79.

Turrow, J. 1997, *Breaking up America: Advertisers and the New Media World,* University of Chicago Press, Chicago.

Umberson, D., Wortman, C. & Kessler, R. 1992, 'Widowhood and Depression: Explaining Low-term Gender Differences in Vulnerability', *Journal of Health and Social Behavior*, vol. 33, no. 1, pp. 10–24.

Verbrugge, L. M. 1990, 'The Iceberg of Disability', in S. M. Stahl (ed.), *The Legacy of Longevity: Health and Health Care in Later Life*, Sage, Newbury Park, New York State.

Vitolins, M. Z., Quandt, S. A., Bell, R. A., Arcury, T. A. & Case, L. D. 2002. 'Quality of Diets Consumed by Older Rural Adults', *Journal of Rural Health*, vol. 18, no. 1, pp. 49–56.

Walker, D. & Beauchene, R. 1991, 'The Relationship of Loneliness, Social Isolation, and Physical Health of Independently Living Elderly', *Journal of the American Dietetic Association*, vol. 90, no. 12, pp. 1667–72.

Weddle, D., Wellman, N. & Shoaf, L. 1996, 'Position of the American Dietetic Association: Nutrition, Aging, and the Continuum of Care', *Journal of the American Dietetic Association*, vol. 96, no. 10, pp. 1048–52.

Wolinsky, F., Coe, R. M., McIntosh, W. A., Kubena, K. S., Pendergast, J. M., Chavez, M. N., Miller, D. K., Romeis, J. C. & Landmann, W. A. 1990, 'Progress in the Development of a Nutritional Risk Index', *Journal of Nutrition*, vol. 120, pp. 1549–53.

Wylie C. 2000, 'Health and Social Factors Affecting the Food Choices and Nutritional Intake of Elderly People with Restricted Mobility', *Journal of Human Nutrition and Dietetics*, vol. 13, no. 5, pp. 363–71.

Yasuda, N., Zimmerman, S. I., Hawkes, D., Fredman, L., Hebel, J. R. & Magaziner, J. 1997, 'Relation of Social Network Characteristics to 5-Year Mortality among Young-Old versus Old-Old White Women in an Urban Community', *American Journal of Epidemiology*, vol. 145, no. 6, pp. 516–23.

Part 5

Food and the Body: Civilising Processes and Social Embodiment

> When you don't have any money, the problem is food. When you do have money, it's sex. When you have both, it's health.
>
> J. P. Donleavy, *The Ginger Man* (1955)

> Certainly these days, when I hear people talking about temptation and sin, guilt and shame, I know they're referring to food rather than sex.
>
> Carol Sternhell, quoted in Rothblum (1994, p. 53)

In developed countries, food is abundant, and food manufacturers, through the media, continuously and persuasively encourage people to enjoy the full pleasures of food consumption. Despite this, a competing trend away from food hedonism emerged in the late twentieth century and continues to this day: the increasing focus on the body has contributed to healthism, an ideology that views health as the primary human goal. The sins of gluttony and sloth have returned and can be seen in secular attitudes of lipophobia (fear of fat). For some people, these attitudes have translated into a lifelong quest for the holy grail of the 'thin ideal'. These attitudes are reflected in the health messages espoused by various health authorities and health 'experts', marketed by corporations, and adopted by consumers. Regimes of body control, particularly through the regulation of food intake, are now common features of Western culture. The chapters in this section deal with such food and body discourses:

- Chapter 15 explores the social construction of the thin ideal in Western societies and how women in particular deal with (adopt, modify, or resist) the social pressure to adopt regimes of body management and dieting.
- Chapter 16 examines eating disorders, highlighting the limitations of the medical model, and discusses the contributions of feminist and social constructionist approaches.
- Chapter 17 provides a sociological analysis of the stigmatisation of obesity.
- Chapter 18 discusses the notion of body acceptance and how women resist the thin ideal.

15

The Thin Ideal: Women, Food, and Dieting

Lauren Williams and John Germov

Overview

- What are the origins of the thin ideal for women and how is it perpetuated?
- How do women respond to the pressure of the thin ideal?
- Why do so many women succumb to the pressure of the thin ideal by dieting?

Gender differences in food consumption remain one of the clearest examples of the social appetite—in short, women often eat differently to men. The social norms governing women's appearance and behaviour result in concern about the implications food consumption has for the look of the body. The thin ideal is the desired aesthetic look for women's bodies in contemporary Western societies and its pursuit—primarily through dieting—significantly influences women's food choices. This chapter examines why dieting is predominantly a female behaviour by exploring the historical, structural, cultural, and critical factors that have contributed to the development of, and resistance to, the thin ideal.

Key terms

agency
anorexia nervosa
body acceptance
body mass index (BMI)
bulimia nervosa
eating disorders
epidemiology
feminist
gender socialisation
maternal ideal
muscular ideal
obesity
patriarchy
post-structuralist
social construction
social control
social determinism
social reconstruction
stigma
structuralist
structure/agency debate
thin ideal

Introduction: The sexual division of dieting

The term **'thin ideal'** refers to the social desirability of a slender body shape in Western societies. A thin body is considered the epitome of beauty and sexual attractiveness, and has been linked to social status, health, and even moral worth. As the overriding aesthetic ideal of female beauty, the thin ideal has significant implications for women's eating patterns. Dieting, or the conscious manipulation of food choice and eating patterns to reduce or maintain weight, is a common behaviour among Western women. It requires a considerable investment of time and money, as well as emotional and physical resources. Kelly Brownell and Judith Rodin (1994) note that the unsuccessful nature of diets can lead to a cycle of 'yo-yo' dieting or 'weight cycling', with detrimental physiological and psychological consequences (see also Berg 1995). Dieting

Table 15.1 Women, weight and dieting: Summary of findings from the Australian Longitudinal Study of Women's Health (in percentages)

Attitude/behaviour	*Young cohort (22–27)** *n = 9683*	*Mid-age cohort (47–52)*** *n = 12,328*
Dieted in past 12 months	50.5	47.0
Wanted to lose:		
1–5 kg	38.3	35.7
6–10 kg	21.0	22.0
>10 kg	16.1	21.1
'Happy as I am'	20.7	19.1
Wanted to gain weight	3.4	1.6
Weight control strategies used in past 12 months:		
Exercise	46.0	53.4
Vomited on purpose	4.8	n/a
Laxatives, diuretics, diet pills	6.2	3.6
Commercial weight loss programs	9.5	8.7
Meal replacements or slimming products	5.0	2.9
Cut size of meals	52.3	59.7
Cut fats and/or sugars	55.1	64.9
Fasting	13.4	3.0
Smoking	8.4	2.9
Vegetarian diet	n/a	7.4

* Data collected in 1998 ** Data collected in 2000

Source: RCGH (2002a, 2002b)

can thus result in a lifelong 'tug of war' with food, and women's food consumption can be plagued with feelings of guilt, anxiety, and deprivation.

Several authors have described the gendered nature of eating, particularly women's ambivalent relationship with food, their bodies, and the provision of food for significant others (Burgoyne & Clark 1983; Murcott 1983; Charles &

Box 15.1 Body Mass Index (BMI) and definitions of overweight

In the health sciences, 'overweight' and **'obese'** are generally defined in terms of **BMI**. A person's BMI is calculated by dividing their weight in kilograms by their height in metres squared:

$$\text{BMI} = \frac{\text{weight (kg)}}{\text{height (m}^2\text{)}}$$

For example, if a person weighed 67 kilograms and was 1.6 metres tall, their BMI would be 26.17 (67 divided by 2.56). The World Health Organization (WHO), using BMI, have defined the following weight ranges for both women and men:

BMI range	*WHO category*
<18.50	Underweight
18.50–24.99	Normal
25.00–29.99	Grade I overweight
30.00–34.99	Grade IIa* overweight
35.00–39.99	Grade IIb* overweight
40+ Grade III*	overweight*

* BMI ≥ 30 is often referred to as 'obese' *Sources:* WHO (2000); Bray et al. (1998)

A 'normal' or 'healthy' weight range is generally considered to be a BMI of between 18.5 and 24.9, 'underweight' is below 18.5, 'overweight' is equal to or above 25, and 'obese' is equal to or above 30. These international standards are relatively new and different cut-offs for each category have been used by researchers in different parts of the world. While BMI can be useful for population-wide **epidemiological** studies, concerns have been raised about the appropriateness of a standard BMI measure for individuals because of the physiological differences between women and men and between some ethnic groups. Some evidence suggests that waist measurement may be a stronger indicator of health risk than BMI (Egger 1992).

Kerr 1988; DeVault 1991). Women often assess food in terms of its dieting value, dividing foods into 'dieting' (good) and 'fattening' (bad) foods (Sobal & Cassidy 1987; McKie et al. 1993; Germov & Williams 1996a, 1996b). Gendered eating behaviour is epitomised by the sexual division of dieting—dieting is primarily a female act. Recent figures, drawn from the longitudinal Women's Health Australia (WHA) study, found that around half the women in the young (22–27) and mid-aged (47–52) cohorts had dieted in the previous year, and that only one in five of these women was happy with her weight (RCGH 2002a, 2002b). The WHA findings on dieting prevalence are summarised in Table 15.1. Of the women reporting dieting behaviour, over a third wanted to lose between 1 and 5 kilograms, a further 20% wanted to lose between 6 and 10 kilograms, and around 16% and 21% of the young and mid-age cohorts respectively wanted to lose more than 10 kilograms. Exercise and cutting down on fats, sugars, and the size of meals were the most popular weight-control strategies used, but of concern was the prevalence of fasting (particularly in young women), diet pills (including laxatives and diuretics), smoking, and vomiting. Such findings indicate the extent of body dissatisfaction among Australian women, and the prevalence of weight-control strategies with detrimental health consequences.

Many women who diet are actually within the medically defined 'healthy weight range' for their height (see Box 15.1) and therefore, according to current medical orthodoxy, do not have health reasons for trying to lose weight (Huon et al. 1990; Tiggemann & Pennington 1990; Banks 1992). Surveys in Australia throughout the 1980s and 1990s showed that more men than women were above their healthy weight range, even though more women diet (National Heart Foundation 1990; Australian Bureau of Statistics 1997). Recent Australian figures showed that 67% of men and 52% of women aged 25 or over were overweight or obese, and only 1% and 2% respectively were underweight—though this rises to 6% for women aged 18–24 (Dunstan et al. 2000; AIHW 2002). The pursuit of the thin ideal underpins the desire of most women for weight loss, and, as Table 15.1 shows, leads some women to consciously adopt unhealthy dieting practices to achieve the goal of slenderness (see Germov & Williams 1996b; Kenardy et al. 2001).

Why is the thin ideal so pervasive?

The controversial question is why so few women resist the thin ideal. **Feminist** writers have generally approached this vexed question from the opposing philosophical perspectives of **structuralist** feminism (liberal, Marxist, and radical feminism) and **post-structuralist** feminism. Structuralist theories assume that the lives of individuals are primarily determined by the society in which they live. The focus is on the large-scale features of society—such as the economy, political system, and dominant culture—and on how these structures shape individual and group behaviour. Post-structuralist theories developed as a critique of structuralist approaches that failed to adequately theorise how individuals shape society. Post-structuralist approaches generally abandon the search for universal, original causes, or for any form of 'objective reality' or overriding logic of social change (Annandale & Clarke 1996). Post-structuralist theorists focus on human agency and **social construction** rather than **social determinism**. Women are not conceived of as passive recipients of the dominant thin ideal discourse, but rather, 'It is women themselves who practise this discipline on and against their own bodies ... This self-surveillance is a form of obedience to patriarchy ... [a woman becomes] a body designed to please or excite' (Wearing 1996, p. 88).

The pressure to conform to the thin ideal clearly has structural elements, perpetuated by various social institutions and commercial interests, such as the media, fashion, and cosmetics industries. The health sector has also played a part, with anti-fat messages often equating health with thinness. These structural factors have clear antecedents in the historical development of **patriarchy**, particularly as represented in various forms of social regulation of the female body (Schwartz 1986; Turner 1992). However, structural factors alone do not provide a complete picture of the contemporary reproduction and pervasiveness of the thin ideal and gendered eating patterns. Post-structural factors, which represent women's subjectivity and **agency**—that is, the way women respond to the social pressure of the thin ideal on a daily basis—also play an important role.

This chapter aims to bridge these two perspectives by discussing the interplay between the patriarchal social structure and female agency: how the thin ideal shapes women's attitudes to food and eating, and how women adopt, modify, or reject these social ideals. Before exploring these issues further, we will look in the next section at the historical antecedents and cultural determinants of today's thin ideal.

Thin ideal antecedents: A brief historical overview

How and why did the thin ideal emerge, and why were women singled out as its subjects? While the thin ideal is a relatively recent phenomenon, the historical antecedents of the **social control** of the female body are well documented (Rubin 1975; Ehrenreich & English 1979; Michie 1987; Eisenstein 1988; Turner 1992; Corrigan & Meredyth 1994; Hesse-Biber 1996). In the nineteenth century, 'women's appearance norms' (Rothblum 1994) reinforced patriarchal beliefs about female sexuality and limited women's participation in public life; for example, corsetry and head-to-toe garments literally constricted the bodies and mobility of women. So the establishment of an ideal shape and size for women as an instrument of social control is not a new phenomenon. The socially desired body ideal may change over time, in terms of size and shape, but the existence of an ideal for women to aspire to has remained constant.

The female ideal of the nineteenth century was a large, curved body, which connoted fertility, wealth, and high status (Bordo 1993; Seid 1994). While poor women were occupied with physical work, the voluptuous women of the middle and upper classes were often viewed as objects of art, luxury, status, virtue, and beauty. Fatness was linked to emotional stability, strength (stored energy), good health, and refinement, to leisure rather than labour. The undergarment industry came to the rescue of the naturally thin woman with products such as inflatable rubber attachments (complete with dimples) to give that rounded, full-figured look (Seid 1994).

The first break with the voluptuous tradition of the nineteenth century came in the 1920s with the 'flappers'—a term used to describe skinny women who were financially and sexually independent, partly as a result of World War I, which left many women in charge of their dead husbands' estates. The word 'flapper' was used to trivialise the 'new independent woman', as Banner states:

> On the one hand, she indicated a new freedom in sensual expression by shortening her skirts and discarding her corsets. On the other hand, she bound her breasts … and expressed her sensuality not through eroticism, but through constant, vibrant movement … The name 'flapper' itself [was drawn] from a style of flapping galoshes popular among young women before the war; it connoted irrelevant movement and raised the spectre of a seal with black flapping paws.
>
> 1983, p. 279

Thus, these women rejected the dominant patriarchal ideal of feminine appearance—and the passivity that went with it—and assumed a more masculine ideal; the new liberated woman was to dress, act, and look more like a man (thin and without curves) (Hesse-Biber 1991, 1996). However, when women lose their curves they tend to become physically smaller and apparently weak. This phase of redefinition of women's bodies occurred during a time of female political activism in the USA and the UK, as the suffragette movement pressed for the vote for women. As women entered the public sphere and increased their profile and power, the ideal female body inversely decreased in size.

Other factors contributed to the emergence of the thin female ideal. The onset of the Great Depression in 1929, followed by World War II, led to austerity measures as a result of food shortages and a subsequent concern with the link between food and health. These decades marked the start of calorie-counting and the using of food for its energy value (Schwartz 1986). Such measures imposed a dieting mentality on the population, especially women, who at that time were the primary gatekeepers of food in the family.

The contemporary thin ideal

The contemporary thin ideal was born in the 1960s and was epitomised by the model Twiggy (whose name alluded to her slight frame) as well as by actresses such as Audrey Hepburn and Grace Kelly. By this time, the Western world was enjoying an era of prosperity and plenty. As prosperity grew and food consumption increased, concern also grew over the increasing weight of the population as medical and epidemiological studies began to find links between obesity and premature mortality. By the 1970s, a rare coalescence of factors emerged to reinforce the thin ideal: medical science, government authorities, and the fashion industry all adopted an anti-fat stance. In Chapter 17, Jeffery Sobal discusses the changing social attitudes towards 'fat' and the growing **stigmatisation** of **obesity**. While dieting and the the cultural aversion to 'fat' have historical underpinnings that pre-date contemporary health warnings (see Schwartz 1986), the well-intentioned anti-fat messages of health professionals and government agencies may have reinforced and legitimised the thin ideal and encouraged unnecessary dieting (Germov & Williams 1996a).

Roberta Seid (1994) argues that the second wave of feminism, in the 1970s, initially embraced a super-fit, thin ideal as a celebration of women's strength and control. Such body control was regarded as a positive symbol of femininity, in contrast to the aesthetics of previous centuries, which conceptualised women as invalids (the 'weaker sex') or as maternal icons (useful for their reproductive capacity); both of these stereotypes were used to support orthodox views that women should be 'protected' from physical and intellectual labour, and that they were dependent on men. Actress Jane Fonda was a vocal feminist in the 1970s, and promoted health and beauty through physical fitness by positing the thin ideal as a break from the **maternal ideal**. Marjorie Ferguson's content analysis of women's magazines (1983, p. 113) notes the influence of the self-help movement on contemporary femininity, bringing about a shift in editorial emphasis 'towards greater self-realisation, self-determination, and the presentation of a more independent and assertive femininity'. This development, which paralleled the growth of consumerism and individualism in advanced capitalist societies, reflected the magazines' successful (profitable) marketing strategy of teaming the thin ideal with women's sexual and economic liberation. As Fonda and various imitators discovered, the focus on female self-help and independence through body discipline tapped into a new market of potential consumers. Fonda, who has suffered from **bulimia nervosa** and has had cosmetic surgery, presents an interesting case study of a celebrity, previously well known as a feminist, who advocated women's emancipation from patriarchy (in terms of economic and sexual liberation) while playing a significant part in reinforcing their subjugation to the patriarchal thin ideal—liberation from the beauty myth was seemingly not part of her agenda.

Box 15.2 The magic pill: The diet drug pushers

The quest for the magic pill or potion that will result in weight loss without effort and irrespective of lifestyle and genetics continues apace, with the commercial 'pay-off' sometimes taking precedence over concern for public health. For example, the 'anti-obesity' drugs Adifax (also known as Redux) and Duramine were withdrawn from the market after a number of recorded deaths associated with their use in the US. Studies have shown that the prescription drugs Xenical and Reductil can achieve a 5–10% weight loss, yet the weight is regained once the drug treatments cease and both drugs have significant side effects. A growing number of prescription and non-prescription drugs have been released in recent years, such as:

- *Dex-fenfluramine (Adifax or Redux) and phentermine (Duramine).* These amphetamine-derived drugs worked as appetite suppressants by raising serotonin levels. The combination of the two drugs (often referred to as phen-fen) was believed to further enhance weight loss. The phen-fen combination, and later the individual drugs, were linked to an increased risk of heart disease (after a number of recorded deaths). A global ban on the drugs was introduced in 1997.
- *Orlistat (Xenical).* This drug works by blocking up to 30% of fat absorption in the lower intestine. Side effects include bloating of the stomach, flatulence and underwear spotting, faecal incontinence (anal leakage), defecation urgency, oily stools, and decreased absorption of fat-soluble vitamins, resulting in the need to take daily multivitamin supplements.
- *Sibutramine (Reductil or Meridia).* This appetite suppressant works by blocking the pre-synaptic re-uptake of the neurotransmitters norepinephrine and serotonin. Side effects include increased blood pressure, headaches, insomnia, and constipation.
- *Non-prescription weight-loss supplements.* There are a wide array of non-pharmaceutical products available that claim to aid weight loss, such as chitosan (powered crustacean shells), chromium picolinate (a type of organic metal chromium), isoflavones (phytoestrogens found in plants such as soybeans), ginkgo biloba (leaves from the maidenhead tree), L-carnitine (an amino acid), and St John's wort (a herb)—all lack supporting evidence for their associated weight-loss claims.

Sources: Egger et al. (1999); Seghatol & Rigolin (2002); Yanovski & Yanovski (2002); Weigle (2003)

The rise of mass production and consumption led the body image industries to develop a 'sure-fire' formula for success: promote a thin ideal of beauty that the majority of women can never attain and thereby create virtually infinite demand among consumers. In the early 1990s, the US diet industry was estimated to be worth US$55 billion per year, with more than 65 million Americans dieting to lose weight (Brownell 1993). The Australian figures are proportionately similar: it was estimated in the early 1990s that over A$500 million per year was spent on commercial weight-loss programs alone (Lester 1994). The weight-loss industry has shown an impressive ability to continually reinvent itself, as witnessed by the emergence of new 'fad diets' (the Zone diet being a recent example) and the resurgence of old fad diets such as the Atkins diet. Moreover, a plethora of 'infomercials' on late-night and daytime TV advertise exercise equipment and diet supplements that promise to give buyers model-like bodies with the minimum of effort. As Box 15.2 indicates, the pharmaceutical industry continues to release so-called 'anti-obesity' drugs, which have significant side effects and only modest results to date. The irony of the weight-loss industry is that its very existence depends on the failure of its products. In what other industry would customers repeatedly pay large sums of money for products and services that do not work? The weight-loss industry has been clever enough to sustain its market share by placing the blame on the consumer, with caveats that their products will only work if used in combination with 'a sensible diet and regular exercise'.

Body backlash: The continued social control of women's bodies

As a number of authors have noted (Beller 1977; Mennell 1985), when food is scarce, cultural ideals favour a large body, whose 'abundance' symbolises wealth and status. Conversely, in times of plenty, social mores shift towards disciplining food intake, and the thin body becomes the ideal. In today's advanced capitalist societies, food is readily available and social worth is increasingly measured by a person's ability to resist excess. This reassertion of moral censure of sloth and gluttony is a remnant of earlier Christian values that focused on purifying the soul and disciplining the body through abstinence and penance, and on purging oneself of excess (Schwartz 1986; Turner 1992). Some authors have also drawn links between religion and the self-starvation diet regimen that is seen at its most extreme in **eating disorders** such as **anorexia nervosa** (see Chapter 16 and Bell 1985; Bynum 1987; Brumberg 1988; Malson 1998; Hepworth 1999).

Susan Faludi (1991) and Naomi Wolf (1990) see a parallel between female sexual liberation and the thin ideal, whereby part of the backlash against the social gains made by women since the 1960s has been a renewed emphasis on women's appearance. Faludi and Wolf argue that it is no accident that the current thin ideal emerged during the second wave of feminism, a period of increased female sexual and socioeconomic liberation. As Sharlene Hesse-Biber states, 'when women are "demanding more space" in terms of equality of opportunity, there is a cultural demand that they "should shrink"... Thinness may be considered a sign of conforming to a constricting feminine image, whereas weight may convey a strong, powerful image' (1991, p. 178). Thus, the thin ideal represents a contemporary example of the social control of women's bodies, reinforced by the commercial imperatives of the body image industries of fashion, cosmetics, fitness, and the media. The thin ideal has also become associated with certain occupations, such as that of female flight attendants, where it is still common to find organisational regulations concerning a woman's figure, make-up, and 'femininity' (Tyler & Abbott 1998).

In the era of the flappers, the rise of women's political and social status resulted in a female body ideal that was diminutive and weak. The increased entry of women into the public sphere directly challenged male dominance, but resulted in a female ideal of physical size that emphasised weakness as opposed to physical strength—the ultimate source of male dominance over women. This time around, the social control over women's bodies has been exercised not through externalised means, such as restrictive clothing, but through the internalisation and pursuit of the thin ideal.

Popular portrayal of the thin ideal

Models and celebrities have been the overt public face of changes in beauty standards over recent decades. Compare, for example, the figure of Marilyn Monroe in the 1950s with that of Elle Macpherson in the 1980s, Kate Moss in the 1990s, and, more recently, Eva Herzigova. Content-analysis studies of magazines, beauty pageants, Hollywood movies, and television programs have consistently found that the female beauty ideal has become thinner with time (Silverstein et al. 1986; Morris et al. 1989). Moreover, experimental studies have found that exposure to media images of thin bodies increases body dissatisfaction (Groesz et al. 2002).

Figures 15.1, 15.2, and 15.3 show three cover designs of Australia's popular women's magazine *Cleo* to trace the presentation of women by the structural interests of the media, advertising, and fashion industries over the past 30 years, from the 'self-help days' of the early 1970s to the engineered 'insecurity' of the early 1990s.

The image on the cover of the January 1973 *Cleo* is a sexual presentation of an attractive blonde model with a plunging halter-top. The picture stops just below the breasts. The woman has her hand to her face in a submissive gesture and is smiling into the camera with a 'knowing' look. This cover shot reflects the

Figure 15.1 *Cleo* magazine cover, January 1973

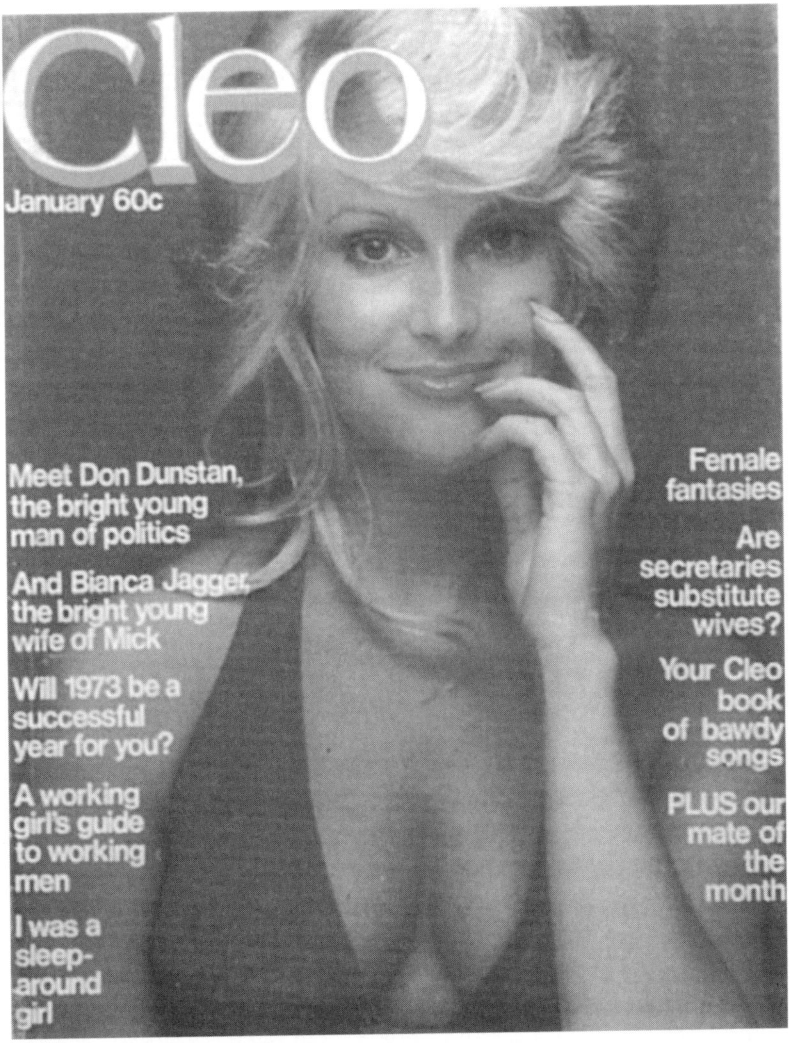

- Meet Don Dunstan, the bright young man of politics
- And Bianca Jagger, the bright young wife of Mick
- Will 1973 be a successful year for you?
- A working girl's guide to working men
- I was a sleep-around girl
- Female fantasies
- Are secretaries substitute wives?
- Your Cleo book of bawdy songs
- PLUS our mate of the month

Figure 15.2 *Cleo* magazine cover, January 1983

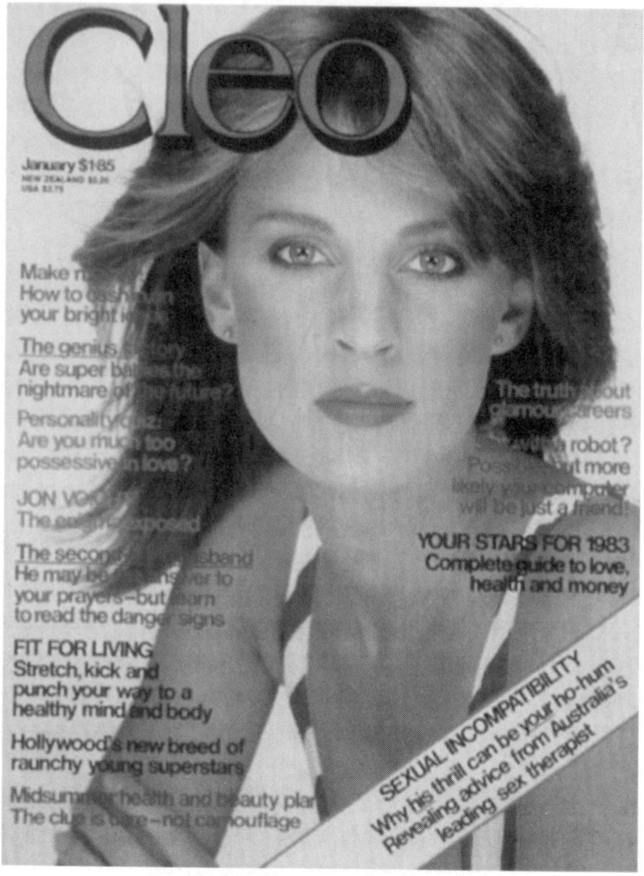

- Make money! How to cash in on your bright ideas
- The genius factory: Are super babies the nightmare of the future?
- Personality quiz: Are you much too possessive in love?
- JON VOIGHT: The enigma exposed
- The second-hand husband: He may be the answer to your prayers—but learn to read the danger signs
- FIT FOR LIVING: Stretch, kick and punch your way to a healthy mind and body
- Hollywood's new breed of raunchy young superstars
- Midsummer health and beauty plan: The clue is care—not camouflage
- The truth about glamour careers
- Sex with a robot? Possible, but more likely your computer will be just a friend!
- YOUR STARS FOR 1983: Complete guide to love, health and money
- SEXUAL INCOMPATABILITY: Why <u>his</u> thrill can be <u>your</u> ho-hum. Revealing advice from Australia's leading sex therapist

Figure 15.3 *Cleo* magazine cover, January 1993

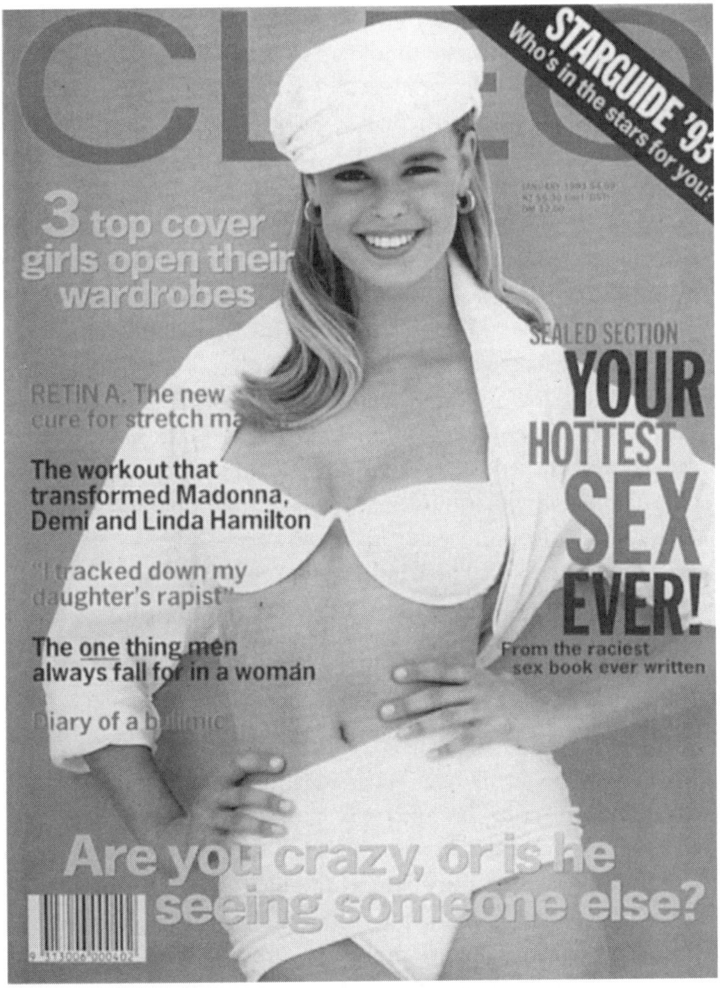

- 3 top cover girls open their wardrobes
- RETIN A: The new cure for stretch marks!
- The workout that transformed Madonna, Demi and Linda Hamilton
- 'I tracked down my daughter's rapist'
- The <u>one</u> thing men always fall for in a woman
- Diary of a bulimic
- Are you crazy, or is he seeing someone else?
- SEALED SECTION: YOUR HOTTEST SEX EVER! From the raciest sex book ever written
- STARGUIDE '93: Who's in the stars for you?

content of some of the headlines, which have an emphasis on sexual liberation. There is a notable absence of articles relating to dieting, exercise, or the body.

The 1983 model is an attractive brunette in a head-and-shoulders shot, turned side-on below the shoulders so that we do not see her breasts. She has an almost vacant, expressionless look on her face. The image is one of attractive wholesomeness, rather than sexuality. By the 1980s, the stories no longer focus on sexual liberation, but on the need for a health and beauty plan. The magazine has learned that encouraging insecurity is the best strategy for ensuring a sustainable readership ('Are you much too possessive in love?'). The emphasis on money in the first-listed headline story reflects both the increased financial independence of women and the rise of the 'decade of greed'.

The January 1993 cover shows a three-quarter body shot in which the model's body is exposed but in a stance that is more athletic than sexy. The model is wearing a white bathing costume with quite full pants rather than revealing briefs. By the 1990s, the focus on body insecurity has intensified: readers are exposed to the wardrobes of models and the workouts of movie stars, neither of which most readers have any hope of attaining. Thus the thin ideal is glamorised and made apparently accessible (if you just read the health and beauty section!). The dangers of body insecurity are poignantly reflected in the 'Diary of a bulimic'. Encouragement of insecurity about men, sex, and life-management continues—you need to read the 'stars' to know how to meet men, and if you already have a man, you need to ask 'are you crazy or is he seeing someone else?'

By 2003, little had changed, with the August issue of *Cleo* headlining stories on 'why sex is the new breakfast' and 'pick up tricks you can learn from a guy', a 'sealed section' on 'tattoos, piercings and designer waxes', and special features on shoes, hair, and weddings. The cover photo shows well-known actor Kate Hudson, who is thin, blonde, and blue-eyed. The use of actors on covers, which has become increasingly common,is, according to Cyndi Tebbel (2000), an attempt by magazines to move away from using supermodels towards what the industry terms 'real women'. Unfortunately, the bodies of these women are no more attainable than those of the models. Early in the twenty-first century, the ranks of thin-ideal role models continue to swell, particularly among actors and pop singers—for example, Calista Flockhart, Courteney Cox, Jennifer Anniston, Lara Flyn Boyle, Nicole Kidman, Kylie Minogue, and Victoria Beckham. In the face of a constant barrage of glamorous images, it is little wonder that cosmetic surgery rates for breast augmentation, face lifts, collagen injections, and liposuction continue to rise. The non-surgical procedure of botox—a wrinkle treatment based on injecting small amounts of the highly toxic botulinum (a product of the bacterium that causes botulism)—has proven to be one of the most popular treatments.

Box 15.3 Men and body image: The muscular ideal

While men are also subject to social pressure regarding their bodies, particularly in the context of obesity stigmatisation, their experience is considerably different to that of women. Even though more men than women are overweight, men report less body dissatisfaction, are less concerned about their bodies, and are less likely to be on a weight-loss diet (Grogan 1999). The social pressure on men is to achieve a **muscular ideal** that indicates strength and masculinity. Rather than promoting weight-loss and slenderness, the male body ideal exaggerates masculine traits to convey power and dominance. Men generally indicate a preference for a larger, more muscular body, and will sometimes undergo cosmetic surgery or take supplements detrimental to their health to achieve it (such as anabolic steroids and human growth hormone). Epitomised by Arnold Schwarzenegger in the 1980s, the muscular ideal has become widespread, as evidenced by the ubiquitous athletic-looking male model sporting highly toned musculature, a defined chest, large biceps, and a 'six pack' of well-defined abdominal muscles.

Mike Featherstone suggests that the representation of the female body in consumer culture, such as in popular women's magazines, 'encourages the individual to adopt instrumental strategies to combat deterioration and decay (applauded too by state bureaucracies who seek to reduce health costs by educating the public against bodily neglect) ... Images of the body beautiful, openly sexual and associated with hedonism, leisure and display, emphasise the importance of appearance and the "look"' (1991, p. 170). Men have also increasingly become subject to social pressure over their bodies, though their experience is quite distinct to that of women (see Box 15.3).

The thin ideal for women and the muscular ideal for men are well entrenched by adolescence (Grogan 1999; Nowak et al. 2001). Women and men are exposed to these body ideals from childhood through the process of **gender socialisation**. Consider, for example, the popular Barbie doll made by Mattel. This doll, with annual sales of US$1 billion (*New York Times Magazine*, 27 May 1994; O'Brien 1997), is blonde, tall, thin, long-legged, and slim-waisted and has a flat stomach, square shoulders, large eyes, and curved red lips. Ken Norton and colleagues (1996) undertook a study in which they scaled the anthropometric measurements of the Barbie doll to adult size, finding that the probability of an adult woman having a Barbie-like body shape is less than one in a hundred thousand. Interestingly, they also scaled the Ken doll (the male equivalent of the Barbie doll, produced and marketed by the same company),

Figure 15.4 The Body Shop's 'Ruby' Campaign (reproduced with permission of The Body Shop International PLC)

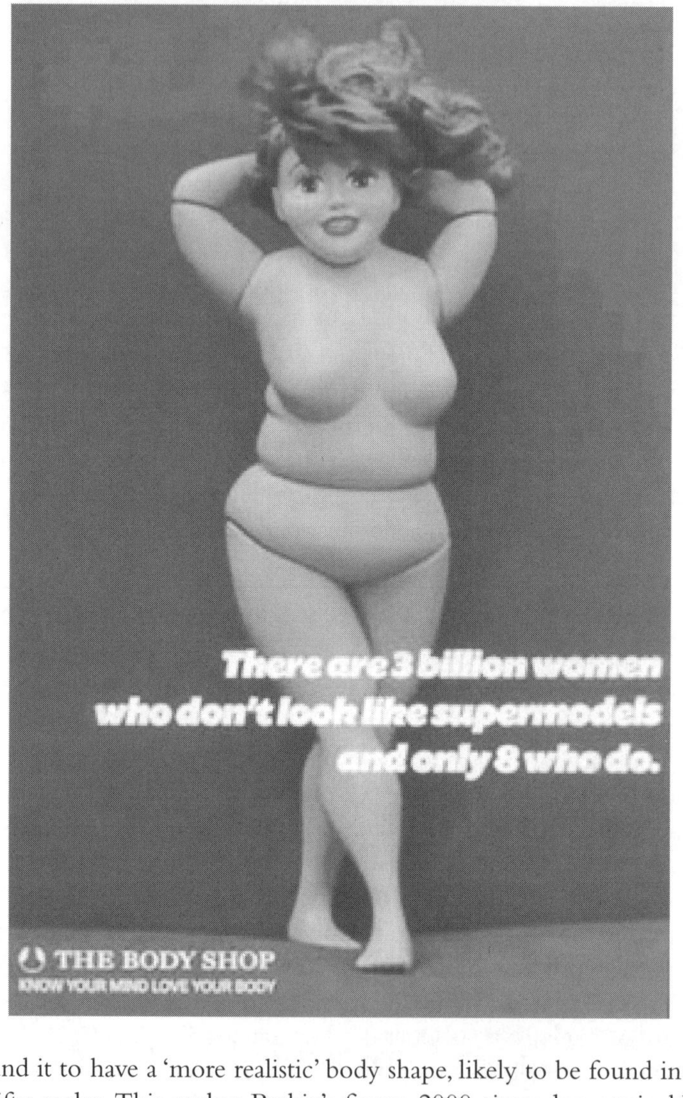

and found it to have a 'more realistic' body shape, likely to be found in one in every fifty males. This makes Barbie's figure 2000 times less attainable than Ken's, reflecting the fact that women are encouraged to aspire to a more unrealistic body ideal than men. The Body Shop produced its own version of Barbie, a full-figured doll named 'Ruby', as part of its campaign for body diversity. The company was initially forced to withdraw the doll as a result of pressure from Mattel, which considered the doll's features to be too similar to those of their idealised blonde best-seller; the Body Shop subsequently released a revised version (Benjamin Smith, pers. comm., 27 May 1998).

Factors influencing the thin ideal today

Structuralist approaches to the thin ideal

In explaining the emergence of the thin ideal, a structuralist would maintain that the thin ideal is the outcome of a patriarchal society, in which powerful men and the various industries and social institutions they control (structural factors) construct the 'beauty myth' for their own material and political benefit (Wolf 1990; Bordo 1993). These structural factors clearly have an impact on cultural beliefs, particularly in terms of gender socialisation, by constructing and promoting a particular ideal of female beauty.

As thinness became synonymous with the powerful combination of health and beauty, the female body became increasingly exploited by both corporate interests and government health authorities. Calls to exercise self-control over one's body for the health benefits and for the sake of social conformity expanded upon the cultural values of individualism and self-responsibility. Women's magazines thus became an important sphere of influence for perpetuating the thin ideal. Those magazines that do not conform to this strategy may not survive. An Australian example of the extent of this control was reported in the *Sydney Morning Herald* by Pilita Clark and Andrew Hornery (1997). In an interview, the former editor of *New Woman* magazine in Australia, Cyndi Tebbel, claimed to have lost her job because the magazine featured a 'Big Issue', which supported International No Diet Day, used size-16 models, and promoted body diversity. According to Tebbel, sales of the magazine were not affected, but advertisers complained and threatened to withdraw, risking up to 50% of the total revenue of the magazine (Tebbel 2000). Consequently, the magazine returned to featuring thin models and to stories promoting body insecurity and promised cures. This illustrates the fact that the cosmetics, fitness, and fashion industries will not tolerate a message that acts against their vested commercial interests—that is, a message challenging the dominant ideal of female beauty.

While gender is clearly a major factor in explaining the cultural preoccupation with the thin ideal, there is conflicting evidence on the role that ethnicity plays, if any. A US study by Sheila Parker and others (1995) examined the body image and dieting behaviours of African–American and white adolescent females. They found that the African–American girls exhibited significantly less body dissatisfaction, and greater appreciation of body diversity and of large female bodies, than their white counterparts, who tended to be rigid adherents to the thin ideal. While the African–American girls studied tended to have a lower prevalence of dieting and were less concerned about body weight and shape than were the white girls, this may not apply to all ethnic groups in the USA. A major US study of over 17,000 adolescent girls found that ethnicity, as opposed to skin colour, did not 'protect' against body dissatisfaction or dieting behaviour, concluding that ethnic subcultures are just as affected by the thin ideal as white mainstream culture (French et al. 1997). Similar findings have been reported in Australia, which show that ethnicity did not mediate the influence of the thin ideal (O'Dea 1998; Ball & Kenardy 2002).

The role of female agency in perpetuating the thin ideal

In contrast to a structuralist analysis, which focuses on the external forces that exert pressure on women to conform to a thin ideal, post-structuralist feminist theorists are concerned with the role played by women themselves in reproducing and resisting the thin ideal (Weedon 1987; Bartky 1990; Barrett & Phillips 1992; Pringle 1995). Post-structuralist theorists do not deny the importance of the historical and cultural factors discussed above, but, rather than viewing these factors as all-determining, they stress the importance of female subjectivity and deal with the complex and subtle facets of the social construction of women's bodies.

It is commonly stated that some women use body control to demonstrate their control over other aspects of their lives. As the January 1993 *Cleo* cover shows (Figure 15.3), the 'successful woman' is financially independent, sexually liberated, and thin. However, Sandra Bartky argues that 'a tighter control of the body has gained a new kind of hold over the mind' (1990, p. 81). The thin body has become an essential symbol of modern femininity and a new form of social control of women's bodies; body regulation is self-inflicted, administered by women on themselves through dieting, starvation, excessive exercise, and, at the extreme, plastic surgery. Therefore, there is a self-imposed component in the pressure to conform. Women are not simply passive sponges of coercive patriarchal structures and cultural stereotypes. In effect, the social control of women's bodies becomes internalised by the women themselves.

In examining female agency, it is important to note that not all women respond to the thin ideal by internalising it and making it an integral part of their identity. Nor do all women perpetuate the thin ideal by reinforcing it in their relationships with and evaluations of other women. Some women reject the thin ideal altogether, as we shall see later in the chapter (Chernin 1981; Orbach 1986; Germov & Williams 1996b). Responses to the thin ideal can be divided into the categories listed in Table 15.2. This categorisation scheme has more to do with whether or not women choose to conform to the thin ideal, and with the subsequent effect on their eating behaviour, than it has to do with actual body weight. *Category 1* refers to the thin ideal 'body conformers' who diet to lose weight, either permanently or on an 'on again, off again' basis, which often results in weight cycling. Women who diet or who consciously restrict their eating (by eating low-fat, low-calorie foods, for instance) may be of any weight, but will probably tend to be thinner than other women. The women in *category 4*, whom we have called 'body acceptors', do not diet, possibly because they have failed to achieve their desired weight and have decided to be unrestrained eaters, or

Table 15.2 Responses to the thin ideal

	Thin ideal acceptors	*Thin ideal rejectors*
Diet to lose weight	*Category 1: Body conformers* Women who diet in pursuit of the thin ideal	*Category 2: Health maintainers* Women who diet for clear health benefits and not for aesthetic reasons
Do not diet	*Category 3: Weight maintainers* Women who are naturally slim and do not need to diet	*Category 4: Body acceptors* Women who accept body diversity and derive their self-identity from factors other than conforming to the thin ideal

because they have consciously rejected the thin ideal and accepted body diversity. As a group, they will tend towards being heavier than the dieters. In *category 3* are the 'weight maintainers', who have never had to diet to stay thin and are unrestrained eaters. These women are able to conform to the thin ideal easily. It is possible that if their weight were to increase, they would move to category 1. A further group are the 'health maintainers' (*category 2*), who do not pursue or conform to the thin ideal, but may seek to lose weight to improve their health or prevent the onset of disease (such as Type 2 diabetes). (These categories are discussed further in Chapter 18.)

The desire to be seen as attractive and the pressure of social conformity are powerful and rational reasons for dieting. The social importance placed on women's appearance (Rothblum 1994) can be so great that some women value weight loss above success in love or work (Charles & Kerr 1988; Wolf 1990). As Edwin Schur argues, 'physical appearance is much more central to evaluations of women than it is to evaluations of men; this emphasis implicitly devalues women's other qualities and accomplishments; women's "looks" thereby become a commodity and a key determinant of their "success" or "failure"' (1983, p. 68). Hesse-Biber (1991, 1996) argues that women are socialised to focus on physical appearance in order to receive social acceptance, while for men public achievement determines social worth and self-image. As Margaret Duncan states (1994, p. 50), women learn to 'compare their appearance with that of the patriarchal feminine ideal and thus become objects for their own gaze'. Pregnancy is a time when women are temporarily relieved from the pressure to conform to the thin ideal (see Box 15.4).

Dieting and pursuit of the thin ideal can thus be viewed as a rational response by women striving for acceptance in the context of the dominant ideals of beauty, sexuality, and femininity. The internalisation of patriarchal norms explains the active role women play in perpetuating the thin ideal (Bartky 1990). Women

Box 15.4 The maternal ideal

During pregnancy, women are encouraged to reject the thin ideal in favour of the maternal ideal; women's bodies are effectively **socially reconstructed** as they are encouraged by family, friends, and medical and health professionals to eat more and eat differently. As Lauren Williams and Jane Potter (1999) note, women respond to the maternal ideal in a number of ways: some renounce it and exhibit body dissatisfaction because their bodies are no longer viewed as attractive, while others embrace the maternal role; those who were overweight prior to pregnancy often experience social acceptance of their size. The maternal ideal has a long historical lineage through cultures that symbolised fertility and maternity with 'Mother Earth' icons. In a society that usually equates attractiveness with slimness, pregnant women's bodies are welcomed and expected—they are, in effect, socially reconstructed (Wile 1994). While the thin ideal represents the social construction of sexual attractiveness, the maternal ideal represents the outcome of the sexual act and the fulfilment of women's biological role—the reproduction of the species and, more specifically, the continuance of the male lineage (Williams & Potter 1999).

police their own bodies and the bodies of other women in a process of constant surveillance. In this way, the thin ideal is reinforced and perpetuated without coercion and often with women's consent. We have described this process of women's body monitoring as the 'body panopticon' effect (Germov & Williams 1999; see also Duncan 1994; Foucault 1979); the pressure to conform to the thin ideal not only stems from structural factors and material interests, but also from women acting as 'body police' for themselves and other women.

Our previous research has documented the myriad responses by women to the thin ideal (Germov & Williams 1996b). The benefit of a post-structuralist approach is that it sheds light on the active role that women play in the social construction of the thin ideal. While such an approach helps to explain the pervasiveness of the thin ideal, self-surveillance does not occur in a social vacuum and is reinforced by structural interests, such as the fashion, weight-loss, fitness, health, and cosmetic industries.

Towards a synthesis of the structuralist and post-structuralist approaches

Both structuralist and post-structuralist perspectives are important in understanding the pressure on women to diet to attain the thin ideal—but can they be reconciled? On its own, neither perspective offers a complete explanation of why women diet. For example, structuralist explanations tend to imply that women are easily duped or even 'brainwashed' by the media, the fashion industry, and men to succumb to the thin ideal. However, such an analysis ignores the fact that not all men act as oppressors of women (either consciously or implicitly) and that some women consciously and effectively resist the pressure to conform to the thin ideal. In an attempt to bridge these two approaches, we suggest that dieting and the thin ideal must be understood within a theoretical schema that acknowledges structural factors and female agency, but that avoids voluntaristic explanations of dieting behaviour as simply a matter of individual lifestyle choice.

Figure 15.5 The social and cultural reproduction of the thin ideal

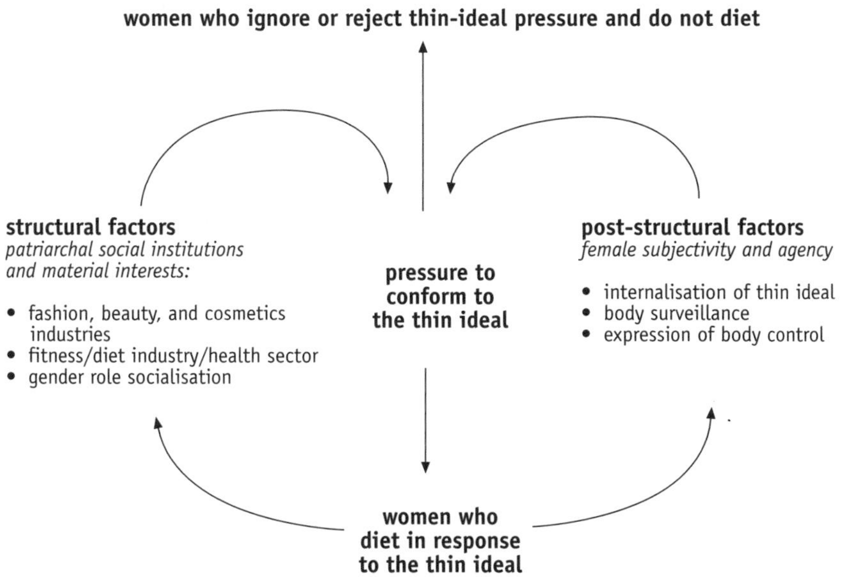

The starting point of Figure 15.5 is the pressure put on women in Western society to conform to the thin ideal. Women can respond to the pressure in one of two ways: by ignoring or actively rejecting the thin ideal, which takes them out of the cycle (as represented by the upward arrow); or, alternatively, by responding to the thin ideal by dieting, which results in gendered food and restrained eating practices. The lists of structural and post-structural factors summarise the key modes by which the pressure to conform to the thin ideal is produced and reproduced (the arrows indicate the direction of influence). Dieting behaviour reinforces both structural interests (for example, the dieting industry) and post-structural factors (for example, self-surveillance), which in turn reinforce pressure to conform to the thin ideal and dieting behaviour, and the cycle continues.

Figure 15.5 provides a helpful starting point for understanding the complex processes involved in the pressure to conform to the thin ideal. It summarises the key structural and post-structural factors and shows how these factors are responsible for the reproduction of the thin ideal and the pressure on women to diet.

Challenging the thin ideal via body acceptance

Incorporating the concept of female agency to understand the production of the thin ideal also allows for the possibility of women rejecting this ideal in favour of an alternative ideal—that of **body acceptance**. Table 15.2 showed that some women ignore the thin ideal as being irrelevant, while others who have tried to conform to the thin ideal in the past have chosen at some point to actively reject it. These women move out of the cycle depicted in Figure 15.5, thereby challenging the dominance of the thin ideal. Enough individuals are choosing this option to constitute an emerging social movement, variously termed the 'anti-dieting', 'size acceptance', or 'fat rights' movement (Sobal 1999).

Occasionally, this anti-dieting sentiment is popularised by the mass media. Figure 15.6 depicts a front cover of the Australian *Who Weekly* magazine. It is one of the few examples of the mass media being critical of the thin ideal. This picture was seized upon by the media in Australia as an example of how the (mid 1990s) trend towards the 'waif look', promoted by the modelling and fashion industry, had pushed the thin ideal too far. More recently, model Sophie Dahl and actor Kate Winslet were touted as successful women who challenged the dominance of the thin ideal. In Dahl's case, this was short-lived, and she now sports the slender look desired by the fashion industry and denies she was ever a role model for body diversity. Kate Winslet has commented on her ongoing struggle to resist dieting to gain more acting work, but has recently embraced a more conformist body shape. Clearly, examples that challenge the thin ideal remain transitory and marginal. Nonetheless, they show that the thin ideal can be undermined.

Promotion of body acceptance offers a mechanism for the dismantling of the thin ideal. In qualitative research conducted with Australian women, we found that body acceptance can be the result of a history of failed dieting, or it can be based on the decision to end the pain of the dieting process and the obsession with one's body (Germov & Williams 1996b). The development of a body-accepting identity poses the analytical question of how some women are able to manage the consequences of rebelling against the thin ideal. While further research into body acceptance is required, our findings suggest that a number of factors are likely to underpin some women's ability to effectively filter out patriarchal influences and construct an identity independent of the thin ideal; these factors are discussed in Chapter 18.

Figure 15.6 *Who Weekly* cover, 27 May 1996, issue no. 222 (reproduced courtesy of WHO WEEKLY)

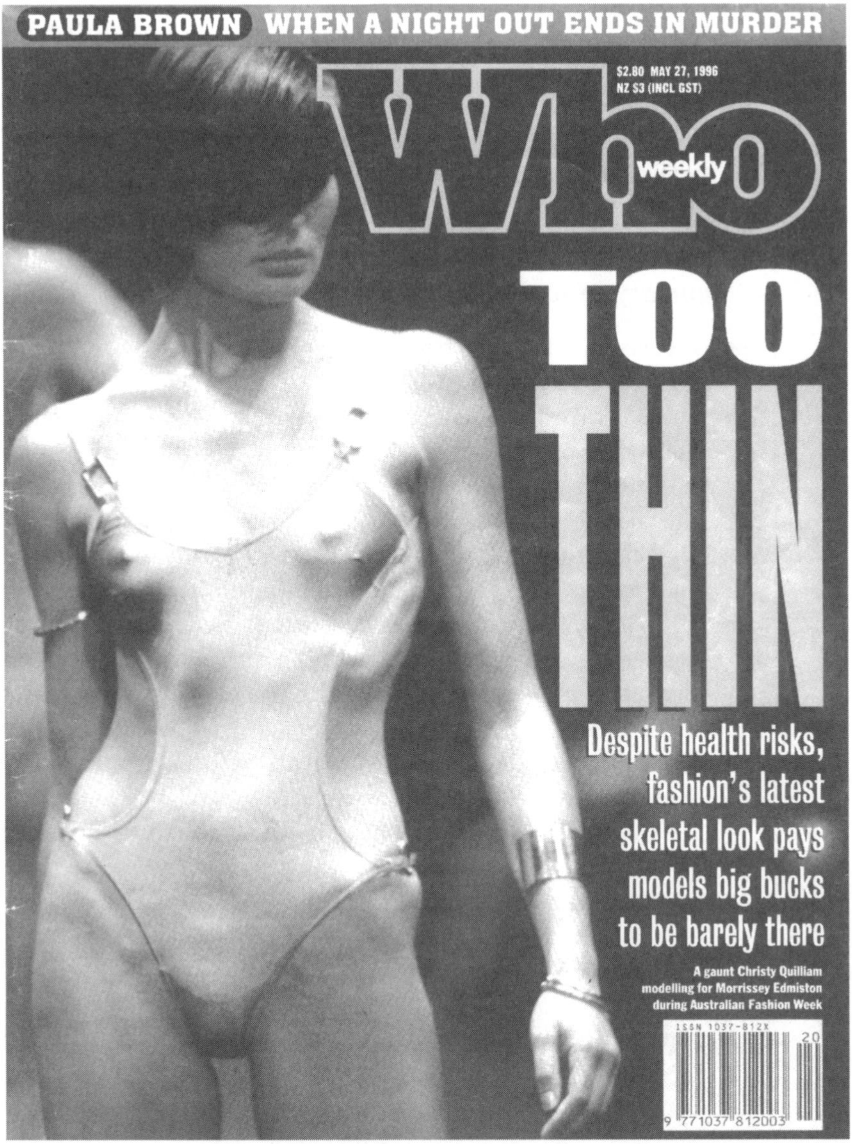

Conclusion

This chapter has outlined the historical, structural, and cultural factors that have generated the thin ideal and the role that women have played in reinforcing or rejecting it. We have also adopted a critical approach in arguing that any understanding of gendered eating habits—particularly an understanding of why women diet and why the thin ideal is so pervasive—requires a conceptual framework that reconciles structuralist and post-structuralist approaches. Women are not merely victims of patriarchal and capitalist imperatives, nor are they simply free to adopt or reject the thin ideal as they please. Some women actively participate in the reproduction of the pressure to conform to the thin ideal, while others resist this pressure by constructing alternative discourses, such as that of body acceptance. The rejection of the thin ideal and the promotion of body acceptance are key strategies through which body dissatisfaction and associated unnecessary and harmful dieting practices can be challenged.

Summary of main points

- A sexual division of dieting exists, in which dieting to lose weight is primarily a female act.
- Sociological explanations of why women diet can be divided into two broad categories: structuralist and post-structuralist.
- An understanding of why women diet and of the persistence of the thin ideal requires a synthesis of structural and post-structural factors.
- The thin ideal has historical origins and is linked to events that have enhanced women's social status and power.
- The representation of women as victims of patriarchal subordination has been successfully critiqued by post-structuralist feminist theorists through a renewed focus on women's agency and subjective experiences of femininity.
- Women react to the thin ideal in a myriad ways—accepting, reinforcing, and resisting the dominant discourse.
- Resistance of the thin ideal through body acceptance is an alternative gaining social momentum.

Discussion questions

1. What are the differences between the structuralist and post-structuralist perspectives on the thin ideal?
2. How did the thin ideal originate, and why did it become so pervasive?
3. How do women perpetuate the thin ideal?
4. If you are a woman, reflect on where you fit into the schema presented in Table 15.2. Are there any responses to the thin ideal that are not encompassed by this table? In what ways do women's bodies undergo a process of social reconstruction during pregnancy?

How may women mediate this process? What might be the implications for the way they eat?
5 What body-ideal pressures are men subject to? Are these pressures equivalent to the pressures on women to conform to the thin ideal?
6 Discuss the potential of the size acceptance movement to dismantle the thin ideal. Do you think this could happen in your lifetime?

Further investigation

1 Some authors argue that there is a parallel between Victorian attitudes to sex and modern attitudes to food, such that 'food rules have become as dour and inhibitory as the sex rules of the 19th century' (Seid 1994, p. 8). Discuss the implications of this quote with reference to gender and food.
2 The media is to blame for the thin ideal and the associated harmful dieting practices and eating disorders of many women. Discuss.
3 How have health professionals contributed to the reinforcement or dismantling of the thin ideal?

Further reading and web resources

Books

Bordo, S. 1993, *Unbearable Weight: Feminism, Western Culture and the Body*, University of California Press, Berkeley.

Cooke, K. 1994, *Real Gorgeous: The Truth about Body and Beauty*, Allen & Unwin, Sydney.

Corrigan, A. & Meredyth, D. 1997, 'The Body Politic', in K. Pritchard Hughes (ed.), *Contemporary Australian Feminism 2*, 2nd edn, Longman, Melbourne.

Davis, K. (ed) 1997, *Embodied Practices: Feminist Perspectives on the Body*, Sage, London.

Fallon, P., Katzman, M. A. & Wooley, S. A. (eds), *Feminist Perspectives on Eating Disorders*, Guilford Press, New York.

Grogan, S. 1999, *Body Image: Understanding Body Dissatisfaction in Men, Women and Children*, Routledge, London.

Hesse-Biber, S. 1996, *Am I Thin Enough Yet? The Cult of Thinness and the Commercialization of Identity*, Oxford University Press, New York.

Schiebinger L. (ed.) 2000, *Feminism and the Body*, Oxford University Press, Oxford.

Schwartz, H. 1986, *Never Satisfied: A Cultural History of Diets, Fantasies and Fat*, The Free Press, New York.

Shilling, C. 2003, *The Body and Social Theory*, 2nd edn, Sage, London.

Sobal, J. & Maurer, D. (eds) 1999 , *Weighty Issues: Fatness and Thinness as Social Problems*, Aldine de Gruyter, New York.

—— (eds) 1999, *Interpreting Weight: The Social Management of Fatness and Thinness*, Aldine de Gruyter, New York.

Tebbel, C. 2000, *The Body Snatchers: How the Media Shapes Women*, Finch Publishing, Sydney.

Weitz, R. (ed.) 2003, *The Politics of Women's Bodies: Sexuality, Appearance, and Behavior*, 2nd edn, Oxford University Press, New York.

Articles

Germov, J. & Williams, L., 'The Sexual Division of Dieting: Women's Voices', *Sociological Review*, vol. 44, no. 4, pp. 630–47.

Journals

Body & Society
Feminist Studies
Gender & Society
Healthy Weight Journal
International Journal of Eating Disorders
Sex Roles

Documentaries

Beyond Killing Us Softly. The Strength to Resist: The Impact of Media Images on Women and Girls, 2000, Cambridge Documentary Films, Cambridge, Massachusetts, 34 minutes.

Killing Us Softly 3: Advertising's Image of Women, 2000, Media Education Foundation, Northampton, Massachusetts, 35 minutes.

The Famine Within, 1990, Kandor Productions, Ontario, with Ronin Films, Canberra, 90 minutes.
An excellent discussion of body image and eating disorders.

Fat Chance, 1994, National Film Board of Canada, 50 minutes.
A riveting and thought-provoking account of fat prejudice.

Fat Files, 1999, BBC/Learning Channel Co-production, four episodes, 153 minutes.

Web sites

Body Icon: nm-server.jrn.columbia.edu/projects/masters/bodyimage/
Body Image & Health Inc.: www.internationalnodietday.com/
Fat!So?: www.fatso.com/
Healthy Weight Network: www.healthyweightnetwork.com/
If Not Dieting, Then What?: www.ifnotdieting.com/
International Size Acceptance Association: www.size-acceptance.org/
Mirror Mirror: www.mirrormirror.com.au
National Association to Advance Fat Acceptance: naafa.org/
NSW Childhood Obesity Summit: www.health.nsw.gov.au/obesity/
Radiance—The Magazine for Large Women: www.radiancemagazine.com/
Women's Health Australia—The Australian Longitudinal Study on Women's Health: www.newcastle.edu.au/centre/wha/

References

AIHW—*see* Australian Institute of Health and Welfare.

Annandale, E. & Clarke, J. 1996, 'What is Gender? Feminist Theory and the Sociology of Human Reproduction', *Sociology of Health and Illness*, vol. 18, no. 1, pp. 17–44.

Australian Bureau of Statistics 1997, *National Nutrition Survey Selected Highlights, Australia 1995* (Cat. no. 4802.0), Australian Bureau of Statistics, Canberra.

Australian Institute of Health and Welfare 2002, *Australia's Health 2002*, Australian Institute of Health and Welfare, Canberra.

Ball, K. & Kenardy, J. 2002, 'Body Weight, Body Image and Eating Behaviours: Relationships with Ethnicity and Acculturation in a Community Sample of Young Australian Women, *Eating Behaviors*, vol. 3, no. 3, pp. 205–16.

Banks, G. G. 1992, 'Culture in Culture-bound Syndromes: The Case of Anorexia Nervosa', *Social Science & Medicine*, vol. 34, no. 8, pp. 867–84.

Banner, L. W. 1983, *American Beauty*, Knopf, New York.

Barrett, M. & Phillips, A. (eds) 1992, *Destabilizing Theory: Contemporary Feminist Debates*, Polity Press, Cambridge.

Bartky, S. L. 1990, *Femininity and Domination: Studies in the Phenomenology of Oppression*, Routledge, New York.

Bell, R. 1985, *Holy Anorexia*, Chicago University Press, Chicago.

Beller, A. S. 1977, *Fat and Thin: A Natural History of Obesity*, Farrar, Strauss & Giroux, New York.

Berg, F. M. 1995, *The Health Risks of Weight Loss*, Healthy Weight Journal, Hettinger, North Dakota.

Bordo, S. 1993, *Unbearable Weight: Feminism, Western Culture and the Body*, University of California Press, Berkeley.

Bray, G. A., Bouchard, C. & James, W. P. T. 1998, 'Definitions and Proposed Current Classification of Obesity', in G. A. Bray, C. Bouchard & W. P. T. James (eds), *Handbook of Obesity*, Marcel Dekker, New York, pp. 31–40.

Brownell, K. D. 1993, 'Whether Obesity Should Be Treated', *Health Psychology*, vol. 12, no. 5, pp. 339–41.

Brownell, K. D. & Rodin, J. 1994, 'The Dieting Maelstrom: Is It Possible and Advisable to Lose Weight?', *American Psychologist*, vol. 49, no. 9, pp. 781–91.

Brumberg, J. J. 1988, *Fasting Girls: The Emergence of Anorexia Nervosa as a Modern Disease*, Harvard University Press, Cambridge, Massachusetts.

Burgoyne, J. & Clarke, D. 1983, 'You Are What You Eat: Food and Family Reconstruction', in A. Murcott (ed.), *The Sociology of Food and Eating*, Gower, Aldershot, UK.

Bynum, C. W. 1987, *Holy Feast and Holy Fast: The Religious Significance of Food to Medieval Women*, University of California Press, Berkeley.

Charles, N. & Kerr, M. 1988, *Women, Food and Families*, Manchester University Press, Manchester.

Chernin, K. 1981, *The Obsession: Reflections on the Tyranny of Slenderness*, Harper, New York.

Clark, P. & Hornery, A. 1997 '"Fat is Fab" Campaign that Ate an Editor', *Sydney Morning Herald*, 18 December.

Corrigan, A. & Meredyth, D. 1994, 'The Body Politic', in K. Pritchard Hughes (ed.), *Contemporary Australian Feminism*, Longman, Melbourne.

Davis, K. (ed) 1997, *Embodied Practices: Feminist Perspectives on the Body*, Sage, London.

—— 1995, *Reshaping the Female Body: The Dilemma of Cosmetic Surgery,* Routledge, New York.

DeVault, M. L. 1991, *Feeding the Family: The Social Organization of Caring as Gendered Work*, University of Chicago Press, Chicago.

Duncan, M. C. 1994, 'The Politics of Women's Body Images and Practices: Foucault, the Panopticon and Shape Magazine', *Journal of Sport and Social Issues*, vol. 18, no. 1, pp. 48–65.

Dunstan, D., Zimmet, P., Welborn, T., et al. 2000, *Diabesity and Associated Disorders in Australia: The Final Report of the Australian Diabetes, Obesity and Lifestyle Study (AusDiab)*, International Diabetes Institute, Melbourne.

Egger, G. 1992, 'The Case for Using Waist to Hip Ratio Measurements in Routine Medical Checks', *Medical Joutnal of Australia*, vol. 156, pp. 280–4.

Egger, G., Cameron-Smith, D. & Stanton, R. 1999, 'The Effectiveness of Popular, Non-prescription Weight Loss Supplements', *Medical Journal of Australia*, vol. 171, no. 6, pp. 604–8.

Ehrenreich, B. & English, D. 1979, *For Her Own Good: 150 Years of the Experts' Advice to Women*, Feminist Press, New York.

Eisenstein, Z. R. 1988, *The Female Body and the Law*, University of California Press, Berkeley.

Faludi, S. 1991, *Backlash: The Undeclared War Against Women*, Chatto & Windus, London.

Featherstone, M., Hepworth, M. & Turner, B. S. (eds) (1991), *The Body: Social Process and Cultural Theory*, Newbury Park, London.

Ferguson, M. 1983, *Forever Feminine: Women's Magazines and the Cult of Femininity*, Heinemann, London.

Foucault, M. 1979, *Discipline and Punish*, Penguin Books, Harmondsworth.

French, S. A., Story, M., Neumark-Sztainer, D., Downes, B., Resnick, M. & Blum, R. 1997, 'Ethnic Differences in Psychosocial and Health Behavior Correlates of Dieting, Purging, and Binge Eating in a Population-based Sample of Adolescent Females', *International Journal of Eating Disorders*, vol. 22, no. 3, pp. 315–22.

Germov, J. & Williams, L. 1996a, 'The Sexual Division Of Dieting: Women's Voices', *The Sociological Review*, vol. 44, no. 4, pp. 630–47.

—— 1996b, 'The Epidemic of Dieting Women: The Need for a Sociological Approach to Food and Nutrition', *Appetite*, vol. 27, pp. 97–108.

—— 1999 , 'Dieting Women: Self-surveillance and the Body Panoptican', in J. Sobal & D. Maurer (eds), *Weighty Issues: Constructing Fatness and Thinness as Social Problems*, Aldine de Gruyter, New York, pp. 117–32.

Groesz, L. M., Levine, M. P. & Murnen, S. K. 2002, 'The Effect of Experimental Presentation of Thin Media Images on Body Satisfaction: A Meta-analytic Review', *International Journal of Eating Disorders*, vol. 31, pp. 1–16.

Grogan, S. 1999, *Body Image: Understanding Body Dissatisfaction in Men, Women and Children*, Routledge, London.

Hepworth, J. 1999, *The Social Construction of Anorexia Nervosa,* Sage, London.

Hesse-Biber, S. 1991, 'Women, Weight and Eating Disorders: A Socio-cultural and Political-economic Analysis', *Women's Studies International Forum*, vol. 14, no. 3, pp. 173–91.

—— 1996, *Am I Thin Enough Yet? The Cult of Thinness and the Commercialization of Identity*, Oxford University Press, New York.

Huon, G. F., Morris, S. E. & Brown, L. B. 1990, 'Differences between Male and Female Preferences for Female Body Size', *Australian Psychology*, vol. 25, pp. 314–17.

Kenardy, J., Brown, W. J. & Vogt, E. 2001, 'Dieting and Health in Young Australian Women', *European Eating Disorders Review*, vol. 9, pp. 242–54.

Lester, I. H. 1994, *Australia's Food and Nutrition*, Australian Government Publishing Services, Canberra.

McKie, L. J., Wood, R. C. & Gregory, S. 1993, 'Women Defining Health: Food, Diet and Body Image', *Health Education Research*, vol. 8, no. 1, pp. 35–41.

Malson, H. M. 1998, *The Thin Woman: Feminism, Post-structuralism, and the Social Psychology of Anorexia Nervosa*, Routledge, London.

Mennell, S. 1985, *All Manners of Food: Eating and Taste in England and France from the Middle Ages to the Present*, Basil Blackwell, Oxford.

Michie, H. 1987, *The Flesh Made Word: Female Figures and Women's Bodies*, Oxford University Press, New York.

Morris, A., Cooper, T. & Cooper, P. J. 1989, 'The Changing Shape of Female Fashion Models', *International Journal of Eating Disorders*, vol. 8, pp. 593–6.

Murcott, A. 1983, 'Cooking and the Cooked: A Note on the Domestic Preparation of Meals', in A. Murcott (ed.), *The Sociology of Food and Eating*, Gower, Aldershot, UK.

National Heart Foundation 1990, *Risk Factor Prevalence Study: Survey No. 3 1989*, National Heart Foundation of Australia and Australian Institute of Health, Canberra.

New York Times Magazine, 27 May 1994, p. 22.

Norton, K. I., Olds, T. S., Olive, S. & Dank, S. 1996, 'Ken and Barbie at Life Size', *Sex Roles*, vol. 34, nos 3 & 4, pp. 287–94.

Nowak, M., Crawford, D. & Buttner, P. 2001, 'A Cross-sectional Study of Weight- and Shape-related Beliefs, Behaviours and Concerns of North Queensland Adolescents', *Australian Journal of Nutrition and Dietetics*, vol. 58, no. 3, pp. 174–81.

O'Brien, S. 1997, '"I Want to Be Just Like You"—Barbie Magazine and the Production of the Female Desiring Subject', *Journal of Interdisciplinary Gender Studies*, vol. 2, no. 2, pp. 51–66.

O'Dea, J. 1998, 'The Body Size Preferences of Underweight Young Women from Different Cultural Backgrounds', *Australian Journal of Nutrition and Dietetics*, vol. 55, no. 2, pp. 75–80.

Orbach, S. 1986, *Hunger Strike*, Faber & Faber, London.

Parker, S., Nichter, M., Nichter, M., Vuckovic, N., Sims, C. & Rittenbaugh, C. 1995, 'Body Image and Weight Concerns among African American and White Adolescent Females: Differences that Make a Difference', *Human Organization*, vol. 54, no. 2, pp. 103–14.

Pringle, R. 1995, 'Destabilising Patriarchy', in B. Caine & R. Pringle (eds), *Transitions: New Australian Feminisms*, Allen & Unwin, Sydney.

RCGH—*see* Research Centre for Gender and Health.

Research Centre for Gender and Health 2002a, *Data Book for the 2000 Phase 2 Survey of the Young Cohort (22–27 Years), Australian Longitudinal Study on Women's Health,* Research Centre for Gender and Health, University of Newcastle, Newcastle, Australia.

—— 2002b, *Data Book for the 1998 Phase 2 Survey of the Mid-age Cohort (47a-52 Years), Australian Longitudinal Study on Women's Health,* Research Centre for Gender and Health, The University of Newcastle, Newcastle, Australia.

Rothblum, E. D. 1994, '"I'll Die for the Revolution but Don't Ask Me Not to Diet": Feminism and the Continuing Stigmatization of Obesity', in P. Fallon, M. A. Katzman & S. A. Wooley (eds), *Feminist Perspectives on Eating Disorders*, Guilford Press, New York.

Rubin, G. 1975, 'The Traffic in Women', in R. R. Rayna (ed.), *Toward an Anthropology of Women*, Monthly Review Press, New York, pp. 157–210.

Schur, E. 1983, *Labelling Women Deviant: Gender, Stigma, and Social Control,* Temple University Press, Philadelphia.

Schwartz, H. 1986, *Never Satisfied: A Cultural History of Diets, Fantasies and Fat*, The Free Press, New York.

Seghatol, F. F. & Rigolin, V. H. 2002, 'Appetite Suppressants and Valvular Heart Disease, *Current Opinion in Cardiology*, vol. 17, no. 5, pp. 486–92.

Seid, R. P. 1994, 'Too "Close to the Bone": The Historical Context for Women's Obsession with Slenderness', in P. Fallon, M. A. Katzman & S. A. Wooley (eds), *Feminist Perspectives on Eating Disorders*, Guilford Press, New York.

Silverstein, B., Perdue, L., Peterson, B., Vogel, L. & Fantini, D. A. 1986, 'Possible Causes for the Thin Standard of Bodily Attractiveness for Women', *International Journal of Eating Disorders*, vol. 5, pp. 135–44.

Sobal, J. 1999, 'The Size Acceptance Movement and the Social Construction of Body Weight', in J. Sobal & D. Maurer (eds), *Weighty Issues: Fatness and Thinness as Social Problems*, Aldine de Gruyter, New York, pp. 183–205.

Sobal, J. & Cassidy, C. 1987, 'Dieting Foods: Conceptualizations and Explanations', *Ecology of Food and Nutrition*, vol. 20, no. 2, pp. 89–96.

Tebbel, C. 2000, *The Body Snatchers: How the Media Shapes Women*, Finch Publishing, Sydney.

Tiggemann, M. & Pennington, B. 1990, 'The Development of Gender Differences in Body Dissatisfaction', *Australian Psychology*, vol. 25, pp. 306–13.

Turner, B. S. 1992, *Regulating Bodies*, Routledge, London.

Tyler, M. & Abbott, P. 1998, 'Chocs Away: Weight Watching in the Contemporary Airline Industry', *Sociology*, vol. 32, no. 3, pp. 433–50.

Wearing, B. 1996, *Gender: The Pain and Pleasure of Difference*, Longman Australia, Melbourne.

Weedon, C. 1987, *Feminist Practice and Poststructuralist Theory*, Blackwell, Oxford.

Weigle, D. S. 2003, 'Pharmacological Therapy of Obesity: Past, Present, and Future', *Journal of Clinical Endocrinology & Metabolism*, vol. 88, no. 6, pp. 2462–9.

WHO—*see* World Health Organisation.

Wiles, R. 1994, 'I'm Not Fat, I'm Pregnant: The Impact of Pregnancy on Fat Women's Body Image', in S. Wilkinson & C. Kitzinger (eds), *Women and Health: Feminist Perspectives*, Taylor & Francis, London.

Williams, L. & Potter, J. 1999, '"It's Like They Want You to Get Fat": Social Reconstruction of Women's Bodies during Pregnancy', in J. Germov & L. Williams (eds), *A Sociology of Food and Nutrition: The Social Appetite*, Oxford University Press, Melbourne, pp. 228–41.

Wolf, N. 1990, *The Beauty Myth*, Vintage, London.

World Health Organisation 2000, *Obesity: Preventing and Managing the Global Epidemic*, World Health Organisation, Geneva.

Yanovski, S. Z. & Yanovski, J. A. 2002, 'Drug Therapy: Obesity [Review Article]', *New England Journal of Medicine*, vol. 346, no. 8, pp. 591–602.

16

The Social Construction of Eating Disorders

Julie Hepworth

Overview

- What are eating disorders?
- What contribution does social science make to our understanding of eating disorders?
- What are some of the limitations of medical models of eating disorders?

The aim of this chapter is to provide an overview of the contribution of the social sciences to our understanding of the field commonly known as 'eating disorders'. Eating disorders, such as anorexia nervosa (AN), bulimia nervosa (BN), binge-eating disorders, and eating disorders not otherwise specified (EDNOS), are described in relation to the historical and social conditions that have shaped and defined them as biomedical and psychiatric phenomena. In addition, the psychological and cultural aspects of eating disorders are briefly discussed. While neurobiological and genetic research on the aetiological factors of eating disorders has attracted considerable interest over the last few years, these areas are not the subject of this chapter. Rather, the historical and social conditions that led to the discovery of anorexia nervosa are examined, as well as how bulimia nervosa was defined much later as a consequence of this earlier discovery. A social constructionist perspective is put forward as being valuable in developing alternative ways of thinking about eating disorders. The various social and cultural explanations proposed by feminist writers are described. Social constructionist and feminist approaches are then taken up later on in the chapter in a discussion of how social constructionism has informed some feminist criticism of the biomedical and pathological models of eating disorders.

Key terms

anorexia nervosa (AN)
biomedical discourse
bulimia nervosa (BN)
culture-bound syndrome
discourse
eating disorders not otherwise specified (EDNOS)
feminism
patriarchy
post-structuralism
social constructionism
thin ideal

Introduction

> Thus the discourse continues, debating whether and to what degree, and in what ways, the body is tomb or temple, loved or hated, personal or state property, machine or self.
>
> Synnott 1993, p. 37

The field of eating disorders originated in the late nineteenth century as a Western medical phenomenon that initially documented the clinical presentation of self-starvation, found almost exclusively in young, white, middle class women. The current prevalence of eating disorders is difficult to estimate, because there are few full-syndrome eating disorders, and much greater numbers of women presenting with eating disorder symptoms. Susan Kashubeck-West and Laurie Mintz (2001) estimated, based on a close analysis of the current research and on information from the *Diagnostic and Statistical Manual-1V* (APA 1994), that full-syndrome eating disorders are rare—the prevalences of **anorexia nervosa (AN)** and **bulimia nervosa (BN)** are 0.5–1.0% and 1–3% respectively—although they are on the rise (see Boxes 16.1 and 16.2). The prevalence of **eating disorders not otherwise specified (EDNOS)** is estimated at 2–5%. Many women (an estimated 19–32%) suffer from only some eating disorder symptoms (Mulholland & Mintz 2001).

One of the major explanations of eating disorders is that changing cultural conditions give rise to concerns, particularly among women, about body size and shape. Cheryl Ritenbaugh (1982) proposed that obesity was a **culture-bound syndrome**; eating disorders can also be seen as culture-bound in the sense that they reflect the dominant ideals of women's slimness in Western societies. The responses to changing eating practices made by the health-related professions have also been linked to the cultural context of Western clinical treatment and management. As Western ideals of the slim female permeate other cultures, especially through mass media representations and changing social roles, these cultural ideals will influence non-Western women's behaviour by encouraging increased surveillance of the body. Indeed, eating disorders are increasingly becoming a global problem, with rising numbers of cases in non-Western countries worldwide—due not only to media representations of

Box 16.1 Diagnostic criteria for anorexia nervosa

A. Refusal to maintain body weight at, or above, a minimally normal weight for age and height (e.g. weight loss leading to maintenance of body weight less than 85% of that expected; or failure to make expected weight gain during period of growth, leading to body weight less than 85% of that expected).
B. Intense fear of gaining weight or becoming fat, even though underweight.
C. Disturbance in the way in which one's body weight or shape is experienced, undue influence of body weight or shape on self-evaluation, or denial of the seriousness of the current low body weight.
D. In postmenarcheal females, amenorrhoea, i.e., the absence of at least three consecutive menstrual cycles. (A woman is considered to have amenorrhoea if her periods occur only following hormone, e.g., oestrogen, administration.)

Specific types:

- Restricting type: during the current episode of anorexia nervosa, the person has not regularly engaged in binge-eating or purging behaviour (i.e., self-induced vomiting or the misuse of laxatives, diuretics, or enemas).
- Binge-Eating/Purging type: during the current episode of anorexia nervosa, the person has regularly engaged in binge-eating or purging behaviour (i.e., self-induced vomiting or the misuse of laxatives, diuretics, or enemas).

Source: APA (1994)

Western ideals but also to familial factors (such as intergenerational conflicts and confusion over racial identity), changes in dietary habits, and increases in obesity (Nasser 1997). The rise in eating disorders among non-Western women is a result of the pressures of moving to the West and adapting to a new culture, or, alternatively, of non-Western women's desire to conform to the norms and values of Western society, including those relating to body shape. However, more culturally sensitive measures of the prevalence of eating disorders are required, especially to facilitate more effective prevention and treatment of eating disorders in women of non-Western cultures who live in the West (Lake et al. 2000).

Also changing are the cultural representations and social conditions of males. Consequently, in the West, increasing numbers of men are being diagnosed with eating disorders. Approximately 10% of individuals who present with AN and BN, and 25% of those with binge-eating disorder, are male (APA

Box 16.2 Diagnostic criteria for bulimia nervosa

A. Recurrent episodes of binge eating. An episode of binge eating is characterised by both of the following:
   (1) Eating, in a discrete period of time (e.g. within any 2-hour period), an amount of food that is definitely larger than most people would eat during a similar period of time and under similar circumstances.
   (2) A sense of lack of control over eating during the episode (e.g. a feeling that one cannot stop eating or control what or how much one is eating).

B. Recurrent inappropriate compensatory behaviour in order to prevent weight gain, such as self-induced vomiting, misuse of laxatives, diuretics, enemas, or other medications, fasting, or excessive exercise.

C. The binge eating and inappropriate compensatory behaviour both occur, on average, at least twice a week for three months.

D. Self-evaluation is unduly influenced by body shape and weight.

E. The disturbance does not occur exclusively during episodes of anorexia nervosa.

Specific types:

- Purging type: during the current episode of bulimia nervosa, the person has regularly engaged in self-induced vomiting or the misuse of laxatives, diuretics, or enemas.
- Non-purging Type: during the current episode of bulimia nervosa, the person has used other inappropriate compensatory behaviours, such as fasting or excessive exercise, but has not regularly engaged in self-induced vomiting or the misuse of laxatives, diuretics, or enemas.

Source: APA (1994)

1994). The increasing problem of eating disorders in men is linked to the rise in media representations of the ideal male body, and the need to exercise to achieve the toned muscular appearance that typifies men's health magazines. While there is clear evidence of an increase in eating distress in males (Petrie & Rogers 2001), eating disorders are still overwhelmingly defined as female conditions and are associated with femininity (Gremillion 2001). For men, this definition of eating disorders as female conditions creates potential barriers to clinical diagnosis. Health professionals may not be as likely to associate symptoms in males with eating disorders, and there is a stigma attached to eating disorders for males, who do not want to be perceived as suffering from a female condition (Hepworth 1999; Petrie & Rogers 2001).

The field of eating disorders is vast, in terms of both aetiological models and treatment approaches. While some explanations remain firmly situated within the disciplinary boundaries of medicine, dietetics and nutrition science, psychiatry, or psychology, most researchers maintain there is multi-factorial causation of eating disorders. Over the last 30 years, particularly within psychology, the contribution of social, cultural, and familial factors to the onset and maintenance of eating disorders has gained recognition (Striegel-Moore & Cachelin 2001; Ogden 2003). Multi-factorial models aim to explain the role played by these factors, and are commonly taught and used in such fields of medicine as primary care, in which eating disorders are understood as constituting more than just biological and pathological processes. These models take into account the multidimensional nature of eating disorders in a way that moves beyond the traditionally dominant **biomedical discourse**.

Interestingly, rather than the last 150 years having produced greater certainty about the nature of eating disorders, through the twentieth century emergence of the social sciences, what has arisen instead is theoretical and explanatory diversity. This diversity has contributed to the vastness of the field by creating competing disciplinary and professional claims, as well as, more positively, interdisciplinary collaboration. Clearly, knowledge in this field has not progressed along a line of increasing certainty; rather, the field incorporates a number of approaches, including medical, **social constructionist,** and **feminist** perspectives, which demonstrate its complexity. These three particular approaches to eating disorders are significant in that they constitute major strands of thought that have shaped current understanding. Through their examination, the field will be revealed as a contested domain in which different disciplines have made various claims to know the aetiological basis of and best way of treating eating disorders, the most long-standing claims being those of clinical medicine.

Biomedical approaches to eating disorders

Despite the proliferation of research on eating disorders over the past century, a specific aetiology or clinical treatment for either AN or BN has not been developed. Characterised still as psychiatric disorders in the DSM-IV (APA 1994), eating disorders were historically defined by medical science and treated within the clinical domain. Current diagnostic and clinical management procedures largely resemble those of over a hundred years ago: medical practitioners manage the conditions within primary care through regular consultations, weight monitoring, and counselling, or in hospitals through re-feeding programs and psychotherapeutic interventions. Eating disorders are commonly seen as something of an enigma, as elusive, in that what precisely causes onset and recovery has not been identified, and, especially in relation to AN, as an intractable problem mostly associated with young women.

In order to understand the significance of biomedical approaches, it is important to know the basic historical background to the emergence of AN and BN as psychiatric disorders and their classification within the DSM-IV. The late-nineteenth-century definition of anorexia nervosa by Sir William Withey Gull was undoubtedly the defining moment when eating disorders became subsumed within biomedical science. William Gull was an eminent British physician; he trained in medicine at Guy's hospital, London, and subsequently worked there as both practitioner and lecturer. Later, in 1872, his career reached its pinnacle when he was made Physician to Queen Victoria. Until the late 1800s, self-starvation had been largely understood through religious ideas about women's sainthood, such as in the case of the seventeenth-century figure of Jane Balan, who reportedly lived without nourishment for 3 years (cf. Morgan 1977); later accounts attributed fasting to an assumed negative spiritual state and inherent wickedness of women. The discovery of anorexia nervosa in 1874 firmly established self-starvation as a disease entity, as a biomedical condition, to be treated within the clinical domain, although Julie Hepworth and Christine Griffin (1990) criticise this discovery, instead arguing that five key discourses—the femininity, medical-scientific, discovery, clinical, and hysteria discourses—gave rise to the social and cultural conditions through which this discovery was made possible.

Here is a typical early case description of anorexia nervosa by Gull:

> Miss B., aged 18, was brought to me Oct. 8, 1868, as a case of latent tubercle. Her friends had been advised accordingly to take her for the coming winter to the South of Europe. The extremely emaciated look, much greater indeed than occurred for the most part in tubercular cases where patients are still going about, impressed me at once with the probability that I should find no visceral disease. Pulse 50, reps. 16. Physical examination of the chest and abdomen discovered nothing abnormal. All the viscera were apparently healthy. Notwithstanding the great emaciation and apparent weakness, there was a peculiar restlessness, difficult, I was informed, to control. The mother added, 'She is never tired.' Amenorrhoea since Christmas 1866. The clinical details of this case were in fact almost identical with the preceding one, even to the number of the pulse and respirations.
>
> Gull 1874, pp. 23–4

With the publication of these kinds of clinical observations, physicians, particularly in Europe, the USA, and Australia, began redefining self-starvation as diagnoses of AN in their patients. Following on from this, the search for the biological causation of AN dominated medical science and psychiatric thinking in this field for a number of decades. The discovery of AN was also influential in the subsequent definition of other eating disorders, especially BN.

The earliest English-language example of BN occurred in 1898 (Parry-Jones 1971) and BN was commonly associated with pituitary insufficiency (studied by Simmonds) from the 1900s onwards. 'Bulimia' comes from the Greek language and means ravenous hunger. One of the earliest clinical case descriptions is found in the work of Hilde Bruch (1974), who described a patient who binged and vomited. However, the term 'bulimia nervosa' was not defined until the late 1970s by Gerald Russell (1979), who acknowledged that BN was not a new disorder and that, indeed, there had been many case histories over the previous 60 years. Although not as much is known about BN as about AN, there are several key similarities and differences in relation to AN. Bulimia nervosa is regarded as often being a 'progression' from AN, and treatment outcomes are more optimistic than for AN. The close connection between the two conditions was recognised some time ago, when Marlene Boskind-White (1987) coined the term 'bulimarexia' to refer to the condition of those people who presented with both AN and BN symptoms, also representing how people alternated between bingeing and fasting.

BN was also primarily diagnosed in young women, and many of the assumptions and practices of the biomedical discourse in relation to diagnosis and treatment were simply enlarged to accommodate what were considered to be new forms of disordered eating. Subsequent to the definition of BN, and notwithstanding the fact that anorexia and bulimia are considered the two major eating disorders, there were further conditions and syndromes, such as binge-eating disorder and EDNOS, that also became diagnostic categories within the field of eating disorders.

What biomedical approaches do not consider are the social and cultural conditions of the body, subjectivity, and sexuality. This has meant that the relationship between the social and cultural contexts of experience and individual behaviour has been poorly understood. Yet these contexts are important to understanding eating disorders precisely because they reflect conflicts that individuals experience about changing societal norms and expectations. Biomedical approaches also do not take into account the dramatic economic, social, and cultural changes in women's lives during the twentieth century, which have given rise to contradictory demands, such as managing the dual roles of career and motherhood, and problematic values, such as the definition of women in terms of the **thin ideal** (Orbach 1986; see also Chapter 15). Through the definition of eating disorders as psychiatric categories, the complexity of social issues, particularly those faced by women but increasingly those faced by men, are individualised as discreet psychiatric conditions to be treated within the clinical domain (Hepworth & Griffin 1995). Consequently, the social and cultural factors that are implicated in the onset and maintenance of eating disorders have remained largely unchallenged.

Social constructionist approaches to eating disorders

The dominance of the biomedical approach to the conceptualisation of eating disorders has been challenged by several authors, and particularly by those using social constructionist approaches since the 1990s. Social constructionism is not a unitary theory but rather is informed by numerous philosophical and theoretical approaches. Key social constructionist writings include the seminal work of Peter Berger and Thomas Luckmann (1967), as well as work by Kenneth Gergen (1985), Henriques and colleagues (1984), and Potter and Wetherell (1987). One of the most common approaches is that informed by the work of French philosopher Michel Foucault (1974), who argues that discourses—regularly occurring systems of language—construct specific concepts. If we take this approach to the field of eating disorders, we can see how eating disorders are socially constructed concepts related to the historical, social, and cultural conditions of the period in which they were defined. If we accept that knowledge is socially constructed, this also allows for the idea that during particular periods of history there are dominant discourses (such as biomedicine today) and competing discourses (such as psychological and feminist explanations) that produce certain kinds of relationships and practices that are reproduced through the use of language. This is why language is central to any analysis in the social constructionist approach known as 'discourse analysis', though 'discourse analysis is best understood as a field of research rather than a single practice' (Taylor 2001, p. 5).

It is precisely by examining the language through which eating disorders emerged and are practised that it is possible to deconstruct or take apart the taken-for-granted meanings and assumptions of the field of eating disorders and identify possibilities for change. As Ludvilla Jordanova (1995) argues, social constructionism enables us to conceptualise, explain, and interpret the processes through which scientific and medical ideas are shaped by given contexts. Psychological uses of social constructionism particularly emphasise the relationship between individual subjectivity and social processes. Discourse analysis provides us with the analytic tools to examine the structures within which certain concepts and conditions such as eating disorders emerged by analysing historical and institutional practices, and to examine the ways in which individual accounts of eating disorders are constructed and reproduced by the linguistic communities to which people belong, such as biomedicine.

Prior to **post-structural** interpretations, identity and self were regarded as being separable from social practices, an idea commonly referred to in psychology as 'individual–society dualism'. Identity *responded to* and was *influenced by* external events; although social and cultural pressures on women to be thin were external, they nevertheless underscored existing intrapsychic problems. In contrast, post-structural approaches maintain that the self is constituted by *multiple* identities, is *constructed through* specific social and cultural conditions, and is *not reified* as an autonomous entity, and that language is the major site in which to analyse and explain the relations between women, food, and subjectivity.

Not least in the contribution of feminist approaches to eating disorders is the work of American feminist Susan Bordo (1988, 1993). Women, food, sexuality, and the body are fundamental to Bordo's writings. In 'Anorexia Nervosa and the Crystallization of Culture' (1988), Bordo argued that AN is a symptom of some of the 'multifaceted and heterogenous distress of our age'. She examined social and cultural images of the female body, 'the political anatomy', and identified slenderness as being significant to the relationship between women's subjectivity and media representations of women's bodies. Drawing on Foucault (1974), Bordo elaborated on a post-structural interpretation of anorexia nervosa by arguing that women achieve power through dieting and that this was a form of 'disciplinary practice' carried out by individual women on themselves in order to maintain and reproduce the thin ideal.

The historical relationship between women's sexuality and food can be seen, for example, in the Victorian era, when women were depicted 'in a sensuous surrender to rich, exciting food' and regarded as a form of taboo (Bordo 1993). The representation of the relationship between women and food often takes the form of exaggerated ideals of the female body. Women are portrayed as succumbing to the gratification of sweet foods, representing their abandonment of self-control over an insatiable desire that is historically linked with sexual desire. In this way, the exaggerated ideal of slenderness, Bordo argues, acts as a contemporary metaphor for desire and the management of female sexuality. One of the major contributions of post-structural feminist writers such as Bordo is theorisation of the discursive nature of the image of slenderness in the context of Western society (Bordo 1993; MacSween 1993).

Using discourse analysis within a feminist framework enables a series of questions to be asked. In the earlier section on biomedical approaches to eating disorders, the historical and social conditions through which the discovery of AN was constructed were identified through post-structural analysis (Hepworth & Griffin 1990). The next section shows how feminist authors uncovered different causes of the onset of eating disorders that challenged the pathologising approach of some mainstream health care practitioners. However, it is important to note that the feminist contributions of Susie Orbach (1978), Kim Chernin (1986), and Sheila MacLeod (1981) were also caught in a discursive dilemma, in that the individual concepts and categorisation of eating disorders as psychiatric problems remained unchallenged.

Feminist approaches to eating disorders

While it is important to recognise that feminist perspectives are informed by diverse theoretical frameworks, by different historical and cultural positions, and by the ethnicity of women, they share a common focus on women, power, and gender relations. These approaches privilege the experiences of women, and address various concerns about power in the onset, duration, and treatment of eating disorders. Fundamental to feminist perspectives is the eschewing, to various degrees, of the medical model of eating disorders. The most common theoretical frameworks and backgrounds that inform feminist perspectives are psychoanalytic theory, existentialism, social and cultural theory, and post-structuralism. In the previous section, examples of post-structural feminist approaches to eating disorders were discussed. This section focuses on early examples of feminist writing about eating disorders and current feminist research in this area.

Feminist perspectives on eating disorders are mostly associated with work during the 1980s by psychoanalytic writers such as Orbach, work that included popular texts such as *Fat is a Feminist Issue* (Orbach 1978 & 1987). Two key themes were expounded through this feminist work: the processes of identity formation and the mother–daughter relationship. Early feminist work on eating disorders also included writing by women who had experienced eating disorders themselves and who wrote about their personal experiences by drawing on various theoretical perspectives, such as Kleinian psychoanalytic theory, in which the mother–daughter relationship is regarded as being fundamental to the conflict experienced in eating disorders (cf. Chernin 1986), and existentialism, which posits that it is a woman's 'being-in-the-world' that creates a sense of tension and conflicts with her developing sense of maturity and womanhood expressed through eating disorders (cf. Macleod 1981). The work of these particular writers was constituted as a series of first moves by feminists working around AN to locate eating disorders in a wider social, political, and historical context (Hepworth & Griffin 1995).

Bruch (1974) is the key figure associated with an early broad interpretation of psychoanalytic theories and also became a significant figure in psychotherapy. Against earlier Freudian ideas about anorexia nervosa, she argued that even though the oral component was important, it was only one factor in the aetiology of AN among many others, such as family dynamics. Another main theme in psychoanalytic approaches was a focus on the mother–daughter relationship. Indeed, by the 1980s there was a shift away from 'oral impregnation theory' towards an exclusive focus on the mother–daughter relationship (Lawrence 1984). Issues relating to identification and separation in the psychosexual development of a young woman became paramount to clinical interventions using psychoanalytic ideas. Furthermore, the social and cultural identities of women, Chernin (1986) argued, constituted ambiguous roles for women, contributing to separation issues between daughter and mother.

Existential approaches to eating disorders focused mainly on female identity and its centrality to AN. Eating disorders were seen as a manifestation of a crisis about 'being-in-the-world'. Sheila MacLeod's (1981) own experience of AN is encapsulated in the statement 'I was free at last!'; she describes herself becoming a 'successful anorexic'. Earlier existential interpretations of AN are found in literature describing AN as a form of asceticism, such as Bell's (1985) book *Holy Anorexia*.

Social and cultural approaches to eating disorders were popularised by Orbach, best known for *Fat is a Feminist Issue* (1 and 2). In these books, body image is regarded as being defined and shaped by **patriarchy** in Western society and by patriarchal power relations. Women are thought to focus on food, eating, dieting, and calorie-counting in order to regain a sense of control over their lives and, to some extent, to reconcile contradictory beliefs about their social position.

Much of this early work has continued through the work of, for example, Katherine Zerbe (1993), who also maintains the significance of the mother–daughter relationship in the onset of a young woman's internal conflicts. On the one hand, a woman increasingly experiences the need to assert her individual identity and act upon the world, and on the other she desires the security offered by her mother. In early adulthood, it is argued by psychoanalytic-informed writers, a young woman can experience guilt at no longer requiring the security offered by her mother and fears about making her mother feel worthless. As Zerbe writes, 'Without individual susceptibility, liabilities imposed by society are less likely to take root' (1993, p. 10). While these lines of feminist thought broaden our understanding of eating disorders by putting them in the context of familial relations—and specifically the mother–daughter relationship—they leave the individual nature of the conditions and pathological processes unexplained.

Conclusion

Using a social constructionist approach, eating disorders and even the seemingly immutable empirical claims of medicine can be understood differently by being evaluated in relation to the broader historical and social context. Through the delineation of the competing explanations of eating disorders it is also possible to examine the relationship between social and cultural conditions and the construction of individual subjectivity. Examining this relationship from a constructionist perspective gives rise to alternative explanations both of why people develop eating disorders (see, for example, the work of American feminist writer Bordo (1993)) and of how the field of eating disorders itself is embedded within historical and social structures of medicine and women's social position (Hepworth & Griffin 1990, 1995; Hepworth 1999).

This chapter has illustrated how the development of the social sciences has included a critical element that deconstructs taken-for-granted knowledge in the field of eating disorders. The range of biomedical theories that emerged from the late nineteenth century onwards assumed that young women had a propensity to develop nervous diseases and that hormonal and psychological changes predisposed them to develop eating disorders. This meant that it was assumed that eating disorders such as AN and BN had a pathological aetiology, thereby rendering them clinical entities to be medically managed within hospitals and/or by doctors in primary care. Alternatively, using a social constructionist perspective informed by the work of Foucault, it is possible to see that these conditions only came about precisely because of the historical context and the social position of women over a hundred years ago.

The contribution of social constructionism to our understanding of the overarching importance of the structures of knowledge about eating disorders was further discussed in the chapter's later section on feminist approaches. These writers, using psychoanalytic, existential, social/cultural, and post-structural explanations made considerable contributions throughout the 1980s and 1990s that challenged the dominance of biomedical explanations of eating disorders. Medical, social constructionist, and feminist explanations, therefore, represent key movements in the knowledge about eating disorders. By considering all three, a broader contextualisation of eating disorders is gained, creating new opportunities to think about how knowledge in this field is reproduced and contested and how different forms of knowledge could be derived.

Summary of main points

- The field of eating disorders originated in the medical discovery of anorexia nervosa in the late nineteenth century.
- A number of eating disorders and eating syndromes have been identified over the last hundred years, including bulimia nervosa, binge-eating syndrome, and eating disorders not otherwise specified.
- Social constructionist approaches explain eating disorders in relation to the social, cultural, and historical structures of knowledge.
- Social constructionist approaches maintain that individual subjectivity is created through the use and reproduction of language within specific contexts.
- Since the late 1970s, feminist writers have challenged the biomedical model, which explains eating disorders as resulting from hormonal, genetic, or psychopathological dysfunction.
- Biomedical, social constructionist, and feminist approaches produce different and conflicting explanations of eating disorders, and challenge us to think about new ways of practising in this field.

Discussion questions

1 Identify three approaches to the explanation of eating disorders and the historical and social contexts in which they emerged.
2 To what extent are criticisms of the biomedical model of eating disorders justified? Reflect on what knowledge and information you use in your answer.
3 The prevalence of eating disorders is markedly different for females and males. What are the main reasons for this difference?
4 What evidence is there that cultural pressures are a major contributory factor in the onset of anorexia nervosa and bulimia nervosa?
5 How can a social constructionist approach to eating disorders make an impact on practice?

Further investigation

1 In what ways do social constructionist approaches to eating disorders differ from biomedical approaches and some feminist approaches?
2 Discuss the contributions made by psychoanalytic, social, and feminist theories to our understanding of eating disorders.

Further reading and web resources

Books

Hepworth, J. 1999, *The Social Construction of Anorexia Nervosa*, Sage, London.

Nasser, M., Katzman, M. A. & Gordon, R. A. (eds) 2001, *Eating Disorders and Cultures in Transition*, Brunner-Routledge, London.

Piran, N., Levine, M. P., & Steiner-Adair, C. (eds.) 1999, *Preventing Eating Disorders: A Handbook of Interventions and Special Challenges*, Brunner/Mazel, London.

Vandereycken, W. & Noordenbos, G. (eds.) 1998, *The Prevention of Eating Disorders*, Athlone Press, London.

Web sites

Eating Disorders Association: www.edauk.com

Health Education Board for Scotland—Talking About Eating Disorders: www.hebs.scot.nhs.uk

References

American Psychological Association 1994, *Diagnostic and Statistical Manual of Mental Disorders (DSM-R)*, 4th edn, American Psychological Association, Washington, DC.

APA—*see* American Psychological Association.

Bell, R. M. 1985, *Holy Anorexia*, University of Chicago Press, Chicago.

Berger, P. & Luckmann, T. 1967, *The Social Construction of Reality*, Penguin, Harmondsworth.

Bordo, S. 1988, 'Anorexia Nervosa and the Crystallization of Culture', in I. Diamond & L. Quinby (eds), *Feminism and Foucault: Reflections on Resistance,* Northeastern University Press, Boston.

—— 1993, *Unbearable Weight: Feminism, Western Culture, and the Body*, University of California Press, London.

Boskind-White, M. & White, W.C., Jr, 1987, *Bulimarexia: The Binge/Purge Cycle*, 2nd edn, Norton, New York.

Bruch, H. 1974, *Eating Disorders: Obesity, Anorexia Nervosa and the Person Within*, Routledge and Kegan Paul, London.

Chernin, K. 1986, *The Hungry Self: Daughters and Mothers, Eating and Identity*, Virago Press, London.

Foucault, M. 1974, *The Archaeology of Knowledge*, Tavistock Press, London.

Gergen, K. J. 1985, 'The Social Constructionist Movement in Modern Psychology', *American Psychologist*, vol. 40, pp. 266–75.

Gremillion, H. 2001, 'In Fitness and in Health: Crafting Bodies in the Treatment of Anorexia Nervosa', *Signs: Journal of Women in Culture and Society*, vol. 27, no. 2, pp. 381–414.

Gull, W. W. 1874, 'Anorexia Nervosa (Apepsia Hysterica, Anorexia Hysterica)', *Transactions of the Clinical Society*, London, vol. 7, pp. 22–7.

Henriques, J. W., Hollway, C., Urwin, C., Venn, C. & Walkerdine, V. 1984, *Changing the Subject: Psychology, Social Regulation and Subjectivity,* Methuen, London.

Hepworth, J. 1999, *The Social Construction of Anorexia Nervosa,* Sage, London.

Hepworth, J. & Griffin, C. 1990, 'The Discovery of Anorexia Nervosa: Discourses of the Late 19th Century', *TEXT: The Journal of the Study of Discourse*, vol. 10, no. 4, pp. 321–38.

—— 1995, 'Conflicting Opinions? Anorexia Nervosa, Medicine and Feminism', in S. Wilkinson & C. Kitzinger (eds.), *Feminism and Discourse*, London, Sage.

Jordanova, L. 1995, 'The Social Construction of Medical Knowledge', *Social History of Medicine*, vol. 8, no. 4, pp. 361–81.

Kashubeck-West, S. & Mintz, L. B. 2001, 'Eating Disorders in Women: Etiology, Assessment and Treatment', *The Counselling Psychologist*, vol. 29, no. 5, pp. 627–34.

Lake, A. J., Staiger, P. K. & Glowinski, H. 2000, 'Effect of Western Culture on Women's Attitudes to Eating and Perceptions of Body Shape', *International Journal of Eating Disorders*, vol. 27, no. 1, pp. 83–9.

Lawrence, M. 1984, *The Anorexic Experience*, Women's Press, London.

MacLeod, S. 1981, *The Art of Starvation*, Virago, London.

MacSween, M. 1993, *Anorexic Bodies: A Feminist and Sociological Perspective on Anorexia Nervosa,* Routledge, London.

Morgan, H. G. 1977, 'Fasting Girls and Our Attitudes to Them', *British Medical Journal*, vol. 2, pp. 1652–5.

Mulholland, A. M. & Mintz, L. B. 2001, 'Prevalence of Eating Disorders among African American Women', *Journal of Counselling Psychology*, vol. 48, pp. 111–16.

Nasser, M. 1997, *Culture and Weight Consciousness*, Routledge, London.

Ogden, J. 2003, *The Psychology of Eating: From Healthy to Disordered Eating,* Blackwell, Oxford.

Orbach, S. 1986, *Hunger Strike: The Anorectic's Struggle as a Metaphor for Our Age*, Faber and Faber, London.

—— 1978, *Fat is a Feminist Issue,* Berkley, New York.

—— 1987, *Fat is a Feminist Issue II: A Program to Conquer Compulsive Eating,* Berkley, New York.

Parry-Jones, W. L. 1971, *The Trade in Lunacy: A Study of Private Madhouses in England in the Eighteenth and Nineteenth Centuries*, London, Routledge and Kegan Paul.

Petrie, T. A. & Rogers, R. 2001, 'Extending the Discussion of Eating Disorders to Include Men and Athletes', *The Counselling Psychologist*, vol. 29, no. 5, pp. 743–53.

Potter, J. & Wetherell, M. 1987, *Discourse and Social Psychology: Beyond Attitudes and Behaviour,* Sage, London.

Ritenbaugh, C. 1982, 'Obesity as a Culture-bound Syndrome', *Culture, Medicine and Psychiatry*, vol. 6, pp. 347–61.

Russell, G. F. M. 1979 'Bulimia Nervosa: An Ominous Variant of Anorexia Nervosa', *Psychological Medicine*, vol 9, pp. 429–48.

Striegel-Moore, R. H. & Cachelin, F. M. 2001, 'Etiology of Eating Disorders in Women', *The Counselling Psychologist*, vol. 29, no. 5, pp. 635–61.

Synnott, A. 1993, *The Body Social: Symbolism, Self and Society*, Routledge, London.

Taylor, S. 2001, 'Locating and Conducting Discourse Analytic Research', in Wetherell, M., Taylor, S. & Yates, S. (eds), *Discourse as Data*, Open University Press, Milton Keynes.

Zerbe, K. J. 1993, *The Body Betrayed: Women, Eating Disorders, and Treatment,* American Psychological Association, Washington, DC.

17

Sociological Analysis of the Stigmatisation of Obesity

Jeffery Sobal

Overview

- Why is obesity stigmatised?
- What sociological approaches are useful in explaining the stigmatisation of obesity?
- How do individuals deal with the stigmatisation of obesity?

Stigmas are attributes of a person that are deeply discrediting, and obesity is highly stigmatised in contemporary post-industrial societies. Obesity is the condition of having high levels of stored body fat. Sociological work on the stigmatisation of obesity can be divided into two major streams: one focusing on documenting the presence, arenas, extent, and sources of stigmatisation, and the other examining strategies for managing and negotiating the stigma of obesity. Prejudice, labelling, stigmatisation, and discrimination based on obesity are very widespread, and occur in many arenas of life (work, family, health, and everyday interactions). Obesity is stigmatised more than some conditions, but less than others. A variety of coping mechanisms are used by obese individuals, including denial, concealment, avoidance, mutual aid, and redefinition of situations. Eating is an especially problematic act for obese individuals, because of the potential for stigmatisation. The coping strategies that obese people use to explain their food choices include providing several types of accounts, making disclaimers, and discounting some eating behaviours. Obese individuals often adopt 'fat' identities as they deal with the stigmatisation of obesity. Sociologists have examined the stigmatisation of obesity from several mainstream disciplinary perspectives, and yet many aspects of the stigmatisation of obesity remain unresolved and need further attention.

Key terms

accounts
attribution
culture-bound syndrome
deviance
disclaimer
discounting
ethnography
functionalism
marginality
master status
obesity
post-industrial society
self-fulfilling prophecy
stigma
stigmatising act
symbolic interactionism

Introduction

A **stigma** is 'an attribute that is deeply discrediting' and that disqualifies a person from full social acceptance (Goffman 1963, p. 3). Stigmatised individuals are seen as blemished, disgraced, and tainted, and routine social interactions become problematic for them. Types of stigma include physical deformities, character blemishes, and group stigmas (Goffman 1963). **Obesity** has become a stigma in contemporary **post-industrial societies**, and sociological perspectives on the stigmatisation of obesity will be the focus of this chapter.

It has been 40 years since Erving Goffman (1963) brought the concept of stigma to the forefront of sociological attention with his classic book *Stigma: Notes on the Management of Spoiled Identity*. Since Goffman's insightful explication of the concept of stigma, the term and idea have diffused widely through sociology, other social sciences, and wider public discourse (Page 1984; Ainlay et al. 1986; Falk 2001; Link & Phelan 2001), with psychologists showing particular interest (Jones et al. 1984; Herman et al. 1986; Heatherton et al. 2000).

In contemporary post-industrial societies, many conditions and characteristics are socially defined as **deviant** rather than being accepted as 'normal'. These conditions are viewed as marginal and labelled as 'deviant', and consequently are stigmatised. The **marginality** of an attribute is not necessarily based on its prevalence or functionality, but instead is based on the social norms and values attached to that particular trait or condition. Individuals who are marginal with respect to one attribute are not necessarily marginal in other respects (Emmons & Sobal 1981; Sobal & Hinrichs 1986). Marginal conditions that are stigmatised in contemporary society include those that are medical (AIDS, cancer, leprosy, physical deformities, infertility, disability), economic (poverty, unemployment, use of welfare, homelessness), sociocultural (ethnicity, homosexuality, prostitution, criminality, illiteracy, substance abuse, divorce), and many other types of conditions. Obesity is a stigma that has received much attention from social scientists.

Obesity is the condition in which a person has a high level of stored body fat. The amount of body fat that people possess varies across a wide continuum.

The leanest individuals carry only a few per cent of their total body weight as stored fat, while the majority of the fattest people's body weight is made up of stored fat. Cut-off points for defining obesity are not absolute and universally agreed upon, and many standards are used in practice (Dalton 1997). For our purposes, obesity can simply be considered as the condition in which an individual has relatively high amounts of body fat (Sobal & Devine 1997; Sobal 2001). Quantitative definitions that specify exactly the level of fat that constitutes obesity are not necessary for examining sociological patterns and processes, despite their emphasis in biomedical work. A relative definition of obesity permits variation among different groups (such as dancers and construction workers) in their evaluations of how much body fat is excessive.

Public beliefs about the cause of obesity tend to focus on the assumption that obese people overeat and consume too much caloric energy, rather than on the role of low activity levels and low energy expenditure in producing obesity. In contemporary post-industrial societies, where the food system provides people with ample access to a wide variety of foods, many of which are high in fat and are calorically dense, there is a strong link between food, eating, and weight. Post-industrial food systems add unnecessary calories at all stages (production, processing, distribution, acquisition, preparation, and consumption) and are therefore labelled 'fattening food systems' (Sobal 2001). Sociologists have commented on how the social system provides easy access to high-calorie inexpensive food, with a consequently high prevalence of obesity and the parallel development of a fear of fatness (Mennell 1985; McIntosh 1996; Beardsworth & Keil 1997).

The stigmatisation of obesity reflects the extent to which high body weight is socially defined as either central or marginal to what is collectively agreed upon and accepted as 'normal' in society (or a portion of society). Thus a person with lower body weight than the average may be defined as socially normal, while someone with a body weight equally far above the average may be regarded as marginal and be stigmatised. Where negative and prejudicial attitudes about obesity exist, obesity is treated as a physical deformity, and obese people are discredited and discriminated against.

Cultural and historical factors

The cultural and historical location of the current stigmatisation of obesity is important to consider in order to gain a broader, relative perspective on how the stigma of obesity is socially constructed (Sobal 2001). Traditional societies, which have not been involved in the modernisation associated with the Industrial Revolution, tend to appreciate and value at least moderate, if not large, amounts of body fat (Brown & Konner 1987). Traditional cultures view stored body fat as a sign of health and wealth, particularly for women (Sobal &

Stunkard 1989). The harsher survival conditions of traditional societies mean that food supplies may be uncertain; moreover, concentrated fat sources are less available in their usual foods and their everyday life involves considerable energy expenditure. Consequently, people who can attain at least a moderate degree of fatness are viewed as attractive; they are clearly not afflicted by a wasting disease or intestinal parasites, and appear to have access to the social resources necessary to obtain food. Cross-cultural data about body preferences for women reveal that over 80% of cultures for which body shape preference data are available prefer a plump shape (Brown & Konner 1987; Anderson et al. 1992). The value of fatness in many African and Pacific cultures is evidenced by the existence of fattening huts (Brink 1989), in which women and men engage in ritualistic ingestion of huge amounts of food and avoid activity to gain large amounts of weight to enhance their beauty and social status (Gaurine & Pollock 1995). The high prevalence of obesity and the strong rejection of body fat in Western, post-industrial nations are very different trends from most other cultures, and anthropologists have described obesity as a **culture-bound syndrome** unique to Western societies (Ritenbaugh 1982).

Historical changes in the evaluation and prevalence of obesity also provide important perspectives on the current patterns of stigmatisation of obesity. Like traditional cultures today and in the past, most Western societies until the late nineteenth century valued at least moderate levels of body fat (Brumberg 1988; Seid 1989; Stearns 1997). At the beginning of the twentieth century, a transformation in values relating to fatness was underway, as modern ideals of thinness were established, promulgated, and widely applied (Stearns 1997). The emphasis on thinness intensified in the second half of the twentieth century, particularly for women. Evidence for this can be seen in the increasingly thinner body shapes of women in idealised social roles, such as beauty pageant winners (Garner et al. 1980; Wiseman et al. 1992) and fashion models (Morris et al. 1989). As pressures towards slimness escalated and intensified, fatness moved from being a social ideal to being rejected as a marginal, deviant, and stigmatised attribute. Most concern about body weight is motivated by appearance, not health (Hayes & Ross 1987).

The stigma of obesity as a master status

Attribution of responsibility for a stigma is a crucial consideration: stigmas that are not considered the 'fault' of an individual are treated differently from those for which personal 'blame' can be attributed (DeJong 1980, 1993; DeJong & Kleck 1986; Weiner et al. 1988; Menec & Perry 1995). The causes of high body weight are currently not established with certainty, with claims and counterclaims about whether obesity is the result of overeating, lack of activity, or genetic or hormonal conditions (Sobal 1995). These disputes about the causes of obesity remain unresolved in the scientific and medical community, as well as among the general public. Stigmatising claims about gluttony and sloth are counterpoised with de-stigmatising claims about inheritance and metabolism. The general orientation in contemporary society is to hold obese individuals personally accountable for their size, and to discredit and reject them as personal failures.

An important aspect of stigma is that it is often incorporated into individuals' identities and involved in their self-evaluations. The impact of stigmas varies, with some stigmas being of only minor importance and others overwhelming a person and becoming a **master status** (Goffman 1963; Hiller 1981). Obese people are often characterised more by their size than by any of their other attributes, being described as simply 'fat' rather than being dealt with on the basis of other qualities. The effects of stigmatisation of obesity are often internalised, particularly by women (Crocker et al. 1993; Sobal & Devine 1997). Negative social stereotypes relating to obesity often become **self-fulfilling prophecies** for obese individuals.

Feminist analysis has shown that some stigmas, particularly obesity, are highly gendered. Stigmatisation of obesity is much more problematic for women because they are evaluated more on the basis of their appearance and weight than are men (Millman 1980). The gendered nature of the stigmatisation of obesity makes weight much more important to women (Tiggemann & Rothblum 1988; Germov & Williams 1996; see also Chapter 15).

Ever since Steven Richardson and his colleagues' (1961) pioneering quantitative research and Werner Cahnman's (1968) interactionist analysis, sociologists have been examining the stigma of obesity. Sociological analysis of the stigma of obesity typically uses two mainstream theoretical perspectives—**functionalism** and **symbolic interactionism**—and has rarely applied other theoretical orientations, such as Marxism or rational choice theory. While a variety of research methods have been applied to the stigmatisation of obesity, the bulk of studies have used the two major sociological data-collection methods of surveys and participant observation. Overall, sociological work on the stigma of obesity has followed two major paths, reflecting two of the most powerful paradigms in the discipline of sociology, functionalism and symbolic interactionism (Ritzer 1975).

Functionalist analysis documents and describes as social facts the presence, arenas, extent, and sources of the stigmatisation of obese individuals. This stream of analysis has involved many disciplines and takes a positivist approach in examining stigma as a barrier to access to social roles and privileges. Analyses are often quantitative, using experiments or surveys to analyse the frequency and extent of stigmatisation.

Interactionist analysis examines the strategies that obese individuals use to manage their stigma and to negotiate their way in a world that values thinness. It does so while considering the construction of social definitions of obesity.

These analyses are primarily done by sociologists and follow the constructionist symbolic-interactionist tradition, often appealing to dramaturgical analyses grounded in the work of Goffman (1959, 1963). These investigations employ **ethnographic** techniques, such as participant observation and in-depth interviews, to investigate stigmatisation as a socially constructed, negotiated, and managed process (Sobal & Maurer 1999a, 1999b). These two lines of analysis will be reviewed in the following two sections.

The presence, arenas, extent, and sources of stigmatisation of obesity

The consensus in the published literature is that severe stigmatisation of obese people exists in contemporary post-industrial societies (Allon 1981; Sobal 1984a, 1991; Goode 1996), though some reviews suggest that the negative effects of the stigmatisation of obesity have not been clearly demonstrated (Jarvie et al. 1983). In addition to establishing the presence of stigmatisation of obesity, studies have examined the arenas, extent, and sources of stigmatisation.

Stigmatisation operates in many arenas, occurring broadly across most domains of an obese person's world—at work, at home, in public life, and so on (Gortmaker et al. 1993). This observation supports the concept that obesity becomes a 'master status' (Goffman 1963) that pervades all aspects of life. Studies of stigmatisation have focused on some areas more than others, with much research having been carried out on stigmatisation in formal roles, such as that of employee. Less research has been done on stigmatisation in informal roles, such as that of friend. The major arenas in which stigmatisation of the obese has been documented are education and work, marriage and family, health and medical care, and interpersonal and social interactions.

Obese individuals in the USA are less favourably evaluated than thinner individuals for admission to the higher education that is essential for entry and advancement in many careers, and receive less financial support when they are admitted to college (Benson et al. 1980; Canning & Mayer 1966, 1967; Crandall 1991, 1995). People who are obese are also less successful in gaining employment and entering the labour force (Roe & Eickwort 1976; Larkin & Pines 1979; Matusewitch 1983). Obese individuals who do become employees receive lower wages than comparable co-workers, are less likely to receive promotions, and experience more discrimination on the job (McClean & Moon 1980; Rothblum et al. 1988, 1990; Register & Williams 1990; Loh 1993; Averett & Korenman 1996). Overall, stigmatisation of obese individuals consistently occurs across the span of educational and work roles.

Weight is an important criterion for dating and mate selection, and obese individuals (women in particular) have a more difficult time dating and finding marital partners than do thinner individuals (Kallen & Doughty 1984; Sobal 1984b; Sobal et al. 1992, 1995, 2003; Gortmaker et al. 1993). Most obese people eventually marry, but their choice of partners is restricted because of their stigmatised condition (Garn et al. 1989a, 1989b). Obese women, once married, may feel they are unable to leave their marriage because they have less value on the marriage market (Sobal et al. 1995). These research findings consistently reveal that stigmatisation of obese individuals occurs in the entry to and maintenance of marital and family roles.

Health professionals frequently stigmatise obese individuals, holding prejudicial attitudes and exhibiting them in discriminatory actions. Health care professionals of many types (including physicians, nurses, counsellors, dietitians, psychologists, health administrators, and others) at many stages of their careers (as students, interns, practitioners, and educators) have negative attitudes and beliefs about obese individuals (Maiman et al. 1979; Benson et al. 1980; Brotman et al. 1984; Blumberg & Mellis 1985; Rand & MacGregor 1990; Agell & Rothblum 1991). The antipathy exhibited by student health practitioners towards obese individuals suggests that their attitudes are based on wider societal values about obesity rather than on actual problems that they have experienced in dealing with obese clients. Prejudicial attitudes towards obese individuals among health care professionals translate into discrimination in the provision of health care services such as diagnosis and treatment (Allon 1979; Young & Powell 1985; Adams et al. 1993). Health care providers are not immune to the stigmatisation of obese individuals as they carry out their professional roles, providing unequal health care service on the basis of body weight.

The everyday interactions of obese individuals also may be hampered by stigmatisation (Pauley 1989). Compared with their thinner counterparts, obese individuals are discriminated against in basic transactions such as renting apartments (Karris 1977). Some investigations report that obese individuals have fewer friends (Harris & Smith 1983), although other studies find this not to be the case (Jarvie et al. 1983; Miller et al. 1995a). Overall, stigmatisation operates as a multidimensional burden on obese individuals, spanning work, family, health, and interpersonal arenas.

A classic series of sociological investigations compared the stigmatisation of physical disabilities with the stigmatisation of obesity by showing participants a series of pictures of children with a variety of disabilities as well as pictures of an obese child and asking who they would prefer as a friend (Richardson et al. 1961; Goodman et al. 1963; Maddox & Liederman 1968, 1969; Richardson & Royce 1968; Alessi & Anthony 1969; Richardson 1970, 1971; Richardson & Emerson 1970; Giancoli & Neimeyer 1983). The striking findings revealed that both adults and children consistently preferred disabled people to obese people, providing clear evidence that obesity is more stigmatised than physical disabilities such as blindness, crippling diseases, amputations, and facial disfigurements. A replication of these studies 40 years after the first ones showed that stigmatisation of obese children by other children had increased significantly over time in the USA (Latner & Stunkard 2003). However, in other cultures, such as Nepal, children reacted positively to the pictures of the obese child (Harper 1997).

Some broader comparative analyses of stigmatisation of different forms of deviant conditions have been done. Several studies reveal that obesity is seen as being as stigmatised as many other deviant conditions, such as AIDS, drug addiction, criminal behaviour, and homosexuality (Spiegal & Keith-Spiegel 1973; Weiner et al. 1988; Schwarzer & Weiner 1990). Stigmatisation of obesity is more severe than that of eating disorders (Brotman et al. 1984; Sobal et al. 1995), although eating disorders are stigmatised and carry negative evaluations (Way 1995; Sobal & Bursztyn 1998). It is notable that in recent years legal measures and social norms have greatly reduced the stigmatisation of many racial, religious, gender, and sexual groups, while prejudice against and derogation of obese individuals are tolerated and even treated as socially acceptable (Solovay 2000; Stunkard & Sobal 1995).

Myriad sources of stigmatisation permeate the lives of obese individuals. In interpersonal interactions, obese individuals are stigmatised by others in a variety of social roles and relationships. The public at large stigmatises obese individuals in informal interactions of many types. The mass media stigmatise obese individuals actively by negatively representing those large people who do appear on television, and passively by not including large people in television, film, and other media in numbers proportional to their presence in the general population (Dyrenforth et al. 1980; Fouts & Burggraf 1999; Fouts & Vaughan 2002). The mass media also present extremely thin people as the ideal, which leads to negative comparisons of obese individuals with media images (Silverstein et al. 1986; Myers & Biocca 1992; Waller et al. 1994). In summary, stigmatisation of obese individuals exists, is prevalent and often intense, occurs in multifaceted ways, and emanates from a variety of sources.

Coping with the stigma of obesity

Goffman (1963) used the concept of stigma within a broad theoretical examination of interpersonal interaction processes, revealing the development and management of deviant identities. The development of the concept of stigma complemented his other sociological work on the presentation of self, dramaturgical role analysis, and impression management (Goffman 1959, 1961; Ditton 1980; Drew & Wootton 1988). Based on the perspectives used by Goffman, many sociologists and psychologists have examined how obese individuals who are stigmatised construct their identities and manage their interactions with others so as to cope with the stigma of obesity (Puhl & Brownell 2003).

Stigmatising acts can be verbal (such as teasing, joking, and negative comments) or non-verbal (such as staring, making gestures, and avoiding a person). Stigmatisation can be active (operating through overt negative behaviours) or passive (occurring through avoidance of interactions with stigmatised individuals).

Everyday life involves the performance of a variety of activities, with individuals operating as actors presenting themselves to actual or imagined others who constitute audiences for their behaviour (Goffman 1959). Stigmatised individuals recognise that their performance of various tasks may be disrupted by negative treatment as a result of their stigma, and attempt to prevent or deal with problems resulting from their stigma. Obese people are treated negatively in social interactions because of their body size and develop many strategies for dealing with the stigmatising acts of others (Sobal 1991).

Gaining and maintaining acceptance is a central feature of a stigmatised person's life. Although legitimacy in interpersonal interactions may be claimed by individuals, it is conferred by others (Elliott et al. 1990). A variety of coping mechanisms exist for individuals with various types of stigma. These include denial, concealment, avoidance, mutual aid, and redefinition of situations (Elliott et al. 1990).

Some obese people, particularly men, use denial to deal with interactional challenges associated with their body weight (Millman 1980). By denying that they are 'really' fat, or denying that the fat they have is their fault, they effectively ignore the stigma of obesity; this strategy offers one way of coping for particular individuals in specific situations. This type of management of stigmatising acts typically involves claims that large size or weight is caused by muscle, large bones, or genetics.

Concealment is a form of strategic impression management whereby a stigma is hidden, disguised, or modified to make it less obtrusive and therefore less likely to be attended to or focused on in a social encounter. Many obese individuals make considerable efforts in concealment, including hiding parts of their bodies by wearing loose or heavy clothing to mask their size. One form of concealment is deflection or distraction, whereby other aspects of appearance, such as hair or jewellery, are used to draw attention away from an obese person's body. 'Passing' occurs when stigmatised individuals successfully conceal their stigma and are accepted as 'normal' (Goffman 1963); passing as 'normal' may or may not be possible for an obese individual, depending on the extent of their weight and their ability to conceal it.

Avoidance and withdrawal are common methods of coping with stigmatisation. Many stigmatised individuals arrange their lives so as to avoid or minimise stigmatising contacts, because of uncertainty about how 'normals' will receive and deal with them (Goffman 1963). Many obese individuals practise selective or widespread avoidance of social settings and individuals where they perceive a likelihood of being stigmatised. This involves outright refusal to enter some situations, particularly those in which their entire body will be on display, such as on a beach, at a swimming pool, or in a locker room. Management of the frequency, content, and extent of interactions with particular individuals is another form of avoidance, with obese individuals eschewing contact with people who have stigmatised them in the past or who are thought to be likely to engage in future stigmatising acts. Self-segregation (Schur 1979) occurs where stigmatised individuals interact with, and accept as 'insiders', only those who are obese or are 'wise' (Goffman 1963) to the plight of overweight people.

By redefining situations, a stigmatised person can steer the topic or subject of interactions away from a stigmatised condition to other more neutral or safe areas. Obese individuals often develop strategies for deflecting or shifting the focus of interactions away from their size to other topics (Sobal 1991). The threat of stigmatisation leads some obese individuals to present themselves in a comedic role, using humour to facilitate and negotiate interactions with people who could potentially discredit them because of their size.

Mutual aid is a strategy whereby communities of stigmatised individuals form to share feelings and resources and provide social support for one another (Goffman 1963). Mutual aid ranges from the exchange of stories and ideas between obese friends to the establishment of national or international organisations to promote size acceptance. While the manifest goal of weight-loss programs is to become thinner through diet and exercise, the latent services often sought and provided through such groups are the sharing of emotional support and the exchange of coping strategies for dealing with being overweight (Allon 1975; Laslett & Warren 1975). Collective behaviour often results from the establishment of advocacy groups and organisations, and the size acceptance movement has established itself as an important force in contemporary public discourse on obesity (Sobal 1995, 1999). Many large people rebel against sizeism, fatism, or weightism and celebrate their bodies (Joanisse & Synnott 1999; Braziel & LeBesco 2001).

Eating is an especially problematic act for obese people (English 1991), because it carries so much potential for critique and criticism by others (Zdrodowski 1996). Several sociological concepts help us to identify some of the special coping methods used by stigmatised individuals when their eating behaviours are scrutinised by others. Even when an obese person eats the same things as a 'normal'-weight companion, the obese person faces the threat of being attacked and criticised for overeating. Stigmatising acts include challenges to, and criticisms of, the eating behaviours of obese individuals. Obese people may avoid food events entirely as a way of coping with the threat of being discredited. Alternatively, they may attend but eat nothing, or they may eat selectively and be prepared to explain their food choices.

Obese individuals may defend the legitimacy of their eating behaviour by providing what Scott and Lyman (1963) term **'accounts'** (English 1991; Orbuch 1997). Accounts can be divided into justifications and excuses (Scott & Lyman 1963). Justifications accept responsibility but deny the negative qualities of the behaviour, as when an obese person eating confectionery claims that it is the only thing that they have eaten all day. Excuses admit the negative qualities of an action, but deny responsibility, and there are several types. Accident excuses deny fault because a behaviour was beyond personal control, as when an obese individual eating ice-cream claims that it was the only food available. Defensibility excuses state that insufficient information was available, as when an obese person claims to have believed that the food being eaten was a reduced-calorie version. Biological-drive excuses explain actions in terms of a lack of control over a behaviour, as when an obese person claims that hormones led him or her to eat a particular item.

There are other ways of managing eating related to accounts. **Disclaimers** (Hewett & Stokes 1975) anticipate challenges to legitimacy, as in claims by obese people that they have adhered to a restricted diet earlier in anticipation of a particular food event. **Discounting** (Pestello 1991) includes several strategies. Coercion discounting occurs when a violation of personal principles is outside a person's control, as when an obese person claims that someone else prepared high-calorie foods for them. Exception discounting involves compromises that are seen as serving a greater purpose, as when an obese person claims not to have wanted to offend someone by refusing to eat high-calorie ceremonial foods that were specially prepared. Denial discounting makes no admission of a behaviour or its meaning, as when an obese person eats what is served at a dinner and makes no comments or explanations about the food. Concealment discounting entails accepting responsibility for a behaviour but denying that the behaviour is negative, as when an obese person reports having eaten a chocolate dessert but claims that the chocolate prevents other food cravings. All of these techniques are used to socially manage eating. They help obese individuals to negotiate a path through potentially precarious social interactions and to ward off threats to their selves.

Often obese individuals develop a 'fat identity' as they accept their weight and as they establish and elaborate a social self that incorporates weight as a personal attribute (McLorg & Taub 1987; O'Brien & Bankston 1990; Degher & Hughes 1991; Hughes & Degher 1993). Attempts to lose weight also involve aspiration to a new, thinner identity. Many obese people perceive this as the attainment of a 'normal' weight status, which will free them from stigmatisation. Often people who do change their weight have to reconcile their social identity with their body size (English 1993; Rubin et al. 1993). Thinner identities may be seen as desirable in that they avoid stigmatisation, but they may also carry undesirable consequences, such as the need to deal with unwanted sexual advances, which did not occur before (Sobal 1984a).

While obese individuals suffer from stigmatisation in contemporary post-industrial society (Millman 1980), they employ many strategies to cope with their stigma and to establish functional life patterns in spite of negative societal attitudes towards them. Psychological strategies are used to compensate for stigma (Miller et al. 1995b), and social relationships are established to buffer against negative experiences (Millman 1980). Organisations and groups help to empower individuals by validating and valorising their struggles against the weight prejudices of many people in the wider society (Sobal 1999). Struggles with negative attitudes and with social avoidance and ostracism are often required throughout an obese individual's life, requiring coping efforts that deeply shape their identities. Sociological analyses that examine how obese individuals construct, negotiate, and manage their lives provide a portrait of the stigmatisation of obesity that differs from, but complements, work describing the prevalence and types of stigmatisation.

Conclusion

Over the past 40 years, stigma has emerged as an important sociological concept, grounded in the pioneering work of Erving Goffman (1963). The concept of stigma has been widely applied to a variety of conditions, stretching and testing the boundaries of its conceptual coverage. Obesity was mentioned as a stigmatised condition in Goffman's seminal book, and it remains a clear case of a stigma in contemporary society.

The examination and elaboration of the concept of stigmatisation in relation to obesity has involved some work in a positivist tradition in social psychology and functionalist sociology. Simultaneously, constructionist work based in the symbolic interactionist tradition of sociological social psychology continued the lines of analysis begun by Goffman. The existing literature on the stigma of obesity reflects a consensus in some areas, but leaves other aspects of the topic to be addressed in future investigations.

Obesity has become a highly stigmatised condition in contemporary post-industrial societies, with obese individuals being labelled negatively and risking a variety of defiling and degrading prejudicial attitudes and discriminatory actions. The social position of obesity relative to other deviant conditions is not currently very clear.

Obese individuals employ several types of coping mechanisms to manage their social interactions with others. However, the frequency and success of different strategies for coping with the stigmatisation of obesity have not been thoroughly researched. Clearly, obesity is a stigma in contemporary society, but it is not clear how obese people can most effectively deal with this stigma.

Summary of main points

- Stigmas are discrediting attributes, and obesity is often stigmatised in post-industrial societies.
- Stigmatisation of obesity is widespread, frequent, and often severe.
- Stigmatisation of obesity occurs in work, family, health, and everyday arenas.
- The mechanisms used to cope with the stigmatisation of obesity include denial, concealment, avoidance, mutual aid, and redefinition of situations.
- Eating is problematic for obese individuals, who use accounts, disclaimers, and discounting to explain their food choices.

Discussion questions

1. How is the stigmatisation of obesity similar to and different from the stigmatisation of other 'deviant' attributes?
2. How would obese individuals be treated in a culture that did not stigmatise either fatness or thinness, or in a culture that highly valued fatness?
3. What types or categories of people in society are least likely to stigmatise obese individuals, and what types are most likely to do so?
4. How do different approaches to sociological analysis (such as functionalist theory using quantitative methods, or symbolic interactionist theory using qualitative methods) provide both incompatible and compatible perspectives on the stigmatisation of obesity?
5. How could society change in order to reduce stigmatisation of obese individuals, and how can obese individuals better deal with stigmatisation?

Further investigation

1. Describe and discuss the medicalisation of obesity.
2. Discuss how the stigmatisation of obesity differs between women and men.

Further reading and web resources

Books

Bryant, C. D. (ed.) 1990, *Deviant Behavior: Readings in the Sociology of Norm Violations*, Hemisphere, New York.

Gaurine, I. & Pollock, N. J. (eds) 1995, *Social Aspects of Obesity*, Gordon & Breach, New York.

Goffman, E. 1963, *Stigma: Notes on the Management of Spoiled Identity*, Simon & Schuster, New York.

Maurer, D. & Sobal, J. (eds) 1995, *Eating Agendas: Food and Nutrition as Social Problems*, Aldine de Gruyter, New York.

Millman M. 1980, *Such a Pretty Face: Being Fat in America*, Norton, New York.

Sobal, J. & Maurer, D. (eds) 1999, *Interpreting Weight: The Social Management of Fatness and Thinness*, Aldine de Gruyter, Hawthorne, New York State.

—— (eds) 1999, *Weighty Issues: The Construction of Fatness and Thinness as Social Problems*, Aldine de Gruyter, Hawthorne, New York State.

Web sites

International Size Acceptance Association: www.size-acceptance.org/

National Association to Advance Fat Acceptance: naafa.org/

References

Adams, C. H., Smith, N. J., Wilbur, D. C. & Grady, K. E. 1993, 'The Relationship of Obesity to the Frequency of Pelvic Examinations: Do Physician and Patient Attitudes Make a Difference?', *Women and Health*, vol. 20, pp. 45–57.

Agell, G. & Rothblum, E. D. 1991, 'Effects of Clients' Obesity and Gender on the Therapy Judgements of Psychologists', *Professional Psychology: Research and Practice*, vol. 22, pp. 223–9.

Ainlay, S. C., Becker, G. & Colemen, L. M. (eds) 1986, *The Dilemma of Difference: A Multidisciplinary View of Stigma*, Plenum, New York.

Alessi, D. F. & Anthony, W. A. 1969, 'The Uniformity of Children's Attitudes toward Physical Disabilities', *Exceptional Children*, vol. 35, pp. 543–5.

Allon, N. 1975, 'Latent Social Services of Group Dieting', *Social Problems*, vol. 23, pp. 59–69.

—— 1979, 'Self-Perceptions of the Stigma of Overweight in Relationship to Weight-losing Patterns', *American Journal of Clinical Nutrition*, vol. 32, pp. 4770–80.

—— 1981, 'The Stigma of Overweight in Everyday Life', in B. J. Wolman (ed.), *Psychological Aspects of Obesity: A Handbook*, Van Nostrand Reinhold, New York, pp. 130–74.

Anderson, J. L., Crawford, C. B., Nadeau, J. & Lindberg, T. 1992, 'Was the Duchess of Windsor Right? A Cross-cultural Review of the Socioecology of Ideals of Female Body Shape', *Ethnology and Sociobiology*, vol. 13, pp. 197–227.

Averett, S. & Korenman, S. 1996, 'The Economic Reality of the Beauty Myth', *Journal of Human Resources*, vol. 31, pp. 304–30.

Beardsworth, A. & Keil, T. 1997, *Sociology on the Menu: An Invitation to the Study of Food and Society*, Routledge, London.

Benson, P. L., Severs, D., Tatgenhorst, J. & Loddengaard, N. 1980, 'The Social Costs of Obesity: A Non-reactive Field Study', *Social Behavior and Personality*, vol. 8, pp. 91–6.

Blumberg, P. & Mellis, L. P. 1985, 'Medical Students' Attitudes toward the Obese and Morbidly Obese', *International Journal of Eating Disorders*, vol. 4, pp. 169–75.

Braziel, J. E. & LeBesco, K. 2001, *Bodies Out of Bounds: Fatness and Transgressions*, University of California Press, Berkeley, California.

Brink, P. J. 1989, 'The Fattening Room among the Annang of Nigeria. Anthropological Approaches to Nursing Research', *Medical Anthropology*, vol 12, pp 131–43.

Brotman, A. W., Stern, T. A., & Herzog, D. B. 1984, 'Emotional Reactions of House Officers to Patients with Anorexia Nervosa, Diabetes, and Obesity', *International Journal of Eating Disorders*, vol. 3, pp. 71–7.

Brown, P. J. & Konner, M. 1987, 'An Anthropological Perspective on Obesity', *Annals of the New York Academy of Sciences*, vol. 499, pp. 29–46.

Brumberg, J. 1988, *Fasting Girls: The History of Anorexia Nervosa*, Harvard University Press, Cambridge, Massachusetts.

Cahnman, W. J. 1968, 'The Stigma of Obesity', *Sociological Quarterly*, vol. 9, pp. 282–99.

Canning, H. & Mayer, J. 1966, 'Obesity: Its Possible Effect on College Acceptance', *New England Journal of Medicine*, vol. 275, pp. 1172–4.

—— 1967, 'Obesity: An Influence on High School Performance', *American Journal of Clinical Nutrition*, vol. 20, pp. 352–4.

Crandall, C. S. 1991, 'Do Heavyweight Students Have More Difficulty Paying for College?', *Personality and Social Psychology Bulletin*, vol. 17, pp. 606–11.

—— 1995, 'Do Parents Discriminate Against Their Heavyweight Daughters?', *Personality and Social Psychology Bulletin*, vol. 21, pp. 724–35.

Crocker, J., Cornwall, B. & Major, B. 1993, 'The Stigma of Overweight: Affective Consequences of Attributional Ambiguity', *Journal of Personality and Social Psychology*, vol. 64, pp. 67–70.

Dalton, S. 1997, 'Body Weight Terminology, Definitions, and Measurement', in S. Dalton (ed.), *Overweight and Weight Management*, Aspen Publishers, Gaithersburg, Maryland, pp. 1–38.

Degher, D. & Hughes, G. 1991, 'The Identity Change Process: A Field Study of Obesity', *Deviant Behavior*, vol. 12, pp. 385–401.

DeJong, W. 1980, 'The Stigma of Obesity: Consequences of Naive Assumptions Concerning the Causes of Physical Deviance', *Journal of Health and Social Behavior*, vol. 21, pp. 75–85.

—— 1993, 'Obesity as a Characterological Stigma: The Issue of Responsibility and Judgments in Task Performance', *Psychological Reports*, vol. 73, pp. 963–70.

DeJong, W. & Kleck, R. E. 1986, 'The Social Psychological Effects of Overweight', in C. P. Herman, M. P. Zanna, & E. T. Higgins (eds), *Physical Appearance, Stigma, and Social Behavior: The Ontario Symposium*, vol. 3, Lawrence Earlbaum Associates, Hillsdale, New Jersey, pp. 65–87.

Ditton, J. (ed.) 1980, *The View from Goffman*, St Martin's, New York.

Drew, P. & Wootton, A. (eds) 1988, *Erving Goffman: Exploring the Interaction Order*, Northeastern University Press, Boston.

Dyrenforth, S. R., Wooley, O. W. & Wooley, S. C. 1980, 'A Woman's Body in a Man's World: A Review of Findings on Body Image and Weight Control', in J. R. Kaplan (ed.) *A Woman's Conflict: The Special Relationships between Women and Food*, Prentice-Hall, Englewood Cliffs, New Jersey.

Elliott, G. C., Ziegler, H. L., Altman, B. M. & Scott, D. R. 1990, 'Understanding Stigma: Dimensions of Deviance and Coping', in C. D. Bryant (ed.), *Deviant Behavior: Readings in the Sociology of Norm Violations,* Hemisphere, New York, pp. 423–43.

Emmons, C. & Sobal, J. 1981, 'Paranormal Beliefs: Testing the Marginality Hypothesis', *Sociological Focus*, vol. 14, pp. 49–56.

English, C. 1991, 'Food is My Best Friend: Self-justifications and Weight-loss Efforts', *Research in the Sociology of Health Care*, vol. 9, pp. 335–45.

—— 1993, 'Gaining and Losing Weight: Identity Transformations', *Deviant Behavior*, vol. 14, pp. 227–41.

Falk, G. 2001, *Stigma: How We Treat Outsiders*, Prometheus Books, Amherst, New York State.

Fouts, G., & Burggraf, K. 1999, 'Television Situation Comedies: Female Body Images and Verbal Reinforcements', *Sex Roles*, vol. 40, pp. 473–81.

Fouts, G. & Vaughan, K. 2002, 'Television Situation Comedies: Male Weight, Negative References, and Audience Reactions', *Sex Roles*, vol. 46, pp. 439–42.

Garn, S., Sullivan, T. V. & Hawthorne, V. M. 1989a, 'The Education of One Spouse and the Fatness of the Other Spouse', *American Journal of Human Biology*, vol. 1, pp. 233–8.

—— 1989b, 'Educational Level, Fatness, and Fatness Differences between Husbands and Wives', *American Journal of Clinical Nutrition*, vol. 50, pp. 740–5.

Garner, D. M., Garfinkel, P. E., Schwartz, D. & Thompson, M. 1980, 'Cultural Expectations of Thinness in Women', *Psychological Reports*, vol. 47, pp. 483–91.

Gaurine, I. & Pollock, N. J. (eds) 1995, *Social Aspects of Obesity*, Gordon & Breach, New York.

Germov, J. & Williams, L. 1996, 'The Sexual Division of Dieting: Women's Voices', *Sociological Review*, vol. 44, pp. 630–47.

Giancoli, D. L. & Neimeyer, G. J. 1983, 'Liking Preferences toward Handicapped Persons', *Perceptual and Motor Skills*, vol. 57, pp. 1005–6.

Goffman, E. 1959, *The Presentation of Self in Everyday Life*, Anchor, New York.

—— 1961, *Asylums*, Doubleday, New York.

—— 1963, *Stigma: Notes on the Management of Spoiled Identity*, Simon & Schuster, New York.

Goode, E. 1996, 'The Stigma of Obesity', in E. Goode (ed.), *Social Deviance*, Allyn & Bacon, Boston, pp. 332–40.

Goodman, N., Richardson, S. A., Dombusch, S. & Hastort, A. H. 1963, 'Variant Reactions to Physical Disabilities', *American Sociological Review*, vol. 28, pp. 429–35.

Gortmaker, S. L., Must, A., Perrin, J. M., Sobol, A. M. & Dietz, W. H. 1993, 'Social and Economic Consequences of Overweight in Adolescence and Young Adulthood', *New England Journal of Medicine*, vol. 329, pp. 1008–12.

Harper, D. C. 1997, 'Children's Attitudes toward Physical Disability in Nepal: A Field Study', *Journal of Cross-cultural Psychology*, vol. 28, pp. 710–29.

Harris, M. B. & Smith, S. D. 1983, 'The Relationships of Age, Sex, Ethnicity, and Weight to Stereo-types of Obesity and Self-perception', *International Journal of Obesity*, vol. 7, pp. 361–71.

Hayes, D. & Ross, C. E. 1987, 'Concern with Appearance, Health Beliefs, and Eating Habits', *Journal of Health and Social Behavior*, vol. 28, pp. 120–30.

Heatherton, T. F., Kleck, R. E., Hebl, M. R., & Hull, J. G. 2000, *The Social Psychology of Stigma*, Guilford Press, New York.

Herman, C. P., Zanna, M. P. & Higgins, E. T. (eds) 1986, *Physical Appearance, Stigma, and Social Behavior: The Ontario Symposium*, vol. 3, Lawrence Earlbaum Associates, Hillsdale, New Jersey.

Hewett, J. P. & Stokes, R. 1975, 'Disclaimers', *American Sociological Review*, vol. 40, pp. 1–11.

Hiller, D. V. 1981, 'The Salience of Overweight in Personality Characterization', *Journal of Personality*, vol. 108, pp. 233–40.

Hughes, G. & Degher, D. 1993, 'Coping with Deviant Identity', *Deviant Behavior*, vol. 14, pp. 297–315.

Jarvie, G. J., Lahey, B., Graziano, W. & Framer, E. 1983, 'Childhood Obesity: What We Know and What We Don't Know', *Developmental Review*, vol. 2, pp. 237–73.

Joanisse, L. & Synnott, A. 1999, 'Fighting Back: Reactions and Resistance to the Stigma of Obesity', in J. Sobal & D. Maurer (eds), *Interpreting Weight: The Social Management of Fatness and Thinness*, Aldine de Gruyter, Hawthorne, New York State, pp. 49–70.

Jones, E. E., Fanna, A., Hastort, A. H., Markus, H., Miller, D. T. & Scott, R. A. 1984, *Social Stigma: The Psychology of Marked Relationships*, W. H. Freeman & Company, New York.

Kallen, D. & Doughty, A. 1984, 'The Relationship of Weight, the Self Perception of Weight, and Self Esteem in Courtship Behavior', *Marriage and Family Review*, vol. 7, pp. 93–114.

Karris, L. 1977, 'Prejudice Against Obese Renters', *Journal of Social Psychology*, vol. 101, pp. 159–60.

Larkin, J. C. & Pines, H. A. 1979, 'No Fat Persons Need Apply: Experimental Studies of the Overweight Stereotype and Hiring Preference', *Sociology of Work and Occupations*, vol. 13, pp. 379–85.

Laslett, B. & Warren, C. A. B. 1975, 'Losing Weight: The Organizational Promotion of Behavior Change', *Social Problems*, vol. 23, pp. 69–80.

Latner, J. D. & Stunkard, A. J. 2003, 'Getting Worse: The Stigmatization of Obese Children', *Obesity Research*, vol. 11, pp. 452–6.

Link, B. G. & Phelan, J. C. 2001, 'Conceptualizing Stigma', *Annual Review of Sociology*, vol. 27, pp. 363–85.

Loh, E. S. 1993, 'The Economic Effects of Physical Appearance', *Social Science Quarterly*, vol. 74, pp. 420–38.

McClean, R. A. & Moon, M. 1980, 'Health, Obesity, and Earnings', *American Journal of Public Health*, vol. 70, pp. 1006–9.

McIntosh, W. A. 1996, *Sociologies of Food and Nutrition*, Plenum, New York.

McLorg, P. A. & Taub, D. E. 1987, 'Anorexia and Bulimia: The Development of Deviant Identities', *Deviant Behavior*, vol. 8, pp. 177–89.

Maddox, G. L. & Liederman, V. R. 1968, 'Overweight as Social Deviance and Disability', *Journal of Health and Social Behavior*, vol. 9, pp. 287–98.

—— 1969, 'Overweight as a Social Disability with Medical Implications', *Journal of Medical Education*, vol. 44, pp. 214–20.

Maiman, L. A., Wang, V. L., Becker, M. H., Findlay, J. & Simonson, M. 1979, 'Attitudes toward Obesity and the Obese among Professionals', *Journal of the American Dietetic Association*, vol. 74, pp. 331–6.

Matusewitch, E. 1983, 'Employment Discrimination against the Overweight', *Personnel Journal*, vol. 62, pp. 446–50.

Menec, V. H. & Perry, R. P. 1995, 'Reactions to Stigmas: The Effects of Targets' Age and Controllability of Stigmas', *Journal of Aging and Health*, vol. 7, pp. 365–83.

Mennell, S. 1985, *All Manners of Food: Eating and Taste in England and France from the Middle Ages to the Present*, Blackwell, Oxford.

Miller, C. T., Rothblum, E. D., Brand, P. A. & Felicio, D. M. 1995a, 'Do Obese Women Have Poorer Social Relationships than Nonobese Women? Reports by Self, Friends, and Coworkers', *Journal of Personality*, vol. 63, pp. 65–85.

Miller, C. T., Rothblum, E. D., Felicio, D. M. & Brand, P. A. 1995b, 'Compensating for Stigma: Obese and Nonobese Women's Reactions to Being Visible', *Personality and Social Psychology Bulletin*, pp. 1093–106.

Millman, M. 1980, *Such a Pretty Face: Being Fat in America*, Norton, New York.

Morris, A., Cooper, T. & Cooper, P. J. 1989, 'The Changing Shape of Female Fashion Models', *International Journal of Eating Disorders*, pp. 593–6.

Myers, P. N. & Biocca, F. A. 1992, 'The Elastic Body Image: The Effect of Television Advertising and Programming on Body Image Distortions of Young Women', *Journal of Communication*, vol. 42, pp. 108–33.

O'Brien, M. S. & Bankston, W. B. 1990, 'The Moral Career of the Reformed Compulsive Eater: A Study of Conversion to Charismatic Conformity', in C. D. Bryant (ed.), *Deviant Behavior: Readings in the Sociology of Norm Violations*, Hemisphere, New York, pp. 774–83.

Orbuch, T. L. 1997, 'People's Accounts Count: The Sociology of Accounts', *Annual Review of Sociology*, vol. 23, pp. 455–78.

Page, R. M. 1984, *Stigma*, Routledge and Kegan Paul, Boston.

Pauley, L. L. 1989, 'Customer Weight as a Variable in Salespersons' Response Time', *Journal of Social Psychology*, vol. 129, pp. 713–14.

Pestello, F. 1991, 'Discounting', *Journal of Contemporary Ethnography*, vol. 20, pp. 27–46.

Puhl, R. & Brownell, K. D. 2003, 'Ways of Coping with Obesity Stigma: Review and Conceptual Analysis', *Eating Behaviors*, vol. 4, pp. 53–78.

Rand, C. S. W. & MacGregor, A. M. C. 1990, 'Morbidly Obese Patients' Perceptions of Social Discrimination before and after Surgery for Obesity', *Southern Medical Journal*, vol. 83, pp. 1390–5.

Register, C. A. & Williams, D. R. 1990, 'Wage Effects of Obesity among Young Workers', *Social Science Quarterly*, vol. 71, pp. 130–41.

Richardson, S. A. 1970, 'Age and Sex Differences in Values toward Physical Handicaps', *Journal of Health and Social Behavior*, vol. 11, pp. 207–14.

—— 1971, 'Research Report: Handicap, Appearance, and Stigma', *Social Science and Medicine*, vol. 5, pp. 621–8.

Richardson, S. A. & Emerson, P. 1970, 'Race and Physical Handicap in Children's Preference for Other Children: A Replication in a Southern City', *Human Relations*, vol. 23, pp. 31–6.

Richardson, S. A., Hastorf, A. H., Goodman, N. & Dornbusch, S. M. 1961, 'Cultural Uniformity in Reaction to Physical Disabilities', *American Sociological Review*, vol. 26, pp. 241–7.

Richardson, S. A. & Royce, J. 1968, 'Race and Physical Handicap in Children's Preferences for Other Children', *Child Development*, vol. 39, pp. 467–80.

Ritenbaugh, C. 1982, 'Obesity as a Culture-bound Syndrome', *Culture, Medicine and Psychiatry*, vol. 6, pp. 347–61.

Ritzer, G. 1975, *Sociology: A Multiple Paradigm Science*, Allyn & Bacon, Boston.

Roe, D. & Eickwort, K. R. 1976, 'Relationships between Obesity and Associated Health Factors with Unemployment among Low Income Women', *Journal of the American Medical Women's Association*, vol. 31, pp. 193–204.

Rothblum, E. D., Brand, P. A, Miller, C. T. & Oetjen, H. A. 1990, 'The Relationship between Obesity, Employment Discrimination, and Employment-related Victimization', *Journal of Vocational Behavior*, vol. 37, pp. 251–66.

Rothblum, E. D., Miller, C. T. & Garbutt, B. 1988, 'Stereotypes of Obese Female Job Applicants', *International Journal of Eating Disorders*, vol. 7, pp. 277–83.

Rubin, N., Shmilovitz, C. & Weiss, M. 1993, 'From Fat to Thin: Informal Rites Affirming Identity Change', *Symbolic Interaction*, vol. 16, pp. 1–17.

Schur, E. 1979, *Interpreting Deviance*, Harper & Row, New York.

Schwarzer, R. & Weiner, B. 1990, 'Die Wirkung von Kontrollierbarkeit und Bewaltigungsverhalten auf Emotionen und Sociale Unterstutzung', *Zeitschrift fur Socialpsychologie*, vol. 21, pp. 118–25.

Scott M. B. & Lyman, S. 1963, 'Accounts', *American Sociological Review*, vol. 33, pp. 44–62.

Seid, R. P. 1989, *Never Too Thin*, Prentice-Hall, New York.

Silverstein, B., Perdue, L., Peterson, B. & Kelly, E. 1986, 'The Role of the Mass Media in Promoting a Thin Standard of Bodily Attractiveness for Women', *Sex Roles*, vol. 14, pp. 519–33.

Sobal, J. 1984a, 'Group Dieting, the Stigma of Obesity, and Overweight Adolescents: Contributions of Natalie Allon to the Sociology of Obesity', *Marriage and Family Review*, vol. 7, pp. 9–20.

—— 1984b, 'Marriage, Obesity and Dieting', *Marriage and Family Review*, vol. 7, pp. 115–40.

—— 1991, 'Obesity and Nutritional Sociology: A Model for Coping with the Stigma of Obesity', *Clinical Sociology Review*, vol. 9, pp. 125–41.

—— 1995, 'The Medicalization and Demedicalization of Obesity', in D. Maurer & J. Sobal (eds), *Eating Agendas: Food and Nutrition as Social Problems*, Aldine de Gruyter, Hawthorne, New York State, pp. 79–90.

—— 1999, 'The Size Acceptance Movement and the Social Construction of Body Weight', in J. Sobal & D. Maurer (eds), *Weighty Issues: Fatness and Thinness as Social Problems*, Aldine de Gruyter, Hawthorne, New York State, pp. 231–49.

—— 2001, 'Social and Cultural Influences on Obesity', in P. Bjorntorp (ed.), *International Textbook of Obesity*, John Wiley and Sons, London, pp. 305–22.

Sobal, J. & Bursztyn, M. 1998, 'Dating People with Anorexia Nervosa and Bulimia: Attitudes and Beliefs of University Students', *Women and Health*, vol. 27, no. 3, pp. 73–88.

Sobal, J. & Devine, C. 1997, 'Social Aspects of Obesity: Influences, Consequences, Assessments, and Interventions', in S. Dalton (ed.), *Overweight and Weight Management*, Aspen Publishers, Gaithersburg, Maryland, pp. 289–308.

Sobal, J. & Hinrichs, D. 1986, 'Bias against "Marginal" Individuals in Jury Wheel Selection', *Journal of Criminal Justice*, vol. 14, pp. 71–89.

Sobal, J. & Maurer, D. 1999 (eds), *Interpreting Weight: The Social Management of Fatness and Thinness*, Aldine de Gruyter, Hawthorne, New York State.

—— (eds) 1999, *Weighty Issues: The Construction of Fatness and Thinness as Social Problems*, Aldine de Gruyter, Hawthorne, New York State.

Sobal, J. & Stunkard, A. J. 1989, 'Socioeconomic Status and Obesity: A Review of the Literature', *Psychological Bulletin*, vol. 105, pp. 260–75.

Sobal, J., Nicolopoulos, V. & Lee, J. 1995, 'Attitudes about Weight and Dating among Secondary School Students', *International Journal of Obesity*, vol. 19, pp. 376–81.

Sobal, J., Rauschenbach, B. & Frongillo, E. 1992, 'Marital Status, Fatness, and Obesity', Social *Science and Medicine*, vol. 35, pp. 915–23.

Sobal, J., Rauschenbach, B.S. & Frongillo, E. A. 2003, 'Marital Changes and Body Weight Changes: A US Longitudinal Analysis', *Social Science and Medicine*, vol. 56, pp. 1543–55.

Solovay, J. D. 2000, *Tipping the Scales of Justice: Fighting Weight-based Discrimination*, Prometheus Books, Amherst, New York State.

Spiegal, D. & Keith-Spiegel, P. 1973, *Outsiders USA*, Rinehart Press, San Francisco, pp. 570–3.

Stearns, P. N. 1997, *Fat History: Bodies and Beauty in the Modern West*, New York University Press, New York.

Stunkard, A. J. & Sobal, J. 1995, 'Psychosocial Consequences of Obesity', in K. D. Brownell & C. G. Fairburn (eds), *Eating Disorders and Obesity*, Guilford Press, New York, pp. 417–21.

Tiggemann, M. & Rothblum, E. D. 1988, 'Gender Differences in Social Consequences of Perceived Overweight in the United States and Australia', *Sex Roles*, vol. 18, pp. 75–86.

Waller, G., Shaw, J., Hamilton, K., Baldwin, G., Harding, T. & Sumner, T. 1994, 'Beauty is in the Eye of the Beholder: Media Influences on the Psychopathology of Eating Problems', *Appetite*, vol. 23, p. 287.

Way, K. 1995, 'Never Too Rich … or Too Thin: The Role of Stigma in the Social Construction of Anorexia Nervosa', in D. Maurer & J. Sobal (eds), *Eating Agendas: Food and Nutrition as Social Problems*, Aldine de Gruyter, Hawthorne, New York State, pp. 91–113.

Weiner, B., Perry, R. P. & Magnusson, J. 1988, 'An Attributional Analysis of Reactions to Stigmas', *Journal of Personality and Social Psychology*, vol. 55, pp. 738–48.

Wiseman, C. V., Gray, J. J., Mosimann, J. E. & Ahrens, A. H. 1992, 'Cultural Expectations of Thinness in Women: An Update', *International Journal of Eating Disorders*, vol. 11, pp. 85–9.

Young, L. M. & Powell, B. 1985, 'The Effects of Obesity on the Clinical Judgements of Mental Health Professionals', *Journal of Health and Social Behavior*, vol. 26, pp. 233–46.

Zdrodowski, D. 1996, 'Eating Out: The Experience of Eating in Public for the "Overweight" Woman', *Women's Studies International Forum*, vol. 19, pp. 665–74.

18

Body Acceptance: Exploring Women's Experiences

Lauren Williams and John Germov

Overview

- What is 'body acceptance'?
- How do some women develop a body-accepting identity?
- How can body acceptance be facilitated?

In this chapter, the concept of body acceptance is explored through the findings of a qualitative study of mid-age women. Women's definitions of, experiences of, and reasons for body acceptance are discussed in terms of life achievements, the influence of significant others, and non-discriminatory personal beliefs. The ability of some women to achieve body acceptance is conceptualised using Anthony Giddens's theory of life politics to explain how certain social processes enable women to exercise their agency. The chapter concludes by highlighting the importance of the findings for health professionals and others seeking to prevent the detrimental health consequences of body obsession and dieting through the promotion of body acceptance.

Key terms

agency	emancipatory politics	post-structuralism
body acceptance	fatism	size acceptance
body image	feminism	social construction
body mass index (BMI)	life politics	stigma
eating disorders	patriarchy	thin ideal

Introduction

A high proportion of Western women experience body dissatisfaction in response to the **thin ideal** of female beauty. Chapters 15 and 17 addressed the **social construction** and commodification of women's bodies, particularly the **patriarchal** and commercial influences on women's **body image** and dieting practices. Much of the literature on women and body image has documented the extent of body dissatisfaction (Grogan 1999), the harmful effects of dieting (Parham 1996, 1999a, 1999b; Dalton 1998; Cogan 1999), obesity stigmatisation and discrimination (Goodman 1995; Sobal 1995, 1999; Solovay 2000), and women's participation in the perpetuation of the thin ideal (Bartky 1990, 1998; Germov & Williams 1999). This vast literature shows how social institutions and cultural values can literally shape women's appearance, behaviour, and identity; many women internalise patriarchal notions and voluntarily impose the thin ideal on themselves and other women (see Chapter 15). However, clearly this does not apply to all women and this chapter addresses how some women are able to resist the thin ideal and develop **body acceptance**. In particular, the chapter highlights the importance of women's **agency** to the construction of a body-accepting identity in the face of the dominant aesthetic ideals.

Do alternatives to the thin ideal exist?

The thin ideal is central to female identity in Western culture, but women are not passive dupes of patriarchal structures and ideologies. **Post-structuralist feminist** authors have emphasised the importance of agency and subjectivity in examining the impact of patriarchy on women's daily lives (Bartky 1990; Butler 1990; McNay 1992; Pringle 1995). These approaches highlight 'women's creativity and agency within social constraints' (McNay 1992, p. 59). While some women conform to the thin ideal, others adopt alternative discourses emanating from the anti-dieting, fat rights, and **size acceptance** social movements (Chrisler 1994, 1996; Sobal 1999; Solovay 2000; Goodman 1995). The leading organisation in this area is the US-based National Association to Advance Fat Acceptance (NAAFA), established in 1969. Its aims include counteracting weight prejudice and exposing the detrimental effects of fad diets, radical medical interventions, and weight-loss programs in general (Fabrey 1995; Stimson 1995). Some corporations have also joined the size acceptance movement—take, for example, the Body Shop's 'Ruby' campaign, which promotes body diversity (see Figure 15.4 in Chapter 15).

Evidence of alternatives to the thin ideal

Few empirical studies have investigated women who have ceased dieting. Those that have been done suggest that the ageing process, life achievements, and self-esteem play a part in the ability of some women to resist the influence of the thin ideal (Blood 1996; Germov & Williams 1996; Tunaley et al. 1999). While body dissatisfaction can afflict women of all ages (Hetherington 1994; Tiggemann & Stevens 1999; Tiggemann & Lynch 2001), Jillian Tunaley and colleagues (1999) report that age may mitigate body dissatisfaction in some women. The researchers interviewed twelve women aged between 63 and 75 and found that even though the women reported some body dissatisfaction, they tended to dismiss the social pressure to be thin by viewing weight gain as an 'inevitable' by-product of ageing and judging the pursuit of a body ideal to be of less importance than the pursuit of their own interests. However, the study focused only on older women and failed to canvass other possible sources of women's resistance of the social pressure to be thin.

Sylvia Blood interviewed six New Zealand women between the ages of 23 and 39 about why they stopped dieting and rejected 'the myth of the "ideal body"' (1996, p. 111). Blood found that the cessation of dieting tended to occur once women developed 'self-acceptance' and countered 'the self-condemnation of body size' through an awareness of the negative influence on body image of external factors such as the media (1996, p. 112). However, Blood tends to privilege voluntarism as the basis for women's ability to reject the thin ideal and hence marginalises the social context in which self-identity and self-acceptance is formed. Blood's conclusions are questioned by the findings of a study of ours that examined women's reasons for dieting to lose weight (Germov & Williams 1996). In this study, participants recognised the unrealistic portrayal of women's bodies in the media, yet they continued to diet because thinness was socially rewarded in terms of sexual attractiveness and **stigma** avoidance. This suggests that awareness of the negative influence of the media, the fashion industry, and other 'body image industries' may be an important factor in the cessation of dieting, but is insufficient grounds for most women to reject the thin ideal. We also found evidence of women who had ceased dieting, rejected the thin ideal, and claimed to be accepting of their body weight (see Chapter 15); these women cited supportive partners and peers as importance influences on their body acceptance.

Body acceptance as life politics

To explore how some women develop a body-accepting identity, a conceptual framework drawn from the work of Anthony Giddens (1991) can be used for viewing the body as both socially constructed and as possessing agency. According to Giddens, we live in an age of 'reflexive modernity' in which social practices are increasingly questioned and changed as alternatives to past actions and beliefs come to light. The body, particularly the female body, has become a 'reflexive project', whereby the appearance of the body becomes a social marker of self-identity. The conscious monitoring and revision of appearance, behaviours, and beliefs produces what Giddens refers to as **life politics**, defined as 'a politics of lifestyle' or a 'politics of self-actualisation' (1991, p. 214).

Critics of Giddens's notion of life politics and reflexivity argue that, when applied to women, such concepts tend to operate in a social vacuum by privileging self-determination and underestimating patriarchy (Tyler & Abbott 1998; McNay 2000). Giddens does acknowledge the limits on lifestyle choice, saying that the existence of 'a multiplicity of choices is not to suppose that all choices are open to everyone ... the selection or creation of lifestyles is influenced by group pressures and the visibility of role models, as well as by socioeconomic circumstances' (1991, p. 82). We argue for a nuanced approach that conceptualises body acceptance as a form of life politics, a 'body project' that accounts for the influence of both social structure and agency on female identity. Robert Connell (2002, p. 47) refers to this process as 'social embodiment'—that is, 'human social conduct in which bodies are both agents and objects'. While some women pursue the life politics of the thin ideal, albeit under significant social pressure, there is evidence that others construct their self-identity through alternative lifestyles. This framework attempts to move beyond both deterministic and voluntaristic assumptions of women's identity formation in order to understand how some women resist patriarchal social pressure and reject the thin ideal.

An empirical study of body acceptance

Our study used the qualitative methodology of in-depth interviews to investigate women's experiences of, understandings of, and reasons for body acceptance. Mid-age women were sought, to increase the chances of gaining alternative responses to the thin ideal, given the consistent findings that younger women are more likely to conform to the pressure to be thin. A sampling method was designed to maximise the proportion of non-dieting women. Participants were drawn from a large established national cohort of mid-aged women (45–50 years in 1996) participating in the longitudinal Women's Health Australia (WHA) survey (see Brown et al. 1996; Brown et al. 1998). All WHA participants who lived within a 90-minute drive of the researchers and who indicated in the 1996 WHA survey that they were satisfied with their weight and had not dieted to lose weight in the previous year were selected. Using **body mass index (BMI)** measures, women who could be medically classified as 'underweight' or 'obese' were excluded from the study in an attempt to minimise the number of participants who had medical reasons to seek weight change. The remaining women were contacted and twenty agreed to participate in interviews, which were conducted between April and September 1998. Their responses are identified in this chapter by self-chosen pseudonyms.

A set of interview questions was developed to investigate the way the participants felt about their bodies and the factors influencing these body-image beliefs.

These questions were derived from factors identified in the literature and from our previous research (Germov & Williams 1996) as potential contributors to body acceptance. Initial questions focused on confirming the non-dieting status and body satisfaction of the participants. Because the participants were within the healthy weight range, we confirmed their non-dieting status by asking 'How would you feel if your weight increased by one stone?' The remainder of the questions identified and explored the reasons for and influences on participants' non-dieting behaviour and body satisfaction. The interviewing was conducted in a semi-structured fashion by a female researcher. While all the questions were covered in each interview, the specific wording and order of questions were altered to suit the circumstances (thereby acknowledging the contingent nature of interviews, in which unforeseen issues can arise) (Denzin 1989).

Findings

The twenty female participants were aged between 47 and 51 years at the time the study was conducted. The women were an ethnically homogenous group, all being from an English-speaking background with the exception of one woman of German origin. Table 18.1 presents detailed information on the demographic and health characteristics of the participants compared to the WHA cohort from which they were selected. The BMI of participants ranged from 20.2 to 24.7, which means that they were all in the medically defined 'healthy weight range'. It is interesting to note that even though women medically classified as 'overweight' (BMI of 25–30) had not been excluded by our selection criteria, there were no women in this category for the specified geographic region who expressed weight satisfaction.

Although all participants had previously reported weight satisfaction and non-dieting behaviour in the quantitative WHA survey, two distinct groups emerged from the qualitative data, groups that we termed 'thin ideal conformers' and 'thin ideal rejectors' (see Table 18.2). The thin ideal conformers can be divided into 'body conformers' (category 1) and 'weight maintainers' (category 3). Twelve of our twenty participants (Tina, Jenny, Joan, Vicki, Emma, Sam, Margaret, Tanya, Olivia, Linda, Kate, and Karen) were weight maintainers—women who remained thin without dieting, valued thinness, and derived their self-identity from their thinness. They reported that they would initiate dieting for aesthetic (and not health) reasons if their weight increased. Most had been 'naturally' thin all of their lives, 'never having what you'd call a weight problem' as one participant, Karen, put it. Thus, if satisfied with their weight, these women would have no cause to diet, but would initiate dieting if their ability to conform to the thin ideal was challenged. For the thin ideal conformers, maintaining a slim body was central to their self-identity. Most of these women expressed a general aesthetic preference for thinness and some even espoused victim-blaming attitudes towards those they deemed overweight:

Table 18.1 Demographic and health characteristics of study participants compared to the WHA cohort in the same geographic area

Characteristic	*Study participants n = 20*	*Mid-aged WHA participants in same geographical area n = 260*
Mean age (SD)	47.6 (1.19)	47.8 (1.5)
Area of residence (%)		
Urban	90	98.8
Rural	10	1.2
Highest qualification (%)		
No post-school qualification	70	62
Trade/apprentice	—	5
Certificate/diploma	20	17
University degree	10	16
Marital status (%)		
Married/defacto	80	77
Separated/divorced	20	17
Widowed	—	2
Single	—	4
Smoking (%)		
Never smoked	50	51
Ex-smoker	35	26
Smoker	15	23
Self-rated general health (%)		
Excellent	20	11
Very good	45	33
Good	25	41
Fair	10	13
Poor	—	02
SF-36 summary score: Mean (SD)		
Physical	55.1 (7.2)	49.7 (9.8)
Mental	51.6 (10.1)	48.7 (11.0)
Anthropometry: Mean (SD)		
Weight	58.4 (5.8)	69.2 (15.1)
Height	164.1 (8.7)	162.8 (7.2)
BMI	21.7 (1.3)	26.1 (5.1)
Menopause status (%)		
Pre-menopausal	50	30.8
Peri-menopausal	15	26.2
Post-menopausal	5	9.2
Surgical hysterectomy	30	31.5

BMI = body mass index; SD = standard deviation

Table 18.2 Typology of participant responses to the thin ideal

	Thin ideal conformers	*Thin ideal rejectors*
Diet to lose weight	*Category 1: Body conformers* Women who diet in pursuit of the thin ideal 0 participants: excluded by selection criteria	*Category 2: Health maintainers* Women who diet for clear health benefits and not for aesthetic reasons 2 participants: Julie, Ruth
Do not diet	*Category 3: Weight maintainers* Women who are naturally slim and do not need to diet 12 participants: Tina, Jenny, Joan, Vicki, Emma, Sam, Margaret, Tanya, Olivia, Linda, Kate, Karen	*Category 4: Body acceptors* Women who accept body diversity and derive their self-identity from factors other than conforming to the thin ideal 6 participants: Jean, Jane, Flash, Mary, Mandy, Maggie

SAM: I don't like the fact of seeing people grossly overweight, you know. This friend I was referring to was really heavy ... I hope I never, ever get like that. She eats the wrong sorts of stuff too, you know; she cooks vegetables and all that sort of stuff, don't get me wrong, but she'll go and buy a hamburger and a bag of chips as a quick meal or something like that. She'll do silly things like that.

KATE: I've got one girlfriend ... she's not happy with her weight but that's her own problem because she sits there and pigs out on junk food all day.

Fat stigma and the social rewards of being thin make dieting to lose or maintain weight a rational response for many women (Germov & Williams 1999). Moreover, because of the strong association of thinness with female beauty in Western societies, the thin ideal is often internalised to such an extent that it becomes an integral part of a woman's self-identity, as shown by the thin ideal conformers in our study. As Giddens states (1991, p. 106), while women have the 'opportunity to follow a whole variety of possibilities ... in a masculinist culture, many of these avenues remain effectively foreclosed'. Writing of the thin ideal, Sandra Bartky (1998, p. 39) notes that 'many women will resist the abandonment of an aesthetic that defines what they take to be beautiful.' The data from these twelve participants adds to what we already know about women who conform to the thin ideal and are not discussed further in this chapter due to our focus on body acceptance.

The remaining eight women espoused attitudes that did not conform to the thin ideal and were identified as thin ideal rejectors; six were in category 4, or 'body acceptors' (Jean, Jane, Flash, Mary, Mandy, and Maggie). These women tended to value body diversity and derived their self-identity from factors other conformity to the thin ideal. If they gained weight, losing it would not be an aesthetic priority, as the responses below show:

> MARY: I've got other things to worry about in my life. If I put on the weight, I put it on ... Hey look, life's too short.
>
> MANDY: I don't think too much about my size … It's not a big part of my life thinking about whether I'm the size that I am … It doesn't worry me, I have lots of other things to think about.
>
> JANE: I'm really happy that I've put on a few kilos in later years as I was always a little bit underweight for my height. I'm very tall and I was always really skinny … so I got really conscious about not wearing things with scoop necks or I wouldn't wear sleeveless things because my arms were always skinny.
>
> JEAN: I'm happy with my weight and I guess like most people, you don't always like what you see in the mirror sometimes, but yeah, I accept the way I am and I would never diet because I thought my waist was too big.

Two of the eight thin ideal rejectors (Julie and Ruth) indicated they would only diet to lose weight for health reasons and only if they gained a significant amount of weight; they are designated as 'health maintainers' (category 2). These women cited weight-related health problems among family members as the basis for that proposed behaviour, reflecting widespread advice from health professionals and health authorities linking excess weight with disease. As Julie commented, 'Health has frightened me a lot I think … All my family are diabetics because of their size. They have all been overweight; I'm the only one that's not.' Ruth stated that 'I wouldn't be happy there [one stone heavier] because … it starts to bring in all sorts of health problems'.

The relationship between individuals' body shape and satisfaction with body weight is complex. Participants were selected for this study on the basis of self-reported weight satisfaction, which is not necessarily the same as body satisfaction. When the women were asked how they felt about their bodies, most stated they were 'quite' happy, but tended to offer qualifying statements, such as that they desired bigger breasts or firmer thighs. Given the rigid aesthetic ideals for women in Western societies, it is likely that few women have complete body satisfaction; hence our preference for the term 'body acceptance'. Indeed, participants who were 'body acceptors' tended to be less concerned with body aesthetics in general and realised that changes to their bodies had occurred with ageing and that this was to be expected. Some had previously been unhappily underweight and a weight increase after menopause had made them feel happier about their bodies. For example, Jean lacked body satisfaction in her 20s because she was underweight: 'I felt that when I looked in the mirror I looked gaunt and horrible and I didn't like the way I felt.'

Components of body acceptance

The responses of the eight thin ideal rejectors were grouped and discussed in relation to the following three themes that arose from the interview findings: self-acceptance based on life achievements, the influence of significant others, and non-discriminatory personal beliefs.

Identity beyond the body: Life politics, life stage, and self-acceptance

Giddens's (1991) notion of the body as a 'reflexive project of the self' acknowledges the potential for self-determination. Among the body-accepting participants, self-determination occurred not through 'body work' and thin ideal conformity, but rather through life achievements and key life events. Given that the participants were in the mid-age range, events such as motherhood, menopause, and workplace achievements were cited as fundamental influences on self-identity. For these women, conforming to the thin ideal was considered unimportant, with a number noting that as they matured, gained more life experience, and achieved more, body satisfaction became less important:

FLASH: Probably by the time I was about 20 or 21, I had this great sort of awareness drop on my head and it was kind of like you don't really give a damn what anybody thinks and you know it was really the growing up … in terms of 'I don't really care, I'll wear what I like, where I like'… and that's just become more pronounced as I've gotten older … As I matured and became prepared to accept myself, then that included my body shape, it included my hair, included my face … it includes like 'This is me, so what, here I am, accept me'.

RUTH: I think when you reach a—I don't know what age it is—certainly in your 40s and you find, well I think this is my theory, you realise your limitations and you've known yourself for 40 odd years, so you make the most of what you've got, you know.

JEAN: I have achieved my goals. I have a husband who loves me, I've got lovely kids and we own our own home and we have plans for the future.

As body weight became less significant in the lives of these women, they became more accepting of their bodies and themselves; this is reflected in comments such as 'I don't think of myself as perfect … but I do accept the way I am. It's me. I'm pleased about what's inside me' (Maggie). For Jane and Mary, the body was not something that was easily malleable, but was the result of genetic predisposition and life processes such as menopause. This view helped them accept their bodies, even if they were not totally satisfied:

JANE: You're a particular body type and I think you're stuck with your body type. I'm an ectomorphic … I think it's probably that a lot of women around the 50 age group … we all put weight on anyway because of the 'change of life' … I only sort of put on about 5 kilos. It wasn't a great deal … I found that 'gee' size 12 didn't fit anymore. You know, it was a good opportunity to get a new wardrobe.

MARY: I'm not happy with the weight I have put on but I accept it 'cause I know why the weight is there … it's menopause and there is nothing I can do about it.

Mary's comment in particular reflects the findings of the study by Tunaley, Walsh, and Nicholson (1999) discussed earlier, which found that even though older women might be dissatisfied with their bodies, they saw weight gain as 'inevitable' and this brought about acceptance.

The ability to mediate or reject the social pressure to be thin tended to be related to the wider issue of what the women termed self-esteem. As the women matured, self-identity was no longer derived from the 'external body', but rather focused on 'internal' factors such as self-esteem and self-worth derived from life achievements. These findings illustrate the reflexive self in action, as some women exercised their agency to construct an alternative life politics to counteract or override the influence of the thin ideal on their self-identity. The ability of some women to accept their weight was summed up by Julie:

JULIE: I think as you mature in life you change … I suppose when you're younger what people think about you really counts, and as you get older you don't really care what people think. It's what *you* think that really counts.

The social context of body acceptance: The influence of significant others

The results summarised above suggest that life course and life achievements were an alternative basis of self-identity for the body-accepting women in our study. Yet life politics need not imply that voluntarism is the basis of body acceptance, because the experiences and choices of individuals are influenced by social practices. Participants commonly cited family members, and particularly partners, as either positive or negative influences on their body acceptance, highlighting that the formation of self-identity is a social process rather than solely a product of self-determination. Mary for example, said that the support of her partner helped her to maintain her body acceptance:

> MARY: My husband's very accepting and it wouldn't worry him if I put on ten kilos, so I don't feel I have to keep slim for his sake. He wouldn't worry about that kind of thing, so I don't think I have ever felt it has been a problem.

Jean developed her body acceptance within a supportive family environment in which body weight and size were not considered priorities:

> JEAN: As a teenager probably my Mum was a big influence. As you're changing and you sort of say I'm too fat or too thin. My Mum is really quite a sensible sort of person that would give you good advice, just point out to you how your body's changing and make you understand what was happening. Things like that, so you did not freak out because your hips were getting broader … when you were 14, because my Mum would explain that those sort of things were normal.

Participants who, like Jean, were exposed to positive beliefs about body acceptance in their early family life maintained these beliefs to mid-life. Other participants had developed body acceptance later in life after conforming to the thin ideal in their youth. For these women, early negative experiences, such as derogatory comments about their weight made by significant others, had led them to be dissatisfied with their weight. Julie expressed how she started dieting at around age 16, when she was a 'very chubby kid'. When asked what prompted her to diet, she replied:

> JULIE: You get rude remarks and you get fed up with people making jokes or whatever … Oh yeah [comments from] family members, cousins, things like that … sometimes it was quite hurtful.

Social relations, such as the influence of parents, siblings, and partners, thus played a role in determining whether or not the women accepted their bodies, but they were not all-determining. Negative experiences early in life were often counteracted by subsequent life experiences, as in Julie's case:

> Julie: Well I certainly think differently now. Your thinking is a lot different now to what it was when you were

young ... The things that you were worried about when you were in your 20s you don't worry so much about in your 50s. As you get older everything changes. I guess I have achieved my goals, you know. I guess my life is generally satisfying ... I've got a career, I've got a family, so I'm happy with myself.

Tolerance of bodies and beyond: Non-discriminatory beliefs and acceptance of diversity

The final theme to emerge from the data was that of non-discriminatory beliefs about others. Participants' acceptance of their own bodies also tended to be extended to the bodies of others:

MANDY: I am what I am and I can't change it ... It's an acceptance. I can't wish that I was 160 centimetres tall, so I have this philosophy towards life that you don't stress over what you can't change; you accept what is ... I think you've just got to learn to live with, you know, the colour of your eyes and the sort of hair you've got and really, if you're a different body shape and structure, well you've just got to be able to put up with that ... I've just accepted that that's the way I am. And once you can do that, you just accept others for what they are. I mean, if you don't judge yourself in that way, it's pretty silly to do it to others, whether it's their body, their skin colour, how they talk ...

Not only did the body acceptors support body diversity as opposed to one ideal body type, but a few participants also went further and drew a link between non-judgmental attitudes about physical features and non-discriminatory views regarding gender and ethnicity:

RUTH: It's more than just the body image ... My friends are all different shapes and sizes and generally speaking we're all fairly comfortable with ourselves. It's something deeper than just body size. It's the way you look at the world, the way you treat other people. And none of us would have anything to do with someone that's sexist or racist ... It's about respect and realising people are different and that's a beautiful thing.

The acceptance of body diversity was characteristic of a broader tolerance of diversity and difference in society. For Jean and Jane, tolerance of a diversity of body sizes was indicative of a political stance of general non-discriminatory attitudes toward people:

JEAN: We have become very conscious of understanding that people can be a different colour, you know, or have different shaped eyes and that's okay ... We can be a different height and that's all right, but we don't accept that the shape can be different ... We concentrate in Australia on accepting people with a disability or a different race or religion, but we are dreadful about accepting people who are overweight or underweight.

JANE: I'm accepting of people. I don't mind what shape or size or colour they are ... I find people interesting and I'd sort of look at them for themselves rather than their shape or size or what country they come from.

Maggie brought this back again to early family influence:

MAGGIE: It goes back to how you're brought up ... It's sort of been built into me by my parents how important it is to feel happy, and not think negatively about anything.

These findings suggest that body acceptance may be related to the general acceptance of others in the form of non-discriminatory values and attitudes towards people. This exposes the social practices and belief systems that underpin an individual's ability to exercise reflexivity and enact a life politics of body acceptance. It may also show how individuals' life politics become the basis of social movements such as the fat-rights and anti-dieting movements.

Life politics, body acceptance, and female identity

The application of Giddens's (1991) concept of life politics to the study of women's body acceptance indicates that certain social relations, values, and practices can facilitate the filtering of patriarchal influences on female identity, enabling some women to exercise agency and construct their identity independently of the thin ideal. For the body acceptors in our study, the external body was no longer a marker of identity or self-worth. These women constructed their identity based on a conception of the 'whole person', whereby life achievements and non-discriminatory values took the place of body image conformity—in Giddens's terms they adopted a 'life politics' that rejected the thin ideal in favour of self-acceptance and diversity. This finding shows the potential women have to resist patriarchal discourses such as the thin ideal and construct alternative forms of femininity, and clearly parallels the postulates of post-structuralist feminist approaches that stress female agency and subjectivity (see Butler 1990; Pringle 1995; Bartky 1998, 1990).

The life politics of body acceptance creates a bridge between the internal and external body—between self-identity and social identity. In an increasingly reflexive society, the conscious monitoring and revision of behaviours and beliefs creates the possibility of a socially reconstructed self-identity derived from life experiences and alternative body discourses. While Blood (1996) concluded that women's self-acceptance was founded primarily on a critical awareness of the negative influence of the media, the women in our study founded their body-acceptance on a more complex constellation of social practices and social relations. The influence of significant others, life achievements, and non-discriminatory attitudes underpinned the development of body acceptance and formed the basis for an alternative, non-aesthetic social construction of female identity.

Facilitating body acceptance: Towards a new body and weight paradigm

While the life politics of body acceptance represents the ability of women to exercise their agency, the ability to exercise this agency appears to depend on the attainment of a certain level of material, personal, and political resources. Furthermore, some women may translate their life politics of body acceptance into what Giddens (1991) refers to as **emancipatory politics**—that is, they may become body-acceptance advocates and engage in public debate to undermine the dominance and salience of the thin ideal. For Giddens, emancipatory politics embodies a commitment to social justice and aims to reduce or eliminate discrimination and exploitation—as evidenced by the non-discriminatory attitudes of the body-accepting women in our study. Emancipatory body politics can be seen in the numerous groups and organisations that have formed to liberate women from the thin ideal. Representative organisations include the International Size Acceptance Association (ISAA), the National Association to Advance Fat Acceptance (NAAFA), and Largesse, the Network for Size Esteem, all of which disseminate information and publicity material that promote body diversity, and lobby governments and corporations about addressing size discrimination and **fatism** (see Box 18.1 and Figure 18.1; Solovay 2000).

In addition to activist organizations, some health professionals are also recommending body acceptance as part of a new health promotion paradigm (Parham 1996, 1999a, 1999b; Kassirer & Angell 1998; Herrin et al. 1999; Higgins & Gray 1999; Ikeda 2000; Ikeda et al. 1999; Jutel 2001; Miller & Jacob 2001; see Strain 1999 for a contrary view). These authors advocate an approach that does not equate thinness with health, and fatness with increased risk of chronic disease. They argue that overweight people can be fit and healthy. While they do not dispute obesity-related health risks, they maintain that there is little evidence to support the position that weight loss *per se* improves health in overweight individuals. They note the continuing high failure rate of weight-loss diets; the

Box 18.1 Body acceptance as a social movement: International No Diet Day

International No Diet Day (INDD) is an annual celebration of body acceptance and diversity. It is observed on 6 May of each year.

What is INDD?

INDD is a day to:

- Celebrate the beauty and diversity of ALL our natural sizes & shapes
- Affirm everyBODY's right to health, fitness, and emotional well-being
- Declare a personal one-day moratorium on diet/weight obsession
- Learn the facts about weight-loss dieting, health, and body size
- Recognize how dieting perpetuates violence against women
- Honor the victims of eating disorders and weight-loss surgery
- Help end weight discrimination, sizism and fat phobia

Does INDD have a symbol?

Yes, the light blue ribbon was designated by INDD's founder, Mary Evans Young, as its international symbol. This year on May 6, we invite you to put on a light blue ribbon and join the celebration!

Who celebrates INDD?

INDD is for everyBODY! Since its origin in 1992, INDD has been celebrated by size acceptance, anti-diet, body image, and eating disorders activists, groups, and individuals around the world who want to empower people of all sizes. Events and activities will be held in cities and towns spanning the globe. Check out the official INDD website for more information: **www.largesse.net/INDD/**

This information is a public service of Largesse, the Network for Size Esteem [http://www.eskimo.com/~largesse/] and may be freely copied and distributed in its entirety for non-commercial use in promoting size diversity empowerment, provided this statement is included.

rising prevalence of overweight, despite the widespread promotion of weight loss by health authorities; the detrimental effects of weight cycling; and the fact that chronic dieting is a risk factor for **eating disorders**.

Debate continues in the obesity literature over paradoxical empirical findings that suggest intentional weight loss is linked to increased mortality (Berg 1995;

Figure 18.1 International Size Acceptance Association poster counteracting the messages of the body image industries

SIZE is relative...
Every
BODY
is
OK!!
The size of YOUR body
should be nobody's
Bu$ine$$
International Size Acceptance Association
P.O. Box 82126
Austin, TX 78758
Web site: http://www.size-acceptance.org
e-mail: director@size-acceptance.org
INTERNATIONAL
Size
ACCEPTANCE
ASSOCIATION

Source: Reproduced with permission of the ISAA (www.size-acceptance.org)

Sørensen 2003; Yang et al. 2003). Given such a situation, some health professionals believe it is inappropriate to promote weight loss, particularly in the context of the social pressure of the thin ideal and the likelihood that many people use unhealthy practices to lose weight for aesthetic reasons. Dietitians such as Joanne Ikeda and Ellen Parham advocate alternative strategies to minimise health risks,

Box 18.2 Ten basic tenets of size acceptance

1. Human beings come in a variety of sizes and shapes. We celebrate this diversity as a positive characteristic of the human race.
2. There is no ideal body size, shape, or weight that every individual should strive to achieve.
3. Every body is a good body, whatever its size or shape.
4. Self-esteem and body image are strongly linked. Helping people feel good about their bodies, and about who they are, can help motivate and maintain healthy behaviours.
5. Appearance stereotyping is inherently unfair to the individual because it is based on superficial factors that the individual has little or no control over.
6. We respect the bodies of others even though they might be quite different from our own.
7. Each person is responsible for taking care of his/her body.
8. Good health is not defined by body size; it is a state of physical, mental, and social well-being.
9. People of all sizes and shapes can reduce their risk of poor health by adopting a healthy lifestyle.
10. Health promotion programs should celebrate the benefits of a healthy lifestyle. Programs should be accepting of and sensitive to size diversity. They should promote body satisfaction and the achievement of realistic and attainable health goals without regard to weight change.

Source: Ikeda (2000).

strategies that promote positive self-esteem, body acceptance, healthy eating, and moderate exercise rather than dieting, weight loss, and an idealised body size and shape (see Box 18.2).

Sobal (1995) notes a division between non-dieting movements that still equate thinness with health—but health achieved through exercise and psychological approaches rather than dieting—and the size acceptance movement, which contests fatism and promotes body diversity. This division exists within the dietetic profession itself, with some dietitians opposing the promotion of body acceptance and others developing health promotion programs based on the new body and weight paradigm (see Box 18.3). These issues have even been acknowledged in the mainstream obesity-research scientific community, with a call for further empirical research to provide evidence to support the efficacy of a 'health at any size' approach (Higgins & Gray 1999; Miller & Jacob 2001).

Box 18.3 An example of body acceptance and health promotion: Body Image and Health Inc.

Body Image and Health Inc. (www.internationalnodietday.com/) is an association of body image consultants, dietitians, and public health workers that highlights the importance of body image issues in the community through research dissemination, training seminars, and public advocacy to counteract body dissatisfaction and promote body diversity. In addition to promoting International No Diet Day activities in Australia, the web site provides access to extensive resources on body image issues for health professionals and the general public, with research summaries and fact sheets on topics such as body image and eating behaviour, body image and ageing, the influence of the media on body image, and fostering positive body image in children.

Conclusion

This chapter has explored how women negotiate cultural prescriptions regarding female identity, to unveil the social processes though which women develop body acceptance. Our qualitative empirical study found that for some women weight satisfaction was derived from being 'naturally' thin and thus from being able to conform to the thin ideal without having to diet (which highlights the limitations of relying on quantitative methods of investigation). However, for other women, body acceptance indicated a rejection of the thin ideal: satisfaction was derived from non-corporeal factors and a non-discriminatory worldview. Our findings suggest that non-aesthetic life priorities, life achievements in the spheres of work and family, the influence of significant others, and non-discriminatory attitudes are likely to be key determinants of body acceptance. The finding that non-discriminatory attitudes contribute to the acceptance of the body in all its diversity adds a new dimension to the literature. Such life politics or lifestyle factors, as Giddens states, create a set of routinised practices that 'give material form to a particular narrative of self-identity' (1991, p. 81). It is worth noting that body acceptance is rare and that age was a factor in the findings reported here, since the research participants were mid-age women who felt they were under less thin-ideal pressure than younger women.

The research results presented in this chapter can inform the efforts of health professionals and others dealing with the detrimental health effects of women's body dissatisfaction. Sharlene Hesse-Biber (1996) suggests that social activism is required to challenge the body image industries, which reproduce the thin ideal, and by so doing to generate new constructions of femininity that value body diversity. Body acceptance is a positive example of the 'reflexive project of the self', and its promotion can set the social context in which diverse female identities, or 'femininities', can flourish, so that women have the social space to construct their own notions of what it means to be female in Western society. The anti-dieting and size-acceptance social movements, which have modelled themselves on the successful civil rights and women's liberation movements, provide an alternative form of social acceptance (of body diversity) by attempting to influence cultural and institutional practices. The extent to which health professions will embrace this movement remains to be seen.

Summary of main points

- Despite the dominance of the thin ideal, some women actively reject it in favour of the alternative body discourses associated with the anti-dieting and size-acceptance social movements.
- The empirical study discussed in this chapter suggests that three key factors underpin the development of body acceptance: self-worth derived from personal achievements rather than body appearance, the influence of significant others in establishing a positive body image, and non-discriminatory social values, which lead to support of body diversity.
- Giddens's concepts of life politics and emancipatory politics provide a useful theoretical framework for understanding the interplay of structure and agency in the social construction of women's bodies and identities in Western society.
- The life politics of body acceptance is an example of how some women resist patriarchal and commercial social pressures and embrace body diversity to redefine ideals of beauty and femininity in their own terms.
- Understanding how some women develop body acceptance can help us to develop intervention strategies to facilitate body acceptance in the wider community.

Discussion questions

1. How would you define 'body acceptance'?
2. Do you accept your own body and other people's bodies?

3 What are some of the key factors that influence whether a person accepts their body?
4 In what ways do you think women's and men's notions of body acceptance differ?
5 Should health professionals in countries with a high prevalence of overweight and obesity promote body acceptance?

Further investigation

1 To what extent could the promotion of body acceptance challenge the thin ideal? What evidence have you seen that an alternative body ideal may be emerging?
2 What are some strategies that could be implemented to facilitate body acceptance in the community?

Acknowledgments

The research reported in this chapter was supported by a grant awarded by the University of Newcastle, Australia. Thanks are due to Michelle Powers for her assistance in gathering and organising the qualitative results into text, Jane Potter for research assistance, and Jean Ball (data manager for the WHA project) for selecting the participants. We also thank the women themselves for giving so generously of their time and of themselves.

The ten basic tenets of size acceptance was developed by dietitians and nutritionists who are advocates of size acceptance; their efforts were coordinated by Joanne P. Ikeda, Department of Nutritional Sciences, University of California, Berkeley, USA. Comments regarding these tenets may be emailed to jikeda@socrates.berkeley.edu.

Further reading and web resources

Books

Sobal, J. & Maurer, D. (eds) 1999, *Interpreting Weight: The Social Management of Fatness and Thinness*, Aldine de Gruyter, New York.

Articles and book chapters

Kassirer, J. P. & Angell, M. 1998, 'Losing Weight: An Ill-fated New Year's Resolution', *New England Journal of Medicine*, vol. 338, pp. 52–4.

Miller, W. C. & Jacob, A.V. 2001, 'The Health at Any Size Paradigm for Obesity Treatment: The Scientific Evidence', *Obesity Reviews*, vol. 2, pp. 37–45.

Parham, E. S. 1996, 'Is There a New Weight Paradigm?', *Nutrition Today*, vol. 31, pp. 155–61.

—— 1999, 'Meanings of Weight among Dietitians and Nutritionists', in J. Sobal & D. Maurer (eds.), *Weighty Issues: Fatness and Thinness as Social Problems*, Aldine de Gruyter, New York, pp. 183–205.

—— 1999, 'Promoting Body Size Acceptance in Weight Management Counseling', *Journal of the American Dietetic Association*, vol. 99, no. 8, pp. 920–6.

Sobal, J. 1999, 'The Size Acceptance Movement and the Social Construction of Body Weight', in J. Sobal & D. Maurer (eds), *Weighty Issues: Fatness and Thinness as Social Problems*, Aldine de Gruyter, New York, pp. 183–205.

Strain, G. W. 1999, 'Response to Promoting Size Acceptance in Weight Management Counseling', *Journal of the American Dietetic Association*, vol. 99, no. 8 , pp. 926–8.

Journals and magazines

Fat!So?

Healthy Weight Journal

Documentaries

Beyond Killing Us Softly. The Strength to Resist: The Impact of Media Images on Women and Girls, 2000, Cambridge Documentary Films, Cambridge, Boston, Massachusetts, 34 minutes.

Fat Chance, 1994, National Film Board of Canada, Bodston, 50 minutes.

Fat Files, 1999, BBC/Learning Channel co-production, 3 episodes, 153 minutes.

Web sites

About-Face: about-face.org/

Adios Barbie: www.adiosbarbie.com/

Body Image & Health Inc: www.internationalnodietday.com/

Fat!So?: www.fatso.com/

Health at Any Size Web Ring: www.bodypositive.com/web_ring.htm

Healthy Weight Network: www.healthyweightnetwork.com/

International No Diet Day resources: www.largesse.net/INDD/

International Size Acceptance Association: www.size-acceptance.org/

Largesse Network for Self-esteem: www.largesse.net/

National Association to Advance Fat Acceptance: naafa.org/

References

Bartky, S. L. 1990, *Femininity and Domination: Studies in the Phenomenology of Oppression*, Routledge, New York.

—— 1998, 'Foucault, Femininity, and the Modernization of Patriarchal Power', in R. Weitz (ed.), *The Politics of Women's Bodies: Sexuality, Appearance and Behavior*, Oxford University Press, New York.

Berg, F. M. 1995, *The Health Risks of Weight Loss*, Healthy Weight Journal, Hettinger, North Dakota.

Blood, K. 1996, 'The Dieting Dilemma: Factors Influencing Women's Decision to Give up Dieting', *Women & Therapy*, vol. 18, pp. 109–18.

Brown, W. J., Bryson, L., Byles, J. E., Dobson, A. J., Manderson, L., Schofield, M. & Williams, G. 1996, 'Women's Health Australia: Establishment of the Australian Longitudinal Study on Women's Health', *Journal of Women's Health*, vol. 5, pp. 467–72.

Brown, W. J., Byles, J. E., Dobson, A. J., Lee, C., Mishra, G. & Scofield, M. 1998, 'Women's Health Australia: Recruitment for a National Longitudinal Cohort Study', *Women and Health*, vol. 28, pp. 23–40.

Butler, J. 1990, *Gender Trouble: Feminism and the Subversion of Identity*, Routledge, London.

Chrisler, J. C. 1996, 'Politics and Women's Weight', Feminism & Psychology, vol. 6, pp. 181–4.

—— 1994, 'Reframing Women's Weight: Does Thin Equal Healthy?', in A. J. Dan (ed.), *Reframing Women's Health: Multidisciplinary Research and Practice*, Sage, Thousand Oaks, California, pp. 330–8.

Cogan, J. C. 1999, 'Re-evaluating the Weight-centred Approach Toward Health: The Need for a Paradigm Shift', in J. Sobal & D. Maurer (eds), *Interpreting Weight: The Social Management of Fatness and Thinness*, Aldine de Gruyter, New York, pp. 229–53.

Connell, R. W. 2002, *Gender*, Polity Press, Cambridge.

Dalton, S. 1998, 'The Dietitians' Philosophy and Practice in Multidisciplinary Weight Management', *Journal of the American Dietetic Association*, vol. 98, pp. 49–54.

Denzin, N. 1989, *Interpretive Interactionism*, Sage, Newbury Park, California.

Fabrey, W. J. 1995, 'A Mini History of the Size Acceptance Movement: The First 25 Years', in *Size Acceptance and Self-acceptance. The NAAFA Workbook: A Complete Study Guide*, 2nd edn, National Association to Advance Fat Acceptance, Sacramento, p. 7.

Germov, J. & Williams, L. 1999 , 'Dieting Women: Self-surveillance and the Body Panopticon', in J. Sobal & D. Maurer (eds), Weighty Issues: Constructing Fatness and Thinness as Social Problems, Aldine de Gruyter, New York, pp. 117–32.

—— 1996, 'The Sexual Division of Dieting: Women's Voices', *Sociological Review*, vol. 44, no. 4, pp. 630–47.

Giddens, A. 1991, *Modernity and Self-identity*, Stanford University Press, California.

Goodman, W. C. 1995, *The Invisible Woman: Confronting Weight Prejudice in America*, Gurze, Carlsbad, California.

Grogan, S. 1999, *Body Image: Understanding Body Dissatisfaction in Men, Women and Children*, Routledge, London.

Herrin, M., Parham, E., Ikeda, J., White, A. & Branen, L. 1999, 'Alternative Viewpoint on National Institutes of Health Clinical Guidelines', *Journal of Nutrition Education*, vol. 31, no. 2, pp. 116–18.

Hetherington, M. M. 1994, 'Aging and the Pursuit of Slimness: Dieting and Body Satisfaction through Life', *Appetite*, vol. 23, no. 2, pp. 198–205.

Hesse-Biber, S. 1996, *Am I Thin Enough Yet? The Cult of Thinness and the Commercialization of Identity*, Oxford University Press, New York.

Higgins, L. & Gray, W. 1999, 'What do Anti-dieting Programs Achieve? A Review of Research', *Australian Journal of Nutrition and Dietetics*, vol. 56, no. 3, pp. 128–36.

Ikeda, J. P. 2000, 'Health Promotion: A Size Acceptance Approach', *Healthy Weight Journal*, January/February, pp. 10–12.

Ikeda, J. P., Hayes, D., Satter, E., Parham, E. S., Kratina, K., Woolsey, M., Lowey, M. & Tribole, E. 1999, 'A Commentary on the New Obesity Guidelines from NIH', *Journal of the American Dietetic Association*, vol. 99, no. 8, pp. 918–19.

Jutel, A. 2001, 'Does Size Really Matter? Weight and Values in Public Health', *Perspectives in Biology and Medicine*, vol. 44, no. 3, pp. 283–96.

Kassirer, J. P. & Angell, M. 1998, 'Losing Weight: An Ill-fated New Year's Resolution', *New England Journal of Medicine*, vol. 338, pp. 52–4.

McNay, L. 1992, *Foucault and Feminism*, Polity Press, Cambridge.

—— 2000, *Gender and Agency*, Polity Press, Cambridge.

Miller, W. C. & Jacob, A. V. 2001, 'The Health at Any Size Paradigm for Obesity Treatment: The Scientific Evidence', *Obesity Reviews*, vol. 2, pp. 37–45.

Parham, E. S. 1996, 'Is There a New Weight Paradigm?', *Nutrition Today*, vol. 31, pp. 155–61.

—— 1999b, 'Promoting Body Size Acceptance in Weight Management Counselling', *Journal of the American Dietetic Association*, vol. 99, no. 8, pp. 920–5.

Pringle, R. 1995, 'Destabilising Patriarchy', in B. Caine & R. Pringle (eds), *Transitions: New Australian Feminisms*, Allen & Unwin, Sydney.

Sobal, J. 1995, 'The Medicalization and Demedicalization of Obesity', in D. Maurer & J. Sobal (eds), *Eating Agendas: Food and Nutrition as Social Problems*, Aldine de Gruyter, New York, pp. 79–90.

—— 1999, 'The Size Acceptance Movement and the Social Construction of Body Weight', in J. Sobal & D. Maurer (eds.), *Weighty Issues: Fatness and Thinness as Social Problems*, Aldine de Gruyter, New York, pp. 183–205.

Solovay, S. 2000, *Tipping the Scales of Justice: Fighting Weight-based Discrimination*, Prometheus Books, New York.

Sørensen, T. I. A. 2003, 'Weight Loss Causes Increased Mortality: Pros', *Obesity Reviews*, vol. 4, pp. 3–7.

Stimson, K. W. 1995, 'A Fat Feminist Herstory 1969–1993', in *Size Acceptance and Self-acceptance. The NAAFA Workbook: A Complete Study Guide*, 2nd edn, National Association to Advance Fat Acceptance, Sacramento, pp. 8–10.

Strain, G. W. 1999, 'Response to Promoting Size Acceptance in Weight Management Counseling', *Journal of the American Dietetic Association*, vol. 99, no. 8 , pp. 926–8.

Tiggemann, M. & Lynch, J. E. 2001, 'Body Image across the Life Span in Adult Women: The Role of Self-objectification', *Developmental Psychology*, vol. 37, no. 2, pp. 243–53.

Tiggemann, M. & Stevens, C. 1999, 'Body Image across the Life Span: The Meaning of Weight at Different Ages', in *The Body Culture: Conference Proceedings, Body Image and Health Inc.*, Victoria, pp. 151–6.

Tunaley, J. R., Walsh, S. & Nicholson, P. 1999, '"I'm Not Bad for my Age": The Meaning of Body Size and Eating in the Lives of Older Women', *Ageing and Society*, vol. 19, pp. 741–59.

Tyler, M. & Abbott, P. 1998, 'Chocs Away: Weight Watching in the Contemporary Airline Industry', *Sociology*, vol. 32, no. 3, pp. 433–50.

Yang, D., Fontaine, K. R., Wang, C. & Allison, D. B. 2003, 'Weight Loss Causes Increased Mortality: Cons', *Obesity Reviews*, vol. 4, pp. 9–16.

Glossary

accounts
Specific claims about the reasons for particular behaviours, used to manage interactions and to gain or maintain acceptance.

active micro-organisms
Organisms that are not visible to the human eye and that have biological activity in humans.

activities of daily living
Activities considered fundamental to an individual's independent existence, including getting out of bed, cooking and eating food, and shopping for groceries.

ageism
Discrimination based on age.

agency
The ability of people, individually and collectively, to influence their own lives and the society in which they live.

agribusiness
The complete operations performed in producing agricultural commodities, including farming, manufacturing, handling, storing, processing, and distributing.

agri-food
The industries involved in the production of food.

alienated labour/alienation
'Alienation' is a Marxist term that refers to the experience of people who have to work for a monetary wage to live. They are alienated from—have no control over—their conditions of work, the process of production, what they produce, and the ownership and distribution of their products.

anorexia nervosa (AN)
A complex eating disorder in which a person severely restricts food consumption to lose or maintain body weight, to such an extent that it is detrimental to normal physiological functioning and life-threatening.

anti-vivisection
A movement that is against the use of animals for laboratory experiments.

appropriationism
The use of manufactured inputs in agriculture (seeds, fertilisers, machinery, etc.) produced by off-farm transnational industries. Compare with *substitutionism*.

attribution
Ascribing a characteristic, quality, or causation to some factor.

biological determinism

An unproven belief that individual, group, and organisational behaviours are ultimately determined by biology.

biomedicine/biomedical model

The conventional approach to medicine in Western societies; based on the diagnosis and explanation of illness as a malfunction of one of the body's biological mechanisms. This approach underpins most health professions and health services, which focus on treating individuals and generally marginalise social, economic, and environmental factors. In terms of diet, eating is conceptualised as a process of sustaining the body as a biological organism by using the nutrients that medical science considers most effective.

biotechnology

The use of molecular biology and genetic engineering to modify plants and animals, including humans, at the molecular level.

body acceptance

A set of beliefs held by those who have a positive body image. These beliefs support body diversity in the community by rejecting conformity to the thin ideal. Also referred to as 'size acceptance', which is promoted by social movements that aim to counteract prejudice and discrimination based on body size and shape. See also *body image*, *fatism*, and *thin ideal*.

body image

The image an individual has of their own body. Body image depends on both the actual shape and size of the body as well as the affective component of how that body is perceived in relation to body expectations. Thus, if the body expectations held by an individual are unrealistic, it is possible for that individual to have a negative body image despite having a body that others would envy.

body mass index (BMI)

A measure of body weight used in the health sciences to determine the prevalence in the population of underweight, overweight, and obesity. BMI is derived by dividing a person's weight in kilograms by their height in metres squared. The World Health Organization has defined the following weight ranges for women and men:

<18.50	Underweight
18.50–24.99	Normal range
25.00–29.99	Grade I overweight
30.00–34.99	Grade IIa overweight
35.00–39.99	Grade IIb overweight
40+	Grade III overweight

A measure equal to or above 30 is also referred to as 'obese'.

bulimia nervosa (BN)

An eating disorder indicated by repeated episodes of binge eating and purging. A person with BN will consume large amounts of food in a short period of time, usually experienced as a lack of control over eating, and will then try to prevent weight gain through self-induced vomiting, misuse of laxatives and medications, fasting, or excessive exercise.

capitalism

An economic and social system based on the private accumulation of wealth; a system in which a relatively small capitalist class own almost all the productive property of a society.

cash crops

Crops produced to be exchanged for cash.

civilising process/civilising of appetite

The 'civilising process' is a concept coined by Norbert Elias to refer to the never-ending social process by which external forms of social control of people's behaviour are replaced by internalised forms of moral self-control. Stephen Mennell has applied this idea to food habits, using the term 'civilising of appetite'.

class (or social class)

A concept used by sociologists to refer to a position in a system of structured inequality based on the unequal distribution of power, wealth, income, and status. People who share a social class typically share similar life chances.

colonialism

A process in which one nation imposes itself economically, politically, and socially upon another.

commodification

A process in which something is converted into a commodity that can be bought and sold in the pursuit of profit-maximisation.

Commodity Systems Analysis (CSA)

Developed by William Friedland, this analytical framework identifies a wide range of factors that contribute to the production of commodities, including production practices, technology, farm and factory labour processes, marketing, distribution networks, and the retail sector.

community-supported agriculture

An organic farming enterprise that is supported by a community group of consumers. The community group is organised to give financial or labour support to the enterprise, which in turn produces food for them.

competencies

'Competence' is the ability to perform activities to the expected professional standard in the workplace. 'Competency standards' are the level of expertise required for professional practice in terms of the unique role and employment context of a particular profession.

conservatism

A political ideology that favours the status quo and a hierarchical society governed by power elites, based on the assumption that social inequality is natural, inevitable, and necessary for social order. Such beliefs often support strict moral regulation of individual behaviour.

continuing competency development
The process of further skill and knowledge development, after an initial professional qualification has been obtained. This usually occurs in the workplace

cosmopolitanism
The global hybridisation of cultures, tastes, and cuisines caused by the globalisation of the media, trade, and travel.

cross-cultural competency
The ability to work effectively with people from another culture, based on an understanding and acceptance of the values, assumptions, beliefs, and practices of that culture.

culinary tourism
The promotion of gastronomic experiences, events, and products (such as food festivals and regional foodstuffs) as a key feature of the travel experience.

cultural capital
A concept that implies that culture can be treated like an economic asset upon which social hierarchies are founded.

cultural economy
An analytical framework that avoids privileging cultural or economic factors by drawing on both, and examining how these factors interact, to understand the way markets and organisations operate.

cultural relativism
The concept that social values and beliefs are culturally specific and are not universal or absolute.

cultural sensitivity
Non-judgmental understanding and acceptance of the values, assumptions, beliefs, and practices of a cultural group other than one's own.

culture
The values, assumptions, and beliefs shared by a group of people, which structure the behaviour of group members from birth until death.

culture-bound syndrome
A health or medical condition that only occurs in particular cultures and is not universal, or culture-free.

developed world/developing world
The developed world comprises the rich countries of the world, in which industrial development is long-standing, and the developing world comprises the poorer countries of the world, in which industrial development is more recent.

deviance
Behaviour that violates social expectations about what is normal.

dichotomous view
A view that stereotypes the diet and food choices of the affluent and better educated as 'healthy' and the diet of the poor and and less educated as 'unhealthy'.

Dietary Guidelines for Australians

Dietary advice for the Australian population. The guidelines aim to reverse those trends in the Australian diet that contribute to chronic disease and disorders.

dietitian

A university-trained health professional with expertise on the relationship between food and health, particularly in terms of illness prevention and treatment for individuals and communities.

disabilities

Limitations on the ability to fulfil role obligations as a result of physical impairments; impairments include limited motion of limbs and generalised muscular weakness, which are usually the result of injury or illness.

disclaimer

An explanation provided in anticipation of challenges to a person's or a behaviour's legitimacy.

discounting

A set of techniques for dealing with violations of personal principles without threatening internal self-definitions or identity.

discourse

A domain of language use that is characterised by common ways of talking and thinking about an issue (for example, discourses about health, disease, diets, and bodies).

DNA

Deoxyribonucleic acid: the molecule within cells that transmits hereditary information.

eating disorders

Generic term for the cluster of disorders including anorexia nervosa, bulimia nervosa, and eating disorders not otherwise specified.

eating disorders not otherwise specified (EDNOS)

Eating disorders that do not fall within the definition of anorexia nervosa (AN) or of bulimia nervosa (BN), in terms of severity or range of symptoms, but that nonetheless may include elements of each.

ecological model

Derived from the broad field of human ecology, which studies the links between human interaction, social organisation, and ecology. When applied to public health, this model explores the determinants of health within a social, economic, and geographic context, rather than simply examining the contribution of medical factors (as in the biomedical model).

economic liberalism/economic rationalism

A general term used to describe a political philosophy based on small government and market-oriented policies, such as deregulation, privatisation, reduced government spending, and lower taxation. See also *neo-liberalism*.

emancipatory politics

A term used by Anthony Giddens to refer to a value-based commitment to reducing or eliminating inequality, discrimination, and exploitation. See also *life politics*.

epidemiology

The statistical study of patterns of disease in the population. Originally focused on epidemics, or infectious diseases, it now covers non-infectious conditions. Social epidemiology is a sub-field, aligned with sociology, which focuses on the social determinants of illness.

ethical responsibilities

Obligations that individuals are required to fulfil on the basis of their cultural or societal position. For example, individuals who are parents have ethical responsibilities concerning the duty of care for their children; these responsibilities form the standards by which individuals judge themselves to be 'good' parents.

ethics

Socially or culturally patterned codes of conduct that oblige individuals to act in particular ways.

ethnocentric

Viewing others from one's own cultural perspective, with an implied sense of cultural superiority based on an inability to understand or accept the practices and beliefs of other cultures.

ethnography

A research methodology based on qualitative experience, detailed observations, and in-depth description of the daily social life of the people under study.

evidence-based medicine (EBM)

An approach to medicine that argues that all clinical practice should be based on evidence from randomised controlled trials (RCTs) to ensure the effectiveness and efficacy of treatments. RCTs are an experiment-based research method used to evaluate the effectiveness of therapeutic interventions by comparing a group that receives an intervention with a 'control' group that does not.

family commensality

Family members preparing, serving, and sharing meals together.

fatism

Discrimination against people with high levels of body fat.

feminism/feminist

A broad social and political movement based on a belief in equality of the sexes and advocating the removal of all forms of discrimination against women. A feminist is one who subscribes to, and may act upon, a body of theory that seeks to explain the subordinate position of women in society.

figurations

A concept developed by Norbert Elias as an alternative to *structure* and *agency*. Figurations represent the nexus of structure and agency, and can be conceived of as networks of people in interdependent relationships. They are the product of individuals but beyond the control of any single individual or group. Elias suggested that figurations could best be imagined as a game in which people must depend on one another within the confines of the rules. Social conflict or competition may result in the rules being changed or may cause new forms of figurations to develop.

flexible accumulation

A general term, often used interchangeably or in conjunction with 'flexible specialisation' and 'flexible production', denoting changes in work organisation. Specifically, it refers to a mode of capital accumulation by corporations that is characterised by an ability to respond quickly to competition and consumer demand by flexibly managing employment (using contract, part-time, or casual labour), by developing staff multiskilling and task flexibility, and by using new technologies that allow production processes to be changed quickly.

food inadequacy/insufficiency

Energy deficiency relative to nutritional needs or the capacity to work. Often used interchangeably with 'undernutrition'.

food safety

The 'safety' of food for human consumption—safe food is free from biological and chemical contaminants (due to food handling, production, or storage) that have the potential to cause illness.

food security/insecurity

'Food security' is the availability of affordable, nutritious, and culturally acceptable food. 'Food insecurity' is a state of regular hunger and fear of starvation.

food system

All the factors that comprise processes of food production, distribution, and consumption—from the paddock and fisheries to the plate—such as agriculture and agri-business, government regulation, marketing, retail preparation, and sales.

food use

A term proposed by Anne Murcott in preference to 'food consumption' to distinguish sociological concerns about the social organisation of food from the nutritional meaning of consumption as eating and the economic meaning of consumption as (food) purchasing.

foodways

Habits and practices relating to food acquisition, food preparation, food storage, distribution of food among family members, meal and snack patterns, food combinations, uses of food, beliefs about food, and identification of core, secondary, and peripheral foods in the diet.

Foucaultian perspective

A theoretical approach drawn from the work of French social theorist Michel Foucault (1926–1984). A Foucaultian (pronounced 'Foo-co-shian') perspective entails a focus on how power is exercised in a multitude of indirect and self-induced forms, particularly in terms of the social control of people's behaviour.

functional foods

Food products that allegedly deliver a health benefit beyond just providing nutrients.

functionalism

Also known as 'structural functionalism', 'consensus theory', or 'systems theory', this theoretical perspective focuses on how social structures function to maintain social order, based on the assumption that a society is a system of integrated parts, each of which has certain requirements that must be fulfilled for social order to be maintained. Key functionalist theorists include Emile Durkheim (1858–1917), Talcott Parsons (1902–79), Robert Merton (1910–2003), and Jeffrey Alexander (1947–).

gender socialisation

The process by which males and females learn the socially constructed behaviour patterns of masculinity and femininity (the cultural values that dictate how men and women should behave).

genetic engineering (or genetic modification)

The alteration of the DNA in plants, animals, and humans to perform new functions, by rearranging or deleting existing genes or inserting genetic material from another species.

genetically modified organisms (GMOs)

Plants, animals, and micro-organisms that have had their DNA altered by human intervention.

gift economy

A proposed utopia in which goods and services are produced by collectives of people and either consumed by the collective or given to other community groups or to the community at large. There is no money and no wage labour in a gift economy: community groups have effective ownership of productive property; individuals, families, or households have effective ownership of personal property.

globalisation

Political, social, economic, and cultural developments—such as the growth of multinational companies, information technology, and international agencies—that result in people's lives being increasingly influenced by global, rather than national or local, factors.

government

In general sociological terms, 'government' is understood as a wide range of practices, strategies, techniques, and programs that influence the beliefs and conduct of the population, rather than simply as a set of centralised state bureaucracies.

greenhouse effect

The gradual but significant increase in the temperature of the planet resulting from an increase in the proportion of carbon dioxide present in the atmosphere—caused by both human and natural activities. Also referred to as 'global warming'.

green revolution

A term originally used in the 1970s to refer to certain technological developments in agricultural production that increased productivity and were heralded as possible solutions to world hunger. Many of the intensive farming methods that were developed and continue to be used have been criticised for damaging the environment.

habitus

An expanded notion of habit, 'habitus' refers to the internalised and taken-for-granted personal dispositions we all possess, such as our accent, gestures, and preferences in food, fashion, and entertainment (among other things).

health claim

A claim made by a food manufacturer that their product or an ingredient in their product directly induces health or combats illness.

healthism

An extreme concern with personal health, which is becoming increasingly common.

health promotion

Any combination of education interventions and related organisational, economic, and political interventions designed to promote behavioural and environmental changes conducive to good health. This may cover a variety of strategies, including legislation, health education, community development, and advocacy. See also *ecological model*, *public health*, *public health nutrition*, and *population health*.

horizontal integration

The purchasing by a company of similar companies to form a larger organisation and reduce competition. Compare with *vertical integration*.

ideological contest

Conflict between different views of social processes, which reflect the goals and interests of different groups and organisations (for example, public health professionals or food producers).

identity

A person's self-conception or self-definition.

individualism

In sociology, the belief that we can explain social phenomena in terms of individual ideas, attributes, and behaviour.

Just-in-Time (JIT)

A system of managing production so that goods are produced as needed to meet market demand by keeping only a minimal amount of stock warehoused.

liberalism

A political philosophy that emphasises individual freedom in all spheres of social life. The meaning of the term tends to vary markedly between countries and contexts—for example, 'social liberalism' supports state intervention to enhance and protect individual freedoms, while 'economic liberalism' views state intervention as an encroachment on individual liberty—see *economic liberalism/economic rationalism*.

life chances

The probability of people realising their lifestyle choices.

life choices

People's choices in their selection of lifestyle.

life politics

A term used by Anthony Giddens to refer to life decisions or lifestyle choices that affect the formation of self-identity, which occurs as a reflexive process in the context of the dynamic nature of social life. See also *emancipatory politics*.

marginality

The socially constructed definition of a characteristic as 'out of the mainstream' or 'abnormal'.

Marxism

A political philosophy and social theory based on the writings of Karl Marx (1818–83). It is founded upon a critique of capitalism in which capitalist society is seen as being dominated by a conflict of interest between two dominant social classes: the capitalist class and the working class. Much of Marx's theory has been reinterpreted and modified, and is now often referred to as 'neo-Marxism'. For example, one version of neo-Marxism is critical theory, which has produced critiques of communist regimes and emphasises the importance of culture rather than the economy (the traditional focus).

master status

The dominant social label applied to an individual, according to which the individual is automatically attributed with a host of stereotyped personality traits commonly associated with the particular status (for example, criminal or homosexual) irrespective of the person's individual personality.

materialism

A cultural ethos that places great value on material goods (and particularly their accumulation). A second meaning refers to the idea that social life is founded in the real, tangible, observable, material reality of everyday life.

maternal ideal

The social construction of the female body that reinforces the desirability of the physiological changes of pregnancy. To conform to the maternal ideal, women should have a large body size when pregnant (as opposed to the thin ideal of female beauty that dominates most Western societies). See also *social reconstruction*.

McDonaldisation

A term coined by George Ritzer to expand Max Weber's notion of rationalisation; defined as the standardisation of work processes through rules and regulations based on increased monitoring and evaluation of individual performance, akin to the uniformity and control measures used by fast-food chains.

medical model

See *biomedicine/biomedical model*.

medical–food–industrial complex

A term adapted from Vincente Navarro and colleagues' (1998) 'medical-industrial complex', coined in 1967 and popularised by Arnold S. Relman (1980); refers to the combination of manufacturing interests, medical scientists, and government agencies that have a vested interest in the development and introduction of functional foods for the purpose of profit maximisation.

medicalisation

The process by which the influence of medicine is expanded by defining non-medical problems as medical problems, usually in terms of illnesses, disorders, or syndromes.

'modern' foods

Those foods for which overall consumption is increasing and that are consumed more by high-status groups than by low-status groups. See also *'traditional' foods.*

modernity

A particular view of society that is founded upon rational thought and the belief that objective realities can be discovered and understood through rational and scientific means—a view rejected by postmodernists. Anthony Giddens has referred to contemporary society in developed countries as high or late modernity, reflecting the advanced and dominant nature of rational and scientific views.

monoculture

The use of a piece of land to produce a single crop.

multinational oligopolies

The control of markets by a small number of international companies, which often have a budget larger than that of many small countries. Such companies are able to act together in pursuit of their mutual vested interests, via price-fixing arrangements, limiting competitors' access to markets, and gaining government concessions (tax breaks, subsidies, and favourable legislation), thereby limiting competition (particularly from local producers).

muscular ideal

The social construction of the male body that reinforces the desirability of a large, muscular body as epitomising masculinity.

neo-liberalism

A philosophy based on the primacy of individual rights and minimal state intervention. Sometimes used interchangeably with *economic rationalism/liberalism.*

neo-Marxism

See *Marxism.*

new public health

A social model of health combining 'traditional' public health concerns about physical aspects of the environment (clean air and water, safe food, occupational safety) with concerns about social and economic factors that affect people's health.

normality

Behaviours, procedures, and practices that conform to certain socially or culturally patterned standards or goals.

novel food

Defined by Standard 1.5.1 of the Australia New Zealand Food Standards Code as 'a non-traditional food for which there is insufficient knowledge in the broad community to enable safe use in the form or context in which it is presented'.

nutritional risk

Factors thought to increase the probability that an individual will develop under-nutrition or malnutrition; risk factors include social isolation and disabilities such as difficulty chewing or swallowing food.

obesity

The condition of having a high level of stored body fat.

organic

Agriculture that makes no use of artificial chemicals as fertilisers, pesticides, or herbicides.

pacifism

Opposition to war and violence in general.

patriarchy

A system of power through which males dominate households. The term is used more broadly by feminists to refer to the preeminence of patriarchal power throughout society, which functions to subordinate women and children.

permaculture

A specific system of permanent, sustainable agriculture.

phytochemicals

Chemicals derived from plants that have biological activity in humans.

placebo/placebo effect

Any therapeutic practice that has no clear clinical effect, but nonetheless results in patient improvement; in practice, it usually means giving patients an inert substance to take as a medication. When a patient reacts to a placebo in a way that is not clinically explicable, this is called the 'placebo effect'.

polyculture

The use of a piece of land to produce a diversity of crops.

population health

The collective health status of a specified population; also referred to as *public health*. A public health approach aims to assess and improve the health status of large groups of people, rather than focusing on the health of individuals at high risk. The strategies used to promote the health of populations are those that tend to have broad effects, such as policy development (for example, legislation for a safe food supply).

post-industrial society

A society in which information replaces property as the prime source of power and social control; in such societies, professionals become powerful social groups and employment is increasingly in service industries rather than manufacturing industries.

postmodern society

A debated concept in sociology that characterises contemporary society as one in which many social institutions, including the state, have lost their power to determine social outcomes. There are no longer clear paths for the individual to influence events by participating in such institutions as political parties, unions, or professional bodies. The result is a society that becomes fragmented as a result of a high level of social differentiation and cultural diversity.

post-structuralism

A term, often used interchangeably with *postmodernism*, which refers to a perspective that is opposed to the view that social structure determines human action, and that emphasises the local, the specific, and the contingent in social life.

primary prevention

Efforts to improve health or prevent disease in those who are essentially well—for example, providing health-promoting foods in school canteens to keep children healthy and prevent the development of coronary heart disease and diabetes in later life.

psychological well-being

A general term used to refer to the ability of people to experience self-acceptance, positive relationships with other people, autonomy, environmental mastery, purpose in life, and personal growth.

public health

Public policies and infrastructure designed to prevent the onset and transmission of disease among the population, with a particular focus on sanitation and hygiene measures, such as clean air, water, and food, and immunisation.

public health nutrition

A population approach to preventing diet-related health problems that addresses the influence of food production, distribution, and consumption on the nutritional status of the population at large and specific subgroups in particular (such as children, the disadvantaged, and indigenous groups). See also *public health*.

public health nutritionist

A professional employed as part of the public health workforce whose efforts are aimed at preventing nutrition-related problems in populations. The majority of –public health nutritionists in Australia are dietitians. See also *dietitian* and *public health nutrition*.

public policy

Policy made by the government or by government agencies.

rational individualism

A view that characterises social life as consisting of the rational choices of individual actors, each motivated to act in his or her own interest.

rationalisation
See *McDonaldisation.*

reflexive modernity
A term coined by Ulrich Beck and Anthony Giddens to refer to the present social era in developed societies, in which social practices are open to reflection, questioning, and change, and therefore in which social traditions no longer dictate people's lifestyles.

risk discourse
'Risk' refers to danger and risk discourse is often used in health promotion messages warning people that certain actions (such as eating foods high in saturated fat and sugar) involve significant risks to their health.

risk factors
Conditions that are thought to increase an individual's susceptibility to illness or disease—for example, abuse of alcohol, poor diet, or smoking.

risk society
A term coined by Ulrich Beck (1992) to describe the centrality of risk calculations in people's lives in Western society, whereby the key social problems today are unanticipated hazards, such as the risks of food poisoning, pollution, and environmental degradation.

role
Behavioural expectations (including duties and rights) associated with a position in society.

ruralisation
A process of relocating urban populations to agricultural regions so that all food is produced and consumed locally.

self-fulfilling prophecy
A concept derived from symbolic interactionist theory that refers to a predicted series of events that unfolds as a reaction to the actual prediction. For example, the labelling of a young child as being of low intelligence may result in a self-fulfilling prophecy, whereby the child chooses to fulfil these low expectations.

self-rationalisation
A concept that draws on Michel Foucault's (1979) ideas of surveillance as a form of social control, and which particularly refers to discourses that attempt to rationally manage and regulate the human body.

shaman
A healer who practices traditional medicine; sometimes described as a 'physician–priest'.

size acceptance
See *body acceptance.*

social appetite
The social patterns of food production, distribution, and consumption.

social class

See *class*.

social control

Mechanisms that aim to induce conformity, or at least to manage or minimise deviant behaviour.

social determinism

The assumption that the behaviour of individuals is shaped by social interactions and social structures. This view tends to neglect the role of biological and psychological factors.

social constructionism

The theory that people actively construct reality and its associated meanings, so that nothing is 'natural' or inevitable and notions of normality/abnormality, right/wrong, and health/illness are subjective human creations that should not be taken for granted.

social differentiation

A trend towards social diversity based on the creation of social distinction and self-identity through particular consumption choices and through group membership.

social isolation

The condition in which an individual both lives alone and has little social contact with other people.

social network

The persons with whom an individual normally has the most contact. These can include friends, immediate family members, more distant relatives, neighbours, co-workers, fellow members of voluntary organisations, and fellow church members.

social reconstruction

A term used to denote the change in societal expectations regarding women's bodies during the period of pregnancy. It is based on the notion of the social construction of women's bodies to conform to the *thin ideal* at all other stages of their lives. These expectations are redefined during pregnancy, thereby reconstructing women's bodies to conform to the *maternal ideal*.

social structure

The recurring patterns of social interaction by which people are related to each other through social institutions and social groups.

social support

Instrumental aid (goods and services) and expressive aid (companionship, comfort, and advice about personal matters) provided by members of a social network.

socialism

A political ideology and system of government with numerous variations, based on the elimination of social inequality, the promotion of altruistic values, and the replacement of private wealth accumulation with state ownership and/or distribution of economic resources.

socioeconomic status (SES)

A measure of social status based on the statistical grouping of people into high-, medium-, and low-SES groups according to certain criteria (usually a composite index of income, occupation, and education); used to gauge social and economic inequalities.

sociological imagination

A term coined by Charles Wright Mills (1959) to describe the sociological approach to the analysis of issues. We see the world through a sociological imagination, or think sociologically, when we make a link between personal troubles and public issues.

speciesism

A term coined by Peter Singer to describe the form of discrimination where one species allows their own interests to justify causing pain and suffering to another species.

spiritual well-being

A general term used to refer to the ability of people to experience meaning and purpose in life, self-awareness, and connectedness with self, others, and a larger reality.

state

A collection of public institutions, including the parliament (government and opposition political parties), the public-sector bureaucracy, the judiciary, the military, and the police.

status

The respect or prestige associated with a particular position in society.

stigma

An attribute of a person that is deeply discrediting and that disqualifies that person from full social acceptance.

stigmatising act

An act of a 'normal' individual that devalues another person, in the process of stigmatisation.

structuralism

A view maintaining that individuals' actions and beliefs are primarily determined by the society in which they live, emphasising that language, culture, and economic organisation pre-exist the individual and limit the possibilities for thought and action.

structure/agency debate

A key debate in sociology regarding the extent to which human behaviour is determined by the social structure.

substitutionism

The use of natural or chemically synthesised 'generic ingredients' in food processing as replacements for original and costly ingredients (for example, sugar from cornstarch rather than cane). Compare with *appropriation*.

sustainable agriculture
Any system of plant and animal production that can satisfy human food needs and maintain or enhance natural resources by maximising the use of renewable resources, conserving and efficiently using nonrenewable resources, and ensuring that the environmental impact of agricultural processes is minimised, so that affected ecological systems survive and prosper.

symbolic interactionism
A theoretical perspective that focuses on agency and how people construct, interpret, and give meaning to their behaviour through interaction with others. Rather than large social structures, small-scale, face-to-face symbolic interactions are studied, as social life is viewed as the cumulative product of human action, interaction, and interpretation. Key symbolic interactionist theorists include George Herbert Mead (1863–1931), Charles Cooley (1864–1929), Howard Becker (1928–), Erving Goffman (1922–82), and Herbert Blumer (1900–1987), who coined the term in 1937.

technologies of government
A range of institutions operating outside state bureaucracy that are able to exert control over the population.

thin ideal
The dominant aesthetic ideal of female beauty in Western societies, which refers to the social desirability of a thin body shape.

time famine
A general term used to refer to the pressure on people's time use in contemporary social life. Being 'time poor' is a common complaint, as people deal with increasingly complex and fast-paced lifestyles, particularly when combining long (and possibly odd) working hours, study, and family and social life.

'traditional' foods
Those foods for which overall consumption is decreasing and that are consumed more by low-status groups than by high-status groups. See also *'modern' foods*.

transgenic organisms
Organisms created through the transferral of genetic information from one species to another by combining DNA molecules from, for example, a plant and an animal into a single 'recombinant' strand to produce a change in the genetic makeup (for instance, transgenic pigs with human growth hormone).

transnational corporations (TNCs)
Refers to companies that have operations in more than one country and no clearly identifiable country as a home base. Often used in preference to the superceded term 'multinational corporations', which tended to refer to companies primarily based in one country, but with subsidiary operations in other countries. See also multinational oligopolies.

unproblematised
Treated as natural and therefore not requiring research or examination.

vegetarianism

The practice of voluntarily refraining from eating meat, chicken, or fish and the beliefs underpinning this practice. There are many variations, but the major sub-categories include lacto-vegetarian (dairy food is still consumed), ovo-vegetarian (eggs are consumed), and vegan (abstinence from eating and sometimes from wearing all animal products).

vertical integration

The purchase by a company of dissimilar companies that can enhance profitability; through vertical integration one company may, for example, acquire a farm, a manufacturing plant, and a supermarket chain. Compare with *horizontal integration*.

Appendix: Key Web Sites, Books, and Journals

Web sites

An up-to-date list of weblinks can be found on the Social Appetite web site: www.oup.com.au/companion

General sociology

American Sociological Association: www.asanet.org

Australian Sociological Association: www.tasa.org.au

British Sociological Association: www.britsoc.org.uk

Canadian Sociology and Anthropology Association: alcor.concordia.ca/~csaa1/

European Sociological Association: www.valt.helsinki.fi/esa/

International Sociological Association: www.ucm.es/info/isa/

Sociological Association of Aotearoa/New Zealand: saanz.science.org.nz/

Sociosite: www2.fmg.uva.nl/sociosite/

Associations

Agriculture, Food, and Human Values Society: www.clas.ufl.edu/users/rhaynes/afhvs/Description.htm

American Dietetic Association: www.eatright.org/Public/

Association for the Study of Food and Society: www.nyu.edu/education/nutrition/NFSR/ASFS.htm

Australian Agri-food Network: www.sct.gu.edu.au/sci_page/research/agri

Australian Consumers Association: www.choice.com.au

British Sociological Association—Sociology of Food Study Group: www.britsoc.org.uk/about/food.htm

Dietitians Association of Australia: www.daa.asn.au

International Commission on the Anthropology of Food: icaf.brookes.ac.uk/

International Food Policy Research Institute: www.ifpri.org/

International Rural Sociology Association: www.acs.ryerson.ca/~isarc40/

Nutrition Australia: www.nutritionaustralia.org/

Nutrition Society of Australia: www.nsa.asn.au/

Research Committee on Food and Agriculture (RC 40): www.acs.ryerson.ca/~isarc40/

Body image and eating disorders

Body Icon: nm-server.jrn.columbia.edu/projects/masters/bodyimage/

Body Image & Health Inc.: www.internationalnodietday.com/

Eating Disorders: www.eatingdisorders.org.au/

Eating Disorders Association: www.edauk.com

Eating Disorders Links: www.uq.net.au/eda/documents/links.html

Health Education Board for Scotland—Talking about Eating Disorders: www.hebs.scot.nhs.uk

International Size Acceptance Association: www.size-acceptance.org/

Mirror Mirror: www.mirrormirror.com.au

National Association to Advance Fat Acceptance: http://naafa.org/

Women's Health Australia—The Australian Longitudinal Study on Women's Health: www.fec.newcastle.edu.au/wha

Food and the environment

David Suzuki Foundation: www.davidsuzuki.org/

Diversitas International (biodiversity): www.diversitas-international.org/

Gastronomy Guide (by Margaret Hosking at Adelaide University): www.library.adelaide.edu.au/guide/hum/history/Gastronomy.html

GeneEthics Network (Australia): www.geneethics.org/community/index.php

GeneWatch (UK): www.genewatch.org/

Global Eco-village Network: gen.ecovillage.org/

Institute for Science in Society: www.i-sis.org.uk/

McSpotlight: www.McSpotlight.org

Organic Consumers Association (USA): www.organicconsumers.org

Organic Europe: www.organic-europe.net/

Permaculture International: www.permacultureinternational.org/index.htm

Slow Food: www.slowfood.com/

True Food Network: www.greenpeace.org.au/truefood/

USDA Alternative Farming Systems Information Center: www.nal.usda.gov/afsic/csa/

Food, culture, and history

Center for Immigration and Multicultural Studies (Australia): cims.anu.edu.au/index.html

Food and Nutrition Information Center—Cultural and Ethnic Food and Nutrition Education (US): www.nal.usda.gov/fnic/pubs/bibs/gen/ethnic.html

Food History News: www.foodhistorynews.com/

Foodways Section of the American Folklore Society: afsnet.org/sections/foodways/

Research Centre for the History of Food and Drink (University of Adelaide): www.arts.adelaide.edu.au/centrefooddrink/

Resources for the Anthropological Study of Food Habits: lilt.ilstu.edu/rtdirks/

World Food Habits Bibliography (Anthropology): lilt.ilstu.edu/rtdirks/

Government and non-government agencies

Australian Bureau of Agricultural and Resource Economics: www.abare.gov.au/

Australian Bureau of Statistics: www.abs.gov.au

Australian Department of Agriculture, Fisheries and Forestry: www.affa.gov.au/index.cfm

Australian Department of Health and Aged Care: www.health.gov.au

Australian Food and Nutrition Monitoring Unit: www.sph.uq.edu.au/nutrition/monitoring/index.htm

Australian Institute of Health and Welfare: www.aihw.gov.au

Codex Alimentarius Commission: www.codexalimentarius.net

Food and Nutrition Information Center (US): www.nal.usda.gov/fnic/

Food and Agriculture Organization of the United Nations: www.fao.org/

Food Standards Australia New Zealand: www.foodstandards.gov.au

National Health and Medical Research Council: www.nhmrc.gov.au

National Institutes of Health: www.nih.gov

Office of the Gene Technology Regulator (Australia): www.ogtr.gov.au

United Kingdom Food Standards Agency: www.food.gov.uk

United States Food and Drug Administration: www.fda.gov

World Health Organization: www.who.org

Public health nutrition—Australia

Acting on Australia's Weight: www.nhmrc.gov.au/publications/synopses/n22syn.htm

Australian Guide to Healthy Eating: www.health.gov.au/pubhlth/strateg/food/guide/index.htm

Dietary Guidelines for Australians: www.health.gov.au/nhmrc/advice/diet.htm

Eat Well Australia: www.nphp.gov.au/signal/natstrat.htm

Food Additive Codes: www.drsref.com.au/foodaddcodes.html

GI Website: www.glycemicindex.com/

HealthWIZ Online—Australia's National Social Health Data Library: www.healthwiz.com.au/online/

National Public Health Partnership (Australia): hna.ffh.vic.gov.au/nphp/

NSW Childhood Obesity Summit: www.health.nsw.gov.au/obesity/adult/summit/summit.html

Nutrition & Healthy Eating (Australia): www.health.gov.au/pubhlth/strateg/food/

Nutrition in Aboriginal and Torres Strait Islander Peoples—An Information Paper: www.health.gov.au/nhmrc/publications/synopses/n26syn.htm

Public Health Association of Australia: www.phaa.net.au

Quotidian—Australian Food and Society (by Pat Crotty): www.quotidian.net

Recommended Dietary Intakes for Use in Australia: www.health.gov.au/nhmrc/publications/diet/n6index.htm

Social Health Atlas of Australia: www.publichealth.gov.au/atlas.htm

Public health nutrition—Global

Cochrane Collaboration: www.cochrane.org/

Cochrane Library: www.update-software.com/cochrane/

Ethnic/Cultural Food Guide Pyramids (US): www.nal.usda.gov/fnic/etext/000023.html

Physicians and Scientists for Responsible Application of Science and Technology: www.psrast.org/

Public Health Virtual Library: www.ldb.org/vl/index.htm

Vegetarianism

Veg Web: www.vegweb.com/

Vegan.com: www.vegan.com

Vegetarian Resource Group: www.vrg.org/

Vegetarian.com: www.vegetarian.com

Vegetarianism and the Social Sciences—A Bibliography by Donna Maurer: academic-editor.com/vegbib.html

World hunger and food security

Andre Gunder Frank Archives: csf.colorado.edu/agfrank/

Centre for Studies in Food Security (Ryerson University): www.acs.ryerson.ca/~isarc40/

FoodFirst: www.foodfirst.org/

The Hunger Site: www.thehungersite.com

The HungerWeb: www.brown.edu/Departments/World_Hunger_Program/

World Hunger Education Service: www.worldhunger.org/

Books

Social science perspectives on food

Atkins, P. & Bowler, I. (eds) 2001, *Food in Society: Economy, Culture, Geography*, Arnold, London.

Bannerman, C. (ed.) 1998, *Acquired Tastes: Celebrating Australia's Culinary History*, National Library of Australia, Canberra.

Beardsworth, A. & Keil, T. 1997, *Sociology on the Menu*, Routledge, London.

Belasco, W. 1993, *Appetite for Change: How the Counterculture Took on the Food Industry*, Cornell University Press, Ithaca, New York.

Belasco, W. & Scranton, P. (eds) 2002, *Food and Nations: Selling Taste in Consumer Societies*, Routledge, New York.

Bell, D. & Valentine, G. 1997, *Consuming Geographies: You Are Where You Eat*, Routledge, London.

Caplan, P. (ed.) 1997, *Food, Health and Identity*, Routledge, London.

Counihan, C. M. (ed.) 2002, *Food in America: A Reader*, Routledge, New York.

Coveney, J. 2000, *Food, Morals, and Meaning: The Pleasure and Anxiety of Eating*, Routledge, London.

Dixon, J. 2002, *The Changing Chicken: Chooks, Cooks and Culinary Culture*, University of New South Wales Press, Sydney.

Dyson, L. E. 2002, *How to Cook a Galah: Celebrating Australia's Culinary Heritage*, Lothian Books, Melbourne.

Fieldhouse, P. 1995, *Food and Nutrition: Customs and Culture*, 2nd edn, Croom Helm, Kent.

Finkelstein, J. 1989, *Dining Out: A Sociology of Modern Manners*, Polity Press, Cambridge.

Gabaccia, D. R. 1998, *We Are What We Eat: Ethnic Food and the Making of Americans*, Harvard University Press, Cambridge, Massachusetts.

Griffiths, S. & Wallace, J. (eds) 1998, *Consuming Passions: Food in the Age of Anxiety*, Mandolin, Manchester.

Harris, M. 1986, *Good to Eat: Riddles of Food and Culture*, Simon & Schuster, New York.

Lupton, D. 1996, *Food, the Body and the Self*, Sage, London.

McIntosh, Wm. A. 1996, *Sociologies of Food and Nutrition*, Plenum Publishing, New York.

Mack, A. (ed.) 1998, Food: Nature and Culture, *Social Research*, vol. 66, no. 1.

Maurer, D. & Sobal, J. (eds) 1995, *Eating Agendas: Food and Nutrition as Social Problems*, Aldine de Gruyter, New York.

Mennell, S., Murcott, A., & van Otterloo, A. H. 1992, *The Sociology of Food: Eating, Diet, and Culture*, Sage, London.

Murcott. A. (ed.) 1983, *The Sociology of Food and Eating*, Gower, Aldershot, UK.

—— (ed.) 1998, *'The Nation's Diet': The Social Science of Food Choice*, Longman, London.

Nestle, M. 2002, *Food Politics*, University of California Press, California.

Probyn, E. 2000, *Carnal Appetites: Food, Sex, Identities*, Routledge, London.

Ogden, J. 2002, *The Psychology of Eating: From Healthy to Disordered Behaviour*, Blackwell, Oxford.

Riddell, R. 1989, *Food and Culture in Australia*, Longman Cheshire, Melbourne.

Ritzer, G. 2000, *The McDonaldization of Society*, 3rd edn, Pine Forge Press, Thousand Oaks.

—— 2001, *Explorations in the Sociology of Consumption: Fast Food, Credit Cards and Casinos*, Sage, London.

—— (ed.) 2002, *McDonaldization: The Reader*, Pine Forge Press, Thousand Oaks.

Scapp, R. & Seitz, B. (eds) 1998, *Eating Culture*, State University of New York Press, Albany.

Schlosser, E. 2001, *Fast Food Nation*, Penguin, London.

Tansey, G. & Worsley, T. 1995, *The Food System: A Guide*, Earthscan, London.

Visser, M. 1989, *Much Depends on Dinner*, Penguin Books, London.

—— 1995, *Why We Eat the Way We Do*, Penguin Books, London.

Warde, A. 1997, *Consumption, Food and Taste*, Sage, London.

Warde, A. & Martens, L. 2000, *Eating Out: Social Differentiation, Consumption and Pleasure*, Cambridge University Press, Cambridge.

Watson, J. L. (ed) 1997, *Golden Arches East: McDonald's in East Asia*, Stanford University Press, Stanford, California.

Whit, W. C. 1995, *Food and Society: A Sociological Approach*, General Hall, New York.

Gender and food, eating disorders, and sociology of the body

Avakian, A.V. (ed.) 1997, *Through the Kitchen Window: Women Explore the Intimate Meanings of Food and Cooking*, Beacon Press, Boston.

Charles, N. & Kerr, M. 1988, *Women, Food and Families*, Manchester University Press, Manchester.

Counihan, C. M. (ed.) 1999, *The Anthropology of Food and Body: Gender, Meaning and Power*, Routledge, New York.

DeVault, M. 1991, *Feeding the Family: The Social Organisation of Caring as Gendered Work*, University of Chicago Press, Chicago.

Featherstone, M., Hepworth, M., & Turner, B. (eds) 1991, *The Body: Social Process and Cultural Theory*, Sage, London.

Gaurine, I. & Pollock, N. J. (eds) 1995, *Social Aspects of Obesity*, Gordon & Breach, New York.

Hancock, P., Hughes, B. Jagger, E., Paterson, K. Russell, R., Tulle-Winton, E. & Tyrler, M. (eds), *The Body, Culture and Society: An Introduction*, Open University Press, Buckingham.

Hepworth, J. 1999, *The Social Construction of Anorexia Nervosa*, Sage, Thousand Oaks, California.

Nasser, M., Katzman, M. A., & Gordon, R. A. (eds), 2001, *Eating Disorders and Cultures in Transition*, Brunner-Routledge, London.

Schwartz, H. 1986, *Never Satisfied: A Cultural History of Diets, Fantasies and Fat*, The Free Press, New York.

Sobal, J. & Maurer, D. (eds) 1999, *Interpreting Weight: The Social Management of Fatness and Thinness*, Aldine de Gruyter, Hawthorne, New York State.

—— (eds) 1999, *Weighty Issues: The Construction of Fatness and Thinness as Social Problems*, Aldine de Gruyter, Hawthorne, New York State.

Turner, B. 1996, *The Body and Society*, 2nd edn, Sage, London.

Weitz, R. (ed.), 2003, *The Politics of Women's Bodies: Sexuality, Appearance and Behavior*, 2nd edition, Oxford University Press, New York.

Public health nutrition

Australian Bureau of Statistics (ABS) (various years) *National Nutrition Survey, 1995*, ABS, Canberra.

—— (various years) *1995 National Health Survey, 1995*, ABS, Canberra.

Australian Institute of Health and Welfare (AIHW) 2002, *Australia's Health 2002*, AIHW, Canberra.

Commonwealth of Australia 2001, *Food Regulation in Australia: A Chronology*, Department of the Parliamentary Library, Canberra.

Crotty, P. 1995, *Good Nutrition? Fact and Fashion in Dietary Advice*, Allen & Unwin, Sydney.

Department of Agriculture, Fisheries and Forestry 2003, *Australian Food Statistics 2003*, Department of Agriculture, Fisheries and Forestry, Canberra.

Food and Agricultural Organisation, 2002, *State of Food Insecurity in the World 2002*, Food and Agricultural Organisation, Rome.

Lee, C. (ed.) 2001, *Women's Health Australia: What Do We Know? What Do We Need to Know?*, Australian Academic Press, Brisbane.

Lester, I. H. 1994, *Australia's Food and Nutrition*, Australian Government Publishing Service, Canberra. Available online at <www.aihw.gov.au/publications/health/afn94/index.html>

National Health and Medical Research Council 2003, *Dietary Guidelines for Australian Adults*, AusInfo, Canberra.

Santich, B. 1995, *What the Doctors Ordered: 150 Years of Dietary Advice in Australia*, Hyland House, Melbourne.

Strategic Inter-Governmental Nutrition Alliance 2001, *Eat Well Australia: A Strategic Framework for Public Health Nutrition 2000-2010*, National Public Health Partnership, Canberra.

Wahlqvist, M. L. (ed.) 2002, *Food and Nutrition: Australasia, Asia and the Pacific*, 2nd edn, Allen & Unwin, Sydney.

World Health Organization/Food and Agriculture Organization 1992, *World Declaration and Plan of Action for Nutrition*, World Health Organization, Geneva.

World Health Organization/Food and Agriculture Organization 2003, *Expert Report on Diet, Nutrition and the Prevention of Chronic Disease*, World Health Organization, Geneva.

Food history and anthologies

Bentley, A. 1998, *Eating for Victory: Food Rationing and the Politics of Domesticity*, University of Illinois, Urbana.

Burnett, J. 1999, *Liquid Pleasures: A Social History of Drinks in Modern Britain*, Routledge, London.

Davidson, A. (ed.) 1999, *The Oxford Companion to Food*, Oxford University Press, Oxford.

—— 2002, *The Penguin Companion to Food*, Penguin Books, Harmondsworth.

Davidson, J. N. 1998, *Courtesans & Fishcakes: The Consuming Passions of Classical Athens*, St. Martin's Press, New York.

Fernandez-Armesto, F. 2001, *Food: A History*, Macmillan, London

Flandrin, J. L., Montanari, M. & Sonnenfeld, A. (eds) 2000, *Food: A Culinary History from Antiquity to the Present*, Penguin Books, Harmondsworth, UK.

Graves, A. 1993, *Cane and Labour: The Political Economy of the Queensland Sugar Industry, 1862-1906*, Edinburgh University Press, Edinburgh.

Katz, S. 2002, *Scribner's Encyclopaedia of Food and Culture*, Charles Scribner & Sons, New York.

Kiple, K. F. & Kriemhild, C. O. (eds) 2000, *The Cambridge World History of Food*, Cambridge University Press, Cambridge.

Kurlansky, K. 2002, *Salt: A World History*, Jonathan Cape, London.

—— (ed) 2002, *Choice Cuts: A Savoury Selection of Food Writing from Around the World and Throughout History*, Ballantine Books, New York.

Lang, T. & Millstone, E. 2003, *The Penguin Atlas of Food: Who Eats What, Where, and Why*, Penguin Books, Harmondsworth, UK.

Levenstein, H. 1993, *Paradox of Plenty: A Social History of Eating in Modern America*, Oxford University Press, New York.

—— 1988, *Revolution at the Table: The Transformation of the American Diet*, Oxford University Press, New York.

Macinnis, P. 2002, *Bittersweet: The Story of Sugar*, Allen & Unwin, Sydney.

Mennell, S. 1996, *All Manners of Food*, 2nd edn, University of Illinois Press, Chicago.

Mintz, S. 1985, *Sweetness and Power: The Place of Sugar in Modern History*, Penguin, New York.

—— 1996, *Tasting Food, Tasting Freedom: Excursions into Eating, Culture, and the Past,* Beacon Press, Boston.

Pendergrast, M. 2000, *For God, Country, and Coca-Cola: The Definitive History of the Great American Soft Drink and the Company That Makes It*, 2nd edn, Basic Books, New York.

—— 1999, *Uncommon Grounds: The History of Coffee and How It Transformed Our World*, Basic Books.

Rowse, T. 2002, *White Flour, White Power: From Rations to Citizenship in Central Australia*, Cambridge University Press, Cambridge.

Smith, J. 1996, *Hungry for You: From Cannibalism to Seduction—A Book of Food*, Chatto & Windus, London.

Symons, M. 1993, *The Shared Table: Ideas for an Australian Cuisine*, Australian Government Publishing Service, Canberra.

—— 1982, *One Continuous Picnic: A History of Eating in Australia*, Duck Press, Adelaide.

Tannahill, R. 1988, *Food in History*, revised edn, Penguin, London.

Food and environment, vegetarianism, and world hunger

Almas, R. & Lawrence, G. (eds) 2003, *Globalization, Localization and Sustainable Livelihoods*, Ashgate, Aldershot, UK.

Boucher, D. H. (ed.) 1999, *The Paradox of Plenty: Hunger in a Bountiful World*, Food First Books, Oakland.

Burch, D., Goss, J. & Lawrence, G. (eds) 1999, *Restructuring Global and Regional Agricultures: Transformations in Australasian Agri-food Economies and Spaces*, Ashgate, Aldershot.

Grigg, D. 1993, *World Food Problem*, Blackwell, London.

Gussow, J. D. 2002, *This Organic Life: Confessions of a Suburban Homesteader*, Chelsea Green, White River Junction.

Hindmarsh, R. & Lawrence, G. (eds) 2003, *Recoding Nature: Critical Perspectives on Genetic Engineering*, University of New South Wales Press, Sydney.

Hindmarsh, R., Lawrence, G. & Norton, J. (eds) 1998, *Altered Genes: Reconstructing Nature—The Debate*, Allen & Unwin, Sydney.

Lappe, F. M., Collins, J. & Rosset, P. 1998, *World Hunger: Twelve Myths*, 2nd edn, Grove Press, New York.

Lappe, M. & Bailey, B. 1998, *Against the Grain: Biotechnology and the Corporate Takeover of Your Food,* Common Courage Press.

Lockie, S. & Pritchard, B. (eds) 2001, *Consuming Foods, Sustaining Environments*, Australian Academic Press, Melbourne.

Martineau, B. 2001, *First Fruit: The Creation of the Flavr savr Tomato and the Birth of Genetically Engineered Food*, McGraw-Hill, New York.

McMichael, P. 2000, *Development and Social Change: A Global Perspective*, 2nd edn, Pine Forge, Boston.

Marcus, E. 2001, *Vegan: The New Ethics of Eating*, McBooks Press, New York.

Maurer, D. 2002, *Vegetarianism: Movement of Moment?*, Temple University Press, Philadelphia.

Nestle, M. 2002, *Safe Food: Bacteria, Biotechnology, and Bioterrorism*, University of California Press, Berkeley.

Poppendieck, J. H. 1998, *Sweet Charity? Emergency Food and the End of Entitlement*, Viking Penguin, New York.

Walters, K. & Portmess, L. (eds) 1998, *Ethical Vegetarianism: From Pythagoras to Peter Singer*, State University of New York Press, Albany.

Essay and study skills

Germov, J. 2000, *Get Great Marks for Your Essays*, 2nd edn, Allen & Unwin, Sydney.

Germov, J. & Williams, L. 1999, *Get Great Information Fast*, Allen & Unwin, Sydney.

Williams, L. & Germov, J. 2001, *Surviving First Year Uni*, Allen & Unwin, Sydney.

Journals

Agriculture and Human Values: www.kluweronline.com/issn/0889-048X

Appetite: www.elsevier.com/locate/issn/0195-6663

American Journal of Public Health

Australian & New Zealand Journal of Public Health

Body & Society

British Food Journal

Critical Public Health

Digest: An Interdisciplinary Study of Food and Foodways: afsnet.org/sections/foodways/digest.htm

Gastronomica: The Journal of Food and Culture: www.gastronomica.org/

Gender and Society

Health Promotion International

Health Promotion Journal of Australia

Health Sociology Review (formerly *Annual Review of Health Social Sciences*)

Healthy Weight Journal

International Journal of Health Services

International Journal of Sociology of Agriculture and Food: www.ryerson.ca/~isarc40/IJSAF/

Journal for the Study of Food and Society

Journal of Health and Social Behavior

Journal of Nutrition Education

Journal of Sociology

Journal of Studies on Alcohol

Journal of the American Dietetic Association

New Internationalist: www.oneworld.org/ni/

Nutrition & Dietetics (formerly *Australian Journal of Nutrition and Dietetics*): www.ajnd.org.au/

Public Health

Qualitative Health Research

Sex Roles

Social Science & Medicine

The Sociological Review

Sociology of Health & Illness

Women & Health

Index

Page numbers in *italics* refer to boxed material.